ICONS OF AFRICAN AMERICAN LITERATURE

Recent Titles in
Greenwood Icons

ICONS OF AFRICAN AMERICAN LITERATURE

The Black Literary World

Yolanda Williams Page, Editor

GREENWOOD ICONS

 GREENWOOD

AN IMPRINT OF ABC-CLIO, LLC
Santa Barbara, California • Denver, Colorado • Oxford, England

Library of Congress Cataloging-in-Publication Data

Icons of African American literature : the Black literary world / Yolanda Williams Page, Editor.
    p. cm. — (Greenwood icons)
    Includes bibliographical references and index.
    ISBN 978-0-313-35203-4 (hardcopy : alk. paper) — ISBN 978-0-313-35204-1 (ebook)
    1. American literature—African American authors—History and criticism.
2. African Americans—Intellectual life.   3. African Americans in literature.
I. Page, Yolanda Williams.   II. Series: Greenwood icons.
    PS153.N5I35   2011
    810.9896073—dc22   2011015377

ISBN: 978-0-313-35203-4
EISBN: 978-0-313-35204-1

15   14   13   12   11   1   2   3   4   5

This book is also available on the World Wide Web as an eBook.
Visit www.abc-clio.com for details.

Greenwood
An Imprint of ABC-CLIO, LLC

ABC-CLIO, LLC
130 Cremona Drive, P.O. Box 1911
Santa Barbara, California 93116-1911

This book is printed on acid-free paper ∞

Manufactured in the United States of America

Contents

Series Foreword

Worshipped and cursed. Loved and loathed. Obsessed about the world over. What does it take to become an icon? Regardless of subject, culture, or era, the requisite qualifications are the same: (1) challenge the status quo, (2) influence millions, and (3) affect history.

Using these criteria, ABC-Clio/Greenwood introduces a new reference format and approach to popular culture. Spanning a wide range of subjects, volumes in the Greenwood Icons series provide students and general readers with a port of entry into the most fascinating and influential topics of the day. Every title offers an in-depth look at 24 iconic figures, each of which captures the essence of a broad subject. These icons typically embody a group of values, elicit strong reactions, reflect the essence of a particular time and place, and link different traditions and periods. Among those featured are artists and activists, superheroes and spies, inventors and athletes, the legends and mythmakers of entire generations. Yet icons can also come from unexpected places: as the heroine who transcends the pages of a novel or as the revolutionary idea that shatters our previously held beliefs. Whether people, places, or things, such icons serve as a bridge between the past and the present, the canonical and the contemporary. By focusing on icons central to popular culture, this series encourages students to appreciate cultural diversity and critically analyze issues of enduring significance.

Most important, these books are as entertaining as they are provocative. Is Disneyland a more influential icon of the American West than Las Vegas? How do ghosts and ghouls reflect our collective psyche? Is Barry Bonds an inspiring or deplorable icon of baseball?

Designed to foster debate, the series serves as a unique resource that is ideal for paper writing or report purposes. Insightful, in-depth entries provide far more information than conventional reference articles but are less intimidating and more accessible than a book-length biography. The most revered and reviled icons of American and world history are brought to life with related sidebars, timelines, fact boxes, and quotations. Authoritative entries are accompanied by bibliographies, making these titles an ideal starting point for further research. Spanning a wide range of popular topics, including business, literature, civil rights, politics, music, and more, books in the series provide fresh insights for the student and popular reader into the power and influence of icons, a topic of as vital interest today as in any previous era.

Preface

Many works and authors enjoy fleeting popularity. They may be included on course syllabi for a while or appear on bestseller lists for a few weeks, but then they fall into obscurity. While few authors and works have enduring, iconic significance, those that do seem to remain recognizable and popular despite the passing of time; they are mainstays in literature classrooms and are continually the subjects of theses and dissertations. From early seminal works such as Booker T. Washington's *Up from Slavery* through contemporary works such as August Wilson's 10-play cycle that documents the African American experience, iconic works and authors such as these have played a tremendous role in the canonization of African American literature.

In fact, the contemporary interest in and recognition of African American literature can be attributed, in part, to several iconic texts, writers, movements, and literary ideals. *Icons of African American Literature* identifies and defines 24 of the most recognizable and popular subjects related to African American literature. The subjects identified as icons are widely regarded and read and are generally considered as canonical. Their appeal crosses literary boundaries; they are not limited to studies of African American literature but can be found in studies of American literature, women, history, and other areas. These subjects have permanence, too; they are just as appealing and insightful today as they were years ago. They continue to be the focus of contemporary research and are the standard to which other works are compared. They are the subjects and basis of film, theatrical productions, and critical texts.

In addition to canonical works and writers such as Toni Morrison, *The Color Purple,* Ralph Ellison, and *Native Son,* movements such as Black Arts and the Harlem Renaissance are also included because many African American writers and texts have been influenced by the cultural and social nuances of those periods. A survey of any number of African American works will reveal that many of them address or use as their subjects pertinent issues from the Black Arts and Harlem Renaissance movements. It can also be argued that many African American literary works are symbolic of the periods. Included, as well, are tropes such as signifying and the blues and jazz aesthetics. The tropes are considered iconic because they are the legs upon which many of the subjects stand, and they serve as the foundation for many other African American works.

Icons of African American Literature has been written so that users will find it helpful no matter their stage of research. Advanced high school students, undergraduates, and users of community college and public libraries will all find the information accessible.

Graduate students and seasoned scholars in the initial stage of research will also find this text useful, for each entry includes primary and secondary sources. Entries are written in chapter format, and vary in length from 5,000 to 10,000 words. The icons fall within three categories: writers/works, literary periods/movements, and forms. Writers/works include **Maya Angelou,** best known for her autobiography, *I Know Why the Caged Bird Sings;* **James Baldwin,** one of the first male African American authors to explore homosexual themes in his work; **Paul Laurence Dunbar,** best known for his use of dialect poetry; **Henry Louis Gates,** the literary scholar and critic who found himself immersed in a national racial drama in 2009; **E. Lynn Harris,** the former IBM salesman who popularized African American gay male fiction; **Langston Hughes,** who is often referred to as the poet laureate of African American poetry; **Zora Neale Hurston,** the major female writer of the Harlem Renaissance; *Invisible Man,* Ralph Ellison's novel that follows the psychological journey of an unnamed narrator; **Terry McMillan,** the wildly popular fiction writer who introduced readers to the independent black woman (IBW); **Toni Morrison,** whose oeuvre earned her a Nobel Prize in Literature; **Walter Mosley,** the mystery writer whose Easy Rawlins series was wildly popular in the mid-to-late 20th century; *Native Son,* Richard Wright's acclaimed protest novel; *A Raisin in the Sun,* Lorraine Hansberry's drama, which was the first play by an African American woman to be produced on Broadway and the first play staged on Broadway with an African American director; *Souls of Black Folk,* W.E.B. Du Bois's prose collection that spurred the genesis of African American literary history; *Up from Slavery,* Booker T. Washington's acclaimed autobiography; **Alice Walker,** the Pulitzer Prize–winning novelist who is credited with rediscovering Zora Neale Hurston; and **August Wilson,** the dramatist from Pittsburgh who won two Pulitzer Prizes for Drama for his 10-play cycle that documents the 20th-century African American experience.

Movements/periods include the **Black Aesthetic,** the post–Civil Rights Movement that encouraged African American writers to reject Western ideology; the **Black Arts Movement,** which was closely associated with the Black Power Movement; and the **Harlem Renaissance,** the early 20th-century movement that took place in Harlem, New York.

Forms include the **Blues Aesthetic,** which takes its inspiration and themes from blues music; the **Jazz Aesthetic,** which includes literature that incorporates the riffs and improvisation of jazz music; **signifying,** a form of verbal play that is widely used in African American literature; and the slave narrative, a literary form that was popularized by former slaves but still influences contemporary African American literature.

While arguably there are other works, writers, movements, and forms that can be considered iconic, the entries that are presented in this book represent the standard by which all others are measured.

Acknowledgments

Many people played a role in this work's completion. First and foremost are the 22 scholars who responded to my call for contributors. I appreciate their willingness to give their time and expertise to write the entries. I thank ABC-CLIO/Greenwood editors George Butler and Kim Kennedy-White: George, for bringing the project to my attention, and Kim for seeing the project to fruition. I appreciate your patience and guidance. Lastly, many thanks to my friends, family, and colleagues for their words of encouragement and support.

Maya Angelou is one of the premier U.S. poets of the 20th century. (National Archives)

Maya Angelou

"I will not allow anybody to minimize my life, not anybody, not a living soul—nobody, no lover, no mother, no son, no boss, no President, nobody" (119). These words spoken by Maya Angelou (1928–) to writer Judith Patterson during an interview in the September 1982 issue of *Vogue* provide the unofficial thesis for the writer's entire career. Heralded as one of the great contemporary writers of African American and women's literatures, throughout her life and career, Angelou has done it all. In a life that has spanned eight decades and several continents, she has been a singer, dancer, actress, director, the first black female railcar conductor in San Francisco, and part-time madam.

The vast majority of what readers know about Angelou stems from her six-volume autobiography that spans the nearly 40 years of her life, from the day she boarded the train for Stamps, Arkansas, to the day she wrote the first line of *I Know Why the Caged Bird Sings*. Angelou has turned the modern autobiography into an art form. She accepted the challenge of friends who encouraged her to write about her life. She set out, determined to bring literary value to the autobiography. She has done so by masterfully using language and speech to articulate identity. Angelou's iconic significance comes from her extraordinary ability to tell her story as a black woman in America in a fashion that validates the experiences of those like her. However, Angelou's writings transcend race, sex, and class and simply speak to the human condition, making her a favorite among scholars and everyday readers.

Angelou was born Marguerite Johnson on April 4, 1928, in St. Louis, Missouri. Angelou was the second child born to Vivian Baxter Johnson and her husband Bailey Johnson Sr. Angelou adored and idolized her brother Bailey Jr., who was only a year older than she. It was her brother who gave her the name Maya, which she would adopt professionally as an adult. As a child, Bailey refused to call his sister Marguerite and usually addressed her as "Mya sister," which was shortened to "My" and eventually "Maya." When Angelou was three, her parents divorced, and she and her brother where sent to live with their paternal grandmother in Stamps, Arkansas. This is where *I Know Why the Caged Bird Sings,* the first of Angelou's six-part autobiography, commences.

I Know Why the Caged Bird Sings, Angelou's most critical and commercial success, chronicles her life from the age of 3 to 16. In addition to telling the story of Angelou's life, the coming-of-age story, whose title derives from a line in the Paul Laurence Dunbar poem "Sympathy," gives insight into the political and social implications of race in the United States in the 1930s and early 1940s. The prologue of the book introduces the reader to the young Angelou. As she tries to recall the lines to a poem during a church program, Angelou wonders how surprised everyone will be when she wakes from her "black ugly dream" and emerges with blond hair and blue eyes (*Caged Bird* 2). Angelou establishes herself as a young girl with troubles regarding her identity, her looks, her purpose, and her place in the world. The young Angelou's desire to be white establishes the prevalence of racism in the rural South and how it affects even the smallest child. The young Angelou equates being white with being better. This questioning battle with race and racism is a theme that is carried out throughout the book.

In *I Know Why the Caged Bird Sings,* a three-year-old Angelou travels from California to Arkansas accompanied by her brother Bailey, armed only with their tickets and a note addressed "To Whom It May Concern." The two make the journey to Stamps assisted by the kindness of the black strangers who watch over and feed them. Upon their arrival, the children are united with their grandmother, Annie Johnson Henderson. The children's grandmother is a hardworking, independent, God-fearing woman. In a television interview for Lifetime Television, Maya once stated that her grandmother talked to God like he was her uncle. She started each day thanking God for allowing her to see the new day.

Annie Henderson owns The Store, which is the center of the black side of Stamps. The family, which also includes Maya's Uncle Willie, lives in the rear of The Store. Willie is partially paralyzed as a result of being dropped as a child. Despite his physical limitations, Uncle Willie is strong and his mother is always sure to tell people that he was not born that way. The importance of family is emphasized in *I Know Why the Caged Bird Sings*. Before long, Maya and Bailey begin calling their grandmother "Momma," and they think of Uncle Willie as a surrogate father. Momma provides Angelou with her moral and spiritual center. She teaches Angelou that she has the power to control her own destiny, despite the personal tragedies life has dealt her.

Life in Stamps consists of working in The Store, going to school, and attending church. The Store itself, always referred to with a capital "S," serves as a symbol of economic independence and prosperity. Although not rich by any means, the Henderson-Johnson family is established and respected. During picking season, Maya watches the pickers enter The Store early in the morning, optimistic and hopeful of the day's work. However, when evening comes around, they are defeated and disappointed, realizing that they cannot possibly pick enough to pay their debts. For Maya, these men represent the cruel reality of black southern life. In *I Know Why the Caged Bird Sings,* Angelou describes the segregation that exists in Stamps. The small town is divided into two separate worlds. Angelou explains that most black children did not even know what whites looked like. She explains that she personally did not believe they were real. The young Angelou does not think of them as people, but rather as "whitefolks" (*Caged Bird* 26). They are not human beings.

In the small town, Angelou comes face to face with the harsh and painful realities of racism. These encounters, which often enrage Maya, also teach her about the prevailing spirit of black people. Momma maintains The Store during the Depression era, providing a sanctuary of sorts for the black community. Her attitudes about whites and how she interacts with them first cause Maya to question her grandmother. In one instance, the young white girls who live on the property come into the front of The Store and proceed to mock and imitate Momma. Momma does not react in the face of the mockery; instead, she stands firm and hums a gospel hymn. Maya is enraged and bursts into tears while watching the scene. However, when she returns to The Store, Maya realizes that a gallant change has occurred in Momma. She realizes that Momma is a survivor who is strategic in the battle she chooses to fight. Later on, when Momma decides to protect a black man from a lynch mob, despite the consequences, she proves herself to be brave and valiant. She is a pillar in the community who is always respectfully addressed by blacks as "Miss," which was uncommon during the 1930s. From Momma, Maya learns a good work ethic, patience, and that she controls her own destiny.

Despite the stable home that Momma provides for Maya and her brother, Maya still has feelings of being unloved, unwanted, and abandoned. This stems from her nonexistent relationship with her parents. As a young child, Angelou has naturally assumed that her parents are dead. Her world is turned upside down when she learned that they are not dead, and her father comes to Stamps to collect Angelou and her brother. Angelou's recollections of her father are less than favorable. Maya describes him as an almost mythical figure that does not belong in the rural South. In addition to being an outsider in Stamps, he is a stranger to Maya. When he arrives in town and then drives Maya and Bailey to St. Louis to live with their mother, she is suspicious and wary of his intentions. In her opinion, she is being shuttled from one stranger to another. However, in St. Louis, Angelou is introduced to the Baxter side of her family. Her mother Vivian Baxter, an outgoing beauty who wears red lipstick, completely enraptures her children. Angelou is almost overwhelmed by the similarities between her mother and brother. She does not believe that she can be related to such a beautiful woman. Maya's disconnection from her parents echoes the feelings of displacement that she alludes to in the prologue of the text. Throughout her life, these feelings continuously resurface.

St. Louis is also the scene of one of the most horrific incidents in Angelou's life. One morning, months after another incident of inappropriate fondling, Angelou is sexually assaulted by her mother's boyfriend, Mr. Freeman. Because she is terrified by his threats to kill her beloved brother, Bailey, the young Maya remains silent about the attack. When she reveals what has happened, her attacker is arrested. During the trial, the attorney asks Maya whether Mr. Freeman ever touched her before the attack. Scared, she replies, "No." After the trial, conviction, and subsequent beating death of her attacker, Maya retreats and enters a five-year-long, self-imposed silence. She believes that her voice and her lie caused the man's death. As a result, from age 8 to 13, Maya refuses to speak to anyone other than Bailey. Maya's self-imposed silence leads to many changes in her life. She and Bailey are sent back to Stamps, Arkansas to live with Momma and Uncle Willie. Maya never knows whether Momma sent for her or whether her St. Louis family sent her away. Regardless, her feelings of being unwanted return. However, in Stamps her silence is more accepted. During this time, a deeper bond and sense of understanding builds between

Maya and Bailey. She understands his newly adopted penchant for sarcasm, a result of his separation from his beloved mother, and he understands Maya's need for silence.

Angelou's lifelong love of learning and literature is birthed while she is living in Stamps. During Maya's period of silence, the written word becomes a needed escape for her. At age nine, she begins her love affair with writing. She becomes a voracious reader and feels connected to the words of William Shakespeare and Charles Dickens. Under the guidance of Mrs. Bertha Flowers, a woman who Maya refers to as an "aristocrat of Black Stamps" (*Caged Bird* 70), Maya reads all of the books in the school library. Starting with A and continuing through Z, she reads for the joy of reading. It is Mrs. Flowers who encourages Maya to use her voice again. After a visit that included cookies baked especially for Maya, Mrs. Flowers assigns her the task of memorizing a poem and reciting it during her next visit. Using the words of others helps Maya to overcome her fear of using her own voice. For Maya, Mrs. Flowers is the first female hero that she has encountered in her life.

Maya's first assertion of self comes when she works for Mrs. Cullinan, a white woman who calls her "Mary" because her name, "Marguerite," is too long. This infuriates Maya because her name is "Marguerite" and Mrs. Cullinan refuses to learn it. The white woman's act of renaming upsets Maya because it shows a lack of respect and is yet another attempt to minimize Maya as a person. She rejects this notion and sets out to reclaim her identity. Although she cannot confront the woman about her name, Maya forces Mrs. Cullinan to fire her by breaking her china. This is just one example of the racism, both overt and covert, that existed in the rural South. At her eighth-grade graduation, Maya expresses displeasure at the speaker's suggestion that blacks succeed predominantly at sports and not in academics. Although saddened by the blemish on her graduation, Maya is left feeling proud after the singing of "Lift Ev'ry Voice and Sing," led by the class valedictorian.

The effects of racism also take their toll on Momma and Bailey. When the white dentist, Dr. Lincoln, refuses to treat Maya, Momma reminds him that he owes her a favor for a loan that she gave him a while back. When the man maintains that he paid his debt, Momma demands interest on the loan. Although she knows that demanding interest after the fact is wrong, she maintains that the man deserved it. Later, when Bailey sees the body of a black man pulled from a pond, he begins to question why white people hate black people so much. Fearing for her grandson's safety in the rural South, Momma makes arrangements for the children to move to California to be with their mother. Living in San Francisco during World War II provides Maya with many new experiences. For the first time, she attends an integrated school. Additionally, Maya studies dance and drama at the California Labor School. During this time, Maya is becoming more aware of herself. In the ever-changing climate of San Francisco during the war, Maya gains a sense of belonging.

Maya enjoys being reunited with her mother and finds her first real father figure in her mother's new husband, Daddy Clidell. She compares the relationship she has with her father and Daddy Clidell. These differences are made more evident after she spends a summer with her father and his girl-friend. Maya eventually runs away after her father's girlfriend stabs her during an argument. Instead of calling her mother and explaining what happened, Maya spends a month in an abandoned junkyard with a multiracial group of runaway teens. Ruled by a system of morals and guidelines, Maya finds a sense of belonging with the group of castoffs. Of her brief time spent in the junkyard, Maya explains, "I was never again to sense myself so solidly outside the pale of the human race. The lack of criticism evidenced by our ad hoc community influenced me and set a tone of tolerance for my life" (*Caged Bird* 254). When she returns to San Francisco, Maya feels as if she has changed.

Bored by school, Maya sets out to get a job as a streetcar conductor. She eventually defies the odds and becomes the first black conductor in San Francisco. Maya suddenly finds herself on the fast track to adulthood when she realizes that she is pregnant at age 16. After her high school graduation, she tells her parents that she is eight months pregnant. Soon after, Maya gives birth to a son. At the conclusion of *I Know Why the Caged Bird Sings*, Angelou is coming to terms with her new role as a young mother. In the closing scene, aided by the guiding wisdom of her own mother, Angelou learns her first motherly lesson as she shares her bed with her three-week-old son.

I Know Why the Caged Bird Sings finds Angelou moving from place to place with no concrete sense of home. Her search for home and belonging is mirrored by her search for self. Angelou sets out to exemplify the feelings of loneliness and confinement that she feels as a child. Her desire to wake from her "black ugly dream" echoes the experience of all blacks in the South during the Great Depression era. Just as Angelou is trapped, the entire black community is trapped by the pains of racism and poverty (*Caged Bird* 2). Although *I Know Why the Caged Bird Sings* is essentially a story about a girl coming into her own and learning what it means to be a black woman in the United States, the book exceeds expectations and transcends racial and gender lines. *I Know Why the Caged Bird Sings* broadens and redefines the American experience. In 1970, Angelou was nominated for the National Book Award for this work.

In 1974, Angelou published her second autobiography, *Gather Together in My Name*. The book follows the three years after the birth of Angelou's son, Guy. The title is taken from the book of Matthew in the Bible, where God states that "where two or three are gathered together in my name, there am I in the midst of them" (18:19–20 King James Version). In the book, Angelou chronicles her experiences through a series of colorful events, jobs, and relationships. Through it all, Angelou continues to explore the issues that arose in *I Know Why the Caged Bird Sings,* including racism, sexism, and the quest for home.

The maturity that Angelou seems to gain at the end of *I Know Why the Caged Bird Sings* is lost in *Gather Together in My Name.* Instead, Angelou is portrayed as a somewhat reckless young woman who has good intentions but oftentimes falls short of her intended mark. As the book opens, Maya is living with her two-month-old baby in San Francisco with her mother and stepfather. Adopting the moniker Rita, she looks for work when she decides not to return to school. She finds work as a Creole cook and rents a room for her and her son. In San Francisco, Rita experiences her first real love and her first heartbreak. These experiences, coupled with the sage advice of her brother, lead her to relocate to San Diego. There, while working in a diner, Rita meets two lesbian prostitutes. This encounter leads her to become their madame for a brief time. However, she soon realizes the legal trouble that she could possibly get into and retreats to the only home she has ever known, Stamps, Arkansas. Rita's big city attitude eventually gets her in trouble with Momma, and she is sent back to San Francisco to her mother. Again, Momma's views and approach to race relations between blacks and whites force her to send her granddaughter away for her protection.

Determined to make a better life for herself and her son, Rita attempts to enlist in the U.S. Army, but her past association with the California Labor School prevents this from happening. The recruiters deny her application, fearing that she may be a member of the Communist Party. Again, Angelou's story reflects not only her personal journey but exemplifies the experiences of others during the time of her writings. This section of Angelou's autobiography evidences the troubles that plagued many perceived communists during the pinnacle of the Red Scare.

After a brief stint as a dancer and another broken love relationship, Rita falls in love with Lou "L. D." Tolbrook, a gambling man who convinces her to work as a prostitute to help get him out of debt. Believing that it is the least she can do for love, she works and spends time with Tolbrook when she can. Rita is then abruptly forced to leave her job and Guy in Stockton while she tends to her ailing mother and her brother, Bailey, who has just lost his wife to tuberculosis. However, she soon realizes that she has been taken advantage of when she returns and discovers that the babysitter has taken three-year-old Guy. She immediately goes to L. D.'s house for help, but before she can explain her situation, he chastises her for coming to his house, where his wife lives. Feeling defeated and rejected, Rita tracks down her son on her own.

At the conclusion of *Gather Together in My Name*, Rita has just witnessed her latest lover shoot up drugs in the bathroom of a drug haven hotel room. Forever changed by the situation, she realizes that despite the various experiences she has had, she is still unaware of many things about the world. Having reclaimed her innocence, she prepares to return to her mother's house and face her uncertain future.

Gather Together in My Name follows Angelou's story as she travels from place to place trying to establish a home for herself and her son, Guy. During the course of the three years in which the story takes place, Angelou drifts between San Francisco, Los Angeles, and Stockton, and even travels back to Stamps, Arkansas. As she travels from each location, she also tries her hand at various careers, although she generally ends up cooking in some sort of diner or greasy spoon restaurant. It is usually in these restaurants that she encounters the characters that lead her down the wrong path. Each character offers promises and opportunities for her to make money and provide for Guy. However, each eventually leads to some sort of pain or heartache for Rita.

In *Gather Together in My Name,* the reader encounters a very different side of Angelou. The Rita portrayed in this volume is more reckless and aimless than the Maya seen in *I Know Why the Caged Bird Sings.* At a time when many of her peers were entering college and discovering who they were as adults, Angelou had to raise and support Guy when she herself was still a child. In the book, her naiveté and lack of experience often affect her decision-making process. Despite this, after each misstep, Angelou seems to learn some life lesson that aids in her maturation.

Thematically, *Gather Together in My Name* focuses on many ideas that will continue to be addressed in the subsequent volumes of Angelou's story. The experiences of motherhood and what it means to be a mother is one such theme. Angelou's desire to provide for Guy motivates her to make questionable decisions and take several unnecessary risks. However, she rationalizes these because she wants to create a better life for him. When he is abducted by the babysitter with whom she has left him for a week, Rita realizes the consequences of her actions. Her ultimate reunion with him changes her perspective on motherhood and brings clarity to their relationship. Angelou writes: "Separate from my boundaries, I had not known before that he had and would have a life beyond being my son, my pretty baby, my cute doll, my charge. In the plowed farmyard near Bakersfield, I began to understand that uniqueness of the person. He was three and I was nineteen, and never again would I think of him as a beautiful appendage of myself" (*Gather* 163). Rita forgives the babysitter and learns a valuable lesson from her mistakes.

Overall, *Gather Together in My Name* lacks the unity exhibited in *I Know Why the Caged Bird Sings.* Angelou adopts a more anecdotal approach to her life story. The episodes are generally short and highlight the more exciting and sensational aspects of Angelou's life after World War II. Several critics have cited the episodic nature and Angelou's changed character as flaws that exist in the text. But Angelou is honest in her accounts and describes both good and bad experiences with equal passion. Despite the oftentimes dark and bleak existence that Angelou recounts, *Gather Together in My Name* concludes in an ambiguous, yet hopeful manner. In the final line, Angelou writes: "I had no idea what I was going to make of my life, but I had given a promise found my innocence. I swore I'd never lose it again" (*Gather* 181). One can assume that as her story continues, she will continue to grow and mature as a woman and a mother.

Singin' and Swingin' and Gettin' Merry Like Christmas, published in 1976, chronicles Angelou's early career as a singer and dancer. In the opening chapter, Angelou proclaims, "Music was my refuge," and she often spends time at a record store and eventually works and meets her husband there (*Singin'* 1). Angelou explains how music allows her to escape her problems. Like the written word served as a healing balm to the younger Angelou, music serves in the same capacity to the older Angelou. The impact of music in her life will be seen throughout her career and manifest itself in her poetry. Angelou oftentimes intersperses lyrics from songs through her text to give specific moments more meaning and subtext.

In *Singin' and Swingin' and Gettin' Merry Like Christmas,* Angelou recounts her marriage to a Greek ex-sailor named Tosh Angelos. During the first year of their marriage, Angelou busies herself with cooking, cleaning, and maintaining a suitable home for her husband and child (referred to in this text by his given name, Clyde). She is happy that her son, Clyde, has a father figure and she cherishes Tosh's presence in young Clyde's life. However, she is aware of the issues that the difference in their race brings into their relationship. Her mother expresses her concern about the relationship from the beginning, stating that the marriage will give them nothing but "the contempt of his people and the distrust of your own" (*Singin'* 25). Angelou also recounts the stares and strange looks she encounters from whites and blacks alike. As a child of the South, Angelou is fully aware of the troubles that could arise as a result of the union. She rationalizes her own concerns by reminding herself that Tosh is Greek, not white.

Although the marriage initially provides Angelou with the stability that she longs for, she begins to have doubts and questions the impact that the union is having on Clyde in terms of the development of his character and the formation of his racial identity. These fears are heightened when he questions when his hair will begin to look like his father's. Additionally, Angelou's relationship with her husband begins to inhibit her independence, and she feels she is being stifled and trapped. Tosh's strong opinions about having people in their house and his disbelief in God leave Angelou questioning herself and the marriage. In a desperate need to free herself from the caged feelings she is experiencing, Angelou leaves her husband and eventually the couple divorces. Consoling Clyde and making him happy again becomes Angelou's top priority after the divorce. He is devastated when Tosh leaves and questions his mother about his father's absence. She answers as best as she can but feels that Clyde questions whether she will stop loving him too. Angelou understands better than most the impact of an absent parent on a child. In an effort to quell her son's fears, Angelou cooks his favorite meals, spends extra time with him, and does only the things he likes. As time passes, Angelou rebuilds the friendship with her son.

Angelou gets a job as the only black entertainer at a local strip club. Angelou, who dances but does not strip, becomes very popular and angers the three white strippers. They accuse her of promising to sleep with the customers in order to earn extra money. Eventually, the women complain to the club manager. Although she proclaims her innocence, Angelou is put on notice of dismissal from the club. An encounter during her last few weeks at the club leads to her next gig. When hired at the Purple Onion as a Calypso singer, she adopts the name that will become her professional moniker, Maya Angelou. At the Purple Onion, Angelou has great success. Several opportunities come her way, including an opportunity to star on Broadway. However, Angelou turns down the offer for a chance to perform in the European touring company production of *Porgy and Bess*.

A significant portion of *Singin' and Swingin' and Gettin' Merry Like Christmas* is dedicated to Angelou's travels with the touring company. In each European country, Angelou chronicles her experiences as a member of the close-knit community of black singers and dancers. As she recounts her journey, Angelou pays special attention to how black Americans are viewed and how they are treated in the various countries. She discusses the treatment of the cast by hotel personnel and the citizens of the countries they visit. Very often, a distinction is made between black and white Americans in the foreign countries. The black cast is often treated with respect, and Angelou also notes that their status as Americans distinguishes them from the African blacks that inhabit the countries, especially France. As with her previous autobiographies, Angelou observes how race and gender affect her interactions with others.

In *Singin' and Swingin' and Gettin' Merry Like Christmas*, Angelou continues to address the theme of motherhood. After the dissolution of her marriage, Angelou again finds herself living as a single mother faced with the challenge of providing for her son, Clyde. As she contemplates taking the *Porgy and Bess* job, she is faced with the decision of whether or not to leave her son. The decision brings up issues with her own feelings of abandonment as a child. Angelou writes: "The past revisited. My mother had left me with my grandmother for years and I knew the pain of parting. My mother, like me, had had her motivations, her needs. I did not relish visiting the same anguish on my son, and she, years later, had told me how painful our separation was to her. But I had to work and I would be good. I would make it up to my son and one day would take him to all the places I was going to see" (*Singin'* 129). For the first time since his kidnapping, Angelou is separated from her son when she leaves him in California with her mother. Angelou continuously struggles with her decision and the impact that it will have on Clyde in the long run.

Throughout the book, Angelou is conflicted between her duties and responsibilities as a mother, her life as an entertainer, and her desire for personal fulfillment. This guilt manifests itself in a state of depression that she goes through upon her return to San Francisco. Nearly driven to suicide by sadness, she seeks the help of a doctor, but feels that he will not understand her. Instead, she goes to see an old friend and vocal coach who reminds her of the many gifts she has been given. She returns home with a renewed sense of self and purpose.

At the conclusion of *Singin' and Swingin' and Gettin' Merry Like Christmas*, a nine-year-old Clyde is coming into his own. In a marked sign of independence, he announces that he wishes to be called Guy and will no longer respond to his given name, Clyde. This act echoes the similar decision that his mother made when choosing her professional name. Just as Angelou rejected the nicknames "Ritie," "Sugar," and "Rita," because they did not represent who she wanted to be, her son takes similar actions.

Singin' and Swingin' and Gettin' Merry Like Christmas, whose title recalls the African American traditions of late partying and early praising, marks the first time an African American female biographer had written a third volume. This distinction would forever distinguish Angelou from all other female autobiographers. The book also marks the emergence of Maya Angelou, the woman. She has reached a level of maturity that had eluded her up to this point. However, she still struggles with finding balance between fulfilling her roles as mother and daughter and her desire to be a satisfied individual.

As the title suggests, Angelou's fourth volume of her autobiography, *The Heart of a Woman,* marks Angelou's transition into full womanhood. The title is taken from a poem by Georgia Douglas Brown, of the same name. In the Douglas poem, a woman's heart is likened to a caged bird. In classic Angelou style, the author begins the book by framing the story both time wise and thematically. In *The Heart of a Woman,* Angelou continues to address issues such as racism in her autobiography. One such encounter occurs when she tries to rent a house in a predominantly white California neighborhood. The owner tells her that the house has already been taken. However, the house miraculously becomes available when her white friend tries to rent it on her behalf, unbeknownst to the owner. Later, when her son Guy is denied school bus privileges because he explained where babies come from to a group of white girls, Angelou decides to move to a more integrated section of town. Angelou refuses to let the school administrators' racist attitudes affect her son.

Although she still stumbles at times during her journey, the woman that emerges in *The Heart of a Woman* is more confident and secure. Angelou decides to dedicate herself to becoming a professional writer and moves with Guy to New York, where she becomes a member of the Harlem Writer's Guild. After her lukewarm reception the first time she shares her work with members of the guild, Angelou works hard at improving her craft. During this time, she interacts closely with members of the black literary world such as John O. Killens and Paule Marshall. Angelou also returns to acting with a role in the Jean Genet play, *The Blacks.* The play explores the idea of reversed racial roles between blacks and whites. Angelou is initially hesitant about taking the role because she feels that blacks would never treat whites as they have been treated. But she eventually recognizes the satirical nature of the play and agrees to play the role of the White Queen.

As her public persona develops, Angelou becomes a more involved political activist. She meets Martin Luther King Jr. and becomes a key member of his Southern Christian Leadership Conference. For the first time in her journey, Angelou emerges as a leader and role model. She organizes fundraisers to benefit the organization and eventually becomes the northern coordinator for the group. Angelou also emerges as a champion of feminist causes when she joins the Cultural Association for Women of African Heritage. She organizes a sit-in at the United Nations General Assembly after the assassination of Patrice Lumumba, the prime minister of Zaire. Angelou's interest in the state of affairs in African countries represents not only her dedication to politics but also her deep interest in the native land of black people. However, Angelou's primary concern continues to be her son Guy and what is best for him. She goes as far as to threaten to shoot an entire family if a young man, the head of a local gang, does not stop harassing her son. In an effort to be more present in Guy's life, Angelou settles down and refuses to tour any more. She finds contentment and stability in her writing and political work.

However, this changes when Angelou meets Vusumzi Make, a South African freedom fighter. She is mesmerized by him and believes he will make a perfect father for Guy. Angelou disregards the fact that she is engaged to another man and the couple joins in a spiritual (never legalized) union. Angelou interrupts her life and joins her husband Vus in Cairo, Egypt. There, she finds work as an editor for the *Arab Observer* newspaper. Professionally, it is here that Angelou hones her skills as a writer. But her new husband is not thrilled that his wife chooses to work. The idea is foreign to him and his traditional African values. Likewise, Angelou soon realizes that her husband has financial problems, and worse, a wandering eye. Angelou is confronted by some of the same issues that ended her first marriage. She struggles with the idea of male domination and is conflicted between being a wife and homemaker and being a professional woman. In addition, Angelou is often left alone due to her husband's travels. It becomes evident that the union is nearing its end and when a job offer comes from Liberia, Angelou jumps at the opportunity.

The theme and motif of motherhood and the "good mother" continue to manifest themselves in this volume of Angelou's story. *The Heart of a Woman* focuses primarily on Angelou's role as mother. The presence of her own mother is limited after Angelou leaves California for New York. Angelou's purpose continues to be caring for her son. She faces her most challenging time as a mother when Guy is involved in a terrible car crash in Ghana. This single experience is so poignant that Angelou revisits the event in her fifth autobiography, *All God's Children Need Traveling Shoes*. After Guy's accident, Angelou keeps vigil at his bedside. He eventually recovers and enrolls in university. Angelou is determined to take care of every part of her son's life. However, he reminds her that it is *his* life and offers her the chance to grow up herself. In *The Heart of a Woman*, like her previous volumes, Angelou examines the plight of the black mother in America. Angelou is forced to come to terms with the idea that her beloved son is growing into an independent man.

The Heart of a Woman captures Angelou's talent as a master of the character sketch, a talent that she is working on at the time the book is set. Throughout the book, Angelou introduces readers to many well-known historical figures and celebrities. Angelou begins with an encounter with the legendarily troubled singer Billie Holiday. Throughout the course of their brief time together, the two women endure several tense moments. Angelou captures the essence of Holiday and portrays her as moody and unpredictable. She presents a woman on the decline with equal empathy and disdain. The section of the book dedicated to Angelou and Holiday's interactions exhibit Angelou's values as a woman and mother. In contrast to Holiday, Angelou is rather serene. Many critics agree that of her subsequent autobiographies, *The Heart of a Woman* comes closest to matching the level of depth and insight initially displayed in *I Know Why the Caged Bird Sings*.

Angelou's physical journey also continues in *The Heart of a Woman*. Angelou travels from Los Angeles, to Harlem, to Egypt, and eventually ends in western Africa. Angelou offers a woman's perspective and view of the world in which she lives. More than in the previous volumes, Angelou reveals her inner hopes, self-doubts, and regrets. Her honesty and pursuit of heart endear her even more to the audience. In *The Heart of a Woman*, Angelou is much more introspective than in her previous volumes. At the conclusion of this volume Angelou finds herself alone, but not lonely.

In 1986, Angelou published the fifth installment of her autobiography, titled *All God's Children Need Traveling Shoes*. The book is written as one long narrative, giving the reader a continuous firsthand account of Angelou's experiences. *All God's Children Need Traveling Shoes* has the same novelesque feel as her previous memoirs. In this chapter of her emotional and spiritual journey, Angelou recounts the four years she spent living in Ghana. Initially, Angelou arrives in Accra, Ghana, in 1962 with the intention of enrolling her son, Guy, at the local university before leaving for a new job at the Department of Information in Liberia. However, he is involved in a car accident that leaves him with a broken neck. A devastated Angelou stays in Ghana and keeps vigil at his bedside. In time, Guy recovers and enrolls at the University of Ghana, where Angelou eventually finds clerical work.

In *All God's Children Need Traveling Shoes*, Angelou explores the black American experience in a global context. Almost immediately, she expresses the sense of happiness and pleasure she feels in Africa. She declares: "We were Black Americans in West Africa, where for the first time in our lives the color of our skin was accepted as correct and normal" (*All God's* 3). For the first time, Angelou is in a place where she looks like everyone else and is not discriminated against or judged based solely on her skin color. With the assistance of friends Julian Mayfield and Efua Sutherland, Angelou comes to terms with all that occurs after she arrives in Ghana. Despite the less than ideal circumstances, Angelou makes the best of her unexpected home. She meets two fellow Americans, Vicki and Alice, and the three become housemates.

The concepts of home and acceptance are recurring themes in *All God's Children Need Traveling Shoes*. Angelou begins to feel more comfortable in her adopted home. She achieves this with the help of the "Revolutionist Returnees," a group that often meets at Julian's house to discuss politics, civil rights, and Africa. The group is comprised of many black Americans who have journeyed to Ghana for political and social reasons. Some have come to Ghana looking to reconnect with their ancestral roots and find true acceptance. Several of the Returnees have come to Ghana specifically in support of the new Ghanaian president Kwame Nkrumah, who supported black American migration to Africa. Despite the feeling of home, Angelou discovers that many Ghanaians do not share the same open door policy as their president. The country is still in its reconstruction phase following its liberation from Britain a mere five years earlier.

While searching for work at the Ghana Broadcasting Office, Angelou encounters a receptionist who openly criticizes black Americans as being crude. As she reflects on the situation, she wonders if she is being discriminated against because her ancestors were slaves. Again, the theme of home as a place of unconditional acceptance arises. Angelou's recognition of the cultural differences between black Americans and Ghanaians comes when she decides to have her hair styled in the same way that the Ghanaian women wear theirs. The woman who comes to style her hair openly laughs when she finds out that Angelou only has one child. Even in Ghana, where she looks like everyone else, Angelou encounters more subtle forms of discrimination.

Racism is another overarching theme that Angelou establishes in *All God's Children Need Traveling Shoes*. In her personal life, Angelou has never been one to tolerate racism against any group, black, white, or otherwise. In the book, she recounts an episode in which an English professor, a Yugoslav woman, and a Ghanaian are discussing the Civil Rights Movement in America. The Englishman expresses his opinion that it is ridiculous that the blacks in America are still upset about their treatment so many years after the end of slavery. He also makes a discourteous remark about the government of Ghana. The Yugoslav and the Ghanaian agree with him. Angelou erupts in anger and tells the group how ignorant she believes them to be. This incident is significant in the narrative for several reasons. First, it once again brings slavery and its effects to the forefront of the memoir. Additionally, it gives the reader insight into attitudes of Europeans regarding the plight of the black American. Lastly, the episode gives insight into Angelou's character and her position on race.

Although not the most prevalent issue in the memoir, the role of women in society is explored in Angelou's relationship with her suitor, Sheikhali. Although Angelou enjoys the company of the man, she cannot understand his attitude toward women. Sheikhali is looking for a traditional, passive African woman. He eventually proposes marriage to Angelou and suggests that she become his second wife and educator to his eight children. The fiercely independent Angelou is understandably outraged and refuses his proposal. Again, Angelou's relationship with the man in her life does not fulfill or satisfy her personal life and goals.

An encounter with the family of Kojo, a boy hired by Angelou to work around the house, gives her a deeper understanding of the Ghanaian and African culture. She has been tutoring the young boy and helping him with his homework since he was hired and expressed to her that he was in school. Angelou had assumed that Kojo came from a poor family. However, upon meeting his family, she learns that his family is actually middle class. He has come to work for Angelou because his family thinks it important for him to have a proper white education. They thank Angelou with crates of fresh fruits and vegetables from their farm. They promise more gifts as long as Kojo works with Angelou. At first, Angelou feels as if she has been deceived, and questions

Kojo about why he had not been honest with her. However, Kojo does not understand her questioning. He never thought to tell her about his family life. To Kojo, it is a non-issue. Angelou immediately realizes the naïveté and innocence of the African country. Once again, Angelou comes to recognize that she is and may always be an outsider. Although Angelou desperately wants to find acceptance in this home away from home and reconnect with her ancestral roots, she realizes that black Americans are perhaps too far removed from their African roots.

The assassination attempt on Ghana's President Nkrumah manages to further drive home the disconnection between Angelou, the black American, and her chosen home of Ghana. Although he is not injured in the attack, accusations are soon being hurled toward the black Americans. Many believe that black Americans had been sent by the American government to infiltrate the country, blend in with other blacks, and destroy the country from the inside. During this volatile time, black Americans are deported, arrested, and some are imprisoned. Many of the Returnees, although not directly implicated in any conspiracy, feel betrayed by their chosen country and lose their desire and passion for Ghana.

In *All God's Children Need Traveling Shoes,* Angelou is forced to confront her feelings about Africa's willing participation in the slave trade. Part of Angelou's inability to truly open up to the Ghanaian culture comes from the nagging knowledge that some of the people sold into slavery from Ghana had been sold by their own family members. Angelou finds it difficult to reconcile this disconcerting fact. On a weekend trip to the village of Dunkwa, she passes Elmina Castle, a known holding spot for captured slaves. Angelou is unable to go near because she is haunted by the thought of her ancestors bound and held captive. Although she longs to know about her past, the experience proves to be too much and she continues to Dunkwa. In the village, Angelou is mistaken for a native African and is pleased by the mistake. The next morning, while showering with the other women in the village, Angelou is again teased for only having one child. However, this time she is less offended by the statement. In fact, she views it as a glimmer of hope that she may be finally accepted unconditionally in Ghana. However, this is a false sense of acceptance because the villagers believe her to be a native African.

The American Civil Rights Movement is discussed throughout *All God's Children Need Traveling Shoes.* Angelou's friends in the Revolutionist Returnees group keep constant watch over the events taking place at home in the United States. In support of Martin Luther King Jr.'s March on Washington, the group decides to march at the American embassy. Just before the march is to begin, news breaks that renowned scholar Dr. W.E.B. Du Bois has died. The group is saddened and sings songs in honor of Du Bois. When the marchers reach the embassy, they are confronted by two marines holding an American flag. The marchers know that the flag and the concepts it is supposed to represent, freedom and equality, are not extended to the blacks in America. Angelou and Julian take a written protest inside. At the conclusion of the march, Angelou leaves feeling dejected.

Shortly thereafter, Malcolm X visits Ghana and speaks to a group at Julian's house. He tells the group of his pilgrimage to Mecca and the changes he has made in his personal philosophy about whites in America. Angelou serves as Malcolm's guide throughout his time in Ghana. His visit challenges her to see the issue of racism from the perspective of someone other than herself. When she is angered by the refusal of Dr. Du Bois's widow to meet with Malcolm and arrange a meeting between him and President Nkrumah until the end of his trip, it is Malcolm who gives her perspective on the situation. He reminds Angelou that Mrs. Du Bois is newly widowed.

Angelou's concept of home is again somewhat shattered when she has a heated discussion with her son Guy. After learning that he has a girlfriend who is older than his mother, Angelou attempts to lay down the law and assert her motherly authority. However, she soon realizes that Guy is no longer a child; he is a man. Guy walks away from the argument. Angelou painfully accepts that she must let him be. The relationship between mother and son has changed forever. Angelou is saddened by this discovery and retreats from Ghana to refocus herself.

Angelou travels to Germany and the trip provides more perspective on the issues of race and racism. She goes to Germany to return to acting in a play titled *Die Negers,* which translates to *The Blacks.* While in Germany, she is invited to share a meal with a German man named Dieter and his wife. He allows her to bring a guest and she invites a black Jewish man that she met during the trip. The breakfast the next morning is tense and uncomfortable. Angelou suspects that Dieter is a Nazi, but the couple stays. As they trade stories to lighten the mood and get to know each other, Angelou is disturbed by Dieter's story of the German worker and the bird (*Gather Together in My Name* 169–71) and insists on leaving. This encounter sheds light not only on racial prejudice, but also on religious prejudice; Angelou has very little tolerance for either of these things. Despite this situation, Angelou experiences a healing moment when she sings in Egypt for the Liberian President. At the end of her performance, she describes a scene where blacks from various places in America and Africa collectively sing "Swing Low, Sweet Chariot." Back in Ghana, Angelou and her son reconcile with a greater understanding of one another. She is finally able to accept that her son is a man with his own life. He assures her that this in no way diminishes his love for his mother.

Angelou receives regular updates about America from Malcolm X. When a job opportunity arises to work with him setting up the office of the Organization of Afro American Unity, Angelou agrees to return to the United States. During her last days in Ghana, Angelou has a full-circle encounter that reinforces her search for home. While in a local market place in the village of Keta, Angelou runs into a woman who becomes visibly upset at the sight of Angelou. Inside the marketplace, another woman appears equally disturbed by Angelou's presence. One of her companions is able to translate and informs Angelou that the women are upset because she reminds them of an ancestor who was kidnapped and taken into slavery. They shower her with gifts as many villagers stare and others cry. Angelou believes that she has finally found her true ancestors, the place from where she came. This experience quells her fears that her ancestors had been betrayed by their own family and cements her feelings for Ghana as home. Upon leaving a few days later, Angelou feels as if she will always have a piece of Africa with her.

As with her other memoirs, in *All God's Children Need Traveling Shoes,* through her personal experiences, Angelou shows the reader greater truths that transcend race and gender. The narrative provides a balanced look at racism and prejudice. In the text, Angelou demonstrates that these things come from both blacks and whites and should not be accepted from either of them.

It would be 15 years before Angelou would publish the sixth and final installment of her autobiography. In 2002, *A Song Flung Up to Heaven* was released. When asked about the lengthy delay between *All God's Children Need Traveling Shoes* and *A Song Flung Up to Heaven,* Angelou responded to interviewer Sherryl Connelly, "I didn't know how to write it. I didn't see how the assassination of Malcolm, the Watts riot, the break up of a love affair, then Martin King, how could I get all those loose with something uplifting in it" (2443). Despite her initial trepidation, Angelou does manage to create a final volume that brings her story full circle. The volume covers the four years that begin with Angelou returning to the United States to work for Malcolm X and ends with her writing the first line of *I Know Why the Caged Bird Sings,* at the place where her literary journey began.

In *A Song Flung Up to Heaven,* Angelou recounts the assassination of Malcolm X and its impact on her and the rest of the black community. Upon hearing the news, she locks herself in her bedroom. Soon, she is coaxed out by her beloved Bailey, who takes her out. Angelou, who believes the world will be angered and devastated to the point of rioting, is shocked by the seeming disinterest of the people they encounter. Angelou, who has returned to the United States to work for the cause and join Malcolm's fight, is baffled by the indifference of her people. Her brother explains that in time, the world will understand what Malcolm has done, and the very same people who did not care now would become his biggest champions.

Angelou then moves to Hawaii and revives her career as a nightclub singer. However, after hearing the legendary Della Reese, Angelou vows never to refer to herself as a singer again. She decides to return to the mainland and move to Los Angeles. There, she works as a surveyor in Watts. Angelou recounts the despair that she observes in the mostly black Watts. As she asks the women mundane questions about the houschold products they use, Angelou gains insight into their personal lives. She encounters the hardworking women, the struggles of their unemployed men, and the sense of hopelessness these two factors breed. Angelou captures the sights, sounds, and smells of the Watts riots with an in-depth, firsthand account of the destruction and the reactions of the people in the midst of the chaos.

Later, Angelou joins the Hollywood production of the play *Medea,* directed by Frank Silvera. The play also features Angelou's neighbor, actress Beah Richards. While working on the play, she meets a man named Phil, who teaches her one of the most valuable lessons of her life. An eternal prankster, one afternoon while out for a drive, he parks the car on the train tracks, just as the train is approaching. A terrified Angelou involuntarily relieves herself on her clothes. She immediately gets out of the car and walks home. From this experience, Angelou learns an important lesson: "Believe people when they tell you who they are. They know themselves better than you" (*Song* 92). This lesson continues to ring true in Maya's life when her "husband" comes to America to collect her. The two share some good times in America, and he even manages to win over her friends and neighbors. However, Angelou soon realizes that old habits die hard when she learns that he has another lover. Ironically, the other woman, named Dolly McPherson, becomes one of Angelou's lifelong friends.

Believing there is nothing else for her to do in Los Angeles, Angelou prepares to move to New York. However, before she can leave, her brother informs her that her son Guy has been involved in another car accident, a mere three days after returning to San Francisco. Feelings of motherly guilt are again awakened in Angelou. Despite having nothing to do with the accident that has broken his neck a second time, she somehow feels responsible. The relationship between mother and son has been somewhat strained in recent times and she looks at him as a man who resembles her son. However, once he is able to sit up, she leaves Guy in the capable hands of her mother and goes to New York.

In New York, Angelou visits the Audubon Ballroom, the site of her friend Malcolm X's assassination. There, she tries to peer into the building as her mind is flooded with "What if?" questions. Angelou does not explicitly state whether she is able to find the peace of mind she seeks by visiting the site of the crime. She simply walks away.

Angelou reconnects with friend Jerry Purcell, who becomes a patron, allowing her to improve her writing skills without the burden of financial responsibilities. Additionally, Angelou has the support of friends Rosa Guy, Dolly McPherson, the members of the Harlem Writers Guild, and her dear friend and surrogate brother James Baldwin. Angelou and Baldwin had met in the 1950s but grown much closer since then. He reminds her of her brother Bailey in physical stature and personality. Angelou becomes a fierce defender of Baldwin and opposes anyone who takes issue with him or his lifestyle. The two remain best friends until his death.

In 1968, at a celebration marking the 100th anniversary of the birth of W.E.B. Du Bois, Angelou hears friend Martin Luther King Jr. speak. Afterward, he approaches Angelou about working with him to garner support for the Poor People's March that he is planning. She agrees to give him a month of time following her birthday. On the day of her birthday, as she is making preparations for her party, Angelou learns that Dr. Martin Luther King Jr.

has been assassinated. As with the death of Malcolm X, Angelou retreats into herself. Similarly, her friend James Baldwin forces her out, just as her brother Bailey had done years earlier. Baldwin reminds Angelou that black people survived slavery and would also survive their current predicament.

In 1968, Angelou writes a series of 10 one-hour documentaries for PBS titled *Black. Blues. Black.* Although she has no formal training in television production, Angelou teaches herself everything she needed to know and returns to San Francisco to begin work on the series. Before leaving, Angelou is contacted by Robert Loomis at Random House publishing. He speaks to her about writing an autobiography. Angelou rejects the idea, believing that at 40, she is too young. After several more attempts, Loomis finally convinces Angelou by challenging her and telling her that it is nearly impossible to create autobiography that is literature. Never one to back away from a challenge, Angelou agrees to give it a try.

In the final scenes of *A Song Flung Up to Heaven,* Angelou sits in her mother's kitchen with her trademark yellow legal pad and ballpoint pen and begins to reflect on the plight of the black woman. She recounts her thoughts as she begins to write: "I thought if I wrote a book, I would have to examine the quality in the human spirit that continues to rise despite the slings and arrows of outrageous fortune" (*Song* 210). Throughout her six-volume autobiography, Angelou manages to do this and much more. She ends her sixth volume with the same line that begins her first "What you looking at me for? I didn't come to stay" (*Caged Bird* 1; *Song* 210).

A Song Flung Up to Heaven provides Angelou's audience with greater insight into the impact of some of 20th-century history's most tragic moments. Angelou personalizes events that many have only heard about in unemotional news reports and history books. Thematically, *A Song Flung Up to Heaven* deals with the state of the black community in the face of the assassinations of Malcolm X and Martin Luther King Jr. Angelou compares the reactions to these events as representations of the status of black people and the condition of the black spirit. When Martin Luther King is assassinated, black people are outraged, and Angelou learns that their reaction is for Malcolm as well as Martin.

Overall, *A Song Flung Up to Heaven* provides a sufficient literary end to Angelou's story. She effectively accomplishes what she set out to achieve. The full-circle ending gives a worthy feeling of completion. And despite the somewhat bleak subject matter of the text, Angelou maintains an air of faith and hope for herself, her people, and all humanity. Angelou's true gift lies in her uncanny ability to recount even the ugliest of situations with a poetic beauty that enhances the urgency of the situation at hand.

Several critics have questioned whether Angelou's texts are actual autobiographies. They prefer to categorize them as autobiographical fiction, citing her abundant use of dialogue. In her book, *Maya Angelou: A Critical Companion,* scholar Mary Jane Lupton outlines the expected tenets of the autobiography. And although Angelou's work exceeds the standard length and thematic format, she does maintain the important tenets of structure. However, Lupton suggests that because of the number of volumes, Angelou's works belong in the subgenre of serial autobiography. Lupton also categorizes Angelou in the genre of literary autobiography. Ironically, that classification is in line with the initial challenge she accepted from editor Robert Loomis. Angelou acknowledges that her books do employ some aspects of fiction writing, but she believes herself to be an autobiographer.

The journey motif is the dominant force that connects all six volumes of Angelou's story. *I Know Why the Caged Bird Sings* begins with Angelou on a physical journey to Stamps, Arkansas. In each subsequent volume, Angelou continues to journey from place to place on a quest for self and home. At the conclusion of *A Song Flung Up to Heaven,* Angelou has literally travelled the world, yet finds herself in a sense back where she started (at the beginning of *I Know Why the Caged Bird Sings*). However, Angelou has morphed from a naïve child to a woman sure of herself and her purpose.

In addition to her autobiographies, Angelou has also written several volumes of poetry including *Just Give Me a Cool Drink of Water 'fore I Diiie* (1971), *Oh, Pray My Wings Are Gonna Fit Me Well* (1975), *And Still I Rise* (1978), *Shaker, Why Don't You Sing?* (1983), and *I Shall Not Be Moved* (1990). Oftentimes, Angelou's poetry combines her musical and her social and political background. She uses both to address the same themes that permeate her autobiographies. Angelou focuses on social and political issues that are pertinent to the black experience in America, such as discrimination, racism, survival, and pride. Angelou primarily writes lyrical poems that are infused with the musical rhythms of jazz, blues, and Calypso. She relies heavily on rhyme and repetition, making her poems well suited for performance. She once told interviewer Lawrence Toppman, "I write for the voice, not the eye" (1).

Angelou's first volume of poetry, *Just Give Me a Cool Drink of Water 'fore I Diiie,* was written at the end of the Civil Rights Movement and at the onset of the Black Arts Movement. In *Just Give Me a Cool Drink of Water 'fore I Diiie,* Angelou divides her poems into two sections. In part 1, titled "Where Love is a Scream of Anguish," Angelou includes 20 poems about the ups and downs of love. In part 2, "Just Before the World Ends," Angelou angrily tackles issues of race and racial oppression in 18 poems. Overall, the collection represents her personal and political experiences in the 1960s. In 1972, Angelou was nominated for a Pulitzer Prize for the collection.

In "Letter to an Aspiring Junkie," featured in her first volume of poetry, Angelou addresses what she perceives to be the contemporary effect of slavery and racism. In the poem, she describes the life of the drug-addicted junkie. The intent of the cautionary poem is to sway those who aspire to escape by using drugs away from this path. In a later poem titled "The Pusher," included in *Oh, Pray My Wings Are Gonna Fit Me Well,* Angelou describes the role of the drug dealer in society. In the poem, the dealer proclaims his powers, and brags about his strength and smarts. *Oh, Pray My Wings Are Gonna Fit Me*

Well is divided into five distinct, untitled sections. In the 36 poems, Angelou continues to explore themes of love, social injustices, and other aspects of black life. In the poems, she addresses growing old, lost love, disconnection and isolation, and the effects of slavery.

In *And Still I Rise,* Angelou injects themes of identity and survival. Even the title suggests an air of perseverance that gives the volume a sense of unity and cohesiveness. The book is divided into three sections: "Touch Me, Life, Not Softly," "Traveling," and "And Still I Rise." In "Touch Me, Life, Not Softly," Angelou exemplifies the black female experience. The poems in this section explore the wants, desires, and triumphs of the black woman. One of Angelou's most popular poems, "Phenomenal Woman," appears in this section. The poem is a celebration of womanhood and female sexuality. In "Traveling," part 2 of the collection, Angelou again addresses the effects of discrimination and racism on black America. Lastly, in part 3, "And Still I Rise," Angelou celebrates the resilience of the human spirit in the face of adversity. She begins this section with the popular poem for which the section and collection are named. The inspirational poem is a celebration of life. "Still I Rise" challenges the world to say what it will about the speaker, because regardless of the outside opinion, she will flourish. The poem echoes the resilience of human spirit that recurs throughout Angelou's autobiographies and poetry.

In "And Still I Rise," Angelou focuses on various aspects of love and the romantic relationship. In "Where We Belong, a Duet," Angelou celebrates the joy and happiness of true love. In this poem, she uses rhymed couplets to give the effect of song. In the end, the persona finds true love in a moment of epiphany. In "Men," she addresses the unpredictable nature of love between men and women. Angelou also adopts several personas in her poetry to convey her message. In the poem "The Memory," Angelou adopts the persona of a slave who has long since died. The poem captures the painful lamentations of the slave and exhibits the dehumanizing effects of slavery. Likewise, in "To Beat the Child Was Bad Enough," Angelou creates the image of a slave master exerting his dominating power over a slave child. *And Still I Rise* is Angelou's most critically acclaimed volume of poetry.

Shaker, Why Don't You Sing? was published the year after Angelou's divorce from her third husband, Paul Du Feu. In this volume, Angelou exudes a feminist perspective of empowerment. Many of the lyrical poems in this collection focus on what it means to be a woman. In one of the highlights of *Shaker, Why Don't You Sing?* Angelou returns to the symbol of the captured bird as a metaphor for the black race and the struggles they face in racist America. In the poem "Caged Bird," Angelou alternates between the images of the free versus caged bird. The caged bird longs for the freedom that the free bird experiences, but remains hopeful. In its allusion to a caged bird, the poem is reminiscent of Paul Laurence Dunbar's poem "Sympathy."

Angelou's poetry has been praised more for its subject matter than its style and structure. Themes of the effects of racism, the joys and pain of love, the importance of family, the need for community pride, and the role of the black woman in regards to each of these themes and how she is impacted by and affects them make her poems accessible to the general public. As a poet, Angelou is influenced by the events and experiences of her own life, as well as the poetic renderings of other black female poets. These influences make Angelou's poetry more suitable for performance. As a poet, Angelou has not experienced the same critical or commercial success as with her prose writings.

Ironically, then, it is for her poetry that Angelou has gained her most significant fame. In late 1992, president-elect William Jefferson Clinton requested that Angelou compose a poem to be read for his inauguration. This marked only the second time in history that a poet, and the first time an African American female one, had been asked to participate in a presidential inauguration. On January 20, 1993, Angelou recited her poem "On the Pulse of Morning" at the inauguration. In the poem, Angelou calls for a nationwide commitment to unity in American society. In 1994, the poem was included in *The Complete Poems of Maya Angelou.*

In 1981, Angelou was appointed the first Reynolds Professor of American Studies at Wake Forest University in North Carolina. Initially, the position was to expire in 1985, but the relationship proved to be so rewarding for both parties that it was turned into a lifetime appointment. In the position, Angelou teaches one semester a year, allowing her ample time to work on her own writing. She has taught a wide range of topics over the years, including poetry, philosophy, and theatre, to name a few. The Maya Angelou Film and Theater Collection is housed at the university and contains the manuscripts of many of Angelou's works. In spite of never attending college, Angelou's prolific career and extraordinary life experiences have led to the bestowing of over 30 honorary degrees from schools such as Wake Forest University, Spelman College, Columbia University, and Howard University. She also speaks six languages.

Over the course of her illustrious career, Angelou's has received many awards and nominations. In 1972, Angelou made her Broadway debut in the play *Look Away,* for which she garnered a Tony Award nomination. She also wrote the screenplay for the film *Georgia, Georgia.* The film was the first original script to be produced by a black woman. In 1977, she played the grandmother of Kunta Kinte in Alex Haley's *Roots* and was nominated for an Emmy. She also has three Grammy Awards: she won for Best Spoken Word Album with *On the Pulse of Morning* in 1993, Best Spoken Word or Non-Musical Album with *Phenomenal Woman* in 1995, and Best Spoken Word Album with *A Song Flew Up from Heaven* in 2003.

Angelou has also written and published two collections of essays: *Wouldn't Take Nothing for My Journey Now* (1993) and *Even the Stars Look Lonesome* (1997), which won the 1997 NAACP Image Award for Outstanding Literary Work, Nonfiction. In 1995, Angelou delivered the poem "A Brave and Startling Truth" at the 50th anniversary of the founding of the United Nations. In 2002, Angelou joined forces with Hallmark to create a signature collection of cards and gifts titled *Maya Angelou's Life Mosaic.* In 2004, at the urging of friends, Angelou penned a cookbook that she titled *Hallelujah! The Welcome Table: A Lifetime of Memories with Recipes*. She has also contributed to such magazines as *Essence, Harper's Bazaar, Ebony,* and *Redbook*.

Important Dates and Information

- *Angelou has recorded two musical albums: 1957's* Miss Calypso *(Liberty Records) and 1968's* For the Love of Ivy *(ABC Records).*
- I Know Why the Caged Bird Sings *was adapted as a television movie for the Columbia Broadcasting System in 1979.*
- And Still I Rise *was adapted as a television special by Public Broadcasting in 1985.*
- *Angelou was a series writer on the short-lived television series,* Brewster Place.
- *Angelou wrote all of the poetry for the 1993 film* Poetic Justice.
- *On October 16, 1995, Angelou delivered the poem "From a Black Woman to a Black Man" at the Million Man March in Washington, DC.*
- *In 1998, Angelou made her feature film directing debut on the film* Down in the Delta, *starring Alfre Woodard, Wesley Snipes, and Esther Rolle.*
- *In 2003, www.mayaangelou.com was launched.*
- *In 2006, Maya Angelou played the role of Aunt May and read her original poem "In and Out of Time" in the Tyler Perry film* Madea's Family Reunion.

In 2006, Angelou became a radio personality as part of the XM Satellite Channel Oprah and Friends. Angelou and talk show host Oprah Winfrey met in the 1980s in Baltimore, Maryland. The two became fast friends and Angelou has served as a mentor to Winfrey throughout her career. Over the years, Angelou has made several appearances on *The Oprah Winfrey Show*. Her books have also been selected for the Oprah Winfrey Book Club. In 2005, Angelou was honored at Oprah Winfrey's Legends Weekend, which celebrated and honored 25 African American women in the arts, entertainment, and civil rights. The weekend consisted of a luncheon, white-tie ball, and gospel brunch. In 2008, in honor of Angelou's 80th birthday, Winfrey hosted a lavish party at Donald Trump's Mar-A-Largo Club in Palm Beach, Florida. Angelou had two other celebrations to mark the momentous occasion. One occurred in Atlanta, Georgia, and raised money for the YMCA in her honor. Lastly, her adopted hometown of Winston-Salem, North Carolina, hosted another birthday celebration.

Throughout her career, there have been several constants that have sustained Angelou. She has followed the same routine when it comes to her writing. As she told interviewer Carol Sarler, she checks into a hotel room and writes in longhand on legal pads while lying on the bed. She keeps a bottle of sherry, a deck of cards (for solitaire), a *Roget's Thesaurus,* and a Bible in close proximity. She writes until the afternoon and edits in the evening. Additionally, Angelou's family and friends continue to be her primary focus and the source of her strength. Both her mother and her brother spent their final days in Winston-Salem with Angelou before their deaths in 1991 and 2000, respectively. Today, Angelou has a grandson, Colin Ashanti Murphy-Johnson, and great-grandchildren Caylin Nicole and Brandon Bailey. Her niece Rosa Johnson Butler, the only child of her brother Bailey, serves as Angelou's archivist.

Angelou's contribution to and role in the establishment of contemporary African American literature has been compared to that of Frederick Douglass in the 19th century. Like Douglass, Angelou has managed to articulate successfully the joys and pain of her life while remaining accessible to a broad audience. Angelou represents not only African Americans or women, but all who are dedicated to creating a moral center for themselves, their people, and their country. She has done this by rising above expectations and defeats by telling her story and fighting for the rights of all. Maya Angelou is indeed an American icon.

BIBLIOGRAPHY

All God's Children Need Traveling Shoes. New York: Random House, 1986.
Amazing Peace. New York: Random House, 2005.
A Brave and Startling Truth. New York: Random House, 1995.
Celebrations: Rituals for Peace and Prayer. New York: Random House, 2006.
Even the Stars Look Lonesome. New York: Random House, 1997.
Gather Together in My Name. New York: Random House, 1974.
Hallelujah! The Welcome Table. New York: Random House, 2004.
The Heart of a Woman. New York: Random House, 1981.
I Know Why the Caged Bird Sings. New York: Random House, 1970.
I Know Why the Caged Bird Sings: The Collected Autobiographies of Maya Angelou.
    New York: Modern Library, 2004.
I Shall Not Be Moved. New York: Random House, 1990.
Just Give Me a Cool Drink of Water 'fore I Diiie. New York: Random House, 1971.
Lessons in Living. New York: Random House, 1993.
Mother: A Cradle to Hold Me. New York: Random House, 2006.
Now Sheba Sings the Song. New York: Random House, 1987.
Oh, Pray My Wings Are Gonna Fit Me Well. New York: Random House, 1975.
Poetry for Young People: Maya Angelou. New York: Sterling, 2007.
Shaker, Why Don't You Sing? New York: Random House, 1983.
Singin' and Swingin' and Getting' Merry Like Christmas. New York: Random House,
    1976.
A Song Flung Up to Heaven. New York: Random House, 2002.

And Still I Rise. New York: Random House, 1978.
Wouldn't Take Nothing for My Journey Now. New York: Random House, 1993.

FURTHER READING

Bloom, Harold. *Maya Angelou's "I Know Why the Caged Bird Sings."* New York: Chelsea House, 2004.

Bloom, Harold, ed. *Maya Angelou.* Philadelphia: Chelsea House, 1999.

Connelly, Sherryl. "Maya Angelou, a Life Well Chronicled." *Knight Ridder/Tribune News Service,* April 10, 2002: K2443.

Elliot, Jeffrey M., ed. *Conversations with Maya Angelou.* Jackson: Mississippi UP, 1989.

Gillespie, Marcia Ann, Rosa Johnson Butler, and Richard A. Long. *Maya Angelou: A Glorious Celebration.* New York: Doubleday, 2008.

Kent, George E. "Maya Angelou's *I Know Why the Caged Bird Sings* and Black Autobiographical Tradition." *African American Autobiography.* Ed. William L. Andrews. Upper Saddle River, NJ: Prentice Hall, 1993. 162–70.

Lewis, David Levering. "Maya Angelou: From Harlem to Heart of a Woman." *Washington Post,* 1991: 1–2.

Lisandrelli, Elaine Slivinski. *Maya Angelou: More Than a Poet.* Springfield, NJ: Enslow, 1996.

Lupton, Mary Jane. *Maya Angelou: A Critical Companion.* Westport, CT: Greenwood, 1998.

McPherson, Dolly A. *Order Out of Chaos: The Autobiographical Works of Maya Angelou.* New York: Peter Lang, 1990.

Patterson, Judith. "Interview: Maya Angelou." *Conversations with Maya Angelou.* Ed. Jeffrey M. Elliot. Jackson: U of Mississippi P, 1989.

Sarler, Carol. "A Day in the Life of Maya Angelou." *New York Times Magazine,* December 1987: 50.

Tate, Claudia. "Maya Angelou." *Black Women Writers at Work.* New York: Continuum, 1983.

Toppman, Lawrence. "Maya Angelou: The Serene Spirit of a Survivor." *Charlotte Observer,* 1983: F1–2.

Kimberly Oden

Portrait of 20th-century African American author James Baldwin. (Library of Congress)

James Arthur Baldwin

Born in Harlem, New York, to his mother, Emma Berdis Joynes, and a father he never knew, Baldwin (1924–1987) grew up with a minister stepfather who adopted him, and was the oldest of nine children. James Baldwin stands out as an icon in American literature because he paved the way for blacks and gays alike. He made it okay to step outside the lines that said black men should be what the majority in society said they should be. He served as a beacon and a voice during a time when it was not cool to be black or gay; the combination of both was completely unacceptable and threatening. He famously said: "The power of the white world is threatened whenever a black man refuses to accept the white world's definition." On the heels of slavery, black men during this time were still in the process of paving their way in a socially unjust society, one where members were threatened by their very existence. As the oldest in his family, it would seem that he was accustomed to carrying the burden and being outspoken. His voice was temporarily muffled by his stepfather, as their relationship was strained, but he reclaimed it for himself when he began preaching at the age of 14. Furthermore, it really came forward when he walked away from the ministry and found it again in New York's Greenwich Village. It was here that he started rubbing elbows with the likes of greats like Richard Wright, who helped him to secure a grant that helped him to travel abroad where he found his writing voice.

Previous to that time, he worked as a freelance writer and editor. One resonating trait that resounded after Baldwin walked away from the ministry was his willingness to stand up and speak the truth and share his opinion, despite opposers and naysayers. James Baldwin made it acceptable to be different. Travelling abroad gave him a perspective and insight to put into words his experience as a black man in white America. He cataloged his experiences in numerous novels, short stories, and essays. The various extremes of emotions and encounters influenced him. Being abroad gave him the leeway to consider his personal convictions and decisions and brought him closer to social concerns in contemporary America. As an author, Baldwin allowed himself the space to question and to show and share his own insecurities and unknowns. Despite his brilliant mind, he did not align himself with haughtiness or arrogance. He surrounded himself with people who questioned and did not conform, like Malcolm X and Martin Luther King Jr. He did not allow himself to be selfish and self-centered; he stayed very connected with the movement and the issues relevant to the times. The unapologetic Baldwin is iconic because he did not seek to be.

Baldwin and His Sense of Responsibility

Baldwin carried a great sense of responsibility. For example, during an interview with John Hall, he very candidly spoke about his personal sentiments concerning his status as a writer. During the initial part of the interview, Baldwin, whose early influences not only included his father, but also the church and Charles Dickens, asserted that the strain as a writer encompasses not only writing in simple terms, but also writing without allowing the audience to lead, or in other words dictate what he is attempting to say. Because Baldwin lived according to his own personal standard, he wrote in an unadulterated fashion and without modification.

Like many of his contemporaries, Baldwin wished to be viewed simply as a writer. He refused to be labeled as an African American writer. For example, in an interview with Francois Bondy, Baldwin frequently distinguished himself as a writer and not simply a Negro writer.

Reading Baldwin's literature, one can see his ongoing dialogue and conversation with himself and simultaneously humanity. Baldwin's use of third-person pronouns helps his readers to become encompassed in his literature and relate to his content. He was not embarrassed to address the matters of the church, as if they were off limits; he did not adhere to social conventions. No one thing was beyond comment if it was in the public space. His iconic status is so appropriate and fitting because he did not seek it. He simply spoke his mind intelligently and through his interactions and personal discourse provoked and propelled original thought and discussion. Baldwin's writings implied and simultaneously declared that it was admissible not to know everything. He rather silently encouraged others to be, to do, and to live who they were in spite of what others deemed appropriate. Baldwin's works are also iconic because he wrote about the human experience, and this is always relevant because there is no experience or emotion that we cannot all relate to or share. Baldwin's traveling abroad released him from the silent, confining lines of social and racial injustice in America; it freed him and simultaneously helped him to write and speak without inhibitions. This is something that a lot of writers had to contend with, especially if they had sponsors or were concerned with community backlash, something Baldwin cared nothing about because he was not writing to be popular. Baldwin was a definite forerunner of individualism.

Not knowing his biological father and having a strained relationship with his stepfather may also have played a major role in his development as a young man. His heavy involvement in the political did not necessarily mean he was a Black Nationalist. He did not favor blacks over whites. He simply spoke his truth and did not show favoritism. He used his experience to say something about the larger society and to highlight the interconnectedness of the human experience. Baldwin was a man who lived in obscurity in regards to private matters in his personal life and was willing to stand in isolation to live according to his personal convictions and standards. The majority of his works cover racial and sexual issues and topics. Other influences include his admiration of Beauford Delaney, Richard Wright, and Philippe Derome. Baldwin met Lucien Happersberger; the two were involved in a close relationship until Happersberger married a woman three years later, which left Baldwin heartbroken. Dealing with his experiences in the pulpit also shaped him as a writer, even in his later years. Before dying of stomach cancer on December 1, 1987, he continued to travel abroad and within the United States, although not as often as he did in his youth, penning and sharing his experiences. His final writings were a collection of essays titled *The Evidence of Things Not Seen* (1985), based on the 1980 Atlanta child murders.

Because of Baldwin's thematic scope, which encompasses identity in relation to being a black man in America, homosexuality, interracial relationships, and brotherhood, his works continue to be widely read and considered in academic circles around the world. Baldwin discusses the plight and condition of the black American, not as a victim, but rather as an active agent who can ascertain his own future despite hardship and socioeconomic status. The underlying theme in Baldwin's work entails a search for identity that essentially leads to one's own personal ideal. Baldwin actively participated in the Civil Rights Movement and interacted with key and various fellow participants of the movement such as Martin Luther King Jr. and Malcolm X. He also participated on the public speaking/lecture circuit. His extensive travel and friendships with other key black leaders gave him a broad and expansive scope. Unlike writers who had sponsors and wrote according to their guidelines, Baldwin wrote unapologetically according to his own personal standard, which displeased his critics, who did not agree with his liberal stance on sexuality. His use of language and diction creates a strong cadence that can be attributed to following in his stepfather's footsteps and serving in the pulpit as a preacher for three years. Until the time of his death, he was working on a tri-biography about Medgar Evers, Martin Luther King Jr., and Malcolm X. Despite the fact that he developed cancer of the esophagus, he continued to interact and spend time with his family, to live, to write, and to work on other projects until his passing. He died on December 1 and was buried in Hartsdale, New York, on December 8, 1987.

Thematically, many of Baldwin's works centered on the church, and the lives his characters led showed the inward and outward manifestation of those caught in confining standards of religion during that time. In his drama *The Amen Corner,* through the creation of Margaret, the initial pastor of the church, and her son, readers are able to view and consider what happens when individuals are not balanced, or as the old saying goes, so heavenly bound that they are no earthly good. Such is the theme in *Go Tell It on the Mountain,* which is a book organized into prayers by each of the main characters. The novel also discusses the hypocrisy of members of the church, who from the outside looking in are supposed to be enlightened and know better. Through dialogue and character description, each section allows the reader to understand the thought process and possible reasons why Florence and Gabriel, for instance, conduct themselves as they do in their adult life. Baldwin speaks to what happens when people use their religion to avoid dealing with their demons and issues of the past. The plot of the novel can be compared to the biblical story of Abraham, Isaac, and Ishmael.

In his essay titled "Everybody's Protest Novel," Baldwin highlights how the canonized novel *Uncle Tom's Cabin* glazed over the truth and the reality of slavery. The absence of characters who exercised agency should be considered because their absence represented the acknowledgment, and the lack thereof, of the black voice. According to Baldwin, author Harriet Beecher Stowe created and constructed black characters according to her personal standards and taste, which left them as a mere servant who had no issue with his station in life. Baldwin contends that the protest novel, the novel that was supposed to speak to the truths American slavery, fails in its purpose because it rejects reality. Similarly, in *Carmen Jones*, according to the majority standard, the Negro is amoral. When paralleled with whites, the Negro always ends up on the extreme that paints him as the bad and unacceptable standard. Baldwin argues that the movie *Carmen Jones* is stereotypical in that the writers, through characterization and music, paint an implied and explicit depiction of the Negro that when considered wholly, reveals the interior of America and how deeply disturbed people are.

In his essay "Many Thousands Gone," Baldwin not only discusses the role of music in Hollywood film during this time but also highlights how the American Negro has been situated in every aspect of life as separate from humanity and thus has a separate dehumanization. Baldwin posits that the Negro is not human because in order for him to become human, he must be tamed in a manner that causes him to be acceptable. He must be tamed and modified according to the majority standard in order to exist. Baldwin continues by asserting that Richard Wright's *Native Son* is the only true celebration of the American Negro.

In "The Harlem Ghetto," Baldwin discusses the overcrowding and congestion of Harlem and personifies Harlem as a careless human, a conundrum of Negro leadership. Baldwin coins the term *Negro leadership* to question how a Negro was to be a leader in the true sense of the word if at any moment he could be confined to standards imposed on him by the majority. Baldwin highlights Negroes' hardships in conjunction with their lasting physical and psychological effects, as well as comparing the plight and condition of Negroes to the lives of the Jewish.

In "Journey to Atlanta," written after visiting Atlanta, Baldwin shares the fact that even though the Negro is not a priority in America, the state of politics shows that change, however slow, is coming to the United States. At this time, Negroes were used as pieces and pawns in the political game, did not have power in the political process, and were not seen as American, but change was still coming. Baldwin acknowledged how political parties, such as the Progressive Party, outwardly embraced the Negro, but only did so in order to push their political agenda. An example of this was the musical group Melodeers, organized by members of the Progressive Party, who sang in various churches on Sunday mornings. The Melodeers primed the hearts of the people so that they would be open and receptive to the smokescreen promises of the party; this is an example both of using the Negro for political gain and giving no consideration to the Negro as an active agent, a human being.

In "Notes of a Native Son," Baldwin recalls being the oldest of nine children and his responsibilities as a child. He talks in depth about his relationship with his father growing up and how the two did not get along because both were stubborn, which is referenced in his novel *Go Tell It on the Mountain*. Baldwin's father, who was a preacher, was a part of the first generation of freed men who moved north in 1919. Just like the children in the novel, Baldwin and his siblings grew up in fear of their father and did not invite friends over because they might encounter his wrath. As a minor, Baldwin did not understand why his father, who died of tuberculosis, was such a bitter man. As an adult, once he traveled overseas and reflected on it, he realized that his father died a bitter man because of his life and the power of white people in the world. Baldwin, too, drank from this bitter cup in his adult life and fully understood his father once he had left the country and returned. His return led to an epiphany about the reality of the American Negro's station in life.

BIBLIOGRAPHY

Another Country. New York: Vintage, 1990.

"Blues for Mr. Charlie." *Contemporary Black Drama: From* A Raisin in the Sun *to* No Place to Be Somebody. Ed. Clinton F. Oliver and Stephanie Sills. New York: Scribner's, 1971.

The Fire Next Time. New York: Modern Library, 1995.

Giovanni's Room. New York: Dell, 2000.

Going to Meet the Man. New York: Dial, 1965.

Go Tell it on the Mountain. New York: Dell, 1981.

If Beale Street Could Talk. New York: Dial, 1974.

Nobody Knows My Name. New York: Vintage, 1993.

Nobody Knows My Name: More Notes of a Native Son. New York: Dial, 1961.

Notes of a Native Son. Boston: Beacon, 1984.

The Price of the Ticket: Collected Nonfiction 1948–1985. New York: St. Martin's, 1985.

FURTHER READING

Eckman, Fern Marja. *The Furious Passage of James Baldwin*. London: Michael Joseph, 1968.

Harris, Trudier. *Black Women in the Fiction of James Baldwin*. Knoxville: U of Tennessee P, 1985.

Harris, Trudier. *New Essays on Baldwin's "Go Tell It on the Mountain."* New York: Cambridge UP, 1996.

Keenan, Randall. *The Cross of Redemption: Uncollected Writings of James Baldwin*. New York: Pantheon, 2010.

Leeming, David. *James Baldwin: A Biography*. New York: Knopf, 1994.

Macebuh, Stanley. *James Baldwin: A Critical Study*. London: Michael Joseph, 1973.

Porter, Horace A. *Stealing the Fire: The Art and Protest of James Baldwin*. Middletown, CT: Wesleyan UP, 1989.

Pratt, Louis H. *James Baldwin*. New York. Twayne, 1978.

Standley, Fred L., and Louis H. Pratt. *Conversations with James Baldwin*. Jackson: UP of Mississippi, 1989.

Sylvander, Carolyn Wedin. *James Baldwin*. New York: Ungar, 1980.

Troupe, Quincy. *James Baldwin: The Legacy*. New York: Simon, 1989.

Jasmin J. Vann

Poet Sonia Sanchez speaks during a news conference at the opening of the *Freedom's Sisters* exhibition at the Cincinnati Museum Center on March 14, 2008. The Smithsonian traveling exhibit tells the story of 20 African American women who helped to shape the Civil Rights Movement. (AP Photo/David Kohl)

Black Aesthetic

The term *Black Aesthetic,* most frequently used in reference to African American literature, was coined during the 1960s, but represents an artistic movement in African American literary history that dates back to writers of the 19th century. The Black Aesthetic is iconic because it has given "value" to artistic elements that are unique to the African American experience, leading to the canonization of writers such as Langston Hughes, Zora Neale Hurston, and Richard Wright. An understanding and appreciation of the Black Aesthetic within the academy has also made it easier for the works of contemporary writers like Toni Morrison to be added to the American literary canon.

"Black Aesthetic" delineates the elements and recurring tropes within African American literature that distinguish it from other racial aesthetics. Broadly speaking, the Black Aesthetic is characterized by the following elements: (1) the black writer speaks directly to a black audience; (2) the work contains a call for revolution; (3) the work emphasizes the rejection of Western ideology; (4) the work rejects the notion of art for art's sake and instead privileges art that serves a social and political function; and (5) the work incorporates African American musical styles and folk culture (i.e., black vernacular, blues, jazz). To fully comprehend the Black Aesthetic, it is important to map its evolution—from its inception in the 19th century to its apex in the 1960s.

Literary scholar Reginald Martin uses the term *original* Black Aesthetic when discussing 19th-century African American writers whose work espoused similar aesthetic qualities to those on which late 20th-century African American writers prided themselves. Martin positions Frederick Douglass and David Walker as leaders in this movement because of the "call to physical resistance of white oppression" within their literary works (21). Martin's assertion subverts the belief that the revolutionary element in African American literature only manifested itself during the mid-20th century. Martin further argues that the difference between 19th-century African American writers and contemporary African American writers was the hope of the former to eventually assimilate into American society. Martin's argument echoes the belief of many contemporary African American writers who, as opposed to Martin, deny the role of late 19th- and early 20th-century African American writers in the Black Aesthetic. These writers usually accused their literary predecessors of being too preoccupied with becoming "American" instead of appreciating their unique African identity. W.E.B. Du Bois's often quoted term "double consciousness" expresses this tension that African Americans have dealt with in regards to understanding their place within American society.

One author to consider when discussing this phenomenon is the 19th-century poet Paul Laurence Dunbar. In his essay "Negro in Literature" (1899), Dunbar expresses the belief that art produced by African Americans will be very similar to art produced by white Americans, since blacks in America are essentially more American than African. When asked by a reporter if there was something native, or African within black art, Dunbar responds by saying, "We must write like white men. I do not mean imitate them; but our life is now the same" (172). Although many African American writers shared Dunbar's sentiment, there were other writers who believed that there was something essentially African about black art and the black experience, and it was this element that empowered it.

Another writer whose work is evidence of the presence of an earlier Black Aesthetic is the prolific author Charles Chesnutt. Chesnutt's book *The Conjure Woman* (1899) is one of the first African American texts that figures a main character who is a positive representation of the African American folk. Uncle Julius, the main character, speaks in black vernacular and uses his superstition as a means to obtain what he wants from the white narrator, John. Chesnutt juxtaposes Uncle Julius's use of black vernacular to John's use of Standard English, and Julius's superstition to John's blatant disregard for black folk beliefs, in order to emphasize the relevance and potency of Julius's folk culture. Julius's blackness does not hinder him but instead gives him agency.

Similarly, many of Pauline Hopkins's texts espouse the Black Aesthetic belief of rejecting Western ideology. Hopkins's *Of One Blood* (1902) subverts the myth of black inferiority by locating African American ancestry in Ethiopia, which Hopkins posits as the original birthplace of civilization. Hopkins urges African Americans to take pride in their rich ancestry instead of disassociating themselves from it. The text ends with the main character settling in Ethiopia rather than returning to the United States. Hopkins uses her text as a way to encourage African Americans to reject Western ideology and to embrace their Africanness.

The Black Aesthetic notion of incorporating African American musical styles was also relevant during these early years. James Weldon Johnson's *The Autobiography of an Ex-Colored Man* (1912) discusses the significance of ragtime in the development of the American musical tradition. Through his novel, Johnson suggests that the innate musical acumen of the African American progenitors of ragtime is equivalent to the extensive training that many classical artists have. In addition, when discussing ragtime, the narrator asserts that it has an international appeal, suggesting that like classical music, it has gained fame among people of all races and nationalities. Essentially, Johnson's text subverts the misconception that black art is lower than white art and instead makes both equivalent.

As the 20th century progressed, African Americans continued to struggle to validate their art in the eyes of white America. There were constant debates within African American literary circles about the role of the black artist. Langston Hughes's seminal essay, "The Negro Artist and the Racial Mountain" (1926), brilliantly addresses the issue of the black artist finding inspiration for his work from within the black race. Consequently, there was a shift among many African American writers toward the incorporation of the folk and African American folk traditions in their work. Additionally, as Alain Locke asserts in "Negro Youth Speaks" (1925), African American writers of this generation became more aware of catering to a black audience. Race pride was seen as essential to uplifting the black race—emotionally, psychologically, spiritually, and socially—and accurate and favorable depictions of the folk were seen as essential to establishing a Black Aesthetic. Writers such as Claude McKay, Zora Neale Hurston, and Sterling Brown positioned the folk as the primary characters in their texts. For example, while McKay's *Home to Harlem* focuses on the role of the folk in the North, Hurston's *Their Eyes Were Watching God* and Brown's *Southern Road*, focused on the folk of the South. Specifically, Brown's *Southern Road* (1932), a collection of poetry, is a call for African Americans to return to their southern roots. He criticizes the mindset of blacks who have migrated north and have espoused the ideals of capitalism. Brown beckons for black people to return to the South—the place he positions as the site of authentic black identity. One of the most powerful and influential poems within the collection is Brown's famous "Ma Rainey" poem. Not only does Brown accurately portray the intense emotion embodied within the folk, but more important, he also elevates the blues singer to the position of messiah amongst her people. Thus, Brown follows in the tradition of black aestheticians like Langston Hughes, who used African American folk music as a medium through which to express the black condition in America.

The rejection of art for art's sake, a critical component of the Black Aesthetic, and an emphasis on the political function of art, were especially prominent during this period. With black people continually disenfranchised and with the Ku Klux Klan in flux, many African American writers believed that "art for art's sake" was not useful in ameliorating the conditions of African Americans. In "Criteria for Negro Art" (1926), W.E.B. Du Bois asserts that his own writing "has been used always for propaganda for gaining the right of black folk to love and enjoy" (259). Poets such as Georgia Douglas Johnson, Countee Cullen, and Claude McKay used their poetry to bring issues about racial identity, segregation, class, and the many other injustices that plagued the black community to the forefront. These writers understood the power of the written word and sought to improve the status of their people by using their work as both a call to revolution among blacks and a wakeup call for whites.

The onset of the Civil Rights Movement created new tensions in America and caused African American writers to take a proactive approach to combating social injustice. Richard Wright's essay "Blueprint for Negro Writing" (1937) was integral in establishing what would develop into the Black Aesthetic commonly associated with the last half of the 20th century. In this seminal work, Wright argues that African American writers of the past were too passive and suggests that they "went a-begging to white America" (1380). Wright set a precedent with his novel *Native Son* (1940) of a militant, proactive literature. Although many African American writers during the 1950s such as Melvin Tolson and Gwendolyn Brooks strayed away from writing "protest" literature as a result of integration (as Arthur P. Davis asserts in his essay "Integration and Race Literature"), social conditions in the United States would prove that despite what appeared to be social progress, there was still much improvement to be made in regard to black/white relations.

Lorraine Hansberry's *A Raisin in the Sun* (1959) is an example of how African Americans still struggled during the time of integration. The play depicts various reasons why the incorporation of a Black Aesthetic was still integral to combating racism in the United States. Hansberry was bold in creating an African American family who, despite their struggles, committed themselves to fighting against racism collectively. The Black Aesthetic idea of embracing one's African heritage is embodied primarily in the character Beneatha. Beneatha's rejection of George's assimilationist ideology, and her admiration and espousal of Asagai's African heritage, challenge the dominant ideology of the time that suggested that beauty and success were synonymous with whiteness. What would follow in the 1960s would be a group of young African American artists who would espouse Wright and Hansberry's militancy and add a new dimension to the Black Aesthetic.

In his essay "The Black Arts Movement" (1968), Larry Neal, one of the prominent voices of this movement, discusses the "new" Black Aesthetic and argues that in addition to art speaking directly to the African American community, participants within this movement would create a "radical reordering of the western cultural aesthetic" (29). Neal further argues that what is different about this generation of writers is that they understood that there were two Americas—one white, and one black. Instead of espousing the hope of their literary predecessors who believed in one united country, this "new breed" of artists believed that their energy should be focused solely on catering to black America. What specifically distinguishes the Black Aesthetic of the 1960s from the original Black Aesthetic is the privileging of the oral and performed (poetry and drama) over the written (prose), the use of a profane and violent rhetoric, and the direct connection to a black political movement.

The privileging of poetry over other literary forms was linked solely to its accessibility to the masses. Artists of this generation believed that the message contained within their work was so critical to the betterment of African Americans that lack of finances and education should not hinder one's access to this material; thus, poetry performances were popularized in order to achieve this goal. The language that was used in poetry was also very distinct to this Black Aesthetic. In addition to the espousal of the language of the everyday black man, these artists also used very violent and profane words. As Larry Neal suggests, this type of language was necessary because "Poems are transformed from physical objects into personal forces" (37). Experimenting with numerous Western forms of poetry was taboo; the artists wanted poetry that would figuratively pierce the listener's flesh. The metaphor of words as bullets was common among the literature of this generation, and Amiri Baraka's (LeRoi Jones) poem "Black Art" is well known for its espousal of this doctrine. Here, Baraka argues that poems are useless unless they "shoot," or are "daggers" or "fists." Similarly, drama was also seen as a more accessible art form than the novel.

During the 1960s, black theatre production groups were on the rise throughout the country, and many African American writers turned to drama as a form of artistic expression. *Black Fire: An Anthology of Afro-American Writing* (1968), co-edited by Larry Neal and Amiri Baraka, is a testament to the influence of drama during this era. Out of the four sections in the anthology, one section is devoted solely to plays written by established as well as up-and-coming playwrights of this generation. The plays included in the anthology depict the tensions between the police force and the black community, criticize the Western construction of black identity, and figure black women as an integral part of the revolution. Similar to Black Arts poetry, the plays are brief (usually one to two acts), espouse violent rhetoric, and call for black people to take up arms in their fight against white America. Characters who are pro-integration or considered Uncle Toms are murdered in the large majority of these plays. Baraka's play *Dutchman* (1964) embodies many of these elements and is one of the central texts of the Black Arts Movement. Clay, the main character, is a 20-year-old, educated, well-dressed African American male who encounters a white woman named Lula on a train in New York City. Lula antagonizes Clay throughout the play, challenging both his identity as a man and as an African American. Clay entertains Lula's games until she calls him an "Uncle Tom"; the result is a long monologue given by Clay that explains why many African Americans present themselves in a manner that is "acceptable" to white America. At the core of Clay's monologue is the chilling reality of the struggle of black artists: Clay argues that artists like Bessie Smith and Charlie Parker used their art as a means to prevent themselves from revolting against white people. Clay asserts "If Bessie Smith had killed some white people she wouldn't have needed that music. She could have talked very straight and plain about the world" (35). Clay's monologue is essential to understanding the Black Aesthetic of the 1960s because through Clay, Baraka suggests that the only way the black community can maintain its sanity is through violence, which he argues is the language of the white Western world. Baraka's *Madheart: A Morality Play* (1967) embodies many of the same elements as *Dutchman* but instead primarily discusses black female identity in relation to the white female body.

The violent rhetoric espoused by black aestheticians reflects their connection to the Black Power Movement. Although the works of Lloyd Brown, Richard Wright, and Ralph Ellison often reflected Communist politics, what distinguishes writers of the "new" Black Aesthetic from these writers is their connection to a politics that, unlike Communism, was exclusively about the improvement of the black race. Larry Neal clearly states that this aesthetic was the artistic component to the Black Power Movement. Black women writers, a central part of the movement, often espoused Black Power politics in their work. The spirit of Malcolm X was often invoked as well as the "black is beautiful" ideology. Two prominent black poets of this era, Sonia Sanchez and Mari Evans, used their poetry as a way to address the issues that plagued the black community. The speaker of Sanchez's poem "Blk/Rhetoric," asks "who's gonna take/the words/blk/is/beautiful/and make more of it/than blk/capitalism./u dig?" (18), ultimately challenging the black community to move beyond the rhetoric of the Black Power Movement and actually yield to its revolutionary cause against "the enemy/(and we know who that is)" (18). Mari Evans's poem "Vive Noir" talks of being frustrated with "hand me downs/shut me ups/pin me ins/keep me outs" (71), and the speaker suggests that instead of accepting things as they are, she is going to "intrude/my proud blackness/all/over the place" (71). In addition to Sanchez and Evans, many of the prominent writers of this new Black Aesthetic were June Jordan, Haki Madhubuti, Ishmael Reed, Alice Walker, Henry Dumas, and Lorenzo Thomas. Poets, dramatists, novelists, and short-story writers, they were all committed to the same goals of revolution.

Many African American novelists did not affiliate themselves with the Black Arts Movement and its understanding of the Black Aesthetic, yet their work was still influenced by it. For example, Toni Morrison was not directly affiliated with the Black Arts Movement; however, Sula, the protagonist in her novel *Sula* (1973), rejects Western standards of beauty and her rebellious black nature influences the people she encounters. The person who is the most influenced by Sula is her best friend Nel. Prior to meeting Sula, Nel would pinch her nose with a clothespin every night so that it would look more "white." However, after Nel meets Sula, she "slid the clothespin under the blanket as soon as she got in the bed. And although there was still the hateful hot comb to suffer through each Saturday evening, its consequences—smooth hair—no longer interested her" (55). Like the work of Morrison's literary predecessors, the espousal of the Black Aesthetic in Morrison's text subverted the ideology of white superiority.

Although Black Aesthetic values were milder in the years following the Black Arts Movement, a Black Aesthetic was still espoused by African American writers in succeeding generations. In his discussion of the Black Aesthetic, literary scholar William J. Harris describes the Black Aesthetic of African American writers from the late 1970s to the 1990s and defines these two groups as the "New Breed" and the "Neo–Black Aesthetic." In short, Harris suggests that the difference between the New Breed writers of the late 1970s and the earlier writers of the 1960s was the incorporation of all marginalized peoples within the New Breed movement—including Native Americans, Asian Americans, and Hispanics. Harris further asserts that the participants within the Neo–Black Aesthetic of the 1980s and 1990s differed from the New Breed because, like their literary predecessors from earlier generations, they saw no problem in finding inspiration from Western culture to include in their work.

There was a shift among writers of the Black Arts Movement toward this New Breed aesthetic, since many writers related their plight in America with the plight of people in the third world, thus furthering the idea of a third world coalition. June Jordan is one poet whose focus shifted at the end of the 1970s from solely addressing the issues of black Americans toward addressing the issues women faced internationally. Jordan's poem "Poem for South African Women," which discusses black femininity and motherhood and paints such images as "mothers/raising arms/and heart," ends with the declaration "we are the ones we have been waiting for," which encourages women throughout the world to unite and fight for their liberation. On the other hand, novelist Andrea Lee represents writers of the Neo–Black Aesthetic. Lee's *Sarah Phillips* (1984) chronicles the life of a middle-class black woman and her journey toward self-discovery. Through her work, Lee criticizes the black middle class yet does not glorify urban black life; instead, Lee's novel challenges the behavior and beliefs of both of these sectors within the black community. Lee also incorporates important nonblack characters such as Gretchen, the protagonist's best friend in high school, a liberal Jewish girl who, along with her family, is radical and opposes the unfair treatment of blacks in America.

Although African American writers of the 1960s denied the participation of their literary predecessors in the Black Aesthetic, it is evident that the history of this revolutionary cultural aesthetic dates back well into slavery. The Black Aesthetic ultimately represents a people who knew that in order to change the plight of black people in America, it would be essential to combine the culture that distinguished them from other Americans with the written and spoken word. These artists refused to espouse any ideology that would misrepresent their abilities as an intelligent people. Ultimately, all of these writers proved that intelligence, excellence, power, and unity can come out of the children of Africa.

FURTHER READING

Baraka, Amiri, and Larry Neal, eds. *Black Fire: An Anthology of Afro-American Writing*. Baltimore, MD: Black Classic, 1968.

Davis, Arthur P. "Integration and Race Literature." *Phylon* 17 (1956): 141–46.

Dubey, Madhu. *Black Women Novelists and the Nationalist Aesthetic*. Bloomington: Indiana UP, 1975.

Du Bois, W.E.B. "Criteria for Negro Art." *The New Negro: Readings on Race, Representation, and African American Culture, 1892–1938*. Ed. Henry Louis Gates Jr. and Jean Andrew Jarrett. Princeton: Princeton UP, 2007. 257–60.

Dunbar, Paul Laurence. "Negro in Literature." *The New Negro: Readings on Race, Representation, and African American Culture, 1892–1938*. Ed. Henry Louis Gates Jr. and Jean Andrew Jarrett. Princeton: Princeton UP, 2007. 172–73.

Evans, Mari. *I Am a Black Woman*. New York: Morrow., 1964.

Gayle, Addison, ed. *The Black Aesthetic*. New York: Doubleday, 1971.

Harris, William J. "The Black Aesthetic." *The Oxford Companion to African American Literature*. Ed. William Andrews, Frances Foster, and Trudier Harris. New York: Oxford UP, 1997. 67–70.

Jones, LeRoi. *Dutchman and the Slave*. New York: Quill, 1964.

Jordan, June. *Passion: New Poems, 1977–1980*. Boston: Beacon, 1980.

Martin, Reginald. *Ishmael Reed and the New Black Aesthetic Critics*. New York: St. Martin's, 1988.

Morrison, Toni. *Sula*. New York: Penguin, 1982.

Neal, Larry. "The Black Arts Movement." *Drama Review* 12 (Summer 1968): 29–39.

Sanchez, Sonia. *I've Been a Woman: New and Selected Poems*. Chicago: Third World, 1978.

Wright, Richard. "Blueprint for Negro Writing." *The Norton Anthology of African American Literature*. Ed. Henry Louis Gates Jr. and Nellie Y. McKay. New York: Norton, 1997. 1380–88.

Lakisha Odlum

Amiri Baraka's commitment to social justice for African Americans is mirrored in his essays, poems, and plays, which seek to describe a coming revolution. (AP/Wide World Photos)

Black Arts Movement

Closely associated with the Black Power Movement of the 1960s, the Black Arts Movement is often cited as beginning with the move of Amiri Baraka (né LeRoi Jones) to Harlem in 1965. Already an established publisher, poet, playwright, and music critic prior to his move, Baraka's split with the Beat poets to work more closely with black writers serves as a symbolic beginning of the movement.

Baraka is credited with founding the Black Arts Repertory Theater/School (BARTS) and giving the movement its formal beginning. Artists who were a part of BARTS, however, also came from an earlier group called Umbra. People such as Askia Touré, Charles Patterson, and Steve Young formed Umbra, which was one of the first post–civil rights literary organizations to present itself in opposition to the white literary establishment. Although Umbra, which produced *Umbra Magazine*, disbanded when members could not agree on allowing the role of their art to be more political or aesthetic, some members carried their ideology and passion to other organizations such as BARTS.

The creation of such organizations proved that African Americans were seeking new ways to express themselves. Life in America was changing and the artistic expression had to evolve as well. The social and political conditions were ripe for the Black Arts Movement. By the mid-1960s, America, especially black America, was at a crossroads. Coming out of the civil rights era, its end marked by the passage of the Voting Rights Act in 1965, many black people were calling for more radical and revolutionary action in the struggle for equality in society. Slogans such as "Arm yourself or harm yourself" were popular among many, demonstrating the favorable reputation of armed resistance. While the nonviolent movement had been popular and effective during the 1950s and early 1960s, many young black people grew disillusioned with these methods of protest and became interested in the Nation of Islam (NOI), the Black Panther Party for Self Defense, and the Black Power Movement, all avenues for more radical activity. Individuals involved in these movements and groups looked to Africa for wisdom and inspiration as they fought for change within the black community through methods of self-empowerment. The NOI, for instance, worked diligently and successfully to reform pimps, gamblers, drug addicts, alcoholics, and ex-cons. This type of reformation provided a real model of community activism. Young people were inspired by the NOI's focus on racial self-determination and the emphasis it placed on black people and black life. They were also influenced by the NOI's newsletter, *Muhammad Speaks*.

Significant Cities, Theatres, and Publishing Houses

Major Locations of Black Arts' Ideological Leadership

- *California Bay Area*
- *Chicago*
- *Detroit*

Black Arts Theatres and Cultural Centers

- *Black Arts Midwest—Detroit, MI*
- *BLKARTSOUTH—New Orleans, LA*
- *Ebony Showcase—Los Angeles, CA*
- *Inner City Repertory—Los Angeles, CA*
- *Kuumba Theatre Company—Chicago, IL*
- *National Black Theatre—New York, NY*
- *New Lafayette Theatre—New York, NY*
- *Organization of Black American Culture (OBAC)—Chicago, IL*
- *Performing Arts Society of Los Angeles (PALSA)—Los Angeles, CA*
- *Southern Black Cultural Alliance—Houston, TX*
- *Spirit House Movers—Newark, NJ*
- *Sudan Arts Southwest—Houston, TX*
- *Theatre of Afro Arts—Miami, FL*

Major Black Arts Presses

- *Broadside Press—Detroit, MI*
- *Third World Press—Chicago, IL*

Most significant from the Nation of Islam to the activists at the time, however, was Malcolm X. Considered the spiritual leader of the movement by some, Malcolm X was fierce, proud, and unafraid to name the wrongs done to blacks by white America. He called for black people to defend themselves against racial tyranny while speaking directly to blacks. Young people were impressed that he did not bother seeking an audience with whites or asking their permission for equality. They were also impressed with his new vision and the skillful and melodic ways in which he spoke about it.

The Black Panther Party for Self-Defense also concerned itself with community activism. Founded in 1966 by Bobby Seale and Huey P. Newton, the Oakland, California–based organization created various programs in the black community that administered free food and free medical and legal aid, as well as service to the homeless and battered women. While a visible preoccupation with weaponry and militancy were a large part of the Black Panthers' national reputation, and an actual part of their tactics, their goal was a free America for the black community. This goal was one that resonated with black youth who were calling for black power.

Black Power became the term for the movement that would grow out of the Civil Rights Movement. Although initially used in the 1950s, it was popularized as a political slogan by Kwame Ture (Stokely Carmichael) after the shooting of James Meredith during the March against Fear from Memphis, Tennessee, to Jackson, Mississippi, in 1966. At the time, Ture was the head of the Student Nonviolent Coordinating Committee (SNCC). Like many of

his young contemporaries, he believed that the integrationist and accommodationist path to liberation was flawed. Through the Black Power Movement
more aggressive tactics were employed to secure equality for blacks. Part of
this was to instill racial pride in black people, as well as to advocate for militancy and in some instances, racial separation.

While the change and turbulence of the 1960s made for a ripe environment
to begin the Black Arts Movement, the groundwork for it had been laid as
early as the 1920s. One can certainly see the correlations between the goals
and impact of the Black Arts Movement and the Harlem Renaissance in that
both promoted the artistic achievement of African Americans and that both
had as its cultural center Harlem, New York. While the Black Arts Movement
had a more nationalist tone, both movements worked to reclaim black culture
as a thing of power and to present opportunities for black artists to produce
and promote black creativity.

Perhaps lesser known, however, are the connections the Black Arts Movement had to the Communist Left. In the 1920s and 1930s, Harlem was the
location of several political organizations such as Marcus Garvey's Universal
Negro Improvement Association (UNIA) and the African Blood Brotherhood,
a black socialist organization with ties to Communism. Involved with these
groups as well as others, artists and other cultural workers purported to have
some ties to the Popular Front well into the 1930s and 1940s.

In the late 1950s, in spite of McCarthy-era persecution, there still remained
African Americans active in leftist politics. Actor, writer, and athlete Paul
Robeson, for instance, produced the leftist journal, *Freedom*, which published
writers and intellectuals such as W.E.B. Du Bois, Lorraine Hansberry, John O.
Killens, John Henrike Clarke, and Julian Mayfield. (Killens, Clarke, and Mayfield
would go on to mentor artists in the Black Arts Movement.) Other cultural leaders such as Du Bois and Benjamin Davis also maintained their ties to Communism despite constant government harassment and internal strife among factions.

Maintaining these ideological ties, many of the leaders formed the Harlem
Writers Guild (HWG), which was responsible for the demonstration protesting Congolese prime minister Patrice Lumumba's assassination (and the
United States' role in it) in 1961. In organizing this demonstration, they connected a wide range of leftist and nationalist activists together. Among the
demonstrators were Baraka and Touré. Calvin Hicks and Sarah Wright, members of HWG, went on to found On Guard for Freedom, which later merged
with Baraka's group, Organization of Young Men. Individuals in this merged
group would go on to form the core of BARTS.

The goal of the Black Arts Movement was to transform the manner in
which African Americans were portrayed in literature. Previously, blacks were
presented in the media as criminal, servile, misfit, or dependent. The image of
the black man and woman was filtered through the lens of the white mainstream and therefore was often considered illegitimate and/or inferior. The
movement sought to valorize African Americans and their cultural practices.
It also sought to bring awareness to the social inequalities of the era.

Incorporating these goals, Maulana Karenga (creator of Kwanzaa) founded The Organization Us, a social and cultural change organization which advocated the philosophy of Kawaida. This philosophy was a multifaceted activist idea that ultimately led to the seven principles, or Nguzo Sabo, associated with Kwanzaa.

Larry Neal, one of the leaders of the Black Arts Movement, stated that the goal of the movement was to create an art that spoke to black America's needs and aspirations. Artists of the movement not only believed it necessary to acknowledge the spiritual and cultural needs of the community but also saw it as their responsibility to respond to those needs through their art. For these artists, one significant need was the re-creation of a standard that was more in line with the black Americans' experience and sensibilities. They saw themselves and the black community in separate terms from mainstream America. Thus, the key concepts of the Black Arts Movement became the reevaluation of Western aesthetics, the traditional role of the writer, and the social function of art. They demanded a separate symbolism and mythology from mainstream art, calling for a critique and iconology that was wholly different. Neal says in his article, "The Black Arts Movement," that the goal of the black artist was to destroy the white way of looking at the world, eliminating white ideas from black art. Unlike in Western ideology, art for these artists was not just for the aesthetic pleasure of the artist or even the audience. For Black Art Movement artists, art had to be functional as well as beautiful. More important, there was little difference between one's ethics and one's aesthetics. The artist had a social responsibility for his/her art and its effect on the community.

Black Arts Movement literary artists used various forms of writing to operate within that social responsibility. Writers such as John A. Williams in *The Man Who Cried I Am* (1969) and James Alan McPherson in his short stories effectively conveyed the message of pride through fiction. Similarly, Baraka revealed the struggles of African Americans and a model for the new Black Aesthetic in his play *Dutchman* (1964), proving that drama could also be a compelling tool in the commission of the movement's goals.

Poetry was viewed by many members of the movement as the most effective means through which to speak to the needs of the people. Because of its succinct structure, poetry allowed for the writer to publish the work him/herself and for the message to be written quickly and conveyed quite forcefully. For instance, in Nikki Giovanni's poem "For Saundra," the poet is able to communicate the disparities in the life situations of black people and white people by writing of her inability to write a nice rhyming poem about nature. Instead, it becomes more important for her to take action with a gun and kerosene. Poets such as Baraka and Haki Madhubuti also recognized the convenience of the poem: a great deal of power could be conveyed in a short space. Largely considered the first publication of the movement, Baraka's volume of poetry *Black Magic* (1969) illustrates the efficacy of poetic expression.

Poetry could also easily incorporate the language of the masses, which writers wanted to include. They used speech from sermons, everyday conversations, and jazz and blues. The folk were a significant part of the movement, and validating their speech as well as their day-to-day life was a key factor in the effort to reframe the picture of African Americans. Poets, as well as fiction writers and dramatists, would also use folk vernacular in combination with standard American forms such as the rhythms of the Beatniks and standard musical strategies or with African forms such as praise poetry or the griot-style of storytelling to create new styles of language.

The new style of language included creating new spellings and usage of punctuation. For instance, in her choreopoem *for colored girls who have considered suicide/when the rainbow is enuf* (1975), Ntozake Shange frequently uses the phonetic spellings of words (as evidenced even in the title with the word "enuf") and avoids using periods, commas, and capitalization. This alteration of standard edited American English was yet another tool that writers, and specifically poets, used in order to distance themselves from Western European standards.

Perhaps because of poetry's usefulness, poets made up the largest group among the artists of the Black Arts Movement. This group included the aforementioned Baraka and Madhubuti, as well as Sonia Sanchez, Askia Touré, Tom Dent, A. B. Spellman, Bob Kaufman, Nikki Giovanni, Jayne Cortez, Ishmael Reed, Raymond Patterson, and Lorenzo Thomas, among others. While many typically associate these poets, as well as the movement, with New York, these writers have a diverse geographical background, coming from the South, the Midwest, the West, and the Northeast. This diversity of background also spoke to the impact of various regions on the movement. Writers immigrating to New York from around the country and New Yorkers emigrating throughout the nation created a sense of national cohesion. Writers were able to learn what was taking place across regional boundaries. Additionally, the regional journals and organizations that maintained longevity (as opposed to those based in New York) helped to establish and promote the work of the artists.

The *Liberator* had a special significance to the Black Arts Movement because it defined the ideology of the movement. Many mark 1965 as the beginning of the periodical's significance, because this is when Baraka and Neal joined the editorial board of the magazine. Prior to Baraka and Neal's commitments to the magazine, however, the *Liberator* was already publishing essays and poetry by Harold Cruse, Ishmael Reed, and Askia Touré. Based in New York and distributed nationally, it aligned itself with domestic and international revolutionary movements.

Other magazines of significance to the movement were *Black Dialogue* and the *Journal of Black Poetry*. *Black Dialogue* began in 1964 and was the first major publication of the Black Arts Movement. It was edited by Arthur A. Sheridan, Abdul Karim, Edward Spriggs, Aubrey Labrie, and Marvin Jackmon (Marvin X). Out of *Black Dialogue* came the *Journal of Black Poetry*. Based in San Francisco, it was founded by *Black Dialogue*'s poetry editor, Dingane Joe Goncalves, and published over 500 poets including Haki Madhubuti, Clarence Page, and Larry Neal. It was in the *Journal of Black Poetry* that Sonia Sanchez published her 1971 epic poem, "Malcolm/Man Don't Live Here No Mo."

Negro Digest (later renamed *Black World*) was a nationally distributed magazine published by the founder of *Ebony* and *Jet*, John H. Johnson. Patterned after *Reader's Digest, Negro Digest* was meant to give a voice to all black people through its poetry, fiction, drama, theoretical essays, reviews, and criticisms. The journal also provided opportunities for writers by hosting literary contests and awarding prizes. Baraka's highly anthologized "A Poem for Black Hearts," about Malcolm X, was first published in *Negro Digest* in 1965.

In addition to providing opportunities for publications, the Black Arts Movement provided the impetus for creative leaders to create their own presses. Nowhere was this more prevalent than in the establishment of publishing houses. Two of the most popular and sustained publishing houses were Third World Press in Detroit and Broadside Press in Chicago. Before its decline, Broadside Press was responsible for publishing over 400 poets in more than 100 books and recordings. It was also instrumental in presenting older writers such as Gwendolyn Brooks, Margaret Walker, and Sterling Brown to a younger audience. While Third World Press continues to produce new material, today Broadside Press mostly distributes older works from its back catalog.

These publications also encouraged mainstream white publishing houses such as Random House and McGraw-Hill to revive out-of-print texts by black authors. Because of the popularity of black writing and black artists, mainstream publishers saw a viable market for such texts. In this way, the Black Arts Movement was yet again responsible for promoting African American writers and encouraging black artistry.

The Black Arts Movement had a significant and lasting impact on the academy. Because of the ideology its adherents maintained and practiced, they were very instrumental in establishing Black Studies programs in the nation's universities and colleges. The first such program was established at San Francisco State in 1969 with the help of Sonia Sanchez and Nathan Hare. Hare, a sociologist from Howard University, was called upon to coordinate the Black Studies program there; after a five-month-long strike that included a multiethnic group of protestors, the university finally instituted the program. Soon, other universities followed suit. That year, Sanchez, after working to establish the program at San Francisco State, was allowed to teach "The Black Woman," the first college seminar ever on African American women's literature at the University of Pittsburgh. The integration of Black Arts principles with academia was not a difficult one, as many proponents of the Black Arts Movement—Addison Gayle Jr., Darwin Turner, Eugenia Collier, Arna Bontemps, Carolyn Fowler, and George Kent—were already academically trained. An example of the synthesis of Black Aesthetics and Western literature and/or criticism can be seen in Gayle's *The Black Situation* (1970).

For all of its positive effects, the Black Arts Movement was not without its controversies. Accusations of anti-Semitism and homophobia were often levied at publications and artists of the movement. While some scholars have attempted to identify the anti-Semitism as a substitute for protest against all white oppressors or a response to wealthy whites who had orchestrated dissension among minorities (to which both blacks and Jews belong), there has been little explanation of the homophobia present in the movement. Similarly, there have also been allegations of misogyny. Such sexism is due in part to the nature of the Black Arts and Black Power Movements. As paramilitary movements, they were often characterized by masculine bravado. (To some extent, this could also explain the pervasive homophobia.) Cultural critic Michele Wallace contends in *Black Macho and the Myth of the Superwoman* that male artists of the movement internalized white American notions of masculinity as sexually aggressive, causing them to enact sexist practices.

In spite of the misogyny present in the work, women's issues were brought to the forefront by the women writers themselves. Audre Lorde, for example, who came into prominence in the Black Arts Movement with her first book of poetry, *The First Cities* (1968), was a lesbian writer who explored issues of sexuality in her work. Poet and essayist June Jordan also examined issues of identity as well as race in her first collection of poetry, *Who Look at Me* (1969). These women and others proved that the female presence was vital to the movement's artistic and political endeavors, from their early involvement in sociopolitical organizations to the second Black Women's Writers Conference at Fisk in 1967 (where many writers met for the first time) to the movement's dissolution and aftermath.

Scholars, critics, and members of the Black Arts Movement have attributed its dissolution, which can be loosely marked as occurring in 1976, to several factors, both external and internal. The federal government in the form of the IRS, the FBI, and the Counterintelligence Program (COINTELPRO) often probed members, conducting numerous intrusive investigations into their lives. COINTELPRO was part of an atmosphere of paranoia and harassment. Artists and activists were taped, surveilled, and unjustly jailed because they were believed to be rebellious and revolutionary. Such government actions undermined the leadership of the movement and encouraged dissent among the members.

Internally, factional beliefs caused problems as well. There was an ideological split between Marxists and nationalists that had its roots in the late 1950s and early 1960s. This split, along with the aforementioned dissension, made it easier for capitalism and commercialization to completely sever the movement. According to Kalamu ya Salaam, poet and cultural critic, mainstream media agents identified the most salable artists and promoted them in a manner that the black presses and theatres were unable to do because they lacked the finances and connections of those mainstream media organizations. In doing so, the mainstream effectively undermined the professional relationships of the artists and aided in the demise of the movement.

Recent critics have denounced the Black Arts Movement as ineffective and short lived. Some even hold little regard for the writing from this literary period. The effects of this era, however, are long lasting. Not only did the artists shape the way society views literature; they also set forth a standard that contemporary writers and scholars are still using to create their works. Furthermore, emerging from this era are the examples of self-determination and racial pride seen in the study of literature and the formation of fields of academic study that other ethnic groups have emulated.

It should also be acknowledged that the Black Arts Movement's focus on orality has proven to be enduring. One of the most notable changes attributed to the movement is the alteration of the use of the word "Negro" to "black." Trying to separate from the racism of the past that caused them to be called "Negro," the artists chose to identify as black in an effort to claim pride in their African-inspired culture and race.

This one example of the transformation of language is indicative of a commonplace but innovative practice found in the literature of the era. This practice can also be found in the written work of contemporary writers and modern spoken word poets such as those one might see at poetry slams or on HBO's *Russell Simmons' Def Poetry Slam*. In addition, this innovation and focus on orality, as well as the integration of politics an aesthetics can be found in the rap lyrics of many artists such as Common, Lupe Fiasco, and Mos Def. In Mos Def's "What's Beef?" for example, the rapper, along with Talib Kweli, tackles the concept of beef, which is commonly assumed to be dissension between various rap artists at any given time. In the song, however, they define beef as the problems the black community faces: "Beef is the cocaine and AIDS epidemic." These artists demonstrate that the Black Arts Movement was a movement that was not only influential in its focus on and inclusion of the oratory power of the masses, but is also iconic in its enduring demand for social change and creation of a nationalist political aesthetic.

Certainly, African American history and literature have benefited from the trials and triumphs of the Black Arts Movement, as has the rest of America.

FURTHER READING

Bambara, Toni Cade, ed. *The Black Woman: An Anthology*. 1970. New York: Washington Square, 2005.

Baraka, Amiri. *Black Magic*. New York: Morrow, 1967.

Baraka, Amiri. *Dutchman and The Slave*. New York: Morrow, 1964.

Baraka, Amiri, and Larry Neal, eds. *Black Fire: An Anthology of Afro-American Writing*. 1968. Baltimore, MD: Black Classic, 2007.

Chapman, Abraham, ed. *New Black Voices: An Anthology of Contemporary Afro-American Literature*. New York: New American Library, 1972.

Conyers, James L. *Engines of the Black Power Movement: Essays on the Influence of Civil Rights Actions, Arts, and Islam*. Jefferson, NC: McFarland, 2006.

Gates, Henry Louis, Jr., and Nellie Y. McKay, eds. "The Black Arts Movement: 1960–1970." *Norton Anthology of African American Literature*. New York: Norton, 1997.

Gayle, Addison Jr., ed. *The Black Aesthetic*. Garden City, NY: Doubleday, 1971.

Giovanni, Nikki. "For Saundra." *Black Feeling, Black Talk/Black Judgment*. New York: Harper, 1970.

Henderson, Stephen. *Understanding the New Black Poetry: Black Speech and Black Music as Poetic References*. New York: Morrow, 1972.

Jordan, June. *Who Look at Me*. New York: Crowell, 1969.

Last Poets. *The Last Poets*. Varese Sarabande, 1970. CD.

Lorde, Audre. *The First Cities*. New York: Poets, 1968.

Mos Def and Talib Kweli. "What's Beef?" *One Million Strong Vol. 2*. Bungalo Records, 2005. CD.

Neal, Larry. "The Black Arts Movement." 1968. *A Turbulent Voyage: Readings in African American Studies*. Ed. Floyd Windom Hayes III and John K. Reed. San Diego, CA: Collegiate, 2000.

Randall, Dudley, and Margaret Taylor Goss Burroughs, eds. *For Malcolm X, Poems on the Life and the Death of Malcolm X*. Chicago: Broadside, 1969.

Redmond, Eugene. *Drumvoices: The Mission of Afro-American Poetry: A Critical History*. New York: Doubleday, 1976.

Ryan, Jennifer Denise. "Black Arts Movement." *Writing African American Women: An Encyclopedia of Literature by and about Women of Color*. Ed. Elizabeth Ann Beaulieu. Westport, CT: Greenwood, 2006.

Shange, Ntozake. *for colored girls who have considered suicide/when the rainbow is enuf*. New York: Scribner Poetry, 1975.

Smethurst, James. "Poetry and Sympathy: New York, the Left and the Rise of Black Arts." *Left of the Color Line: Race, Radicalism, and Twentieth-Century Literature of the United States*. Ed. Bill V. Mullen and James Smethurst. Chapel Hill: U of North Carolina P, 2003.

Smith, David Lionel. "The Black Arts Movement and Its Critics." *The American Literary History Reader*. Ed. Gordon Hunter. Oxford: Oxford UP, 1995.

Williams, John A. *The Man Who Cried I Am*. 1969. New York: Overlook, 2004.

ya Salaam, Kalamu. "Black Arts Movement." *The Oxford Companion to African American Literature*. Ed. William L. Andrews, Frances Smith Foster, and Trudier Harris. New York: Oxford UP, 1997.

ya Salaam, Kalamu. *The Magic of Juju: An Appreciation of the Black Arts Movement (BAM)*. Chicago: Third World, 2007.

RaShell R. Smith-Spears

Portrait of blues musician Muddy Waters in 1964. (Library of Congress)

Blues Aesthetic

The Blues Aesthetic, as defined by Kalamu ya Salaam, "is an ethos of blues people that manifests itself in everything done, not just music" (Moses 623). As an African American literary motif, the Blues Aesthetic is grounded in the blues tradition and fortified by its connection to African American culture. In fact, the blues has become emblematic of the modern African American experience, giving a voice to the hardships of slavery, the challenges in adjusting to life beyond the plantation, of the Great Migration, of cultural immersion, and of finding a place and space within contemporary American society—all set against the backdrop of a guitar-laced melody. The blues is also known for, and in earlier years, was criticized for, addressing subjects considered taboo by mainstream society. Promiscuity, addictions, and criminal acts (such as murder) have, at times, been metaphorically addressed within the more worldly blues lyrics; however, as it grew in popularity and began crossing over onto mainstream musical charts, critics and audiences alike began to recognize the blues as a vehicle for the artistic expression of life's complexities rather than a conduit for the dangers of immorality.

Indeed, blues lyrics alternately celebrate and mourn the joys, sorrows, highs, and lows of life in the same way that blues musicians draw from a variety of musical traditions to create the accompanying melody. Similarly, by honoring the oral tradition in African culture while adapting to the form and structure of the Western written tradition, African American literature (which includes an emphasis on local dialect found within the African American vernacular, audible rhythmic variances, and lyrical intonations) has undoubtedly been shaped by the Blues Aesthetic.

The Blues Aesthetic in literature is a reflection of its association with the musical genre. Originally called the "folk blues" by southern musicians, it would ultimately be referred to as simply "the blues" in later years, as its format changed along with its geographical location. The musicians migrating to northern states during the Great Migration of the early 20th century introduced the blues to newer and more diverse audiences, and its popularity grew among both whites and blacks in major metropolitan cities. Classic blues, the genre encapsulating the newer era of blues music, is a product of the post–Civil War, post-slavery era in modern American culture, when African Americans were adjusting to the changes accompanying life beyond the plantation. This period in American history is reflected in the history of the blues largely because it represents a musical transition from the group ethos of oppression to the individual's societal plight.[1]

As an outgrowth of several musical forms popular in the American South (including spirituals and folksongs), the blues emerged in the African American community during the late 19th and early 20th centuries, although no exact date or point of origin has been identified (Baraka 101). However, the first official blues recording was George W. Johnson's "Laughing Song," recorded in 1895 in the Mississippi Delta. Later, this branch of blues music became known as the "Delta blues" and would remain consistent with its distinct artistic standards, namely the heavy reliance on the guitar and harmonica for musical support, as well as the accompanying lyrics, which frequently center on themes of promiscuity and travel (the journeying theme). In the early years, from about 1890 to 1920, the blues was a dominated by musicians from the South; as such, most of the lyrical content was grounded in the local perspective. Its growth necessitated the creation of additional branches within the blues umbrella, including those identified by region (such as the Memphis blues and the swamp blues), instrument (piano blues, electric blues), and style (jump blues and boogie-woogie). The emergence of the blues in the country's urban centers, particularly during the war years, was both a welcome and painful reminder of the past for many artists, thus prompting many of these transplanted artists to pay homage to both their past and present experiences. This included an increased presence of more modern musical instruments like electric guitars, as well as a more vibrant lyrical content, reflecting city life as well as life back home. Developments in the music industry further distinguished the various branches; however, despite the changes that would mark the blues' evolution as a genre, the basic structure and form would remain relatively consistent.

Structurally, blues music incorporates features of traditional slave work songs, field hollers, and Negro spirituals. The most frequent element is the call and response technique common to most early forms of black music. This component of the blues, however, is limited solely to the singer (or speaker) of the song (or narrative)—starting a new trend in secular African American music of the period that focused on the individual rather than the group performance. The most standard lyrical structure of the blues as a genre of music is the 12-bar progression. The term *12 bar* refers to the numerical structure of a blues song: there are four beats in every line, four lines in every stanza, and three stanzas in every section of the song. A 12-bar progression is the standard rhythmic appropriation for conveying the theme of a blues song, and each stanza contains a measure of repetition in order to fully articulate the singer/speaker's particular message. The repetition often occurs in what is referred to as an AABA pattern: The first two lines of the song are the same, and the third line differs from the first two as a form of response to the first two lines. The fourth line is typically a repetition of the first two lines. There are many variations on this arrangement within the broad context of blues music; however, the 12-bar format is at the core of its foundation and has also proven influential in other musical genres, such as jazz, folk, country, and rock and roll.[2] Blues musicians such as W. C. Handy, Bessie Smith, and Muddy Waters used this format to compose some of their more popular songs.

William Christopher Handy, known professionally as W. C. Handy, is often credited as the father of the blues, as well as the architect of contemporary blues lyrical form. He was also known for infusing his work with folksongs, creating a unique sound that established him as an innovator among other musicians. Some of Handy's songs include "Memphis Blues" and "St. Louis Blues," which established the standard that would be followed by legions of blues musicians in subsequent years. "St. Louis Blues" is a song about the pain experienced by a woman whose husband has been stolen by another woman; "Memphis Blues" was a song inspired by a Memphis-based political boss. Like Handy, Bessie Smith gained extreme and lasting popularity as one of the most popular figures in blues history. Known as the Empress of the Blues, Smith gained fame with songs such as "Downhearted Blues" and "Empty Bed Blues," as well as her own version of "St. Louis Blues." Regarded as one of the best singers in the era of classic blues, Smith's vocal innovations had a major impact on several notable jazz singers in later years. Similarly, McKinley Morganfield, better known as Muddy Waters, was perhaps one of the most genre-spanning and influential blues musicians, leaving an imprint on artists ranging from Chuck Berry to Eric Clapton. Gaining early popularity in the 1950s with songs like "Rollin' Stone" (from which the legendary rock and roll group, the Rolling Stones, derived their name) and "Hootchie Cootchie Man," Waters, who is credited as the father of Chicago blues, maintained a consistent presence on the American musical landscape even during the late 1940s and early 1950s, when the blues appeared to have reached its peak on the musical charts. However, its presence on the literary scene was still rising in popularity—beginning in the 1920s during the Harlem Renaissance, with the introduction of blues poetry.

Blues poetry was ultimately the gateway for blues-inspired fiction, as the latter category appeared much later within the historical timeframe. It is widely accepted that blues poetry is an integral part of the history of African American literature, and although most black poets have at some point addressed the blues in their work, not all of these works follow the traditional blues form (the AABA format). Essentially, blues poetry, although most recognizable when constructed according to the traditional stanza and meter of blues music, is not required to follow this pattern in order to be qualified as blues poetry. Further, although the blues stanza used in select blues poetry is symbolic of the blues in structure and meaning, relatively few African American literary poets actually utilize this device.[3] As a literary motif, however, the blues signifies the larger African American experience via the African American oral tradition, which is based on the oral tradition of storytelling and historical preservation in African culture.

In terms of literary analysis, according to Kalamu ya Salaam, the Blues Aesthetic requires a "condensed and simplified codification" that includes the following elements: a "stylization of process," which signifies the transition from communal to collective; "the deliberate use of exaggeration" that calls attention to central thematic issues; "brutal honesty clothed in metaphorical grace," a strategy used to address oppressive social conditions for African Americans such as racism; "the acceptance of the contradictory nature of life," such as the balance between good and evil; "optimistic faith in the ultimate triumph of justice, and celebration of the sensual and erotic elements of life" ("It Didn't Jes Grew" 357). In short, the narrative structure of a blues novel would "follow a pattern common to traditional blues lyrics: a movement from an initial emphasis on loss to a concluding suggestion of the resolution of grief" (Moses 623).

The blues singer is comparable to the African griot (storyteller); the literature characterized by the Blues Aesthetic is often narrated from the first-person perspective. Though most literary critics, scholars, and poets cite the presence of iambic pentameter in blues poetry, the aesthetic shift in African American culture that coincided with the publication of early works in this genre requires a greater emphasis on the inclusion of the 12-bar lyrical structure. The classical iambic pentameter, often found in poetry and dramatic verse, contains five syllabic groupings within each line of a stanza. To establish the rhythm in the iambic pentameter, an alternating emphasis is placed on each syllabic group (with the short syllabic group preceding the longer unit). Though the alternation in emphasis varies depending upon the specific work or the culture from which it emerges (e.g., English vs. Greek poetry), the structure of the iambic pentameter is relatively consistent, as is its function as one of the more common forms used in poetry. Coincidentally, the alternating rhythmic scheme of the iambic pentameter can be easily likened to the 12-bar structure adopted by the blues, in large part because of the challenge in making a literal transcription of the blues.

On the one hand, critics often cite the difficulty of transposing the essence of blues music into literary form, finding that the true value of a Blues Aesthetic is located solely in the performance. On the other hand, many of the lyrics to blues songs are written down and can thus be as easily articulated in poetic form, using literary tools (such as alliteration) to compensate for the absence of an oral component. Examples of this audio-scribal transcription can be identified in the blues poetry of writer Langston Hughes.

Hughes, prominent among the group of avant-garde artists whose aesthetic influences were taken from the culture at large, captured the essence of the blues music popular among both black and white audiences, and his works were among the first blues poems ever written. "The Weary Blues," which describes an evening spent listening to the blues in Harlem, integrates lyrics of blues songs with the elements characteristic of the genre, including the repetition of lyrics and the down-home language of blues musicians. Hughes also articulates the emotion of the speaker in this poem—which, consequently, is one of disillusionment. This feeling of inertia is a frequent component of both blues poetry and blues music, and in "The Weary Blues," the speaker chooses to identify his feelings of weariness with the lyrics performed by a blues musician.

In other works, such as "Blues Fantasy" and "Red Clay Blues," Hughes explores the blues as it reflects the emotional experience involved in moving from South to North. This is symbolic of the Great Migration—the period during the late 19th and early 20th centuries when millions of African Americans migrated from the South to the North (and in some cases, the West) in search of greater opportunities for employment and social acceptance.[4] The mode of transport in many instances was by train, a symbol in blues music representing a means of escaping the oppression prevalent in the American South, as well as the angst caused by the separation from loved ones left behind. The train as a symbol is also found in many fictional works by African American authors; most notably among these are Zora Neale Hurston and James Alan McPherson. For example, in Hurston's first novel, *Jonah's Gourd Vine* (1934), the train symbolizes many things for the protagonist, John Pearson—including, but not limited to, his lust for "power, dynamism, and mobility" (Washington 101). However, within the overall context of both the novel itself and the period in which it was written, the train is a symbol of the Great Migration and the blues, supported by the constant coming and goings of the citizens of Eatonville, Florida (the town in which the bulk of the novel takes place), the "worldly" behavior of the promiscuous protagonist, and the songs being sung by the workmen. The short stories by James Alan McPherson celebrate another aspect of the train in African American culture.

The train as both a symbol and a metaphor is prevalent in McPherson's works, recalling the people and experiences he encountered during his employment as a dining car waiter for the Great Northern Railroad (circa 1962). McPherson (along with poet Miller Williams) famously related some of his experiences as a railroad employee in his book of short stories, *Railroad: Trains and Train People in American Culture* (1976). Though he aligned his writing style with mainstream American literary tradition and rejected the notion that literature should necessarily retain cultural influences, the recounting of his experiences as an African American can be clearly linked with those of other writers of the African American literary tradition whose works clearly embodied the stylistic influences attributed to the Blues Aesthetic.

In blues-inspired works, the audience can be exposed to the inner dialogues of the speaker via the expressions of the artists, and these dialogues contribute to a larger, ongoing conversation between African Americans in rural and urban settings. The blues connotes a collective feeling of confrontation "with the self, with the family and loved ones, with the oppressive forces of society, with nature, and, on the heaviest level, with fate and the universe itself" (Henderson 32). Through this confrontation, the artist seeks to find a level of inner solace that can be transformed into a story to which anyone facing similar experiences can relate. Generally, the writer is most successful in articulating the artistic ideal encompassed within the Blues Aesthetic if the work follows a structural pattern similar to that of the music.

The Blues Aesthetic in literature is also found in the overall narrative structure—how it compares to blues lyrics, as well as in how it manifests the relevant thematic content. Further, many of the writers whose works are characterized by the Blues Aesthetic are also avid blues enthusiasts; through their writings, authors such as Nikki Giovanni, John Oliver Killens, James Baldwin, Richard Wright, Toni Morrison, Ralph Ellison, and Amiri Baraka establish a strong link to the blues, the tradition of black music, and the social-cultural evolution of African American culture.

Many of Nikki Giovanni's writings, for example, have been dedicated to the celebration of African American culture and identity. In her first two collections of poetry, *Black Feeling, Black Talk* (1968) and *Black Judgment* (1969), Giovanni salutes the sometimes militant segment of the African American community during an era in American history when African Americans were ferociously rebelling against the racism of U.S. society. While these works are most recognized for their revolutionary qualities, they also noted for the recurrent themes of love, loss, and loneliness—key thematic influences found in the blues and works characterized by the Blues Aesthetic. Poems such as "Nikki Rosa" and "Knoxville, Tennessee" are among the most popular of Giovanni's early works, offering both an introspective and observational assessment of the state of the black community at large and the accompanying feelings of joy and pain. Community is also a focus in the fiction of writer J. O. Killens.

John Oliver Killens's work runs the gamut in its representation of the black experience: *Youngblood* (1954) is the story of a poor, black family struggling to survive in the South during the Jim Crow era, and of its primary protagonist, Joe Youngblood, who mirrors the tragic male hero archetype found throughout the canon of African American literature; *And Then We Heard the Thunder* (1962) is a novel about the challenges for African Americans in the military during the war years; *The Cotillion; or, One Good Bull Is Worth Half the Herd* (1971) explores the intraracial conflicts arising from assimilation and classicism, and their effects on the black community; and finally, the novel *A Man Ain't Nothing but a Man: The Adventures of John Henry* (1975) is a retelling of the ballad of John Henry. *A Man Ain't Nothing but a Man* was written for a young adult audience; however, it is perhaps one of the best examples of the Blues Aesthetic in his body of work due to its adaptation of the folk ballads about John Henry, the mythical figure of heroic strength prevalent in many African American folk tales. In many ways, the John Henry–esque archetype is central to the blues tradition through its connection to the folk genre and culture of the American South, as well as its representation of black masculinity. Blues has also been a conduit for black masculinity, frequently serving as a vehicle for bemoaning the challenges for black men in societies divided by racism or becoming the tool for empowerment. Writer James Baldwin's works typically revolve around a number of themes associated with black manhood, as expressed through the blues.

The Blues Aesthetic in the work of writer/poet James Baldwin can easily be identified in several of his most popular works. *Go Tell It on the Mountain* (1953), a semi-autobiographical account of his own experiences as a teenaged minister, highlights the age-old conflict between guilt, sin, and religion that serves as inspiration for many musicians—particularly in the blues genre. Later works such as *Another Country* (1963), *If Beale Street Could Talk* (1974), *Just Above My Head* (1979), and the short story "Sonny's Blues" (1965) pay homage to the African American musical tradition. Baldwin's one-time friend and mentor, Richard Wright, also incorporates the African American musical tradition in his early poetry; his fictional offerings contain elements of the Blues Aesthetic largely from thematic, rather than structural, influences.

Though known largely for his novels, *Native Son* (1940) and *Black Boy* (1945), Richard Wright is also notable for his incorporation of the African American musical tradition in some of his early poetry. For example, the poems "King Joe I" and "King Joe II" (in honor of boxer Joe Louis) merge the folkloric tradition of southern culture with the societies of the urban northern cities—one of the primary characteristics of the Blues Aesthetic. These poems were written in a musical format and later recorded by Paul Robeson and the Count Basie Orchestra. Wright's fiction narrated the challenges that accompanied the assimilation process (or lack thereof) for southern-born black men living in northern societies typically dominated by racism. This experience, rife with travail and disparity, is also clearly articulated in the blues music produced during the first half of the 20th century, and can be located in the works of several other writers in the same period. For example, Ralph Ellison's seminal novel, *Invisible Man* (1952), narrates the journey of a young black man through early to mid-20th-century America. The novel's journeying theme, moving from South to North and exploring all of the varying degrees of selfhood ostensibly defined for black men (also reiterating the theme and construct of black masculinity), becomes a metaphor for the challenges faced by all African Americans in the years prior to and immediately following the Civil Rights Movement. The Black Arts Movement, which began during the 1960s (at the height of the Civil Rights Movement), celebrated black culture in all manifestations, and writers/poets such as Amiri Baraka, one of the leaders of this movement, wrote extensively both on the African American experience and the evolution of black music.

Baraka's *Blues People* (1963) speaks directly about the ethos of the Blues Aesthetic in literature as a representation of the collective African American experience as articulated through blues music. An avid music fan, Baraka has written extensively on the intersections between music and literature; much of his work, particularly his early poetry, is reflective of a connection to the African American musical tradition. Indeed, he is known to have hosted poetry readings that consisted of works being read to the accompaniment of blues or jazz music. He has also written several books about the influence of black music, including *The Music: Reflections on Jazz and Blues* (1987). Though he has written works of fiction (including plays) that encapsulate blues-related themes, most of Baraka's work on the blues is written from a theoretical and/or rhetorical perspective. Other writers, such as Toni Morrison, have explored the subject largely through fictional narrative.

Many of Toni Morrison's novels have been linked with the Blues Aesthetic, namely *Sula* (1973), *Jazz* (1992), *The Bluest Eye* (1970), and *Song of Solomon* (1977). Sula, one of the primary protagonists in the novel of the same name, represents the "promiscuous woman" scorned in many blues songs. She and the other protagonist, Nel, were bound by a friendship that changes following a tragedy occurring during their youth. Despite the differences in the socioeconomic statuses of their families (Sula's mother was a loose woman, while Nel came from an upstanding family), this bond initially seemed to transcend these temporal barriers; however, as is often the case, the two girls eventually drift apart and go on to become the women that society expected them to be. Nel leads a traditional life, complete with husband and family, and Sula thwarts social convention and moves away from the Bottom, going on to have several affairs with several men, both black and white—including Nel's husband. She ultimately takes up her mother's social position in the Bottom (which is the name of the community in which they live) and becomes their collective target—uniting them in their hatred. The Blues Aesthetic in this novel is heightened by Sula's character and experiences. Sula is characterized as a woman of ill repute, despite the inherent hypocrisy of this label, and it is only after she dies and the community (including Nel) has to face their own culpability in the evil surrounding them that she can achieve some level of redemption. *Jazz* has a similar basic plot structure in that the story revolves around a single female figure; however, its location (in Harlem) and more modern approach creates a marked difference between the two novels—much like the difference between down-home folk blues and the city blues.

Jazz tells the story of a couple, Violet and Joe Trace, who are haunted by the spirit of a young girl, Dorcas, who was Joe's mistress and the object of his obsession. As is common in many blues songs about domestic disharmony, Joe ultimately kills Dorcas out of extreme jealousy—he fears that her youth and appeal will lead her to leave him. Adding a strange twist to the plot, Violet (also known as Violent) becomes obsessed with Dorcas, mimicking her hairstyle and exploring the various aspects of her life in search of some answers for herself (Violet). The Blues Aesthetic in this novel is further emphasized in the narrative structure in that Dorcas's life and death are relayed in brief flashbacks; the reader is not fully aware of exactly what happened to Joe and Violet, or for that matter, to Dorcas, until at least mid-way through the novel. A similar strategy is implemented in *The Bluest Eye*, where, notes writer Cat Moses, "the catharsis and the transmission of cultural knowledge and values that have always been central to the blues form thematic and rhetorical underpinnings...the narrative's structure follows a pattern common to traditional blues lyrics: a movement from an initial emphasis on loss to a concluding suggestion of resolution of grief through motion" (623).

Blues Aesthetic in Film and Television

The Blues Aesthetic in film can be found in both early and contemporary motion pictures, including, but not limited to, Lady Sings the Blues *(1972) starring Diana Ross, Richard Pryor, and Billy Dee Williams,* The Blues Brothers *(1980) starring Dan Aykroyd and James Belushi,* O Brother, Where Art Thou? *(2000) starring George Clooney,* Ray *(2004) starring Jamie Foxx, and* Black Snake Moan *(2007) starring Samuel L. Jackson, Christina Ricci, and Justin Timberlake.* Lady Sings the Blues *is a musical biography of Billie Holiday, the iconic yet tragic blues singer who is regarded as a legend in both the genres of blues and jazz music.* The*

Blues Brothers is a unique commentary on the evolution of the blues in the overall American musical landscape (circa 1980) through the two main characters, who, ironically, are Caucasian musicians.[†] A modern satire of Homer's Odyssey, O Brother, Where Art Thou? *is the story of three prisoners who escape the chain gang and end up becoming folk/blues musicians.[‡]*

The battle between good and evil is a common aspect of any blues-inspired work, and Ray, *the musical biography of blues musician Ray Charles, highlights the singer's struggle with his childhood demons and a drug addiction.[§] This aspect of his life was not as publicized as was his amazing musical talent; however, the story alone follows the structure of any blues song, and the movie is clearly influenced by the Blues Aesthetic—particularly in the search for redemption, which is a critical thematic issue in this movie and many others (including* Black Snake Moan). Black Snake Moan *is the story of a burned-out blues musician who crosses paths with a troubled nymphomaniac, and somehow, they save each other's lives. Writer and director Craig Brewer, a blues enthusiast, was criticized for his seemingly stereotypical portrayal of the characters in this film; however, when analyzing the film from the blues perspective, it is clear that the plot possesses many of the same ingredients that comprise any work of art influenced by the Blues Aesthetic.*

---

[*]Holiday is famous for many blues songs that speak to the highs and lows of heartbreak, loneliness, and life in America for African Americans, such as the legendary song "Strange Fruit," which was written in response to the practice of lynching in the South. The most fascinating aspect of this movie is that it gives an insight into Holiday's life, which seemed to be the inspiration for her songs.

[†]Though the genre has many practitioners of all different ethnicities, it is largely regarded as the territory of African American musicians, and this movie comically explores the adventures of two white blues musicians.

[‡]Though the musical influences in this film are largely linked with the folk genre, it is closely related to the Blues Aesthetic in the large number of similarities between the blues and folk genres—particularly with regard to the storytelling within the lyrics. In addition, the film is set in the American South, and the plot revolves around the strange, yet good luck of three prisoners who are also forced to reconcile their good fortune and their troubled pasts with elements of spirituality (i.e., good vs. evil).

[§]Ray Charles witnessed the death of his younger brother, lost his sight, and was sent away from home to find a better life at a young age, and he never really recovered until much later—despite his natural and extremely powerful musical talent. In order to cope, he took heroin and was an addict for many years until he was forced to either go to rehab or face jail time.

The Bluest Eye has one narrator, Claudia, and she assumes the role of storyteller for all of the trials and tribulations of the other characters. Though not the main character—the protagonist of the novel is actually Pecola, who, though largely silent throughout the narrative, is central to the plot—according to Moses, Claudia is "the narrative's blues subject, its bluest 'I' and representative blues figure, and Pecola is the abject *tabula rasa* (blank slate) on which the community's blues are inscribed" (626). Claudia's function in this novel can be likened to the speaker and/or singer in a blues song, where the speaker may be telling the story of one person but linking his/her experience with that of the surrounding community. For example, the character archetype commonly known as a "Jody" in several blues songs typically refers to a local Casanova, someone who has affairs with married or otherwise committed women. While the song may make reference to one particular kind of man, the narrator is typically addressing all persons involved in the Jody's adventures—including the woman and her significant other.

By first isolating the Blues Aesthetic in *The Bluest Eye*, Moses succeeds in locating the essential blues ideology that both drives the narrative and invites the reader to participate in what Ropo Sekoni, author of *Folk Poetics*, calls an "aesthetic transaction"—where both writer and audience engage in an informal contract stipulating a mutual recognition of the writers "claim to a communal ethos shared with the readership" (qtd. in Akoma 5). In further explanation of her argument, Moses writes that "the novel's central paucity is the community's lack of self-love, a lack precipitated by the imposition of a master aesthetic that privileges the light skin and blue eyes inherent in the community's *internalization* of a master aesthetic. Claudia (the narrator) is the voice for the community's blues, and Pecola (the main character) is the site of inscription *of* the community's blues" (634). Basically, the Blues Aesthetic in *The Bluest Eye* lies within Claudia's perception of both Pecola and her community at large.

Song of Solomon (1977) is another one of Morrison's novels that encapsulates several blues-related themes, specifically the challenges of geographical displacement and black masculinity. The story revolves around Milkman Dead, the primary male protagonist, and his search for identity—undertaken via an exploration of his family's history. Milkman must confront the lasting impact of slavery on his society through several painful encounters with his immediate family—and this leads him to determine that the past is essential in determining the future. Though Milkman is the general focus of the novel, the most pivotal character is actually his father's sister Pilate. Indeed, Pilate is born without a navel: in the African American literary tradition, a character with no navel is the carrier of history (Traylor 43). In addition to providing the insight that will propel Milkman's journey, Pilate is symbolic of the griot and/or mystic in traditional African culture—the living and breathing testament to history critical to uncovering the past as a means of moving forward. The blues is a genre of music that relies on its history as a way of creating new forms and techniques; the Blues Aesthetic in other art forms can also be identified by their celebration of the past. As such, the Blues Aesthetic in *Song of Solomon* is most evident by its use of folklore, travel, and history as tools in one man's search for identity.

There are many similarities between the analyses of blues in literature and music, and the academic consideration of this genre has risen steadily over the past three decades. Though nearly a century has passed since the blues first appeared on the American musical landscape, after catching the attention of musician W. C. Handy in a Mississippi train station, and over this period, this unique musical genre has experienced a number of structural transitions and settled into a comfortable niche that often borders other musical genres with similar historical groundings—namely those of folk, soul, and gospel music. The blues as a musical genre has remained popular since it was formally introduced to American audiences; however, during the 1950s, its presence seemed to plateau on the record charts. In the 1960s, following a period marked by a sharp decline in popularity, blues music was revitalized by several British rock and roll groups (such as the Rolling Stones). This reemergence brought even greater attention to both the genre and the musicians who were still writing and performing the blues in small clubs across America.

Though the blues maintains a stable contingent of ardent followers—composed of fans and musicians alike—it fails to command the type of attention that it once did, largely due to the later appearance of musical forms such as jazz, R&B, rock and roll, and hip-hop. However, the spirit of survival characteristic of the blues, as well as the history of the community from whence it comes, is still imbedded within each 12-bar progression. And contemporary music—and African American literature—owes its popularity, in large part, to the path laid by the Blues Aesthetic.

The blues, a universally representative art form,[5] works as a literary aesthetic for precisely this reason: what can be articulated through the music can also be derived from the writing. From the dawn of slavery to the post-slavery/Reconstruction era, through the Civil Rights Movement, and up to the present day, the blues has survived the shifts in American society by chronicling the evolution of black culture, both psychologically and artistically. As an aesthetic principle, the blues initially symbolized the way in which African Americans saw the world (and vice versa) during the most transitional periods in American history. Later, the Blues Aesthetic would articulate the experiences of African Americans in more modern societies, juxtaposing the feelings of joy at the luxuries of the city with the sorrows of a lingering sense of oppression experienced during the more devastating periods in rural southern America. This blue mentality—which was not always downtrodden—would ultimately impact mainstream American culture through its innovative techniques for cultural expression. Through mediums of art, music, literature, and poetry, the cultural backdrop of the United States experienced a significant shift in the racial climate, from the time of its first emergence in the late 19th century to the present day, and the contributions of its most noted artists would be memorialized within the canons of both American and African American culture.

Blues Documentaries

The blues has been the subject of many documentaries, including Red, White, and Blues, Godfathers and Sons, The Soul of a Man, *and* Warming by the Devil's Fire. *These documentaries are among the seven produced by director Martin Scorsese focusing on the role of the blues in the evolution of American musical culture. Filmmaker Robert Mugge has directed and produced numerous tributes to the genre, including* Blues Divas *(2004), a series of documentaries featuring footage of well-known female blues singers at the Ground Zero Blues Club in Clarksdale, Mississippi, which is co-owned by actor Morgan Freeman. The continued, celebrated presence of the blues in American society is evidenced through these various enterprises and artistic expressions.*

In response to the growing influence of the blues as a literary aesthetic, several volumes of criticism have been penned by scholars of both literature and music. Most prominent among these scholarly texts are *Blues, Ideology, and Afro-American Literature: A Vernacular Theory* (1984), *Langston Hughes and the Blues* (2001), and *The Blues Aesthetic and the Making of American Identity in the Literature of the South* (2003). *Blues, Ideology, and Afro-American Literature*, written by Houston A. Baker, explores the relationship between the blues, American history, and African American literature from the linguistic (language) perspective, citing the significance of African American vernacular in storytelling. In *Langston Hughes and the Blues*, Steven C. Tracy explores the presence of blues structures in the work of Langston Hughes. Finally, in *The Blues Aesthetic and the Making of American Identity in the Literature of the South*, writers Barbara Baker and Yoshinobi Hakutani analyze the works of writers such as George Washington Harris, Charles Chestnutt, and Zora Neale Hurston, among others, finding the links between many of their central themes: racial identity, the place of the blues in the lives of the characters, and the culture of the South. Amiri Baraka's *Blues People* (1963), *Black Music* (1968), and *The Music: Reflections on Jazz and Blues* (1987) can also be referenced for further theoretical consideration on the topic of blues and its aesthetic value.

James Cone's *The Spirituals and the Blues* (2009), a comparative study on these two genres of black music that were important in African American cultural history, also examines the language (code-words) and other survival tools of African Americans during pivotal eras in American history (such as slavery, Reconstruction, and the Civil Rights Movement). Both of these works help to fill in some of the existing gaps in the social history of the blues in earlier texts. Another aspect of blues history that the writer found central to its development of the genre was the impact of location and/or migration. Robert Palmer's *Deep Blues* (1981), for example, narrates the rise of the blues tradition from the Mississippi Delta to the South Side of Chicago through some of its best known practitioners (such as Muddy Waters and Robert Johnson).[6]

NOTES

1. A broader review of blues history can be found in *The History of the Blues: The Roots, the Music, the People* (2003) by Francis Davis, which, in addition to a historical overview, also assesses the ways in which racial tensions altered the perception of the blues and its successes/failures within the larger American musical culture.
2. Jazz is one of the earliest cited musical descendents of the blues; legendary performers such as Duke Ellington, Ella Fitzgerald, Billie Holiday, Dinah Washington, and Charlie Parker are among the many noted practitioners of this art form during the early 20th century.
3. Among the writers who use this device are Langston Hughes, Sterling Brown, Amiri Baraka, and Sonia Sanchez.
4. *The Selected Poems of Langston Hughes*, first published in 1959, has a number of blues poems that elaborate on the same (or similar) themes as expressed in those listed in the text of this analysis.
5. For further discussion, please see *Shadow and Act* by Ralph Ellison (1953).
6. Lyndon and Irwin Stambler's *Folk and Blues: The Encyclopedia* (2001) is an informative contemporary index of musicians and movements that have defined both folk music and the blues. Debra DeSalvo's *The Language of the Blues from Alcorub to Zuzu* (2006), an exhaustive dictionary of blues terms/phrases, is quite useful in the interpretation of most blues lyrics and related conversations. The writer believes that interpreting the blues requires an emphasis on local dialect found within the African American vernacular, audible rhythmic variances, and lyrical intonations, as well as an allegiance to the art of storytelling. These academic texts represent only a small sampling of the available literature on the blues and its broad influence in a very wide range of fields.

FURTHER READING

Akoma, Chiji. *Folklore in the New World Black Fiction: Writing and the Oral Traditional Aesthetics*. Columbus: Ohio State UP, 2007.

Baldwin, James. *Another Country*. New York: Dial, 1963.

Baldwin, James. *Go Tell It on the Mountain*. New York: Doubleday, 1953.

Baldwin, James. *If Beale Street Could Talk*. New York: Dial, 1974.

Baldwin, James. *Just Above My Head*. New York: Dial, 1979.

Baldwin, James. "Sonny's Blues." *Going to Meet the Man*. New York: Dial, 1965.

Baraka, Amiri. *Blues People*. New York: Morrow, 1963.

Baraka, Amiri. *The Music: Reflections on Jazz and Blues*. New York: Morrow, 1987.

Black Snake Moan. Dir. Craig Brewer. Perf. Christina Ricci, Samuel Jackson, and Justin Timberlake. Paramount, 2007. Film.

The Blues Brothers. Dir. John Landis. Perf. John Belushi, Dan Aykroyd, John Candy, and Carrie Fisher. Universal, 1980. Film.

Davis, Francis. *The History of the Blues: The Roots, the Music, the People*. Cambridge: DaCapo, 2003.

DeSalvo, Debra. *The Language of the Blues from Alcorub to Zuzu*. New York: Billboard, 2006.

Ellison, Ralph. *Invisible Man*. New York: Random House, 1952.

Giovanni, Nikki. *Black Feeling, Black Talk*. New York: Afro-Arts, 1968.

Giovanni, Nikki. *Black Judgment*. New York: Afro-Arts, 1969.

"Godfathers and Sons." *The Blues*. Dir. Mark Levin. Prod. Martin Scorsese. DVD. PBS Home Video; Vulcan Productions, 2003.

Handy, W. C. *Memphis Blues*. Indie Sounds, 1994. MP3.

Handy, W. C. *St. Louis Blues*. Indie Sounds, 1994. MP3.

Henderson, Stephen E. "The Heavy Blues of Sterling Brown: A Study in Craft and Tradition." *Black American Literature Forum*, 14.1 (1980): 32–44.

Hughes, Langston. "Blues Fantasy." *Selected Poems of Langston Hughes*. Vintage Classic Edition. New York: Vintage, 1990. 91.

Hughes, Langston. "The Weary Blues." *Selected Poems of Langston Hughes*. Vintage Classic Edition. New York: Vintage, 1990. 33.

Hurston, Zora Neale. *Jonah's Gourd Vine*. 1934. *Zora Neale Hurston: Novels and Stories*. Ed. Cheryl Wall. New York: Literary Classics, 1995. 1–172.

Jimoh, Yemisi. *Spiritual, Blues, and Jazz People in African American Fiction*. Knoxville: U of Tennessee P, 2002.

Killens, John O. *And Then We Heard the Thunder*. Washington, DC: Howard UP, 1984.

Killens, John O. *The Cotillion; or, One Good Bull Is Worth Half the Herd*. New York: Trident, 1971.

Killens, John O. *A Man Ain't Nothing but a Man: The Adventures of John Henry*. New York: Little Brown, 1975.

Killens, John O. *Youngblood*. Re-issue. Athens: U of Georgia P, 2000.

Lady Sings the Blues. Dir. Sidney J. Furie. Perf. Diana Ross, Billy Dee Williams, and Richard Pryor. Paramount, 1972. Film.

McPherson, James. *Railroad: Trains and Train People in American Culture*. New York: Random House, 1976.

Morrison, Toni. *The Bluest Eye*. New York: Holt, 1970.

Morrison, Toni. *Jazz*. New York: Alfred A. Knopf, 1992.

Morrison, Toni. *Song of Solomon*. New York: Knopf, 1977.

Morrison, Toni. *Sula*. New York: Knopf, 1973.

Moses, Cat. "The Blues Aesthetic in Toni Morrison's *The Bluest Eye*." *African American Review* 33.4 (Winter 1999): 623–37.

O Brother, Where Art Thou? Dir. Joel and Ethan Coen. Perf. George Clooney, John Turturro, Tim Nelson, and John Goodman. Touchstone, 2000. Film.

Palmer, Robert. *Deep Blues*. New York: Penguin, 1981.

Powell, Richard J. *The Blues Aesthetic: Black Culture and Modernism*. Washington, DC: Washington Project for the Arts, 1989.

Rampersad, Arnold. "Red Clay Blues." *The Collected Poems of Langston Hughes*. New York: Random House, 1994. 212.

Ray. Dir. Taylor Hackett. Perf. Jamie Foxx and Regina King. Universal, 2004. Film.

"Red, White, and Blues." *The Blues*. Dir. Mike Faggis. Prod. Martin Scorsese. DVD. PBS Home Video; Vulcan Productions, 2003.

Smith, Bessie. *Downhearted Blues*. Columbia, 2003. MP3.

Smith, Bessie. *Empty Bed Blues*. Columbia, 2003. MP3.

"The Soul of a Man." *The Blues*. Dir. Wim Wenders. Prod. Martin Scorsese. DVD. PBS Home Video; Vulcan Productions, 2003.

Stambler, Irwin, and Lyndon Stambler. *Folk and Blues: The Encyclopedia*. New York: St. Martins, 2001.

Traylor, Eleanor W. "A Blues View of Life (Literature and the Blues Vision)." *The Blues Aesthetic: Black Culture and Modernism*. Ed. Richard J. Powell. Washington, DC: The Washington Project for the Arts, 1989.

"Warming by the Devil's Fire." *The Blues*. Dir. Charles Burnett. Prod. Martin Scorsese. DVD. PBS Home Video; Vulcan Productions, 2003.

Washington, Mary Helen. "'I Love the Way Janie Crawford Left Her Husbands: Zora Neale Hurston's Emergent Female Hero." *Invented Lives: Narratives of Black Women 1860–1960*. New York: Anchor, 1988: 237–54.

Wright, Richard. *Black Boy*. New York: Harper, 1945.

Wright, Richard. *Native Son*. New York: Harper, 1940.

Lynn Washington

Paul Dunbar was one of the most popular American poets of the late 19th century and the first African American poet to become known internationally. In his poetry, Dunbar focused on the experience of African Americans in an effort to humanize his people in the eyes of whites. (Ohio Historical Society)

Paul Laurence Dunbar

Part of the first generation of African Americans born after the end of slavery, Paul Laurence Dunbar (1872–1906) was the son of two former slaves who moved to Dayton, Ohio, after the Civil War. Though he wrote plays, novels, and short stories, he made his greatest impact as a writer of poetry, particularly poetry in dialect. While Dunbar was the most successful and popular African American poet before the Harlem Renaissance, several decades after his death, his work was overshadowed by the work of Langston Hughes, Sterling Brown, and others. His work remained popular with readers of poetry, however, and while at the beginning of the Black Arts Movement of the 1960s, his reputation was as an old-fashioned, dialect poet, he was nonetheless influential on poets associated with this movement, including Nikki Giovanni and Maya Angelou; by the 100th anniversary of his birth in 1972, his reputation was on the rebound. Since then, critical interest in his work has continued to grow, as evidenced by the organization of a Paul Laurence Dunbar Centennial Conference at Stanford University in March 2006, marking the century since his death; many of the papers at this conference were later collected in a special edition of *African American Review* in 2007.

Born on June 27, 1872, in Dayton, Ohio, Paul Laurence Dunbar was the son of former slaves Joshua Dunbar and Matilda Murphy. Joshua was Matilda's second husband; an escaped slave from Kentucky who served in the Civil War as part of the Massachusetts 55th Regiment, his marriage to Matilda would not last long. Married in 1871, the couple separated in 1874, filed for divorce in 1876, and officially divorced the following year. Joshua died in 1885 in a home for disabled soldiers. Matilda supported the family by doing laundry, including working for the family of Orville and Wilbur Wright. The only black student in his class at Central High in Dayton, Ohio—where the Wright brothers were his friends and classmates—Dunbar excelled as a student. He was editor-in-chief of the school newspaper, president of both the school's literary society and debating society, and the class poet who wrote the lyrics for the graduating class of 1891.

Dunbar: Little Known Facts

- *Both of Dunbar's parents were born in slavery—one reason, perhaps, that the conditions of the slave were a continuing inspiration to him.*
- *Dunbar's mother, Matilda, was a fine artist in her own right, one whose fine voice and love of music not only served as the basis for Malindy in "When Malindy Sings," but who no doubt inspired the love of music that is evident in his poetry.*
- *Dunbar's father, Joshua, was born a slave and trained as a skilled plasterer. Joshua's story of escape was the inspiration for the "The Ingrate." Like the character in the story, Joshua would do skilled labor not only for his master, but also for neighboring plantations to which his master*

would rent him out. To ensure that he would not be cheated, Joshua's master taught him some fundamentals of math and reading. He later used these skills to plan and enact an escape to Canada on the Underground Railroad. When the Civil War broke out, he enlisted in the 55th Massachusetts Colored Infantry. While stationed on Folly Island, South Carolina, with duties that mostly consisted of support duties for white soldiers, Joshua was discharged due to varicose veins. Several months later, he re-enlisted, this time in the 5th Massachusetts Calvary, a combat unit. His company was active in the campaign against Petersburg of 1864–1865, and Joshua received two promotions, first to corporal, and then to sergeant.

As a student, he had published some poems in the *Dayton Herald*; after graduation, he applied for a job as a reporter there, but without luck. Instead, he found a job as a hotel elevator operator. He continued to read and write widely, including during slow times on his job, and sold two stories to a newspaper syndicate, which encouraged him to believe in himself as a writer capable of professional sales. When a former teacher asked him to address the Western Association of Writers meeting in June 1892, he wrote a poem as a welcoming address, which led to his invitation to join the association. During this time, he also founded a black newspaper, the *Dayton Tattler*.

In 1893, he published a collection of 56 of his poems titled *Oak and Ivy*; selling copies himself for $1 apiece, he quickly recouped the $125 printing cost. The same year, he was invited to recite his poetry at the World Columbian Exposition, where he met Frederick Douglass, who became a strong supporter, hiring the young writer as a clerk in the Haitian Pavilion and declaring that he was the most promising young colored man in America. While in Chicago, he also had the chance to meet some of the other leading black writers of his day, including Ida B. Wells and James Campbell, a poet who, like Dunbar, frequently worked in dialect.

Upon Dunbar's return to Dayton, he again suffered financial challenges. Two friends and supporters of his work, psychiatrist Henry A. Tobey and attorney Charles A. Thatcher, encouraged him to move to Toledo and not only arranged for him to recite his poems at libraries and literary gatherings but also funded the publication of Dunbar's second book, the one that was to win him a national audience, *Majors and Minors* (dated 1896 but published 1895).

In the June 1896 issue of *Harper's Weekly*, William Dean Howells, the novelist and critic who was perhaps the leading tastemaker of his day, favorably reviewed *Majors and Minors* but with a reservation that was to come back to haunt the poet. Explaining that the "Majors" of the title were the poet's Standard English poems, he declared that while none of them are "despicable," most are not especially notable. By contrast, in the dialect "Minors," he found, "a man with a direct and fresh authority."

The positive publicity led directly to his first commercial publication, *Lyrics of Lowly Life* (1896) by Dodd, Mead and Co. A collection of 105 poems, most of which had been previously published in *Oak and Ivy* and *Majors and Minors,* the volume contained an introduction by William Dean Howells in which he again especially lauded Dunbar's dialect poetry and repeated from his earlier review the importance of such an accomplishment by a man of "pure African blood."

Buoyed by this success, Dunbar embarked on a reading tour of England in 1897. At his going away party, he met a woman, Alice Moore, with whom he had been exchanging letters for months; the daughter of middle-class parents, a graduate of Straight University (later known as Dillard University), Moore was a teacher and short-story writer whose *Violets and Other Tales* had been printed in 1895. He asked her to marry within hours of first meeting her. Though his tour of England was not to prove to be the financial success he had hoped for, while there he did begin writing his first novel, *The Uncalled* (1898).

On returning home in 1898, he moved to Washington, DC, took a clerical job at the Library of Congress, and married Alice Moore in secret because her family disapproved of him. He published both his first collection of stories, *Folks from Dixie* (1898), and his novel, *The Uncalled,* and collaborated with Will Marion Cook on the first African American musical to be presented to a primarily white audience, *Clorindy; or, The Origin of the Cake Walk* (1898), a collection of songs and sketches. After quitting his job to focus on writing, Dunbar suffered a near fatal case of pneumonia in 1899, which did not stop him from publishing his next collection of poems, *Lyrics of the Hearthside* (1899).

Despite persistent ill health, Dunbar continued to publish at a rapid rate. In 1900, he published a collection of short fiction, *The Strength of Gideon and Other Stories.* Three novels in three years followed: *The Love of Landry* (1900), a Western novel; *The Fanatics* (1901), a Civil War novel; and *The Sport of the Gods* (1902), the novel which continues to attract the most acclaim, about a black family who leaves the South for the North, only to run into a new set of problems.

In 1902, Alice and Paul separated. His health continued to be a problem. He began drinking heavily, in part hoping to control his coughing. Yet even as his health deteriorated, he kept up his prolific authorial pace. Several more books of poetry followed; in 1903 he published a well-received book of plantation stories, *In Old Plantation Days,* which relied heavily on the established conventions of the plantation tradition, with varying degrees of success; in 1904, he published another collection of stories, *The Heart of Happy Hollow.* By the end of 1905, his health grew worse, and he returned to Dayton, Ohio, where he died in his mother's house on February 9, 1906.

After his death, his reputation initially grew. As Lillian and Gregg Robinson pointed out in a 2007 article, his widow, Alice Dunbar, promoted readings of his works, and black schools and churches would frequently include works by Dunbar as part of their programs. Starting with the Harlem Renaissance, however, an intellectual reevaluation of Dunbar began, and this followed up on the criticism implicit in Howell's early praise. Comparing him to Robert Burns (a comparison many others have since made), Howells had said that Dunbar and Burns were least like themselves when they wrote literary English. Following this comparison further, a line of criticism developed that disparaged Dunbar for trying to write like an English Romantic poet. In the breakthrough anthology *The New Negro,* published in 1925 as the Harlem Renaissance was beginning to define itself, William Brathwaite accused Dunbar of writing from a general folk sensibility rather from a specifically racial one. Several years later, in *Negro Poetry and Drama,* Sterling Brown (1937) repeated and amplified this charge, claiming that in Dunbar's writing, "Old slaves grieve over the lost days, insisting upon the kindliness of old master and mistress, and the boundless mutual affection. Treated approvingly, they grieve that the freedmen deserted the plantation" (32). The suffocating influence of dire poverty gets played down, he asserted, in favor of a sentimental assertion of pastoral values.

While Brown nonetheless lauded Dunbar for the fullness with which he treated black folk life, some later critics were not so kind. Melvin Tolson thought that Dunbar's writing was emblematic of plantation stereotypes that had held back black writing. Ralph Ellison declared that Dunbar had repeated the stereotypes of the minstrel tradition that came from white writers. Edward Margolies declared flatly in 1968 that "No white racist has ever caricatured Negro folk more grossly than Dunbar. His slaves are docile children" (29). Nor are these critiques isolated events; during the 1960s and 1970s, such critics as Jean Wagner, Robert Bone, and Henry Louis Gates Jr. all expressed severe limitations on the value of Dunbar's writing. One of the key moments in beginning a reevaluation of this trend was a 1972 centennial celebration of his birth sponsored by the University of California at Irvine. Several years later, in 1975, came the publication of *A Singer in the Dawn: Reinterpretations of Paul Laurence Dunbar* (ed. Jay Martin). In the Afterword by Nikki Giovanni, a poet of the generation that had generally found Dunbar's work wanting, she declared that Dunbar "is peerless. There is no poet, black or nonblack, who measures his achievement" (245).

Central to almost any discussion of the permanent value of Dunbar's poetry has to be a consideration of his use of African American dialect. Toward the end of his life, Dunbar wrote a short poem, "The Poet," which seems to summarize his deep ambivalence about the success of his dialect poetry at the expense of his other writing. "He sang of life supremely sweet/With, now and then, a deeper note," Dunbar wrote, apparently of himself, and, "He voiced the world's absorbing beat" (1–2). "But ah," he reflects, "the world, it turned to praise/A jingle in a broken tongue" (7–8). The tone of the poem is ironic and amused, but certainly reflects the frustrations that the author had felt in trying to get his Standard English literature to be taken seriously. When Dunbar was writing, use of dialect was very much a literary vogue; one of

America's enduring classics, *Adventures of Huckleberry Finn*, makes extensive use of it. Joel Chandler Harris, a white reporter for a southern newspaper, had become one of America's best known writers by retelling African American folk stories he had heard as a child and as an adult in his popular Uncle Remus stories, some of which faithfully recreated, to the best of the writer's ability, the various shades of dialect he remembered from childhood. Minstrel shows, which featured white actors in blackface singing dialect songs of pathos and comedy, had become one of America's favorite forms of entertainment. Thomas Nelson Page, a white writer who wrote dialect-heavy stories, was leading a literary movement that was known as the *plantation school*, in which the old South of slavery was sentimentalized. In African American writing, William Wells Brown had made heavy use of dialect in his first novel, *Clotel; or, The President's Daughter*; and though he had yet to make an impact, Dunbar's contemporary African American writer Charles Chesnutt had already begun to write his early dialect stories. Nor were the only dialects that were popular necessarily southern or black; James Whitcomb Riley, a writer who had directly influenced Dunbar, had frequently featured Hoosier dialects in his writing.

By the time Dunbar started writing his poetry, dialect writing had already developed a few conventions. Among these were phonetic spelling; words would be deliberately misspelled to suggest the way the word might be pronounced; often, these printed distortions would become so extreme as to be almost unrecognizable to the eye, but not when read aloud, providing a source of easy humor. Nonetheless, even the most authentic dialect writing only suggests spoken language rather than completely reflecting it; dialect writing rarely reflects the stammers, the false starts, the irrelevant interjections that are a part of true human speech. This can especially be seen in poetry, where the art of the dialect poet gives poems the shape and compression that poetry demands, while still suggesting sounds and word choices close to how a dialect speaker might sound. Because of the nonstandard nature of dialect writing, certain themes tended to dominate, chiefly humor and pathos. Love, too, was a common theme of dialect poetry, but with the lover often viewed in a comic light. This limitation of theme led to the proliferation of certain recognizable stereotypes, such as ex-slaves remembering the simpler days of slavery, or ridiculous looking young men overdressing to impress a lady. Mark Twain's *Huckleberry Finn* was relatively unusual in its use of a dialect character to voice a theme of common, shared humanity. During the Harlem Renaissance, Langston Hughes and Sterling Brown, especially, would expand the thematic range of dialect poetry in part by severely restricting the use of deliberate misspellings, focusing instead on word choice to suggest dialect. Similarly, Richard Wright would use dialect in fiction to voice the anger of racial inequality, but this, too, was a 20th-century innovation, several decades in the future for Dunbar.

To understand what Dunbar could do in dialect, and why all but his harshest critics concede that he elevated the genre, there is no better poem to start with than one of his most reprinted dialect poems, "An Ante-Bellum Sermon." Told from the perspective of a slave preacher speaking to his flock about Moses and the Exodus, the poem's speaker adopts a rhetorical trickster's strategy to assure his congregation that God hates slavery, and that he will end it, even while he declares, in case anyone reports back to the master about him, that he's not "preachin' discontent" (48) but only speaking "de' fac's" from "scriptuah" when he says "a servant/Is a-worthy of his hire" (59–60; a line taken from Luke 10:7). The Pharaoh of old had to come to learn that "Evah mothah's son" that God gave breath to was free, and that God's "almighty freedom/Should belong to evah man" (67–68). So if God sent a Moses once to save people from slavery, he will again, because "his ways don't nevah change" (44). Many critics have found in this poem evidence of what W.E.B. Du Bois, writing in *The Souls of Black Folk,* would come to call "double-consciousness," by which he meant an African American awareness of oneself both as a self and as viewed by the white world. When used by this preacher as a deliberate rhetorical strategy, this double consciousness creates a kind of circle around those of his audience who understand that he is indeed saying that African American slavery is against God's law as he understands it, and the distant white overseers who only see a slave preacher talking somewhat comically about the Bible. In Dunbar's own day, slavery had been over for 30 years; however, the racial discrimination of Jim Crow was on the rise. Though Dunbar was popular among both black and white readers, it is not hard to see that this poem may have held different meanings among these audiences. The white audience might well have seen a comic presentation of a slave preacher using dialect and the Bible to hearten his congregation, whereas the African American audience would more likely have seen the implied comparison between the battle against slavery and the battle against Jim Crow discrimination. If one was wrong, so was the other; if God opposed slavery, he'll oppose segregation.

In interviews, Maya Angelou has often cited the percussive rhythms of Dunbar's poem "A Negro Love Song" as a 19th-century forerunner of 20th-century rap. Whether one agrees with this or not, her observation does call attention to the importance of music to Dunbar's poetry. The narrative of "A Negro Love Song" tells of a young man walking his lady home, hoping and planning to steal a kiss—which he does. The percussive refrain, "Jump back, honey, jump back," besides suggesting dance, serves to heighten and punctuate the feelings of anticipation and accomplishment. Music, particularly in its ability to alleviate misery, but also its ability to celebrate good times, is one of the most common themes in Dunbar's poetry, evident in some of his best loved poems, like "A Banjo Song," and in numerous of his lesser known works—"Hymn," "Dirge," "The Song," and many others—especially in "When Malindy Sings."

Widely considered to have been inspired by the singing of his mother, Matilda, "When Malindy Sings" begins with the narrator telling "Miss Lucy" to stop practicing her singing; she'll never be as good as Malindy because she does not have the "nachel o'gans." When Malindy sings, fiddlers stop fiddling, birds stop whistling, and banjo players stop their fingers. Singing "Come to Jesus," she causes sinners to repent; when she sings "Rock of Ages," the audience breaks into tears. Her singing is sweeter than the music of the most educated band, and holier than the music of church bells. The poem ends with the narrator hushing his household, because he thinks he can hear the echoes, through the breath of "angel's wings" of "Swing Low, Sweet Chariot"—"Ez Malindy sings." Besides being a moving tribute to the power of one woman's singing, such a poem calls attention to the importance of the African American church traditions in celebrating and developing individual talent.

The way Dunbar celebrated music and its importance to black spiritual and social life led many critics to find fault with his writing. The slave speaker in "A Banjo Song," for instance, begins by complaining about all of the worldly aches and sorrows he has to swallow down—and then announces that to feel better, all he needs to do is to take "My ol' banjo f'om de wall." Where a sympathetic reader might see a celebration of culture as a survival strategy, critics have sometimes seen a trivialization of black pain at a time when direct confrontation was called for. Worse, these images of slave life are very similar to the images of African Americans that were being presented in minstrel shows, where white actors would appear in blackface makeup and perform comic or pathetic songs about life on the slave plantation. The stereotypes promoted by such songs, the vast majority of which were written by white writers, were frequently mistaken by white audiences as authentic expressions of black life. It is clear that Dunbar was influenced by this tradition, in both his poetry and his writing for musicals. The important issue, however, is what new perspectives he brought to the material (such as the slave's legitimate complaints about having to bear the pains of slavery) to make it fresh and vital, which most critics now believe he did.

Perhaps the best poem to turn to for clues in understanding his use of dialect is his Standard English poem, "We Wear the Mask." The double consciousness evident in "An Ante-Bellum Sermon" gets a full treatment herein one of his best-loved Standard English poems. It begins,

> We wear the mask that grins and lies,
> It hides our cheeks and shades our eyes,—
> This debt we pay to human guile;
> With torn and bleeding hearts we smile,
> And mouth with myriad subtleties. (1–5)

The initial "we" is unstable. Is the "we" the sum total of humanity, and the poem therefore a poem about people's inability to reveal themselves to one another simply and directly? Is the "we" of the poem the collective voice of slaves? Is it the collective voice of African Americans? All of these interpretations are possible. The later lines,

> We sing, but oh the clay is vile
> Beneath our feet, and long the mile;

But let the world dream otherwise,
We wear the mask! (12–15)

strongly suggests the experience of slaves, but without excluding other interpretations. One way of interpreting the poem is as a statement of the human
experience drawn especially from the experience of slaves. Another interpretation sees a key to his dialect poetry: The dialect tradition he will spend much
of his career working in is a mask, a survival strategy inherited from slavery,
and he is appealing to the reader to consider what lies beneath it.

There is no doubt that Dunbar's writing, taken as a whole, conveys rural,
pastoral values as opposed to urban ones. In "At Candle-Lightin' Time," for
instance, a slave, Ike, comes in from working the fields to eat supper and
make shadow puppets on the wall to entertain his children. Even though set
during slavery, there is no hint of protest or anger at the brutality of the system; instead, the poem celebrates hard work and simple pleasures, describing
details of life that would have been very familiar to the African American
sharecropping tenant farmers who were many of Dunbar's contemporaries.
Rather than detailing the grievances of slavery, Ike, like the speaker in "When
De Co'n Pone's Hot," finds solace in the simple pleasures that life offers. Dunbar's critic J. Saunders Redding finds such poems to depict "Negroes as folksy,
not-too-bright souls…whose problems can be solved by the emotional and
spiritual equivalent of sticks of red peppermint candy" (Redding, qtd. in Robinson and Robinson 219). Such a critique, however, depends upon looking at
a few of his pastoral poems in isolation, and then projecting that they are to
stand in for Dunbar's whole statement on the reality of the African American
experience. Such is clearly not the case. Instead, Dunbar's pastoral poetry reflects small corners of the lived reality of black men and women of Dunbar's
time, and their enduring popularity is in part testament to his success.

If some of these poems fail to break with the traditions of plantation writing, the same cannot be said of all his rural-themed poetry. Dunbar was very
capable of voicing protest, and he does so nowhere more lyrically than in his
ballad, "The Haunted Oak." Written after a decade in which well over a thousand black men had been lynched, often for false crimes or trivial offenses that
crossed the boundaries of Jim Crow standards, Dunbar adapts the traditional
English ballad form to dramatize this politically volatile topic. Based on a
story he had heard about a tree where one branch had withered and died after being used to hang an innocent black man, his poem begins with the tree
being asked why one particularly branch is bare. The tree answers with the
story of a man falsely accused of a crime who was forcibly removed from the
jail by a lynch mob, led by the judge wearing "a mask of black," the doctor
wearing "one of white," and the minister and his son dressed "curiously," that
is, in disguise. The mob hanged the weeping man from the bough in question.
To this day, the oak says,

I feel the rope against my bark,
And the weight of him in my grain,

I feel in the throe of his final woe
The touch of my own last pain. (49–52)

Whenever the judge rides by, the tree sees the soul of the innocent man haunting the judge, and every night feels the same soul haunting the tree. Perhaps
because the overriding mood of the poem is one of sorrow and the uncanny, as
opposed to anger, this poem has often been overlooked by critics who accused
Dunbar of being too accommodating to the politics of segregation. However,
in 1939, Billie Holiday would record the remarkable protest song "Strange
Fruit," a song similarly detailing the uncanny horror of hanging black men
from trees; this has been rightfully recognized as a breakthrough development
in popular music and American culture in general, and we can now recognize
Dunbar's achievement in "The Haunted Oak" as being an important precursor to Holiday's recording.

Dunbar's dialect poem "When Dey 'Listed Colored Soldiers" provides
another interesting challenge to the plantation tradition, in part because it
uses many of the conventions of plantation poetry while avoiding some of
the worst stereotypes. Told from the perspective of a slave woman living
on a plantation, the poem tells the story of 'Lias, who, upon hearing that
the Union is accepting colored soldiers, immediately declares he will enlist;
the refrain at the end of each stanza repeats variations of "W'en dey 'listed
colo'ed sojers an' my 'Lias went to wah" (8+). The narrator begs and pleads
for 'Lias not to go, but he is determined, and when she sees him in his blue
uniform, she can't help but get caught up in pride. After he leaves, she recalls
how her mistress and her mistress's daughter had reacted when the master
and his son went off to war: "I did n't know dey feelin's is de ve'y wo'ds dey
said" (26). At the time, she felt she did; now she realizes she didn't know half
of how they felt till her 'Lias left. This stanza is crucial to understanding the
poem's depth. On the one hand, it establishes a shared bond between the
women, based on their similar experiences of watching a beloved man go off
to war; on the other hand, it is a bond that only the narrator acknowledges.
The constraints of race and class are very much in place, even if the narrator
is able to see beyond them.

At the end of the poem, the father comes home sick and broken. The son
has died, and was left on the roadside. The narrator feels keenly the pain of
the white women of the house, because she has a man in danger. Then she
learns that 'Lias has died, but unlike the young master, was buried with full
military honor. She accepts his death because "dat's whut Gawd had called
him for" (39), to fight and die for his freedom. Remarkably, the poem asserts
the value of cross-racial sympathy, even while it celebrates the struggle for
freedom from race-based slavery.

Perhaps the greatest expression of the importance of pastoral themes for
Dunbar comes in his poem "Sympathy," in which he imagines what a caged
bird looking at open fields must feel. A poem whose popularity has increased
since Maya Angelou used a line from it for the title of her autobiography,

I Know Why the Caged Bird Sings, it suggests in three successive stanzas that the writer (and therefore the reader) knows what the caged bird feels as he looks out at woods and streams, why he beats his wings flying against bars again and again, and why he sings. The extreme anthropomorphism demands that we see the bird not as a bird at all but as a slave. After the wistful sadness of the first stanza and the extreme pain and frustration of the second, the singing in the third stanza is surprising:

> I know why the caged bird sings, ah me,
> When his wing is bruised and his bosom sore,—
> When he beats his bars and he would be free;
> It is not a carol of joy or glee,
> But a prayer that he sends from his heart's deep core,
> But a plea, that upward to Heaven he flings—
> I know why the caged bird sings! (14–21)

This final stanza can in many respects be characterized as a poetic rendering of what Frederick Douglass said about slave singing in chapter 2 of his first autobiography, *Narrative of the Life of Frederick Douglass, an American Slave.* Explaining that slaves sing most when they are unhappy, he declared that slave singing is "a testimony against slavery, and a prayer to God for deliverance from chains," exactly as it is for the bird in the poem (*Narrative* 11). While the song may be an articulation of the slave's experience, the feelings, Dunbar's poem suggests, are well within the range of all human sympathy.

Dunbar's most complex break with the literary tradition of plantation writing probably comes in his best-known and most critically acclaimed novel, *The Sport of the Gods.* By 1902, when Dunbar published this novel, the theme of young people moving to the city only to be seduced into immorality had been developed in the naturalistic fiction of Stephen Crane's *Maggie* and Theodore Dreiser's *Sister Carrie;* Dunbar's novel develops a similar theme, but with the important distinction that he is focusing on an African American family, the Hamiltons.

At the beginning of the novel, the Hamiltons, led by Berry Hamilton, have achieved apparent economic security through decades of loyal service to the family of the former slave owning Maurice Oakley. As the Oakleys' postwar affluence increases, so do the material conditions of Berry and his family, all of whom work for the Oakleys, and to an extent they grow apart from the black community, who look with envy at their success. When Maurice's half-brother Francis takes money from Maurice, Berry is accused of stealing the money, based solely on his race. After Berry is sentenced, his family, led by the mother Fannie, decides to go to New York, a place none of them has been and where they know no one, because what they have heard seems to offer hope and glory.

The children, Joe and Kitty, immediately fall in love with city life. Joe becomes part of a drinking crowd, the Banner Club. Kitty uses her singing talent to break into Vaudeville Theatre and becomes a rising starlet. Joe falls in love with a chorus girl and friend of Kitty's, Hattie Sterling, whom he murders in a jealous rage; like his father, he goes to prison. Fannie (believing she is divorced from Berry) marries a gambler named Gibson who becomes abusive.

Eventually, Francis Oakley confesses his guilt and Berry's innocence to Maurice. Although Maurice tries to suppress the truth to maintain the family name, a reporter named Skaggs working for the New York *Universe* discovers the truth, and manages to get Berry free. Berry travels to New York to reunite with his wife, and learns about his son's imprisonment, his daughter's life as chorus girl, and his wife's marriage to Gibson. Taking a job with the *Universe*, he plots Gibson's murder, but Gibson's sudden death in a fight at the racetrack frees Fannie. Fannie and Berry reunite, and take up residence in their old cottage near the Oakleys', listening at night to the shrieks of the now-mad Maurice. Their life, the narrator informs us, was not a happy one, but was all that was left to them.

Many critics have viewed the *The Sport of the Gods* in the tradition of naturalism. The Hamiltons are buffeted by socioeconomic forces far beyond their control, and often beyond their understanding. Even Berry's eventual freedom is a quirk of fate; Skaggs is not presented as high minded but as ruthless, and his ability to bring down Maurice is due to his lack of scruples and his employer's deep pockets; it is a triumph of northern capital over southern agrarianism. Another important touchstone for interpretation is Booker T. Washington's 1895 Atlanta Exposition (aka Atlanta Compromise) address, in which he asserted deep skepticism about the promise of northern cities, saying that only in the South are blacks given a "man's chance" to succeed. Though the novel does not express Washington's hope for a harmonized South, it clearly does share his suspicions about the North. Bridget Harris Tsemo, however, reads the Hamiltons' migration to and from the North against the confinement of slavery dramatized in the poem "Sympathy," and concludes that the novel is ultimately about the inevitable conflicts African Americans would face in the North or the South, but also the importance of having the choice of how to face them, and the courage to face them with dignity, as the Hamiltons do in the end. Certainly, the novel is a major break from the plantation tradition; the Hamiltons start out as true believers in the bonds between wealthy white aristocrats and their black servants, and are betrayed for their loyalty. In addition, as the first African American novel to take the obstacles of northern, urban life as a theme, the novel serves as an important forerunner to Richard Wright's *Native Son* (1940) and Ralph Ellison's *Invisible Man* (1953).

By contrast, two stories from *The Strength of Gideon and Other Stories*, the title story and "Viney's Free Papers," are notable for maintaining some of the conventions of the plantation tradition while still trying to create depth of character. In "The Strength of Gideon," Gideon, a loyal slave, makes a deathbed promise to look after the family if anything should happen to the son. When the son goes off to war, Gideon determines to make good on his promise. A year later, most of the slaves have left, and a nearby Union army camp is looking for servants to hire. His fiancée Martha intends to leave to work as a nurse's aid. Won't Gideon leave too? Gideon is faced with the choice: Go to freedom, or stay and fulfill his promise. He chooses to stay. It is not that Gideon does not want his freedom; he does, and he expects it will come eventually, and he certainly wants to marry Martha, but he needs to be true to his promise. The point of the story is not to suggest that Gideon is making the right or wrong choice, but to portray the dignity of a man making a hard decision to be loyal to his word.

A variation on the same theme is "Viney's Free Papers," from the same collection. In it, Ben Raymond, after working to save money to buy freedom for himself and his wife, Viney, discovers he can only afford one; he buys freedom for Viney. Almost immediately, Viney begins to change. She changes her last name from Raymond to Allen. Casting off a slave name upon achieving freedom was an important passage for many former slaves (Sojourner Truth and Frederick Douglass being two notable examples); in this case, it becomes a point of derision among the slave community. Viney soon decides that she is now better than her fellow blacks—"I ain' goin' 'sociate wid slaves!" (65) she tells Ben—and determines to go north. When Ben says he won't go with her, she plans to leave without him. Eventually, though, as she is packing to leave, Viney realizes how much she has hurt Ben, and determines not only to stay, but to burn her free papers, over her husband's gasping objection. The story ends with singing and banjo music coming from Ben's cabin. In much of Dunbar's writing, music is presented as the soothing balm of a slave seeking after a distant freedom; in this case, it is the celebration of having renounced freedom. The story offers an interesting contrast to "The Strength of Gideon" in that, although Viney's choice is similar, the reasons are different; this time, the personal loyalty is to her husband. Though set during slavery, stories like "Viney's Free Papers" and "The Strength of Gideon" do represent struggles that African Americans of Dunbar's time were facing, namely the difficult transition from slavery to freedom, and the struggle between conflicting loyalties during a time when many were fleeing north, leaving behind defining roots to family and community.

Two stories from the same collection that stand in stark contrast to the plantation tradition are "The Tragedy at Three Forks" and "The Ingrate." Of these, the first is a bitter protest story about lynching. After a deliberate fire is set, destroying one of the wealthiest men in Barlow County, a group of citizens decide that this must be the work of black men. A newspaper headline helps to stir up passions. Two blacks are arrested for the crime; the prosecuting attorney tells them that if they persist in swearing their innocence, the mob outside will lynch them, whereas if they confess, the law will see that they are put in jail. They confess, word of their confession soon spreads, and a lynch mob drags the men out to be hanged. After the hanging, a fight breaks out between two men who are also rivals for the affections of the same girl over the rope they each wants as a souvenir; one kills the other. The story ends with an editor thinking, comparing Salem and its witches to the South and its lynching. In a collection that brings depth and dignity to slaves making complex decisions, this story stands out for the sharpness of its anger over white citizens taking foolish, brutal actions without depth or reflection.

While "The Tragedy at Three Forks" is about an issue contemporary to Dunbar, "The Ingrate" goes back into slavery and family history. "The Ingrate" of the story is Josh Leckler, a skilled plasterer on the Leckler plantation. Eager to earn $2,000 to buy his freedom, Josh has been doing side jobs locally, giving most of his money to his master and saving the rest. When Mr. Leckler discovers that some people may have been underpaying Josh, he determines to teach Josh the basics of math and reading, so he will be able to tell if his employers are being honest. Josh takes to the new learning with zest for a year, until Mr. Leckler determines he can read and add, and on his next job Josh points out that the employer, Mr. Eckley is $2 short in his payment; of this, Josh himself only gets to keep 20 cents.

Soon after that, Josh is slow to return from a job; when Leckler goes to look for him, he discovers that Josh used a pass—one he obviously forged using his new skills—to board a railroad train. From there, he is smuggled into Canada and, when the Union begins to recruit colored soldiers, he makes his way to Boston to enlist, and is shortly made a soldier. The story ends with Mr. Leckler reading the rolls of a colored regiment and seeing the name of his old slave; "oh, that ingrate, that ingrate!" (681) he complains to his wife. The ironies in this story go beyond the obvious, that Mr. Leckler's clear motivation for teaching Josh is for his own wealth, which is what empowers Josh to escape, but also go to the less obvious story-telling strategy; the emphasis of the story is not on the accomplishment of a slave planning and achieving his escape to freedom, but rather on the greedy narrow-mindedness of the slave owner who didn't see it coming.

Throughout his career, Dunbar wrote a number of sonnets on men who were important to African American history—"Booker T. Washington," "Robert Gould Shaw," and "Frederick Douglass." Of these, his poem to Washington is probably the most straightforward, as it is a celebration of racial uplifting as epitomized by the life story of the best known race leader of his day. "A poor Virginia cabin gave the seed" (5) he writes, from which came the "peer of princes" (7). Washington moves on, without looking back at braying hounds, like the front of a forward-moving ship. As glimpsed in this poem, Dunbar's Washington is a heroic leader who will not waver from leading the race forward.

The other two sonnets are somewhat less optimistic. "Robert Gould Shaw" is his poem to the white, Ivy League–educated colonel who led the black 54th Massachusetts Volunteer Infantry. Why, he asks, did fate call you from the "classic groves" (2) to lead the "unlettered and despised droves" (7)? Dunbar is writing an elegy to the dead, but not simply to eulogize him; his model for the elegy is Milton's "Lycidas" in which the poet not only laments the death of a noble spirit but also the conditions of the present time. "In Robert Gould Shaw," Dunbar tells Shaw and those who died with him, "the Present teaches, but in vain!"—a remarkable line, one of Dunbar's full-throated expressions of disappointment with the developments of the Jim Crow era. Similarly, his sonnet to Frederick Douglass, one of several poems he wrote to Douglass, not only mourns the loss of the great man, but of the "evil days" but that have followed his passing, a clear reference to the atmosphere of inequality and racial violence. Now more than ever, the country needs someone from the "harsh long ago," whose voice once amazed the country and even not might sound over the storm and provide comfort "through the lonely dark" days that lie ahead (14).

Dunbar's ability to write poems in African American dialect better than anyone before had ever done may have been a mixed blessing; it certainly provided him an audience for his writing, but it made the audience unreceptive to much of his output. Nonetheless, his achievements in that area can be seen not only in the enduring popularity of some of his best-loved poems, but in the ways in which subsequent generations of poets, including Langston Hughes, Maya Angelou, and Nikki Giovanni, have built on his work. Moreover, as the debate over the lasting value of his work in this specific area has receded, readers have come to realize that he was a writer of diverse talents and serious ambition who died in full bloom.

BIBLIOGRAPHY

The Best Stories of Paul Laurence Dunbar. Ed. Benjamin Brawley. New York: Dodd, 1938.
The Collected Poetry of Paul Laurence Dunbar. Ed. Joanna Braxton. Charlottesville: UP of Virginia, 1993.
The Paul Laurence Dunbar Reader. Ed. Jay Martin and Gossie H. Hudson. New York: Dodd, 1975.
The Sport of the Gods. New York: Dodd, 1902.
The Strength of Gideon and Other Stories. New York: Dodd, 1900.

FURTHER READING

Brown, Sterling. *Negro Poetry and Drama.* 1937. Reprinted in *The Negro in American Fiction and Negro Poetry and Drama.* New York: Arno, 1966.
Gayle, Addison, Jr. *Oak and Ivy: A Biography of Paul Laurence Dunbar.* New York: Anchor/Doubleday, 1971.
Giovanni, Nikki. Afterword. *A Singer in the Dawn: Reinterpretations of Paul Laurence Dunbar.* Ed. Jay Martin. New York: Dodd, 1975.
Margolies, Edward. "History as Blues: Ralph Ellison's *Invisible Man.*" *Native Sons: A Critical Study of Twentieth-Century Negro American Authors.* Philadelphia: Lippincott, 1968.
Martin, Jay, ed. *A Singer in the Dawn: Reinterpretations of Paul Laurence Dunbar.* New York: Dodd, 1975.
Paul Laurence Dunbar. Spec. issue of *African American Review* 41.2 (2007).
Revell, Peter. *Paul Laurence Dunbar.* Boston: Twayne, 1979.

Robinson, Lillian S., and Greg Robinson. "Paul Laurence Dunbar: A Credit to his Race?" *Paul Laurence Dunbar*. Spec. issue of *African American Review* 41.2 (2007): 215–25.

Tsemo, Bridget Harris. "The Politics of Identity in Paul Laurence Dunbar's *The Sport of the Gods*." *Southern Literary Journal* 41.2 (2009): 21–37. Web. 2 Sept. 2010.

Thomas Cassidy

Henry Louis Gates Jr. is an English literature and African American studies professor who has taught at Yale, Cornell, and Duke Universities and is currently teaching at Harvard. (Justin Ide/Harvard News Office)

Henry Louis Gates Jr.

One of the scholars/pubic intellectuals most responsible for establishing African American literature and culture as a professionally respectable field of academic study in the 1980s, Henry Louis "Skip" Gates Jr. (1950–) is the chair of the W.E.B. Du Bois Institute for African and African American Studies at Harvard University. He is a prolific author of monographs and scholarly articles, editor of many essay collections and anthologies, and contributor to magazines such as *The New Yorker, Time,* and various online journals. He received his BA from Yale, and his MA and PhD from Clare College at Cambridge University in England.

Professor Gates was born on September 16, 1950, in Keyser, West Virginia. He was born to a family of modest means four years before *Brown v. Topeka Board of Education,* and as a result, Gates lived through one of the most transformative periods in American race relations. In his memoir, *Colored People,* Gates describes the biographical and historical background that has clearly informed much of his later work. The small community of Keyser was located far enough away from the larger southern cities that were at the center of the Civil Rights Movement that the changes convulsing the nation came slowly, which means that many of Gates's childhood memories feature a racially segregated but close-knit community. Although not without the occasional rumor of adultery and other scandals one might expect in any extended family rooted in one location, both the class-conscious Colemans, on his mother's side, and the fun-loving Gates families as a whole appear to have been well regarded in their local communities. It seems that one of the implicit aims of Gates's memoir is to re-create this sense of family for other African Americans, if seemingly more for well-educated and middle-class African Americans who may find life in the integrated professional classes sterile and alienating.

Significant Events

- *1987 and 1988: Publishes* Figures in Black *and* Signifying Monkey, *two texts that bring postmodern theory in conversation with African and African American vernacular culture and helps to bring the study of that literature into the mainstream of academic discourse and thrusts Gates into national prominence.*
- *1990: Called as an expert witness in the case against rap group* 2 Live Crew *where he testifies that the group's lyrics employ language games that are common in African American oral traditions, which qualifies their music as art and not obscenity.*
- *1991: Becomes the chair of the African American Studies Department at Harvard University and begins transforming it from a small department to a national and international powerhouse.*
- *1994: Publishes* Colored People: A Memoir, *an autobiography that charts Gates's life and thought over the course of his life up to that point.*

- *1998: Begins a series of documentaries for PBS,* Wonders of the African World, *that explores the contributions of Africa and people of African descent to the world.*
- *2003: Begins a series of documentaries for PBS,* African American Lives, *that traces the family trees of famous Americans.* African American Lives *first focus on African Americans, but* Faces of America, *released in 2010, includes a greater diversity of Americans*
- *2009: Arrested for causing a disturbance after being locked out of his own house. After a series of widely publicized events, he and the arresting officer, Sergeant James Crowley, are invited to the White House to meet with President Barack Obama.*

Gates's father worked in the local paper mill during the day and as a custodian at night. His mother, Pauline, did domestic work in addition to looking after her two sons. She instilled in her sons a sense of self-confidence, and Gates proclaims himself to have been a momma's boy. She was very involved in her sons' lives, even becoming the first black member of the local PTA. However, it was to get closer to his father that Skip joined the little league baseball team. He quickly discovered that he was not an athlete and became a manager, then a sports reporter for the school paper. (This was the beginning of a path that led him to become staff correspondent for *Time* magazine for two years after graduating from Yale.) It was while playing touch football at a church camp that Gates felt a pain in his knee; this turned out to be a symptom of a slipped epithesis, or disconnected hip. He was taken to a doctor who concluded that the pain was a psychosomatic symptom of Gates's being an overachiever because of his desire to be a medical doctor. The doctor asked him to walk and the pressure of his weight sheared away the ball of his hip. His mother then rushed him to the university hospital, but it was too late. As a result, one of his legs is two inches shorter than the other, which is why he walks with a cane to this day.

Because Gates came of age when the walls of segregation were coming down, he was one of the first wave of children bussed to schools in order to integrate them. Gates took advantage of the opportunities, developing a schoolboy crush on a white classmate who eventually rejected him, but who along the way introduced him to reading literature, and rising to the top of his class academically. He was offered a scholarship to the prestigious Exeter Academy in New Hampshire, but he soon dropped out of the school due to homesickness. After graduating from high school, Gates started at Potomac State University, where he was strongly advised to take a class with a Mr. Whitmore, who turned the young man away from his lifetime ambition to be a medical doctor and toward a life of scholarship. This professor urged Gates to go to an Ivy League university, and Gates chose Yale.

While a student at Yale, Gates became involved in the Black Power Movement that roiled the campus, and he reports that he was one of the brothers who policed the blackness of his fellow students. He reveled in the us-ness of black identity, yet rebelled against the determinism implicit in much Black Nationalism. As Gates puts it, he "can't construct identities through elective affinity, that race must be the most important thing about me" (*Colored People* xv). While at Yale, Gates decided that he would not get caught up with complaining about how the man has kept him down or robbed him of his humanity. He argued that those who engage in excessive black radicalism abdicate their responsibility by implicitly accepting the charge that they lack humanity in order to lay the blame for their depravity at the feet of whites. He attributes this perspective to his parents in that they were skeptical about America, but they still deeply believed in its ultimate values. They denied that antiblack racists had all the control of the nation's wealth and opportunities, which meant that there was a great deal of agency left for black people to exert in the country and the world, a view denied by a victim mentality.

Interestingly, Gates appears to criticize the revolutionary spirit he celebrated in *Colored People* by suggesting that as a black radical, he and others like him were looking for a definite opponent, such as Bull Connors, and this political agenda did double work for them. On the one hand, having a definite opponent gave them a real target to direct their outrage and indignation for the continuation of segregation, but on the other hand it was a distraction from the real work of trying to figure out who they were individually. Looking back, Gates muses that much of the revolutionary rhetoric demanded an ideological purity that would have ensured that he remained an alienated and angry intellectual, and "as one for whom the warmth of a village was sustenance, I couldn't begin to afford its ideological membership fee" (*Future of the Race* 18). Gates notes the findings of Jennifer Hochschild's study, which reported that poorer African Americans were just as likely to attribute economic success to political connections and gender preference as they were to attribute it to racial preference, which is in contrast to wealthy African Americans, who are more likely to focus on the race and poverty of less successful African Americans. In his view, cynicism has become institutionalized among African American elites because professional blacks have to interact with elite whites more often, particularly at the higher levels, which means they are more often exposed to subtle expressions of racism. Finally, since upwardly mobile African Americans may feel stigmatized by both the larger African American community and their white peers, they are more likely to develop a psychological defense against the sense of isolation they feel.

In all of his major works, Gates touches on the theme of black struggle to achieve some sort of middle-class respectability in the face of oppression, whether through the mastery of the language of the written word or the assertion of one's self through political or financial success. Gates focused on mastery of language earlier in his career as he sought to establish his reputation as a scholar of literature, and he appears to have incorporated other indices of success in the documentaries where he traces the genealogies of people, mostly famous ones.

In the introductory essay to *"Race," Writing, and Difference* (1988), Gates lays out the history of the perceived (non)relationship between black people and literature. As Gates will repeat many times again in *Figures in Black, The Signifying Monkey, The Norton Anthology of African American Literature,* and elsewhere, the Enlightenment began with the privileging of reason over other forms of human feeling, and the mastery of writing became the clearest sign of not just one's own ability to reason, but the abilities of any given race. Gates notes that even the most careful philosophers like Hume, Kant, and Hegel fell into the trap of promoting the alleged inferiority of people of African descent. This bias coincided with the early European experiences in colonialism around the world, and it was deployed to help rationalize the increasingly systematic oppression and exploitation of all nonwhite people, but particularly people of African descent (*Figures* 3–41; *Norton* xxxviii–xli; *"Race," Writing, and Difference* 9–11; *The Signifying Monkey* 13, 127–32).

In *Figures in Black,* published the year after *"Race," Writing, and Difference,* Gates argues that when America was still a colony, there were those who experimented with the notion of black inferiority by attempting to educate black children. The idea was to test the assumption that black people could not reason and that the lack of a body of written works was proof of that inability. If that were the case, the logic went, it would be impossible to teach them how to write. Many of those who undertook this experiment quickly discovered that there was little difference between black children and white children. Yet, the myth of black inferiority continued unabated, and black writers were repeatedly put into the position of having to prove their humanity through their writing. As a result, each time that a black writer sat down to write, the act itself was overdetermined. Not only was the rhetoric profoundly influenced by the need to directly address white supremacist assumptions that blacks couldn't write or that slavery was justifiable, but the mere act of writing itself was to act as an index of black intelligence.

At the dawn of the Enlightenment, those who wondered if people of African descent could be educated and some families attempted the experiment. What black people actually wrote was of little consequence at this time; what was significant was the mere act of writing itself. Gates uses examples of how literacy affected the treatment of some blacks, such as Amo, who got a PhD from the University of Wittenberg in 1734 and proved to some that sub-Saharan Africans had superior minds. This was an onerous task because these writers were not competing with Newton, but were rather struggling to prove that they were better than apes. In Gates's view, this is the origin of the black literary tradition: To use literacy to argue for and to prove one's humanity. As Gates puts it: "What an ironic origin of a literary tradition! If Europeans read the individual achievements of black in literature and scholarship as discrete commentaries of Africans themselves upon the Western fiction of the 'text of blackness,' then the figure of blackness as an absence came to occupy an ironic place in the texts of even the most sober European philosophers" (*Figures* 14).

For Gates, efforts for black political organization and artistic production represent the "nether side" of the Enlightenment. Gates argues that the early African American texts largely "signified" on three other texts in the Western tradition, namely Peter Heylyn's *Little Description of the Great World* (1633), Willem Bosman's *A New and Accurate Description of the Coast of Guinea* (1705), and Kant's *Observations on the Feelings of the Beautiful and Sublime* (1764). Heylyn is the first to write that because Africans have little wit and lack the sciences, they should not be considered human. Gates claims that most writings about people of African descent through the early 20th century have been variations and elaborations on this theme. In his text of 1705, Bosman relates a story about how black and white people were given the choice between gold and literacy. Blacks chose gold first, leaving literacy to whites, and God was so upset with black avarice that he made the black an illiterate slave. In *Observations on the Feelings of the Beautiful and Sublime,* an anecdote is told about a black man who observed that white men give women too much power then complain that they drive them mad; this seemed reasonable until Kant realized the man was black and therefore what he said had to be stupid. Gates maintains that for W.E.B. Du Bois and others writing through the beginning of the 20th century, literature lost its metaphoricity and allegoricity in order to become social commentary or outright propaganda. Du Bois makes this explicit in his address, "Criteria of Negro Art," delivered before the Chicago branch of the NAACP in 1926. In that address, Du Bois famously declares that "all Art is propaganda and ever must be, despite the wailing of the purists.... I do not care a damn for any art that is not used for propaganda" (*Crisis* 290–97). In making this stand, Du Bois implicitly restricts the creative range of the artist, specifically the black artist, to producing art with an explicit political agenda. In other words, for a writer who happens to be black, skin color defines what one can or should write about, and even the meanings available for interpreting those texts. Gates then criticizes three contemporary texts—Stephen Henderson's *Understanding the New Black Poetry* (1973), Houston Baker's *Blues, Ideology and Afro-American Literature* (1984), and Addison Gayle's *The Black Aesthetic* (1971)—that attempt to formalize this kind of black theory. Gates criticizes Henderson's *Understanding the New Black Poetry* for its section on structure, which posits a literal reading of texts that is belied by the existence of multiple meanings, irony, and the like. Had Henderson discovered black vernacular forms, identified them as black, and then shown how they impress themselves on black literature (which is what Gates does himself), then he would have made quite a contribution, as far as Gates is concerned.

Gates criticizes Houston Baker for essentially claiming that blackness is the repudiation of whiteness, and Addison Gayle for arguing that one must be black in order to properly read black texts. These are what he calls race and superstructure theorists, and what Gates finds so galling about them is that their approaches are reductionist in that they hold to the theory that race determines scholarly interest as well as the capacity to understand literature. Baker's approach makes blackness simply a reaction to whiteness, while Gayle's approach makes it a matter of biology. Gates himself is interested in blackness as a metaphor, as something that is rooted in the black vernacular but is not determined by it, as the ability of race to incorporate other languages makes perfectly clear. Black literature, therefore, signifies on other black texts as well as white texts, which makes it double voiced. Gates is therefore a genuine scholar, interested in literature as literature that pursues a particular trope that suggests blackness. As Gates himself puts it:

> We urgently need to direct our attention to the nature of black figurative language, to the nature of black narrative forms, to the history and theory of Afro-American literary criticism, to the fundamental relation of form and content, and to the arbitrary relationships between the sign and its referent. Finally, we must begin to understand the nature of intertextuality, that is, the nonthematic manner by which texts—poems and novels respond to other texts. After all, all cats may be black at night, but not to other cats. (*Figures* 41)

Here, Gates shifts the theory of one's capacity to recognize and understand blackness to the disciplining of literary scholarship itself. That one is born black or that one has had a range of experiences based on being perceived as black can provide a useful background that one can employ in unpacking black literature; however, what is most important is the study of black-authored texts, vernacular language, and academic theory.

The following year, Gates published *The Signifying Monkey* in which he explains that it is his mission "to enhance the reader's experience of black texts by identifying levels of meaning and expression that might otherwise remain mediated or buried beneath the surface" (xx). He not only wants to challenge the conception that theory does not apply to noncanonical texts, but at the same time seeks to establish a theory that is organic within African American literature itself and just as distinct as he believes African American literature to be. This is why he argues that black vernacular offers insight into a theory that is autonomous from Western traditions. To establish how the vernacular is rooted in Africa, Gates turns to "two signal figures, Esu-Elegbara [Yoruba character] and the Signifying Monkey [African American character]," as representing language games (xx). Gates argues that both are related as diasporic phenomena, and that he does not create a canon and merely select texts based on their suitableness for his aims. Instead, this is an attempt to come to a theory of the tradition of African American literature. Gates wants to show how the black vernacular "informs and becomes the foundation for formal black literature" (xxii). He states:

> It is probably true that critics of African and Afro-American literature were trained to think of the institution of literature essentially as a set of Western texts. The methods devised to read these texts are culture-specific and temporal-specific, and they are text-specific as well. We learn to read the text at hand. And texts have a curious habit of generating other texts that resemble themselves. (xxii)

Here, Gates seems to suggest that he hasn't been influenced by those texts; they're texts by and about others that are irrelevant to his own experience. Yet, all his values are of the bourgeoisie. He later accepts this critique, but says that black texts register a difference in specific language use—the source of which is, of course, the black vernacular. As Gates states, "To rename is to revise, and to revise is to Signify" (xxiii); he sees the "proper work" of black criticism to "define itself with—and against—other theoretical activities" (xxiv). Black critics must always be comparativists because, free of the white man's gaze, black people created their own unique vernacular structures using repetition and revision, which are fundamental to the black artistic forms. As he puts it, "Whatever is black about black American literature is to be found in this identifiable black Signifyin(g) difference" (xxiv).

To identify these differences, Gates goes on to discuss the black tradition being double voiced and identifies four versions of double-voiced textual relations: tropological revision, the speakerly text, the talking text, and re-writing the speakerly. Tropological revision is a trope that is repeated (and revised) from text to text. Examples of these tropes include the protagonist's descent underground, the vertical ascent from South to North, and figures of the double, including double consciousness. The "talking book" is the first major trope, starting with Gronniosaw's 1770 slave narrative; this shows up at least four times by 1815. The speakerly text is characterized operating in the vernacular mode to speak to the reader, thereby deploying hybrid narra-tive voices that are not exclusively that of the narrator or the protagonist. The talking texts are texts that speak to each other, but indicate a shift from the mimetic to the diegetic; or a shift from an effort to render life as accurately as possible to one where the narrator asserts self-conscious control over the narrative. Finally, rewriting the speakerly text refers to how Alice Walker's embrace of the diary form in *The Color Purple* is distinguished from Ishmael Reed's "motivated" effort to parody or critique the black tradition. In *The Color Purple*, Walker uses the traditional white epistolary form to tell the story of poor, black Celie; whereas Reed's poetry uses the traditional styles that were popularized by black poets of his day. Gates argues that literary discourse is the most black when it is the most figurative, and that modes of interpretation that are most in accord with the vernacular tradition direct attention to the manner in which language is used.

Gates lays out a range of definitions of signifying, all of which turn on the notion of language play, playing the dozens—a ritualized form of insult—and the like. It is supposed to be a deferral of meaning, yet it is tied to a sense of meaning that those in the black community get, but whites do not. He distinguishes between signifyin(g) and playing the dozens in that the dozens are always about bringing someone down by insulting one's opponent or a family member, but signifying can serve to build up an interlocutor as well as to tear him down. There's an example where he relies on an early rapper, H. Rap Brown, who gives a rap that Gates seems to read merely as expressing one's feelings; however, he somehow fails to discuss the obvious turn to a "you," presumably white, that the rap castigates for not doing more to help the less fortunate like himself. What Gates misses here is that there is less of a rhetorical wordplay going on and more of a direct plea for the recognition of humanity and expression of charity (*Signifying* 74).

Gates also promotes the notion of signifying as linguistic wordplay that operates as competition, which is perfectly in line with a capitalistic society, and even goes so far as to refer to the "ironic" leisure class of black Americans that are without gainful employment, a "leisure class with a difference" (*Signifying* 76). Gates observes that much of the black tradition of criticism has focused too much on treating language as transparent, rather than noting its use of trope. Thus, signifying does not always simply mean wordplay; it also means ways of meaning rather than meaning itself.

Metaphorical signifying is when the interlocutor gets the indirect message implied by the speaker, while third-person signifying is when the interlocutor is excluded from the message, but third party "insiders" listening in on the exchange "get it." Gates takes his eight characteristics of signifying from sociolinguist Geneva Smitherman: indirection, circumlocution; metaphorical-imagistic (images of everyday world); humor, irony; rhythmic fluency and sound; "teachy but not preachy"; directed at person(s) in a situational context; punning, play on words; and the introduction of the logically or semantically unexpected (*Signifying* 94).

Gates maintains that the slave narratives are "the most obvious site to excavate the origins of Afro-American literary tradition" (*Signifying* 127), and stresses the importance of literacy in those texts. He notes the irony of the "literature of the slave" because slaves were not supposed to be "human" to the extent of being able to publish literature. They "stole" literature, therefore making their learning "impolite learning": "the texts of the slave could only be read as testimony of defilement: the slaves *representation* and reversal of the master's attempt to transform a human being into a commodity, and the slave's simultaneous verbal witness of the possession of a humanity shared with the Europeans" (*Signifying* 128). The text then explores several different early slave narratives that use the theme of the talking book (in addition to other objects, such as gold), and how each of these writers use that trope to signal their elevation from slavery to humanity in their own eyes, as well as in those of their captors. There is also an evolution away from religious import, though most of these texts retain a strong religious element.

In his discussion of Zora Neale Hurston, Gates notes that with the collapse of slavery, black writers were left to address the scattered effects of a splintered racism between the Civil War and the Jazz Age (*Signifying* 171). A central concern is with the idea of an authentic black voice that could challenge de facto and de jure segregation with its exceptionality, while at the same time making a case for everyone caught behind the color line. Black writers were forced to confront entirely new circumstances, yet had to revise and rework many of the tropes from the antebellum period. Gates starts with Hurston's revision of Douglass's dream of freedom as he stares longingly at the sails of ships in the harbor. Here, Gates credits Douglass with contributing the important rhetorical of the "chiasmus" (*Signifying* 172) to the slave narrative tradition, in this instance when Douglass tells his reader that the reader have witnessed how a man has been made a slave, but he will show how a slave will become a man. It is repetition and reversal. By the end of the Civil War, black writers wrote almost exclusively about their social and political position, but by the turn of the century another issue comes to the fore, namely, how the black voice would be best represented in print. Here, there is a question about what to do with the dialectical poetry written by Paul Laurence Dunbar, especially as writers like F.E.W. Harper begin to argue that black writers are about more than just their plight—that they are also human and can talk about other issues as well.

In 2003, Gates began making documentaries for PBS in which he looks into the family trees of African Americans by examining birth certificates, property deeds, and the like. He begins with the two-part *African American Lives* series and explores the genealogies of famous African Americans, including comedian Chris Rock, actors Don Cheadle and Morgan Freeman, Nobel Laureate Maya Angelou, radio talk-show host Tom Joyner, legendary singer Tina Turner, and others. Gates traces the genealogies of these individuals back in time, in some cases to before the Revolutionary War. In his research, Gates discovers that many of these individuals, some of whom knew nothing about their family histories, had ancestors that were historically significant, such as Chris Rock's great-great-great-grandfather, who had been a slave, joined the Union, and fought in the Civil War. He was elected to the state senate during Reconstruction and was reelected in 1876, only to be ousted when the Hayes-Tilden Compromise ended Reconstruction. He then went on to become a property owner. By the end of his life he owned a lot of property valued at thousands of dollars. Upon learning of all this, Rock claims that if he had been told about it in his childhood, it "would have taken away the inevitability that I was going to be nothing."

The next step in Gates's larger goal of demonstrating the centrality of the African American experience to the American experience as a whole was his 2009 documentary, *Looking for Lincoln*, which commemorated the bicentennial of Abraham Lincoln's birth. Gates begins the documentary with a series of man-on-the-street interviews in which he asks passersby who their favorite president is and why. As expected, the interviews establish that Abraham Lincoln is still the most popular president, in large part because of his reputation as "The Great Emancipator," and because he successfully prevented the United States from being torn asunder. Gates recalls his own childhood admiration for the man "who set my people free," but now recognizes that a larger-than-life myth can obscure as much as it reveals about an individual. The documentary challenges many prevailing myths about Lincoln, but in the end asserts that understanding the full complexity of Lincoln's life, that he was someone who struggled to find the right way rather than someone who just knew it, makes him even more heroic.

Gates's ideas have been controversial from the start. In terms of the collection of essays originally published in the journal *Critical Inquiry* that were repackaged as an edited volume, *"Race," Writing, and Difference,* Tzvetan Todorov takes issue with Gates's focus on how Enlightenment thinkers like Hume, Kant, and others, implicitly or explicitly provided the intellectual framework for the degradation of Africans and people of African descent. Todorov contends that this amounts to a selective reading because these writers also provided the universalist perspective for which the Enlightenment is famous, and that provided the intellectual framework and political platform to launch an effective assault on slavery and racism. Moreover, in Todorov's view, Gates implicitly argues that black-authored texts require a specific set of critical (indigenous) theories that only an indigenous critic with the experience of blackness can provide, in spite of Gates's protestations to the contrary. Houston Baker, on the other hand, chastises Gates for claiming to privilege African American vernacular speech as the source for his indigenous theory when he does not include one essay in the collection that actually does so.

Gates has been criticized by those who insist that African American elites have a special obligation to directly address and to counter political and social realities faced by other African Americans, especially the "underclass." Perhaps the most famous exchange between Gates and one of his interlocutors took place in the journal *New Literary History* in 1987, when Joyce A. Joyce criticized Gates for his embrace of poststructural theory at the expense of more radical politics. This exchange between Joyce and Gates, as personal and vitriolic as it turned out to be, touched on many of the objections that have since been raised about Gates's scholarship and his impact on literary and cultural studies over the years.

Joyce maintained that poststructural theory is irrelevant for black literature because it divides the signifier of race from the signified of racial discrimination and oppression, turning the former into mere metaphor operating in the abstracted worlds of literary and cultural production. This turns race into more of a linguistic puzzle that black literary scholars try to solve in discourse. She regards this as at best an unintentional evasion of the political imperatives of black literature and pedagogy, and an outright rejection of that responsibility at worst. Joyce begins her indictment of the state of black scholarship with an anecdote about an African American student who challenged James Baldwin for publishing the article "On Being White…and Other Lies" in *Ebony* magazine. The student could not imagine how a lay audience would be able to understand the article, and Joyce relates that she sorted through the standard responses she was trained to offer as a literary scholar and found herself unable to offer a response worthy of the question. Joyce decided that she was indeed guilty of the elitism that her student implicitly charged her with, and identifies Gates as the scholar most responsible for making black scholarship less sensitive to the immediate needs of the black community, contributing at least in part to her own failure of this particular student.

Joyce observes that up to the 1980s, publishers did not rely on black academics, but instead relied on black creative writers to comment on black social issues. After the 1980s, however, publishers started to look to black academics, turning them into public intellectuals, including Gates, and Joyce apparently feels this was a bad move. Joyce claims that Gates denies the political and social fact of race as an important use of literary analysis, and she cites *Figures in Black* as evidence of how he focuses on literary texts and their formal features. Where earlier efforts at canon building—such as the anthologies of Stepto, Fisher, and Harper—privileged works that directly challenged white oppression, Gates privileges those aspects of African American culture that developed ways of evading social, political, and economic realities at a time when there were few options for direct engagement. That is, where other critics focus on how texts directly challenged Jim Crow segregation and explicit racism, Gates now wants to focus on the covert linguistic strategies as evidence of creativity, while downplaying the centrality of the oppression that forced the writer to adopt it. Now that black critics can directly confront the lingering effects of slavery and Jim Crowism, glorifying and even reproducing those evasive strategies makes one complicit in the ongoing oppression of other African Americans. These critics, she insists, recognized that "the function of the creative writer and the literary scholar was to guide, to serve as an intermediary in explaining the relationship between Black people and those forces that attempt to subdue them" ("The Black Canon" 338–39). In the next sentence, Gates and others are found wanting:

> The denial or rejection of this role as go-between in some contemporary Black literary criticism reflects the paradoxical elements of Alain Locke's assertions and the implicit paradoxes inherent in Black poststructuralist criticism: for the problem is that no matter how the Black man merges into American mainstream society, he or she looks at himself from an individualistic perspective that enables him or her to accept elitist American values and thus widen the chasm between his or her worldview and that of those masses of Blacks whose lives are still stifled by oppressive environmental, intellectual phenomena. ("The Black Canon" 339)

That is, black critics like Gates believe that their plight is not tied to that of the race as a whole and begin to adopt the elitist perspective of the academy and utilize its linguistic tools. Oddly enough, she then quotes Richard Wright, who seems to have felt this would be a good thing, before she goes on to mention some other texts that give the same sense of estrangement that Ellison's article in *Essence* did. She clearly misreads Wright, who thought that blacks writing as humans and not just as black people (which he regarded as an estrangement) would have a "healthy effect" on the culture of the United States, to be saying that such a move would be an estrangement the critic perhaps "never wanted" ("The Black Canon" 340). She assumes that the primary goal of adopting a poststructuralist methodology was political.

Joyce acknowledges that such estrangement from the masses is true for white critics as well, but the stakes are higher for black critics because the black masses suffer more when the black critic fails to directly confront the structures of white power. She argues that structuralism attempted to counter the existentialist view of isolated humans by revealing how language binds all of us together, and that it and poststructuralism recreate alienation by suggesting that the words on the page have no relationship to the external world. She uses some of the technical terminology to make her point. She agrees with Gates when he claims that the social and polemical functions have "'repressed'" the structure of Black literature, but says she must part ways with him when he outlines the methodology he uses to call attention to what he refers to as 'the language of the black text" ("The Black Canon" 342). She seems to suggest that Gates approves of the way that blackness and absence have been paired in Western thought.

For Joyce, the black creative writer has always attempted to bridge the gap between self and other through shared experiences of blackness and the language that was supposed to convey those experiences directly, and which was intended to promote black pride and dissolve double consciousness. She insists that black people are structuralists in that the signifier and signified are linked, and she takes issue with poststructural theorists like Terry Eagleton who claim that poststructuralism separates the two when he maintains that nothing is ever fully present in signs—that the self is always dispersed in the language trails one leaves behind. She asserts that the "'poststructuralist sensibility' does not apply to Black American literary works" (341–42). She reads Eagleton as claiming that "meaningful or real communication between human beings is impossible" and such a stance contradicts the "continuity embodied in Black American history" ("The Black Canon" 342). Because in her view African Americans are always trying to overcome the failure of language to convey meaning directly, she implicitly charges Gates with acting white when he privileges the language games he argues is the hallmark of African American literature.

Ironically, Gates, who has long represented himself as a trickster figure in academic life, takes Joyce's critique at face value when he could have simply seen it as her calling him out, à la "the dozens," and "paid her b(l)ack." But he doesn't. Gates begins his two-pronged response by taking issue with her implicit distrust of theory. In arguing for the primacy of uninterrogated experience, he suggests, critics like Joyce fail to understand how language operates in delineating subjectivity. He takes aim at Joyce by distinguishing between "the critic of African American literature" and the "black critic" ("What's Love Got to Do with It" 346). The former is any critic who takes an interest in exploring how race functions in the texts produced by and about African Americans; the latter are those critics marked as black; who therefore posit a shared experience and deploy a particular set of assumptions about how literature should be read and what criticism should do to advance the cause of black Americans in general. Joyce and critics like her, he argues, are ethnocentric in that they assume that critics who are marked as "black" have a responsibility to engage in scholarship that is political or even polemical ("What's Love Got to Do with It" 354). Joyce, on the other hand, implies that scholars who privilege Western theory accept a type of "indenture" and adopt a pose of isolation from the community that art is supposed to nourish and liberate ("What's Love Got to Do with It" 349).

Gates counters that he has been using Western theoretical traditions to help create a theory or set of theories that are responsive to the black texts under consideration, not just to apply an existing theory and force black texts to fit. By engaging in this double voicing of theory, he wants to defamiliarize the text from the sense in which it is commonly understood—to lay bare its workings to understand it better and give it the proper respect it deserves. He maintains that "we have more in common with each other than we do with any other critic of any other literature" ("What's Love Got to Do with It" 353). Gates argues that the critic of black literature makes a fatal mistake in racing language and theory as "white" and then avoiding it for that reason, but he also recognizes the danger of "indenture" if one becomes too beholden to it ("What's Love Got to Do with It" 353).

In "A Tinker's Damn," published in *Callaloo,* Joyce updates her criticism of Gates to include *Signifying Monkey,* which was published right after the previous exchange appeared in *American Literary History.* She begins by calling into question Gates's interpretation of his central figure of Esu, the Yoruban Monkey, that plays on words. She cites a scholar who studies and practices Yoruba in order to show that Esu is not about trickery, as Gates maintains, but that he is a more straightforward character in Yoruban myth. She sees literature as having a direct impact on black lives in a way that is presumably different from the way literature operates for white people, and ends the article by suggesting that Gates might be a little more responsive to the plight of actual black people if he experienced black oppression himself, especially at the hands of white law enforcement officers.

Other critics like Eric Lott, Kenneth Warren, and Adolph Reed criticize Gates less from the position that he is in effect betraying "the race" than from the position that he is in effect using the discourse of race as a way to secure his own professional status as an academic and a public intellectual. Unlike critics like Joyce who suggests that black scholars should be political advocates for other African Americans, Lott, Warren, and Reed reject blackness as having any claims on scholars, particularly those identified as African American. At the same time, however, they share Joyce's concern with what they see as Gates's embrace of a culture of celebrity and his implicitly conservative attitude toward notions of success.

In 2008, the 20th anniversary of Gates's *"Race," Writing, and Difference,* the Modern Language Association published a special edition of *PMLA* on "Comparative Racialization," and contributors were asked to comment on the enduring legacy of that work. While the contributions included two laudatory essays by Farrah Jasmine and Valerie Smith that describe the enduring impact of *"Race," Writing, and Difference* and Gates's impact on the study of literature and race, respectively, Eric Lott argues that Gates's recent turn to DNA testing in his PBS videos reveals a larger conservative pattern that was always implicit in his earlier work, including *"Race," Writing, and Difference.*

Also in 2008, Kenneth W. Warren delivered the annual Du Bois lecture at Harvard University in which he credits Gates with creating a space for African American studies but names him as one of the scholars who have deprived African American literature of some of its potency by focusing on it as an aesthetic product rather than understanding it in terms of the moments of its historical and political production. For Warren, Gates's continuing efforts to appeal to a sense of blackness, even a blackness that is largely metaphor, gets in the way of current efforts to come to grips with and effect change in the current historical moment. That race still matters is not disputed by many on the left or right, Warren argues, so to insist that it does matter is not especially illuminating.

The following year, in 2009, Gates became the center of a national controversy when he was arrested for disorderly conduct after breaking into his own house. Gates had returned from a trip abroad and discovered that he had locked himself out of his house in Cambridge; he asked his driver to help him get in. A neighbor spotted the pair and called police. Two police officers, Sergeant James Crowley and Officer James Figueroa, arrived on the scene and demanded proof that Gates was indeed the rightful owner of the house. Gates produced the documentation, but he was also combative and loudly insisted that the officers were being more aggressive because Gates and his driver were black. This led to Gates's arrest. In the ensuing media storm, President Barack Obama, who is usually circumspect on issues of race, was quoted as saying that Sergeant Crowley and Officer Figueroa "acted stupidly." In an effort to stem the tide of racial tension, Obama invited Sergeant Crowley and Professor Gates to the White House for what has since become known as "the Beer Summit."

The fact that Gates's work has generated so much criticism and attention is evidence of the importance of that work in the study of African American literature and culture. As noted at the beginning of this essay, Gates's work has fundamentally transformed not just studies of African American literature and culture, but also the study of American literature and culture as a whole. When Gates first took over the African American Studies Department in 1991, it was very small. In a few short years, he turned it into perhaps the most prestigious program in the country by luring luminaries in the field to Harvard, such as Cornel West from Princeton and William Julius Wilson from the University of Chicago, among many others. The scholarship produced by these academics has had an impact on virtually every discipline in the humanities and social sciences. The study of race has become central in many of these fields, and scholars of all phenotypes can now be found who explore issues pertaining to race. Gates's tireless efforts to bring marginalized art forms to the margin has had a significant impact on other critics, such as those who study hip-hop culture, a field that has rapidly expanded over the past two decades. Gates has also singlehandedly recovered a range of lost black-authored texts, including his detective work that determined that Harriet Wilson's *Our Nig* was indeed written by Harriet Wilson, and the discovery of Hannah Craft's *The Bondwoman's Narrative*. Gates has become what is now called a public intellectual because of his willingness to address the nation at large rather than just other scholars. He writes blogs and has been a frequent contributor to numerous newspapers and magazines, but the PBS documentaries have dramatically increased Gates's public profile. For instance, the success of *African American Lives* surely helped in NBC's decision to air the similarly formatted *Who Do You Think You Are?*

BIBLIOGRAPHY

Monographs

The African American Century: How Black Americans Have Shaped Our Country. Co-written with Cornel West. New York: Free Press, 2000.

Afro-American Women Writers. New York: Macmillan Library Reference, 1998.

Black Literature and Literary Theory. Co-written with Catherine R. Stimpson. New York: Routledge, 1990.

Colored People: A Memoir. New York: Knopf, 1994.

Figures in Black: Words, Signs and the Racial Self. New York: Oxford UP, 1987.

Finding Oprah's Roots, Finding Your Own. Phoenix, AZ: Crown, 2007.

The Future of the Race. Co-written with Cornel West. New York: Knopf, 1996.

Loose Canons: Notes on the Culture Wars. New York: Oxford UP, 1992.

The Signifying Monkey: Towards a Theory of Afro-American Literary Criticism. New York: Oxford UP, 1988.

Speaking of Race: Hate, Speech, Civil Rights and Civil Liberties. New York: New York UP, 1995.

Thirteen Ways of Looking at a Black Man. New York: Random House, 1997.

Edited Works

Africana: The Encyclopedia of the African and African American Experience. Ed. with Anthony Appiah. Boulder: Perseus, 1999.

African American Studies: An Introduction to the Key Debates. Ed. with Jennifer Burton. New York: Norton, 2002.

The Classic Slave Narratives. New York: New American Library, 1987.

The Norton Anthology of African American Literature. Ed. with Nellie Y. McKay. New York: Norton, 1997.

Race, Writing, and Difference. Chicago: U of Chicago P, 1986.

Schomburg Library of Nineteenth-Century Black Women Writers. New York: Oxford UP, 1991. (A 10-volume supplement.)

Articles

"Academe Must Give Black Studies Programs Their Due." *Chronicle of Higher Education* 36.3 (1989): A56.

"The African American Century: A Reality That Is More Complicated and More Heroic Than the Myth." *New Yorker,* April 29, 1996: 9.

"American Letters, African Voices: History of African American Authors." *New York Times Book Review*, December 1, 1996: 39.

"Black Creativity: On the Cutting Edge." *Time,* October 10, 1994: 74.

"Blacklash? African Americans Object to Gay Rights–Civil Rights Analogy." *New Yorker,* May 17, 1993: 42.

"Delusions of Grandeur: Young Blacks Must Be Taught That Sports Are Not the Only Avenues of Opportunity." *Sports Illustrated,* August 19, 1991. http://sportsillustrated.cnn.com/vault/article/magazine/MAG1139954/1/index.htm.

"The Fire Last Time: What James Baldwin Can and Can't Teach America." *New Republic* 206.22 (1992): 37–43.

"How Do We Solve Our Leadership Crisis?" *Essence,* June 1996: 42–44.

"Introduction: 'Tell Me Sir,... What is 'Black Literature?'" *PMLA* 105.1 (1990).

"The Master's Pieces: On Canon Formation and the African American Tradition." *South Atlantic Quarterly* 89.1 (1990): 11.

"Our Next Race Question: The Uneasiness between Blacks and Latinos." *Harper's,* April 1996. http://www.highbeam.com/doc/1G1-18170233.html.

"What's Love Got to Do with It?" *New Literary History* 18 (1986–87): 345–62.

"Words that Wound: Critical Race Theory, Assaultive Speech and the First Amendment." *New Republic* 209.12–13 (September 20, 1993): 37.

Videography

African American Lives. Kunhardt Productions and Thirteen/WNET. PBS, 2006. DVD.

African American Lives 2. Kunhardt Productions and Thirteen/WNET. PBS, 2008. DVD.

America: Beyond the Color Line. Dir. Dan Percival and Mary Crisp. PBS, 2003. DVD.

Faces of America. Kunhardt Productions, Inkwell Films, and Thirteen/WNET. PBS, 2010. DVD.

Looking for Lincoln. Kunhardt Productions, Inkwell Films, and Thirteen/WNET. PBS, 2010. DVD.

FURTHER READING

Appiah, Kwame Anthony. "The Conservation of 'Race.'" *Black American Literary Forum* 23 (1989): 37–60.

Bentsen, Cheryl. "Henry Louis Gates: Head Negro in Charge." *Boston Magazine* July 23, 2009.

Fuss, Diane. "'Race' under Erasure? Poststructuralist Afro-American Literary Theory." *Essentially Speaking: Feminism, Nature and Difference.* London: Routledge, 1989. 73–96.

"Henry Louis Gates." Answers.com. Web. 9 Jan. 2011. http://www.answers.com/topic/henry-louis-gates-jr.

Joyce, Joyce A. "The Black Canon: Reconstructing Black American Literary Criticism." *New Literary History* 18.2 (1987): 335–44.

Joyce, Joyce A. "A Tinker's Damn: Henry Louis Gates, Jr., and *The Signifying Monkey* Twenty Years Later." *Callaloo* 31.2 (2008): 370–80.

Lott, Eric. "Criticism in the Vineyard: Twenty Years after '*Race,' Writing, and Difference.*" *PMLA* 123.5 (2008): 1522–27.

Mason, Theodore O., Jr. "Between the Populist and the Scientist: Ideology and Power in Recent Afro-American Literary Criticism; or, 'The Dozens' as Scholarship." *Callaloo* (Summer 1988): 606–15.

Reed, Adolph. "Tradition and Ideology in Black Intellectual Life." *W.E.B. Du Bois and American Political Thought: Fabianism and the Color Line.* New York: Oxford UP, 1996.

Warren, Kenneth W. *What "Was" African American Literature?* Cambridge, MA: Harvard UP, 2011.

Mark S. James

Many literary critics consider Jean Toomer's *Cane* as the first text of the Harlem Renaissance. (Library of Congress)

Harlem Renaissance

African American literature can conceivably be divided into three chapters to which the Harlem Renaissance acts as the introductory agent of the last chapter: the literature of self-identity and individual freedom. The first chapter of African American literature—the literature of African aptitude—shows the intellectual capacity of Africans through the use of English as a means of expression. The primary writer of this chapter, Phillis Wheatley, ushered in this period with her poetic volume, *Poems on Various Subjects, Religious and Moral* (1773) with poems of perfectly crafted neoclassical European verse. Because English neoclassical poetry relies heavily on the use of metrics, proficient execution of the poetic form is not easy, and her masterful completion of the task was exponentially more difficult because it required near-native familiarity in a second language. Wheatley's volume addressed not only those who declared African Americans as subhuman, but it also spoke to other African Americans who followed her. Her example of literacy and language acquisition inspired them to narrate tales that absolutely needed to be told.

Important Events Related to the Harlem Renaissance

- *1919: 369th Regiment marched up Fifth Avenue to Harlem.*
- *1919: Marcus Garvey founded the Black Star Shipping Line.*
- *1920: Universal Negro Improvement Association (UNIA) Convention held at Madison Square Garden.*
- *1921: The New York Public Library at 135th Street holds an exhibition of African American art, including Henry Tanner, Meta Fuller, and Laura Waring.*
- *1922: Lynching becomes a federal crime.*
- *1923: Bessie Smith records "Down-Hearted Blues" and "Gulf Coast Blues."*
- *1923: Mobster Owney Madden opens the Cotton Club.*
- *1924: Paul Robeson stars in Eugene O'Neill's* All God's Chillun Got Wings.
- *1925:* Survey Graphic *issue, "Harlem: Mecca of the New Negro," edited by Alain Locke and Charles Johnson.*
- *1926: The Carnegie Corporation buys Arthur Schomburg's collection of African American artifacts, which function as the foundation for the Schomburg Center.*
- *1926: Savoy Ballroom opened in Harlem.*
- *1927: Harlem Globetrotters established.*
- *1927: Lois Armstrong and Duke Ellington gain recognition.*
- *1928: The Lindy hop is made famous at the Savoy Ballroom.*
- *1929: Negro Experimental Theatre founded.*
- *1930:* The Green Pastures, *with all-black cast, opens on Broadway.*
- *1934: W.E.B. Du Bois resigns from* Crisis *and the NAACP.*
- *1934: Apollo Theater opened.*

The second chapter of African American literature—literature for freedom— is that of slave narratives, abolitionist novels, essays, and speeches against slavery and included authors Olaudah Equiano, Frederick Douglass, Harriet Jacobs, William Wells Brown, Harriet Wilson, Frances Harper, David Walker, George Washington Williams, and others. They recounted the horrible experiences plaguing Africans snared within the institution of slavery, and they reflected the humanity of the victims by giving the enslaved a collective voice and removing faceless sufferers from a faraway land to pages perused by white readers in their own homes. These tales told not of slaves but fathers and husbands who were unable to protect their wives and daughters from lascivious lechers, of mothers who witnessed their children taken from them and sold away into slavery, and of children who saw their mothers and/or their fathers taken away never to be seen again. The second chapter of African American literature shows how African Americans moved from a collective bondage to a collective freedom.

Where the canonical works of the 18th and 19th centuries spoke of progress, the third chapter of African American literature—the literature of self-identity and individual freedom—is best characterized by the newly found freedom that African American authors explore in their literature. The turn of the century brought the last great slave narrative, Booker T. Washington's *Up from Slavery* (1901), and W.E.B. Du Bois's forward-looking treatise, *The Souls of Black Folk* (1903). Du Bois's work set the cornerstone for the literature of self-identity and individual freedom with his description of how whites viewed African Americans, as well narrating the African American experience from the perspective of the African American living in America. The work that Du Bois began eventually manifested itself specifically within the Harlem Renaissance; his consideration of double consciousness and understanding of what it was like to be perceived as a problem led many African American artists to question who they were and their purpose within American culture. This realization and discussion largely describes what the Harlem Renaissance was: an exercise in self-discovery that manifested itself in the arts that also offered whites an opportunity to see how African Americans saw the world and their place in it.

Artists from this period produced works that discussed grand and philosophical questions as well as everyday experiences. The movement produced high and low art that genuinely reflected the community, and the works revealed a people who were truly coming to see themselves as the determiners of their destinies and not simply the victims of an awful fate. The Harlem Renaissance was the introductory agent that led not only to self-discovery but also to greater artistic works that would populate the canons of African American and American literature later, throughout the 20th century.

The Harlem Renaissance—also known as the New Negro Movement— was a cultural phenomenon that arose from specific historical and political events culminating in the self-definition and further development of African

American through literature, music, and theatre. The Harlem Renaissance was not limited to Harlem, New York, but much of the demonstrable outgrowth from the movement was found there. From this movement came some of America's most distinguished and influential African Americans, including W.E.B. Du Bois, Alain Locke, Jessie Redmon Fauset, Marcus Garvey, Langston Hughes, and Zora Neale Hurston. While much of the scholarship concerning the Harlem Renaissance focuses on the literature and its authors, it is important to note that the Harlem Renaissance was composed of political, musical, and theatrical experiences along with the quotidian experiences of Harlemites.

At the heart of Americanism is the Declaration of Independence's proclamation—"We hold these truths to be self-evident, that all men are created equal, that they are endowed by their Creator with certain unalienable Rights, that among these are Life, Liberty and the pursuit of Happiness." And as fundamentally understood as these rights are to anyone connected with the country, so too is the fundamental understanding of the requirement of economic prowess and sustentation for the procurement, concretization, and maintenance of these rights. While life, liberty, and the pursuit of happiness were said to be unalienable, it was not until African Americans experienced postbellum freedoms and the power to personally control and benefit from the outcome of their labor that they obtained those rights and established their new place within the American landscape.

Where the antebellum South had not been a great place for African Americans, it was not much better afterward. During the new postbellum reality, many whites occupied different socioeconomic lots in life. General William T. Sherman with his field order number 15 took all lands from Charlestown, South Carolina, to Jacksonville, Florida, and gave them to the slaves who had been freed resulting from the North's winning of the war. Whites who were rich suddenly found themselves with little or no real estate and with a very small and finite labor force. Wealth that seemed inexhaustible very quickly saw its limits, and many southern whites became furious with their new plights. Even though General Sherman's order was countermanded, with the lands being returned to its white owners only a few short months later, southerners had to deal with the new Freedmen's Bureau. This organization sought to systematically deconstruct southern culture to create a new paradigmatic structure that set both whites and blacks as equals. That aim was fundamentally antithetical to southern culture, which had well established that pigmentocracy was its supreme maxim.

Some thought that the best means for improving the South was through the economic upward mobility of African Americans. Theoretically, it was a sound idea, because numerous ex-slaves had to support themselves; food and shelter that had always been provided suddenly came with a cost. Former slaves and slave owners entered the financial relationship of sharecropping, where former slaves leased land from former slave owners and paid the lease with a portion of the harvested crops.

While the outward interactions changed, things beneath the surface remained the same. Multiple factors, including unfair trade practices, land contracts, and landowners' outright stealing, prevented the two races from ever coming to be counterparts. Sharecropping became another legally sanctioned means of slavery. African Americans often found themselves attempting to pay off debts that they could never pay, and land acquisition proved to be nothing more than a dream. Furthermore, the initial goals of the Freedmen's Bureau never truly came to fruition, as the federal government later decided that the project was worth neither the economic nor political capital needed to complete the mission. The federal government no longer actively tried to enforce equal protection laws, and the old paradigm of pigmentocracy returned.

Southerners needed to return to the antebellum status quo, where African Americans were reassigned to subhuman ranks. Intimidation through violence and Jim Crow laws were the preferred tools of choice. In the latter portion of the 1800s, deaths by lynching rose dramatically for African Americans in the South, reaching an apex of approximately 150 per year during the 1890s. Augmented by Jim Crow laws that produced unjust trials for African Americans, the South was a dangerous and unfriendly place for African Americans. Beyond that, there was a massive boll weevil infestation that led to the repeated destruction of cotton crops during the summers of 1915 and 1916. The infestation's result was a financial loss so significant that many African Americans realized that there was little or no economic future for them in the rural South. So, they moved north to its industrial cities and its neighborhoods.

The failure of Reconstruction, the inhospitable South, along with the chance of greater economic fortunes and a better way of life in the North, in addition to other drawing factors, fueled the Great Migration of African Americans. With World War I came a halt to European immigration and its supply of labor. The sudden void in cheap labor was something that African Americans gladly filled. African Americans were going to change the landscape of America in a big way. While many African Americans traveled to the Ohio Valley, a great number made their way to a small section of Manhattan, New York known as Harlem.

Even before the Great Migration, there were many African Americans in New York City. During the antebellum period, the North was known as a place of personal freedom. This sovereignty not only included unfettered movement and independence of thought, but also involved the necessary means of self-sufficiency in the way of paid labor. While the North was by no means perfect, with African Americans suffering northern forms of racism and prejudices, it offered more opportunity than what could be expected in the South. In the North, African Americans had access to education, freedom of religion, and a voice—be it a small one—in the political process. The North, even with its shortcomings, was far better for African Americans than the South.

Wages for African Americans in the North were sometimes two to three times higher than wages in the South. Combined with the growing recession that the cotton industry produced for southern workers, the North seemed considerably better. While some African Americans worried about their fates in the North, periodicals such as the *Defender* painted pictures that made dying free in the North sound better than dying oppressed in the South. For many, this was the catalyst necessary for the exodus out of the South. And while southern blacks were heading north of the Mason-Dixon Line, the communities that housed other African Americans in the North were swelling almost to the point of rupture.

In New York City, most African Americans resided in Manhattan's small crowded communities of Tenderloin and San Juan Hill. A segregated area, it continued to grow in population with each passing year and with every new round of southern migrants. While this area was breaking at the seams, other areas in New York were suffering with real estate depression. In Harlem, landlords owned apartments that desperately needed tenants. All that mattered to landlords was profit; they cared about races only in so much as that they knew that they could charge African Americans more rent. African Americans, desperate to leave the overcrowded neighborhoods, willingly paid the higher prices. The work that Phillip A. Payton, an African American realtor, started with a single residence at West 133rd Street in 1905 produced an incalculable and unimaginable outcome.

Payton found a reliable group of tenants—most of whom were African Americans looking to further improve their lots—and his filling of the apartment house began a predictable pattern. When African Americans moved into the neighborhood, the property value began to decline. Harlem, which was originally named after the Dutch town Harlaam and once the home to many rich whites and Jews, soon became the place for upwardly mobile African Americans. Harlem's current residents objected to the new neighbors because they saw a direct correlation between the presence of African Americans and the loss of property values, but it was too little too late. And true to what many thought, with one group came another and another until the demographic nature of Harlem changed.

Where all of New York City consisted of a little more than 20,000 African Americans between 1890 and 1900, it contained more than 220,000 by 1930. Where the African American population once occupied only two small sections of Manhattan and a single apartment house in Harlem, by the end of the 1930s the black portion of Harlem included almost two square miles concentrated between 114th Street and 156th Street and St. Nicholas Avenue and the East River (Wintz 14). Harlem had exploded to become a metropolis for African Americans, a city within a city. It had its own businesses, churches, recreation, and its own social structure; Harlem became a Mecca for African Americans seeking an experience in self-determination. With the establishment of the new metropolis came politics, arts, and the life of the quotidian man. However, the glory of Harlem began to decline with the fallout of the Great Depression, and it all but came to an end in 1935 with the city's race riots.

The Harlem Renaissance was not without its own movers and shakers. The period contended with issues within the African American community, as well as issues beyond it. Because the Renaissance spontaneously occurred, having its participants arrive at a specific point was not an easy task. Some members of the African American community thought the Renaissance was a great opportunity for African Americans to become more greatly accepted in mainstream America, while others thought the time was a great opportunity for African Americans to assert a greater independence. These ideas were set against the backdrop of white America's appointment of Booker T. Washington as the recognized leader of the African American community.

Washington, race leader and educator, was born a slave on a Franklin County plantation in Virginia circa 1856. Because his mother was a plantation cook and his white father unknown to him, Washington had a real and intimate knowledge of the South's relationship with its African American residents. While he missed the harshest elements of slave life with the emancipation of 1865, Washington did not miss the callous life of Reconstruction. After his family moved to West Virginia in 1865, Washington worked hard in salt and coal mines as a preteen.

Enriched by his mother, who bought him his first spelling book, and further educated at the local elementary school that he attended while working in the mines, Washington came to be literate and quite interested in procuring the best life that his education could offer him. To that end, he took a position as a domestic in the home of Viola Ruffiner. Her persistent demands of industry, frugality, and cleanliness were enough to drive other youths away, but not Washington. He embraced her maxims, and she came to respect him and his hard work.

In 1872 at age 16, Washington enrolled in the Hampton Normal and Agricultural Institute. Some 500 miles away from home and with only enough money to cover half of the traveling expenses, Booker T. set off on the month-long journey determined to gain admittance at the new school, which was less than five years old. When he arrived he had only 50 cents, and with that money he asked for admission. It was at this moment that his previous life experiences with Ruffiner demonstrated their greatest usefulness. Before he would be accepted, Washington was given a task of cleaning a specific room. Suspecting, but unsure, that his success would be the criteria for entrance, he cleaned the area until it was spotless (Washington 28). His suspicions were confirmed; after his successful completion of this task, he was indeed a Hampton student.

He did well at Hampton, not only mastering the labor skills of brick masonry and agriculture, but also the school's academic curriculum. Beyond simply learning skills, Washington totally absorbed the philosophy of General Samuel Chapman Armstrong—the school's founder. Armstrong believed the freedman's future rested with a practical education as well as a strong moral fiber. This philosophy would become the cornerstone for Washington and his future work as an educator and race leader. And when Alabama's education commissioners approached Armstrong seeking a white principal for the new school for Negroes, he persuaded them to employ Washington. Upon arriving, he discovered that he had only enough money for salaries; there were no facilities, nor was there any campus. Washington assuaged the concerns of whites in the area and recruited African American students. He taught his first class in a shack, and with help from his white connections at Hampton, Washington learned how to fundraise in general and specifically how to court white benefactors. With these skills and funding, he bought the land on which the Tuskegee Institute would later stand. On that land, students built the first buildings of the institution, as well as growing the food necessary to feed those in the new territory of learning.

Tuskegee grew to have 2,000 acres of land, 100 buildings, and a distinguished faculty composed of the black intelligentsia. The all-black faculty and administration of Tuskegee were the products of Hampton and Fisk University. Some of these great minds were the scientist George Washington Carver, the sociologist Nathan Work, and the educator Olivia Davidson. By all accounts, Tuskegee was a success, and syllogistically, so too was Washington. As the institute expanded beyond its original goals, it began to encompass aiding poor black farmers and encouraging business ventures. By the mid-1880s, Washington had established great popularity on the lecture circuits. His appearances secured additional funding for Tuskegee and granted him more power. Washington slowly became the accepted voice for African Americans in the United States (Muggleston 847–49).

In 1895, Washington made his most famous speech, the "Atlanta Compromise," where he masterfully painted a picture of the state of affairs in the South. He reminded southern whites that they needed African Americans, especially in the labor market, and he encouraged blacks to remain in the South, become educated, and be accepted by their white neighbors. Washington also included the powerful trope of a hand; he noted as the separate fingers make up the entire hand, so too was the capacity of the society to be truly separate yet unified and equal. He argued that attempting to force changes in the law with respect to segregation was unwise and dangerous for African Americans in the South. Some critics suggest that Washington's speech provided a tacit agreement from African Americans that separate but equal was an acceptable posture; furthermore, some believe that his speech affected the outcome of *Plessy v. Ferguson* (1896) (850–51).

In 1903, an African American scholar from the north—W.E.B. Du Bois—publicly challenged Washington's beliefs in his philosophical treatise, *The Souls of Black Folk*. In this work, Du Bois pressed for the necessity of black scholars to fight against the racial injustices suffered by African Americans in the country. He believed that having black thinkers was just as important as having black laborers. Du Bois was interested in forcing Justice to release her spoils to the forgotten and mistreated Negro rather than offering small tokens from time to time.

Du Bois, scholar and race leader, was born in 1868 and reared in Great Barrington, Massachusetts. In Great Barrington, there were fewer than 5,000 people, and Du Bois was one of the no more than 50 black members of that small community (Du Bois, *Autobiography* 83). Du Bois tells conflicting stories about the exact moment of his racial self-discovery, but his epiphany unquestionably sets Du Bois's life apart from that of Washington, who knew suffering from the earlier moments of his consciousness. After the realization of his racial identity, Du Bois claimed that he committed his life to the advancement of his race. After finishing high school, Du Bois was further educated at Fisk University; his educational voyage to Fisk was Du Bois's first experience with the South and its African American population.

This experience was significant because it gave Du Bois an opportunity to connect with a part of the black experience that he never knew. He went from a community of being one of 50 in 5,000 to being surrounded by an entire community of people who looked like him. While they did look like him, however, they were definitely from a culture that was foreign to him. His experiences during the three years that he was in the South led to Du Bois's further appreciation of the racial divide and injustice that existed in the country, and it motivated him to continue his work for the advancement of African Americans. He returned to the North and entered Harvard. There, he earned another bachelor's degree and completed his master's work in 1891. Afterward, he studied abroad at the University of Berlin in Germany.

During his time in Europe, he had the chance to see how its development and the further development of the United States with its practices of systematic racism in the North American continent, as well as that on the continents of Africa and Asia, were all interrelated. Only a single semester away from finishing a doctoral degree at the University of Berlin, Du Bois was forced to return the United States because of financial limitations. He returned to the United States to become the first African American to graduate with a PhD from Harvard; his dissertation, "The Suppression of the African Slave Trade in America," was an important new contribution to the world and specifically the American Negro.

After Harvard, Du Bois spent two lackluster years at Wilberforce teaching. In 1896, he conducted research through a grant-funded project for the University of Pennsylvania. Scientifically studying the habits and patterns of African Americans in Philadelphia's seventh ward, Du Bois authored *The Philadelphia Negro* (1899), which discussed the lives and the lifestyles of the African Americans living there. Beyond being subjects in a study, Du Bois's study subjects became a means by which he himself came into contact with other African Americans. This was an important opportunity for him to spend time with African Americans of the metropolitan North.

Du Bois finished this project and returned to the South, where he taught sociology at Atlanta University for 13 years. It was then that he had his initial contacts and philosophical differences with Booker T. Washington. Washington promoted moderate social advances with a concentration on limited knowledge acquisition specifically focusing on agricultural and domestic skills, while publicly discounting the need for higher scholastic and political advancement for African Americans. Du Bois, in contrast, saw those ends as quintessential to the survival of the black race. In 1903, Du Bois publicly challenged Washington in "Of Booker T. Washington and Others" in *The Souls of Black Folk,* where he analytically and systematically dissected, discussed, and deconstructed Washington's philosophical positions and arguments. Simultaneously, Du Bois was taking on the old paradigmatic power structures of the old and slowly evolving South. Du Bois did not stop there; he continued to use the power of the press to push his point further.

In that same year, Du Bois contributed an essay to another work titled *The Negro Problem,* where he discussed his Talented Tenth—that small group of intellectually curious and gifted African Americans whose abilities could help to propel the rest of the race forward. Du Bois believed that the training that this group of educators, clergy, doctors, businessmen, and editors should be for the betterment of the community, specifically demonstrating the value, contribution, and significance of African Americans within the American landscape. In a sense, he proposed that African Americans should reshape the old paradigms (Du Bois, *Tenth* 851).

In 1909, Du Bois joined with white liberals to form the National Association for the Advancement of Colored People (NAACP), where he served as the editor-in-chief to its magazine *Crisis: A Record of the Darker Races.* As the editor, Du Bois directly used the publication to not only lift up African Americans, but also to publicly condemn bigotry and racism. Indirectly, Du Bois became the means for literary success within the African American community. Through the book reviews and nurturing hands of Du Bois and his staff at *Crisis,* many of the Harlem Renaissance writers came to the attention of their community. In this role, Du Bois became an icon of the new African American and his culture.

While Du Bois attempted to save the African American race with his Talented Tenth, he inadvertently but ostensibly alienated many of the people whom he wished to help. Many African Americans coming to the North were not elite or privileged; furthermore, most of those from the North themselves were not elite. Insomuch as the working class may have appreciated the efforts of Du Bois, his theoretical applications did not always resonate in their lives, and the manifestations of his work were sometimes nebulous or marginal in their immediate effects on their quotidian experiences. That reality played a role in Marcus Garvey's (1887–1940) success as an African American leader. Garvey recognized the obvious exclusion of the masses in Du Bois's model, and used this shortcoming to appeal to the everyday person's needs.

Garvey, Black Nationalist and race organizer, was born in St. Ann's Bay, Jamaica, in 1887. Born into a family of very modest means, he found himself employed at the age of 14 as a printing apprentice. By 1904, Garvey was a foreman at the P. A. Benjamin Limited printing company in Kingston, where he involved himself in local union activities. In 1907, he participated in an unsuccessful printers' strike, and by 1910 he was in the employ of the Jamaican government printing office. Holding a variety of jobs in Costa Rica and Panama, Garvey moved to London where he continued his work as a printer.

In England, Garvey studied at Birkbeck College, where he had two important encounters. First, he came across Booker T. Washington's philosophy through his autobiography, *Up from Slavery* (1901), where he discovered Washington's beliefs about African Americans' need to be self-sufficient for the procurement of self-advancement. He also met with Duse Mohamed Ali—a Sudanese-Egyptian working to change the political landscape of Egypt to include more Egyptian powerbrokers. Ali operated a small newspaper for which Garvey came to write. His experience with the periodical and other Africans committed to Ali's ideas inspired Garvey greatly. He left London believing that African Americans would only free themselves from outside oppression if they became self-supporting and freed themselves universally.

He returned to Jamaica in 1914 and founded the Universal Negro Improvement and Conservation and African Improvement Association, more commonly called the Universal Negro Improvement Association (UNIA). When the UNIA failed in Jamaica, Garvey moved to Harlem to try again. In New York, the UNIA was a great success because Garvey seemed to easily connect with the average African American from the beginning. His organization addressed the concerns of returning African American World War I veterans; he acknowledged their disappointment in returning to a country that promoted democracy abroad but maintained a super-restrictive racial caste system at home. Beyond that, he focused on the sentiment of Pan-Africanism that was growing in the Harlem community.

He promoted ideas such as Black Nationalism in ways that encouraged people to follow not only with their hearts but also with their wallets. During the 1920s, Garvey's UNIA had an estimated 70, 000 dues-paying members, and there were throngs of other members worldwide who numbered into the millions. In the summer of 1920, he held an international convention that lasted a month and included thousands of delegates, along with parades and other public ceremonies. With this, Garvey became a very popular character. He was self-aware and very knowledgeable about the press's power to propagate his position; and like Du Bois, he used his organization's weekly periodical, *Negro World,* to further his agenda. From *Negro World,* he not only promoted Black Nationalism and separation, but also further promoted the business of the UNIA.

Having interests that extended beyond the geographic boundaries of Harlem, Garvey had several business ventures that included a steamship company— the Black Star Line—which was his grandest venture in every sense. It was his largest undertaking, and it was his greatest subsequent failure. The all-black company was supposed to aid in trade with diasporic countries, as well as being a means for African Americans' repatriation to Africa; however, the line was plagued with problems before its start. The adventure ended when one ship sank, another was abandoned in Cuba, the last was sold by U.S.

marshals in an effort to cover unpaid debts, and Garvey was tried for mail fraud. In the same way that the UNIA provided public showings of parades and pageantry marking the zenith of its success, its antipodal demise was also a public spectacle for the masses. Garvey's business dealings were adjudicated in the federal courts, as well as in the court of public opinion. The U.S. justice system convicted Garvey, sentenced him to prison, and later deported him.

The dynamic interactions and exchanges among Washington, Du Bois, and Garvey, who did not always like each other, were greatly analogous to the overall experience of the Harlem Renaissance. They were three completely different individuals with different life experiences directing their good intentions. Their ideas working in concert with one another rather than in competition with one another are what ultimately provided the best environment for growth. Whether it was Washington's model of slow progress and self-provision, Du Bois's model of integration via intellectual advancement, or even Garvey's separatist nationalism, each man in his own way contributed a necessary element for the furtherance of the community. In some instances, tweaking old paradigms was sufficient, and in other cases completely overthrowing old patterns was necessary, but history shows that the advancement of African Americans would not have progressed as it did without Washington, Du Bois, and Garvey.

It is rather difficult to think of the Harlem Renaissance without considering the profound effect that the arts produced during this time had on the United States of America and beyond. To do so would be like discussing Europe's Renaissance while omitting Da Vinci's *Mona Lisa,* Shakespeare's *Hamlet,* or Cervantes's *Don Quixote* and their long-lasting impression on Western culture. And just as the European Renaissance was a means of moving from a tradition of theocentrism to the tradition of anthrocentrism, this was the case with the African Americans of the 1920s. The African American quite simply moved from being the subject of the past to an agent of the present. Through the use of the arts—specifically literature—African Americans helped to change their place in the world. With their penned and published words, they began to carve out a new niche in the world. Their works endured to challenge some of the old narratives and inspire other people to create new ones.

The role of literature and written text was not exclusively left to the poets, novelists, and playwrights; some of the first works that function as the foundation to the movement include the philosophy of W.E.B. Du Bois in *The Souls of Black Folk* (1903) and those of Alain Locke in his 1925 work, *The New Negro: An Interpretation of Negro Life.* With *The Souls of Black Folk,* Du Bois published some of his previously published articles along with new essays to further treat the issue of race in America. His essays discuss events from his own life as well as events in history, but all of the articles ultimately center around illuminating and improving the problems that result from race prejudices. Du Bois believed that the problem of the 20th century was the problem of the color line (359); and beyond that—to improve the issues of the grand 20th century problem, one would need to erase or attempt to blur the line in such a way that it was less obvious and thereby less problematic. The group who would be tasked with this very important job would unquestionably be the Talented Tenth.

One person who fell into the category of Du Bois's Talented Tenth was James Weldon Johnson (1871–1938), an educator, writer, musician, race leader, and the first African American admitted to the Florida Bar Association (Skerrett 219–21). As a musician, Johnson's most celebrated work is "Lift Every Voice and Sing," and his most celebrated literary work is the 1912 novel *The Autobiography of an Ex-Colored Man*. While Du Bois provided a philosophical foundation for the movement with his *Souls of Black Folk* and "The Talented Tenth" essay, James Weldon Johnson's work can be said to have provided a literary foundation for the Harlem Renaissance.

In his novel, the protagonist, a fair-skinned black—who does not know that he is black—grows up financially secure with only his mother in an environment of whites and upper-class African Americans. After his mother's death during his high school years, he finds himself in the most socioeconomically depressed regions of the African American community. While his transition goes well, he comes to be liberated from poverty through his ability as a musician in a white man's employment. After working for this man and his friends, the protagonist is motivated to return to the black world to improve it through his music. But while studying, he observes a lynching that provokes him to want to pass (a term referring to a fair-skinned African American pretending to be white). He makes the decision, commits to the idea, and consummates his choice with a marriage to a white woman with whom he has children. He continues his ruse and later writes his autobiography.

The novel's significance comes in two parts. First, the novel did not experience great success when it was first published, even though it was well written; Johnson believed that the work was unsuccessful in large part because it was before its time (Wintz 60). Supporting that idea is the fact that the work's most significant impact came almost a decade later during the Harlem Renaissance; the text really seemed to resonate among the young talent, who began to understand what Johnson was saying. Second and most importantly, the novel began to change the course of the conversations and paradigms. No longer simply discussing the travesties experienced by African Americans at the hand of white Americans, Johnson began to pose new questions: Who are we now? What does it really mean to be black? Can I use my artistic ability to explain and/or express the reality of being an African American in America (Wintz 67)?

If Johnson can be said to have laid a foundation for the prose of the Harlem Renaissance, then Claude McKay (1889–1948) can be said to have provided the poetic foundation for the movement. McKay was born to a middle-class Jamaican family where he was the youngest of 11 children, and he was first educated by his brother, who was a teacher. During his early teen years, he was composing his own poetry, and it was then that he had his first contact with Walter Jekyll, a British folklorist who mentored McKay in many things.

Jekyll provided McKay with additional literary works beyond what his brother's school could provide, and he encouraged him to write dialect poetry. By age 22, McKay had published two volumes of poetry, *Songs of Jamaica* (1912) and *Constab Ballads* (1912), which were greatly received in Jamaica. While he enjoyed his success, he was interested in traveling to the United States to broaden his horizons.

Initially interested in Booker T. Washington's philosophy, McKay enrolled at the Tuskegee Institute planning to study agronomy. However, it was in Alabama that McKay experienced American racism, and the experience motivated much of what McKay would later write. After holding several jobs, and having experienced a failed marriage lasting less than a year, McKay eventually found himself in Harlem. Doing menial jobs for survival's sake, it was not until 1917 that he published again; his poems "Invocation" and "Harlem Dancer" appeared in the *Seven Arts* magazine. This reality of publishing in white periodicals became a recurring event with McKay during the Harlem Renaissance. After finding a friend in magazine publisher Max Eastman, McKay published almost exclusively in white publications during the Renaissance. However, it should be noted that McKay submitted his protest poetry to black periodicals, and it was frequently deemed too militant for publication within their pages. "To the White Friends" was rejected by Du Bois's *Crisis;* and ironically, McKay's most famous poem, "If We Must Die," was rejected from Alain Locke's *The New Negro.*

By 1922, McKay had left Harlem, and his mark as a protest poet was already established. Many of the younger writers found inspiration in McKay's willingness to challenge the old paradigmatic structures, along with his introspective glances at the African American self. While his poetry was greatly in the style of the European models, his legacy lived on. Of all of the Harlem Renaissance poets, his body of work continues to be some of the most discussed. At the time, his contemporaries were split on how they viewed the significance of his work. Some thought that his work was inconsistent and reflective of a writer willing to write anything for a profit, while others saw it as bold and rich in depth.

As McKay was exiting the scene, another young writer poet was taking center stage, Langston Hughes (1902–1967). Hughes was very different from McKay in many ways: He came from a relatively unstable family from the Midwest that did a significant amount of traveling. When his father was not admitted to the Kansas Bar, he relocated the family to Mexico where he practiced law and operated a mine. At the age of seven, Hughes returned to Kansas to live with his grandmother, Mary Sampson Langston. She frequently told him stories of slavery and the changes in the world. These stories helped to create a palette on which Langston's imagination could paint. Furthermore, with his love of reading and his access to the public library, Hughes, from an early age, was well on his way to the successful literary life that he would live.

At the age of 15, Hughes's grandmother died, and he went to live with his mother and stepfather in Illinois. It was there that he began to write his poetry and develop a passion for writing. With high school graduation being an immediate reality, Hughes went to Mexico to ask his father for the necessary funding for his college education. Hughes's father disliked the idea of Langston staying in the United States to study writing, and he tried to persuade him to study science in Europe. Hughes rejected the offer, but they compromised and arrived at an agreement—Langston would remain in the United States, but he would study engineering at Columbia. Hughes accepted, but had no intention of following through. He attended Columbia, but within a year he dropped out. While he was there, he did manage to publish several poems for *Crisis,* and he laid the groundwork for a career in writing.

Primarily, Hughes wrote about themes that evolved from or centered on the more common and everyday experiences of the African American. Being an outsider—a non–New Yorker—it is reasonable to believe that he was more aware of everyday things in the city than the jaded natives. It may very well have been this perspective that allowed him to give life to common things, because for him they may not have been common at all. Furthermore, Hughes had the privilege of being the first Renaissance writer to be discovered and promoted by the black literary establishment of the early 1920s (Wintz 75). The literary editor for *Crisis* not only published his work, but also introduced him to the great patriarch, W.E.B. Du Bois (Watson 51).

Du Bois's unique role as editor of *Crisis* made him extraordinarily influential in promoting the new talent of the movement. It was *Crisis* that presented Jean Toomer's (1894–1967) first printed poem "Song of the Son" to the world in 1922, while Du Bois himself praised Toomer's *Cane* (1923), the experimental novel treating race and the legacy of slavery that fascinated the young writers of the Renaissance movement. However, Du Bois could not have done it without Jessie Fauset (1882–1961), who was essential not only to promoting but also nurturing new talent from the period.

Unmistakably a member of the Talented Tenth, Fauset was Ivy League educated and a pioneer in African American accomplishments. The first African American woman to graduate Phi Beta Kappa from Cornell University, Fauset earned a bachelor's degree in classical and modern languages in 1905, and a master's degree in French from the University of Pennsylvania in 1919 (Smith 293). At the personal invitation of Du Bois, Fauset came to work as the literary editor for *Crisis* in 1919. During her seven years at that post, she was responsible for the initial publishing of some new artists along with the subsequent publishing and promoting of many of the authors associated with the Harlem Renaissance: Langston Hughes, Claude McKay, Jean Toomer, and Countée Cullen. Not only an editor and a mentor, Fauset was also a talented writer; first coming to the attention of Du Bois through her submissions to *Crisis,* she came to the attention of the world with her novels.

Her first novel, *There Is Confusion* (1924), was partly inspired by T. S. Stribling's *Birthright* (1922), in which the white author attempted to treat black themes utilizing the archetypal pattern of the old Negro. Fauset, knowing that she could tell the African American story better than Stribling, penned a tale of African American experiences that are complex and multifaceted, yet interrelated and simultaneously independent. Coming from a modest background in Philadelphia but later ascending the socioeconomic ladder, it seemed appropriate that her tale included black people in a variety of circumstances; in many ways, the tale may be laced with tidbits of her own experiences. Her work was well received, and Fauset continued to produce other works that made her one of the most prolific novelists of the period (Myree-Mainor 194).

Following with the works: *Plum Bun* (1929)—her most highly celebrated work—*The Chinaberry Tree* (1931), and *Comedy: American Style* (1933)—her least critically acclaimed work, Fauset very concretely added to the depth and dimension of the African American literary canon. Her novels ostensibly treated the themes of African Americans at many different levels. In *There Is Confusion*, Fauset deals with the themes of self-identity, upward social mobility, and the self-empowerment of women through their choices of relationships and reproduction. In that novel, the heroine Joanna Mitchell usurps the traditional power structure, and Fauset has Joanna acting rather than waiting to be acted upon. She takes the prevailing theme of the Renaissance and stretches it to the point that it also includes women. Her heroine creates a new archetypal pattern for African American women in which they do not wait to be made complete through marriage and a man's choice of a mate, but rather make decisions for themselves and choose what will make them whole—marriage and motherhood, or careers.

In her second and most celebrated work, *Plum Bun*, Fauset treats another important idea for African Americans during the front end of the 20th century—passing. In this novel, Fauset masterfully explores the complexity of passing, including both its benefits and its detriments. While her protagonist, Angela Murray, believes that she ultimately will be rewarded with an elevated socioeconomic lot as a result of passing and marrying a white husband, she discovers that the improved station comes with a greater cost than what she anticipates. While Angela acquires more material possessions, she loses all contact with her family. The special bond that exists between Angela and her darker-skinned sister is severed because she can have no contact with her. The notion of marrying in order to gain a family is negated in this instance, because Angela must completely deny her own family and accept that of her husband. When the matters finally resolve, Angela discovers that the cost of passing is too great, and she decides to return to the African American world where she is content to remain.

While *Confusion* and *Plum Bun* both discuss issues surrounding race, they also take on feminists issues. Long before feminism and feminist literature became established in American culture, Fauset challenged some of the norms of the American patriarchal society. She gives two examples of two very different women who are deciding how to lead their lives. In the first text, she shows a woman who recognizes the importance of deriving pleasure and self-fulfillment from within. Joanna does not passively wait for things to happen; she makes things happen and is happy at the end of her tale. Her counterpart, in contrast, tries to derive happiness externally. Angela not only waits for someone else to be the catalyst for her fulfillment, but also actively abandons what has made her happy in the past—her family—to obtain this external happiness. In the end, she realizes what her predecessor already knows. It may be reasonably concluded that Fauset very quietly offers a warning to African Americans and women about the dangers of trying too hard to assimilate into mainstream culture.

Confusion not only had the privilege of being first novel within the new movement; it also had the distinction of functioning as the inducement of the birth of the Harlem Renaissance proper. For many years, Du Bois and Fauset functioned as the gatekeepers to African American culture because they largely controlled what was published and presented to the African American community. As such, Du Bois could unilaterally direct the literature of the time. When he said that all literature should be propaganda (Du Bois, *Art* 1000), he not only meant it for himself and the novels that he wrote but also meant that literature published in *Crisis* would meet that criterion. However, by 1924, the access to the printing press was opening to more people; Charles S. Johnson (1893–1956), University of Chicago PhD and founder and editor of *Opportunity,* the periodical of the National Urban League, began to assume an interesting position within the community.

Where *Crisis* had functioned as the single lens concerning arts and politics through which many African Americans viewed the world, *Opportunity* wished to offer another perspective on art. Du Bois had always been the great philosopher on race, and no one challenged him in that arena, but the matter of what constituted art and its true purpose was offered time and space for further discussion. *Opportunity* presented a place for many young writers to express their creativity and publish their work. On March 21, 1924, Johnson took a major step in concretizing *Opportunity*'s place within the African American literary community. That evening, Johnson gave a dinner at New York's Civic Club to celebrate the success of Jessie Fauset's *There Is Confusion.* Invited to the dinner were the literati from both the black and white worlds, and the event gave Paul Kellogg, the editor of *The Survey Graphic,* and Alain Locke an opportunity make an important connection.

Howard University professor Alain Locke, a philosopher and literary critic who was a pioneer in African American history, held an undergraduate degree as well as a PhD from Harvard, while also being the first African American Rhodes scholar at Oxford University. That evening, he functioned as the master of ceremonies, and in a manner of speaking, all but announced the birth of the Harlem Renaissance to a small group of friends. In doing so, he helped to move *Opportunity* into the status of the citadel of African American literature in the same way that *Crisis* was the citadel of African American politics. Beyond that, the evening's events prompted Kellogg to dedicate an entire issue of his magazine to African American literature, Professor Locke serving as the guest editor on the project.

From that project, another much larger one grew; later that year, Locke assembled, edited, and contributed to the multidimensional work, *The New Negro*. This work was an amalgamation of different types of art, including renderings of African artifacts, essays, original poetry, and biographies. The list of contributors was a virtual who's who of Harlem Renaissance artists; that exclusive company included visual artists Winold Reiss and Aaron Douglass along with essayists E. Franklin Frazier and W.E.B Du Bois, and poets Countée Cullen, Langston Hughes, and Angelina Weld Grimké.

If the March 21 dinner was the birth announcement to a group of friends, then Locke's *The New Negro* project was the birth announcement of the Harlem Renaissance to the entire world. His work at its quintessence was not only about redefining the image of the African American, but also an act of African American self-definition; beyond this defining, there was the ever important presentation of the new self to the world. The old mythical and archetypal Negro was gone; exposed for what he was—a stock character and a stereotype—he would remain a literary creation of fiction. But the new or present Negro was not the flat, fictional stock character that everyone knew: He was a live, intricate, multidimensional person full of real life and often-times dealing with real-life issues just like his white counterparts. Locke gave the very best and the brightest the opportunity to show the Western world what African Americans were capable of doing when provided with adequate resources and opportunity (Harris 539).

During the Harlem Renaissance, from Jessie Redmon Fauset's *There Is Confusion* (1924) until Zora Neale Hurston's *Their Eyes Were Watching God* (1937), there was an explosion of literary art in, around, and from Harlem. The themes and the genres differed as much as the writers themselves. At one extreme, there was Countée Cullen, a classically trained poet with membership to Phi Beta Kappa, along with degrees from New York University and Harvard. His poetry was much in line with the classic form similar to that of McKay's mimicking of the British models, but it was brilliant. By Cullen's senior year at New York University in 1925, he had published his first volume of poetry, *Color,* which was highly praised. Having already received national attention from his poems published in multiple periodicals, both black and white, he was well on his way. In 1927, he published his next volume, *Copper Sun,* which again did very well. While Cullen's first volume treated race more than his second volume did, it was his magnificent use of the classical poetic structures more than his themes that established his greatness within the movement. He was doing what the patriarchs wanted; he took the models and morphed them to include the removed African American.

At the other extreme was Zora Neale Hurston, who was writing a novel in dialect about the everyday life of a small all black community in Florida. Hurston, a native of Eatonville, Florida, set out on life's journey relatively young. At the age of 14, after her mother's death, and finding herself unable to get along with her new stepmother, Zora joined the Gilbert and Sullivan Theater Company. After traveling with the company for about 18 months, she left them when they arrived in Baltimore, Maryland (Luker 426). With very little money in her pocket and a single dress, she enrolled in Morgan Academy (the preparatory division of the present day Morgan State University), did well, graduated, and then went on to study at Howard University.

Hurston met and studied with Alain Locke in 1921, shortly after entering Howard University, where he taught literature and philosophy. As a member of the literary club, she went on to publish her first short story, "John Redding Goes to Sea" (1921) in the university's magazine *Stylus;* three short years later, she was publishing in *Opportunity.* In 1925, Hurston moved to New York City where she was in the employ of Jewish novelist Fannie Hurst. Working as her secretary and chauffer, Hurston came into contact with many influential whites. The result of these contacts was the procurement of a scholarship to Columbia University's Barnard College. At Barnard, she studied with the esteemed anthropologist Franz Boas, whose encouragement led her to focus on and appreciate the richness of her own community. In 1928, when she graduated from Barnard, she was the first African American to do so.

From 1930 until 1937, Hurston engaged in and published a significant quantity of writing projects that included an unfinished collaborative work with Langston Hughes, *Mule Bone* (1931); anthropological works *Mules and Men* (1935) and *Tell My Horse* (1938); novels *Jonah's Gourd Vine* (1934) and *Their Eyes Were Watching God* (1937); and her 1942 autobiography *Dust Tracks on the Road.* Hurston's works of varying genres speak to the depth of her ability, while the contents of those texts speak to her artistry. Without question, her novels demonstrate Hurston's artistic creativity along with her craftsmanship.

In *Jonah's Gourd Vine,* the reader meets John "Buddy" Pearson—a young African American who is coming to understand himself and the world in the post-slavery era. After seeing his father frequently brutalize his mother, he has failed relationships with women. He enters would-be monogamous relationships, but he frequently has affairs. After marrying, he travels to the budding community of Eatonville, Florida, alone. John sends for his family; and while he is a good financial provider, he is not a good husband. His wife Lucy is aware of the extramarital affairs, but she quietly endures them.

When Lucy is no longer willing to suffer silently, she confronts John about his behavior. Convicted and guilty, he promises to improve, and he seeks God's help. With Lucy's aid, he comes to pastor a local Baptist church; and just when it seems like he has overcome his weakness of lust, he reverts back to his familiar behavior. His wife becomes sick and dies, and he is guilt ridden. His guilt shows itself during his second marriage, when he is discovered in an extramarital affair and physically assaults his new wife when she confronts him about his behavior. Public knowledge of the event forces him out of the church and the town.

In the next town, John begins to recapture parts of his old life. He marries again and leads another Baptist church. He experiences success at the local and state level, and all seems to be on the mend in his life until a return trip to Eatonville. There, John finds himself following his lust and afterward being guilt ridden. While returning home with the knowledge of what his self-destructive behavior has done to so many women who have loved him, he is struck by a train.

In Hurston's second and most celebrated novel, *Their Eyes Were Watching God,* the reader encounters Janie Crawford's coming of age tale. Initially set in a West Florida town, the reader finds Janie living with her grandmother, the only parent she has ever known. When her grandmother suspects a budding attraction to a local youngster, she arranges a marriage for Janie to a considerably older, more financially secure man of the community. Janie goes along with the wedding, but she is disgusted by her husband and her new life on the farm.

Soon, she finds herself in a relationship with a man named Jody (Joe) Starks, who is traveling from Georgia to Eatonville. In leaving her first husband for Jody, she takes a huge gamble, and at first it seems that she wins. Quickly, Joe is seen as a leader, especially after he concretizes the town's desire to have street lights. In what seems to be no time at all, Joe is elected mayor. Janie goes from being a farmhand, or at least a farm wife, to a town's first lady. But as Joe's clout grows, so does his objectification of Janie; their relationship declines and finally deteriorates to the point that Janie has a difficult time properly mourning his death.

This truth manifests itself in Janie's new younger love interest—Tea Cake Woods—shortly after Joe's death. Even against community advice, Janie gambles again and leaves Eatonville with Tea Cake. They marry and move to the Everglades, where they live and work. While there, they live through a hurricane during which Tea Cake is bitten by a rabid dog while attempting to save Janie's life. Tea Cake saves Janie, but it comes at an extraordinary price. His mind is overtaken by rabies so that he attacks Janie, and she has to stop him with lethal force. Having known true love and true loss, she returns to Eatonville to live out the rest of her life as a truly free woman.

These two works show the nexus of Hurston's abilities as a novelist as well as an anthropologist. In the *Jonah's Gourd Vine,* the reader sees Hurston's extraordinary command of Eatonville dialect and proverbs, along with her ability to seamlessly convey them in a lengthy narrative. While her characters are from the South and are more common than Fauset's Joanna Mitchell and Angela Murray, they are nonetheless complex and multifaceted in their dealings with one another. In *Their Eyes Were Watching God,* Hurston shows not only her mastery of dialect writing, but also a greater appreciation for the epic as a literary model along with the call to rework the classic paradigms to include African Americans. Even beyond that, she makes a deliberate point to discuss women's issues. Where Fauset subtly treats the matters, Hurston overtly makes her point about the trials of African American womanhood. Not only preaching about the joys of freedom, she also shows women that the experience comes with cost. While Janie is free to love and live, she is also responsible for making the sometimes hard decisions that come with life. Janie is not only an African American hero: She is also a hero for women. At its best, the novel transcends race and gender and becomes a prophetic word that reminds all readers about the truest realities of living.

While the approach and writing styles of Fauset and Hurston are dichotomous, there are plenty of other fine examples of what Harlem Renaissance literature was to the different writers of the movement. Walter White's *Fire in the Flint* (1924) tells the tale of an African American doctor who returns to the South only to discover that the world has not changed nearly as much as he thought. This works tells of and about the group of African American professionals who do not find it easy to practice their professions during the first part of the 20th century. James Weldon Johnson's *God's Trombones* (1927) poetically treats the African American preacher and his relationship with his sermon and his congregation; very much like Geoffrey Chaucer's *Canterbury Tales* (c. 1390) or Samuel Taylor Coleridge's *Rime of the Ancient Mariner* (1789), these poetic narratives are meant to be heard as well as read.

Du Bois's *Dark Princess* (1928) continues his theory of literature as propaganda functioning as the second part to the 1911 propaganda novel, *Quest of the Silver Fleece,* where he advocates meritocracy trumping pigmentocracy and the need for the true principles of capitalism to ultimately make ineffective the baseless practices of racism. In *Dark Princess,* Du Bois promotes Pan-Africanism as a means of redirection of the global markets and extrication from the white oppressor. James Weldon Johnson's *The Autobiography of an Ex-Colored Man* (1927), Nella Larsen's *Quicksand* (1928) and *Passing* (1929), and Jessie Fauset's *Plum Bun* (1929) explore the issue of pigmentocracy and passing within the African American community. At the same time, Wallace Thurman's 1929 novel *The Blacker the Berry* discusses the issue of pigmentocracy within the African American community, specifically treating the challenges that dark-skinned African Americans face within the African American community. Arna Bontemps deals with the themes of financial success and self destruction in his novel *God Sends Sundays* (1931).

While there were many great artists who were esteemed for their contributions, there were two particular works that drew extreme praise from some, while receiving great condemnation from others. One novel that split community opinion was Carl Van Vechten's *Nigger Heaven* (1926). Van Vechten was seen as someone who was genuinely interested in the advancement of Harlem Renaissance writers and African Americans as a whole. He was not only a helpful publisher, but also someone who invested his time and reputation in his friends. It was common for him to have parties at his home where African Americans as well as whites were invited guests; likewise, it was common for him to be in the Harlem clubs and speakeasies. Furthermore, he had very close personal relationships with writers, including James Weldon Johnson and Zora Neale Hurston in particular (Rampersad 934). Thus, the characters that he speaks of in his book are more or less real characters that he had met. They are not the stereotypical, stock characters from fiction like those found in Stribling's book, but they are reasonably (with a little latitude for artistic license) the sum of his observations as a newspaper reporter and critic.

Nigger Heaven is the tale of two young people struggling to maintain a relationship while the elements of racism permeate and slowly suck the life out of their dream of happiness. The story, which encompasses everything from elite blacks appreciating the finer things in mainstream life to common folks who drink and party their sorrows away, created a stir in Harlem and beyond. Many African Americans, offended by the title alone, rejected the book without even reading it.

Most first-generation Renaissance writers, such as Du Bois, Locke, and Fauset, rejected the novel, while the younger writers like Hughes, Thurman, and Hurston embraced it. The division came in part because of the generation gap, as well as the relationships that Van Vechten formed with the writers of the period. While Van Vechten's novel had a polarizing effect in the African American community, however, the white audience loved the work. It was like a traveler's guide through Harlem. Whites looking for some excitement started to come to Harlem for entertainment in large part because of the novel.

Nigger Heaven gave space to dissention among the ranks of Renaissance writers who thought that all art need not be propaganda. The younger generation of writers thought that the restrictive nature of the first generation writers was as impeding in artistic freedom as being limited to the old paradigms of white writers. Being forced to write about one thing or with only one objective was not seen as a liberating experience. Many of the young writers saw the March 21 dinner at the Civic Club as their opportunity to truly express their artistry, but they ultimately found that to be untrue.

In order to wrest control of the arts from the powerful hands of the patriarchs, the second-generation writers tried to publish their own periodical, *Fire*. Functioning as both contributors and editors, Wallace Thurman, Gwendolyn Bennett, Langston Hughes, Zora Neale Hurston, and others significantly changed the direction of the Harlem Renaissance. While their periodical only produced one edition, it did allow the authors to break away from the control of Du Bois and others. Their experiment with control allowed them to say that they would write, discuss, and explore whatever they chose. It was after *Fire* that novels discussing the internal events of the African American and Harlem communities began to surface. From issues of passing to interracial prejudice, the themes appeared; and in some cases, they did so in spite of the disapproval of the elders. However, it was the venturing beyond the conventional themes of race and advancement that really helped to progress the cause. African Americans saw themselves, in their best and at their worst, reflected in the literature they read, and it helped the community to grow.

Another text that split the community's opinion was Claude McKay's *Home to Harlem* (1928), which takes its themes from the common man's world just as his poetry had done. Discussing the world and life of Harlem, McKay penned a tale in which Harlem's more sordid happenings are shown and almost praised. Within his novel, McKay's more common man finds a way to survive and enjoy life while his college-educated counterpart all but implodes with his self-destructive behavior. Accordingly, there were some—especially first-generation Renaissance writers—who thought that the work not only lacked substantive contribution to the improvement of the race, but actually denigrated it. Other members of the literati had varying opinions. While some criticized the work, others praised it.

One author in particular who commended the work was Wallace Thurman (1902–1934). In the following year, 1929, he published *Infants of the Spring*, in which he satirically discussed the first generation leaders of the Renaissance and their thoughts concerning the arts of the movement. Thurman—different from the first generation of Ivy League–educated writers—believed that the arts existed for everyone, and that art should be produced for art's sake. While *Infants of the Spring*, needless to say, did not earn the praise of everyone, it did speak of the African American community's ability to appraise and discuss itself. Thurman's work was not the last of the movement, but it was a definite beginning of one school of thought and the ending of another.

Whites came to enjoy Harlem's nightlife in terms of the theatre, music, and clubs. With the exception of Eubie Blake and Noble Sissle's *Shuffle Along* (1921), starring an all–African American cast, a lot of African American drama went unviewed by whites. During the later 1920s, there were African American–themed dramas, but they were written by whites who did not really know or understand African American culture. Plays like Charles MacArthur's *Lulu Belle* (1926), DoBose and Dorothy Heyward's *Porgy* (1927), and Mar Connelly's *Green Pastures* (1930) relied heavily on stereotypes and archetypal paradigms with which the authors were familiar (Watson 106–7); however, in 1923, Willis Richardson's one-act play *The Chip Woman's Fortune* was the first production in which white audiences actually saw a drama about African Americans written by an African American performed on Broadway. Garland Anderson's 1925 *Appearances* was the first full-length play by an African American on Broadway, while Wallace Thurman and white author William Rapp's *Harlem* gave white audiences a glance within the veil of Harlem life (Chambers 108).

As much as anything, the venues were in some cases as important as the works. It is difficult to discuss the arts of Harlem without considering the historic building standing at 253 West 125th Street—the Apollo Theater. In that venue, many popular and important musicians performed and springboarded into stardom. The building has endured to be one of the last concrete reminders of the glory of the Harlem Renaissance. It continued afterward to launch new performers into the public's view. Beyond giving talents such as Billie Holiday and Ella Fitzgerald a place to start, it was later the stage on which performers such as Sarah Vaughan, James Brown, the Jackson Five, and countless others performed.

Another important venue that has lasted in the annals of history, while not standing today, is the famed Cotton Club. A safe haven for whites wishing to travel into Harlem, the Cotton Club—on Lenox Avenue and 143rd

Street—was a segregated establishment catering exclusively to its white clientele. From its the all-black servers to its fair-skinned chorus line, this establishment's objective was to give customers the feeling that they had traveled to an exotic location where the primitive still existed—from a safe distance. The house band played the lively authentic rhythmic tunes that patrons expected to hear, while the chorus line performed the wild and exotic dances that added to the experience. The Harlem club experience was important because it helped to move jazz into the American mainstream. Just as much as the literature of the Harlem Renaissance serves as a record of its greatness, so too does its music. And while the music was important, it would not have been the same without its colorful composers, conductors, and performers such as Duke Ellington, Louis Armstrong, Josephine Baker, Ella Fitzgerald, and Billie Holiday.

Duke Ellington (1899–1974), composer, conductor, and pianist was a major force in the development of American jazz. Taking jazz from the nightclubs to Carnegie Hall, he more than any other single musician did more to make it a part of American culture. From band leader at the Cotton Club (1927–1931) to orchestra conductor on a European tour (1931), Ellington and his music were known worldwide. Associated with Ellington and his band are the songs "Mood Indigo" (1931), "Sophisticated Lady" (1933), "Take the 'A' Train" (1941), and a host of others. It was through his formal presentation of jazz music that this genre came to the masses (Collier 271–74).

Also playing in the Cotton Club was another of the greatest jazz musicians of the Renaissance, trumpeter and vocalist, Louis Armstrong. First learning to play in New Orleans, Louisiana, his talent began to shine most when he moved to Chicago, Illinois in 1922 to play with his idol Joe "King" Oliver in Oliver's Creole Jazz Band. It was then that he met his second wife, Lilian Hardin, who encouraged Armstrong to consider playing in the Fletcher Henderson Orchestra. Armstrong was a member for 14 months, and then returned to Chicago in 1925, where he made his first recordings as a leader with the group the Hot Five and later Hot Seven; some of those works are considered classics among traditional jazz enthusiasts, and others have become standard pieces for serious musicians of the genre. In 1929, Armstrong moved his band to Harlem to perform in the theatrical work *Hot Chocolates* (1929). It was also during the late 1920s that Armstrong introduced scatting—an improvised vocal styling—to jazz. Ultimately, Armstrong went on to be one of the most lucrative jazz performers of his time. Some of the songs associated with Armstrong are "Rhapsody in Black and Blue" (1932), "Pennies from Heaven" (1937), and "New Orleans" (1946) (Tirro 29–31).

Josephine Baker (1906–1975), dancer and singer, began her public career in the Harlem theatrical classic, *Shuffle Along* (1921). Baker was originally a dresser for the company; but when a dancer from the chorus line became sick, she stepped into the role and performed in the play until its curtain call in 1923. Continuing to work with Blake and Sissle on other projects, in 1925 Baker was recruited to leave Harlem and work in Paris, where she experienced great success for about three years. When she returned to Harlem, she was not greeted with the reception she expected as a result from the stardom she achieved in Paris, and when she traveled to other places in Europe, she was not a well-received artist. Her truest successes in life came toward its end, but her phenomenal performances during the Harlem Renaissance are what brought her to the world's attention (Peterson 38–39).

Another great female presence that resulted from the Renaissance was Ella Fitzgerald. Her first major appearance was a victory in an amateur night competition at the Apollo Theater in 1934. Three months later, she won another competition at the Harlem Opera House, and later that year she teamed with the Chick Webb Orchestra. From there, her career did very well; she worked with many other famous jazz musicians, including Charlie Parker and Dizzy Gillespie, leaving a lasting impression on them as well as on jazz history. Classics associated with her career include "Sing Me a Swing Song," "Flying High," "Lady Be Good," "How High the Moon," and others. Her career extended into the 1980s, and she died from complications of diabetes in 1996 (Pellegrinelli 295–97).

Billie Holiday (1915–1959)—singer and songwriter—was an iconic figure of the Renaissance for some. Her unique sound with the slightest southern drawl, most likely from her time spent in Baltimore, was classic. Much like Fitzgerald, she entered the Renaissance at the tail end of the movement, but unlike Fitzgerald she did not live a long, productive life. Her career included musical rendezvous with Duke Ellington, Benny Goodman, Count Basie, and countless others, as well as producing more than 300 recordings. Some of her most influential work includes, "Strange Fruit," "Don't Explain," "Lover Man," and "My Man." However, her life—especially toward the end—was plagued with abuses; as a child, she suffered through sexual abuse, and as an adult she dealt with the demons of substance abuse; in 1959 she died from a drug-related illness (Griffin 405–7).

While the average Harlemites did not see their favorite bands or singers at the Cotton Club, they may have seen them just a few blocks away on 140th and Lenox Avenue at the Savoy Ballroom. Known for its integrated crowd and its lively music, this was a great place to dance, have a good time, and meet people. Another place that Harlemites would have met people and enjoyed great music was at rent parties. Frequently, someone in the city held a party on Friday or Saturday night in an effort to pay the above-average cost for rent. Opening one's home for a small admission and the cost of food was a pretty sure way to make the rent; however, there came a time when it was just an opportunity to party. It was at some of these parties that Harlemites might run into some of their favorites participating in a jam session or coming through for some good food or fun.

While the other great artistic expressions from the period tend to be well remembered, sometimes the Harlem Renaissance visual and plastic arts are overlooked. Many of the images that the Western world has of African Americans during the period can be attributed to one major photographer—James Van Der Zee (1886–1983)—a self-taught artist who kept his studio in Harlem for nearly 50 years. Similar to Addison Scurlock of Washington, DC, Van Der Zee worked in thriving, middle-class African American communities;

both figures not only tried to document the history of the African American progression, but also functioned like a Greek chorus, providing a narrative voice that told the African American story (Patton 114–15). In addition to the photographers, there was also the very prolific graphic artist Aaron Douglass (1899–1979), whose work graced the front pages of African American periodicals, as well as the covers of some influential African American novels, including Alain Locke's *The New Negro* and James Weldon Johnson's *God's Trombones*. While he contributed widely to numerous projects, Douglass's most noted work is *Crucifixion* (1927) which calls the role of the North African Simon of Cyrene to the foreground. His artistic view and style coupled with themes of Africa and the African American experience won him the praise of many associated with the Harlem Renaissance, as well as establishing his place within art history.

Other important painters include Palmer Hayden (1890–1973), Archibald J. Motley Jr. (1891–1981), and Hale A. Woodruff (1900–1980). Just as the writers sought to express the African American experience in a fashion that would be appreciated by the white Americans, so did these painters. Hayden aimed to subtly integrate aspects of the African experience into his art. In *Fétiche et Fleurs* (1926), Hayden creates a still-life of a beautiful room with a table at its center. On the table rest a bouquet of flowers in the foreground and an African statue on top of a Kuba cloth in the middle plane; in the background there is a very period-appropriate curtain and a lightly colored wall. This work, through its subject as well as its composition, reveals Hayden's desire to integrate the African presence into the mainstream; his work does not demand that a viewer appreciate the African art, but it does invite viewers to enjoy good art that includes African elements.

Motley took a different approach as a portraitist; he primarily presented middle-class African American women at different stages of life. His most famous work *Mending Socks* (1924) offers a realistic rendering that features his paternal grandmother in front of a table in a delightfully decorated home, presumably mending socks, while his proudest work, *The Octoroon Girl* (1925), portrays a beautiful light-skinned woman wearing a black hat and black dress with striking red trim at her neck and wrist collars in a dimly lit room, with a single source of light illuminating her seven-eighths white skin. While *Mending Socks* offers a glimpse of the quotidian life of some African Americans, *The Octoroon Girl* silently discusses the evolving history of African American women, as well as the relationship between skin color and socioeconomic status within and beyond the African American community. The fine artwork is simply magnificent to see; it has a prolific message, and invites viewers to witness an amazing reality of the African American experience.

Woodruff's work seems vaguely familiar to white audiences because he amalgamated the styles of Pablo Picasso and Paul Cézanne and superimposed African subjects into those styles. Using Cézanne's *Card Players with Pipes* as a point of departure, Woodruff reproduced the works with obvious cubist influences while using blacks as the subjects; the effect of this was that African

Americans artists were shown to be able to contribute to art even in the most sophisticated spectrums, and they could do it without sacrificing their commitment to advancing black art and culture. Other artist who took themes and familiar motifs included Palmer Hayden with his *Midsummer Night in Harlem* and Horace Pippin with *John Brown Going to His Hanging*. And just as these painters morphed common Western motifs to include the African and African Americans, so too did Harlem Renaissance sculptors. Augusta Savage's *The Harp* (1939) reshaped the classic image of the harp and to include a choir of African American women while *Gamin* (1930)—a bronze bust of her nephew—shows the beauty of the common African American. Where Savage used traditional occidental themes, sculptors Richmond Barthé's *Fera Benga* (1935) and Edna Manley's *Pocomania* (1936) focused on the beauty of African imagery.

FURTHER READING

Anderson, Paul A. *Deep River: Music and Memory in Harlem Renaissance Thought.* Durham, NC: Duke UP, 2001.

Baker, Houston A., Jr. *Afro-American Poetics: Revisions of Harlem and the Black Aesthetic.* Madison: U of Wisconsin P, 1996.

Banks, William H., Jr., ed. *Beloved Harlem: A Literary Tribute to Black America's Most Famous Neighborhood, from the Classics to the Contemporary.* New York: Harlem Moon, 2005.

Bassett, John E. *Harlem in Review: Critical Reactions to Black American Writers, 1917–1939.* Selinsgrove, PA: Susquehanna UP, 1992.

Bontemps, Arna. *God Sends Sundays.* 1931. New York: Washington Square, 2005.

Boyd, Herb, ed. *The Harlem Reader: A Celebration of New York's Most Famous Neighborhood, from the Renaissance Years to the Twenty-First Century.* New York: Three Rivers, 2003.

Campbell, Mary S., ed. *Harlem Renaissance: Art of Black America.* New York: Abrams, 1987.

Carroll, Anne E. *Word, Image, and the New Negro: Representation and Identity in the Harlem Renaissance.* Bloomington: Indiana UP, 2005.

Chambers, Jewell. "African American Theater." *Humanities in the Modern World: An Africana Emphasis.* Ed. Wendell Jackson et al. Boston: Pearson, 2001.

Chaucer, Geoffrey. *The Canterbury Tales.* Oxford: Oxford UP, 1998.

Coleridge, Samuel Taylor. "Rime of the Ancient Mariner." 1798. *Coleridge's Poetry and Prose.* Norton Critical Edition. New York: Norton, 2004.

Collier, James Lincoln, Duke Ellington. *African American Writers.* Ed. V. Smith. New York: Scribner, 1991.

Cullen, Countée. *Color.* New York: Harper, 1925.

Cullen, Countée. *Copper Sun.* New York: Harper, 1927.

Dawahare, Anthony. *Nationalism, Marxism, and African American Literature between Wars: A New Pandora's Box.* Jackson: UP of Mississippi, 2003.

Doyle, Laura, and Laura A. Winkiel, eds. *Geomodernisms: Race, Modernism, Modernity.* Bloomington: Indiana UP, 2005.

Du Bois, W.E.B. *The Autobiography of W.E.B. Du Bois.* New York: International, 1997.

Du Bois, W.E.B. "Criteria of Negro Art." *Du Bois Writings*. Comp. Nathan Huggins. New York: Library of America, 1986.

Du Bois, W.E.B. *Dark Princess: A Romance*. 1928. New York: Oxford UP, 2007.

Du Bois, W.E.B. *Quest of the Silver Fleece*. 1911. New York: Oxford UP, 2007.

Du Bois, W.E.B. *The Souls of Black Folk*. 1903. Norton Critical Edition. New York: Norton, 1999.

Du Bois, W.E.B. "The Talented Tenth." *Du Bois Writings*. Comp. Nathan Huggins. New York: Library of America, 1986.

Edwards, Brent H. *The Practice of Diaspora: Literature, Translation, and the Rise of Black Internationalism*. Cambridge: Harvard UP, 2003.

Fauset, Jessie Redmon. *The Chinaberry Tree*. New York: Stokes, 1931.

Fauset, Jessie Redmon. *Comedy: American Style*. 1933. College Park, MD: McGrath, 1969.

Fauset, Jessie Redmon. *Plum Bun*. 1929. Boston: Beacon, 1990.

Fauset, Jessie Redmon. *There Is Confusion*. 1924. Boston: Northeastern UP, 1989.

Floyd, Samuel A., ed. *Black Music in the Harlem Renaissance: A Collection of Essays*. New York: Greenwood, 1990.

Franklin, V. P. *Living Our Stories, Telling Our Truths: Autobiography and the Making of the African American Intellectual Tradition*. New York: Oxford UP, 1995.

Goldsby, Jacqueline. *A Spectacular Secret: Lynching in American Life and Literature*. Chicago: U of Chicago P, 2006.

Griffin, Farah Jasmine. "Billie Holiday." *African American Writers*. Ed. V. Smith. New York: Scribner.

Hamalian, Leo, and James V. Hatch. *The Roots of African American Drama: An Anthology of Early Plays, 1858–1938*. Detroit: Wayne State UP, 1991.

Hatch, James V., and Leo Hamalian, eds. *Lost Plays of the Harlem Renaissance: 1920–1940*. Detroit: Wayne State UP, 1996.

Hughes, Langston, and Zora Neale Hurston. *Mule Bone*. 1931. New York: Harper, 1991.

Hurston, Zora Neale. *Dust Tracks on the Road*. 1942. New York: Harper, 2006.

Hurston, Zora Neale. *Johan's Gourd Vine*. 1934. New York: Perennial Library, 1990.

Hurston, Zora Neale. *Mules and Men*. 1935. New York: Perennial Library, 1990.

Hurston, Zora Neale. *Tell My Horse*. 1938. New York: Perennial Library, 1990.

Hurston, Zora Neale. *Their Eyes Were Watching God*. 1937. New York: Perennial Library, 1990.

Johnson, Eloise E. *Rediscovering the Harlem Renaissance: The Politics of Exclusion*. New York: Garland, 1997.

Johnson, James Weldon. *The Autobiography of an Ex-Colored Man*. 1912. New York: Penguin, 1990.

Johnson, James Weldon. *God's Trombones: Seven Negro Sermons in Verse*. New York: Viking, 1927.

Kellner, Bruce. *The Harlem Renaissance: A Historical Dictionary for the Era*. Westport, CT: Greenwood, 1984.

Keresztesi, Rita. *Strangers at Home: American Ethnic Modernism between the World Wars*. Lincoln: U of Nebraska P, 2005.

Larsen, Nella. *Passing*. New York: Knopf, 1929.

Larsen, Nella. *Quicksand*. New York: Knopf, 1928.

Lewis, David L. *When Harlem was in Vogue*. New York: Knopf, 1981.

Lewis, David L., ed. *The Portable Harlem Renaissance Reader.* New York: Viking, 1994.

Locke, Alain B. *The New Negro: An Interpretation of Negro Life.* 1925. New York: Macmillan, 1992.

Luker, Ralph E. "Zora Neale Hurston." *African American Lives.* Ed. H. Gates and E. Higginbotham. New York: Oxford UP, 2004.

Martin, Tony. *African Fundamentalism: A Literary and Cultural Anthology of Garvey's Harlem Renaissance.* Dover, MA: Majority, 1991.

McKay, Claude. *Constab Ballads.* London: Watts, 1912.

McKay, Claude. *Home to Harlem* .1928. Boston: Northeastern UP, 1987.

McKay, Claude. *Songs of Jamaica.* 1912. Miami, FL: Mnemosyne, 1969.

Muggleston, William F. "Booker T. Washington." *African American Lives.* Ed. H. Gates and E. Higginbotham. New York: Oxford UP, 2004.

Myree-Mainor, Joy R. "Jessie Redmon Fauset." *Encyclopedia of African American Women Writers.* Ed. Y. Page. Westport, CT: Greenwod, 2007.

North, Michael. *The Dialect of Modernism: Race, Language, and Twentieth-Century Literature.* New York: Oxford UP, 1994.

Osofsky, Gilbert. *Harlem: The Making of a Ghetto. Negro New York, 1890–1930.* Reprinted 2nd ed. Chicago: Dee, 1996.

Patton, Sharon F. *Oxford History of Art.* Oxford: Oxford UP, 1998.

Pellegrinelli, Lara. "Ella Fitzgerald." *African American Writers.* Ed. V. Smith. New York: Scribner, 1991.

Peterson, Bernard. "Josephine Baker." *African American Writers.* Ed. V. Smith. New York: Scribner, 1991.

Rampersad, Arnold. "Harlem Renaissance." *The Norton Anthology of African American Literature.* Ed. Henry Louis Gates and Nellie Y. McKay. New York: Norton, 1997.

Reid, Margaret A., and Nikki Giovanni. *Black Protest Poetry: Polemics from the Harlem Renaissance and the Sixties.* New York: Lang, 2001.

Roses, Lorraine E. *Harlem Renaissance and Beyond: Literary Biographies of 100 Black Women Writers, 1900–1945.* Boston: Hall, 1990.

Schwarz, A. B. Christa. *Gay Voices of the Harlem Renaissance.* Bloomington: Indiana UP, 2003.

Sherrard-Johnson, Cherene. *Portraits of the New Negro Woman: Visual and Literary Culture in the Harlem Renaissance.* New Brunswick, NJ: Rutgers UP, 2007.

Skerrett, J. T., Jr. "James Weldon Johnson." *African American Writers.* Ed. V. Smith. New York: Scribner, 1991.

Smith, Erin A. "Jessie Redmon Fausett." *African American Writers.* Ed. V. Smith. New York: Scribner, 1991.

Spencer, Jon Michael. *The New Negroes and Their Music: The Success of the Harlem Renaissance.* Knoxville: U of Tennessee P, 1997.

Stribling, T. S. *Birthright.* New York: Century, 1922.

Sudhalter, Richard M. *Lost Chords: White Musicians and Their Contribution to Jazz 1915–1945.* New York: Oxford UP, 1999.

Thurman, Wallace. *Infants of the Spring.* 1929. Boston: Northeastern UP, 1992.

Thurman, Wallace. *The Blacker the Berry.* 1929. New York: Scribner, 1996.

Tirro, Frank. "Louis Armstrong." *African American Writers.* Ed. V. Smith. New York: Scribner, 1991.

Toomer, Jean. *Cane.* 1923. Arion, 2000.

Van Vechten, Carl. *Nigger Heaven*. 1926. Urbana: U of Illinois P, 2000.

Washington, Booker T. *Up from Slavery*. 1901. Norton Critical Edition. New York: Norton, 1996.

Washington, Mary H. *Invented Lives: Narratives of Black Women, 1860–1960*. New York: Anchor, 1987.

Watson, Steven. *The Harlem Renaissance: Hub of African American Culture, 1920–1930*. New York: Pantheon, 1995.

White, Walter. *Flint in the Fire*. New York: Knopf, 1924.

Wintz, Cary D. *Black Culture and the Harlem Renaissance*. Houston, TX: Rice UP, 1988.

Wintz, Cary D., and Paul Finkleman, eds. *Encyclopedia of the Harlem Renaissance*. London: Routledge, 2004.

Ordner W. Taylor III

E. Lynn Harris poses in the living room of his Atlanta home, 2008. (AP/Wide World Photos)

E. Lynn Harris

E. (Everett) Lynn Harris (1955–2009) is best known for his fiction series about African American homosexual men in the late 20th and early 21st centuries. A 10-time *New York Times* bestselling writer, Harris has carved his niche as a literary icon because his catalog of novels is dedicated to giving voice to the marginalized experiences of gay black men. Harris's writing, though often controversial because of its sensitive subject matter, attempts to help his readership deconstruct heteronormative understandings of sexuality and identity.

Awards and Recognitions

Blackboard Novel of the Year, Just as I Am *(1996)*
Sprague-Todes Literary Award (1998)
James Baldwin Literary Excellence Award (1997)
Distinguished Alumni Award, University of Arkansas at Fayetteville (1999)
Induction into the Arkansas Black Hall of Fame (2000)
Blackboard Novel of the Year, Any Way the Wind Blows *(2002)*
Savoy *magazine "100 Leaders and Heroes of Black America" (2002)*
Blackboard Novel of the Year, A Love of My Own *(2003)*
Lambda Literary Award, Freedom in the Village *(2005)*
Ebony *magazine, "Most Intriguing Blacks" (2006–2009)*

Harris ventured into literature after a 25-year career as a salesman at IBM. He published his first book, *Invisible Life,* independently in 1991 and sold copies of the novel out of his car trunk. In 1994, Harris was discovered by Anchor Books, which reprinted *Invisible Life* the same year. His literary career then took off: the popularity of Harris's stories earned him the nickname "the male Terry McMillan" among his fans. A frequent trend of Harris's writing is the relationship between his personal experiences as a gay man and his characters. The conflict Harris faced initially in his career of being closeted about his homosexual orientation is reflected in his characters and storylines, often opening conversation about constructions of masculinity and normalcy in the African American community over the last two decades. In his 2003 autobiography, *What Becomes of the Brokenhearted,* named after singer Jimmy Ruffin's song, Harris reflects upon a particularly painful incident where his father refers to him as a sissy on Easter Sunday because of how he presents himself: "Look at you. You fuckin' little sissy with this coat all buttoned up. Don't you know better? Men don't button their coats up all the way" (11). Harris then proceeds to talk about his father's violent reaction to his twirling to show his Easter outfit in similar fashion to his sisters. Harris's father, afraid that Harris's twirling indicated softness and femininity, curses and beats him. After his mother quickly changes him so that he can deliver his church speech,

Harris's perfect delivery is overshadowed by a lack of understanding and fear of his father's outburst: "All I recall is that I wasn't wearing a dress, and I remember what my daddy had said to me. I didn't know what a sissy was and why Daddy despised them so. All I knew was that I was determined never to be one" (13). The violent reproach of Harris's father represented a widely accepted understanding of manhood within the African American community—hardness, no indication of sensitivity, and straightness. Any behavior or action that challenged these indicators was a threat to the little perceived normalcy black men enjoyed for following the widespread sexual identity practices of American society. Harris's father viewed his twirling as a hindrance to any opportunity to function as a member of not only white American society, but also the African American community. These battles for self-definition and an understanding of acceptable practices of manhood framed Harris's adult experiences, as well as his plots as a writer.

It is important to point out the significance of Harris's work to a more contemporary (post-1980) canon because of his willingness to engage with the intersections of gay culture, blackness, and manhood in a post–civil rights era. Unlike predecessors Richard Bruce Nugent (1906–1987) or James Baldwin (1924–1987), Harris is afforded the opportunity to actively engage in creating an updated identity of gay black men in America. While discussions of homosexuality in the African American community are certainly not new, references to gay culture are often allegorical or inferred. Nugent, a Harlem Renaissance artist and one of the organizers of the short-lived *Fire!!* magazine, captured the affliction of being gay in an intolerant society during the early half of the 20th century in his much-discussed short story "Smoke, Lilies, and Jade." The abstractedness of Nugent's writing style, exhibited through the use of heavy ellipses and seemingly erratic thoughts, reflects the conflicting emotions and expectations of normalcy and self-desire as a (black) man. Nugent's protagonist struggles between heteronormative expectations of his family to marry a woman and his own inner desires to stay with his gay lover, simply referred to as "Beauty." Stories like "Smoke, Lilies, and Jade" attempted to normalize the gay experience within the African American community, but often used a cloaked discourse to approach this taboo subject. More specifically, black men were often at the center of these conversations, expected to lead and be the face of a changing black experience in American society.

Black masculinity as a gauge of the black experience is especially prevalent in the hypermasculine era of the 1950s and 1960s, the same era as Harris's childhood. Writers took cues from Richard Wright (1908–1960), who embodied and legitimized black masculine rage in his creation of the character Bigger Thomas in *Native Son* (1940). African American literature's focus on manhood spoke to the call to arms that positioned African American men in the forefront of the community's uplift. Critics and theorists of the Black Power Movement and its sister Black Arts Movement often shunned the participation of gay men. There was little room for varied interpretations of gender and identity. Alternative views of manhood spearheaded by Wright's one-time mentee James Baldwin found these static representations of African American masculinity problematic and ostracizing. In his essay "Everybody's Protest Novel" from his collection of essays *Notes of a Native Son,* Baldwin uses theological reasoning to pinpoint the peculiarity of American racial politics and identity: "theological terror, the terror of damnation…this panic motivates our cruelty, this fear of the dark makes it impossible that our lives shall be other than superficial" (18). While initial analysis of Baldwin's arguments suggests a strong critique of racial politics in mid-20th-century American society, Baldwin's observations are also applicable to notions of sexuality and identity. Baldwin's writings constantly fuse religion with constructions of blackness, a nod to his zealous Christian upbringing. One of the primary foci of Christian damnation is homosexuality, which Baldwin attempts to deconstruct in many of his novels, including the most blatant engagement with male same-sex relationships, *Giovanni's Room.* The cruelty Baldwin addresses in "Everybody's Protest Novel" can also mean cruelty to those who are not heterosexually oriented and that unfamiliarity with gay culture results in violent reparations against it.

Ironically, many of the forerunners of critical thought and creative expression during the Black Liberation era were openly gay. Bayard Rustin, a close associate and advisor of Dr. Martin Luther King Jr. was openly gay yet actively engaged in civil rights protests. Rustin had a heavy hand in the organization of the March on Washington. Other gay men of color like choreographer Alvin Ailey and cultural theorist Hoyt Fuller also contributed to a shifting paradigm of blackness through cultural outlooks that helped expand understanding of the African American experience.

Harris pulls from personal experiences like his Easter Sunday run-in with his father to help formulate an approach to making homosexuality in the black American community less taboo and more visible in a nonstereotypical manner. Harris's iconoclastic writing carves a niche for collapsing outdated representations and imagery of a homosexual experience in the late 20th century. Most striking in Harris's characterization of gay black men is his use of what is considered the down-low trope, or engaging in closeted sexual trysts with men while (re)presenting heterosexual and often highly homophobic public lives. Harris's down-low characters branch from his own initial denial of his sexuality in order to be considered normal. Harris's approach is additionally intriguing because of his layering of closeted gay African American men's troubled constructions of gender politics and identity in popular culture. While there is an outward push for tolerance of racial and sexual orientation, African American men exist within a vacuum. As Mark Anthony Neal astutely states in his essay "A (Nearly) Flawless Masculinity?": "Black men do not live in polite society—however effectively they earn their keep within those spaces." African American men exist on the fringes of polite or acceptable white notions of society and are constantly in search of the means to balance their expected behaviors and their actual existence. This understanding is further complicated with regard to African American gay men, which Harris uses to frame his work.

Harris's main characters are often professional athletes or successful professional men. They are in the American public spotlight, and because of their fame, are often under heavier scrutiny than their counterparts. Furthermore, many of Harris's characters exist in uncontested heterosexual spaces where a difference in sexual expression from the heterosexual norm is interpreted as weak and signifying the inability to function properly (normally). One of Harris's most popular recurring characters, John "Basil" Henderson, for example, is a successful businessman and former professional football player. Although unapologetically bisexual, Basil keeps his male trysts out of conversation and the public light because of his high-profile image and brand. Harris's intentionally high-profile male characters shed light on the difficulty of masculine expression for black men in this present moment of social-cultural history.

With the 2004 release of author J. L. King's book *On the Down Low,* Harris's work catapulted to the center stage of American public attention. A hyperawareness of gay black men in America became a pulse point of racial paranoia about such men as predatory. African Americans, particularly women, were engulfed with fear and the assumption that *all* black men were down-low and seeking homosexual relationships. Harris became an even more public advocate of gay rights in the black community, continuing to write and even appear on *The Oprah Winfrey Show* to dispel some of the misunderstandings about homosexuality in African American culture. Given that Harris's audience consisted primarily of women of color, Harris's speaking out about the problematic absorption of down-low culture as an indicator of the gay community as a whole merited some alleviation of their fears. And as his career certainly displays, Harris discussed closeted homosexual black men way before the down-low phenomenon ever hit public American culture. The difference, however, is that Harris's characters kept their sexual orientations private as a coping mechanism instead of a predatory weapon. At the height of the down-low paranoia, Harris himself became a target of harsh criticism, with many suggesting that his work glorified down-low behavior instead of clarifying or offering insight into it. Harris spoke to close friends about the hurt of such criticism but utilized critics' outcries to release *Freedom in this Village* (2005), an edited anthology dedicated to writings by African American gay men.

E. Lynn Harris's sudden death in July 2009 stunned fans and the literary world. Harris's novels arguably created a space for insight into African American gay men's lives that would lead to a more widespread acknowledgment and consumption of their image in popular cultural expression. His bold and at times controversial explorations of nonheterosexuality and African American men opened doors for conversations about gay culture in the black American community and were means to learn to tolerate and ultimately accept their contributions to the contemporary African American experience.

BIBLIOGRAPHY

Novels

Abide With Me. New York: Anchor, 2000.
And This Too Shall Pass. New York: Anchor, 1997.
Any Way the Wind Blows. New York: Anchor, 2002.
Basketball Jones. New York: Anchor, 2009.
I Say a Little Prayer. New York: Anchor, 2007.
If This World Were Mine. New York: Anchor, 1997.
In My Father's House. New York: St. Martin's, 2010. (Posthumously released)
Invisible Life. 1991. New York: Anchor, 1994.
Just as I Am. New York: Anchor, 1995.
Just Too Good to Be True. New York: Doubleday, 2008.
A Love of My Own. New York: Anchor, 2003.
Mama Dearest. New York: Simon, 2009. (Posthumously released)
Not a Day Goes By. New York: Doubleday, 2000.
What Becomes of the Brokenhearted. New York: Doubleday, 2003.

Collections and Anthologies

Gumbo: A Celebration of African American Writers. New York: Broadway, 2002.
Freedom in this Village. Cambridge: Da Capo, 2004.

Regina N. Bradley

For more than five decades, Langston Hughes wrote poetry, fiction, and plays that were meant to capture the essence of the black experience in America. A prolific writer of rare versatility, he wrote for the men and women he saw struggling first for survival and then for equality from the 1920s through the 1960s. (Library of Congress)

Langston Hughes

Poet laureate, dean of black American writers, a self-proclaimed literary share-cropper, and radical socialist were terms used to describe Langston Hughes (1902–1967) at some point during his literary career. All apply to the man, and in subtle ways, they underscore the vision he had for his corpus. More than an American poet, Hughes successfully wrote and published short stories, novels, two autobiographies, children's books, critical essays, and editorials. He also translated the works of Jacques Romain, Nicolas Guillén, Leon Damas, Gabriela Mistral, and Jean-Joseph Rabearivelo (Miller 114). He collaborated with musical composers, working as a lyricist and writer of librettos; and as a dramatist, he designed plays that were performed on Broadway and in smaller venues—the Karamu House in Cleveland, Ohio, and New York's Harlem Suitcase Theatre. In addition, Hughes also edited definitive collections that helped lay early foundations for appreciating the African American literary canon. He partnered with his best friend Arna Bontemps to publish *The Poetry of the Negro, 1746–1949* (1949) and *The Book of Negro Folklore* (1958). Independently, he compiled anthologies such as *Poems from Black Africa* (1963), *New Negro Poets: U.S.A.* (1964), *The Book of Negro Humor* (1966), and *The Best Short Stories by Negro Writers* (1967). These translations, works of fiction, essays, anthologies, poems, and theatrical pieces cemented his stature as a writer and literary critic, but Hughes's scholarly pursuits and creative interests also included the mentoring of a younger generation of black writers, people such as LeRoi Jones (né Amiri Baraka; 1934–), Gwendolyn Brooks (1917–2000), Ralph Ellison (1914–1994), Richard Wright (1908–1960), Margaret Walker (1915–1998), and Paule Marshall (1929–), to name a few. Of course, Hughes offered this tutelage to the next generation of black American writers while concurrently developing professional relationships with his contemporaries: Alain Locke (1886–1954), Countee Cullen (1903–1946), Zora Neale Hurston (1891–1960), Carl Van Vechten (1880–1964), Wallace Thurman (1902–1934), Nicolas Guillén (190–1989), Arthur Koestler (1905–1983), and Ernest Hemingway (1899–1961), for example. His rapport with these professional writers led to Hughes being given the titles of "poet laureate" and "dean" of African American letters, for his diverse body of work, and his influential prominence impacted members of the literary intelligentsia and black literati alike. Yet his career achievements are outmatched only, perhaps, by his social visions and political convictions; such convictions wedded him to the proletariat classes as well, for he was consummately concerned about human rights and civil liberties for all people.

Traveling the world as a young adult, Hughes gained an international perspective and in doing so adopted a worldview that respected and sought a more equitable society for all marginalized individuals. Although his travels were often dictated by a need to pursue fiscal opportunities that he could not find as a black man in America, these journeys endowed him with a foresight that is widely embraced in the 21st century: a global perception that civil liberties must be preserved for all people regardless of race, ethnicity, religion, or national origin. His examination and articulation of these ideas can best be found in his two autobiographies, *The Big Sea* (1940) and *I Wonder as I Wander* (1956). In these texts, he recounts his travels across America, Africa, Mexico, Europe, Russia, parts of Asia, and the Caribbean, voicing a deeper recognition of global perspectives in a world that was inevitably evolving in the midst of burgeoning postcolonial moments (e.g., the fact that sovereign nations were forming as colonizing influences returned to their imperial hubs—as was the case in the Caribbean and parts of Africa— or that civil infrastructures were defying imperial dictatorships within their borders—as occurred in Spain and parts of the Soviet Union/Central Asia). Of course, Hughes acquired material and/or sources of inspiration for his work during these trips. He produced, for example, a travel book about his experiences in central Asia and a volume of radical poems; both texts were rejected by Knopf, but some material was integrated into *The Ways of White Folks* (Hill 72). Most importantly, these journeys enabled him to interact with representations of the upper and lower echelons of these societies; he mingled with the layperson and the socialite, artist and worker, government official and political activist.

A chameleon of sorts, he was able to adapt to any situation and felt comfortable in all settings. In other words, Hughes was adept at communicating with a diverse community of individuals, comfortably engaging people across economic, political, cultural, and ethnic divides. This ability to relate to divergent perspectives was most likely influenced by the man's migratory lifestyle, a transitional way of being that began during the writer's formative years. For example, whether living with his grandmother in Kansas, her neighbors and elderly friends, the Reeds, after her death, or his parents in various locations in the American Midwest and Mexico, Hughes found it necessary to quickly adapt to changing environments, and in each new location, he typically needed to negotiate relationships with a diverse group of individuals (adults and members of his own peer group, as well as black, white, Christian, Jewish, American, and/or Mexican perspectives). Thus, Hughes developed a tolerance for others. He also observed his parents' divergent lifestyles, especially his father's frugal but well-to-do existence in Mexico in opposition to his mother's inability to save, which contributed to the family's impoverished condition: "The opposite of my father, my mother was very generous and kindhearted with everyone around her.... [My father, h]e was very penurious" (*I Wonder* 307–8).

It should be no surprise that Hughes was comfortable with any layperson or the sophisticate, a paradoxical fact reflected in his inability to position himself above the poverty line despite his literary success and worldwide notoriety. He would write to Arna Bontemps in 1951 that he was a "literary sharecropper," for example (qtd. in Rampersad, *Vol. II* 187–89). On the one hand, Hughes is referencing the limited income he was attempting to live off of, while also conveying his frustration over an inability to reap the financial benefits of his published work. These latter points—Hughes's ability to identify with the pluralism he found abroad, his connection with educated and uneducated black

Americans, and his professional rapport with America's white intelligentsia—denote the radical foresight he had about a more egalitarian world, one that would evolve once European imperialism was dismantled in many third-world countries and blacks were no longer treated as second-class citizens in the United States. When traveling in Japan, for example, Hughes wrote: "How wonderful,...it would be if all the colonies and color lines in the world were wiped out. Meanwhile, I am glad that Japan is able to enjoy her ceremonial tea without the unwelcome intrusion of the imperialist powers of the West who brought the color line to Africa and Asia" (*I Wonder* 243). Statements such as these led to Hughes being labeled a radical socialist, a term that followed him during and after his travels through Russia and Asia during the 1930s. He was, as Richard Wright praised, "a cultural ambassador" (qtd. in Rampersad, Introduction, *The Big Sea* xvi), a world-traveled individual who respected not only his own but also other cultural identities.

Chronology

1902   *Born in Joplin, Missouri.*

1903   *Parents' marriage disintegrates, father moves to Mexico.*

1909   *Carrie Langston Hughes sends young Langston to live with his grandmother in Lawrence, Kansas.*

1915   *Lives with Mr. and Mrs. Reed, following his grandmother's death; moves to Lincoln, Illinois to join his mother and her second husband.*

1916   *Finishes his middle-school education in Lincoln before the family relocates to Cleveland, OH; there he attends Central High School.*

1919   *Visits his father in Mexico, summer before his senior year of high school.*

1920   *Graduates from Central High School.*

1921   *Enrolls in Columbia University, New York City and publishes "The Negro Speaks of Rivers" in the NAACP's* Crisis *magazine.*

1922   *Drops out of Columbia University.*

1923   *Seeks maritime work, first working in a shipping graveyard on the Hudson before heading to Africa; lives in Paris where he works as a dishwasher and bouncer in jazz clubs.*

1925   *Meets poet Vachel Lindsay while working at a hotel in Washington, DC; Lindsay reads his poetry and introduces him to the literary world as the busboy poet; wins Urban League's* Opportunity *magazine poetry prize.*

1926   *Publishes* The Weary Blues, *his first collection of poetry, and enrolls in Lincoln University.*

1927   Publishes his second book of poetry, Fine Clothes to the Jew.

1929   Graduates from Lincoln University.

1930   Co-writes Mule Bone, an African American folk drama, with Zora Neale Hurston; both are receiving patronage from widowed philanthropist Charlotte Osgood Mason. Also publishes his first novel, Not Without Laughter. Drives from New York to Florida en route to Cuba and Haiti; along the way, visits Bethune-Cookman College, which he revisits after returning from the Caribbean. Mary McLeod Bethune accompanies him and his travel companion on the drive back to New York.

1931   Receives a Harmon Foundation grant to tour the South, lecturing and reading his work mostly at historically black colleges and universities, churches, and in the community; Mrs. Bethune advised him to design this tour.

1932   Travels to the Soviet Union as an actor, assistant script coordinator for Black and White, and journalist. Publishes The Dream Keeper and Popo and Fifina, two children's book that he co-wrote with Arna Bontemps.

1933   Crosses the Soviet Union from Moscow to central Asia by train; he returns to the United States via Hawaii.

1934   Publishes The Ways of White Folks, a collection of stories; father dies in Mexico.

1935   When he returns to New York, he discovers that his play, Mulatto, is being rehearsed for its Broadway release.

1936   Mulatto becomes the longest-running Broadway play authored by an African American.

1937   Covers the Spanish Civil War for the Associated Negro Press.

1938   Creates the Suitcase Theatre in Harlem, New York; his mother dies.

1940   The Big Sea, his first autobiography, is published.

1942/ Introduces Jesse B. Semple in a column he writes for Chicago's
43   black-owned newspaper, Defender.

1947   Works on a musical adaptation of Elmer Rice's Street Scene with Kurt Weill; Weill is the composer for the production, while Hughes writes the lyrics.

1948   Invests in a permanent home, buying a townhouse in Harlem with the Harpers.

1949   Takes a job as a visiting poet at the Laboratory School of the University of Chicago.

1950   First bestseller, Simple Speaks His Mind, is published.

1953   Forced to testify before Joseph McCarthy and his Senate committee.

1956 Simply Heaven, a play developed from his Jesse B. Semple stories, debuts at an off-Broadway theatre; I Wonder As I Wander, his second autobiography, is also published.

1957 Releases The Book of Negro Folklore, which he co-edited with Arna Bontemps.

1960 Awarded the NAACP Spingarn Medal by friend and colleague, Arthur Spingarn.

1961 Ask Your Mama, a book of satirical verse, is released, and Hughes is inducted into the National Institute of Arts and Letters.

1966 Journeys to Dakar, Senegal to attend the First World Festival of Negro Arts.

1967 Dies from complications following surgery for prostate cancer in New York City.

Born in Joplin, Missouri, on the February 1, 1902, Langston Hughes inherited a rich African American family history. His maternal grandmother, Mary Patterson Leary Langston, was the first black woman accepted to attend Oberlin College (Lawrence 71). While living in Ohio, she met and married her first husband, Lewis Sheridan Leary. Leary stood with John Brown at Harpers Ferry. His bloodstained shawl, worn the night of the failed assault, was mailed to Mary, letting her know that her husband would not be returning home to her (Hughes, *Big Sea* 12). Before her death, she sent the shawl to Hughes, who treasured the memento as a memorial of his family's participation in an antebellum fight to liberate enslaved Africans in America (Hill 16). Her second husband, Hughes's maternal grandfather, Charles Harold Langston was also committed to the abolitionist movement and was Virginia's first black congressman (Otfinoski 33). A graduate of Oberlin College, Charles helped lead a daring slave rescue called the Oberlin-Wellington Raid, was active in Republican politics after the Civil War, and was an editor for an African American newspaper in which he advocated for equal rights and better educational resources for black Americans. His two brothers, Gideon and John Mercer Langston, also graduated from Oberlin. Gideon was an affluent Virginia businessman and John Mercer went on to become a prominent lawyer, a congressman from Virginia, the first dean of Howard University's Law School, the first president of Virginia State University, and an ambassador to Haiti (Hill 17; Hughes, *Big Sea* 13). Charles also published an autobiography, *From the Virginia Plantation to the National Capital* (1894), in which he recounted his personal achievement and inspirational family history (Miller 115).

Considering this ancestral legacy, it should come as no surprise that Hughes would have such reverence for his African American roots or that he would pursue writing as a vocation. Not only was he born into a highly educated and socially conscious family, but his great uncle John Mercer and grandfather Charles enjoyed careers as eloquent orators and published writers. Mary Leary Langston, Hughes's grandmother, shared this love of literature and orature, which she passed on to her daughter, Carrie, and to her grandson, Langston. Mary told him African American folklore and stories about the family's history, while Carrie, a novice poet during her college years, read to him and frequently took him to movies, theatre performances, and community plays and recitals in order to broaden his appreciation of the arts (Hill 17–19; Lawrence 71). Add this artistic dimension to his ancestors' political commitments, and no one should be surprised that Hughes became the iconic writer, folk artist, and scholar that he did.

The only unexpected turn in his career may be the fact that he did not enjoy the wealth of an earlier generation of Langstons or the financial success of his father, James Nathaniel Hughes. John Mercer, Hughes's maternal great uncle, enjoyed a wealthy lifestyle and was able to leave his descendants with a financially secure inheritance (Miller 115). Charles Langston, Hughes's grandfather, also attempted to secure his family's future prior to his death. The son of Ralph Quarles—a wealthy Virginia plantation owner who had what would be recognized today as a common-law marriage with his black housekeeper—Charles Langston inherited part of the estate his father bequeathed to Lucy, his mother, a former slave and mother of three (Hill 16–17). Mary, Charles's wife and Hughes's grandmother, presumably owned her home during Hughes's childhood. However, as her fiscal security declined, Mary Langston found it necessary to rent her home to roomers in order to supplement her income; she was too proud to work as a housekeeper or nanny, and perhaps having taken out another mortgage (or mortgages) on the home—although no documentation has been found to prove this fact—the house was taken by a mortgage collector upon her death (Hill 17). As a result, Hughes moved into the home of his grandmother's best friends, the Reeds. They cared for Hughes until his mother sent for him in 1915. She moved him to Lincoln, Illinois, making arrangements for him to live with her, her new husband, Homer Clark, and his son Gwyn from another relationship (Hill 21). In Lincoln, Hughes was voted class poet and required to write a poem for his graduating class (Hill 22). However, the newly formed family's time in Lincoln was short lived. They relocated to Cleveland, Ohio, in 1915, where Hughes attended Central High School.

Hughes enjoyed his time at Central. He was a popular student and talented athlete. Moreover, while at Central, Hughes met Helen Chesnutt (Hill 22), daughter of Charles W. Chesnutt, one of the most important and influential African American authors of the late 19th and early 20th centuries. Under Helen Chesnutt's tutelage, Hughes found the inspiration he needed to explore his literary inclinations. He contributed poems to the *Belfry Owl*, a student magazine, edited the school yearbook, and discovered his talent for short fiction. Some stories written during this period are archived in Yale's Beinecke Library. These became accessible to the greater public arena in 1996, when Akiba Sullivan Harper published an edited collection of Hughes's short fiction. Three of these stories are "Mary Winosky," "Those Who Have No Turkey," and "Seventy-five Dollars." "Mary Winosky" is archived at Yale's Beinecke Library in the Langston Hughes Papers of the James Weldon Johnson collection

(Harper 299). "Those Who Have No Turkey" was first published in the school's *Monthly* in December 1918; it was published again in *Brownies Book 2* (November 1921). "Seventy-five Dollars" was also published in *Monthly* (1919; Harper 299).

"Mary Winosky" was written for a 1915 Central High School English assignment, and prior to Harper's publication, the story had remained un-published. This "dull tragedy" documents the life of a Russian immigrant, who worked as a scrubwoman in America and died alone and depressed after amassing a sizeable savings account (*Short Stories* 275). Although she lived most of her life as a single woman, she was once married, and even after her husband abandoned her, maintained hope that he would someday return. Her death occurs immediately after she learns that her husband—who she has not seen for years—was killed in the war (*Short Stories* 275–78). The story ends with the statement: "Many parents read it [the obituary byline] to their children as an excellent example of thrift and economy" (*Short Stories* 278), a statement that endorses the misappropriation of this woman's life. Few seem to realize the tragedy of this woman's circumstance: "A drab-colored life of floors to scrub and rags to pick, having at its end eight thousand dollars as a result of the drudgery" (*Short Stories* 275), money that neither she nor the one person she loved would ever spend. In essence, the story questions the precepts of the American dream, that freedom and opportunity in the United States actually denotes success, happiness, and social freedom for all its citizens, for nothing in Mary Winosky's story implies that she was or perceived herself to be happy, successful, and/or free at her life's end. The tenet of this story is fascinating when one considers Hughes's particular interest in social-ism later in his life, an interest in Marxist ideals that led him to visit the Soviet Union during the 1930s. Certainly during his time at Central, he was exposed to working-class immigrant families, whose struggles and successes added a nuanced perspective to a white, American story, a view of poverty in America to which Hughes could relate.

"Those Who Have No Turkey" is another story about class and an Ameri-can immigrant experience. The protagonist, Diane Jordan, is a midwestern teen from the farmlands visiting her aunt's family in Cleveland, Ohio, for the Thanksgiving holiday. Accustomed to roaming the outdoors, Diane can-not remain in the house as everything is being prepared for the dinner, so she decides to take a walk through the neighborhood. Along the way, she meets Tubby Sweeney, a red-haired little boy who is selling newspapers on the corner. When she discovers that he has no plans for Thanksgiving, let alone an expectation of enjoying a turkey dinner, she invites him and his fam-ily to her aunt's home for the holiday. Tubby explains to an innocent Diane: "We ain't got nothin' yet…and we won't have much if dere's not enough pennies in my pocket to get somethin'" (*Short Stories* 281). The narration explains: "She had never heard of anybody having nothing for dinner except the poor war-stricken Belgians, and that was because the Germans had eaten up everything" (*Short Stories* 281). But the Germans have certainly not eaten everything on American soil, and yet this immigrant family is starving as they endure poverty in America. In essence, the young Hughes again incorporates irony and an interest in economics and American social issues into his early fiction, perhaps relating to the experiences of some of his classmates, while also universalizing an experience of inequity that was all too familiar to him and to members of the African American working community. He further explored these motifs in another story, written while a student at Central High School.

Poverty and hunger are major themes for "Seventy-five Dollars." In this tale, Hughes relates the sacrifices and the financial or emotional hardships of six children who survive their mother's death, a single woman who "worked herself to death" in an effort to provide her children with a better life (*Short Stories* 285). Martha, the oldest, becomes the primary breadwinner and disciplinarian in the family; Tough, the second-oldest brother, aspires to leave his delinquent ways behind him, when Martha explains that the welfare of their younger siblings really depends upon them and their diligent work ethic. Joe, the third oldest, has always loved learning and yearns to graduate from high school and complete a college degree. To meet the family's basic needs, however, Joe is forced to drop out. Yet all agree that their mother did not want him to accept the working-class lifestyle that she was forced to endure. In a compromise, the older siblings decide that Tough and Martha will carry the major expenses, allowing Joe to save while he works so he can return to school; he accumulates 75 dollars toward this venture. Unable to completely distance himself from the street life, however, Tough steals and spends 75 dollars from old-man Steiner, who demands that he be repaid or the perpetrator, Tough, will be incarcerated for the crime. Joe discovers that his treasured savings for school will have to be spent to save his older brother. Ultimately, the crux of the issue is whether to lose the third family income and see a sibling sent to jail, or have Joe sacrifice his life's aspiration—one that might ultimately improve the entire family's circumstances. Therefore, Joe accepts the fact that "he couldn't go back to school, because they were too poor," and in essence, always would be (*Short Stories* 291). Yet again, Hughes writes about poverty, an issue that clearly affected black and white students alike in his Ohio school district. Thus, during these pubescent years in Cleveland, Hughes not only better understood his penchant for writing, but also acquired a cultural awareness and multicultural sensitivity that enabled him to interact freely and positively with first-generation white immigrant teens, Jews, and other working-class midwestern teens who also attended the school. This exposure to cultural diversity prepared Hughes to visit with his father in Mexico between 1919 and 1921.

James Nathaniel Hughes met and married Carrie Mercer Langston when she was teaching school in Guthrie, Oklahoma, a frontier town. In Oklahoma, J. N. Hughes owned a 160-acre homestead. However, because of his business ambitions, he had no intention of keeping his family in this prairie state. Born a slave, the elder Hughes refused to remain relegated to a secondary status in a country that proclaimed to be the land of the free, and the home of the brave. Two of his brothers rode with the legendary African American squadron known as the Buffalo Soldiers in the American Civil War, and before leaving Indiana, he was venerated as a successful farmer and church official, acclaim he maintained during his life in Oklahoma with his wife, Carrie. Upon receiving a job opportunity at the Lincoln Mining Company, he moved his family to Joplin, Missouri. But after confronting years of discrimination in America, he eventually relocated, first to Cuba, and then Mexico, to pursue his legal interests and business ventures (Hill 26).

Having been denied the opportunity to sit for the bar exam by an all-white examination board in Oklahoma and tired of fighting against the Jim Crow biases that pervaded America at the turn of the 20th century, the older Hughes became an émigré, pledging never to reside in the United States again (Hill 13). In Mexico, Hughes's father reaped the financial fruits of living in a country that was not as markedly racist and subordinating to people of African descent. Once there, he was able to establish himself as a successful businessman, owning land, a ranch, and rental properties; he brokered some international business deals and litigated minor matters for local denizens who sought his advice and legal aid. James Nathaniel Hughes was also fluent in three languages: Spanish, German, and English (Hill 26). When he sent for his son in 1919, the year before Hughes would begin his senior year at Central High, the elder Hughes's behest to his son was that the younger Hughes move to Mexico and assist his father with his bookkeeping. Ultimately, he hoped that his son would pursue a college degree in Germany, develop his accounting skills, and inherit the father's property. Of course, that did not happen.

Although Hughes reveled in the thrilling adventures he had in Mexico— riding horses, traveling through the open country, and being exposed to a frugal but wealthier lifestyle than what he was accustomed to in America—he quickly became dismayed by his father's prejudiced opinion of black Americans and Mexican peasants. Thus, when he returned to Mexico the year after he graduated from Central High School, he soon discovered that he could not endure a life in Mexico with his overly materialistic and racist parent. He would rather battle the transitory lifestyle and impoverished conditions with which he was familiar and pursue a career as a writer. For even without the riches of his father's inheritance, Hughes knew that he could survive as he had seen his mother, grandmother, and the Reeds do for so many years (*Big Sea* 39–49). Also, having penned "The Negro Speaks of Rivers" during his first train ride to Mexico that summer of 1919, and having continued to develop his love of literature and writing the following year in Mexico, the burgeoning writer confessed an unwavering desire to become a professional writer (*Big Sea* 54).

Despite Hughes's dreams, however, his father had different aspirations for the son, ones driven largely by the father's own hopes and dreams. Not only did J. N. Hughes want his son to avoid the dehumanizing obstacles he experienced as a young man, but he also wished for his son to enjoy the comforts of a professional career that neither he nor Hughes's mother had been able to eke out for themselves. So the elder Hughes adamantly demanded that his son consider a college career abroad, pursuing a math or science major—preferably engineering, accounting, or business administration. However, when the younger Hughes refused, asserting his interest in Columbia University's literature programs, Nathaniel acquiesced, agreeing to pay for his son's attendance at the Ivy League school (Otfinoski 34–35). He may have been persuaded by the fact that his son's poem, "The Negro Speaks of Rivers," had been published in *Crisis* that summer (Hughes, *Big Sea* 72). Certainly, the father was not inveigled by his son's enthusiasm; he was a thrifty worker who expected Langston to be pragmatic in his vocational pursuits. Nonetheless, the discovery that Hughes's work had been well received in the public arena helped to coax the father into supporting the son's interests in a humanities degree from Columbia University.

The reality of being a matriculated African American student at Columbia, however, was dynamically—and problematically—different from what Hughes had imagined. Unlike his experience at the predominantly white Central High School, students were not friendly to him and did not welcome him into the university's social echelon. For that matter, due to the segregated atmosphere of the campus, he found it impossible to create the extracurricular niches he so successfully navigated at Central (Hill 33–35). Therefore, although his first semester academic grades were adequate, by the second semester, Hughes was not attending his classes but rather choosing to spend more time with the black bohemians of Harlem. Consequently, as his grades weakened, his father refused to continue paying tuition. As a result, Hughes dropped out of Columbia, forever fracturing his relationship with his father. Although they wrote to each other occasionally, throughout the remainder of the elder Hughes's life, the young author would never see his father alive again, and the rift between them concerning the son's vocation and the father's hopes for his child's career expectations would never be healed. The writer returned to Mexico in 1934, after coming back to the United States from his travels abroad in Asia, when news of his father's death reached him (*I Wonder* 287–91).

Without his father's financial support, Hughes found himself economically disenfranchised in New York and in desperate need of employment. He was a 20-year-old black man, struggling to find work in a country where it was virtually impossible for any black male to secure reputable employment, especially if he had no training in a trade. Thus, Hughes experienced tremendous disappointment when seeking employment after withdrawing from Columbia. The only work he initially found was working at a truck-garden farm in Staten Island (*Big Sea* 86). During this time, he also continued writing, sending his work to Jessie Fauset, editor of the *Crisis* magazine. Next, Hughes became a delivery man for a provident florist, a man who reminded him of his father: "My father would have loved his efficiency. He and Mr. Thorley could have been good friends" (*Big Sea* 89). Thus, when a rift formed in his relationship with Mr. Thorley—Hughes wanted to be paid overtime for additional work that he had done but Thorley refused—the aspiring author abandoned his job. Hughes decided that he would simply not show up for work one day. But because he had little savings and knew he needed a job in order to survive he decided to become a seaman: "It seemed to me now," he commented, "that if I had to work for low wages at dull jobs, I might just as well see the world, so I began to look for work on a ship" (*Big Sea* 89).

The first shipping job he found was that of a mess boy on a freighter that was docked in a shipyard on Jones Point in the Hudson River (*Big Sea* 90–91). It was during the time that Hughes was trapped in this anchored line of decommissioned ships that he wrote "The Weary Blues," a poem about a Harlem piano player (*Big Sea* 92). It is also during this time that Hughes was sought out by Alain Locke, professor of English and philosophy at Howard University and the soon-to-be founding father of the Harlem Renaissance in America. According to Hughes the noted scholar was fascinated by the "merits of [Hughes's] poems" and interested in coming to meet him at Jones Point (*Big Sea* 92–93). Embarrassed perhaps by the decaying atmosphere of his maritime surroundings or the homoerotic overtures of the older scholar, Hughes declined the invitation. Arnold Rampersad puts a different spin on this chain of events in the first volume of his biography on Hughes. In *The Life of Langston Hughes,* Rampersad explains that Hughes and Locke had begun corresponding in 1921. They were introduced to each other by Countee Cullen who, perhaps, had unrequited affections for Hughes (Rampersad, *Vol. II* 66–72). Hughes, however, does not mention this correspondence between himself, Locke, and Cullen in *The Big Sea*. Soon after Locke's attempted visit, Hughes decided "to leave the dead ships and find a vessel that was moving" (*Big Sea* 97). He signed on to work the S.S. *Malone*, which took him from America to the continent of Africa:

> I was a seaman going to sea for the first time—a seaman on a big merchant ship. And I felt that nothing would ever happen to me again that I didn't want to happen. I felt grown, a man, inside and out. Twenty-one. (*Big Sea* 3)

This journey to Africa marked Hughes's voyage into manhood—a journey that would culminate in his artistic maturation as a writer and in his intellectual curiosity and respect for global perspectives. During these travels, he not only identified with an African diasporic sense of identity, but he was also exposed to other writers and marginalized experiences, all of which had an indelible role in broadening his understandings of political and economic struggles throughout the world.

Prior to launching from New York Harbor in 1923 Hughes threw his books overboard—texts he had accumulated during his first year at Columbia. Many scholars note the fact that Hughes refrained from throwing one book overboard: Walt Whitman's *Leaves of Grass* (Hill 1997; Rampersad 1986). Whether his holding onto this volume of verse conveys any concrete relevance concerning Hughes's hopes for his own poetry or his efforts to reconcile his sexual identity, all underscore the ways in which this gesture of exorcising himself from books and the academy liberated the artist. Thus, when Hughes began his journey to Africa, he felt free to see the world as a man not shackled to American ideals but rather as a seeker who aimed to see the world with fresh, unadulterated eyes.

It is 1923 and Langston Hughes, who had already begun thinking about the world in global and economic terms—as shown in his Central High stories and revealed in his writings about his experiences in Mexico—is paying attention to his environment and keenly querying his position as a black American man living in a global world. For him, this sense of placement and identity had to begin with his grounding in an African diasporic context. Aptly, then, he mentions Marcus Garvey (1887–1940) in the opening pages of *The Big Sea* (102). Garvey was a Pan-African liberation leader of the early 1900s who advocated for the reverse migration of black Americans from the United States to Africa (Gates and McKay 995):

> The white man dominates Africa. He takes produce, and lives, very much as he chooses. The yield of earth for Europe and America. The yield of men for Europe's colonial armies. And the Africans are baffled and humble.... At that time, 1923, the name of Marcus Garvey was known the length and breadth of the West Coast of Africa. And the Africans did not laugh at Marcus Garvey, as so many people laughed in New York.... They only knew the white man was there in Africa, heavy and oppressive on their backs. And they wanted him to go away. (*Big Sea* 102)

These mentions of Garvey in the opening chapter of this section of *The Big Sea*, which is about his voyage to Africa, allow the reader to speculate about Hughes's own socialist views, especially an anticolonial perspective about the dehumanized ways in which the bodies and goods produced by people of color have been commodified in many countries. There are two compelling ideas in the above quotation: one is Hughes's clear, anti-imperialist statement about a need and desire for blacks to own their resources and be seen as sovereign individuals; the second is the notion that "white m[e]n" are the oppressors and an entity Africans wanted to see removed from their country. The former, Hughes will return to later in the chapter, comparing a colonized African position to the second-class struggles black Americans had been experiencing in America since slavery. The latter exploits the paradox of Hughes's own mixed-race ancestry, which historically ensued once America was colonized and Africans were deported from their continent as a labor source for those Europeans who had relocated to the Americas. For example, in *The Big Sea,* Hughes immediately follows his allusion to Garvey with a statement about how he attempted to identify racially with the Africans he met: "'Our problems in America are very much like yours,' I told the Africans, 'especially in the South. *I am a Negro, too*" (102). The African response was "You, white man! You, white man!" (*Big Sea* 103), and as noted above, for Africans, "the white man was...heavy and oppressive.... And they wanted him to go away" (*Big Sea* 102). Clearly, if the Africans wanted all white men to leave their continent, they also wanted people like Hughes to depart.

One might imagine that this response from "his African brothers" might have disillusioned the author and encouraged him to view the blacks he met in Africa as the other—in the marginalized ways in which many of his fellow crewmen interacted with them—but he did not. For example, Hughes describes George, a dark-skinned African American from Kentucky. When a Kru man, a local tribesman hired to work on Hughes's boat, explains that Hughes is not black because of his "copper-brown skin and straight black hair," he readily points to George, who worked in the pantry on the ship, as if to say, "now here is a Black man." George immediately refutes the implication with a retort, "I'm from Lexington, Kentucky, U.S.A. And no African blood, nowhere." The Kru man responds, "You black" (*Big Sea* 103). In essence, although Hughes was rightly recognized throughout his career as a "Negro poet" and dean of black American writers, because he valorized the black American experience in his writing, he also appreciated his connection to black Africans, a connection that a person like George disavowed. Thus, not only did Hughes relate to this African Kru man, a man he encountered on his first shore leave in Africa, but he also related to Edward, a biracial young man born to an African mother and a British father, a "[p]oor kid" that Hughes consistently describes as lonely and marginalized in his African village (*Big Sea* 105).

Hughes could relate to this teenager, who felt caught between two worlds, for he too had to navigate the displacement he felt as a result of his own parents' failed union and the subsequent loneliness and isolation he experienced because he was never quite at home with either parent. Thus, the imprint of his own marginalization in America—spawned by familial tensions and American racial discrimination and financial duress—forced Hughes to continue articulating the similarities between himself and his African kinsmen and women throughout the duration of his sojourn on the continent. He even mentioned seeing signs of segregation in some of the 32 ports he visited while in Africa, where inns and taverns toted signs that read "Europeans only" (*Big Sea* 106). Despite the apparent presence of racism in Africa, however, Hughes enjoyed his adventures, safely returning to New York via Puerto Rico and the Virgin Islands six months later. Upon leaving, he vowed to return, which he did, four decades later, shortly before his death in 1966, when he traveled to Dakar, Senegal.

Back in New York City, with very little money and finding it difficult to rent a room—primarily due to the fact that he now owned a rare species of red monkey, Jocko—Hughes visited his family: his mother, stepfather, and younger, stepbrother Gwyn, or Kit, as he called him; they now lived in Washington, DC (*Big Sea* 134). Unable to stay with his family due to arguments over the monkey and Hughes's lifestyle—his mother wanted him to secure a permanent income and abandon his commitment to writing—he traveled south via train before quickly returning to New York (*Big Sea* 134–37). There, he signed on to work a boat that was traveling from Hoboken to the Caribbean, but soon quit that job and joined a freighter that carried cargo between New York and Holland (*Big Sea* 139–40). He arrived in Holland on Christmas Eve 1923, and when the ship returned to port in New York, he decided to remain with the crew. Difficult peregrinations, however, plagued the crew, and after multiple bouts with seasickness, pneumonia, and other misfortunes, Hughes surmised that the ship was jinxed and chose to catch a train from Rotterdam, Holland to Paris, France (*Big Sea* 143).

Once in France, Hughes struggled to find work. Shortly upon his arrival in the city, he learned from another African American émigré, who worked as a doorman, that the only work for blacks in the city involved music and dance: "Less you can play jazz or tap dance, you'd just as well go back home" (*Big Sea* 146). Of course, Hughes did not have these talents, but with only 25 dollars in his pockets, he couldn't afford to fund his way back to the United States. The doorman told him that he might find inexpensive housing and menial work in Montmartre, a black American section of Paris. Along the way, he met a Russian dancer, Sonya, who was also hard on her luck; the two roomed together, but because neither was able to secure work at the same time, they struggled although they did make ends meet. They parted ways a month or so later (*Big Sea* 156). With Sonya gone, Hughes needed to procure an income. As luck would have it, he found work as a bouncer-doorman outside a night club; because this profession really did not suit the man, who "didn't like the task of fight-stopping" (*Big Sea* 156), Hughes looked for another job, which he discovered through Rayford Logan, an ex-serviceman who had remained in France after the war. Logan would later become a revered professor of history at Howard University.

Hughes met Logan on the streets of Montmartre and because Logan had read Hughes's poetry in the *Crisis,* the man was all too happy to help the writer find employment. When Logan learned that a black-owned nightclub, Le Grand Duc, was hiring a second cook—really a dishwasher—he quickly shared the news with Hughes. Rayford Logan also introduced Hughes to his first love, a young woman named Mary, or Anne-Marie Coussey, an English-educated young woman of African and Scottish descent (Hill 41). Mary, so named by Hughes in *The Big Sea,* is also described as an "English-African" whose family divided its time between Lagos, Nigeria, and London (*Big Sea* 164–65). The two were determined to be together, until Mary's father first ended her allowance and then sent someone to bring her back to London, forcing her to end her relationship with a broken-hearted Hughes. In his first autobiography, he explained that he dedicated a poem to this first love, "The Breath of a Rose." Later, Hughes set music to the lines of verse (*Big Sea* 168–70). Although the rights of the song belong to G. Schirmer, Inc., the poem is reprinted in its entirety in *The Big Sea* (170–71).

While working at Le Grand Duc, the locale where all the black American musicians and artists congregated after their performances at local white clubs, Hughes heard the familiar blues of which he was so fond. He was also introduced to jazz there, a new improvisational form borne out of the more traditional blues. Hughes felt at home in the Duc and found the inspiration he would so adeptly incorporate into his poetry: African American dialect (e.g., "Lawd," "Goin' up de wall," "Is you ever seen…?"), the rhythms of the jam sessions, as well as engrossing characters and topics (e.g., describing a cabaret singer or jazz musician while exhorting the passion, beauty, and joy these characters can express despite their heartache and painful lives). At this point in the autobiography, Hughes recounts a song about a one-eyed woman; the verse suggests the songwriter's intrigue with a heart-wrenching, albeit beautiful, image of watching this woman's emotion; also, because he is writing about a song that would have been performed at Le Grand Duc, readers are invited to imagine the pace and ingenuity of the popular songs that would have been sung at this time (*Big Sea* 163). As a result, Hughes goes on to write: "That room was right out of a book, and I began to say to myself that I guess dreams do come true.… here I am living in a Paris garret, writing poems and having champagne for breakfast" (*Big Sea* 163).

Prior to Hughes meeting and dating Mary, and in the month after Sonya moved out of their shared room, the writer met a young man named Bob. Bob had worked at one of the cabaret jobs Hughes took before he began working at the Grand Duc. Another displaced American immigrant in Europe, Bob had difficulty finding employment. Thus, when Hughes encountered Bob, who explained that he was unable to replace the job he lost to Hughes, the charitable author extended a similar courtesy to Bob that he had shared with Sonya: he invited the homeless man to sleep in his attic room (*Big Sea* 164). Despite this generosity, it did not take Hughes long to discover that Bob was nursing a heroin addiction. Rather than deal with the hassle, Hughes decided to move. However, before he actually vacated his room, he was surprised by an early morning caller, Alain Locke:

> Dr. Locke of Washington, a little, brown man with spats and a cultured accent, and a degree from Oxford. The same Dr. Locke who had written me about my poems, and who wanted to come to see me almost two years before in the fleet of dead ships, anchored up the Hudson. He had got my address from the *Crisis* in New York, to whom I had sent some poems from Paris. Now, in Europe on vacation, he had come to call.
>
> I was covered with confusion at finding so distinguished and learned a visitor in my room and me groggy with sleep, and Bob likely to enter at any moment groggy with dope. (*Big Sea* 184–85)

In *The Big Sea*, Hughes explains that Dr. Locke was interested in seeing Hughes's new poems and invited him to hear *Manon* at the Opéra Comique.

Many may wonder why such a distinguished scholar would seek Hughes out so ardently. Arnold Rampersad suggests that Hughes's relationship with Locke and Countee Cullen provides evidence of Hughes's homosexual leanings (*Vol. I* 66–72). Other scholars and many of Hughes's colleagues and friends, Carl Van Vechten and Louise Thompson—Hughes and Hurston's secretary when working on *Mule Bone*—for example, all describe Hughes's sexuality as androgynous (Rampersad, *Vol. I* 20, 45, 133, 196, 289). Whether Locke sought Hughes out in an attempt to develop an intimate relationship or not, Hughes and Rampersad concur that nothing physical transpired between the two men. Rather, Hughes aspired to forge a bond with someone he hoped would ensure his enrollment at Howard University, where Locke taught. Locke remained in Paris for a few days and then traveled to Germany. The writer never joined the professor at the opera, nor did he travel with the noted scholar to Germany. Instead, Hughes remained in France until July (*Big Sea* 184–86).

Because business at the Grand Duc had declined, Hughes voyaged to Italy, but quickly returned to Genoa, France. After being pickpocketed on the train ride from Italy, he became a beachcomber and considered becoming a seaman again (*Big Sea* 190–96). However, the color line was so stringent among the American ships in Europe that he could not acquire a position (*Big Sea* 196–97). The best job offer he received was to paint the hull of a ship docked at the harbor. Eventually, Hughes did secure a post on an American boat en route back to the United States. He traveled from Genoa to Livorno, Naples, Pompeii, Catania, Valencia, past Gibraltar, across the Atlantic Ocean, and back to Manhattan (*Big Sea* 197–201). It was now November 1924, and the Harlem Renaissance was in full swing.

The first person Hughes visited when he returned to New York was Countée Cullen; he visited him to share some of the most recent poetry he had written during his time abroad. Cullen invited Hughes to an NAACP fundraiser that was to occur that evening. At the benefit, Hughes was introduced to James Weldon Johnson and Carl Van Vechten. Hughes also discovered that the *Crisis* magazine had attempted to cable him 20 dollars when he was in Paris; he had written them when he had had difficulty finding employment in Genoa, asking for a commission for the work the magazine had published. Because the cable was returned, they still had the money for him, which staff members gave him the next day (*Big Sea* 201–3).

He used these monies to travel to Washington, DC, where his mother and Gwyn were living with distant cousins. Hughes had a dual motivation, however. Certainly he desired to see his mother and younger sibling. More importantly, however, was his imperative to pursue a degree at Howard University (*Big Sea* 204). Rampersad explains that one of the reasons Hughes may have entertained Alain Locke's overtures was due to his efforts to get assistance with gaining admissions to the historically black university (*Vol. I* 94). However, Rampersad argues, because Hughes neglected to return the older gentleman's advances, he never received the desired assistance: Hughes avoided Locke when he traveled to the dead ship yard at Jones Point, and he neglected to meet the man at the theatre in France. Thus, Locke did not support Hughes's application, and the writer never enrolled at the elite university.

Finding himself unemployed with no prospect of registering for college, Hughes had to work when he moved to DC. He did "wet wash laundry," wrote poetry, and mingled with cultured black Washingtonians who were keeping the New Negro Movement vibrant and evolving in this mid-Atlantic region. He acquired a job at an African American newspaper and worked, for a very short time, as Carter G. Woodson's (1875–1950) personal assistant. Woodson is known as "the father of Black history," due to his investment in encouraging African Americans not only to know their history, but also to pursue education as a vehicle for teaching themselves in order to enlighten others about the contributions people of African descent have offered the world (Brown). Hughes, however, did not enjoy his work with Woodson. In particular, he noted that reading Woodson's proofs hurt his eyes (*Big Sea* 211).

Hughes decided, then, to become a busboy at the Wardman Park Hotel. There, one evening, he passed three of his poems to Vachel Lindsay (1879–1931), a popular American poet. Lindsay was giving a reading in the hotel theatre that night and Hughes hoped to solicit feedback on his work from the famous poet. The poems were "Jazzonia," "The Weary Blues," and "Negro Dancers." Each speaks to the Blues Aesthetic he was exposed to while working at Le Grand Duc in France: for example, "Jazzonia" describes six players in a Harlem cabaret, and "The Weary Blues" talks about the "syncopated tune…[he] heard a Negro play" (1.1–3). Lindsay enjoyed the lines of verse and not only mentioned but also read the unknown poet's texts during his presentation. The next morning, Hughes learned that newspapers were referring to him as the busboy poet and when he arrived at work, he was greeted by reporters and their cameras (*Big Sea* 212). Due to this reception, Lindsay advised Hughes to pursue his craft, deeming that the writer would become an exceptional poet for the 20th century, someone who would revive an otherwise dying canon of contemporary American poetry (*Big Sea* 213).

Following Lindsay's advice, Hughes submitted "The Weary Blues" to a poetry contest at *Opportunity* magazine, which was published by the Urban League—a prominent civil liberties union for African Americans. He won first prize and had the pleasure of meeting James Weldon Johnson, again, as well as Zora Neale Hurston and Eric Walrond at the award banquet. He had met Johnson initially at the NAACP *Crisis* event in New York, November 1924. Carl Van Vechten was also at the event, and at their second meeting—he, too, had been at the New York *Crisis* event—he asked Hughes whether he had written enough poetry to publish a book. Hughes sent Van Vechten what he had, and Van Vechten passed the material on to his publisher, Alfred A. Knopf. The book of verse was published under the title *The Weary Blues,* what Hughes described in *The Big Sea* as his "lucky poem" (214–16). Also, with Van Vechten's help, Hughes published poems with *Vanity Fair* magazine. He joined the young writers who met and read their works daily at Georgia

Douglas Johnson's salon sessions in DC, and he won another literary prize from *Crisis* magazine.

Hughes also liaised with a student who attended Lincoln University, Waring Cuney (1906–1976). Cuney introduced Hughes to a woman—who remains unnamed in *The Big Sea*. She offered the writer a scholarship to Lincoln University, which enabled Hughes to pursue his dream of completing a college degree (*Big Sea* 218–19). He enrolled at Lincoln that spring, February 1926. The following summer, he collaborated with Bruce Nugent, Hurston, Wallace Thurman, Aaron Douglas, John P. Davis, and Gwendolyn Bennett to found *Fire!!*, "a Negro quarterly of the arts" (*Big Sea* 235–41). Although they only raised enough money to produce one issue, the vision for the publication is revered in most scholarly anthologies about the origins and innovative developments of contemporaneous movements within the African American literary canon.

For the next three years, Hughes traveled between Pennsylvania and New York, completing his undergraduate degree and avidly interacting with New York's black literati and those participating in the city's underground art scene (*Big Sea* 256). During these weekend romps and summer vacations in New York, Hughes enjoyed the city's theatre and night life. Much of what he saw and experienced was incorporated into his poetry, and one might argue that this period provided him with the inspiration to start exploring drama and musical lyrics as another outlet for his creativity. He wrote the poem, "Mulatto," for example, during the summer of 1926 that he spent in New York. The play rendition of the poem became the longest-running African American play on Broadway when it was produced in 1936. Dealing with interracial relationships, "Mulatto"/*Mulatto* provided the impetus that compelled Hughes to write additional works about desired and forced race relations. His first collection of short stories, *The Ways of White Folks,* was published in 1934. "Father and Son," a short story version of "Mulatto"/*Mulatto,* is anthologized in this collection, as well as stories such as "Cora Unashamed."

Keith Lawrence describes Cora, the protagonist in this story, as "a simple yet noble black woman who is mistreated and ignored by the surrounding white community" (75). Cora Jenkins is a "maid of all work" for the Studevant family; she does the housework, cares for the old and young, carries water, makes fires, and so on, and for all intents and purposes, finds herself to be a modern-day slave in the early 20th century (*Short Stories* 40). She is caught "in the trap of economic circumstances that kept her in their [the Studevants] power practically all [of] her life" (*Short Stories* 41). There is only one shining light in Cora's life: the youngest Studevant descendant, Jessie, a young woman deemed slow or intellectually impaired (*Short Stories* 44). When Jessie becomes pregnant at the age of 19, her parents arrange for her to have an abortion, which causes her death. After Jessie and the baby die, Cora finds the strength to free herself from the Studevant family, and although she and her parents live in poverty on the outskirts of Melton—a rural midwestern town where the story is set—they "somehow manage to get along" (*Short Stories*

49). In other words, they survive without being yoked to an oppressive and prejudiced domestic labor system. "Cora Unashamed" and other stories from *The Ways of White Folks* received critical acclaim (Hill 72).

Hughes is best known for his poetry, however, and especially his texts about an African American sense of self and history, such as *The Weary Blues* (1926) and *Fine Clothes to the Jew* (1927). The latter text, *Fine Clothes,* did not receive the positive response given to *The Ways of White Folks* or the earlier volume of poetry, *The Weary Blues*. Hughes speculated that black reactions were poor because African American critics "were very sensitive about their race in books" (*Big Sea* 267). White critics, on the other hand, praised Hughes for the blues inflections found in the volume, but often did not see any intellectual grit in the lines of verse (see Robert Young's *Poetry Criticism* 1991). No matter what the reviews, however, Hughes remained undaunted and more firmly committed to his writing endeavors.

Thus, despite the mixed reception of *Fine Clothes,* Hughes sustained his success, and after graduating from Lincoln in 1929, he decided to travel again, going to Fisk University to read his work to a live audience. From there he went to Baton Rouge, Mississippi, to help inspire and assist the relief workers and survivors of flooding in the area. From Baton Rouge, he visited New Orleans, and when standing on the docks, decided to sign on to work as a seaman again. He voyaged to Havana, Cubab and back to New Orleans (*Big Sea* 285–93). While in Louisiana, visiting with the Creoles, he again crossed paths with Zora Neale Hurston. Hurston was actively collecting folklore and conjure stories (*Big Sea* 296). Similar to Hurston, Hughes was also drawn to these southern folk communities. As a result, he was ready and interested to accompany Hurston on her drive through the South on her way back north. Along the way, Hurston continued to collect material that she would incorporate into her own writing and anthropological interests (*Mules and Men* [1935], *Tell My Horse* [1938], and *Their Eyes Were Watching God* [1937], for example). Hurston and Hughes also visited the farm that inspired Jean Toomer's *Cane* (*Big Sea* 299), and they shared a patron, Mrs. Charlotte Osgood Mason. Hughes met Mason in 1927 (Hill 52), and her patronage enabled him to fund some of his (and Hurston's) travels through the South (*Big Sea* 296–99).

Once back in Pennsylvania, Hughes started writing his first novel, a semiautobiographical work titled *Not Without Laughter;* the memoir was published in 1930. Over the course of the year and a half that it took Hughes to finish this piece of nonfiction, he developed and distributed a survey at Lincoln. He used the survey as a catalyst for petitioning the all-white faculty at the historically black university to diversify its staff. After compiling and submitting his results to the board, the trustees acted on the findings, realizing that the school was unsuccessful in reaching the institution's mission of "instilling [the] quality of self-reliance and self-respect" into its students, preparing "leaders of the colored people." How could this mission be successful, if those leaders could not be employed at their own alma mater? (*Big Sea* 310). Hence, Hughes proudly concluded in *The Big Sea* that the Lincoln University of the

1940s was certainly "not the Lincoln of my survey" (310). In other words, the board had acted on the findings of his survey, changing the student-faculty racial representations. While in Pennsylvania, Hughes also befriended and strengthened his relationships with Joel and Amy Spingarn; they offered him some patronage during the late 1920s (*Big Sea* 311–13), and some speculate that Amy was the unknown benefactor who helped fund Hughes's scholarship to attend Lincoln (Hill 49).

By the winter of 1929, Hughes lost his primary support from Mrs. Mason. Earlier that year, following their trip through the South, he and Hurston had begun working on *Mule Bone*—a play they were co-authoring about the black southern folklore and culture they observed during their journey (*Big Sea* 320). However, after having an unresolved disagreement with Hurston, Hughes also experienced a falling out with Mason. In need of a change, he traveled to Cuba that winter (*Big Sea* 326–27). Hughes tells his readers in *The Big Sea* that he and Hurston argued over *Mule Bone* and Hurston's apparent jealousy over Hughes's friendship with Louise Thompson, their office secretary. Deceitfully, Hurston told Mrs. Mason that she was doing all the work while Hughes and Thompson were having an affair (Hill 58). Rampersad infers that Hurston might have expected Thompson to be fired. Instead, Mrs. Mason decided to let Hughes go. Eventually, Hughes acknowledged that he was angry with his benefactor, feeling overwhelmed by a debilitating and unexplainable illness immediately following the incident: "Violent anger makes me physically ill…for I had loved very much that gentle woman who had been my patron and I wanted to understand what had happened to us that she had sent me away as she did" (*Big Sea* 327). Despite his disappointment, though, he was far more dismayed over the loss of his camaraderie with Hurston. He always regretted their broken partnership: "I never heard from Miss Hurston again. Unfortunately, our art was broken, and that was the end of what would have been a good play had it ever been finished—the first real Negro folk comedy—*Mule Bone*" (*Big Sea* 334). The tragic outcome was that he lost a rapport with an important artist of his day, someone who most readily appreciated the direction, diversity, and interdisciplinary nature of his own artistry. Although the pair never worked together again and *Mule Bone* remained an unfinished text, a version of the play was performed in 1991. Henry Louis Gates and George Houston Bass edited the original play, based on archival information, and Gregory Mosher directed the "comedy of negro art" that premiered at the Ethel Barrymore Theater on Broadway (Gates, "Why the *Mule Bone* Debate").

The Big Sea ends with Hughes explaining that Harlem was no longer in vogue. Yet with the end of the Harlem Renaissance, which coincided with the stock market crash of 1929 and the ensuing Great Depression, he announced that he was still determined to be a writer. Aware that he would probably no longer enjoy the scholarships, patronage, and literary awards that he had received for most of the 1920s, especially the later part of that decade when he became recognized as an important literary voice of the Harlem Renaissance,

Hughes concludes the volume by explaining that "Literature is a big sea full of many fish. I let down my nets and pulled. I'm still pulling" (*Big Sea* 335). Readers would not understand the magnitude of these words until the release of his second autobiography, *I Wonder as I Wander*. In this second autobiography, Hughes revealed the travails he endured during the decline of the Harlem Renaissance and the temerity he needed to exude in order to continue maturing and sustaining his notoriety as an American writer.

I Wonder as I Wander chronicles Hughes's life between 1930 and the early 1950s. In this volume, he highlights his disparaging break with Mrs. Mason, explaining that after the stock market crash of 1929, he encountered his "personal crash" (*I Wonder* 3). He was depressed, estranged from his patron, confronting a depreciated job market, and scholarships, fellowships, grants, and literary prizes were scarce. A recent college graduate, coming to grips with bleak job prospects, Hughes wrote that "of necessity, I began to turn poetry into bread" (*I Wonder* 3). This initial attempt at commodifying his craft took the form of him touring America's historically black colleges and universities; along the way, he also spoke at local churches and community events.

Margaret Walker describes *I Wonder as I Wander* as a "picaresque journey," an "episodic book of travel scenes, people, places, and happenings." She also suggests that "it is a piece of social history," an important part of Hughes's writing, "a social fabric of the times" reflecting his thoughts and efforts during the 1950s and 1960s (Walker xi). In her assessment, Hughes "was one of the most prolific writers of this [the 20th] century," a man who left an indelible mark on the black world and broader international community. Walker talks specifically about Hughes's "immense and profound" influence on "the Black World in Africa, Latin America, the Caribbean Islands, and in Black America" (xii), but it is also important to stress the socialist and anti-imperial movements that were equally influencing Hughes during these decades: the communist movements transpiring in Russia and Europe and the postcolonial efforts beginning and/or continuing throughout parts of Africa and the Caribbean, for example.

Before beginning his 1930 tour of predominantly black colleges and universities throughout the American South, Midwest, and West Coast states, Hughes traveled to Haiti and Cuba. In Cuba, he was able to distinguish the color lines that were either blurred or highlighted, depending on where you were on the island. He faced discrimination at a Havana beach resort, for example, but also enjoyed the cultural diversity of the island, where its music, cuisine, and dance mirrored the country's hybridized history (*I Wonder* 6–15). This heterogeneity is equally commented on when Hughes traveled to Haiti, where despite letters of introduction that he could have used to mingle with the country's political and artistic elite, he concentrated on spending time with Haiti's lower-class citizens (*I Wonder* 15). Thus, while visiting this Francophone country, Hughes took it upon himself to interact with "native life," which he concluded would be "more interesting than that of the capital"

(*I Wonder* 17). In doing so, he became riveted by the ways in which Haitians "seem[ed] to remember Africa in their souls," practicing voodoo rituals and dance routines that had their foundations in African cultural expression and spirituality (*I Wonder* 22). What disheartened Hughes, however, were the intraracial divisions among light- versus dark-skinned blacks and economic hegemonies that dictated immutable social norms and boundaries that should never be crossed (*I Wonder* 24–25). For Hughes, these disparaging tensions began with the colonization of the island:

> But perhaps a coat and a pair of shoes had more meaning than that inherent in their mere possession. And perhaps that meaning was something carried over from the long-ago days of the white masters, who wore coats and shoes—and had force and power. Perhaps they were symbols. (*I Wonder* 28)

These material assets, used to demonstrate income and social status, were the basis for surmising whether an individual was literate or not. Hughes continued, "Most of Haiti's people without shoes could not read or write, and [therefore] had no power" (*I Wonder* 28).

Thus, in Haiti, before returning to Cuba en route to the United States, Hughes "realized how class lines may cut across color lines within a race, and how dark people of the same nationality may scorn those below them" (*I Wonder* 28). In essence, his encounter with people living in a postcolonial moment enticed him to think about class and racial identity in newer and different terms. For "in this all-black atmosphere, rich with history, music, and folk art, he shook off the hurt of his manipulation by Charlotte Mason" and "renewed his social conscience" while enabling himself to connect the economic subjugation he saw in Haiti and Cuba to a "racist exploitation of African American labor in the South" (Hill 59–60). Hughes's enhanced perception of social identities as predominantly defined according to class and not race was reinforced and further elucidated when he traveled to Russia and Spain. While in these countries, Hughes became interested in socialism, particularly the ways in which governments appeared to be striving to create more egalitarian societies in their countries.

This fascination with socialism led Hughes to travel to Russia in 1932. He joined a group of African American writers, performers, and filmmakers in an effort to produce the first Russian film about life in the South for black Americans (Hill 63). Ironically, many of the American cast and crew members joined the venture in order to escape the discrimination and absence of opportunities they encountered in America, and paradoxically, one such member was Louise Thompson, the only true actress in the group, and the woman with whom Hurston accused Hughes of having an affair. Although the production was never completed, due to problems with the "absurd script" and improved relationships with America whereby the Russian government decided that it was no longer interested in any negative propaganda about the United States, Hughes was forever changed during his time in the Soviet Union (Hill 65; *I Wonder* 76–78, 96–99). Thus, when the film company disbanded, he decided to tour the interior of the country, especially central Soviet Russia/Soviet Central Asia (Hill 69–70).

While touring Soviet Central Asia, visiting Tashkent, the Uzbek Republic/Uzbekistan, Samarkand, and cities like Ashkhabad, Hughes met and forged a fraternity with Arthur Koestler, a Hungarian-born British Jew (Miller 125). Not only did they share and comment on each other's writing, but they also worked together in Ashkhabad and other places, spreading a socialist vision for the confederacy of Soviet nations. They were joined by Shaarieh Kikilov, head of the Turkoman Writers Union, who often frequented Hughes's hotel room in Ashkhabad (*I Wonder* 113–15). In 2002, David Chioni Moore shared some of his research about this period in Hughes's life, especially the "Hughesian perspective," or "Hughes-based bridge of understanding" that can help broaden American perceptions of civil liberties within a global context (1115). For Moore, the poems Hughes wrote while on the Uzbek border demonstrate the worldview he was able to adopt as a result of his traversing the "global crossroads" that intersected in central Asia, a geographic site where Asian and Western worlds have historically met. Moore discusses Alexander the Great's ride through Samarkand, Chingiz (Genghis) Khan's empire, the reign of Tamerlane (or Timur the Great), and the Indian Mughal dynasty, as well as the silk trade that extended across this area, connecting medieval Europe to China (1117). Thus, Moore argues, "Russia and then Russo-Soviet control of Central Asia [presents] a chapter in the world's colonial and now *post*-colonial history which has been terribly neglected" (1117). Consequently, Hughes's interests and work in the country during the 1930s also reflects an insightful postcolonial moment, whereby Hughes can be deemed a predecessor of later revolutionary visionaries, who saw the world in international terms and gravitated to those initiatives that sought to dismantle imperial hegemonies throughout the globe. Moore, for example, suggests that 20 of the poems published in *Langston Hyuz She'rlari/Poems by Langston Hughes* "were revolutionary, focusing on the hoped-for worldwide revolution and its benefits for colored people" (1124).

What is most seminal about Hughes's travels through Soviet Central Asia was the ways in which political developments within the Soviet alliance broadened his own understandings about the human condition. For example, he continually explained to Koestler that his reactions to the things they saw in Ashkhabad were directly contingent upon his perspective as an American Negro:

> There were among the students, one patriarchal old man with a splendid white beard, and a brown young girl with a desert tribal mark on her head. This interested me enormously because here were *colored* people being taught by *white men*, Russians, about the making of films from

the ground up—the building of sets, the preparation of scenarios, acting, camera work—and I could not help but think how impregnable Hollywood had been to Negroes, and how all over America the union of motion-pictures operators did not permit Negroes to operate projection machines, not even in theaters in Negro neighborhoods.... When I told this to Koestler, he said he could hardly believe it. But I was trying to make him understand why I observed the changes in Soviet Asia with *Negro* eyes. To Koestler, Turkmenistan was simply a *primitive* land moving into twentieth-century civilization. To me it as a *colored* land moving into orbits hitherto reserved for whites. (*I Wonder* 116)

When traveling through other areas of Turkmenia, Hughes observed the fact that "all forms of minority discriminations were abolished" (*I Wonder* 135). For example, when traveling through Tashkent, he discussed the "old partitions" found on street cars that had previously been used to segregate "natives from Europeans, colored from white" (*I Wonder* 172). Thus, diverse ethnic groups with different religious affiliations were expected to enjoy equal liberties within the Soviet Republic.

Of course, Hughes discovered that this was not necessarily perceived by some Jews and Muslims, who did not feel that party antics respected their religious tenets (*I Wonder* 136). In particular, some Russians, Koestler included, embraced the prejudice that Jews were stealthy manipulators who would trick anyone out of his or her wares if it would increase the Jew's material assets. Hughes specifically described an encounter with a Jewish reporter. The American writer gave his pencil to the reporter as a foreign souvenir. Koestler explained that the embarrassing Jew swindled the naïve visitor out of a valuable commodity that was difficult to come by in Russia. Russian pencils were frail and the lead wore down quickly. Hughes was quick to denounce any prejudices on his part, but he did indicate that Koestler believed that the man wanted a better "tool of [their] trade" and not a memento from America (*I Wonder* 137–38). Koestler and Hughes parted ways once they reached Tashkent. Ironically, Hughes would meet him again once Koestler achieved world acclaim and broke his affiliation with the Communist movement (*I Wonder* 143).

While in Russia, Hughes learned that his third book, *The Dream Keeper*, had been published in the United States (*I Wonder* 122). This collection of poems was specifically written for young people and received high praise from critics when first published in America (Hill 66). Hughes also allowed *The Weary Blues* to be translated into Uzbek, and wrote articles for the Soviet Union, having been appointed an interpreter and translator by the Soviet Writers Union (*I Wonder* 144, 170). Moreover, Hughes began experimenting with short fiction again, returning to a form that he had not written since his high school days. Part of his renewed interest in the short story stemmed from his exposure to D. H. Lawrence's prose, for after returning to Moscow from Central Soviet Asia, Marie Seaton gave him Lawrence's *The Lovely Lady* to read. The title story reminded Hughes of his patron, Mrs. Mason (*I Wonder* 213), who had ironically started him on this journey to the East when she decided she would no longer support his creative endeavors; upon reading the entire collection, Hughes wondered if he, too, could "write stories like [Lawrence's] about folks in America" (*I Wonder* 213). The first tale he penned was "Cora Unashamed," originally published in *The Ways of White Folks* (1934) and printed again in Akiba Sullivan Harper's edition of *Langston Hughes's Short Stories* (1996).

Thus, while the Depression ended the New Negro Movement in America, impoverishing many black writers who had previously enjoyed a promising and lucrative exposure to an American literary circuit and artistic arena, some—like Hughes—were still able to publish their material both in and outside of the United States. Therefore, Hughes "made enough to travel all over the Soviet Union, [and] to come home via Japan and China." In essence, he continued his world travels and sightseeing, for "writing in the USSR was one of the better-paid professions" (*I Wonder* 196). All in all, Hughes was privileged during his time in Asia, appreciating the opportunities women and people of color could find in this new "Union [that] was then only fifteen years old" (*I Wonder* 210).

From Russia, Hughes voyaged to Japan. However, during his short stay, he was ousted from the country. In Japan, the government identified him as a "persona non grata" and expelled him from their borders (*I Wonder* 271). The government was especially interested in black left-wing, or liberal, American writers and Hughes's connection with these propagandistic writers. In addition, he was seen, perhaps, as a threat to the country's evolving democracy, particularly in light of his Communist affiliations, shown during his visit to the Soviet Union and in his travels to China (*I Wonder* 263–76).

However, Hughes, as Arthur Koestler would eventually do, found it necessary to distinguish himself from socialist rhetoric and from his early associations with the Soviet Union. He first avowed that he was not a Communist, despite his affiliation with proponents of the philosophy prior to his expulsion from Japan (*I Wonder* 276). He again denied any direct associations with Communist activities when questioned by Joseph McCarthy and his Senate committee in 1953. Although Hughes did not discuss his appearance at the McCarthy hearings in *I Wonder as I Wander*—the text was written prior to this turn of events in the man's life—there are other useful sources that elucidate this period. Christine Hill writes that the momentum of American anti-Communist sentiments led to Hughes's appearance before the subcommittee that was investigating Communist activity within the borders of the United States (96). Noel Sullivan explains that, as a black man, Hughes "was bait for the Communist trap and, at least partially, fell into it" (qtd. in Rampersad, *Vol. I* 375). Biographer Keith Lawrence writes that Hughes became increasingly enamored with communist theory as he was distressed with capitalism, "which he saw as the primary instrument by which whites oppressed blacks and other minorities" in America (75). Steven Otfinoski goes so far as to suggest that Hughes's interest in socialism and communism was what took him to the Soviet Union in the first place (38).

When Hughes met before the Senate subcommittee on Un-American Activities he acknowledged the social nature of his poetry but refuted any notion that he was ever a member of the Communist Party (Rampersad, *Vol. II* 213, 215). Rather, he argued his idealism concerning a free America, "where people of any race, color, or creed may live on a plane of cultural and material well-being, cooperating together unhindered by sectarian, racial, or factional prejudices and harmful intolerances that do nobody any good, an America proud of its tradition, capable of facing the future without the necessary pitting of people against people and without the disease of personal distrust and suspicion of one's neighbor" (Hughes qtd. in Rampersad, *Vol. II* 215). Apparently these statements, made during the Senate hearing, disarmed the committee and much of the nation's suspicions. Hughes was exonerated and perceived as having "preserved something of his dignity," but his "passive, perhaps supine" responses were also interpreted by some as an indication of his endorsement of McCarthy's blacklisting of other artists (Rampersad, *Vol. II* 219). Therefore, although Hughes emphasized race during this period in order to distance himself from Communism, he avoided repudiating the Soviet Union. Rampersad explains that Hughes "had no intention of attacking the Soviet Union; his belief in radical socialism had become clandestine but remained strong. The basis of his faith remained vested in the progressive treatment of the darker minorities in the Soviet Union, as compared to overt racism and segregation in the U.S.A." (Rampersad, *Vol. I* 375). He stood by his position of wanting to bring about social change as an artist (Rampersad, *Vol. II* 191).

Later, as an American correspondent for the *Baltimore Afro-American*, Hughes demonstrated his non-Communist leanings, writing about black American participation in the Spanish Civil War; African American recruits were active in the International Brigades, fighting to prevent Franco's socialist regime from gaining ground in the European nation (*I Wonder* 315, 323–32). Again, during this time abroad, Hughes contended with postcolonial or antihegemonic initiatives that deemphasized race and class distinctions in the interests of human, social movements. While in Valencia, he discussed the postcolonial ramifications of this diverse presence and involvement in Spain's political affairs:

> I asked this young African what he thought about the war. He said, "I hope the government [the Spanish loyalists] wins because the new Republic stands for a liberal colonial policy with a chance for my people in Africa to become educated. On Franco's side are all the old dukes and counts and traders who have exploited the colonies so long, never giving us schools or anything else. Now they are making the Africans fight against the Spanish people—using Moors and my own people too,

to try to crush the Republic. And the same Italians who dropped bombs on Ethiopia now come over here to help Franco bomb Spaniards." (*I Wonder* 329)

Hughes would go on to counter that these colored soldiers were well aware of the tragic paradox of their circumstances: "The International Brigaders [*sic*] were, of course, aware of the irony of the colonial Moors—victims themselves of oppression in North Africa—fighting against a Republic that had been seeking to work out a liberal policy toward Morocco" (*I Wonder* 353). Hughes wrote a poem to express his sentiments and the feelings of those American blacks fighting in this war. The piece was scripted as a letter from an American Negro Brigadier to a relative in Dixie. It imagines a wounded Moor, captured by the loyalist army, who dies trying to explain his plight as an imprisoned soldier, forced to fight for the Fascists, when he only wanted to return to a free Africa that was no longer colonized by Spain (*I Wonder* 353–54).

In the years leading up to and following Hughes's appearance at the Senate hearings, the writer continued playing with multiple forms of fiction. During the Christmas holiday of 1931, he co-wrote a children's book, *Popo and Fifina*, with his good friend Arna Bontemps. Hughes was vacationing with Bontemps and his family at Oakwood Junior College in Alabama, where Bontemps was teaching. *Popo and Fifina* was published the following year and marked the first of many collaborative projects the two would undertake together (Hill 62).

Hughes also indulged his interests in theatre. Inspired by the theatrical performances he had seen during his travels, he founded the Suitcase Theater when he returned to New York in January of 1938. On the one hand, he wanted to showcase how productions could be derived from the mere contents of a single suitcase; on the other, he wanted to experiment with the collapsing of stage-audience spaces, allowing his actors to enter both locations during their performances. His first play, *Don't You Want to Be Free?* was a smash hit. It consisted of dramatic scenes, the reading of his poetry, and traditional African American music. It also starred Robert Earl Jones—the father of the now famous actor James Earl Jones—and was performed on and off the Harlem stage for three years (Hill 79).

During the 1940s, Hughes joined Yaddo, an annual retreat in Saratoga Springs, New York, where writers, musicians, and other artists came together to share and collaborate on their work. Hughes was the first African American invited to join the group. He attended the summer retreat in 1941 and 1942 (Hill 86). He also published *Shakespeare in Harlem* (1941) and introduced Jesse Semple to the American public. *Shakespeare in Harlem* is a collection of verse that candidly examined the malaise caused by the Great Depression (Young 234). Jesse B. Semple was serialized in the Chicago *Defender*. Following in the humorist tradition of Mark Twain (Hill 86–87), Hughes used the anecdotes to create a black "everyman," and through the voice of Semple (or Simple, as he became known), he "commented wryly on everything from racist Southern politicians to everyday life in Harlem" (Otfinoski 40). Hughes also taught during the 1940s, joining the faculty at Atlanta University in 1947 and teaching at the Laboratory School of the University of Chicago in 1949. While working these teaching jobs, he completed and published two additional volumes of poetry: *Fields of Wonder* (1947) and *One Way Ticket* (1949) (Hill 93). In 1948, he wrote *Montage of a Dream Deferred,* integrating bebop—jazz's newest innovation—with his poetic verse. It was published as a book in 1951 and included one of Hughes's most reputable poems "Harlem" (Hill 93).

By 1950, Hughes was able to purchase a three-story brownstone at 20 East 127th Street in Harlem. Using the proceeds he reaped from the four-month success of *Street Scene* (1947), which debuted on Broadway, he was able to invest in the down payment on the home, which he co-owned with Ethel "Toy" Harper, a friend of his mother Carrie Clark, and her husband Ernest (Hill 89–90). For the first time in his life, since the death of his grandmother, Hughes enjoyed the permanency of a "home." Although he continued to travel, he no longer restricted himself to provisional housing; with the Harpers, he had a home to return to, one where he was always welcomed with a warm meal (Hill 89–90). Thus, during the 1950s, Hughes truly lived the life of a professional writer. He sometimes wrote for an average of 18 hours a day, published widely in a variety of genres, and toured the country on speaking engagements (Hill 95). Yet, despite this literary success, he still did not enjoy a wealthy lifestyle; the royalties he received for the work he was doing were certainly not lavish.

However, with the advent of the 1960s and the success of the Civil Rights Movement, Hughes finally received the accolades that he deserved. With a developing market for African American literature came a resurgence in the publishing of texts that spoke to and about the black American experience. Publishers sought Hughes out, soliciting his work and supporting most of his publishing ideas. As a result, he edited the *Book of Negro Folklore* (1958) with Bontemps and co-authored *A Pictorial History of the Negro in America* (1956) with Milton Meltzer; both are landmark texts in black American cultural and literary studies (Hill 101).

The year 1961 was exceptionally significant for Hughes, as this is when he published *Ask Your Mama,* a book of satirical verse on contemporary race relations. In the words of Steven Otfinoski, the book "showed [that] the old master had lost none of his bite," reflecting "a half angry and half derisive retort to the bigoted, smug, stupid, selfish, and blind" (41). "A sly parody of academic white poetry," *Ask Your Mama* was read with jazz playing (Hill 103). Furthermore, in terms of awards, Hughes received the Spingarn Medal in 1961, as well as being the second African American to be inducted into the National Institute of Arts and Letters; W.E.B. Du Bois was the first. Carl Van Vechten was also inducted in 1961. This select group, limited to 250 lifetime members, represents the most highly accomplished Americans in the fields of literature and the fine arts (Hill 104). Hughes was also invited to the White

House and enjoyed lunch with President John F. Kennedy in November: "The occasion was a small gathering in honor of President Leopold Sedar Senghor of Senegal. The African president, a poet himself, had corresponded with Hughes for a number of years. Senghor, in his after-luncheon speech, praised Hughes as an inspiration" (Hill 104). Perhaps the invitation to this dinner with Kennedy led Lyndon B. Johnson to appoint Hughes as the leader of an American delegation sent to Dakar, Senegal in 1966. The team was assembled to attend the First World Festival of Negro Arts. There, Senghor praised Hughes and his writing, and after his death, Senghor would say, "He will always be a model not only for the United States but for the world" (qtd. in Hill 107). This festival presented an opportunity for black American artists to give a tribute to their African peers; it also afforded them the diasporic opportunity to examine and dialogue about the similarities and differences in their cultural archetypes and communal sources of inspiration (Rampersad, *Vol. II* 347).

Langston Hughes died shortly after his return from Senegal. Rushed to the hospital with abdominal pain, he went into surgery and was released only to die shortly thereafter (Otfinoski 41). His last collection of poems, *The Panther and the Lash,* appeared that same year, 1967, and *Black Misery,* another children's book—although the wit, humor, and racial commentary may be better absorbed by an older audience—was published posthumously in 1969 and again in 2001. Hughes's ashes are entombed in the lobby of the Langston Hughes Auditorium at New York's Schomburg Center for Research in Black Culture (Hill 112).

Hughes's seminal achievement mark him as an important black American writer among his biographers; they also acknowledge his political activism, and especially a personal pledge to support civil liberties for all humans, particularly those who were treated as second-class citizens within the United States (see Keith Lawrence [1994], Trudier Harris [1987], Robert Young [1991]). Thus, in the course of moving from place to place, Hughes adopted a worldview that many new millennial scholars and teachers encourage their students to recognize today. He was a product of globalization and could conclude at the end of his second autobiography that his world would never end:

> The year before, I had been in Cleveland. The year before that in San Francisco. The year before that in Mexico City. The one before that in Carmel. And the year before Carmel in Tashkent. Where would I be when the next New Year came, I wondered? By then, would there be war—a major war?…Would civilization be destroyed? Would the world really end? "Not my world," I said to myself. (*I Wonder* 405)

Because of his worldview and the ability to comprise a diverse corpus of work, a body of literature that reflects his artistic and political hopes for the world, his legacy is assured. For, as Steven Otfinoski wrote, "Langston Hughes's reputation as a writer is secure today. No other black poet is as widely read and appreciated" (41). Thus, although his first and possibly the most cited biographer on his life, Arnold Rampersad, concedes that Hughes's "creative identity, in spite of his plays, fiction, and essays, remained that of a poet" (*Vol. II* 193), it is impossible to negate the broad scope of his aesthetic interests. The legacy of Hughes's life and work lives on today in the promise of young artists and scholars. An elementary school in Lawrence, Kansas was named after him in 2000 (Toplikar), and Kansas University proffers a visiting professorship named for the writer. This teaching fellowship was established in 1977 and rotates among departments at Kansas University; it was founded as an effort "to bring prominent scholars to the university," and was so named "to honor the late playwright and historian who lived in Lawrence as a child ("KU News Release"). Hughes's dramatic legacy also continues through performances at Cleveland, Ohio's Karamu House (Mitchell) and through productions shown at the annual Langston Hughes African American Film Festival, which provides an outlet for black independent filmmakers to debut and discuss their works with other screenwriters and performers (*LHAA Film Festival*). Hughes is truly an icon for African American letters, as well as a paragon for literary achievement within the broader American canon.

Bestsellers	*Critically Acclaimed Works*
Ask Your Mama: 12 Moods for Jazz *(1961)*	Mulatto *(1935)*
The Big Sea *(1940)*	Mule Bone *(1930) debuted in 1991*
Black Misery *(1969, 1994)*	Simply Heavenly *(1957)*
Black Magic, *with Milton Meltzer (1956, 1967)*	
The Collected Poems of Langston Hughes *(1994)*	
The Dream Keeper and Other Poems *(1932)*	
I Wonder as I Wander *(1956)*	
Montage of a Dream Deferred *(1951)*	
Not Without Laughter *(1930)*	
The Panther and the Lash: Poems of Our Times *(1967)*	
Popo and Fifina, *with Arna Bontemps (1932)*	
The Return of Simple *(1995)*	
Selected Poems *(1959)*	
The Ways of White Folks *(1934)*	
The Weary Blues *(1926)*	

BIBLIOGRAPHY

The Big Sea. 1940. New York: Hill, 1998.
I Wonder as I Wander. 1956. New York: Thunder Mouth, 1988.
Short Stories. Ed. Akiba Sullivan Harper. New York: Hill, 1996.

FURTHER READING

Bloom, Howard, ed. *Langston Hughes*. New York: Chelsea House, 1988.
Callaloo: An Afro-American and African Journal of Arts and Letters 25.4 (2002). Baltimore: Johns Hopkins UP.
DeSantis, Christopher C, ed. *Dictionary of Literary Biography: Langston Hughes, a Documentary Volume*. Detroit: Gale, 2005.
Gates, Henry Louis. "Why the *Mule Bone* Debate Goes on?" *New York Times*, February 10, 1991. Web. 10 Jan. 2009. http://nytimes.com.
Gates, Henry Louis, and Nellie Y. McKay, eds. *The Norton Anthology of African American Literature*. 2nd ed. New York: Norton, 2004.
Hill, Christine M. *African American Biographies-Langston Hughes: Poet of the Harlem Renaissance*. Berkeley Heights, NJ: Enslow, 1997.
"KU News Release." University of Kansas. February 8, 2008. Web. 10 Apr. 2008. http://www.news.ku.edu.
Langston Hughes African American Film Festival. Langston PAC. n.d. Web. 10 Apr. 2008. http://www.langstonarts.org.
Lawrence, Keith. "Langston Hughes." *Authors and Artists for Young Adults*. Vol. 12. Ed. Kevin S. Hile. Detroit: Gale, 1994.
Meltzer, Milton. *Langston Hughes: A Biography*. New York: Harper, 1988.
Miller, R. Baxter. *The Art and Imagination of Langston Hughes*. Louisville: UP of Kentucky, 1989.
Moore, David Chioni. "Colored Dispatches from the Uzbek Border: Langston Hughes' Relevance, 1933–2002." *Callaloo* 25.4 (2002): 1115–35.
Myers, Elizabeth P. *Langston Hughes: Poet of His People*. Portland, OR: Garrard, 1970.
Osofsky, Audrey. *Free to Dream, the Making of a Poet: Langston Hughes*. New York: Lothrope, 1996.
Otfinoski, Steven. "Langston Hughes: Dean of Black Writers." *American Profiles: Great Black Writers*. New York: Facts on File, 1994. 32–43.
Rampersad, Arnold. *The Life of Langston Hughes*. Vols. I & II: 1902–1941: I, Too, Sing America. New York: Oxford UP, 1986.
Walker, Alice. *Langston Hughes, American Poet*. New York: Crowell, 1974.

Karima K. Jeffrey

Zora Neale Hurston was an American novelist, folklorist, anthropologist, and prominent member of the circle of writers associated with the Harlem Renaissance of the 1920s. (Library of Congress)

Zora Neale Hurston

Zora Neale Hurston (1891–1960), a leading novelist, dramatist, folklorist, and short-fiction writer during the Harlem Renaissance, was born in Nota-sulga, Alabama, the daughter of John and Lucy Potts Hurston. When she was very young, the family moved to the all-black town of Eatonville, Florida, where Hurston grew up. Eatonville became a fixture in her artistic vision and much of her work is set there. As well, many of her characters are based on Eatonville persons and many of her fictive situations are drawn from real-life occurrences there.

As a child, Hurston lived a rather carefree and happy life surrounded by a large family, including her grandmother. Her father was a local minister and mayor of Eatonville; her mother was a schoolteacher and housewife. Hurston received her early education at the Hungerford School in Eatonville, a normal school patterned on the model of Booker T. Washington's Tuskegee Institute. Her later schooling took place at a boarding school in Jacksonville, Florida, until she left school altogether after the death of her mother and her father's remarriage.

For a time, Hurston lived with relatives, worked a variety of odd jobs, and ultimately obtained work as a lady's attendant in a traveling show. When the show reached Baltimore, Maryland, Hurston left the show and entered the high school department of the Morgan Academy (now Morgan State University). Upon completion of her high school diploma, Hurston entered Howard University in Washington, DC. While a student at Howard, she studied English with the noted scholar Lorenzo Dow Turner and took classes with Dr. Alain Leroy Locke, the first black Rhodes scholar, who taught literature and philosophy at Howard and also advised the literary magazine *Stylus*. While it is not known exactly when Hurston began writing, she had managed to place several poems in Marcus Garvey's newspaper, *The Negro World,* and enjoyed the publication of her first short story, "John Redding Goes to Sea," in the 1921 issue of *Stylus,* the Howard University literary magazine. In addition, Hurston published several works in the annual yearbooks for the Zeta Phi Beta Sorority, which she joined while at Howard. Impressed by her creative abilities, Alain Locke brought her to the attention of Charles S. Johnson, editor of *Opportunity* magazine, the official publication of the National Urban League. *Opportunity,* along with the NAACP's *Crisis* magazine, were instrumental in jumpstarting the Harlem Renaissance by sponsoring literary contests to identify and foreground young African American writers and provide them with publishing venues for their works. Hurston moved to New York where she soon became a prizewinning author and one of the Harlem Renaissance's most celebrated personalities.

Throughout the remainder of the 1920s, Hurston's reputation grew. She published a number of important short stories, including two of her most well known works, "Spunk" and "Sweat." She also published several short plays and presented several revues—programs that featured folk music, dance, and storytelling, told in dialect, in an effort to recreate and celebrate black folk

Hurston Interesting Facts

1. *Though born in Notasulga, Alabama, Hurston was raised in all-black Eatonville, Florida, from age three and considered it her home.*
2. *Hurston was encouraged by her mother to "jump at the sun."*
3. *Hurston completed her high school requirements at the Morgan Academy in Baltimore, Maryland, in 1919 before transferring to Howard University.*
4. *While a student at Howard University, Hurston pledged the Zeta Phi Beta Sorority, Inc., and helped found the student newspaper* The Hilltop.
5. *Hurston won several second place awards for her short works in the annual* Opportunity *contests during the mid-1920s.*
6. *Hurston graduated from Barnard College in New York City in 1927, the institution's first black graduate.*
7. *In 1934, Hurston's first novel,* Jonah's Gourd Vine, *was published and was named a Book-of-the-Month Club selection.*
8. *During 1935 and 1936, Hurston was awarded coveted Rosenwald and Guggenheim Fellowships to collect folklore in the South and the Caribbean.*
9. *In 1939, Hurston was awarded an honorary doctorate from Morgan College in Baltimore.*
10. *In 1943, Hurston was awarded the Anisfield-Wolf Award in Race Relations by* Saturday Review *for her autobiography* Dust Tracks on a Road *(1942).*
11. *In 1943, Howard University presented Hurston with a Distinguished Alumni award.*
12. *Alice Walker spurred a revival of interest in Hurston in 1975 with an article published in* Ms. Magazine *titled "In Search of Zora Neale Hurston."*
13. *The Zora! Festival, an annual Zora Neale Hurston Festival of the Arts, was begun in Eatonville, Florida, in 1990.*
14. Mule Bone, *a play authored by Hurston and Langston Hughes in 1930, premiered at the Ethel Barrymore Theater in New York on February 14, 1991.*
15. *In 2002, the USPS issues a 37-cent stamp celebrating Zora Neale Hurston.*
16. *In 2005, an Oprah Winfrey–produced television adaptation of* Their Eyes Were Watching God *aired.*

life as she knew it from growing up in the South. In addition, Hurston entered Barnard College, the women's division of Columbia University, on a scholarship. There she studied anthropology with the famed Franz Boas and began her work as a collector of African American folklore. She became the institution's first black graduate in 1928.

In the early 1930s, Hurston turned to the novel as her preferred artistic form, beginning with the publication of *Jonah's Gourd Vine* in 1934. The story, loosely based on her parents' lives, confirmed Hurston's mastery of dialect writing and further established her as a leading voice in African American fiction. In 1935, Hurston published *Mules and Men,* a collection of folklore she had collected throughout her expeditions to the south. Although it was an artistic rather than a scientific presentation of her research, the book nevertheless gained an appreciative audience for Hurston. In 1937, Hurston published her most important work, the novel *Their Eyes Were Watching God.* This novel, destined to become a classic in African American and women's fiction, was published to mixed reviews, but even the stingiest reviewer had to acknowledge that Hurston was a master of her art.

In 1938, a second collection of folklore, *Tell My Horse,* appeared. Unlike *Mules and Men, Tell My Horse* focused largely on folklore and folk life in Haiti. Hurston closed out the busy 1930s with the publication of a third novel, *Moses, Man of the Mountain,* in 1939. A retelling of the Moses myth from an African American perspective, the novel often shows Hurston at her comic best.

Hurston began the 1940s with the same energy with which she closed the previous decade, by publishing an autobiography, *Dust Tracks on a Road*, in 1942. An unconventional autobiography, it revealed little about her personal life, but did offer her opinions on any number of other matters. With the publication of *Seraph on the Suwanee* in 1948, Hurston's career came to a painful and unfortunate close. Though she lived for more than a dozen years more, she was never able to recapture her own artistic energy or the interest of publishers in her work.

Throughout the 1950s, Hurston's life was in constant decline. She was discovered working as a maid in the early 1950s and wrote only occasionally, oftentimes for black newspapers like the *Pittsburgh Courier.* Though she continued to write, most of her work was rejected by publishers. Hurston soon began to suffer from the ravages of hypertension and advanced age and suffered a series of strokes. The last stroke, late in 1959, left her debilitated and she entered a welfare home in Ft. Pierce, Florida, where she died penniless in 1960. After a funeral, paid for largely with solicited funds, Hurston was buried in an unmarked grave in Ft. Pierce's Garden of Heavenly Rest. A marker was erected in the early 1970s by Alice Walker, who called her "a genius of the South" (Walker 85).

Hurston came to critical notice during the 1920s with the publication of a number of short stories. These stories often had a southern setting; in fact, many of them were set in Eatonville, Florida, and were peopled with characters

Hurston had known while growing up there, and whose stories were far more entertaining than any Hurston could have contrived. Her first published story was titled "John Redding Goes to Sea." It appeared in *Stylus,* the Howard University student literary magazine, in 1921. It is the story of a young man, John Redding, who puts his dreams on hold while he lives up to the expectations of his mother and wife by staying at home and being the dutiful son and husband. The Florida setting, strong elements of folklore and folk life, and the prominence of a theme that Hurston was to use repeatedly make this an important first story. Although "John Redding Goes to Sea" has a predictable plot, the story does much to establish Hurston as an artist who has a keen ear for dialect speech patterns and a sharp eye for character traits.

Two other stories published during the mid-1920s, "Spunk" and "Sweat," are among Hurston's finest stories. "Spunk" is the story of a bold, brassy, uncompromising individual, Spunk Banks, whom Huston admires because he has *spunk,* an attitude toward life that Hurston herself held. Having been encouraged by her mother to "jump at the sun" (*Dust Tracks*), Hurston clearly admired those who dared to demand to be accepted on their own terms. Spunk Banks is by no means a positive character in the usual sense; in fact, he is probably more precisely an antihero. Indeed, he is a philanderer who preys upon a weak Joe Kanty, not only because Spunk wants Joe's wife Lena, but also because he knows that Joe does not have the courage to challenge him. Spunk parades around town, even in Joe's presence, with Lena on his arm, much to the displeasure of the townsmen. When Joe does muster up the courage to demand that Spunk leave Lena alone, Spunk kills Joe with a pistol. Spunk suffers revenge by being cut with a circle saw at the sawmill where he works. To his dying breath, he blames it on Joe's making an appearance as a black bobcat and pushing him into the saw. This inclusion is more evidence of Hurston's use of African American folk beliefs and how they inform the everyday lives of the people. As well, Hurston presents the vibrant community of Eatonville and foregrounds the interactions among its residents as they go about their individual and communal lives. Not the least of these are the men who gather at Joe Clarke's store, functioning as a moral center of the community. Hurston would include these men on the store porch in a number of her works, so much so that their inclusion becomes vintage Hurston.

"Sweat," published in 1926, is arguably Hurston's finest short story. It is the story of Delia Jones, a longsuffering washerwoman who suffers verbal, emotional, and physical abuse from Sykes Jones, her brutish husband of 15 years. This story, too, is set in Eatonville, with the townspeople gathered on Joe Clarke's store porch serving as a backdrop and moral voice for the story. Delia works all week long, including Sundays, to earn money by washing clothes for white customers. When the story opens, on a Sunday evening following church services, Delia is sorting clothes to soak for the next day's wash. Sykes, considering Delia and her work with great disdain, preys upon her fear of snakes by letting his bullwhip slither down her back. An argument ensues and Sykes makes his usual threats and insults.

It soon becomes clear that Sykes wants to make Delia so uncomfortable that she will leave her home, but Delia firmly informs him that she has worked long and hard for that house and has no intentions of leaving it to him and his mistress, a large, dark woman aptly named Bertha. Sykes further resolves to frighten Delia into leaving by placing a large rattlesnake in a box just outside the door to the house, an act of which the community clearly does not approve. When Delia grows accustomed to the snake and its mere presence no longer frightens her, Sykes takes his determination to rid himself of his wife a step further by placing the snake in the clothes hamper where he knows Delia will reach to sort her wash. Delia, however, discovers this trap in time to save herself and escapes the house unharmed.

Sykes, though, is not as lucky. In an ironic twist, he stumbles into the house with a hangover from a night of carousing and falls into the clutches of the snake, which bites him. Whether paralyzed from fear of the snake or hatred of her husband, Delia is unable or unwilling to come to Sykes's aid. He dies, knowing that Delia is fully aware of his dying and is refusing assistance.

"Sweat" offers a number of tragic dimensions, not the least of which is Delia's transformation from an essentially good, Christian woman to one who refuses to offer compassion to the dying, although we certainly understand the reasons for her refusal. "Sweat" also plays on the folk adage that the trap you set for others may just as well ensnare you. This truism is particularly applicable to Sykes, a ne'er-do-well who is intent on destroying a good woman in favor of one who has few if any admirable qualities. The story further shows Hurston's adept handling of a familiar setting, familiar characters, and familiar dialect. Although Hurston was sometimes accused of pushing off folklore as imaginative literature, "Sweat" demonstrates her growing expertise in developing dramatic characters and sustaining credible action throughout the plot.

Another important short story is "The Gilded Six-Bits," which was published in 1933 in *Story* magazine. This story also pivots on the relationship between a black man and woman, but instead of focusing on hatred as in "Sweat," "The Gilded Six-Bits" posits the enduring and healing power of love. Joe and Missie May Banks are a young couple clearly in love as the story opens. They frolic in their youthful expressions of love and lust and everything around them is clean, bright, and fresh. A trip to a newly opened ice cream parlor, however, proves disastrous for the couple. Both Joe and Missie May succumb to their own naiveté and unsophistication, and are taken advantage of by a newcomer in town, Otis D. Slemmons, who seduces Joe emotionally and Missie May physically. One night, Joe comes home early from work and discovers Missie May and Slemmons in a compromising position. Slemmons barely escapes with his life, and Missie May says in her own defense that she was doing it for Joe's sake. Joe is both hurt and incredulous.

Joe's attitude toward and treatment of Missie May change dramatically. For a while, he acts as if nothing is the matter and in a moment of physical attraction they make love. Much to Missie May's horror, however, Joe pays her for her services with the gold-plated coin that he snatched from Otis Slemmons on the night of their altercation. Missie May is devastated and, to add more to her fears of losing Joe, she discovers she is pregnant.

In the conclusion of "The Gilded Six-Bits," Joe acknowledges that the child Missie May has borne is his; according to his own mother who served as midwife for the child, the child is the "spitting image" of Joe. Because they love each other, and because they now have a child that serves as a bridge between the two of them, Joe and Missie May are able to reconcile their differences and resume their lives together just as much as in love as before. Once again, Hurston shows herself as a clever manager of artistic detail. As well, she has drawn superb characters and has plotted the action with extreme care.

"The Gilded Six-Bits" not only solidified Hurston's reputation as a talented short story writer but also launched her career as a novelist. In response to an editor's query as to whether she might have a novel in the making, Hurston, ever the opportunist, responded in the affirmative and set about writing what became her first novel, *Jonah's Gourd Vine,* published in 1934. This novel is based loosely on the story of her parents, John and Lucy Potts Hurston (Pearson in the novel), and, as such, provided Hurston the opportunity to demonstrate that she could handle the longer narrative inasmuch as she had already mastered the short story. Also, writing the novel gave Hurston the opportunity to reconcile some of her feelings about her father's philandering.

Jonah's Gourd Vine opens in southern Alabama shortly after slavery and concerns the coming-of-age of John "John-Buddy" Pearson, a mulatto field hand known for his physical prowess and his big voice. His father is not known, but is suspected to be the white landowner; this suspicion, coupled with his stepfather's brutal treatment of John-Buddy's mother, causes considerable difficulty in the household. As John Pearson grows into a handsome young man, many young women seek him out, but he is attracted to Lucy Potts, the young daughter of the landowning Potts family. After they marry, against the advice and preference of the Potts family, John-Buddy goes to Eatonville, Florida, an emerging all-black town, and soon sends for his wife and children to join him. Although Pearson works to support his family, he is unable to contain his sexual appetite and is often involved with other women. Lucy is aware of his philandering but often suffers in silence.

After a particularly pointed confrontation over his many affairs, John, in a fit of guilt, gives himself over to God and promises to do better. Assisted by his wife, he becomes the pastor of a local Baptist congregation. For a while, all seems to have changed, but then John Pearson falls victim to his previous sexual urges. Subsequently, his wife, the long-suffering Lucy Potts Pearson, becomes ill and dies, and his life and the lives of his children are thrown into greater turmoil. Shortly after Lucy's death, John remarries a woman with a questionable reputation and further damages what is left of his paternal relationship with his children.

Sometime later, again responding to the guilt over the ill treatment of his now dead wife Lucy, and his less than supportive role as a father to his children, Rev. Pearson beats his new wife, blaming her for his many failures and shortcomings, and sets in motion his dismissal as the pastor of the church. He later leaves town, having felt the wrath of those whom he has betrayed.

John Pearson travels to a neighboring city where he hires himself out as a carpenter. He meets a widow and they subsequently marry. With her assistance, John becomes the pastor of another church and grows into a powerful Baptist leader at both the local and statewide level. For a time, all of his past indiscretions seem to have disappeared and John actually prospers in the company of his new wife and the people of Zion Hope Baptist Church. However, on a trip back to Eatonville to visit old friends, John finds himself enamored of a young woman who awakens in him those same old urges. Although he is warned against pursuing these feelings by one of his old friends, it is as though John cannot help himself. In the aftermath of the affair, however, as John Pearson is reeling from the guilt of betraying yet another good and supportive wife, and no doubt remembering his betrayal of his first wife as well, he is struck and killed by a train.

Besides being a compelling story, *Jonah's Gourd Vine* shows that Hurston can ably manage a longer narrative. The pacing of the events is particularly well handled and she maintains a remarkable consistency in point of view, particularly when one considers that this must have been an especially difficult story to write. Of course, the fact that Hurston's recounting of her parents' lives was, at best, barely fictionalized, gave critics reason to be stingy in their reception of her first novel. However, there is so much that is done well, including the handling of the dialect, the detailed presentation of the physical settings, the precise, nonjudgmental capturing of the lives of black folk of the rural South, and the careful and refreshing placement of humor and pathos throughout the work, that it is a work to be reckoned with even by the most demanding of critics.

In 1935, Hurston published *Mules and Men,* a book of folklore that she collected from across the South while she was a student at Barnard College and while she was employed briefly by Dr. Carter G. Woodson's Association of the Study of Negro Life and History. Because she elected to present her findings artistically instead of from a social science perspective, *Mules and Men* is quite a different kind of collection of folklore. Because Hurston immerses herself in both the collection and reporting of her findings, *Mules and Men* indeed reads like a collection of stories. In fact, Hurston was frequently criticized for presenting folklore as fiction. As narrator of the collection, Hurston establishes herself as part and parcel of the larger community from which she collects these tales. This act gives her greater authority to comment on African American folklore and folk life as not just a subject for the social scientist, but as a vibrant entity deserving of both attention and respect. Because Hurston was interested in the black diaspora, she also forayed into Haiti, Jamaica, and South America to uncover African retentions and particular cultural phenomena of these native populations. These trips to the Caribbean and South America provided the material for her second collection of folklore, *Tell My Horse,* published in 1938.

Their Eyes Were Watching God, without question Hurston's most iconic and most critically acclaimed work, appeared in 1937. Although chronologically, it is a post–Harlem Renaissance work, it nevertheless captures Hurston's lifelong concern with the presentation of the life of the folk, or as she aptly phrased it, "the Negro farthest down" (*Mules and Men* introd.). Written in a very short timeframe, as is most of Hurston's best work, *Their Eyes Were Watching God* concerns the life of Janie Crawford and her quest for freedom and womanhood.

The novel opens in West Florida in the years following emancipation. Janie Crawford, who never knew her mother and father, has been raised by her now aging maternal grandmother, whom we know as Nanny. The narrative opens on a beautiful spring day. As Janie observes the business of nature, with honeybees pollinating pear blossoms, she experiences her sexual coming of age. In an attempt to divert her attention from the flirtatious young Johnny Taylor, Nanny announces that she has decided to marry Janie off to a much older man, Logan Killicks, who owns considerable property and his own house. Although Janie protests against the selection of her husband, she ultimately acquiesces in the face of a determined Nanny who tells her she wants her to have "protection," ostensibly from the Johnny Taylors of the world who would make a "spit cup" out of a beautiful young woman like Janie (*Their Eyes* 13). Nanny knows what it is like to suffer as a black woman, and she knows what it is like to be marginalized as well. Therefore, she does everything she knows how to spare Janie from experiencing any of the physical abuse and emotional turmoil that she herself had to endure. In her well-meaning efforts to make life better for her granddaughter, however, Nanny in effect projects her own dreams of marriage and respectability and her aspirations to be a woman of some consequence upon Janie. These early episodes, therefore, constitute the first of Janie's accepting the dreams of others as her own and also set in motion her life of disappointment, a pattern that will remain until she seizes the opportunity to live her own life on her own terms.

Janie's marriage to Logan Killicks is doomed from the beginning. Not only is Killicks much older than Janie, but he is not her idea of how "a bee for her blossom" looks or acts. To be sure, Killicks is respectable in the sense that he owns 60 acres of land, works hard, and lives well, and has a considerable reputation—all this for a black man who survived slavery. But he is clearly a mismatch for the young, beautiful, and spunky Janie Crawford. The honeymoon is indeed short-lived, and Janie soon realizes that she is expected to work both inside and outside of the house; moreover, Killicks expects Janie to do as he says, to which Janie responds, "Ah'm just as stiff as you is stout," in an early assertion of her spunk and independence. Moreover, Janie has no intention of becoming a farm worker and when Killicks goes to a neighboring town to purchase a mule for her to plow with, Janie knows that it is just a matter of time. In the meanwhile, Joe Starks enters the picture. He is from Georgia and is passing through West Florida on his way to Eatonville, Florida, where he has heard the residents are in the process of starting an all-black town. With little persuasion, he convinces Janie to come with him. She leaves Logan Killicks behind and marries Joe, thereby casting her lot with another man who has dreams of his own.

When Joe and Janie arrive in Eatonville, they find only the rudiments of a town, but this gives Joe the opportunity to put his considerable and varied business skills to work and soon he becomes the "big voice" around town (*Their Eyes* 43), indeed, the mover and shaker in Eatonville. He establishes a general store and a post office and goes about developing Eatonville into a real town. As Joe prospers and becomes more influential, he becomes mayor and announces that Janie is now "Mrs. Mayor Starks," an identity that she neither relishes nor understands fully. What Janie does realize is that this distinction separates her from the regular folk of Eatonville, and she begins to feel isolated. Then, too, there is no room for Janie's own dreams in this scheme of things, and Janie begins to feel marginalized and unfulfilled.

The years draw on and Joe continues to be financially successful, even though his health begins to fail. Because Janie is considerably younger than Joe, she holds on to a degree of youth that Joe cannot appreciate, and he takes all of his frustrations out on Janie by being both verbally and physically abusive. Perhaps the most frequently cited episode in all of Hurston is when Janie stands up to Joe when he berates her for her inability to cut a piece of tobacco straight. Clearly tired of the abuse and even more tired of masking her pain and humiliation with a smile, Janie mounts a spirited defense, deflecting Joe's abuse with insults of her own, challenging his sexuality in front of a male audience. As a result, Joe enters a period of decline in both his standing in the community and his health. At the time of his death, he and Janie are estranged, even though they still share the house. Janie goes through a very brief period of mourning and then elects to move on with her life.

Shortly after Joe Starks's death, Janie is visited at the store by a much younger man, Vergible "Tea Cake" Woods, described as "a glance from God" (*Their Eyes* 94), who begins to woo her to a much-scandalized Eatonville; the townspeople warn Janie that Tea Cake is only after her money. Tea Cake and Janie soon leave for Jacksonville, where they are married, and later go to the Everglades to live and work among the migrant workers. Though Janie is considerably older than Tea Cake, theirs is a youthful sort of love—they live fast, they work hard, and they love as hard as they work. When their lives are disrupted by a powerful hurricane, Janie learns the true meaning of love and loss. While trying to save Janie's life, Tea Cake is bitten by a rabid dog and descends into madness. In his derangement, he tries to kill Janie and she shoots him in self-defense.

After she is acquitted by a jury of white men, Janie decides to return to Eatonville to live out the rest of her life. While she is met with scorn and derision from some of the older women of the town, her "kissing friend" (*Their Eyes* 7), Phoeby, receives her with open arms. It is to Phoeby that Janie tells the story that forms the novel.

Their Eyes Were Watching God is a masterpiece of fiction and there is little wonder that it holds such an iconic place in African American literature. It is cleverly plotted and infused with emotion on every page. The characters are realistic, as are the situations, and Hurston handles both with exceeding care. In addition, *Their Eyes Were Watching God* is made great by many of the best elements of Hurston's previous works—an expert rendering of dialect speech, a careful and precise inclusion of elements of black folklore, a heartfelt appreciation of the lives of black folk, a comfortable knowledge of setting and a deep sense of place, and a careful balance of humor, tragedy, and pathos that propel the narrative forward in a way that few have matched. Indeed, Janie's journey from the physical beginnings of womanhood all the way to the attainment of the spiritual and emotional maturity of full womanhood is a celebratory journey, one that firmly establishes Hurston as an icon and the matriarch of many black women writers.

While Janie is without question Hurston's most solid character of all, *Their Eyes Were Watching God* no doubt confirms that Hurston is equally talented in drawing male characters. Glimpses of this talent were seen in the character of John Pearson in Hurston's first novel, but now in her masterpiece, Hurston presents three male characters with outstanding clarity and conviction. Not only does she represent these men in a range of ages and colors of the race, but more importantly in a range of psyches that demonstrate the myriad concerns and conflicts present in the lives of African American men. While Logan Killicks represents the black man who pulls himself up by his bootstraps in the aftermath of slavery and reconstruction, Joe Starks represents the entrepreneurial spirit in pursuit of middle-class respectability. Joe Starks is endowed with spunk, initiative, and black pride, and he puts these energies to work in building of Eatonville, where he and others, but especially he himself, could be a "big voice." Starks possesses a native intelligence and remarkable business acumen, and these bring him financial success if not the same measure of happiness in his personal life.

Tea Cake Woods represents yet another dimension of the African American male, that of the bluesman. Tea Cake approaches life from a carpe diem perspective, feeling that life is for living and enjoying in the moment. Thus, he works whenever it is necessary, loves whenever he wants to, and lives as fully as he can, without explanation or apology. Tea Cake moves from one adventure to the next, and one conquest to the next. And then there is his music to make everything all right. Tea Cake holds no illusions about class respectability and he enjoys life far too much to be concerned with what people think of him or his lifestyle.

Taken together, these characters demonstrate Hurston's powers of observation and keen insight into the behaviors and motivations of black men. In addition, in writing Janie's interactions with a range of male types, Hurston shows a genuine regard for the back male-female relationship and reveals a strong talent for placing on the page what is felt in the heart.

In 1942, Hurston published *Dust Tracks on a Road,* an autobiography. While it did not meet the expectations that most readers have of an auto-biography, it is significant because it was one of very few autobiographical statements written up to that point by an African American woman. While it revealed very little about Hurston's personal life, much to the annoyance of those who wanted the whole story, it did catalog her attitude toward a number of issues and concerns, including how black people are regarded by whites and by each other. The original manuscript of *Dust Tracks on a Road* also included Hurston's critiques of America's imperialist behavior, but these were removed from the book by the publisher in the aftermath of the bombing of Pearl Harbor in 1941. The sections that were removed have since been restored and thus provide a more complete reflection of Hurston's views. Even without those sections, though, *Dust Tracks on a Road* won the Anisfield-Wolf Award given by the *Saturday Review* for the most significant work published in the area of race relations.

Hurston published two additional novels, *Moses, Man of the Mountain* (1939) and *Seraph on the Suwanee* (1948). *Moses, Man of the Mountain* continues Hurston's interest in biblical lore and in an African presence in the Bible, while one of the most significant aspects of *Seraph on the Suwanee* is that its principal characters are white southerners. While these works round out Hurston's canon, neither of them reaches the magnificence of *Their Eyes Were Watching God* and the early short stories. Although Hurston continued to write until her last years, she published very little after 1950.

Considering the iconographic position that Hurston occupies today, and while she was recognized as a leading personality by her contemporaries of the Harlem Renaissance, there is not a large body of criticism available from the early period of her career. This is due in part to the fact that literary criticism, as we know it today, was still a fledgling industry in the 1920s; thus, many writers received scant mention in an occasional review but very little sustained study. Those critics and reviewers who did write about Hurston were often ambivalent: They recognized her energy, but they were often unsure what to make of her use of dialect, her southern folk settings, her characters drawn from "the Negro[es] farthest down" (*Mules and Men* introd.), or her humor. Many were put off by her portrayals of characters and situations that they would just as soon forget in a time when they were trying to be recognized for their *American-ness* instead of their *blackness.* Richard Wright was particularly dismissive of Hurston's talent, complaining that she seemed more of a minstrel type who was intent on entertaining white people instead of advancing the cause of African Americans. Likewise, Alain Locke was critical of her use of folklore. Indeed, whatever merit these two critics' positions may have, it is clear that they sought to diminish Hurston's contributions because she would not follow their separate agendas for black writing.

For many years following the 1930s, the critics were largely silent on Hurston. When she died in 1960, for example, her works were out of print and very little was known about her or her writing. In the early 1970s, however, critic Larry Neal wrote a new introduction to *Jonah's Gourd Vine* that attempted to rescue Hurston from oblivion; still it was not until a few years later that novelist Alice Walker launched a full-scale Hurston revival with an essay titled "Looking for Zora," published in *Ms. Magazine.* Over the span of the last three decades, not only has Hurston been rescued from oblivion, but she has also been afforded a prime seat at the table where the best of the world's literature is served. It is difficult to imagine in this day and time that Hurston was ever unheard of or forgotten. Her works are the centerpiece to any number of literary canons, from Harlem Renaissance literature to African American literature in general, to women's writing, to American and world literature proper, to all points between and among these lines of demarcation. It is difficult to find a college literature course that does not include some Hurston material; this is particularly true of *Their Eyes Were Watching God,* now regarded as a classic novel of American literature. Another telling factor is the number of sustained studies of her work that are produced by graduate students in this country alone. For example, up until 1981, only 10 doctoral dissertations focused on Hurston's work; by the one year period from 1993 to 1994, there were 26 such dissertations, and the numbers have remained consistently high for every year after that, now numbering in the hundreds. Clearly, Hurston's work has been scrutinized from every possible vantage point and has not come up lacking in critical regard.

Similarly, there are a number of scholarly works that have been published by academics and activists alike, including a new biography and a collection of Hurston's letters. Hurston herself is celebrated in any number of ways, including the issuance of a postage stamp bearing her likeness in 2003, the annual Zora Neale Hurston Festival of the Arts and Humanities held in Eatonville each January, having her name attached to the Hurston/Wright Foundation that supports young writers, being the subject of several plays, and so on. In addition, there is a Zora Neale Hurston National Museum of Fine Arts, and her life and works have been the subject of a PBS American Masters documentary and a California Newsreel documentary titled *Jump at the Sun.* Her most iconic work, *Their Eyes Were Watching God,* was made into a film in 2005, solidifying her place in the realm of popular culture. Fictional characters in other works by African American female writers have named their central characters Zora in homage to the great writer/icon and several, including Bernice L. McFadden in *Glorious* (2010), have borrowed details from Hurston's own life story to inform a fictional tale. Feminist and womanist scholars and activists have found a matriarch in Hurston and hold her up as one who often squared off against patriarchy in her personal and professional life and overcame it. One of the more surprising developments in recent years is her embracement by the political right for her outspoken conservative views during the 1950s, especially her criticism of the 1954 *Brown v. Board*

of Education, Topeka, Kansas Supreme Court decision that led to the deseg-
regation of schools. However, evidence of these conservative leanings can be
found in a much earlier essay, "How It Feels to Be Colored Me," published
in 1928, in which she rejected what she called "the sobbing school of Negro-
hood." Even so, Hurston could be as militant as any civil rights crusader and
therefore resists any easy political categorization. For a writer who came from
rather humble beginnings, who struggled mightily to carve a place for herself
in the world, and who died nearly forgotten, this recent restoration of Hurston to a place of critical honor in the literary world and the continued raising
of Hurston to the status of icon certainly speak volumes for her writing and
for the person she was.

BIBLIOGRAPHY

"Color Struck." *Fire!! A Quarterly Devoted to the Younger Negro Artists* 1.1 (1926):
    7–14.
The Complete Stories. Intro. by Henry Louis Gates Jr. and Sieglinde Lemke. Afterword
    by Henry Louis Gates Jr. New York: HarperCollins, 1995.
Dust Tracks on a Road. 1942. 2nd ed. Ed. Robert Hemenway. Urbana: U of Illinois
    P, 1984.
Jonah's Gourd Vine. 1934. New York: Harper, 1990.
Mule Bone: A Comedy of Negro Life. With Langston Hughes. New York: HarperCol-
    lins, 1991.
Mules and Men. 1935. Bloomington: Indiana UP, 1978.
Their Eyes Were Watching God. 1937. Urbana: U of Illinois P, 1978.

FURTHER READING

Bloom, Harold, ed. *Zora Neale Hurston.* New York: Chelsea, 1986.
Boyd, Valerie. *Wrapped in Rainbows.* New York: Macmillan, 2003.
Carby, Hazel V. *Reconstructing Womanhood: The Emergence of the Afro-American
    Woman Novelist.* New York: Oxford UP, 1987.
Chinn, Nancy, and Elizabeth E. Dunn. "'The Ring of Singing Metal on Wood': Zora
    Neale Hurston's Artistry in 'The Gilded Six-Bits.'" *Mississippi Quarterly* 49 (Fall
    1996): 25–34.
Crabtree, Claire. "The Confluence of Folklore, Feminism and Black Self-Determinism
    in Zora Neale Hurston's *Their Eyes Were Watching God.*" *Southern Literary
    Journal* 17.2 (1985): 54–66.
Harris, Trudier. *The Power of the Porch: The Storyteller's Craft in Zora Neale Hur-
    ston, Gloria Naylor, and Randall Kenan.* Athens: U of Georgia P, 1996.
Hemenway, Robert E. *Zora Neale Hurston: A Literary Biography.* Urbana: U of Il-
    linois P, 1977.
Hill, Lynda Marion. *Social Rituals and the Verbal Art of Zora Neale Hurston.* Wash-
    ington, DC: Howard UP, 1996.
Jones, Evora. "Ascent and Immersion: Narrative Expression in *Their Eyes Were
    Watching God.*" *CLA Journal* 39.3 (March 1996): 369–79.

Kaplan, Carla, ed. *Zora Neale Hurston: A Life in Letters.* New York: Doubleday, 2002.

Lowe, John. *Jump at the Sun: Zora Neale Hurston's Cosmic Comedy.* Urbana: U of Illinois P, 1994.

Lupton, Mary Jane. "Zora Neale Hurston and the Survival of the Female." *Southern Literary Journal* 15.1 (1982): 45–54.

McWhorter, John. "Thus Spake Zora." *City Journal* 19.3 (Summer 2009).

Plant, Deborah. *Every Tub Must Sit on Its Own Bottom: The Philosophy and Politics of Zora Neale Hurston.* Urbana: U of Illinois P, 1995.

Walker, Alice. "In Search of Zora Neale Hurston." *Ms. Magazine,* March 1975: 74–79, 84–89.

Warren J. Carson

Ralph Ellison, whose novel *Invisible Man* has become a classic of modern American fiction, wrote compellingly of the experience of African Americans in a society that has tended to ignore their problems. (National Archives)

Invisible Man

Invisible Man (1952) is Ralph Waldo Ellison's semiautobiographical novel. Ellison was born on March 1, 1913 (although Ellison always insisted on 1914 as his correct birthdate) in Oklahoma City, Oklahoma, to Lewis Alfred and Ida Millsap Ellison. Although Lewis Alfred—a veteran of the Spanish-American War—earned his living as a common laborer, at the time of his untimely death, he was a well-respected construction worker and tradesman in coal and ice. After an accident with an ice delivery, Lewis Alfred died in 1916, leaving behind a grieving widow with two small boys to care for. The loss of his father had a profound influence on Ellison, but it was Lewis Alfred who bequeathed to his young son a love of books and a passion for poetry. As a construction worker in the racially segregated city, Alfred often gathered with other black veterans to drink and discuss the politics of the day beyond the white eyes and ears of Oklahoma City. The young Ellison listened to the stories of these black veterans who fought for American democracy, but came back to an America which denied them the equal rights for which they had bravely fought. One point of their political discussion, perhaps, was the hope for a golden day when racial segregation would be a thing of the past. Lewis's (and his fellow veterans') club is reflected in his son's creation of The Golden Day saloon and madhouse in *Invisible Man,* where "Many of the men had been doctors, lawyers, teachers, Civil Service workers; there were several cooks, a preacher, a politician, and an artist" (Ellison 73). This scene in *Invisible Man* completely captures a racist America as the "madhouse" that Lewis Alfred and his fellow black veterans know, but his son—like the young narrator—feels is "a game…whose rules and subtleties I could never grasp" (Ellison 73).

   More importantly for the young Ellison, Lewis Alfred had the hope that his first surviving son would have a life that was unlimited due to race, and like many black parents, he saw hope for the plight of black Americans in the fight for literacy and social justice. As a future artist, Ellison did manage to form a complex psychological identity forged in the scant memories of an adored father, and a sense of abandonment from Lewis Alfred's early death. But the absence of Lewis Alfred created a Ralph Waldo Ellison eager to establish his own identity separate from the influence of Lewis, or what the absence would mean to him. As a teen, Ellison was embarrassed about the name of Ralph Waldo; it was a name he felt was too pretentious for a black youth whose chances in life were hemmed in by the racial segregation of the time. However, in a letter to literary critic Alfred Kazin (1987), Ellison finally appreciated what the New England writer—Ralph Waldo Emerson—meant to Lewis Alfred and other blacks. It was Emerson's spiritual and intellectual messages of the American quest for personal freedom that resonated with Lewis Alfred and his contemporaries. Coming to terms with his name (Ralph Waldo) as his writing career began to flower, Ellison saw his own connection (and that of all African Americans) in the legacy of abolitionism, and the moral fervor of the New England Transcendentalists. For the adult Ellison, his name would always remind him of the shared cultural heritage on which his own nonfiction always insisted.

Perhaps as a way to help the new widow cope with the death of her husband, the three-year-old Ralph was taken by cousins to visit his paternal grandfather Alfred Ellison in South Carolina, a visit that would prove to be fortuitous for the adult writer. Alfred Ellison (1845–1918) may have been one of the models for the grandfather in the adult Ellison's *Invisible Man*. A wiser Invisible Man (and perhaps the young Ralph Ellison) recalls: "I am not ashamed of my grandparents for having been slaves. I am only ashamed of myself for having at one time been ashamed" (Ellison 15). A proud man, born a slave, and illiterate throughout his life, Alfred was politically active in his small southern community during the years of Reconstruction. But he soon found that his position as town marshal came with an exacting price. Hired to keep the peace in tiny Abbeville, South Carolina, Alfred was also expected to enforce the local laws that prohibited black voting rights, and in the midst of renewed hostility and violence toward blacks, Alfred lost his job at the risk of losing his life. Even after blacks were stripped of social and civil rights in 1877, Alfred managed to maneuver around the violence directed toward blacks in the area: "I never told you, but our life is a war and I have been a traitor all my born days, a spy in the enemy's country" (Ellison 15). It is hard to believe that Alfred's presence is not behind these words that Ellison places in the mouth of the grandfather in the first chapter of the novel. "Live with your head in the lion's mouth. I want you to overcome 'em with yeses," the grandfather continues on his deathbed, "undermine 'em with grins, agree 'em to death and destruction, let 'em swoller you till they vomit or bust wide open" (Ellison 15–16). But the sense of hopelessness for black life in the South was too much for Alfred's son Lewis (born in 1877), who left Abbeville in 1898 for a better life.

The loss of the family breadwinner was incalculable to the small Ellison family, and Ida was forced into domestic work in order to sustain the household. Fortunately, the young Ralph was befriended by two prominent black families in segregated Oklahoma City. Jefferson Davis Randolph (who Ellison affectionately called Grandpa) was a respected black leader in the community who—along with Grandfather Ellison—became important role models in living "in the lion's mouth" (Ellison 15). Highly adept in the most arcane points of U.S. law, Randolph—the former principal of the black high school—was barred from the profession because of his race, and later found work as the janitor at the local law library, a job considered more prestigious than his job as the black principal of an all-black school. Years later, in a moving tribute to Grandpa Randolph, Ellison recounts how white lawyers would often come to Randolph for answers on certain aspects of the law, which gave him an "another example of white folks taking advantage of black folks. This was a tantalizing mystery, but the fact that white men of power would show no shame in exploiting the knowledge of one far beneath them in status aroused my sense of irony" (*Perspective of Literature* 322). But the impetuous and impatient teenager resented the trading of black dignity for survival; for the young Ralph Ellison, patient endurance and humility would not solve the unjust racial inequalities with which blacks were forced to live.

However, in spite of his defiant opinions, Randolph, especially, impressed the young Ralph with his gift for language, and his humorous tales of myth and legend told in a unique blending of black and white *American* vernacular. Randolph's storytelling style contributed to the novelist's love of language in many ways, and his insistence that African Americans were also the inheritors of a rich cultural heritage that equally blended the tragic with the comic had a lasting effect. African American folk tales handed down by plantation slaves figure prominently in *Invisible Man*. Many of these tales act as metaphors or commentary on slave life; on the other hand as they traveled North during the years of black migration, they continued to express the lives of modern black folks living under racial segregation. Some of the more familiar tales Ellison no doubt heard from Randolph were the trickster tales about Jack the Rabbit and Jack the Bear. Jack the Rabbit and Jack the Bear (along with Brer Rabbit and Brer Fox) were all familiar tales told by slaves not only to entertain children, but also to instruct young blacks on how to behave in the lion's mouth. A "jack" also referred to a con man or trickster: Jack or John could be either black hero or white villain. In *Invisible Man*, Ellison uses Jack the Rabbit and Jack the Bear (as Randolph did) as elements of cultural survival and folk wisdom whose meanings are often overlooked by the narrator.

As the Invisible Man walks along the busy streets of New York, he marvels at the impersonal manners of white New Yorkers who brush up against him, but never seem to see him: "they would have begged the pardon of Jack the Bear, never glancing his way if the bear happened to be walking along minding his business" (Ellison 171). Later, the narrator runs into a man singing the blues who tells him that "this Harlem ain't nothing but a bear's den. I tried," recalls the narrator, "to think of some saying about bears to reply, but remembered only Jack the Rabbit, Jack the Bear" It is this "bear's den" that the narrator has escaped in order to "hibernate"; as he explains in the prologue: "A hibernation is a covert preparation for a more overt action" (Ellison 13). However, the same black man the narrator meets recalls another significant figure in African American folklore: Petey Wheatstraw, a black man so cunning that he married the devil's daughter. The man introduces himself as the legendary figure who promises to teach him "some good bad habits." The startled narrator remembers: "I'd known the stuff from childhood, but had forgotten it; had learned it back of school.... He was the Devil's son-in-law, all right, and he was a man who could whistle a three-toned chord.... God damn, I thought, they're a hell of a people! And I didn't know whether it was pride or disgust that suddenly flashed over me" (Ellison 174).

Equally significant, perhaps, were the tales of runaway slaves, both real and mythic. Running away from impossible situations—from slavery to the migration away from the Jim Crow South—would later figure in Ellison's life and in his fiction. Lewis Alfred set the pattern for Ellison when he left South Carolina; later, Ellison would flee the South for New York to get away from the limited possibilities for young black men. Ellison captures the theme of running early in *Invisible Man* when the narrator recounts a dream where his stern grandfather orders him to open the fine briefcase he receives for winning the battle royal. Inside the briefcase, the narrator finds an official envelope: "and inside the envelope I found another and another...Them's years, he said. Now open that one" (Ellison 33). The last envelope reads: "To Whom It May Concern...Keep This Nigger-Boy Running" (Ellison 33). Later, after his expulsion from the Negro College, the narrator is given seven letters by Dr. Bledsoe to present to friendly white employers in the North, but he is ordered not to open them ("White folks are strict about such things" [Ellison 147]). The letters fail to win him a job, until he visits the son of one of the college's benefactors who gives him one of the letters to read; in essence, Dr. Bledsoe has suggested to the whites the College depend on to consider the narrator as one who has fallen. "Please hope him to death, and keep him running" (Ellison 190–91). And the narrator runs from one situation to another in his endless quest to find himself. Like his narrator, Ralph Ellison and his family would run from one desperate situation to another as the threat of poverty and disaster followed on their heels.

After a brief stay in Gary, Indiana, the Ellisons remained proud (an inheritance from Alfred Ellison), but continued a life of desperate poverty. To aid the family, the young Ralph began work at 12 as a shoeshine boy; his tips kept the family from complete destitution. The young Ellison had to face the hostile attitude of the other black shoeshine boys who resented Ellison's sense of superiority and reluctance to swallow racial humiliation. Moreover, the proud Ellison soon gave up his menial job because of the racial arrogance of the white men whose tips depended on black subservience, although the Ellisons desperately needed the extra money. The racial arrogance of his white customers (and the psychological blow to his own sense of pride) is reflected in "The Battle Royal" of *Invisible Man* where the protagonist is forced to fight other young, black men ("like crabs in a barrel") in an exhibition before the town's prominent white citizens. Praised as an example of "desirable conduct" by the white citizens of his town, the narrator recalls the theme of his graduation speech, "On my graduation day I delivered an oration in which I showed that humility was the secret, indeed, the very essence of progress" (Ellison 17). The speech is far from the intent of his grandfather's dying wish: that humility must be disguised as treachery to the racial expectations of whites. Invited to give his speech to a gathering of the town's most prominent white men, the narrator finds himself expected to perform in the battle royal with other young, black men; but he has "misgivings" about participating: "Not from a distaste for fighting, but because I didn't care too much for the other fellows who were to take part" (Ellison 17). Not unlike the young shoeshine boy, Ralph Ellison, the narrator feels himself above the common black boys who debase themselves for tips.

For the young Ellison, survival in segregated Oklahoma City (he later recalled) was little more than a battle royal for African Americans, who were too often forced to fight blindly for an equality that eluded them—like a prize of "gilded coins on an electrified carpet" (Ellison 27). However, it was during this period of the Ellison's reduced circumstances that he developed his life-long passion for music. In Oklahoma City, Ellison was surrounded by music: from the holiness churches to the professional blues, and later the music of the jazz musicians who entertained for segregated (and sometimes integrated) audiences. Ellison's first formal education in music began with his introduction to European classical music, where he learned the type creative discipline that he would employ in his writing. But Ellison—like many young people—was fascinated and exhilarated by the new music. The music of the blues and jazz was an entirely original musical form born from the vernacular experiences of African Americans. That these new forms appeared oppositional to Western musical forms made the new music more attractive. As a young trumpeter trained in the Western tradition, Ellison soon found himself torn between the traditional European form and the new—especially at a time when jazz horn players were devising innovative techniques in expressing the new music: "I had been caught actively between two," Ellison recalls in "Living with Music," "that of the Negro folk music, both sacred and profane, slave song and jazz, and that of Western classical music" (190). Ellison, however, was more impressed by how jazz musicians sacrificed a part of their personal lives for their art through a strict discipline that seemed out of bounds for a young man impatient with the racial boundaries of Oklahoma City in the 1920s. Still, as a writer who traded one dream for another, a much older Ellison became one of the more astute essayists on jazz. In a moving tribute to jazz guitarist Charlie Christian, Ellison wrote in 1958: "Jazz, like the country which gave it birth, is fecund in its inventiveness, swift and traumatic in its developments and terribly wasteful of its resources. It is an orgiastic art which demands great physical stamina of its practitioners and many of its most talented creators die young" ("The Charlie Christian Story" 233). Although at one point in his musical education, the young Ellison desired a life as a professional musician, he was too impatient to endure the hours of discipline dedicated to technique; still, Ellison learned an important lesson about combining the sacred (Western music) and the profane (jazz) that is reflected in the narrative structure of *Invisible Man.*

Ralph Ellison graduated from Douglas High School in 1932 after working at a series of menial jobs to raise money for college. Ellison had not given up on his dream to be either a professional musician or high school music teacher, and after hearing the brilliant musicianship of the Tuskegee choir broadcast from New York's Radio City, the young Ellison decided that Booker T. Washington's Tuskegee Normal and Industrial Institute was the place to nurture his musical ambition. After the death of its founder (Booker T. Washington) Robert Russa Moton became head of the school, and although the academic emphasis at Tuskegee (instituted by Washington) was on the domestic sciences and vocational and agricultural training, Moton encouraged the growth and autonomy of its celebrated music school. The school's professional music program—under the leadership of William Dawson—although relatively new, excited Ellison, who dreamed of the social cachet a degree in music from

Tuskegee would give him. Dawson was the only faculty member at Tuskegee allowed to hire his own instructors, and many of his carefully handpicked faculty could boast musical training from an elite corps of European musicians. Happily for Ellison, Dawson could also offer a much-needed scholarship to cover the costs of the school—but only after an initial audition before the fall term began. Faced with the requirement of an audition, the problem for the near penniless Ellison was how to travel to Tuskegee, Alabama.

The requirement of an audition in front of Tuskegee's music faculty posed a dilemma for Ellison, who had planned to work during the summer in Oklahoma in order to survive as a student in the fall. With his future career as a musician stalled in its tracks, Ellison's options were limited. He could spend the year working instead, sell the new cornet he desperately needed for the train fare, or do what many Americans were forced to do for transportation during the Great Depression: illegally ride the rails. Full of youthful optimism (and enamored by the adventures of Huck Finn, Jack London, and Carl Sandburg), Ellison chose what he thought would be a grand adventure. However, the experience for a lone, black youth hopping boxcars through southern states under the mean and watchful eyes of brutally racist freight detectives was anything but youthful adventure; the era of the brutal beatings and lynching of black bodies was still evident in 1933 whenever the line of racial etiquette was crossed.

Unfortunately, Ellison's adventure took place while the case of the Scottsboro Boys continued to rage in the courts, and in the fervid racial fantasies of southern whites. Riding the rails in 1931—like many other men and women during the Depression—nine young, black men were charged with the rape of two young white women who were in the same boxcar. Although the charges were false, and one of the white women finally recanted, racial etiquette had been breached and the penalty was lynching. As civil rights groups and black churches held fundraisers to support their legal defense (even the American Communist Party played a big part in the boys' defense), Ellison's relatives pleaded with him to forgo the foolish and dangerous notion of hopping freight cars. But an older Ellison recounts the terror of the times when the naked blond is ushered into the presence of the narrator and the other young, black boys during the battle royal of *Invisible Man,* while the jeering white men laugh at the boys' discomfort: "Some threatened us if we looked and others if we did not" (Ellison 19). Caught by rail detectives with a gang of fellow hoboes (white and black) in Decatur, Alabama, Ellison faced the reality of the treatment of black men at the hands of racist detectives. The adventure quickly turned to nightmare, as Ellison—taking advantage of the mass confusion—ran for his life until he found a hiding place underneath a railroad shed. He remained in his hiding place until it was safe the next morning. But the nightmare—the chase, finding safety in a hole—would never leave him.

While *Invisible Man* does contain some elements from Ellison's life, the novel is not (strictly speaking) autobiographical. His experience at Tuskegee is a case in point; in the novel, Ellison perfectly captures the divided reputation among blacks about the school, which he satirizes in the novel as "The State College for Negroes." Although Ellison had a pleasant relationship with Morton and his family, the character of Dr. Bledsoe (the founder's former office boy) reads as a combination of Dr. Emmett Jay Scott (Washington's personal secretary) of Howard University and Washington himself. It was the speech given by Scott on Founder's Day in 1936 extolling Washington's genius and the generosity of wealthy whites, however, glossing over the petty realities that Ellison experienced at Tuskegee, that convinced him that it would be better to leave the institute than continue under its rank hypocrisy. But the incident—replicated in *Invisible Man*—also comments on the divided reputation of Booker T. Washington, as the narrator points out: "He was our leader and our magic, who kept the endowment high, the funds for scholarships plentiful and publicity moving through the channels of the press. He was our coal-black daddy of whom we were afraid" (114).

Even before Ellison's arrival, the school's very existence—and what it stood for—was a contentious point of debate among black political and social activists, since the conservative had Washington decided that the school would focus on the industrial to the detriment of the liberal arts. Dependent on the good will of neighboring whites in the area, and the philanthropic contributions of wealthy northern whites (represented in the novel as Mr. Norton), Washington assured his white benefactors that the school would always aid and support the inherently subservient role of blacks in America. In his speech at the International Exposition at Atlanta, Georgia in 1895, Washington assured the gathered white businessmen that "the agitation of questions of social equality is the extremist folly." American "privileges," he continued, would be won by "constant struggle rather than of artificial forcing" (*Up from Slavery* 101). Ellison first hints at the negative reaction of many black political and social leaders to Washington's speech when the narrator is finally called to give his speech. He begins his speech with Washington's call for his fellow blacks to "cast down your bucket where you are" (Ellison 29) and advocating getting along with whites as the highest "social responsibility" for blacks. But after repeated calls for his phrase "social responsibility," the narrator slips and instead mentions "social equality." The jocular attitude quickly dissipates: "Sounds of displeasure filled the room. They shouted hostile phrases at me" (Ellison 31). After assuring the men that the phrase "equality" was a mistake, the whites praise his speech: "We mean to do right by you, but you've got to know your place at all times" (Ellison 31) However, one black who refused to know his "place" forcefully disagreed with Washington.

W.E.B. Du Bois forcefully objected to Washington's accommodation to white anxiety over black political and social equality in his essay: "Of Mr. Booker T. Washington and Others," collected in *The Souls of Black Folk* (1903). In his famous essay, Du Bois publically takes Washington to task for his submission to white political and social supremacy: "It has been claimed that the Negro can survive only through submission. Mr. Washington distinctly asks that black people give up, at least for the present, three things,—First, political power, Second, insistence on civil rights, Third, higher education of Negro youth,—and concentrate all their energies on industrial education, the accumulation of wealth, and the conciliation of the South" (40). Thus, Du Bois—with his advocacy for black voting rights—set himself at odds with Washington's accommodation to white racism—although to be fair to Washington, soothing the fears of lynch-happy southerners who surrounded Tuskegee may have seemed a pragmatic necessity at the time. But Ellison replicates this political division in his young narrator, who is eager to convince the white men gathered for the battle royal that he is an example of desirable conduct.

Ellison managed to find an intellectual respite from the dreariness of Tuskegee in a small group of fellow students who shared his curiosity about life outside of the school's militaristic structure of rigid rules, and anti-intellectualism. There were also some teachers at Tuskegee who were a welcome oasis for the imaginative Ellison, and decades later he would remember a handful of these teachers whose influence on his writing was incalculable. Morteza Drexel Sprague taught Ellison's English class the best in British and American literature, and encouraged Ellison's beginning critical judgment in literature. As a celebrated writer and critic, Ellison would later dedicate a collection of essays—*Shadow and Act* (1964)—to Sprague in appreciation. Another influential teacher was Hazel Harrison, head of the piano department, who inspired one of Ellison's most famous essays, "The Little Man at Chehaw Station," on the need to always adhere to the highest standards, no matter the listener or (in Ellison's case) reader. The head librarian at Frissel—Walter Bowie Williams—quickly found in the young Ellison a student to nurture in his cloistered world of art, music, and literature. Williams (only seven years older than Ellison) introduced him to the small group of campus aesthetes who made the young Ellison's stay at Tuskegee bearable. More importantly, Williams allowed Ellison the run of the library. Providing the library shelves with stock was the purview of its head librarian, and Williams, reared and trained in northern colleges was not prepared for the literary indifference and the anti-intellectual ethos of Tuskegee. Happily, the conservative administrators did not check the shelves too carefully, and Ellison was able to read the types of European modernist texts that routinely appeared on lists as censorable, or not taught in the majority of Tuskegee's English classes. It was at Tuskegee that Ellison first came into contact with *The Waste Land* by the modernist poet T. S. Eliot, which would have a lasting effect on his writing.

For the future writer of *Invisible Man*, the most influential modernist text Ellison came across was the Anglo-American T. S. Eliot's book-length poem *The Waste Land* (1922). With its dizzying array of mythological and literary allusions, and copious footnotes, *The Waste Land* captured the imagination of many young writers (most notably F. Scott Fitzgerald) because of its startling rhythmic and tonal structure. Tackling the poem was clearly an endeavor not for the casual reader, and as an avid reader, the young Ellison was drawn to the poem in the same ways he was drawn to jazz. The poem's myriad literary and mythological allusions may have eluded the young Ellison, but for the aspiring musician, Eliot's structure was rhythmically familiar: "Somehow its rhythms were often closer to those of jazz than were those of the Negro poets, and even though I could not understand them, its range of allusion was as mixed and as varied as that of Louis Armstrong. Having given so much attention to the techniques of music," he recalls in the essay "Hidden Name and Complex Fate," "the process of learning something of the craft and intention of modern poetry and fiction seemed quite familiar" (*Shadow and Act* 160). Morteza Sprague encouraged Ellison not only to study Eliot's sources but also to read the literary criticism about the artistic and literary effects of the poem. "That really was a beginning of my literary education," he writes later in "On Initiation Rites and Power." But the poem inspired something else: his transformation "from a would-be composer into some sort of novelist" (*Going to the Territory* 40). Although the impact would involve years of study and practice, the early transformation would result in an American literary classic.

Ellison finally left Tuskegee Institute in the spring of 1936 with vague plans for the fall semester. On a conscious level, Ellison planned to work during the summer as a hotel porter in order to earn extra money, but subconsciously Ellison became dispirited with the college's cultural backwardness. Equally disappointing was the attitude of his musical hero, William Dawson, who refused to bend any of the rules to benefit Ellison. Dawson, similar to the other conservative faculty members, truly believed that the strict and puritanical rules against drinking and rowdy behavior would reflect badly upon Tuskegee, set as it was among the bucolic scenery that barely contained the itchy rope-wielding hands of the county's white population. Eager to find quick employment, Ellison left the South for Harlem—the capital of Afro-America, where he would be able to enjoy "a summer free of the South and its problems" ("An Extravagance of Laughter" 147). The older Ellison recalls that he considered Harlem "as the site and symbol of Afro-American progress and hope" (147), and *Invisible Man* captures Ellison's marvel at the sense of a black freedom he had never known in segregated Oklahoma, or at Tuskegee. The narrator of *Invisible Man* shares Ellison's wonder: "There were even black girls behind the counters of the Five and Ten as I passed. Then at the street intersection I had the shock of seeing a black policeman directing traffic—and there were white drivers in the traffic who obeyed his signals.... Sure I had heard of it, but this was *real*" (156–57).

But what was also real was the effect of the Great Depression on Harlem. Although Harlem was the epitome of black urban living, with its numerous black owned institutions, the Depression hit the black poor, who continued a migration that began at the turn of the century. Overcrowding, rapacious landlords, and the scarcity of employment soon took its toll on Harlem—even the fabled Renaissance was over as its white patrons could no longer indulge their support for African American artistic pursuits. Harlem was also becoming home to the free-styling public rhetoric of black political separatists and religious cult leaders, who took advantage of the freedom to rail against racial injustice with a freedom of black speech unknown in the South. Ellison would later use the background voices of various strains (and clashes) of Black Nationalists, Marxists, and storefront religious leaders to effective use in *Invisible Man*. Upon his arrival, the young narrator hears a voice, "angry and shrill" (157), that comes from a "short, squat man, yelling something in a staccato West Indian accent" (157). He comments, "I had never seen so many black men angry in public before, and yet others passed the gathering by without a glance" (157). The speaker is Ras the Exhorter/Destroyer, who will reappear in the life of the Invisible Man, but he is also Ellison's parody of the real-life Black Nationalist Marcus Garvey, a Jamaican national who at the time challenged the traditional civil rights organizations because of their inclusion of white members. After the narrator joins The Brotherhood, he and Todd Clifton get into a street fight with Ras's supporters; reluctant to end Todd's life, Ras cries and pleads with Todd: "Why you with these white folks?…You *my* brother, mahn. Brothers are the same color; how the hell you call these white men *brother*?" (363). Ras's question would later be asked of an older and celebrated Ralph Ellison by younger black writers during the late 1960s, but in 1930s Harlem, a much younger Ellison was just coming to terms with the complicated political and artistic landscape there.

Moreover, Ellison could also see the lasting evidence of the Harlem Riot of 1935, and the increased racial animosity between blacks and white business owners, as well as the hostility of white police officers, which would again erupt in 1943. It was the 1943 riot that Ellison would use later in the novel, and which forces Invisible underground. However, Harlem still held on to its luster as the center for black music and dance, which was a welcome relief for a young musician who had long been chastised by puritanical teachers for his love of jazz. Although Ellison may have been too late for the best of the Harlem Renaissance, he did form a friendship with Langston Hughes. Introduced by Alain Locke, the young Ellison and the established poet quickly formed a bond based on their shared admiration for T. S. Eliot. Hughes quickly introduced Ellison to black and white artistic and literary circles, while Ellison worked at the small jobs he could find to support himself. But Ellison also wanted Hughes to provide him with the latest literature from the radical left, which he was unable to obtain in the segregated South, and certainly not at Tuskegee. Closely reading the proletariat literature of writers like Nelson Algren and the political writings of Andre Malraux, Ellison prepared to share his insights with Hughes's coterie of likeminded intellectuals, and he was taken up by the small group of black American Communists. Overlooking the fact that the American Communists frequently fought with the Black Nationalist Garvey movement, Ellison—who never overcame his family legacy of pride—nevertheless felt comfortable with the proletarian Communists as an African American of working-class roots. Hughes encouraged Ellison's study of radical theory and literature, and encouraged his embrace of the American Communist Party, whose white leadership was eager to increase party membership among black intellectuals. Hughes also encouraged Ellison to read the literary journals that specialized in proletarian literature and pointed him to an especially effective poem by a young black writer named Richard Wright.

"Between the World and Me" expressed a different approach to the possibility for black writing; the poem combined both the experimental daring of T. S. Eliot with the racial situation experienced by southern blacks. Richard Wright's explosive poem conjured the horrific images of the brutalities of lynching and the cries of a black body tormented by the literal and metaphorical fires of race hatred. For Ralph Ellison, the poem by the young Richard Wright acutely rendered everything that "stood between a black person's apprehension of the self and individual existence in society" (Jackson 175). Agreeing with Langston Hughes that Wright was a formidable talent, a meeting was arranged by Hughes between the two when Wright left Chicago for New York in 1937. Determined to found a literature that would reflect both a black psychology and a folk consciousness, Wright would later sum up his ideas for the social function of black writing in his influential essay "Blueprint for Negro Writing," which marked him as a formidable literary critic of contemporary black writing. Wright's themes would later prove to be influential in Ellison's own craft, first attempted in his short stories. However, the theme of the struggles between the liberation of the black self and a cry for black individualism against a hostile society would be the framework of his highest fictional achievement in *Invisible Man*.

Although he never officially joined the American Communist Party, Ellison used his and Richard Wright's experiences with the party to good effect in *Invisible Man*. In the novel, the party is The Brotherhood—a sly comment on the party's mandate of brotherhood and equality for all working people, which made the racism of American unions an attractive target for infiltration. The Invisible Man comes across (by accident) a clandestine union meeting at the paint factory where he lands his first job; at first, he is hailed as "brother" (214), until the members find out that he works with the black Mr. Brockway—then he is labeled "a fink" (215), an informer for management. However, the chairman reminds his fellow workers: "It's our task to make friends with all the workers. And I mean *all*. That's how we build the union strong." But the cries of "fink" grate on the Invisible Man—"the hoarsely voiced word grated my ears like 'nigger' in an angry southern mouth" (215). But when he is asked if he wants to become a member, the narrator is rejected: "They had made their decision without giving me a chance to speak for myself. I felt that every man present looked upon me with hostility; and though I had lived with hostility all my life, now for the first time it seemed to reach me, as though I had expected more of these men than of others" (218).

Among themselves, Ellison and Wright had their doubts about the brotherhood of the American Communist Party; while there were a handful of African American members, the increasingly suspicious Wright strongly believed that he was recruited solely based on his race. There were also the mundane tasks of political rallies and demonstrations that Wright felt took up too much of his time as a serious writer. Ellison saw the party as a vehicle for his own literary pursuits, but Wright's bitterness with the Communists was put to use by Ellison in *Invisible Man.*

However he may have felt about Wright's denunciation of communist dogma against individual artistic pursuits, Ellison quickly raised his stature among left-wing intellectuals with his insightful literary criticism. In "Richard Wright and Recent Negro Fiction," Ellison set the intellectual themes for his later essays and for *Invisible Man,* where he criticized black writing for ignoring Negro folklore. Ellison also began to practice in fiction what he advocated; struggling financially as a budding writer, Ellison worked on establishing his fictional art while his critical reviews paid the bills.

Encouraged by Richard Wright, Ellison used his own experiences of riding the rails on his way to college in order to save money, when the racism of the 1930s curtailed his youthful adventure. The young Ellison soon found that black skin could be detrimental to the inviting freedom of hopping trains and outwitting the brutality of the railroad detectives. Although Ellison never wrote about getting caught and beaten by vicious white railroad detectives, the episode was used in his first foray in writing fiction, where he utilized the first-person narrative, a technique which would later anchor *Invisible Man.* The short story "Hymie's Bull" reflects some of the terror of Ellison's youthful experience of riding the rails. The story's narration is coolly told by an unnamed black narrator who recounts how "an ofay bum named Hymie" fights with one of the detectives, kills him and then vanishes into the night. But while the white Hymie is able to directly fight one of the bulls, the black challenger sees this type of direct challenge to white authority as risky for blacks: "Once a bull hit me across the bridge of my nose and I felt like I was coming apart like a cigarette floating in a urinal" (83).

The year 1944 saw a writer more assured of his narrative talents, as Ellison became renowned in elite literary circles as an astute (Negro) literary and social critic; but while he basked in the admiration of white intellectuals, Ellison (like many blacks at the time) could feel the coming destructive eruption of racial hostility in American cities. Ignited by war fever, military authorities made Harlem off limits to white women as racial violence engulfed the nation. Since the 1935 riot, Harlem had held its collective breath, but based on a rumor that a black serviceman had been shot and killed by white racist cops while defending his mother and wife, Harlem exploded for a second time. Contacted by the mainstream conservative tabloid *New York Post* to cover the riot, in his article, Ellison tried to explain the causes of the black violence while simultaneously reassuring apprehensive whites that many blacks were not inherently violent. The *Post* paid well, but Ellison believed that the situation needed a further critical analysis that the newspapers did not want but fiction could provide.

The short stories: "King of the Bingo Game" and "Flying Home"—both published in 1944—satisfied Ellison's artistic and critical skills in thinking about the racial condition in America. "King of the Bingo Game" contains many elements that Ellison would later use for *Invisible Man:* an unnamed character who leaves the South for fortune in the North, fractured identity, and the surreal scenes of high dramatic tension coupled with black comedy. The idea for "Flying Home" was grounded on the mixed reception of the (now celebrated) Tuskegee Airmen. The announcement that the U.S. Army Air Corps would train black pilots at Ellison's old college was met with a mixture of racial pride and suspicion by many African Americans, and especially by Ellison. But Ellison saw the chance to combine myth and history in the figure of an urban black character who could voice the complexities of modern black identity. The title "Flying Home" was from a Charlie Christian solo that the musician in Ellison highly admired for its musical innovation; this would prove to be a useful device (for *Invisible Man,* Ellison would use a popular Louis Armstrong tune as a theme). Ellison named his central character "Todd," a name he would use again for another conflicted character in *Invisible Man.* Todd, an ambitious Tuskegee Airman, is diametrically opposed to Jefferson—a poor black sharecropper—who reminds Todd of the limits of race. Jefferson argues that a college education and the opportunity to fly—the means of ascending racial stereotypes—will fail without the wisdom of the folk—another idea that would be elaborated in *Invisible Man.* The reconciliation between the modern African American desire for individuality, and the pull of the communal black folk (like the poor sharecropper and Mary Rambo) would be one of the most compelling tensions in *Invisible Man.* Showered with praise for the short stories (even by Richard Wright), Ellison finally felt free from the anxiety of following in Wright's considerable artistic shoes. The success of "King of the Bingo Game," combined with the equally successful "Flying Home," convinced Ralph Ellison that he was ready to tackle a larger form.

Appearing two years before the first decision in *Brown v. Board of Education of Topeka* (1954), *Invisible Man* (1952) was born from the frustrations of racial segregation at a time when African Americans were virtually invisible in the social and political landscape; they would remain so until the Civil Rights Movement of the mid-1950s. In many ways, Ellison's literary style was a deliberate act of cultural integration between cultural high art and the African American folk culture he knew so well. Thus, the novel can be read as universal *and* specific to the African American experience in that it pleads the cause of social integration. Although black America continued to face tough racial barriers, many were optimistic about American democracy due to several successful challenges in federal courts and the end of segregation in the Armed Services. The mood of optimism, especially in the postwar period, was also reflected by many black writers who, like Ellison, mirrored the new optimism in their work. Ralph Ellison was not the only black writer who insisted that he shared an integrated literary history; writers like Lorraine Hansberry joined him in refusing to be labeled as *black* writers—instead, they were writers who *happened* to be black.

Hailed on its appearance by contemporary critics as an American classic of "near genius," *Invisible Man* was chosen as the most outstanding novel of 1952, awarded the National Book Award in 1953, and has since been translated into over 15 languages. Not only does *Invisible Man* continue to receive extensive critical attention, but the novel remains a staple on American college reading lists, and is widely recognized as an exemplar of American literature. Influential literary critics quickly recognized Ellison's wide reading of classic and modernist texts as disparate as Homer's *Odyssey,* Herman Melville's *Moby Dick,* and William Faulkner's *Light in August,* whose influences can be traced in *Invisible Man*'s thematic structure. Ellison, a perfectionist, worked on the novel for seven years, and before completing it published what became the first chapter: "Battle Royal." Ellison also added a chapter that would become the prologue in the completed novel; both chapters (and the completed novel) received enthusiastic reviews from international and American critics. In many ways, *Invisible Man* made the struggling writer a very visible man as Ellison achieved literary and academic honors, and became a much sought-after lecturer and essayist on jazz, literature, and race relations.

Although the novel's larger themes of human individuality and alienation during the second half of the 20th century resonated with many intellectuals, Ellison's weaving of these heady questions with the African American experience was quickly recognized as another exploration of modern anxieties. But for the legacy of African American writing, *Invisible Man*'s enduring search for an identity not shaped solely by sociohistorical circumstances, although an often elusive goal, keeps the novel in the canon of African American literature. Similar to those of many African American writers before him, Ellison's work argues for—what he believed—is a black identity beyond the borders of racial stigma and degrading stereotypes that rendered African Americans virtually invisible to a wider American society. Moreover, *Invisible Man* offers a more complex view of black humanity as the novel moves from rural tenant farmers to northern tenement dwellers; from the uplift ethos of black southern colleges to the strident political tones of Black Nationalism—the novel captures a dizzying array of one man's psychological journey in his search for himself. Ellison also uses the novel to question contemporary political ideology as the Invisible Man struggles to find a self-identity between the accommodationist ideology of Booker T. Washington and the new spirit of Black Nationalism.

Often read as a universal character, the unnamed protagonist of *Invisible Man* is closely aligned with the bildungsroman tradition, where the building of character in a naïve young man is highly contingent on his interactions with an often hostile world. Ellison's work, however, recognizes this same foundation in black creativity; notwithstanding his staunch argument for the universality of *Invisible Man* (with its numerous allusions to Euro-American texts, scenes of surrealism, satire, and rowdy comedy), the novel cannot escape the Africanist improvisatory elements of jazz and blues forms as Invisible is forced to create meaning at each turn in his journey. The improvisatory nature of black music is thus added to a complex literary style as Ellison employs a number of striking literary techniques such as allegory, metaphor, symbolism, evocative imagery, and surrealism in his portrayal of African American life, from destitute black sharecroppers to urban black trickster figures from the 1930s, and the urban unrest that struck Harlem in the early 1940s. Ellison's unique, innovative narrative style and technique combine European literary forms with the unique African American vernacular of myth and music; in the process, *Invisible Man* has shown younger black writers—such as Ishmael Reed, Amiri Baraka, Alice Walker, and Toni Morrison—a wealth of possibilities for complexity in modern black literature.

The unnamed narrator of *Invisible Man* reveals a journey through a series of episodes that take place in a racist South, and continues north as he attempts to find himself as an individual. His journey, however, reveals several faults—not only in himself, but also in American society. "What Did I Do to Be So Black and Blue?"—also the name of a popular Louis Armstrong recording—he cries in the prologue as he declares himself to the world as an invisible man after his underground hibernation. The prologue represents the conclusion of a journey where the narrator belatedly recognizes the existence of his own invisibility. In many ways, the journey of the Invisible Man is symbolic of the sociopolitical journey of African Americans in the early 20th century; thus, as an unnamed and *invisible* narrator, he symbolizes African American identity as more fluid and fractured than fixed and restricted by racial ideology. Even though the narrator recounts the various stages in his journey, and his reactions to the betrayals he experiences at the hands of others, readers learn very little about the narrator himself in the way of physical description. In effect, he remains physically invisible to the reader and to himself as he finally understands that invisibility is not only the condition of blacks in American society, but also offers a space for creative hibernation and a reclaiming of self. It is also important that although others give him names (which are never revealed), personal identity only comes to him when he finally takes control of his destiny and names himself: "I am an Invisible Man."

Often anthologized as a stand-alone chapter, "Battle Royal" begins the Invisible Man's journey through a nightmare landscape. Throughout the narrator's journey to find himself, he repeatedly fails to see the true motives of the people he encounters. Significantly, Ellison uses various terms for sight and vision throughout the novel—from the blind Reverend Homer A. Barbee to the one-eyed Brother Jack; the motif of blindness is repeated throughout the novel, where the most compelling instance of blindness is the narrator's own inability to see himself.

The first lesson of blindness occurs when the young narrator is forced by the town's most influential white men to participate in a "battle royal" with other young black men. To influence the young men, a tawdry, half-naked white woman with an American flag tattoo on her thigh is paraded in front of the boys to remind them of what white power denies them. The narrator, invited because he has given a speech that endorses the values of Booker T. Washington, cannot understand why he is thrown in a ring to fight with a group of common young blacks. The jeering white men *blindfold* the group, who are then forced to compete for money. The narrator tries to convince the others to cooperate and work together instead of being divided by the power of whites, but the others only think of the prize—a clutch of fake coins. Connected to the theme of "blindness" is Ellison's severe critique of Booker T. Washington's ideological stance of black accommodation to white racism. The argument here concerns the young narrator as he models himself on Washington; what he fails to see is the betrayal by the Washingtonian model for American success symbolized by the false front of the College and its administrators. The visiting Reverend Homer A. Barbee praises the vision of the god-like founder of the College, a veiled allusion to Booker T. Washington and his famous college at Tuskegee. The fact that Ellison gives Barbee the name of the blind Greek poet is significant, since Barbee is blind to the realities of the College, and the selfish aims of Dr. Bledsoe. Not until he learns the truth about Dr. Bledsoe does the Invisible Man learn that he and the Reverend Barbee are both blind to the truth about the aims of the College.

Mr. Norton, the College's white benefactor, is also blind to his own racial paternalism as he fails to really see his own part in a racial system that educates black students to know their place. Ellison clearly uses Norton as a stand-in for the wealthy whites who contributed generously to Tuskegee after they were persuaded by Booker T. Washington that blacks were quite happy to remain subservient. Mr. Norton also fails to see his own contribution to the degradation of Jim Trueblood, and the supposed insanity of the black patrons at the Golden Day, who are revealed as former veterans of World War I that fought for a democracy denied to them at home. Some of the patrons are professional men, representing the results of a blind system that refuses to accept their gifts in the way that they help Mr. Norton, who has fainted. Another blind figure, later in the novel, is the white Brother Jack, who is half blind. Brother Jack is the leader of the Brotherhood, and preaches an ideology that purports to transcend race while in fact using race to further the aims of the organization. As a critique of the Communist Party, Ellison firmly allies their brand of blind paternalism with that of Mr. Norton, where the blindness of the party is symbolized by Brother Jack's glass eye and his callous disregard for the fate of Tod Clifton.

The opening cry of the narrator in the prologue, "I am an invisible man," recalls W.E.B. Du Bois's concept of "double consciousness" from *The Souls of Black Folk* (1903). The feeling of "twoness"—"an American, a Negro... two souls, warring in one dark body"—(*Souls* 8), argues Du Bois, is at the forefront of African American writing. This twoness, the reconciling of black identity, assures the iconicity of Ralph Ellison's *Invisible Man* in the long tradition of African American writing. In *The Souls of Black Folk,* Du Bois argues that African Americans are forced to see themselves through the eyes of others, whereas the world refuses to see them as individuals. There is a veil between the black and white worlds, Du Bois states, where African American cultural contributions are invisible assets to American democracy. But Ellison also places the task of tearing away the veil as a responsibility of blacks who blindly follow a narrow racial ideology—not of their making—which limits their range of possibilities. Thus, Ellison positions the theme of blindness, which runs throughout the novel, both literally and metaphorically. In the "Battle Royal" chapter, the young narrator is forced to compete for a worthless prize while he is blindfolded with other young black men for the amusement of whites. At each point in his continuing journey, the gullible narrator blindly believes in the vision of others who try to thwart his goal of individuality: from the accommodationist Dr. Bledsoe of the southern black college, to the false class ideology of the Brotherhood, and finally to the Black Nationalism of Ras the Exhorter.

More direct influences on *Invisible Man* can be found in Jean Toomer's *Cane* (1923), a work that is evocative of the fragmented lives of the black rural South. Toomer's slender work mixes poetry and prose with the lasting effects of slavery in a daring experiment that reflects—like Ellison's purpose—a nonstatic definition of black identity. Similar to Ellison, Toomer's work also argues that black writers could share in a European literary inheritance by adopting a variety of narrative strategies and experimental techniques, regardless of the race of the author. Moreover, *Cane* mourns what Toomer sees as a valuable folk culture vanishing in the face of urban migration, while Ellison charts its migration and continued wisdom even in the face of modern urbanity. Ellison's unnamed narrator gives truth to Toomer's fears, as the Invisible Man is unable to read the signs familiar to southern blacks on the ways of white folks, or the devices used to survive them.

One of the hallmarks of African American writing has been (and continues to be) one of identity, especially the debate over racial authenticity. As Ellison argued, his work should not be judged by rigid ideology, especially the increasing debates over whether or not Invisible is as black as Wright's Bigger Thomas—a debate that would dog Ellison throughout the 1960s and 1970s. *Invisible Man*—in the debate over a racial essentialism—joins James Weldon Johnson's *The Autobiography of an Ex-Colored Man* (1912). Although a novel of racial passing, Johnson's work is also one of cultural passing, where the narrator exchanges black culture for a Euro-American one in a world that does not allow him an identity free from stereotypes about blackness. While Johnson's unnamed narrator disappears down a hole of whiteness because of his color, Ellison's unnamed narrator goes underground in order to survive with his blackness intact. Furthermore, Ellison does not see black authenticity as limiting; he sees the degradation and humiliation in political invisibility, but he also maintains that that same invisibility presents limitless creative possibilities and avenues for self-definition.

In a lecture delivered at the University of Iowa's Institute for Afro-American Culture in 1971, Ellison finally came to terms with the author and friend whose literary influence almost overshadowed his own: Richard Wright. In the lecture—collected in *Going to the Territory*—Ellison offers "the memories of a middle-aged man" of a writer who "was sometimes too passionate." Ellison finally joins himself with Wright when he sums up the demands that both writers shared: "But at least Wright wanted and demanded as much as any novelist, any artist, should want: He wanted to be tested in terms of his talent, and not in terms of his race or his Mississippi upbringing. Rather, he had the feeling that his vision of American life, and his ability to project it eloquently, justified his being considered among the best of American writers" (216).

Notwithstanding the recognition that the National Book Award gave him as an artist, Ellison could not escape the fact that in many circles he was a black writer who had written what many considered to be another facet of the black experience. As one of the major African American authors of his time, white publications and publishers both sought Ellison's critical pronouncements on the latest black novel, which he invariably refused to do. For a writer who insisted that the racial novel did not exist and that black writers should stay away from racial polemics, his position only exacerbated what would much later become a contentious relationship with younger, black writers. Ellison's refusal to support talented black writers would haunt his reputation—and that of the book—for decades to come with succeeding generations of young African American writers. While *Invisible Man* did have its white detractors, whose criticism was largely stylistic, the criticism of the novel from the African American community was based on what was perceived as Ellison's black self-hatred.

Although Ellison did receive a modicum of praise from Langston Hughes and Richard Wright, the negative criticism from the black community recorded in black-oriented publications puzzled Ellison. African American reviewers (who Ellison dismissed as lacking the proper literary credentials) veered from pride that a black writer had achieved such an honor based solely on artistic merit to disgust for what many believed was another traitorous depiction of the African American male begun by Richard Wright's *Native Son* (1940). There were still other voices who were equally dismayed at Ellison's portrayals of African American rural life. Many middle-class blacks were not only outraged at the incestuous character Jim Trueblood, but also his criticism of the black colleges that had educated them. Still, Ellison steadfastly insisted that his work transcended race, and that the acceptance of his work by the National Book Award judges meant that America's race problem was much better than activists wanted to admit. Comparing Bigger Thomas with the Invisible Man, many critics (black and white) faulted Ellison's lack of rage at American racial injustice, but Ellison refused to compromise his artistic goals within—what he felt—were the too-narrow restrictions of racial ideology, and later disparaged Wright for compromising his own intellectual gifts in *Native Son*. However, there is a rage in *Invisible Man* that too many readers in their criticism of the novel overlooked: that not all black men were Bigger Thomas, and that African Americans could be as psychologically complex as other groups of Americans.

One of Ellison's closest friends—critic Stanley Hyman—completely misread Ellison's use of familiar African American folk figures and customs when he summed up the trickster figure (the unnamed narrator) as the darky entertainer. Hyman's criticism stung Ellison's pride: "Hyman's favorite figure is the trickster, but I see a danger here," he wrote in answer ("Change the Joke and Slip the Yoke" 46). While Ellison granted the fact that popular entertainment had a hand in creating the comic darky, Hyman was inescapably wrong about the use of the mask by performers/minstrels, whites whose ritual mask of grotesque black features and dialect vernacular created the comic darky. But for African Americans, hiding feelings behind a "mask that grins and lies" was not a joke: "The mask was an inseparable part of the national iconography. Thus, even when a Negro acted in an abstract role the national implications were unchanged" ("Change the Joke and Slip the Yoke" 48). In essence, Ellison was incensed that Hyman had reduced *Invisible Man* to black folk custom and the blues—or another example of Negro literature, a designation that Ellison fought against throughout his writing life. Furthermore, the two men disagreed on the use of folklore in literature; however, Ellison's essay "Change the Joke and Slip the Yoke" remains as one of his most insightful and influential essays.

To the dismay of many college-educated African Americans, Ellison used his protagonist to critique the class and accommodationist strictures of black college life in the Jim Crow South, and the fate of black World War I veterans who expected to participate in the real democracy for which they fought. Publically, however, Ellison remained socially conservative and refused to lend his name to racial causes. Part of Ellison's hesitancy may have been due to the postwar preoccupation with communist infiltration in American popular culture. The Red Scare of the 1950s was especially hard on black entertainers and writers, and Ellison, busy with *Invisible Man,* was careful with any public attacks on American racial policy. While Ellison (like Richard Wright before him) flirted with the American Communist Party, his sly, satirical criticism of the party (the Brotherhood) generated overwhelmingly negative reviews from the party's book reviewers. Liberal white critics steeped in Marxist theory attacked *Invisible Man* for its lack of a violent, class-bound militancy, and its indifference to the theme of African American modern protest and social realism initiated by Richard Wright's *Native Son* (1940). Not only was the novel unfairly compared to *Native Son,* but the tone of the negative remarks appeared to be a reaction to Ellison's stinging rebuke of the racial politics of the American Communist Party. In 1963, the influential (and staunchly socialist) literary critic Irving Howe unfavorably compared *Invisible Man* (again) to *Native Son;* even worse for Ellison was the fact that Howe rated the younger writer James Baldwin's explosive *Another Country* even higher (Ellison detested Baldwin). But Howe took issue with Ellison's transparent depiction of the American Communist Party (the Brotherhood) as "gross caricature" and the ending as "vapid and insubstantial." The judgment sums up Arnold Rampersad's opinion of the text, who said that "Wright wrote fiction as a Negro should. Ellison had shirked his responsibilities" (401). Incensed by the attack, Ellison responded in another brilliant essay, "The World and the Jug," where he argued that *Invisible Man* was not ideological in nature but expressed a more varied and complex reality of the black experience that many white liberals refused—or could not comprehend—and that the novel should be judged solely on its artistic merits.

Later, Ellison's insistence on black individuality, disdain for the back-to-Africa Garvey movement, and the new Black Nationalist/Arts agenda would earn him the wrath of black cultural nationalists during the late 1960s. Instead of the expected black anger from a novel like *Native Son*, Ellison's white admirers who were influential critics focused on the narrative technique and the universality of alienation as the condition of modern man. However, later critics of African American writing—especially the group of younger black writers during the Black Arts Movement of the 1960s—preferred the social realism of Richard Wright's *Native Son* over the lack of any racial anger in *Invisible Man*. According to Ellison biographer Arnold Rampersad, black critical assessment at the time of the novel's publication—except for a favorable review by Langston Hughes—was that for all of its European and white American literary influences, *Invisible Man* only slandered the African American experience by shamelessly dealing in vicious black stereotypes in a tradeoff for the approval of white critics.

Disillusioned by the nonviolent (and bourgeois-led) Civil Rights Movement, adherents of the new black cultural nationalism that rose in the mid-1960s derided the work as not black enough—*Invisible Man* did not value a common cause with the black masses, and Ellison's achievement was an instance of a literary racial integration. In turn, Ellison challenged these critics on the grounds that, as a creative artist, he was also an inheritor of *both* European literary and African American cultural traditions, and that the themes and structure of the novel demonstrated a belief in a racially unified American democracy. Unfavorable criticism by younger black writers was no doubt due to generational differences between older assimilationist goals and the impatience of youth, but another factor had to do with Ellison's personality. His lectures to black college students incorporated a grudging admiration for their political courage and dismay at their growing militancy, which he warned them "could be counterproductive." Significantly, Ellison "stressed the need to keep politics and art separate, and warned of the dangers of political fantasy" (Rampersad 385).

Ellison rarely championed any of the younger black writers who came to critical attention in the aftermath of the laudatory praises for his own novel. The sense that he had finally laid the shadow of Richard Wright behind him was upset when James Baldwin (1924–1987) replaced him in black cultural relevancy. To Ellison's great indignation, the foremost literary critic "Edmund Wilson hailed Baldwin as the greatest African American writer ever" (Rampersad 389). His often violent and vitriolic condemnation and dismissal of fellow black writers, such as Ishmael Reed (1938–), Melvin Kelley (1937–), and John Edgar Wideman (1941–), for example, contributed to the continuing lack of black critical support, which hindered the initial acceptance of the novel as an exemplar of African American writing. However, while Ellison's novel and his own personal disdain for younger black writers may have tempered youthful criticism, there was overwhelming respect and admiration for Ellison's nonfictional prose collected in *Shadow and Act*.

The literary legacy of Ralph Ellison continues as successive generations have evaluated and reevaluated the breadth and scope of his literary intellect. Every year brings a new perspective on *Invisible Man* in the forms of dissertations and critical essays and a scholarly appreciation of his essays on jazz and African American culture. After the era of black militancy, *The Craft of Ralph Ellison* by Robert O'Meally in 1980 was one of the first critical works to usher in the type of academic attention that Ellison craved; unfortunately, the text was full of errors, not only about the facts of his life, but—as Ellison angrily pointed out to the young author—misquotes attributed to Ellison himself. Ellison was also wary of Kimberly Benston's *Speaking of You*, until Benston assured him that the collection would include critical essays by writers Ellison admired—especially those who compared *Invisible Man* favorably with the European masters Ellison liked. Although Ellison was notorious for his disdain of young, black writers, he did manage to form friendships with a select group of black males who tended to share Ellison's political—often reactionary—views on African American culture.

Biographer Rampersad also notes Ellison's pointed antipathy directed toward the emergence of African American female writers during the 1970s who severely criticized the depiction of black women in *Invisible Man*—especially his depiction of the wife and daughter of the incestuous sharecropper Trueblood, and the Mammy-like figure of Mary Rambo. As many black feminists began to challenge male authority, they created "a literary country Ralph [Ellison] seemed to have little interest in visiting" (Rampersad 547). A decade after his death, Toni Morrison explicitly captured Ellison's standing among a younger generation of African American writers where she notes Ellison's "narrowness of his public encounters with blacks," while praising *Invisible Man* as a "spectacular novel." "For him," she writes to Arnold Rampersad, "in essence, the eye, the gaze of the beholder remained white. But if the ideal white reader made sense for *Invisible Man* in 1952, he or she made less sense for the black writer by the seventies and eighties.... He saw himself as a black literary patrician, but at some level this was a delusion" (549). *Invisible Man*, perhaps, makes more sense today than it did in 1952 because its scope and structure was unknown territory for African American writing; although the work has been hailed as an exploration of universal modern man—it is unmistakably *black* in its use of signification, African American folk customs, and musicality. However, due to the maturation of their own critical skills, many of the young writers who had earlier disparaged *Invisible Man* have come to an understanding of Ellison's literary skill in terms of many of the work's literary strategies and themes, and newer black critics of African American literature—Henry Louis Gates Jr. and Houston Baker—have reappraised the novel as an icon in the African American literary canon.

Additional Works by and about Ralph Ellison

Fictional Works by Ralph Ellison

Flying Home. *New York: Vintage, 1998*
Invisible Man. *New York: Vintage, 1972.*
Juneteenth. *New York: Vintage, 2000*

Ellison never lived to see the publication of his second novel, which he had been working on in fits and starts since the 1950s. Pieced together from Ellison's voluminous notes by his literary executor, John F. Callahan, the novel was published after Ellison's death.

Short Stories from Flying Home

"Flying Home"
"Hymie's Bull"
"King of the Bingo Game"

Nonfictional Works by Ralph Ellison

"Change the Joke and Slip the Yoke." Shadow and Act
Going to the Territory. *New York: Vintage, 1987.*
"Living with Music." Shadow and Act
"Perspective of Literature." Going to the Territory
"Richard Wright and Recent Negro Fiction," Direction *4 (Summer 1941): 12–13.*
Shadow and Act. *New York: Vintage Books, 1964.*

Biographies of Ralph Ellison

Jackson, Lawrence. Ralph Ellison: Emergence of Genius. *New York: Wiley, 2002.*
Rampersad, Arnold. Ralph Ellison: A Biography. *New York: Knopf, 2007.*

FURTHER READING

Benston, Kimberly W., ed. *Speaking of You: The Vision of Ralph Ellison.* Washington, DC: Howard UP, 1987.
Bloom, Harold, ed. *Modern Critical Views: Ralph Ellison.* New York: Chelsea House, 1986.
Busby, Mark. *Ralph Ellison.* Twayne: Boston, 1991.
Callahan, John F., ed. *Ralph Ellison's Invisible Man.* New York: Oxford UP, 2004.
Graham, Maryemma, and Amritjit Singh, eds. *Conversations with Ralph Ellison.* Jackson: UP of Mississippi, 1995.

Morel, Lucas E., ed. *Ralph Ellison and the Raft of Hope: A Political Companion to Invisible Man*. Lexington: UP of Kentucky, 2004.

Nadel, Alan. *Invisible Criticism: Ralph Ellison and the American Canon*. Iowa City: U of Iowa P 1988.

O'Meally, Robert, ed. *New Essays on Invisible Man*. Cambridge: Cambridge UP, 1994.

Sundquist, Eric J. *Cultural Contexts for Ralph Ellison's Invisible Man*. Boston: Bedford, 1995.

Dolores V. Sisco

Gayl Jones, whose work is associated with the jazz aesthetic, is a novelist, poet, playwright, professor, and literary critic. (Courtesy of Profile Books)

Jazz Aesthetic

Jazz is more than a name: it is a sound, a nebulous musical current whose history stretches from the 19th century to the present. Its etymology is as mysterious as that of the blues and many interpretations have been made about its origin: an American one (jazz referring to the words "gism"/"jasm," bearing sexual connotations), an African one (according to an African dialect, "jasi" means living fast), and French ones (jazz sounds like "jaser," i.e., gossiping; but "jazz-belles" was also the nickname of New Orleans prostitutes, called Jezebel women). Anyway, all of these associations have something in common: The impulse of jazz is full of vitality.

Like the blues, jazz was born in the South; if Mississippi represents the symbolical home of blues music, then Louisiana is the home of jazz. The geographic situation is always important in the shaping of a musical form; as the blues developed in the country, jazz made its first steps in a city. But not any city: New Orleans—"The Crescent City"—in the Storyville district, more precisely. Historically, New Orleans was a city bound to multiculturalism; it was formerly inhabited by Native Americans, then occupied by French people (Louisiana became one of Louis XIV's settlements), which explains why it bears the French name *Orléans*.

For Further Reading and Listening Pleasure

Jazz Music

Shadwick, Keith. The Illustrated History of Jazz. *New York: Crescent Books, 1991.*

Stearns, Marshall W. The Story of Jazz. *New York: Oxford UP, Inc., 1956.*

Discography Jazz Music

Bessie Smith, Billie Holiday, Ella Fitzgerald, Peggy Lee, Lena Horne. Ladies Sing the Blues, *Soho Collection, Union Square Music, 2003. CD.*

Billie Holiday. Billie Holiday Sings Her Favorite Blues Songs, *Disky Communications Europe B.V., 2006. CD.*

Cab Calloway. Hi de Ho Man. *Sony Music Entertainment Inc., Columbia, 1974. CD.*

Cotton Club, Harlem 1924-Broadway 1936. *Frémeaux & Associé S.A, DADC Sony, 1998. CD.*

Dr. John. The Dr. John Anthology. *Rhino Records Inc., 1993. CD.*

Duke Ellington. All Star Road Band. *EPM Musique, 1985. CD.*

Duke Ellington. The Blanston-Webster. *RCA/Ariola International, New York, 1986. CD.*

Duke Ellington and His Orchestra. Such Sweet Thunder. *Sony Music Entertainment Inc., Columbia, 1957. CD.*

Ella Fitzgerald, 1918–1996. Going for a Song Ltd., London UK, 2004. CD.

Jimi Hendrix. Experience. *L.L.C., MCA Record, A Universal Music Company, 2000. CD.*

Magnificent Seventh's Brass Band. Authentic New Orleans Jazz Funeral. *Mardi Gras Records Inc., 1991. CD.*

Louis Armstrong and His Orchestra. 1929–1930. Classics Records, 1990. CD.

Louis Armstrong. Great Original Performances 1923–1931. *1985. BBC Enterprises Ltd, 1986. CD.*

Miles Davis. Kind of Blue. *Sony Music Entertainment Inc., Columbia, 1997. CD.*

Nina Simone. The Greatest Hits. *BMG UK & Ireland Ltd, 2003. CD.*

Nina Simone. 2 CDs. Recording Arts, Dejavu Retro Gold Collection, 2003. CD.

Filmography

Bluesland, Masters of Jazz. *Toby Byron. Multiprises, 2002. DVD.*

Louis Armstrong, Masters of Jazz. *Toby Byron, Multiprises-EDV 1284, 2002. DVD.*

Cotton Club. *Francis Coppola. ITC Entertainment Group Ltd., Studio Vidéo, 1993. Film.*

Godfathers and Sons. *Marc Levin. Martin Scorsese Présents The Blues collection. Vulcan Production Inc., 2003. DVD.*

The Soul of a Man. *Wim Wenders. Martin Scorsese Présents The Blues collection. Vulcan Production Inc., 2003. DVD.*

New Orleans is a port city; a place of trade and travel; the meeting point of people coming from Great Britain, France, Spain, or Africa (Louisiana relied on slave labor). Geographically, New Orleans is a city bound to cosmopolitism, too; it is part of a gulf that communicates with Cuba, Mexico, Jamaica, and Haiti—countries that have brought along their own religion and tradition. New Orleans, then, quickly became a place at the junction of many influences, where identity was of a hybrid and creole type. Voodoo beliefs that developed there exemplify the encounter of Haitian Vodun and Christianity; the African animist approach to life and the monotheist world crossed with each other. If Vodun bases its faith on the forces of nature (stressing its healing quality), Christianity brings the notion of good and evil, which is why New Orleans voodoo is characterized by the presence of black and white magic. New powers, new saints, and new spirits appeared: Marie Laveau, or "Marie the Sainted," witch doctors like Doctor Jim, and medicinal remedies, or gris-gris, like snake Root or high John root.

In this mosaic of languages, cultures, and beliefs, how do people communicate? When words prove insufficient, what other media do people have to express themselves? Art. For example, the music of the famous musician Dr. John (born Mac Rebennack), an artist of multiple identities, is Creole; he illustrates the syncretism of genre and mood, languages and beliefs. His songs contain French influences, like in "Loop Garoo," Voodoo tones, like in "Gris-Gris Gumbo Ya Ya" and "I Been Hoodood," as well as blues notes, like in "Travelling Mood." Meandering piano rhythms and dizzy melodies inhabit colorful and dark songs—songs that prompt you to dance. Dancing is an important aspect of jazz music; as Gospel music aims to free the mind, jazz liberates the body. This aspect is primarily due to the influence that ragtime had on jazz; ragtime is a musical genre with spirited rhythms, and was developed at the end of the 19th century by the famous pianist Scott Joplin. Cakewalk, juba, and quadrille dances were very popular at the time. Dancing helped slaves' survival, enlightening their pains and misfortunes; but it was also one of their favorite pastimes.

Technically, New Orleans jazz took the emotional dimension of the blues, and the dancing rhythms of quadrilles, ragtime, marching bands, and Spanish and other African dances. Jazz music, then, is a complex art form, since it is made up of multiple rhythms. Life is at the heart of jazz, and even more so as the music was played on many occasions, during carnivals, political meetings, or funerals; on such occasions, marching (or military) bands were called to parade in the city. The most famous jazz bands and leaders at the time were King Oliver's Creole Jazz Band, Louis Armstrong's Hot Seven, and Jelly Roll Morton's Red Hot Peppers. Like Dr. John, Louis Armstrong exploited the aesthetic dimension of Creole-ness. "Basin Street Blues," "C'est Si Bon," and "Tiger Rag" also play on the amalgamation between different musical genres, languages, and dance. When this music was played, New Orleans honky-tonks began to swarm with people.

The need to celebrate life was getting even more appealing, particularly when World War I came to an end. People, especially African American people, decided to try their fate and leave the South; in the beginning of the 20th century they massively took Highway 61 and migrated to northern towns like New York City and Chicago, hoping they could work, love, and live for themselves. New York City, now representing the capital of jazz music, looked ideal for those in search of a new life. An important black population settled in Harlem and a jazz microcosm was created. Emblematic places like the Apollo Theater, the Cotton Club, and the Savoy Ballroom became the symbols of jazz music. New icons like Duke Ellington, Billie Holiday, Count Basie, or Charles "Yardbird" Parker made their appearance. Orchestras and big bands started to be formed. The geographical change marked an evolution in the music, now known as middle jazz; however, the piano and brass instruments remained key (both providing melody and harmony), and became important means for virtuosity. Improvisation was still at the heart of creation.

The basic pattern of middle jazz answers two basic dynamics: a horizontal one that corresponds to the development of the theme, also called the "chorus," and a vertical one, the rhythm section. However, technical transformations occurred and musicians began to arrange their pieces. The soloist artist, playing within and against the group emerged, his voice sometimes imitating the instrument through scat and growl. The players' instruments were also treated as an extension of the human voice—a technique known as wha wha. The blues or spiritual's pattern of call and response, which represents a real act of communication, also remained. Blues music, then, adapted to urban life, and was still influential—let us not forget Willie Dixon's phrase: "The Blues is the roots, everything else is the fruits." Bessie Smith and Billie Holiday's songs, for example, were full of blues tone, including "Blue Moon," "Solitude," and "Travelin' Light." The blues pose seems to betray disappointment on the part of African American people, who, despite the vogue they were experiencing in Harlem, had still to struggle for their rights.

African American artists never forgot their musical heritage, since they managed to use it again and revive it according to circumstances. Jazz music evolved from Charlie Parker's bop to Miles Davis's cool jazz, and orchestras eventually took the shape of other types of ensemble, like the quartet or quintet.

Jazz music as a literary strategy raises many technical questions: How can the writer handle the story and plot, the role and relationships between characters, the narration and motifs?

Reading a Jazz novel requires being all ears and eyes to make Jazz music happen. The external composition of a novel tinged with jazz music does not answer strict rules; the length and chapter structure vary a lot. The general form of the novel does make sense; following the nature and working of jazz music, the novel is on the whole freely arranged. The structure of *Jazz* is not built with chapters, but rather a blank page separates one section from another; Stanley Crouch's novel *Don't the Moon Look Lonesome,* on the contrary, is divided into numbered parts and titled chapters—often making reference to blues and gospel songs like "Me and the Devil [Blues]" or "Amazing Grace." It is also not unusual to find a prologue (or prelude) in which the narrator gives the outlines of the story, the same way bluesmen or jazzmen would introduce their piece. The device recalls the minstrel's art of storytelling. That is what Lead Belly did in a version of "Rock Island Line," or Cab Calloway in "Minnie the Moocher" when he begins his song with "folk's here's the story 'bout Minnie the Moocher."

The internal composition of a jazz novel, however, reflects the principal techniques of jazz music which is based on the dynamic of theme and variations. The City and Bailey's Café are the background and frame of *Jazz* and *Bailey's Café,* the starting place and last décor that regularly appear throughout the story. They are the structure and pattern of the novel; each section of *Jazz* and *Bailey's Café* actually opens on a new scene that introduces the weather and season in the place before it focuses on the character(s). Practically all section titles in *Bailey's Café* bear the name of the main protagonists. The framed story structure of *Jazz, Invisible Man,* and *Bailey's Café* also lies in the fact that the work is "wrap[ped]" (*Jazz* foreword) by a prologue and an epilogue; the prologue is voiced by the narrator who, like a minstrel, gives the key tune of the story. The tone in *Jazz* is set from the beginning but upset in the end, contrary to *Invisible Man* and *Bailey's Café* in which the mood remains the same in the beginning and in the end.

The plot is more like a "narrative line" (*Jazz* foreword), a "drift" (*Bailey's Café* 35), which starts with a particular situation and involves several protagonists whose interactions, sometimes clashing at first, eventually lead them to adapt their individuality into the collective. Communication and exchange also keeps characters from being invisible to others and to themselves. Yet, harmony is not easy to find; understanding remains a gradual and active process that is possible through the mediation of at least one other person. Paule Marshall's novel *Praisesong for the Widow* (1984) proves that understanding takes at least two people; would Avey Johnson have understood herself had she not providentially met a Caribbean juba dancer? Would she have made sense of her own past and realized what had been happening in her mind had she not let herself go and trusted the Carriacou stranger?

Place in *Jazz, Invisible Man,* and *Bailey's Café* is not a simple backdrop. The stories, frequently located in New York surroundings, remind the reader that jazz music has evolved in urban areas—only *Bailey's Café* is apparently situated on the edge of nowhere, "on the margin between the edge of the world and infinite possibility" (*Bailey's Café* 76). But locations are symbolic; one person points out the historical and geographical evolution of jazz music, another its conception and meaning as it stresses possibility and the freedom of composition in a jazz suite. Nevertheless, Harlem and Bailey's Café above all represent the principal stage where a group of characters, like a Greek chorus, gathers and learns to live together—"together" being the very last word in Stanley Crouch's novel *Don't the Moon Look Lonesome.* In *Bailey's Café,* the acting arena consists of a café where regulars meet and talk about their life. In musical terms the place stands for the theme; it plays an important part in the plot, since its recurrent appearance becomes the "drift" Gloria Naylor refers to in the novel.

The place is generally endowed with a mysterious power of attraction as well. If Bailey asserts himself to be "a very captivating fella" (*Bailey's Café* 16), he cannot really tell why people are appealed to by the café; "I'm at this grill for the same reason that they keep coming. And if you're expecting to get the answer in a few notes, you're mistaken" (*Bailey's Café* 4). There seems to be something unspeakable about the forces that draw the characters there and drive them to action. Like a magnet, Harlem represents for the narrator in *Invisible Man* the absolute place of success; an inescapable place for Joe and Violet, the two main protagonists in *Jazz,* who have been snared by the city as "the minute the leather of their soles hit the pavement—there was no turning around" (*Jazz* 32).

Once the theme is exposed, variations occur. These variations betray African American writers' main literary strategies: movement/deconstruction in terms of space and time, and the interplay of voices.

Digressions, shifts in point of view, distortions, and monologues, are all literary devices that are used to move from the theme. The very first type of variations that should strike the eyes of the reader in African American literature is a graphic one: the lexical constructions or the frequent use of words in italics. In *Invisible Man,* the passage in italics that almost fills the prologue appears like a translation of jazz into words, since the passage renders the inflections of the music. Only after that strange and sudden experience does the narrator feel himself "ascending hastily from this underworld of sound" (*Invisible Man* 14). Visual variations are much used in Stanley Crouch's, Ralph Ellison's, and Gloria Naylor's novels. The textual organization in *Bailey's Café*—short paragraphs, isolated and indented lines, and capital letters— seems to reproduce the different sequences and pauses found in a jazz suite.

The story is also significant in that it conveys the musical shifts that often happen in jazz. Like blues music, jazz works on tension and slackening, pitch and low notes; in the text, this aspect is translated into movements of whatever kinds. Exodus and migration, trip down into the South, fall, flight, resurfacing past, are in African American literature recurring patterns which might well actualize the rising and falling notes of a musical scale. Migration to the North is a frequent motif, for example, especially in novels set in New York City and Chicago—places where African American people migrated, especially in the 1920s. It is Joe and Violet's prospect in *Jazz* on coming to the city. Social ascension and visibility, which belong to the American mainstream culture, are precisely what the narrator in *Invisible Man* is looking for when he decides to leave the South. He, however, ironically ends up in "a hole in the ground" (*Invisible Man* 9).

Soaring and falling are the opening actions of Toni Morrison's novel *Song of Solomon;* in an attempt to "fly away" from his dull life, an insurance agent decides to jump from the roof of a building (3–9). The scene recreates a musical experience: a witnessing crowd, songs and silence, roaring, guitar, suspense, tension, then release. A similar scene is presented in the beginning of Ralph Ellison's novel *Juneteenth;* Sunraider, wounded by an assassin's bullet, falls like "a bird in soaring flight" (*Juneteenth* 38) from a high chamber in the Senate. The dynamic of soaring and falling makes the scene tense and confusing. Before his fall Sunraider goes into a sort of trance on seeing a blazon tumbling to the ground (*Juneteenth* 38). However hard he tries to struggle against the hallucinations provoked by the picture of the eagle, Sunraider almost loses self-control. He finds himself in a strange state of both distress and exhilaration, feeling "a surge of that gaiety, anguished yet wildly free" (38); the tension here in the character's unstable emotions gives way to virtuosity. Sunraider's experience at this stage of the book reminds the narrator's in *Invisible Man* as he makes a "hasty ascension" on listening to Louis Armstrong (Ellison 571).

At a more abstract level, the notion of a fall and redemption is very present in these works; it is not unusual to meet characters who consider themselves damned. Jazz music has frequently been qualified as Devil's music, which might explain why atmospheres of danger and temptation are to be found in the novels. For example, in *Invisible Man,* the experience the Invisible Man goes through is described as a journey through Hell. There is something infernal about it, since the narrator seems to be enmeshed in a whirl of events. Yet, he begins and ends in a hole; such a circular motif recalls Dante's circles. The prologue actually makes this comparison: "I not only entered the music but descended, like Dante, into its depths" (Ellison 8). On the other hand, we guess that redemption is what awaits the narrative voice at the end of *Jazz,* who, in a state of dejection and loneliness, appeals to the reader in the final prayer "make me, remake me. You are free to do it and I am free to let you because look, look. Look where your hands are. Now" (*Jazz* 229). Generally speaking, love, friendship, and brotherhood enable people to redeem and fulfill themselves—these are all forms of human bonds that African American people were deprived of when they were enslaved.

Such disruptions that breach the theme inevitably generate tension. Tension and suspense are already set from the beginning of *Jazz* by the narrative voice's shocking statement about Dorcas's death: "what turned out different was who shot whom" (*Jazz* 6). The dramatic tone used obviously betrays a taste for scandal. Suspense and mystery are equally conveyed in Bailey's puzzling statement about life and its unspeakable experiences: "most of what happens in life is below the surface" (*Bailey's Café* 19); or in the Invisible Man's strange assertion "the end is in the beginning" (Ellison 5). Because they are quite intriguing, these different statements are meant to catch the reader's attention.

Multiplicity is another cause for tension. Shocking scenes like those of falling, murder, or suicide often appear before a group of people; this occurs in *Jazz* before a church congregation at the time of Dorcas's funerals, or before guests during a party; it happens in *Juneteenth* before an audience in the Senate. To make the situation exciting, African American writers pack characters, mixing colors, places, and times: this mix almost becomes a mess. Crashing, clashing, and conflict create uneasy atmospheres. Crowded scenes often alternate with chaotic pictures or moments of loneliness, which slacken the pace of narration. *Invisible Man* plays with this contrast: either the narrator is withdrawn from the rest or finds himself in "complete anarchy" (*Invisible Man* 23). Lonely within a group, or lonely against a group, that is how the character in African American literature has become the novel bluesman, preacher, or jazz leader.

Besides distortions and verticality, variations are also produced by the characters and narrator's parts, which take place in chapters or sections. Their interweaving speeches break from the main theme and create different moods or atmospheres.

The concept of jazz characters does not mean that characters in jazz novels are necessarily musicians, though this is sometimes the case. Bluesmen and preachers are sometimes present in African American novels and may occupy a leading role, like Reverend Hickman, a former jazz player who has quit the profane world to embrace the sacred one; he is above all the key actor in

Senator Sunraider's redemption. Other musicians can have their part in the novel, since we also find intertextual references made to genuine bluesmen and jazzmen such as Muddy Waters in *Mama Day,* or Louis Armstrong in *Invisible Man.*

Furthermore characters and narrator's relationships, actions and interactions, are quite disconcerting. There are so many voices in a jazz novel that the reader sometimes gets the impression of witnessing a jam session.

The role of the narrator is in fact a key one; as a maestro, he is supposed to conduct the whole story. His or her position is quite subtle. "The jazz soloist works with and against the group at the same time" (*Liberating Voices* 48); according to Gayl Jones, he is both *in* and *out* of the story. The role of the narrator is therefore worth observation.

The narrator in *Jazz* is a tricky question, for example; both in and out, male and female, the narrator's gender is difficult to decipher. Is it a man or a woman? Nothing is revealed. Who hides behind the "disembodied voice," the nameless "I" (*Invisible Man* 468)? Is it the voice of the book or the eye of the Divinity suggested in the epigraph from the *Nag Hammadi,* a goddess who creates, "the name of the sound and the sound of the name" but also someone who destroys "the designation of division" (*Jazz* 216)? Is she a Devil's agent, someone who manipulates, makes and remakes? Like a snake, the hissing *sth,* she might provoke discord and temptation; after all, she asserts her power to divide in the epilogue: "I break lives" (*Jazz* 219). Does this not betray some devilish pose and purpose? A snake narrator could also explain her invisibility; she is someone who can see without being seen. At any rate, this reveals a duality about this narrator. Whatever the mask, one thing is certain: the narrative voice has a part to play with the other characters, and the quotation from the *Nag Hammadi* in the first person pronoun inevitably makes her a female character.

She also represents the jazz leader: she knows, she comments, and judges. a real viper's tongue sometimes. She is very skilful at minstrelsy too; not only the one who introduces the story and its characters at the beginning of each section, she also presents things in a subjective way or in a parody form, like a masquerade. For example, the interjection "sth" (*Jazz* 3) that starts the novel betrays a scorning attitude toward Violet, as if already exasperated with that character. The way she mocks Violet's dancing steps by comparing her to an "old street pigeon pecking the crust of a sardine sandwich the cats left behind" (*Jazz* 6) testifies to her particular taste for caricaturing people. Another example is the manner in which she tells Golden Gray's story, a sort of mock-epic of a boy passing for white who tries to perform one of the most important deeds in his life, that is, going to Virginia to kill his father, "the blackest man in the world" (*Jazz* 157). In this account, the narrator makes him out to be cowardly and timorous person.

The frontier between trick and truth is blurred; all of these interpretations make it hard to see how plain the narrator is, whether she is playing or acting. Does she not sometimes try to entertain, divert the attention from what is really going on? Her lack of objectivity induces the reader to question her reliability, and even more so, because if she delights in playing the characters like jazz instruments, she does not have total control over them either: Sometimes she is confident and spontaneous—almost overdoing it when she exclaims "I'm crazy about this city"—or sometimes put out, "disturbed" (*Jazz* 198) at some character's reactions. She is the soloist, the solitary one from beginning to end. And as we have seen previously, at the end of the novel, the playful tone gives way to a completely crushed mood when she seems to crack and admits having been outplayed by the characters, repeating "I missed it altogether" (*Jazz* 220). How unusual it is for a narrator-goddess who starts the story as if owning the main theme, thinking, like the narrator in *Invisible Man,* that she can influence people's destiny—but finally ends so helplessly, entreating the reader to "make me and remake me" (*Jazz* 229).

Things must have got out of hand; it did not turn out as expected. Did she plan Joe and Violet's final reunion? Did the two people just suddenly fall in love again? What is the part of predictability and improvisation in the novel? All of this looks so *jazz:* There is an artful leader, sometimes misleading and misled, directing and nondirecting, interrupting and disrupting; she asserts things in the same way as she doubts and wonders. She likes digressions, passing from one subject to another. Digressions and improvisation are important aspects in the novel. And is not the art of improvisation held by Violet?

Another great maestro in term of improvisation has marked jazz history: Duke Ellington, the principal inventor of the jungle style—a pictorial approach to jazz music adapting complex and colorful suites according to the musicians' individuality. Gloria Naylor appears to approach her novel the same way in personality is in fact a very important aspect in a jazz novel, since colorful characters are led to get along in a heterogeneous space, in "the jungle of Harlem" (*Invisible Man* 9) or in places encapsulating "a whole set" of people (*Bailey's Café* 4). Some characters not only present diverse skin complexions, varying from black to beige, but they also have a specific aura that is also quite colorful. *Bailey's Café* almost re-presents Eve's garden, with its flower-like boarding-girls, or Jezebel girls, composed by Sweet Esther, a white rose, Mary/Peaches, a daffodil, and Jesse Bell, a dandelion. All of them have got a personality of their own; for the narrator, each of them is a "special case" (*Bailey's Café* 117).

We have seen that one of the major techniques in jazz music is scat. Jazz novels work on that same technique; some characters seem to imitate the sound or the beat produced by the instruments. Rhythm, for example, is provided in *Jazz* by the character of Violet, one of the "crazies" to be found in jazz novels (*Bailey's Café* 101). Quite abrupt in her manners, she is very hard to handle at first; her punctual cracks, similar to Jazz pulsations, make her do unexpected things, like stealing a baby or stabbing a corpse in a sort of improvised gesture.

Madness is an interesting feature as far as cadence is concerned, because when one is mad, he is more liable to impulsions. This is both the means and the end of the music: unpredictable in a way and intoxicating in effect. There are wild and hot-tempered characters in jazz novels—characters prey to fits of violence that prompt them to act, to fight, in an impulsive way. *Invisible Man*'s narrator experiences that sensation when he explains in the prologue how he once came to "mug" a blond man in a frenzied and "outraged" manner (*Invisible Man* 8). Unpredictability characterizes the world of *Invisible Man;* it is worth noticing how recurrent the words "sudden" and "suddenly" are. Violence/self-violence is experienced in *Bailey's Café,* too, by Mary/Peaches, who suddenly rips her right cheek in a surge of self-hatred, or by Jesse Bell, who, under the effect of heroin, "banged her own head against the wall" (*Bailey's Café* 132). There is so much sound, fury, and anger within all of these characters, making them lose control of themselves easily. Their deeds, however, provide the twists and turns of the story; like drums, they beat time and push the action.

In jazz music, the tension is softened with the interruption of bluesy notes. When that melancholy melody is played, you step into another sphere; a mood-indigo sphere that is certainly mastered by Sadie, the wino woman in *Bailey's Café,* or by Joe Trace, the brooding man introduced as such at the very beginning of *Jazz*. Love is their principal cause of unhappiness (solitude, loneliness, or departure); Joe is suffering because torn between lacking or pent-up love in a way, and Sadie is incapable of fulfilling her "dreams of love" (*Bailey's Café* 44). Both journey into their past to understand their fragmented selves. In the section "Mood: Indigo," which obviously recalls Duke Ellington's suite, Bailey presents Sadie's past on the South Side of Chicago. Hers is a sad story, similar to Janie's in *Their Eyes Were Watching God*. She goes through hard times—violence, poverty, prison—which have made her an alcoholic. Yet, she still wishes to one day love and be loved. It seems that Sadie has been doomed by her name to such a life.

In section 5, Joe Trace is expressing his thoughts. His blues part comes after a brief introduction by the narrative voice, as if setting the tone, in which she makes direct allusion to blues music:

Blues man. Black and bluesman. Black therefore blue man.
Everybody knows your name.
Where-did-she-go-and-why man. So-lonesome-I-could-die man.
Everybody knows your name. (*Jazz* 119)

The passage is full of intertextual elements; first it echoes Louis Armstrong's bluesy song "What Did I Do to Be So Black and Blue," then he signifies on James Baldwin's novel *Nobody Knows My Name*.

Blues is above all black country music, evoked with the earthy characters of Jim Trueblood, the black farmer in *Invisible Man*, or Joe Trace, a hobo-like character educated in the woods by a *houngan* father figure qualified "witch doctor" Both Jim and Joe are regarded as brogues, tramps, people with country manners. Joe takes to fighting and hunting in his youth—first his mother, then his lover. Trueblood's sexual appetites and incestuous lifestyle are blamed by the Invisible Man for having "brought disgrace upon the black community" (*Invisible Man* 42). Violence boils within these characters—violence so hard to repress for Joe that it spurs him on to shoot at Dorcas. Both loners after all, Jim and Joe have got the blues; one "don't eat nothin' and … don't drink nothin' and caint sleep at night" (*Invisible Man* 58); the other is crying all day and night.

Like in blues songs the train theme regularly appears in Sadie and Joe's account; their story keeps on buzzing with trailing and tracking movements. In the blues, the sound of the train can be imitated by the guitar—mostly via the techniques of slides—or alluded to as a symbol of migration and freedom. Joe is characterized by movement; he was used to making tracks, and is now roaming the Harlem streets. His job as a door-to-door salesman of beauty products makes him a walking man. His tracking his mother and Dorcas makes him a hunting man. As for Sadie, she spends most of her life on the hunt for money, wandering from place to place to find work. Joe's narrative passage, in which he explains himself, has a cathartic effect on his mind, since he allows the melancholy that weighs him down to resurface. It is a key moment when he manages to express himself with his own, down-home words and images. Joe Trace and Jim Trueblood use evocative language that is very concrete, full of imagery, and close to the senses, to better convey their emotion: Dorcas is for Joe as sweet and soft as honey—"I never knew the sweet side of anything until I tasted her honey" (*Jazz* 129), or as tempting as an "Apple" (*Jazz* 129). Jim Trueblood's depiction of the flesh is based on visual impressions: "dark, plum black. Black as the middle of a bucket of tar" (*Invisible Man* 48). Both use animal imagery—"roosters," "chicks," "cocks" (*Jazz* 132–33) and "geese" (*Invisible Man* 52)—to describe their environment, and sometimes the references are not without double entendre, like "juicy gal" or "low-down dog" (*Invisible Man* 50, 56).

For blues characters, freedom is all. Sadie would rather defer her dreams of love than corrupt herself with bargain or deal of any kind, despite the secure life Jones offers to give her. On the other hand, murder represents a liberating deed in *Jazz*; it has an existential scope. Even if he does not suit the words to the action, Golden Gray plans to kill his father "to be a free man" (*Jazz* 173). A similar motive impels Joe to shoot at Dorcas. He does it in a state of confusion and intoxication, driven by the city train buzz and the streets, loaded with the memory of his mother and the fear of losing Dorcas. Looking for the latter with a gun in his hand, he finally catches her "messin' 'round with another man" and shoots her. Given that jazz was born in the South, it contains important composite or Creole elements, such as voodoo, which brings magic, mystery, and mysticism to the general atmosphere. This is represented by the "primitive" character of Wild, the hobgoblin figure in *Jazz*, the "used-to-be-long-ago-crazy girl" children are warned against (*Jazz* 167); or symbolized by Sambo, the "grinning doll of orange-and-black tissue paper…mov[ing] up and down in a loose-jointed, shoulder-shaking, infuriatingly sensuous motion" (*Invisible Man* 347). Dances and rituals are also important voodoo elements;

the section "Lavé Tête" in *Praisesong for the Widow* presents a Creole man—an ageless rum shopkeeper and Carriacou juba dancer—who attends and performs night ceremonies located up on a hill, past a crossroads, in a yard. Avey Johnson eventually takes part in one of these ceremonies, "And as suddenly he began singing in a quavering, high-pitched voice, his eyes transfixed, '*Pa' doné mwé/Si mwé merité/pini mwê . . .*' His arms opened wide in a gesture of supplication: '*Si mwé merité/Pa'doné mwê*'" (*Praisesong* 165). This mystic ceremony during which people go into a trance—"eyes transfixed" and "quavering" voice—participates in Avey Johnson's redemption. We have seen that voodoo spirituality never parts with Christianity; the character of Mama Day (in another Gloria Naylor novel), a conjure woman or *manbo,* uses both herbal medicines and prayers to heal people. Like Avey Johnson, Mama Day manages to cross the frontier between the living and the dead, and communicate in her dreams with Sapphira Wade, one of her ancestors. Death has become part of her existence, just as the spirit of Beloved in *Beloved* and Dorcas in *Jazz* represent a "living presence" (*Jazz* 11) that shares other characters' life. And as for the Invisible Man, even if he denies in the prologue that he is some Edgar Allan Poe spook, that narrator speaking from his hole in *Invisible Man* looks like the living dead. He is very strange, quite deceptive, asserting himself in the prologue as "a man of substance, of flesh and bone, fibre and liquids," and confessing in the end to "being invisible and without substance, a disembodied voice" (*Invisible Man* 468).

Moreover drawing from the blues and the gospel, jazz music plays with the tension between high and low notes, as well as between "hot" and "sweet tempo" (*Invisible Man* 11). Romance never parts with violence. Though some characters are associated with flowers in *Bailey's Café,* they are none the sweeter. Eve's boarding girls show that contradiction: Many are full of romantic ideals, yet resort to prostitution. Mary/Peaches, though "plump and sweet" (*Bailey's Café* 102), hates herself so much that she mutilates her own face; "Sweet Esther" is raped in a cellar by a man she has been forced to marry. But neither violence nor disgrace are conveyed in the narration, only the riff-like sentences, "*We won't speak about this, Esther,*" which are suggestive enough (*Bailey's Café* 95). As for Sadie, her "dreams of love" are not likely to be fulfilled on giving up Jones, the man who is apt to offer true affection. Love is a central question for the characters. If Sadie is lucky enough to have had "a real kiss" from Jones (*Bailey's Café* 76), Esther is still puzzled about the meaning of love, especially when she listens to music: "The songs speak of making love. I [Esther] cannot imagine what that is and I grow irritated by the songs. The music causes me to ache in a way I cannot understand" (*Bailey's Café* 98).

Dorcas, the city girl in *Jazz,* also represents a blend of sweetness and violence. There is something glamorous in her that may be connected with her hot lips. Red is her symbolic color. Many references are made to her "rouge" lips and fingernails (*Jazz* 65). She is also compared by Joe to the Garden of Eden's red apple. This characteristic gives her the power of tempting people, like a foxy lady, or a candy. However, she pays the price for this, since her charms finally drives Joe mad to the point of killing her. Tragically, her sudden fall takes place at a moment of fleeting happiness, during a sense of romance and felicity she feels in Acton's arms. The blood flowing across her face sadly represents the last touch of red.

Musically speaking, it is hard to decide on Dorcas's possible role. She may sound like a trombone or a trumpet—instruments expressing the glamour and the pathos, the whining or voluptuous notes which can be produced via the *wha wha* technique.

All of the instruments, found in a specific order within an orchestra, actually make the music polyrhythmic; the brass generally at the back, then the rhythm section, and the narrator-soloist in front, revealing his or her emotions, allowing others to respond. Solo, duo, and trio are found in an orchestra in the same way as many kinds of alliances are made in jazz novels; friendship, love, and enmity, for example, provide duos. A triangle of characters—Joe/Dorcas/Violet in *Jazz,* or Bailey/Nadine/Eve in *Bailey's Café*—can represent the core of the novel. And the minor voices like Golden Gray, Sugar Man, Jim Trueblood, and so on, can be considered *sidemen,* that is, participants who make their contribution to the piece. We can ask if there is a narrator/reader duo as well. The last words in the novel *Bailey's Café*, "When you have to face it with more questions than answers, it can be a crying shame" (229); *Invisible Man*, "Who knows but that, on the lower frequencies, I speak for you?" (572); and *Jazz*, "Say make me, remake me. You are free to do it and I am free to let you because look, look. Look where your hands are. Now" (229) all include the personal pronoun "you," inevitably involving the reader in the story.

Expression or expressiveness is an important aspect in a jazz novel, as it is in jazz music. The aim is to be as meaningful and spirited as possible. This may explain why jazz narration contains strange lexical constructions like "things-nobody-could-help stuff" (*Jazz* 7), "the usual how-much-I-miss-and-love-you's" (*Bailey's Café* 13), and "the old down-to-earth, I'm-sick-and-tired-of-the-way-they've-been-treating-us approach" (*Invisible Man* 276); or words associations like "ping of desire" and "gash of a ruby horizon" (*Jazz* 29, 105). In these expressions, connotation is emphasized and sound helps to support meaning. To increase diversity in form and language, the writers also use foreign words: the Ethiopian "*injerra*" (*Bailey's Café* 148), or the Native Indian "*N'ya-hap me-ye- moom*" and "*e hotche*" (*Bailey's Café* 168). The register also varies from the vernacular—one might think about Zora Neale Hurston's works—to the colloquial or slang. The narrator in *Invisible Man* keeps on saying "to hell with," and the words "suck," "bitch," "shits," and "fuck" repeatedly appear in Stanley Crouch's *Don't the Moon Look Lonesome.*

Expressiveness also betrays a search for virtuosity, the intention to convey a strong feeling in whatever way; for example, in her song "I Wish I Knew How It Would Feel to Be Free," Nina Simone, emotionally carried away, progressively sings higher notes as if expressing and attaining freedom and ecstasy. Jazz was not a scored music at first, and in literature this idea could be translated into the absence of a destiny that shapes the characters' lives. As a collective art, jazz music suggests freedom and possibility; in literature, this could mean that the story can take any direction.

"If life is truly a song, then what we've got here is just snatches of a few melodies" (*Bailey's Café* 219): Jazz music is made up of the superimposition of rhythms and melodies which eventually form a whole. Jazz novels work in the same way. However misfit the protagonists may appear, they "aren't as far apart as they sound" (*Bailey's Café* 33); however discordant their relationships seem at the beginning, they may find the unison out of the cacophony. Like blues novels, jazz novels deal with the reconstruction of the self, but also harmony within diversity.

African American novels often demonstrate that the other is essential in the creative process and in the building of oneself, that two are better than one. The reader's participation is quickly solicited, who is often drawn out or dared by the narrator through rhetorical questions and direct addresses: this makes it possible to respond to the work, go further, imagine new things, or simply repeat the story like "an abused record" (*Jazz* 220). An act of communication then occurs between the writer and reader. This is how an experience can be shared and art can be collective: You add your own view and work your own facet of the prism.

In jazz novels, neither fate nor destiny can condition the characters' lives, given that the story takes place in spaces of "infinite possibility" (*Bailey's Café* 76; *Invisible Man* 464). The world of a jazz novel, with its mosaic of voices and maze of possibilities, quickly appears as a jammed one; this is probably what gives the jungle style to the story. The plot, or story line, is not easy to grasp at first, and you can get easily lost in *Jazz, Invisible Man,* or *Bailey's Café.* Appearances may prove deceitful, and names and narration do not necessarily reflect the truth. Is Violet that madwoman the narrative voice describes at the beginning of *Jazz*? Is the Brotherhood in *Invisible Man* a cheerful and friendly society of brothers?

Reading a jazz novel is disconcerting at first and shakes traditional literary conceptions. The relationships between narrator, character, and reader are quite unusual; the narrator rarely has the upper hand, so that some characters become rather opaque, almost unreal, if not surreal, and the reader is invited to join the stage. Spaces and time are also surreal, especially if one considers place and displacement in jazz novels and the way in which chronology works. Because it is based on deconstruction, the novel knows no geographical or human boundary.

Jazz, Invisible Man, and *Bailey's Café* share a basic theme: Each novel deals with the life of a people in a given city/community. The city, in the characters' dreams, represents a place of new possibilities; yet most of them realize they do not own the rules, and some come to think they are "playing a part in some scheme" (*Invisible Man* 140). Since freedom is also at stake in a jazz novel, characters have to learn not to be slaves of others, of themselves, or of their past. Some characters try to hold the power; for example, Bledsoe is directing the Invisible Man's destiny with the letter he sends to his school friend, Mr. Emerson, instructing on what "shall" happen (*Invisible Man* 156), or the narrative voice in *Jazz* who thinks she can "manage" her characters (*Jazz* 220). Such dominations are obstacles to bliss and happiness, while characters' felicity is reached through knowledge and understanding. The epiphany phrases "now I know" and "I know now" actually represent the recurrent comments and the characters' understanding at the end of *Jazz* and *Invisible Man*. The epilogue is a moment when the narrator thinks his or her story out, drawing lessons from what has passed, musing on mistakes; the sense of failure that Ellison's Invisible Man and the narrative voice in *Jazz* feel may be due to their vain attempt to gain power and glory; they have in a way missed themselves in the hollow pursuit of the American dream of success. Thus, the epilogue represents a moment of truth and recognition for the narrator who is now able to "shake off the old skin" (*Invisible Man* 468). Yet no answer is given, no resolution is attained.

If questioning reflects the protagonist's feeling of loneliness and lack of control over her environment, communication becomes a way to make sense and escape solitude. Speaking from a literary standpoint, this happens through dialogue, whether mental or actual. Musically speaking, the characters can be released thanks to the blues and spirituals. Whether sacred or profane, music is a way to overcome and transcend times of crisis. Beyond expression, it becomes a powerful means of communication. African American music works on the call-and-response technique. The bluesman howls his melancholy at the guitar sound, singing songs of sadness, separation, frustration, deception, yearning, and questioning. On the other hand, in spirituals, which include gospel music, jubilees, and sermons, the technique remains the same, but the exchange happens between a preacher and a congregation.

In *Jazz,* Violet's memory of the past—of her mother Rose Dear—which has been so far kept at bay, wells up after a tense conversation with Dorcas's aunt, Alice Manfred, during which the latter has to curb any thirst for revenge. Both of them confront their own thoughts. Sullen at first, Alice Manfred manages to control her anger and gradually opens herself up, speaking what is to her unspeakable—Dorcas's death—and listens to someone she does not want to hear about—Violet. The latter has to make sense of a past situation that the dialogue recreates, and figure out what went on in Violet's mind at one point. Understanding does work out in the following section (section 4), especially through Violet's stream of consciousness, during which she keeps rehearsing her past. The meditation arouses the memory of her lost mother, Rose Dear, who mysteriously committed suicide in a well; of an absent, "phantom father" (*Jazz* 100), who deserted the family; and of her grandmother, True Belle, who took up her education. In this silent recollection, Violet is gradually remembering herself, since she finally manages to coincide with her other self: "[she] left the drugstore and noticed, at the same moment as Violet did, that it was "spring in the City" (*Jazz* 114). The acts of communication that occur between Alice and Violet make it possible for Violet to face what has haunted her mind. The catharsis is of a blues type at first; she remembers True Belle's philosophy "that laughter is serious" (*Jazz* 113), and starts laughing—a way, according to Langston Hughes, to "keep from cryin'." Her symbolic rebirth is later completed in the course of her conversation with Joe and Felice at the end of the novel, when she admits her mistakes and realizes how absurd the world is, wondering "what's the world for if you can't make it up the way you want it?" (*Jazz* 208). Is there no catharsis of a jazz type when she finally dances with Joe, on hearing a music coming through the window?

Other characters are there to join people together, characters like Eve, the host who boards lost women in *Bailey's Café*. Moreover, it is with the help of Reverend Hickman that Senator Sunraider makes sense of his past and retraces his childhood and moments of "bliss" he has experienced in the South (*Juneteenth* 38). Joe Trace's mental dialogue with Dorcas represents a first step toward reconstruction; after having conjured up his fragmented self, Joe now finds himself able to love Violet again. The duo, or double, Dorcas/Felice can stand for the bridging girls who prompt Joe and Violet to confront and reunite with one another; if Dorcas's love affair with Joe signals their estrangement, Felice's questioning attitude at the end of the novel brings them together.

It seems that Joe and Violet's final reunion thwarts the narrator's plans. Characters in jazz novels often act in an unexpected manner to counteract tight situations. That is how the Invisible Man's "sudden impulse" (*Invisible Man* 25, 77) manages to reverse an appalling spectacle; outraged by the eviction of an old couple from their apartment, he suddenly makes an improvised speech on the street in which he defends the dispossessed. The narrator's spontaneous performance, which preludes his commitment to the Brotherhood, makes him a preacher figure, comprehending and understanding, addressing people, quoting the Bible, and reflecting on the law. The cold organization, instructions, and omnipotence of the Brotherhood, however, turn out to be an obstacle to the Invisible Man's freedom, as it runs counter jazz philosophy that "you could never tell where you [are] going" (*Invisible Man* 308).

Jazz music, which is concerned with the here and now, is full of unpredictability, vitality, and optimism, which also may explain why Joe and Violet eventually manage to mend their love in time—a love that has finally survived all temptations of the city. Contrary to expectations, fragmentation and cacophony are replaced at the end of *Jazz* by love and "whispers" (*Jazz* 228). Even the narrator surrenders: "I envy their public love" (*Jazz* 229).

Like the music, a jazz novel works on polyphony and antiphony. In *Jazz*, the epigraph from the religious text *The Nag Hammadi* somehow gives the tune, and one might ask what gospel the reader is going to hear. The multitude of voices mixing present and past tense, mental conversation, thoughts, dialogues, and monologues inevitably challenge the almighty role of the narrator. As we have seen before, the palette of characters brings a specific tint to the story their different parts, most of them in the first person, add to the meaning. The narration is therefore an interesting field to explore; the point is not only *what* the story is about, but *how* it is told.

To be the most evocative possible in his prose, Ralph Ellison arranges his narration in a very personal manner, making a collage of words in italics, capital letters, and snatches of songs. Silence is also reproduced through suspension points, as if to visually translate the speed of delivery. On his techniques of narration, he stated:

> I was to dream of a prose which was flexible, and swift as American change is swift, confronting the inequalities and brutalities of our society forthrightly, but yet thrusting forth its images of hope, human fraternity and individual self-realization. (Jones 140)

Likewise, Toni Morrison, wanting to unchain language, works her manner of writing, saying in her essay "Playing in the Dark" that her purpose is to "to manoeuvre ways to free [it] up from its sometimes sinister, frequently lazy, almost always predictable employment of racially informed and determined chains" (29). She explained during her conference in Le Louvre (Paris) in 2006 that she tries to bring out the "meaning of language," to make it "emotional and powerful"; to her, "music can be sister to language" (62), which means that music has a complementary function to fulfill, being a good way to empower language and express what words fail to convey.

The polyphonic aspect in jazz novels stresses the importance African American writers attach to the oral African tradition of storytelling, which is embodied in the griot figure, for example. Listen to the text and you might hear things you have not read or come across without noticing. African American novels resonate with echoes and sounds of all kinds. Writers often use the technical words belonging to jazz music to compose their novel—"stomp" (*Bailey's Café* 87), "fox trot" (*Bailey's Café* 126), "jam" (one of *Bailey's Café*'s chapters), "stride piano" (*Jazz* 64), "combo" (*Jazz* 23), "breaks" (*Invisible Man* 11), "rag" (*Invisible Man* 349), let alone the numerous occurrences of "hot" and "sweet" scattered here and there in the texts. Snatches of jazz songs might even resound to the ears of the reader; it sometimes seems to me that I am hearing a woman singing in *Jazz*, "the music is faint but I know the words by heart" (*Jazz* 193), especially during the (gin) house party in section 8 when Dorcas tells Joe to stay away from her, when she reproaches him in that he "just don't care for her clothes and style," and not to mention Violet's revealing her need for "some fat in this life" (*Jazz* 110), some sugar in her bowl. Were the intertextual references to Nina Simone's songs Toni Morrison's intention?

The intertextual references become more explicit when real bluesmen and jazzmen are part of the story. Sometimes they are integrated as mere characters who, like Muddy Waters in *Mama Day* and Peter Wheatstraw, "the Devil's son-in- law," in *Invisible Man*, give performances. One might also find samples of bluesmen and jazzmen's songs slipped into the narration—very frequently Louis Armstrong's song "What Did I Do to Be So Black and Blue" which is played in the prologue of *Invisible Man*, or signified on by the narrative voice in *Jazz* and by Bailey in the epilogue to *Bailey's Café*.

Music also lies in the phrasing of the novels, in which rhythm and melody are combined. Jazz music, also called "symphonized syncopation" by LeRoi Jones, is full of riffs. If Louis Armstrong's song is echoed in many texts, it is also regularly alluded to in the Invisible narrator's frequent "what did I do?" questions, which recur in the story. In *Jazz* and *Bailey's Café*, some expressions or small sentences are repeated twice or more, betraying, for example, Violet's obsessive reflections on the death of Rose Dear, who "jumped in the well and missed all the fun" (*Jazz* 99, 102). The changing lights of the posts "from red to green to red again" (*Bailey's Café* 63) that match Sadie's nervousness as she walks away from a soldier give a dizzy impression. The narrative voice's fascination for jazzmen on rooftops playing music "pure and steady and kind of kind" (*Jazz* 196–97) betrays her exuberance. In *Bailey's Café*, the repetition of one-syllable words even reproduces sound effects; "*stomp, Billy*" (*Bailey's Café* 87) recalls the muffled sounds of stamping feet, while the phrases "sweet sweet voice" (*Bailey's Café* 101) and "my words were lost, lost" (*Bailey's Café* 128, 130) have a lilting quality.

The swinging quality of jazz novels is created by a certain rhythm/pace in the narration. This is first suggested by the punctuation. Periods, commas, and the absence of commas articulate and modulate the fluidity of a sentence. Furthermore, the sentences in *Jazz* are based on a binary structure, often divided by the conjunctions *and, but, or,* and *nor:* "convinced that he alone remembers those days and wants them back, aware of what it looked like but not at all what it felt like" (*Jazz* 36). Rings of voices are also formed, which shows that in jazz, everybody is free to communicate and participate in the musical experience; "men groan their satisfaction; women hum anticipation" (*Jazz* 189).

Besides the recurrent sound of Violet's cracks and Joe's tracings, which punctuate the novel, the rhythm is mostly provided by the one-syllable words that fill the book, and isolated words coming after more or less long sentences, like syncopations or finger snaps: "A city like this one makes me dream tall and feel in on things. Hep. It's the bright steel rocking above the shade below that does it" (*Jazz* 7). In *Bailey's Café,* Gloria Naylor makes use of hyphens to syncopate the rhythm: "This summer the talk in here is all about Dewey's upcoming election—and Eve. The Indians closing in on the pennant—and Eve. The first new line of Chevys since the war—and Eve" (*Bailey's Café* 79).

The rhythm of jazz music has traces of the blues. Albert Murray manipulates the narration in *Train Whistle Guitar* by alternating long and sometimes meandering paragraphs with shorter sentences made up of one-syllable words, which creates a particular pace and maintains the beat. The preposition "up" in *Jazz* suggests the same usage and even speeds up the rhythm. The sensation of accelerando is also rendered by broken sentences accumulating verbs, adjectives, or nouns: "one week of rumors, two days of packing, and nine hundred Negroes, encouraged by guns and hemp, left Vienna, rode out of towns on wagon or walked on their feet" (*Jazz* 173–74), or by breathless sentences, often maddeningly long:

> there was no place to be somewhere, close by, somebody was not lick-
> ing his licorice stick, tickling the ivories, beating his skins, blowing off
> his horns while a knowing woman sang ain't nobody going to keep me
> down you got the right key baby but the wrong keyhole you got to get it
> bring it and put it right here, or else. (*Jazz* 60)

Such running sentences convey the velocity of jazz music. In *Invisible Man*, Peter Wheatstraws makes it even faster as he pronounces the breathtaking "I'maseventhsonofaseventhsonbawnwithacauloverbotheyesandraisedonblac kcatbonehighjohntheconquerorandgreasygreens" (*Invisible Man* 144).

Jazz, Bailey's Café, and *Invisible Man* are approached like jazz pieces since they are built on one theme—living in a city/ community—to which the writer has arranged his or her story in a personal manner, varying style and expression, characters and action. Jazz music actually works that way, and "Trouble in Mind" is an example of this; the song, originally written by Richard M. Jones, has been taken up and performed and recorded over time by hundreds of people in a style all their own.

Every artistic creation remains the work of one person and one sensibility; *Jazz* betrays Toni Morrison's chief concerns and favorite literary themes of love, madness, and violence, in the same way that *Train Whistle Guitar* seems to display Albert Murray's partiality to color and atmosphere, as the novel is filled with touches of blue varying from "sky-blue" to "blue steel," thus making the work a piece in blue major.

Ellison's statement "music is heard and seldom seen, except by musicians" (*Invisible Man* 15) points out the magic of a great composition, which becomes powerful when it works on artistic correspondences. Does this mean that a jazz novel tends toward pure art? Or does a jazz novel simply stand at the crossroads of genres?

Color and cadence are the principal modes of expression in a jazz novel, and represent the aesthetic translations of the music. Yet a jazz novel also manages to recapture a whole state of mind—"to reproduce the flavor of the period" (*Jazz* foreword)—since it displays, or rather plays, jazz music often reminiscent of Duke Ellington's art: jungle, creole, colorful, expressionist. In that manner, all jazz novels could become in turn "samplings of Negro music proper to whatever moment of the Negro's social history."

The idea of a jazz novel inevitably creates a new concept of literature, almost a new genre, more evocative and meaningful—a conception in which music guides the words. Words and sounds, together, become the appropriate media to tell a story, or a people's history. In this way, not only do African American writers keep a record of a traditionally oral style, jazz music, but they also pass it on in a novel form.

FURTHER READING

Baker, Houston A., Jr., *Blues, Ideology, and Afro-American Literature, A Vernacular Theory*. Chicago: U of Chicago P, 1984.

Baldwin, James. *Notes of a Native Son*. 1949. London: Corgi, 1969.

Bass, George Houston, ed. *Selected Poems of Langston Hughes*. 1959. New York: Vintage Classics, 1987.

Crouch, Stanley. *Don't the Moon Look Lonesome, A Novel in Blues and Swing*. New York: Pantheon, 2000.

Ellison, Ralph. *Invisible Man*. 1952. London: Nicholls, 1976.

Ellison, Ralph. *Juneteenth*. New York: Random House, 1999.

Gaines, Ernest J. *In My Father's House*. 1978. New York: Vintage, 1992.

Gates, Henry Louis, Jr., and Nellie McKay, eds. *The Norton Anthology of African American Literature*. New York: Norton, 1997.

Hurston, Zora Neale. *Their Eyes Were Watching God*. 1937. Chicago: U of Illinois P, 1978.

Jones, Gayl. *Liberating Voices, Oral Tradition in African American Literature*. Cambridge: Harvard UP, 1991.

Marshall, Paule. *Praisesong for the Widow*. New York: Plume, 1983.

Montgomery, Maxine Lavon, ed. *Conversations with Gloria Naylor*. Jackson: UP of Mississippi, 2004.

Morrison, Toni. *Playing in the Dark, Whiteness and the Literary Imagination* (1992). New York: Vintage, 1993.

Morrison, Toni. *Jazz*. 1992. New York: Vintage, 2004.

Morrison, Toni. *Beloved*. 1987. New York: Vintage, 1997.

Morrison, Toni. *Song of Solomon*. 1977. New York: Penguin, 1987.

Murray, Albert. *Train Whistle Guitar*. 1974. New York: Vintage, 1998.

Naylor, Gloria. *Mama Day*. 1988. New York: Vintage, 1993.

Naylor, Gloria. *Bailey's Café*. 1992. New York: Vintage, 1993.

Taylor-Guthrie, Danielle, ed. *Conversations with Toni Morrison*. Jackson: UP of Mississippi, 1994.

Wilson, Sondra Kathryn, ed. *The Crisis Reader, Stories, Poetry, and Essays from the N.A.A.C.P.'s* Crisis *Magazine*. New York: Modern Library, 1999.

Karine Bligny

Terry McMillan accepts the award for outstanding literary work, fiction, for *Getting to Happy* at the 42nd NAACP Image Awards in Los Angeles, 2011. (AP/Wide World Photos)

Terry McMillan

Literary icon and pop culture figure Terry McMillan was born on October 18, 1951 in Port Huron, Michigan. McMillan has received national acclaim as the author of best-selling novels: *Waiting to Exhale* (1992), *How Stella Got Her Groove Back* (1996), *Disappearing Acts* (1989), *Getting to Happy* (2010), *Mama* (1994), and *A Day Late and a Dollar Short* (2004). McMillan, the oldest of five siblings and witness to domestic violence, found refuge in education. Her mother often worked two jobs as a domestic and an auto factory worker, but maintained high academic expectations for all of her children. McMillan fulfilled those expectations by graduating from the prestigious University of California at Berkeley. Prior to that, McMillan's family life profoundly influenced her as a writer; moreover, her parents' divorce undeniably impacted her worldview, and quite possibly influenced her depiction of black male characters in her novels.

Her novels *Mama, Waiting to Exhale,* and *Getting to Happy* are peppered with unredeemable black male characters, who often serve as the major antagonist. One could argue that her parents' divorce and the absence of her father shaped her view of male and female relationships, and that perspective was frequently expressed in her literary works. In her other novels, black females tend to be the stronger sex and black males the weaker one, as illustrated in *A Day Late and a Dollar Short, Waiting to Exhale,* and *How Stella Got Her Groove Back.* Despite the absence of their father or perhaps because of it, McMillan's mother instilled strength, self-reliance, and determination in all of her children. These qualities were later conceptualized in the female characters in McMillan's novels, who are generally the protagonist, again demonstrating how her upbringing has influenced her creative works.

After completing her secondary education in Port Huron and earning a bachelor's degree in journalism from the University of California at Berkeley, McMillan continued to follow her mother's dictates and pursued a master's of fine arts degree at Columbia University. McMillan further distinguished herself as a visiting professor at two other well-known universities: Stanford University and the University of Wyoming. She also served as a tenured professor at the University of Arizona–Tucson while writing her *New York Times* bestseller *Waiting to Exhale.* Although McMillan found fulfillment in lecturing, she found even greater fulfillment and success as a writer.

In her novels, Terry McMillan, the quintessential everywoman, reveals the complex internal struggle of the individual woman caught between society's projection of the ideal woman and a woman's own emotional reality. McMillan's language, symbols, and characterizations do more than reflect the experience of group life: They create it. McMillan's influence on popular culture and African American contemporary literature is realized in her promotion of the independent, intellectual middle-class African American woman. These women present as a "viable racial subject that becomes a regularized norm that has been recited to the degree that they are recognizable; it is the very repetition of these acts that makes it seem as if the identity being expressed is natural" (Ehlers 155). McMillan purposefully creates recognizable characters to weave her fictional narratives into the lives of her respondent readers. This act proves significant because it advances issues specific to contemporary women rather than those issues representative of a postmodern era in which contemporary women cannot add testimony. Despite lingering, historical stereotypes of the black woman, McMillan rewrites the norm, and according to Ehlers, "norms can be reworked, but pure resistance is impossible" (155). McMillan's characters explicate the truth of Ehlers's argument. Her characters present as nurturing mothers and highly educated, successful career women, yet they each wrestle with their identities, which are firmly rooted in American culture. Middle-class, 30-something *Waiting to Exhale* characters Savannah, a senior underwriter, Bernadine, a former real estate controller, Robin, a high-powered executive, and Gloria, a salon owner, wrestle with their reality and ideologized notions of a perfect life, complete with the perfect man, perfect relationship, and perfect marriage. In contrast, divorced, 40-something, *How Stella Got her Groove Back* character Stella confronts societal stereotypes and taboos and unexpectedly finds personal happiness and fulfillment in her relationship with a younger man, Winston Shakespeare. Similarly, in the *Waiting to Exhale* sequel *Getting to Happy,* mature, 50-something characters Savannah, Bernadine, Gloria, and Robin have experienced life and its unexpected joys and misfortunes, and make a concerted effort to get back to happy.

Terry McMillan's female characters share common threads of existence, persistence, strength, and presence, despite the divergent stereotypical idealizations of African American women. McMillan depicts those reworkings in her novels and invites reader response, which allows McMillan to talk back to her readers in "speech which usually must be written (in order to become history), that transcends and transforms the barriers of race, class, and sex to address the world" (Wallace 19). McMillan's talk back lends an authentic authorial voice to her novels. And for McMillan, the construct of the perfect middle-class African American woman allows for "transformative practices... ones that alter or rework the conventional injunctions of any given identic position" (Ehlers 155). Consequently, Terry McMillan's diverse characterizations dispel the myth of the powerless African American woman; it is through her silent self-knowledge, fortitude, and strength that she is able to reject current ideologies and past presupposition of womanhood.

Fittingly, Terry McMillan's fictitious representation of the contemporary African American woman has contributed to new images of the African American woman and her presence in relation to others in both popular culture and contemporary literature. The new image of the contemporary black woman in literature is vastly different from her earlier 19th-century depictions. Her transformation into the new contemporary middle-class black woman has provided others with content in which to create and promote new stereotypes. The new contemporary middle-class black woman, known as an IBW (Independent Black Woman), is now cast as a strong, insensitive, demanding, no nonsense, bitchy, man-bashing spinster; these stereotypes are perceived as both refractory and fallacious. McMillan's novels are worthy of literary and interdisciplinary discussion in the examination of the contemporary middle-class black woman, specifically, how her being and her womanhood both coincide with and subvert notions of identity preservation within 21st-century American literature. Professor Paulette Richards agrees that McMillan's works are of great literary significance and her novels "stand at an important juncture in the evolution of African American literature" (20). Furthermore, "They provide a body of popular fiction to nourish the creative imagination along with the oral traditions" (20). While Richards asserts that McMillan's novels are important to the literary world, few scholars have addressed McMillan's novels in a serious, sustained manner because of their popular elements. Representing a new subgenre, popular black women's literary fiction, *Waiting to Exhale, How Stella Got Her Groove Back,* and *Getting to Happy* are uniquely different from other African American literary fiction and are of significant literary and cultural importance.

First, it is important to recognize the ambiguity of the term *pop culture.* Since the concept of culture is relative and subject to multiple interpretations, it is doubtful that there exists a single agreed-upon definition of what society considers popular. However, to limit the discussion to understanding the influence of literary icon Terry McMillan, the term must be simplified. To understand the influence of Terry McMillan and her fiction on pop culture and African American popular fiction, a Lipsitz deterministic pop culture framework is utilized. According to George Lipsitz, "pop culture can be defined as all cultural artifacts or expressions that speak to both residual memories of the past and emergent hopes for the future, which allows consumers of pop culture to move in and out of subject positions in a way that allows the same message to have widely varying meanings at the point of reception" (13). Even in an adoption of a Lipsitz framework, it is important for readers to remember that popular culture is also inextricably "inscribed with history of political and cultural struggles" (qtd. in Bourdeui). McMillan has benefited from the transformation of whiteness in pop culture, for "a white face is no longer mandatory to make an artist or performer or product 'pop'" (Wynter 37). According to literary critic Leon Wynter, "Popular forms of entertainment (media and literature) are inexorably shifting from what is 'white' to what is 'real'" (37).

Terry McMillan's use of literary conventions such as satire, literal and figurative language, and stream of consciousness, provide agency for McMillan to bridge the "residual memories of the past" (Lipsitz 13) with the collective consciousness of a new intellectual readership. While McMillan does not explicitly make reference to the Harriet Jacobses, A. J. Coopers, or Alice Walkers of the world in her earlier novels, in *Getting to Happy,* she makes subtle didactic references to the past as a means to explicate the black female experiences of the present. *Getting to Happy* is contextually different from her earlier novels in that she specifically makes reference to the past and prolific African American poets like Langston Hughes, Sonia Sanchez, Gwendolyn Brooks, Nikki Giovanni, and Mary Oliver. McMillan's *Getting to Happy* is representative of a mature, spiritually salient Terry McMillan, who recognizes the positive and negative influence of pop culture on African Americans and the African American literary canon. She couples these concerns with residual memories of the past, and in doing so, McMillan solidifies her canonical significance in African American popular fiction, particularly in the black literary world.

Inspired by Zora Neale Hurston, McMillan has created her own reality and has carved a distinct niche in the African American literary canon. For McMillan, the contemporary middle-class black woman is no wishful illusion she is a real life participant in the formation of America, American pop culture, and African American literary fiction. The relationship between black women and society is one of the overarching issues in McMillan's works *Waiting to Exhale, How Stella Got Her Groove Back,* and *Getting to Happy.* McMillan's characters depict a delicate balance between conformity and resistance, falling prey to the ideologies of popular culture and abandoning their disillusionment through reinvestment of the self.

Despite McMillan's growing reputation, some critics argue that her works are terminable, suggesting a temporal value to the literary canon. Those critics contend that her work is not transcendent because her novels are too grounded in popular culture. Themes such as politics or inequality do not occupy space in McMillan's novels, and for this reason, critics contend that her works lack longevity. Again, while McMillan's influence on pop culture literary fiction has been qualified, some critics continue to argue that the canonical significance of Terry McMillan's novels has yet to be evidenced. Critics remark that McMillan's work is centered exclusively in the present, and therefore lacks true literary value and relevancy to past and ongoing black experiences. However, for critics to characterize McMillan's work as terminable is to invalidate the importance of the contemporary black woman's experience, a distinctively new black experience that is not grounded in a slave-master genre or struggle for civil rights. Manning Marable, in "Living Black History: Resurrecting the African American Intellectual Tradition," identifies three standard characteristics of African American literary work of canonical significance: "It is 'descriptive,' presenting the reality of black life and experience from the point of view of black people; it has been 'corrective,' a concerted attempt to challenge and to critique racism and stereotypes that have been ever present in the main discourse of white academic institutions; it has been 'prescriptive,' an intellectual orientation which consistently connected scholarship with collective struggle, social analysis with social transformation" (7). McMillan confronts each of the aforementioned elements, yet her approach is distinctly different from those of Alice Walker and Toni Morrison.

McMillan's *Waiting to Exhale,* depicting a new black experience, is recognized as a central text in the African American literary canon, due in part to its unprecedented success in the literary marketplace. McMillan markets her work as a competing and complementary discourse, a discourse that seeks both to adjudicate competing claims and witness common concerns. Fabrication of the contemporary black woman requires reexamination, recycling, and rewriting the "conventional and canonical stories as well as revising the conventional generic forms that convey these stories" (Henderson 903). McMillan rewrites the "conventional story and dismisses its generic form" (903) in favor of a uniquely different reader experience. J. C. Charles, author of "Desire, Agency, and Black Subjectivity," in his analysis of Robert Reid-Pharrs's *Once You Go Black: Choice Desire and the Black American Intellectual*, asserts that African Americans have always made the conscious choice to self-identify, despite some African American authors and critics' decision to limit their discussions to the influence of the white patriarchal society on the African and African American and Africans and African Americans' lack of agency. The critical importance of Charles's observation reveals "the undecided concept of black subjectivity" (270), for Charles asserts:

> Black identity and culture are not simply thrust whole-cloth onto a passive "African" mass by an all-powerful white culture. Nor is it mystically transmitted from ancient African beginnings. Instead, Black American individuals have always on some level chosen, or at least negotiated, the nature of their affiliation with the communal—the race and the nation—and in this choosing they make and remake the communal. (270)

Despite Charles's observation, some African American authors have found it necessary to establish a certain level of stability, and therein sublimate black identity and the black experience. McMillan's aim to supplant the black identity and the black experience has proven a source of contention for other authors. McMillan's work is representative of the undecided concept, and this allows her greater narrative space and affords her a larger readership. McMillan's everywoman archetype represents the familiar in pop culture and that motif has solidified her pop status.

McMillan's Stella Payne in *How Stella Got Her Groove Back* and Bernadine Harris, Robin Stokes, Gloria Matthews, and Savannah Jackson in *Waiting to Exhale* represent the familiar in pop culture, insomuch as McMillan's readers catapulted her to stardom and her novels remained on the *New York Times* bestseller list for 38 consecutive weeks. This was a feat not accomplished by any other contemporary African American author. In pop culture America, consumers have demonstrated their affinity for brand-name items, symbols of quality, dependability, and superior craftsmanship, or items with which they are familiar or want to be associated. Representing the familiar, McMillan's brand of literature "is a form of cultural expression and a useful source for understanding how a group of people perceives itself and the world around it at a specific period in time" (Falola and Agwuele 13). McMillan's novels also serve as "products of a specific culture, literary works frequently containing the cultures' ideologies and values, and expressed either implicitly or explicitly within the themes the authors employ" (Falola and Agwuele 13). Popular culture images such as those depicted by Terry McMillan emerge as particularly powerful agents in time and space, as were images depicted by Toni Morrison and Alice Walker, which are representative of another era.

McMillan writes about her heritage, her identity, her story, her essence, echoing Barbara Christian's argument, "if black women don't say who they are other people will and say it badly for them" (xii). McMillan realizes that writing is a necessary mechanism in foregoing one's own epistemology of what it means to be a black woman in America, a necessary mechanism to create communal change. By examining the plight of women and their relationships to others, as she does in *Waiting to Exhale* and *Getting to Happy,* McMillan revalues the context of the self through vocalized and nonvocalized dialogue. McMillan's pop culture novels are artifacts that have been commodified and commercialized, like testimony-driven reality television. McMillan's novels are highly autobiographical and representative of the African American tradition of testifying and signifying. McMillan testifies the truth, and therein, embraces crisis exclusive to women and those who are privy to the black experience while simultaneously using tactics of resistance, exploring provocative subjects such as black sexuality and romance, the Black Aesthetic, hidden meaning and messaging in black lexicon, slang, and African American Vernacular English (AAVE).

McMillan's tactics of resistance serve as an inspiration for many new contemporary writers. Her characterizations of the educated upper-middle-class African American protagonist has influenced contemporary African American authors, like E. Lynn Harris, Zane, Omar Tyree, and Susan Miller, who, like McMillan, found success in publishing authentic characterizations of African Americans and for their audacity to confront community taboos, particularly the black community's taboos such as homosexuality, elitism, and erotica. McMillan's style has inspired new contemporary African American novelists who have found sanctuary and narrative space in which to reexamine stereotypes, the black identity, black sexuality and romance, the Black Aesthetic, and new constructs of the black family and community in contemporary literature.

Not all of the issues that McMillan presents are uniquely representative of African American culture, but can apply to mainstream American culture as well. Terry McMillan is successful in creating contemporary identities to which other Americans can relate, namely those of educated, middle-class African American women. While this is true, her aim to redefine the contemporary African American woman is not limited to her novels, but resonates in the media and American culture in general. This cross-cultural acceptance accounts for the marketability and success of her novels and film adaptations, like *Waiting to Exhale* and *How Stella Got Her Groove Back.* As a consequence of McMillan's relatable characters, her popularity as a novelist is acknowledged by a universal audience, once again evidenced by her time on the *New York Times* bestseller list. The publication of her novels and screenplay adaptations have allowed McMillan a worldwide outlet in which to construct new images of sexually liberated womanhood. This concept, in some of her novels, was the precursor to the popular television shows *Girlfriends,* in which single, sexually liberated black women endeavor to find the perfect mate, and *Sex in the City,* in which sexually liberated white women explore their independence. Consequently, McMillan's influence on pop culture literature is undeniable and the significance of her novels in the African American literary canon is qualified by its prescriptive and corrective intentionality.

In *Waiting to Exhale,* Savannah ritualistically recites the contemporary black woman's national anthem, "I can take care of myself." McMillan's middle-class women are financially independent, mobile, educated, career-oriented elitists who present with dual consciousness. Former It girls and Boston University graduates Savannah, Bernadine, Robin, and Gloria are financially independent, narcissistic women who embody pop culture consumerism. Savannah, a business controller, Robin, a public relations executive, Bernadine, an entrepreneur, and hair salon owner Gloria are representative of McMillan's middle-class black women. McMillan meticulously provides readers with the distinction between other black women and the middle-class black woman. Thematically, they are in this life together; however, McMillan is compelled to share the inimitable experiences of the middle-class black woman in pop culture America, an experience markedly different than those of other blacks.

McMillan is suggestively unapologetic in her depictions of the financially independent middle-class woman. Her characters are embodiments of pop culture consumerism in that they find value in their career-earning potential, their license to be highly discriminating when it comes to possible suitors, where they live, and how they live. By contrast, Savannah's Mama is representative of the other blacks. Other blacks are generally not self-sufficient or discriminating when pursing relationships with the opposite sex. The distinction McMillan makes between the middle class and others suggests that other blacks are not confined to ghettos; rather, their otherness stems from a predisposed state of mind. The other blacks, like Savannah's Mama and sister, Shelia, are devout members of the patriarchal society. And, as devout members, Mama and Shelia seem pledged to maintain relationships with men in order to receive validation as women within the society, maintain their financial dependency on the men or other agency, and promote dissension within the larger black community if the aforementioned conditions are not met.

A key characteristic of McMillan's middle-class woman is mobility. Her notion of mobility is not limited to the physical body, but extends to mobility of the mind. Her middle-class characters are both physically mobile and psychologically mobile. Other black women like Shelia and Mama have limited psychological mobility and virtually nonexistent physical mobility, as Savannah observes. They are trapped physically and financially, so they stay trapped mentally. In a conversation between Savannah and Shelia, Shelia remarks, "this will make the fourth city you've lived in fifteen years" (4) in comparison to Shelia's one, Pittsburgh, suggesting mobility is a privilege exclusive to the middle-class black woman. U.S. labor statistics suggests a direct correlation between education and mobility; educated individuals advance at a progressively higher rate than their undereducated counterparts, therein accounting for their ability to relocate, advance their careers, and benefit from new cultural experiences. Although other blacks maintain an awareness of these statistics, they are culturally brainwashed by the ideologies perpetuated by popular culture and the patriarchal society of which they willingly remain a part. Cultural patriarchic brainwashing is not exclusive to other blacks, but is an inherent part of the black experience. Despite the middle-class black woman's mobility, financial independence, and sentient awareness of sameness and difference both within and outside of her community, she occasionally will buy and invest her stock in popular culture, conforming to the rules of investment and trading at will.

McMillan's knowing thinking middle-class black women are subliminally aware of the historical theme of mobility, an invariable part of the African American oral tradition. Lyrics from Negro spirituals such as "Swing Low, Sweet Chariot" and the slave narratives of Frederick Douglass and Harriet Jacobs are rich with images of movement, both physical and psychological. Generally, most movement depicted in 19th- and 20th-century African American literature served as a form of escapism, whereas 21st-century African American literature generally presents mobility as a form of physical and psychological advancement, a conscious choice to improve one's quality of life. Frequent relocation is not characteristic of many African Americans' lifestyles, but is distinctly representative of the contemporary middle-class African American woman's disposition. McMillan's 36-year-old Savannah remarks that she has lived in Boston and Denver and is relocating to Phoenix, Arizona, signifying the middle-class black woman's increased economic independence and willful abandonment of her family and larger African American community. McMillan's theme of mobility, physical or psychological, is important to maintaining and advancing oral traditions in the African American community and advancing its prescriptive and descriptive relevance in the African American literary canon.

Black middle-class mobility has caused tension between the black middle class and others, both black and white. Within the black community, there is dissension between different classes of African Americans, the ones are who identified as *all that* and who live in predominately white suburbs, and the ones who are in the hood, even though "we are all out here knee-deep together" (*Waiting to Exhale* 32). Stella's dual consciousness, full of contradiction, acknowledges that she is a part of corporate and suburban white America and a migrant in black America, suggesting that the black middle class is both separate and a part of a larger black community. Savannah is keenly aware of the underlying tension in her community; her sister has three kids and doesn't work, and their mother lives in Section 8 housing, getting $407 per month in social security and $104 in food stamps, while Savannah pays a portion of her mother's rent and provides her with additional money each month. And yet, when Savannah confesses she is taking a $12,000 pay cut by accepting a new job in Arizona, she is concerned, like an anxious henpecked husband, that her mother would disapprove of such actions, particularly since she is dependent on Savannah for financial support. Seventeen years of manlessness has caused Savannah's mother to view Savannah as the surrogate man of the house, and she is quite capable of fulfilling those responsibilities: Savannah is financially independent, methodical, and mobile, qualities usually reserved for men, the historic wage earners of the house. McMillan's recurrent theme of change serves to reposition the middle-class black woman in a place of power, permitting her to exert power over others and exercise governance over herself.

Themes of change saturate all of McMillan's novels, and she distinguishes herself from other contemporary writers in that she does not aggregate the black woman's identity, but rather recognizes her complexities, all of her identities, racial, sexual, and social. McMillan is uniquely instrumental in creating authentic contemporary characterizations of the black woman that have been accepted in popular culture and widely adopted in contemporary African American literary fiction. Terry McMillan has mastered art imitating life, and her novels serve as a point of departure from highly romanticized relationships between men, women, and society.

McMillan effortlessly refabricates and reinvests the black woman's image. This reinvestment has increased her stock in popular literary circles and the media, consequently attracting new investors from the publishing world. The new investors welcome McMillan's middle-class African American characters, especially since they have proven to be a valuable commodity in the marketplace. Success by pop culture standards is quantified by one's material possessions and qualified by one's access and use of power. Stella is a woman who makes a six-figure salary, owns her own home and a luxury vehicle, and can take exotic trips on a moment's notice, clear signification of her economic power. Stella is also presented as her own woman, both voiced and voiceless, a state which allows her to peregrinate between the black and the white world.

McMillan is an agent of reconciliation, a subject's ability to come to terms with her surroundings, however imperfect or ideal these surroundings may be. And, as an observer of life, McMillan reveals those imperfections through her characters while simultaneously and effectively satirizing societal stereotypes. In her signature, matter-of-fact tone, McMillan says that she is a woman who is "willing to take action, who is responsible for her own happiness, and who is willing to take risks" (Interview Bookpage), for "when we speak and answer back," according to Christian, "we validate our experiences. We say we *are* important, if only to ourselves" (xii). Even though most of McMillan's protagonists are single and independent, McMillan is careful not to generalize, for she recognizes there are some black women, like Bernadine, who suffer from the "true all American girl" syndrome, whose symptoms include wanting the perfect marriage and 2.5 kids (McMillan, *Exhale* 21). Although McMillan sanguinely speaks for herself, and claims not to speak for all black women, she does provide black professional middle-class woman with a voice, and recognizes her place and struggles in the literary canon.

McMillan's discourse of sexuality "is not a power which 'represses' a 'natural' sexuality" but instead produces effects of power which organize and produce what sexuality is in specific historical and geographical contexts (Foucault 101, qtd. in Hollows 74). McMillan's 21st-century characters are portrayed as women who are keenly aware of their own sexuality and who intentionally and unintentionally romanticize their relationships and sexual encounters. McMillan has repositioned the black woman in a position of power, a stark contrast from the black woman's more oppressive and repressive past. Consequently, Stella's sexual assertiveness and Savannah's anticipatory longings are of particular importance, since McMillan uses the transformative power of sex, intimacy, and sexuality to dismiss the neutrality of the black woman's sexual desire, dismiss stereotypes, and chronicle a new era of female sexuality.

For the black woman, sexuality and romance have always been associated with the body. Images of the violated black female body abound in American literature; images of sex, rape, and abuse are depicted by both black and white writers. Consequently, it is important to recognize the significance of the black female body in pop culture literature. In most cases, control of the body serves as a means to establish authority over others, and more recently, governance of oneself, thus extending the concept of sexuality to move beyond the body to include psychology. While the body often signifies people's place in the world, McMillan is successful in deconstructing sociopolitical constructs of place. According to Oyeronke Oyewumi, "the body is the bedrock on which social order is founded, the body is always in view and on view, and invites a gaze, a gaze of difference and differentiation" (164). Early African American writers did not promote differentiation of the black female body, for black female bodies shared the experience of victimization, objectification, and exploitation that served to unite and vilify their presence, their existence. Early American literature promoted a myriad of stereotypes about the black woman, most of which placed emphasis on the black female body. As a result of patriarchal manufactured stereotypes, many African American authors made great effort to neutralize black female sexuality; as a result, African American literature was virtually void of romance and love and fertile with sexual violence. Images of black romance and intimacy, sexual awareness, and Black Aesthetics have changed as a result of Terry McMillan's 21st-century romantic realism.

McMillan's novels explore the boundaries of African American womanhood, and she challenges some of the most confining structures defining female sexuality. McMillan's thinking, knowing, articulate African American female characters, like Stella Payne and Savannah Jackson, are not passive, and are in control of their bodies, signifying self-governance. As symbols of sexual freedom and empowerment, Savannah and Stella exercise their female power over others and their relationships with them, no matter how loving or licentious they are. McMillan's representation of the empowered African American woman has given rise to black love and romance, which has subsequently influenced other contemporary writers like Zane and Jerome Dickey, to further advance the sexuality and sensuality of the middle-class black woman, exploring her place in exotic and erotic fiction.

McMillan's intention "seems to be to remove the stigma, the mark of shame from the collective flesh of her race" (Putzi 3). To remove this stigma, there must be the acknowledgment that intimacy, the act of evidencing close personal relations, can exist between the black man and black woman:

> He is standing there so tall and beautiful and as he walks over toward me I smell his Escape and feel my shoulders drop and when he put his arms around me I feel so relieved so grateful that he is live and not Memorex anymore and I put my arms around him and clutch him tight because I want him to know how happy I am to feel him see him smell him … and he presses those Easy-Bake oven lips against mine and I absorb them as long as I can stand it and then I back away. (McMillan, *How Stella* 337)

After Winston's arrival in the United States, he and Stella share an intimate moment at the airport. Winston's gentle embrace of Stella conveys the power of black love through his protective feelings toward her, while her arm tightly clutched around him signifies her physical and emotional attachment, her dependency upon him for strength, comfort, and emotional security. Although Stella is not fully convinced of a happily ever after, she does savor the moment, a moment that McMillan captures with sensory details that evoke all of the senses, suggesting a close relationship between the two characters that resonates with readers.

McMillan's characters, middle-class black women, do not entirely invest in the notion of the perfect ending. Distinctively different from popular Harlequin Romance novels, McMillan's heroes are fallible and her heroines are not in distress. Her male characters present as severely flawed heroes with few redeeming qualities. McMillan's romantic realism is a negotiation between women's expectations, previous experiences, and obligatory optimism for future happiness. McMillan's characters are keenly aware of the emotional investment required to maintain relationships, and therefore they maintain psychological distance from prospective suitors. McMillan's depiction of black romance serves to redefine the contemporary African American woman's identity in relation to herself and her significant other.

The novel *How Stella Got Her Groove Back,* set in Northern California, captures the complex taboo relationship between characters Stella, a successful older woman, and Winston, her younger beau. It is through this very construct that McMillan influences change in contemporary American literature, particularly African American literature. The courtship between Stella Payne and Winston Shakespeare is presented in a first-person stream of consciousness and that invites the reader into Stella's world, full of insecurities, uncertainties, skepticism, and hope. McMillan pioneered the expression of what a woman wants, the hope of meeting the perfect man who makes her lips tremble, her breasts throb, who makes her wet with anticipation, and who can take her worries away (McMillan, *How Stella* 11). McMillan made it possible for new contemporary African American writers like Zane and Jerome Dickey to create a new genre: black erotica. Like McMillan, Zane's use of first-person stream of consciousness in her novel *Afterburn* draws the reader into Roxi's mind and takes him on an adventure in eroticism, experimentation, and sexual fulfillment. McMillan's work is significantly important to the African American literary canon, for she has reaffirmed the black woman's presence as a woman and as a sexual being, therein contributing to the transformation and uplifting of her identity.

Stella and Winston's waltz-like courtship, three steps forward and three steps back, provides readers with a view of the complexities of contemporary dating. McMillan dispels the notion of the perfect courtship in favor of an authentic, loving, multilayered, conflict-ridden relationship between the black woman and black man. "In regaining her virginity," so to speak, McMillan's Stella is unreserved in telling Winston how she feels about him; she finds him refreshing in that "he is still fascinated and overwhelmed by things," and he "makes her feel good about being who she is" (306). He is enthralled with her beauty, the sound of her voice, her smile, her kisses, her very essence. Unlike some early American and African American authors, McMillan meticulously humanizes her male and female characters, depicting all of their faults, uncertainty, hope, truths, and love. Appealing to her readers' complex lives, McMillan, filled with certainty and indecision, like Stella, speaks truth, the truth that she has fallen in love with Winston despite their age difference, feels like herself when she is with him, and contends with the scrutiny of others.

Terry McMillan's works are excellent examples of socioculturally conscious texts in that, unlike many of the novels by 20th-century female authors, her works are anchored in society and the stability of her characters, while simultaneously exploring the dichotomy of dependence and independence in her characters' relationships. Terry McMillan's penchant for pairing spoken discourse and silent thought within her novels is revealed through her use of lexicon, theme, symbolism, and consciousness.

Writing about Stella's temporal shame, McMillan recalls her visit to a nudist beach in Jamaica, where she covers her breasts with her hands, but in another instance, sets them free, squeezes them, and turns around and smiles, as if to hearten the "gaze" of the white man (*How Stella* 109). Stella's vulnerability to the gaze of others is temporal, for in a calculated act of rebellion and assertion of her womanhood, Stella invites the gaze, superimposing her black sexuality on pop culture. The black female characters manifested in McMillan's novels are representative of the contemporary woman's difference; they are atypical women who are vocal, independent, willful, complex, and contradictory. Although there is no all-representative model of the new black woman, McMillan deploys politically neutral archetypes and icons as a strategy for rehabilitating and representing late 20th-century African American identities; these women reclaim their individuality, maintain access to power, wrest control of their body, and by extension their selfhood, from the overarching ideology of group identity.

Pop culture once associated sexual deviance and perversion with the black woman and man. The rhetoric of black intellectual inferiority served to promote black stereotypes relative to the body, that of the loose woman and the well-endowed black man. To counter the misconceptions of promiscuity, African American authors avoided testifying to the sexual awareness, sexual desire, and sexual assertiveness of the black woman. Contemporary writers, starting with Zora Neale Hurston and Toni Morrison, are more reserved in revealing the black woman's sexuality, but Terry McMillan is more forthcoming, more explicit in revealing her characters' sexuality and sexual desire. As a part of the sexual revolution, Terry McMillan draws upon her own life-changing experiences to promote themes of independence and liberation. Contemporary authors like McMillan provide pop culture with strong, outspoken black women, and her sexually liberated characters Savannah and Stella provide readers with uncensored insight into the black middle-class woman's sexuality and desire.

McMillan acknowledges an awareness of past ideologies of African American women as wives, mothers, and slaves to societal expectations and imposed cultural norms. In protest of these presuppositions, McMillan creates iconic characters such as Stella, Bernadine, Savannah, Robin, and Gloria, who allow her greater narrative space in which to write beyond stereotypical and past ideological images of the African American woman. Despite McMillan's successful commodification of the contemporary black woman, this idyllic existence is disputed by critics who classify McMillan's characters as bossy, demanding, atypical man bashers, yet another stereotype that serves to neutralize their sexuality. While McMillan does not consider herself a man basher, feminist critic Layli Phillips contends that a black male-bashing attitude only perpetuates popular media sensationalization of black life grounded in the myth of a black gender war (85). Though *Waiting to Exhale* characters like Bernadine, Savannah, Robin, and Gloria may be viewed as strong, determined women, they also display their insecurities and vulnerabilities, which contradicts their bossy, man-basher image.

In "Cultural Mulatto," Terry McMillan suggests that African American women can be strong, vulnerable, insecure, sensual, and independent around-the-way girls in the 21st century, similar to the popularized female images in *Girl Friends and Soul Food* and distanced from images of victimization like those presented in *Push* by Sapphire and *For Colored Girls* by Tyler Perry (Ellis 235). McMillan is keenly aware of her associations and disassociations with society, for as a "cultural mulatto," she is one who does not forget that despite her ability to communicate and borrow from white culture, she does not have to please both the white and black worlds, but only herself (Tudorica 8). To further authenticate and empower the black woman, McMillan establishes the African American female character as a sexual being rather than a sexual object:

I've been divorced now for almost three years and haven't been on a legitimate date in almost a year even though I have a number to call when I just have to have some sex even though it's not passionate but purely maintenance-oriented sex and thank God he's married because I wouldn't want him any other way and these last few months have been tough because he has turned into such a lazy @#$* and he is pissed at me for not returning his calls. (McMillan, *How Stella* 40)

McMillan utilizes stream of consciousness to illustrate Stella's sexual awareness. She evokes themes of independence, power, and self-governance as Stella remarks that she is in need of sex for her own gratification, and when in need, she wills it. McMillan transposes gender roles; Stella, in an authorial voice, readily admits she is sleeping with a married man of whom she has no further interests other than sex; she doesn't reveal any emotional attachment. She presents as a liberated woman, rejecting fake courtly courtesies in favor of objectifying her lover, for she knows the number to call for sex, yet chooses not to return her lover's calls. Stella's bravado is revealed in the critique of her lover's sexual performance, an unfathomable feat in late 19th- and early 20th-century literature, with the exception of Zora Neale Hurston's Janie in *Their Eyes Were Watching God*. Stella's action, however, begs the question: Is sleeping with a married man really liberating or independent? This feeds into the belief that black women must share men or be hypercompetitive. In theory, she could have the same relationship with a single man and maintain more control over the relationship. However, the notion of sharing a man is not a new phenomenon, for the black slave woman and her white mistress regularly shared a white master. The legacy of slavery inscribed on the black woman has resulted in her need for liberation, and McMillan is cognizant of this fact and creates independent black women who subscribe to their own level of engagement with their male counterparts.

True to her narrative voice and matter-of-fact tone, McMillan depicts women as sexual beings in favor of portraying men as sexual objects. McMillan writes, "all I was doing was trying to preserve my right to my own self-image, but I am here to be whoever I am" (Interview Winfrey). Like her unapologetic characters, McMillan finds satisfaction in revealing life's truths and her audience is favorably responsive to those revelations. McMillan's testimonial of life's truths, as characteristic of the African American tradition, is significant, for Stella is an embodiment of the black woman's dueling personas: woman as a sexual being and woman as a black lady. McMillan's phrase, "I just have to have some," places Stella in a precarious position—she is both in a position of power and moral decadence. The tension is of great canonical importance because it speaks directly to the reader and allows the reader to subjectify her position. Popular culture manufactures life truths for mass consumption, and Terry McMillan is influential in its production of contemporary black sexuality and liberation.

The sexual assertiveness of McMillan's characters presents as controversial in the black community and in contemporary African American literary fiction. Although the topic of white female sexuality has found narrative space, there remains limited discourse about the black woman's sexuality. The literary discourse that is present provides readers a limited scope of black female sexuality, and yet, when it is presented, discussion is highly exaggerated, unnaturally reserved or limited to sexual perversion. Noted sex therapist and professor of psychiatry and biobehavioral sciences at the University of California at Los Angeles (UCLA), Dr. Gail E. Wyatt, finds that "sexuality is still a taboo subject for most people" (67), but although sexuality remains a taboo subject, stereotypes about black female sexuality abound. Through Dr. Wyatt's curiosity and interest in black female sexuality, her research revealed that the data did not support the myth of the black woman's sexual appetite. Dr. Wyatt's data reported that 56 percent of the black women studied had only one sexual partner from the time they initiated sexual intercourse until age 17; whereas only 36 percent of white women reported a long-term relationship during adolescence. Additionally, the study showed "African American women were less likely to have participated in multiple-partner sex than White women" (Wyatt 68). To write is to write or rewrite history, and McMillan's contemporary characters serve this purpose. Her foray into women's sexuality serves to delineate issues central to society, issues of sexism, ageism, and objectivism. But again, in the case of Stella, she is sharing a man, which feeds into a newer stereotype.

McMillan rejects manufactured symbols of purity and pure womanhood. She mocks the very concept of such an artificial state of being through the exchange of dialogue between Stella and her sister Angela, where Stella refers to Angela as Mrs. Cleaver. She is making reference to the ideological sitcom matriarch, the quintessential white lady, June Cleaver from *Leave It to Beaver*. In the 1950s and 1960s, June Cleaver embodied the perfect woman: She was a domestic, dutiful wife and mother who lacked economic independence, sexuality, voice, or presence of her own, and her identity was crafted by a patriarchal society. McMillan's characters are truly authentic in that McMillan parodies the life of the historically subservient dutiful black lady, quasi–June Cleaver, Angela, with that of Stella, the liberated, empowered 21st-century woman, to explicate the myriad of black identity.

"The Black lady," according to Dr. Lisa B. Thompson, "is so morally upright she is almost inhuman. It's time to break the mold" (3). McMillan's novelistic realism stands in agreement with Thompson, for McMillan's characters do not deny their sexual agency in favor of a more confining, restrictive identity," to do so would "merely add to the litany of misrepresentation" (Thompson 10). McMillan's authenticity has influenced other African American women writers to write more realistic, assertive, and particularly sexually assertive, reflexive characterizations of women. Having at her disposal language as the main medium, McMillan decides to focus on its ability to generate new events and perspectives. This operation amounts to setting free the immense capacities of language to freely associate—and thus redefine, which ultimately accounts for McMillan's nonimitative style. McMillan's literary style, however, is inspired by black writers such as Zora Neale Hurston, Toni Morrison, and

Alice Walker, authors who have no reserve in exploring the depths of the African American experience in nontraditional ways.

In early literature, black women were characterized as voiceless, both within society and within their relationships. Often objectified, the black female character was subjected to the injustices of a patriarchal society, a society that did not allow women to have control over themselves or their level of engagement with others. In Alice Walker's *The Color Purple,* Celie, the main character, is subjected to the abuses of her stepfather and husband, thereby rendering her voiceless. Celie's "sistah-girl" relationship with Sugg Avery gives her the courage to reject her oppressive state. Celie understands her role as the perfect obedient wife, resigning herself to being a submissive domestic, caretaker, and concubine, a state that McMillan identifies as unsustainable. Similarly, Angela "handed her entire soul over to Kennedy, her husband, for safe keeping when she married him; he is only the second man she has ever slept with" (*How Stella Got Her Groove Back* 22) unlike Stella, who identifies her lovers, Chad, Nathaniel, and Dennis, suggesting a possible army of former lovers. McMillan presents Angela as the foil to contemporary women like Stella, who once, like Angela believed marriage could be the "end of the rainbow," only to discover that "something is inherently wrong with the whole notion" (*How Stella Got Her Groove Back* 22). McMillan's characters, like modern-day women, have higher expectations of their male counterparts than ladies of previous generations, insomuch that when their expectations are not met, they find the relationship intolerable and sever the relationship or divorce. Stella's financial independence possibly accounts for her inability to compromise and her inability to relinquish her own identity, not as a wife, but as a "fancy smancy analyst who makes a shit load of money" (*How Stella Got Her Groove Back* 16). McMillan's use of language and strong sentiment casts Stella in a male-gendered role rather than that of an obedient, compromising wife.

Popular sentimental novels of the 19th and early 20th centuries featured the "perfect black lady," a woman committed to maintaining patriarchal values and whose identified "prime objective is to obtain a husband and then keep him pleased, duties focused entirely on the bearing and rearing of heirs and caring for the household, marital 'duties that wear you out'" (*How Stella* 11). Stella's younger married sister, Angela, has decided to play the part of the dutiful, "predictable," "perfect lady." Angela's "worship of her husband" represents an antiquated ideology, an ideology that even Angela's mother does not buy into anymore. Angela and Stella's mother, the mature woman, recognizes the time for change and suggests that her daughters should "never let a man run the whole show; never let him know how much money you got and keep some of your business to yourself" (*How Stella* 21). In reality, today's middle-class woman is self-sufficient and financially independent, with a business of her own. Although stereotypes do not reflect or represent reality, as illustrated by Walker's Ms. Celie, stereotypes do function as a disguise or mystification of objective social relations; McMillan's novels not only serve to demystify ideologies of African American womanhood and such women's relationships with others but act as a means by which to explicate issues central to the human condition, issues that transcend culture.

Pop culture's preoccupation with perfection—the perfect house, perfect life, and perfect marriage—has placed the perfect body at the center of controversy. Even the Commodores' lyrics to "Brickhouse" promote contradictory images of beauty, for being "built like an amazon," a tall, strong and often masculine woman warrior, and body measurements of "36–24–36" represent two distinctly different body types. Statistics show that the average woman is a size 12; her waist circumference is 27 inches and she weighs 164.7 pounds. Furthermore, black women only make up 12.9 percent of the U.S. female population. These data suggest that white Americans do not epitomize their own ideological creations (Centers for Disease Control and Prevention). McMillan's characters confront society's contradictory images of beauty, an issue relative to all women, but particularly black women.

Beauty, typically defined by white society, with the white woman setting the standard, is reconceptualized by McMillan who even takes a jab at the white woman and "her breasts that are the same size as her stomach" (*How Stella* 168) and "who envies the black woman," who again serves as the object of the white man's desire (*How Stella* 168). In a mix of contradiction, McMillan uses objectification and subjectification to inform the reader of the contradictory messages of beauty that bombard society. Stella is keenly aware of the standard of beauty established by society. She fights against it (talking critically about white women) but falls prey to it as well (plastic surgery and insecurities). She takes pride in her appearance but has been made to feel insecure because of the impossibility of achieving the standards that society in general has established. To Stella, society says the white woman is the epitome of beauty, but here she is with sagging breasts, a big gut, trying to bake herself black. Society criticizes the black woman but secretly lusts after her. This has ties to the old slave quarters, where the white wife was treated a like a virgin queen, an object of near worship, but the slave master lusted after the black slaves and used them as sexual objects. It serves as a reminder that the new standard of beauty looks like her, Stella, a shapely, voluptuous tan-skinned woman who presents as another standard of beauty in pop culture and contemporary literature.

Reminiscent of other established authors like Toni Morrison and Alice Walker, McMillan's ability to recall past experiences into present consciousness is extraordinary. Contemplating taking her clothes off "in front of a bunch of old alcoholic-looking white men," Stella rethinks her decision, "considering what 'they' used to do to us during slavery and all" (*How Stella* 44). McMillan is a sensitive critic of society, but her approach to it is almost exclusively through interior consciousness, illustrating McMillan's power with words and the voiceless power of the contemporary African American woman. McMillan's depiction of romance, particularly between characters Stella and Winston in *How Stella Got Her Groove Back* and Savannah and

Kennedy, serve to recycle ideologies of womanhood, thereby fabricating a new sexually liberated woman within contemporary African American fiction.

McMillan's characters are iconic in that they inform society of a new aesthetic, black beauty. McMillan has carved space for black beauty to be defined by black women, an image seemingly void of patriarchal influences and ideologies. Thematically, McMillan's novels propose an alternative way of solving the conflicts between the self and acceptable notions of society. An astute business professional, Stella is plagued with contradictory images of beauty and finds herself both loving and hating her body. At this point, the story captures the typical narration of vexation and uncertainty. What follows is a complete surprise: Instead of engaging society in a war of words or ideology and being victorious or defeated, Stella is presented with the alternative of self-acceptance. In an ironic turn, however, McMillan positions Stella as the symbol of beauty and sets for herself a level of acceptance, through which she reconciles age, gender, and the body. This reconciliation is meant to inspire and empower other writers, particularly African American ones, by challenging ideological ideas of beauty.

Stella fights against perfect ideologies in her observation of ugly white women but falls prey to it as well as demonstrated in her insecurities and her consideration of plastic surgery. She has pride in her appearance, but is frustrated by societal norms. She is especially frustrated because part of the white standard is white skin, which she can never have. It is not that she hates herself or her complexion; rather, society is telling her that she is not the standard (despite the fact that white women tan themselves). This makes her lash out at the ugly white women, pointing out how they are not as attractive as she is, despite their whiteness. McMillan purposefully depicts white women who do not represent their society's aesthetic of beauty, a jab in which McMillan uses pop culture as a means to debunk the beauty myth—an ideology that does not even exist in the white patriarchal society itself.

An image of a younger man and older woman invokes curiosity in pop culture and uncertainty in other communities. In pop culture, the cougar is a woman age 40 or over who dates significantly younger men. McMillan's depiction of the black cougar in *How Stella Got Her Groove Back* resonates with popular culture and the "realities facing mature women, particularly black women, for they are aging, female, and nonwhite in a society defined by youthfulness, patriarchy, and White dominance" (Dickerson and Rousseau 316). Images of the older man and younger woman are normative, whereas images of the mature woman and younger man are seen as atypical. Relationship expert and author of *Cougar: A Guide for Older Women Dating Younger Men*, Valerie Gibson posits "aging isn't so awful"; it is incorrect that "aging is always a dreadful thing and women were supposed to shut down and be invisible and go away and drop off a cliff" (interview). Stella laments the fact she is 42, and yet she cannot articulate what 42 looks like or feels like. And, in an increasingly superficial society, McMillan recognizes and exposes pop culture's conflicted images; Stella is determined to maintain her youthful looks, no matter what her age and no matter what the cost, and yet, ironically, she has reservations about dating a younger man. McMillan places the younger, youthful woman at odds with the older, mature woman. Both are competing for the young, virile Winston Shakespeares of the world, a tension less likely to be revealed in both contemporary American and African American literature but can be found in pop culture. Shifting skillfully between voices and perspectives, McMillan recognizes the black woman's realities and consequently presents pop culture with alternative images of the contemporary black senior woman, for she is physically fit, sexually active, and more spiritually sentient than her younger counterparts.

McMillan directs society to look at itself and consider the implication that such an ideology has for society; Stella recognizes this implication and tries, unsuccessfully, to avoid the hype. Stella is confident in her appearance, but there are these nagging things that she wants to fix in order to reach the unobtainable goal of physical perfection. According to black community standards, Stella and Savannah are attractive women, but they remain dissatisfied with their looks and occupy their time with both admiring and loathing their body. Stella is so preoccupied with her body image, namely her breasts, that she undergoes breast lift surgery. In *Getting to Happy,* McMillan's Savannah not only directs society to reconsider the standard of beauty, but also exposes pop culture's obsession with youthfulness and intolerance of those considered aged. The underlying theme of the story suggests one of sameness, for many blacks and whites have conflicting images and/or messages concerning beauty and the body, and to guard against any single standard of beauty, particularly from the media marketed and broadcast by popular culture. As a writer born before the civil rights era and raised in after the 1960s, McMillan is aware of the trap of dichotomous thinking about race in society; as a result, she chooses issues that relate to all women.

Rita Dandridge credits Terry McMillan with "debunking the beauty myth" (32) in *Waiting to Exhale*. Protagonists Bernadine Harris, Robin Stokes, Savannah Jackson, and Gloria Matthews recognize each other's beauty, and yet lament the fact they do not and will not possess features representative of their European counterparts. Even when the characters are told they are beautiful, they reject the notion that black is beautiful. Black beauty is not an ideology frequently found in contemporary African American literature, and McMillan, a witness to the Black is Beautiful movement, presents the characters' dueling persona and anima through stream of consciousness. As the younger Savannah looks in the mirror, she "thought she looked pretty good" (*Getting to Happy* 10). Isaac, the mature Savannah's love interest and future husband, remarks that she is "absolutely beautiful" (5). Yet, in response, Savannah "blushed brick red because he was lying through his teeth" and she claimed "she was not then, nor will she be even remotely close to beautiful" (5). Like the mature Savannah portrayed in McMillan's *Getting to Happy,* women of all races and ethnicities have experienced poor body image and conflicting images of beauty. Even more so, the contemporary black woman's perception of her body is distinctively animus. And, Savannah remarks, "I'd buy me some new breasts instead of walking around all these years with this big ass and big legs and these little sunny-side-ups on my chest" (15). African American authors of the past inextricably associated the black identity with the body. Black thought, love, beauty, and talk originate from the body, the site where perceptions begin. However, characters soon discover that perfected bodies do not guarantee personal happiness and fulfillment. McMillan's sociocultural consciousness resonates with popular culture, and like her characters, more than half of women in a 2009–2010 *Cosmopolitan* magazine poll reported being dissatisfied with their bodies and considered breast augmentation or another plastic surgery procedure. Unfortunately, society's quest for the perfect body is wrought with the unrealistic expectation of a perfect ending. Skillfully, McMillan further strengthens her relationship with her readers through Bernadine, Robin, Gloria, and Savannah, whose unrealistic expectations align with middle-class audiences.

The *Waiting to Exhale* sisterhood serves as an embodiment of tensions between individual realities and society's expectations. By revealing these tensions, McMillan is able to record the evolution of women, for she believes women evolve with age. Like the characters portrayed in *Waiting to Exhale,* women in their 30s are obsessed with men; on the other hand, women in their 50s, like the characters portrayed in *Getting to Happy,* are concerned with other things according to McMillan (*GMA* interview). The other things McMillan refers to include her personal journey of getting to happy, particularly after her painfully public divorce from spouse Jonathan Plummer. *Getting to Happy* is concerned with the mature woman and her reconciliation of the mind, body, and spirit. In writing *Getting to Happy,* McMillan testifies she lost her center, her identity, based on someone else; and in an epiphany, realized she had to get back to happy. In an interview with *Good Morning America* anchor Robin Roberts, McMillan discussed the novel and asserted that "we all go through our own personal hell that allows us room to recover and reinvent ourselves." And, in a sagacious narrative voice, the reinvented 51-year-old Terry McMillan provides readers with testimony of how 50-year-old Bernadine, Savannah, Gloria, and Robin get to happy. Contrary to popular opinion, McMillan asserts 50 is not the end of the world and issues that seemed important will not be as important as they once were (interview Roberts). Most importantly, McMillan's positioning of the mature woman at the center of narrative discourse is unconventional, thus making all of McMillan's novels, particularly *How Stella Got Her Groove Back* and *Getting to Happy,* of great canonical significance.

Most contemporary women consider discussion about age to be a taboo subject, but the discourse of ageism is central to McMillan's novels. Recent marketing campaigns have promoted images of youthfulness and agelessness, leaving the mature woman with few identifiable pop culture images. Pop culture's inability to categorize or define the look and behavior of the mature

40-something woman has proven problematic, insomuch as such women have been marginalized. Media images of youthfulness and virility or longevity and decline pervade American culture, and like most middle-class Americans, many 40- and 50-something black middle-class women are in a precarious position because they do not definitively belong to one group or the other. Like tweens, adolescents between the ages of 12 and 13, who do not quite identify with young children or young adults, 40-somethings cannot quite identify with those of childbearing age or those of retirement age. McMillan presents the unique dichotomy of the black middle-aged woman in pop culture, and she exposes society's biases against those 40 and over; she counters the notion of the useless, sexually inactive and unattractive, matronly middle-aged woman in favor of a sexually and physically active, attractive, mid-career woman and mother who is optimistic about her future and who clearly has a sense of her own identity.

McMillan finds fault in pop culture's treatment of middle-aged women; however, she is also acutely aware of the image she must maintain in order to fit into the popular culture image and reap the tangible and intangible benefits of a narcissistic, materialistic, image-driven society. She also aims to dispel stereotypes associated with the mature woman, the notion that she is unattractive, unhealthy, overweight, and undesirable:

> I was totally unable to resist those bright yellow luscious orange sweet pink ensembles in the windows of those specialty boutiques where mostly teenagers and young girls in their twenties with high-performance bodies shop but I went in with a young attitude and bought some of the hottest outfits a woman my age could tolerate because in the so-called misses sections of the department stores all they had was that senior citizen type resort wear...with sailboat and starfish appliqués. (*Getting to Happy* 29)

Ageism is apparent in pop culture and McMillan is cognizant of that fact in her observation of clothing marketed for young 20-somethings and clothing marketed for 50-somethings. Bright colors are often associated with youthfulness; whereas the heavily appliquéd misses sportswear signifies the inherent conservatism of the mature woman. McMillan's middle-class, middle-aged black woman is contradictory, for she maintains a young attitude and yet purchases outfits a woman her age can tolerate, suggesting her awareness of society's stereotypes of the middle-aged woman and its manufactured images of acceptability. Pop culture ideologies of the mature woman present her as useless to mainstream society; she is no longer a viable part of the workforce, no longer a viable host for procreation, and the allure of her youthful femininity no longer exists:

> Women over fifty who usually hide under their umbrellas and use number 80 sun block and wear cheap straw hats and loud bathing suits with

flared skirts and they usually have varicose veins and gigantic breasts
and they watch children play in the sand or they stare at young women
with perfect magazine bodies and remember when they used to look like
this...but I am not there yet. (*Getting to Happy* 30)

Most women are concerned with aging and its effects, and even though Mc-
Millan's characters are equally concerned with this, her middle-class, middle-
aged black women find themselves in a unique position in an image-conscious
society. McMillan's middle-aged black women continue to maintain a youthful appearance despite their age, allowing the author narrative space in which
to challenge pop culture images of beauty and aging. McMillan's characters
acknowledge themselves to be physically attractive, and thereby allow themselves to become observers of society's mixed messaging, which identifies the
white woman as *the* standard of beauty, a standard with infinite privisos:
young and white, 20-something and physically fit, well endowed (bosom)
and blonde, attractive and sexually active. Society continues to contradict
itself, negating the presence of the mature white woman in society: the one
who sits under the umbrella, wearing a gaudy bathing suit while showcas-
ing her varicose veins, as if she is invisible. The middle-aged white woman
does exist and McMillan methodically presents the white woman for further
analysis, comparing and contrasting her with the black middle-age woman
whose 40-something-year-old breasts still stand at attention and whose ass, as
Savannah remarks, is her best asset. Physically fit Stella and her lamentation
about detectable cellulite is of a shared concern among most women, but the
contemporary 40-something-year-old white woman's surrender to heavily appliquéd fashions, longing for her youthful past, and defunct sensuality serves
as an epoch to countermand contradictory images of black beauty in popular
culture.

While Brookshas identified the oral tradition as a signifier of African American literary canonical merit (169), McMillan not only makes reference to the
oral traditions of the African American community, but also advances the notion that it is near extinction. Once a distinct signifier of the African American
literary tradition, storytelling is changing. In presenting the evolution of the
oral tradition through her character's stream of consciousness, McMillan's
novel serves as a concerted effort to preserve it. According to a mature Savannah, "times have certainly changed. We're all busy. We don't hangout like we
used to, don't run our mouths on the phone half the night the way we used to,
don't gossip about each other the way we used to...we send email or text"
(*Getting to Happy* 9). McMillan signifies a change in the African American
oral tradition, thereby suggesting that the written word, storytelling, is even
more important to the African American literary world than ever before. Pop
culture, a culture of technology and impersonal relationships, has virtually
abandoned the oral traditions, storytelling, folk tales, and legends of past
generations in favor of a new historical record, email and text messaging.
In the African American literary world, electronic media are a double-edged

sword: They serve to undermine the African American oral tradition and yet also serve as a means in which to recover it, further supporting the notion that stories can and will be told through various means, distinctly different from the traditional.

McMillan's voice has served to rewrite literary history as we know it. In 19th- and 20th-century African American literature, many female novelists' characters not only speak with a voice of strength and determination, but also a voice of victimization. Terry McMillan, in a Time.com interview, rejects the narrative of victimization as an unidimensional approach to the African American experience; McMillan develops her own manner of relating to official history, for she writes her novels as events that "create and rewrite history though the medium of literature" (Time.com interview). As such, McMillan rediscovers the performative power of language, which prevents her from falling into the trap of mimicking or responding in a victimizing voice. In *Mama*, Mildred is subjected to the abuses of her husband, and yet, despite her harsh reality, Mildred is transformed by the experience and presents as more resilient than before. Like McMillan, Sapphire's protagonist in *Push* (1996), Claireece "Precious" Jones, is transformed by her experiences and breaks the cycle of abuse and self-hate. Although Mildred and Precious do not represent educated, middle-class women, they do present as strong women, a unifying quality of all women, particularly African American ones.

Diane Patrick, author of *Terry McMillan: The Unauthorized Biography*, recognizes the effects of McMillan's work on her readers. Patrick remarks that McMillan learned that her books affected her readers in a number of ways, even influencing their relationships with others and providing them with a venue for self-reflection and understanding. Patrick calls McMillan a "fearless and well seasoned interviewer" (148) who uses the coarse street language and smartass attitude that her inner circles already knew. McMillan's reality resonates with readers insomuch as, Patrick remarks, they often responded to McMillan by testifying, "you tell it girl and ain't that the truth" (165). The African American tradition of the testimony is not a new phenomenon; however, McMillan's influence on contemporary African American literary fiction has afforded American culture, particularly African American literary circles, a venue in which to revivify black slang and Black Vernacular English (BVE).

Many critics have praised McMillan for the authentic voice she has given to her characters; however, other critics have lamented the fact that McMillan elected to use three- and four-letter words to add authenticity, seeming street credibility, to her characters. McMillan is successful in commodifying her characters' authenticity through her use of language, for according to Lisa Savan, author of *Slam Dunks and No Brainers: Language and Your Life, The Media, Business, African American Vernacular English*, has undeniably impacted society.

McMillan's lexicon reveals a tension between pop culture mainstream American ideologies and the revalued, refabricated identity of the African American woman, an identity that McMillan purposefully distances from the norm. The norm is identified as an alignment with middle-class white American values and talking white, the use of standardized English. Because of the power of words, McMillan influences society and other literary forms in not only contributing to pop language, but also in revealing the underlying meaning of her word choice. McMillan's characters are in essence bilingual; they are able to talk white and talk black, signifying their dual consciousness. Being both separate and a part of American culture, McMillan's characters navigate the predominately white workplace and neighborhoods while simultaneously maintaining and cultivating the relationships in their own communities. Being bilingual is critical to the middle-class black woman's economic prosperity and continued financial independence. McMillan shows society that the African American female is different in regards to how she positions herself within society. McMillan's characters routinely code switch, talking white, talking black, and using profanity, a universal language.

Because the middle-class black woman is predictable, particularly in literature, she is recognized for her alignment and resemblance to middle-class white women. McMillan presents language as a creative manifestation of the instinct for survival, for if it were not for the language difference, how would McMillan's characters vary from those of other contemporary American female authors? McMillan recognizes her words as a power construct, for her three- and four-letter words symbolize opposition, a means to advance the underlying themes of liberation, opposition, empowerment, and independence.

Antonio Brown asserts it is the intentionality of the speech act that gives the individual power, the power to identify oneself as a person. While many critics have stated that McMillan's works are not intellectually challenging, her works are worthy of intellectual discussions due to the myriad complex issues that McMillan addresses through her characters. The suggestively titled novels *How Stella Got Her Groove Back* and *Waiting to Exhale* chronicle lists of events and provide alternative readings of African American culture, allowing McMillan a certain ethos in promoting the exceptionality of a people—who invented new identities, new dances, new slang, and ultimately new fictional worlds. To advance the notion of the black woman's dual persona, McMillan animates her characters through black talk. McMillan can be credited with contributions to the African American slang and AAVE.

Writers who stand free from stereotypical approaches to culture, race, literature, or music are McMillan's ultimate heroes and companions, the ones with whom she feels solidarity and engages in a complex cultural project. McMillan's nonimitative writing and freedom of mind allow her to blur the boundaries between cultures and race, thereby cross-pollinating them. Moreover, McMillan's writing induces in her readers the desire to read critically and engage in critiquing stereotypical representations that pervade pop culture and mass media. According to Tom Dalzell, "one cannot help but be struck by the powerful influence of African American vernacular on the slang of all 20th century American youth" (258). Author of "Slang and Sociability," Connie Eble calls the black influence on the American language "overwhelming"

(258). Leslie Savan argues that the black vernacular has undeniably influenced pop culture, insomuch as white America has unofficially adopted this quasi-language.

Savan argues that "white people (and not just the young) draw from a black lexicon every day, sometimes unaware of the words origins, sometimes using them because of their origins" (258). Savan cites three ways in which the black vernacular has influenced pop culture: The "language of outsiders has given Americans cool, has affected the broader pop in that black talk has operated as a template for what it means to talk pop in the first place, and… is an important piece of identity-and-image building for individuals and cooperation" (258). McMillan's blockbuster film and book titled *How Stella Got Her Groove Back* contributed to the African American vernacular, which unequivocally informs pop culture.

The term *groove* means movement; thus, in the context of McMillan's title, readers gain a sense of McMillan taking them on a journey in the black experience. As with many American English terms, there are often two definitions for a single word. The second definition of groove is to dance, to make fit, to do, get into a routine of something. McMillan uses the terms equally; however, in relation to her characters, it is a term that signifies getting out of a rut and moving. McMillan is skillful in conjuring the black tradition of dance. She reminds the black readership of the power of dance as an intricate part of the black experience. For others, the term *groove* simply allows, according to Savan, "the language of an excluded people to be repeated by the nonexcluded in order to make themselves sound more included" (258). The irony of McMillan's word choice is that it is actually exclusive in a symbolic sense, for historically, Africans communicated with each other through the art of dance, the groove.

McMillan artfully plays up the stereotype that white people can't dance, for getting our groove back is exclusive to black culture. More importantly, it is particularly exclusive to the black woman, in that to get her groove back she must undergo a transformation that is exclusive to the individual. Stella must rid herself of her insecurities to get her groove back, which means letting go of pop culture ideologies and societal taboos. And for Stella, her intimate encounter with Winston proves transformative, enabling her to get her groove back. McMillan's catchphrase has elicited several pop culture variations, such as "get my groove on," "get my swerve on," and "I'm in the groove," all of which connote movement, physical and mental. "Cultural skin is always permeable, absorbing any word that has reached critical mass of usefulness or fun" (263), Savan asserts, for that is how languages develop.

McMillan's iconic characters serve as conductors of American slang and AAVE, for their dialogue and McMillan's written word contribute to the marketability and promotion of the black experience in pop culture and the maintenance of the oral tradition found in canonical African American literature. McMillan constructs less than perfect characters. They are far from depictions of the traditional lady, and their use of language challenges the patriarchal authority of the community, along with the ideologized manner of legitimizing African American characters in literature.

MCMILLAN FAMILY VALUES

Statistics reveal that 4.1 million households are managed by women. McMillan's novels reflect the reality of a changing society and in doing so she forgoes the promotion of an infallible Cosby image, an image unrealistically devoid of conflict or struggle. McMillan does not promote artificial images of black womanhood; instead, she elects to record and package her personal experiences and life observations as a consumable product, a cultural artifact, which readers can readily purchase, demonstrating their affinity for her brand. Although McMillan's novels reflect the changing values of pop culture society, she also presents the changing values of the contemporary black woman through her characters' rejection of societal norms, for her characters are single by choice, able to take care of themselves and their families emotionally and financially, and able to maintain healthy relationships with sistahs as a means to strengthen family bonds and maintain community connections.

Another characteristic of the contemporary middle-class black woman is her status as a bachelorette. Noted sociologists and economists have observed a decline in marriages among African Americans since the 1960s. In the past, the allure of marriage "provided women with a kind of social respectability, and it served as protection from sexual exploitation" (Dubey, qtd. in West 231). The legacy left by slavery resulted in the white woman seeking liberation from her ladylike behavior and the black woman opting for sexual conservatism, a seeming swap of positions between the two (Genevive 235). McMillan disposes of the black woman's sexual conservatism and her inherent dependence upon her male counterpart.

McMillan is a facilitator of change, particularly in the African American community. Her characters are representative of the middle class, for past narratives situated black women in lower classes or in abject poverty. McMillan's depiction of the sexually liberated, educated, financially independent, mobile black woman is a stark contrast to the sexually repressed, domesticated, churchgoing, Christian woman revered in the black community. Stella, a successful middle-aged professional, is the perfect embodiment of the modern woman according to present-day societal ideologies. Pop culture recognizes success by material wealth; thus, Stella represents the pop culture ideal with her BMW, six-figure salary, and homeownership in a predominately white suburb. "You can have it all images," like the iconic Stella, resonate with pop culture (Hollows 201). The "women in sistah-lit novels (novels about and primarily for black women), like McMillan's, define themselves in opposition to a history of domestic servitude and pressures of class and race" (Henderson 903).

Unlike Savannah, Bernadine marries, pursues a career, and creates a family. Robin, Savannah, and Gloria, in *Waiting to Exhale,* embark on a quest to find the perfect partner, marry, mate, and start a family, or alternatively, mate, start a family, and marry. Bernadine recollects her past and present existence with bitterness and resentment. She realizes, however, through her silent inner reflection, that she is to blame for her fragmented life in her unspoken pledge to her family. Stella, like Bernadine, recognizes that in order to reconcile her dual personas as a black woman and ex-wife, she must forgive and forget her resentment of the past. McMillan's ability to express Stella's resentment through stream of consciousness, her inner voice, reveals the power of silence. McMillan's desire to redefine contexts of power through voice and voiceless-ness serves to broaden traditional canonical definitions of power and presence in pop culture.

THE MATRIARCHAL FAMILY

McMillan's families are not without a traditional family construct, a formu-laic composition of a husband, wife, and child(ren). However, her depictions of such unions between the black man and black woman appear to be bad investments, particularly to the black woman. Perhaps in part due to Mc-Millan's upbringing, the black matriarchal family is a staple in her novels. McMillan's portrayal of the black matriarch is not a new phenomenon; the black matriarch is recognized in countless works of literature. McMillan also recognizes sistahs as a means to acknowledge the shared experiences and struggles of all women while stressing the importance of culture and language as contexts for understanding definitions of man and woman, particularly as a means through which to explore the advancement for black women in terms of white American values. McMillan's new genre is of significant canonical importance, for according to Kenneth Burke, once immersed as a member of a society, we do not see our common culture (29), and McMillan is successful in promoting the common culture. McMillan slowly shifts the family dynamic, from a core, nuclear family, to single mothers, a population that represents 43 percent of the black population. This also leads to a closer union of women into a sistah-hood of shared frustrations and triumphs. Terry McMillan has popularized waiting to exhale parties, similar to the '70s women's liberation rallies, where women vent these frustrations and share these victories.

Many critics, including Bill Cosby, have noted that the black middle-class family is in a state of crisis. Several factors have contributed to the dissolution of the black family. And like Savannah, "we don't know why we stopped be-ing social creatures" (McMillan, *Exhale* 10). Acknowledging the increasingly materialistic, individualistic, and narcissistic lifestyle of pop culture society, McMillan shows readers how technology, media, and shifting cultural values have changed the way we live and think. McMillan purposefully presents the ideology of marriage in each of her novels, an ideology to which most Americans can relate, whether single, married, or divorced. She captures a broad audience of readers and consumers who find the new image of the single African American female character relatable and authentic. McMillan skillfully acknowledges the early societal constructions of the perfect wife, for she writes, "it seems like everyone is striving for perfection" (*Exhale* 12). In this context, perfection is understood as a social construct in which the perfect family unit is comprised of a loving wife, doting husband, and obedient child. In the early 1800s, slaves were encouraged to strive for perfection, and perfection was usually achieved through marriage. White slave owners encouraged marriage among slaves as a means of control. Slaves who were married were loyal to their family and least likely to leave the plantation, whereas those who were single, without families of their own, were likely to seek freedom and run away. Perfection (marriage), as McMillan posits, is a dead institution, as is slavery (*Exhale* 11). McMillan finds marriage to be highly restrictive, despite ideologized notions of the knight in shining armor who is sworn to protect and provide.

McMillan's multigenerational images of women, particularly in *Getting to Happy,* are representative of collective history between mothers, daughters, sisters, and aunts, real or fictive. Women are central to families' survival; the black man's absence, physical or psychological, has resulted in the black woman's dual existence, as both mother and father, nurturer and provider, giving life to the family matriarch motif. In McMillan's novels, her family matriarchs serve as a prescriptive in which to accurately depict the single black middle-class mothers' struggles, triumphs, desires, and self-sufficiency, a means in which to counter stereotypical images of other contemporary single black mothers, who appear as uneducated, drug-using, welfare-dependent, baby-making video-hoes who will do anything to support their habits and families, an easily commodifiable image by popular culture standards. Postmodern and contemporary black women, like Bernadine, Gloria, and Stella are often depicted as powerful and strong, in part because of their resiliency, their ability to endure stereotypes, economic inequities, male abandonment, and single motherhood. McMillan's depictions of the strong black woman is central to the African American tradition of storytelling, and she will continue to evolve and tell her story to future generations, thereby contributing to the African American literary canon.

BIBLIOGRAPHY

Fiction and Nonfiction

Breaking Ice: An Anthology of Contemporary African American Fiction. Editor. New York: Viking, 1990.
A Day Late and a Dollar Short. New York: Penguin, 2001.
Disappearing Acts. New York: Viking, 1989.
Getting Back to Happy. New York: Penguin, 2010.
How Stella Got Her Groove Back. New York: Viking, 1996.
The Interruption of Everything. New York: Penguin, 2005.
Mama. Boston: Houghton Mifflin, 1987.
Waiting to Exhale. New York: Viking, 1992.

Films

Waiting to Exhale (1996)
How Stella Got Her Groove Back (1998)
Disappearing Acts (2000)
Getting Back to Happy (in progress, 2011)

Interviews

"Exclusive Interview with Best-Selling Author, Terry McMillan." MackeyMedia. February 20, 2008. Web. 15 July 2010. http://www.youtube.com/watch?v=YVK jaAfjV2Q.

Interview. BookPage. Web. 18 Aug. 2010. http://www.bookpage.com/0102pb/.Terry_ mcmillan.html.

Iverem, Esther. Interview with Terry McMillan. Seeingblack.com. September 26, 2002. Web. 4 Sept. 2010. http://www.seeingblack.com/x092602/mcmillan.shtml.

Winfrey, Oprah. Interview with Terry McMillan. *Oprah Winfrey Show*. Web. September 28, 2010. http://www.oprah.com/oprahshow/Author-Terry-McMillan-and-Her-Ex-Jonathan-Plummer.

Winfrey, Oprah. Interview with Terry McMillan. *Oprah Winfrey Show*. Web. September 28, 2010. http://www.oprah.com/oprahshow/Terry-McMillan-Lets-Her-Anger-Go-Video (viewed September 28, 2010.

Roberts, Robin. "10 Questions for Terry McMillan." *Good Morning America*. McMillan, Terry. Interview by Rebecca Keegan.

TimeMagazine. September 9, 2010. Web. 25 Sept. 2010.

FURTHER READING

Agwuele, Augustine, and Toyin Falola. "Definition of Nature and Culture." *Africans and the Politics of Popular Culture*. Rochester, NY: U of Rochester P, 2009.

Andrews, William L., Frances Smith Foster, and Trudier Harris. *The Concise Oxford Companion to African American Literature*. New York: Oxford UP, 2001: 284–85.

Bass, Patrik Henry. "Terry McMillan's Triumphant Return." *Essence* January 2001: 62.

Bennett, Michael, and Vanessa D. Dickerson. *Recovering the Black Female Body: Self-Representations by African American Women*. Piscataway, NJ: Rutgers UP, 2001.

Bourdieu, Pierre. *Language and Symbolic Power*. Cambridge, MA: Harvard UP, 1993.

Brooks, Daphne. "'It's Not Right but It's Okay': Black Women's R&B and the House that Terry McMillan Built." *The New Black Renaissance: The Souls Anthology of Critical African American Studies*. Ed. Manning Marable. Boulder, CO: Paradigm, 2005: 168–79.

Brown, Antonio. "Performing 'Truth': Black Speech Acts." *African American Review* 36.2 (2002): 213.

Burke, Kenneth. *On Symbols and Society*. 2nd ed. Ed. Joseph R. Gusfield. Chicago: U of Chicago P, 1989.

Bush, Vanessa. "Getting to Happy." *Booklist* 106.21 (2010): 7.

Carroll, Denolyn. "A Short History of Contemporary Black Erotic Fiction." *Black Issues Book Review* September 2004: 22–23.

Charles, John C. "Desire, Agency, and Black American Subjectivity. Once You Go Black: Choice, Desire, and the Black American Intellectual by Robert Reid-Pharr." *Twentieth-Century Literature* 55.2 (Summer 2009): 269–80.

Christian, Barbara. *Black Feminist Criticism: Perspectives on Black Women Writers.* Elmsford, NY: Pergamon, 1985.

Dandridge, Rita. *Black Women's Activism: Reading African American Women's Historical Romances.* New York: Lang, 2004.

Dandridge, Rita. "Terry McMillan." *Contemporary African American Novelists: A Bio-Bibliographical Critical Sourcebook.* Ed. by Emmanuel Nelson. Westport, CT: Greenwood P, 1999. 319.

Dickerson, Bette, and Nicole Rousseau. "Ageism through Omission: The Obsolescence of Black Women's Sexuality." *Journal of African American Studies* 13.3 (2009): 316.

Dodson, Angela P. "McMillan's Wit and Wisdom." *New York Amsterdam News* 97.48 (2006): 9.

Drew, Bernard A. *100 Most Popular African American Authors.* Westport, CT: Libraries Unlimited, 2007.

Dunn, James L., Jr. "Our Own Erotica." *American Visions* 12.5 (1997): 31.

Eaton, Kalenda C. *Womanism, Literature, and the Transformation of the Black Community, 1965—1980.* New York: Routledge, 2008.

Ehlers, Nadine. "'Black Is' and 'Black Ain't': Performative Revisions of Racial Crisis." *Culture, Theory and Critique* 47.2 (2006): 149–63.

Ellerby, Janet Mason. "Deposing the Man of the House: Terry McMillan Rewrites the Family." *MELUS* 22.2 (1997): 105.

Ellis, Trey. "New Black Aesthetics." *Callaloo* 38 (1989): 235.

Foucault, Michel. *The History of Sexuality.* Vol. 1. New York: Penguin, 2008.

"Getting to Happy." *Publishers Weekly* 257.26 (2010): 24–25.

Gibson, Valerie. Interview. *January Magazine.* February 2002. Web. http://january magazine.com/profiles/vgibson.html.

Grimes, Tresmaine R. "In Search of the Truth about History, Sexuality, and Black Women: An Interview with Gail E. Wyatt." *Teaching of Psychology* 26.1 (1999): 66–69.

Henderson, Mae G. "Speaking in Tongues: Dialogics, Dialectics, and the Black Woman Writer's Literary Tradition." *African American Literary Theory: A Reader.* Ed. Winston Napier. New York: New York UP, 2000. 903.

Hollows, Joanne. *Feminism, Femininity, and Popular Culture.* New York: St. Martin's, 2000.

Johnson, Kayln. "Zane, Inc." *Black Issues Book Review* September 2004: 17–18.

Lipsitz, George. *Collective Memory and American Popular Culture.* Minneapolis: U of Minnesota P, 2001.

Nunez, Elizabeth, and Brenda M. Greene, eds. *Defining Ourselves: Black Writers in the '90s.* New York: Peter Lang Publishing, 1999.

Odhiambo, Tom. "The Black Female Body as a 'Consumer and a Consumable' in Current Drum and True Love Magazines in South Africa. *African Studies* 67.1 (April 2008): 78.

O'Keefe, Mark. "Foul Words Permeate Pop Culture Lexicon, Eliciting a Backlash." *Christian Century* 121.7 (2004): 14–15.

Okeowo, Alexis. "McMillan Brings Her Groove to Harlem." *New York Amsterdam News* 96.30 (2005): 8.

Oyewumi, Oyeronke. "Visualizing the Body: Western Theories and African Subjects." *The Feminist Philosophy Reader*. Ed. Alison Bailey and Chris Cuomo. New York: McGraw-Hill, 2008. 163.

Patrick, Diane. *Terry McMillan: The Unauthorized Biography*. New York: St. Martin's, 1999.

Phillips, Layli. *The Womanist Reader*. Routledge: London, 2006.

Presler, Andrews B. "Terry McMillan." *American Ethnic Writers*. Vol. 2. Ed. Danvid Peck. Pasadena, CA: Salem, 2000.

Putzi, Jennifer. "'Raising the Stigma': Black Womanhood and the Marked Body in Pauline Hopkins's Contending Forces." *College Literature* 31.2 (Spring 2004): 3.

Richards, Paulette. *Terry McMillan: A Critical Companion*. Westport, CT: Greenwood Press, 1999.

Savan, Leslie. "Black Talk and Pop Culture." *Slam Dunks and No-Brainers: Language in Your Life, the Media, Business, Politics, and Like…Whatever*. New York: Knopf, 2005.

Scott, Whitney. "*Getting to Happy.*" *Booklist* 107.5 (2010): 37.

Smith, Jessie Carney. "Terry McMillan." *Notable Black Women*. Vol. 2. Farmington Hills, MI: Gale, 1991.

Springer, Kimberly. Rev. of *Longing to Tell: Black Women Talk about Sexuality and Intimacy* by Tricia Rose. *SIGNS* September 2005: 231–32.

Stein, Ruthe. "Stella's Stuck in a Groove: McMillan Adaptation Overemphasizes Age." *San Francisco Chronicle*. August 14, 1998. Web. June 28, 2010. http://www.sf gate.com/cgi-bin/article.cgi?file=?chronicle/archive/1998/09/14/DD31545.DTL.

"Terry McMillan." *Contemporary Novelists*. 7th ed. Detroit, MI: St. James, 2001.

"Terry McMillan." n.p. Web. 18 Aug. 2010. http://us.penguingroup.com/static/html/author/terrymcmillan.html.

"Terry McMillan." *UXL Encyclopedia of World Biography*. Vol. 7. *Gale Virtual Reference Library*, n.d. 1273–75.

Thompson, Lisa B. *Beyond the Black Lady: Sexuality and the New African American Middle Class*. Champaign: U of Illinois P, 2009.

Tudorica, Letitia Guran. "Reconsidering African American Identity: Aesthetic Experiments by Post-Soul Artists." Thesis. University of Richmond, 2008.

Wallace, Michele. *Black Popular Culture*. Ed. Gina Dent. New York: New Press, 1998.

Weir-Soley, Donna A. Rev. of *Eroticism, Spirituality, and Resistance in Black Women's Writings* by Esther Clark. *Multi-Ethnic Literature of the United States* 35.3 (September 2010): 234–36.

West, Genevieve. *Zora Neale Hurston and American Literary Culture*. Gainesville: UP of Florida, 2005: 231–35.

Whitaker, Charles. "Exhaling! Terry McMillan Hits Jackpot in Romance and Finance." *Ebony* 56.6 (2001): 154.

Williams-Page, Yolanda. "Terry McMillan." *Encyclopedia of African American Women Writers*. Vol. 1. Westport, CT: Greenwood, 2007.

Wynter, Leon. *American Skin: Pop Culture, Big Business, and the End of White America*. New York: Crown Publishers, 2002.

"Zora Neale Hurston." The Official Zora Neale Hurston Website. http://www.zora nealehurston.com/biography.html.

Marian C. Dillahunt

Toni Morrison is one of the most significant American authors of the 20th century. She was awarded both the Pulitzer Prize and the Nobel Prize for Literature. (Olga Besnard/Dreamstime)

Toni Morrison

Toni Morrison (1931–) was born Chloe Anthony Wofford to parents who had settled in Lorain, Ohio, where her father worked in a steel factory. She grew up, the second of four children, in a joyful, strong-willed family. Her mother, Ramah Willis, sang all the time, jazz as well as opera, and according to Morrison "never entertained fragility or vulnerability." Toni was devoted to her father, whose courage and determination she admired. Brought up among musical people who kept telling stories, she turned to books very early and was the first of her family to graduate from college. She earned a degree in English literature and classics from Howard University in 1953. She went on to pursue a master's degree at Cornell in 1955 and started teaching English at Texas Southern University, then taught back at Howard until 1963. In the meantime, she had married Jamaican architect Harold Morrison, with whom she had two sons: Ford in 1961 and Slade in 1964. By then, she had obtained a divorce and begun writing. She became an editor, holding various university teaching positions while steadily writing her way to success and recognition. She not only found who she was, but provided her whole community with a new pride and self-esteem, paving the way for many more African American women writers whom she encouraged and edited. With *Beloved,* she gave her own people a new perspective on their own tragic history, lifting the veil on what had hitherto been hidden and giving words to the unspoken. Her work suddenly became the concrete embodiment of all that her predecessors had dreamed of achieving during the New Negro Movement, but were unable to do because they were still a long way away from civil rights.

When Toni Morrison reigned over the Louvre in Paris during the fall of 2006, she acquired full recognition as one of the major intellectual figures of our time. She had not been invited as an icon of African American culture only, but as an artist and a critic whose thoughts were challenging and eagerly sought after in the cultural world. Here was a woman who had spent her life trying to investigate the many shapes of the hydra discrimination, a woman who now embodied the spectacular breakthrough of a community that had not only managed to survive 200 years of slavery, but had finally succeeded in stifling the demons of shame and self-deprecation in order to claim its place within American society and in the world. Her work, whose main purpose has been devoted to refiguring African American history and identity, is eminently relevant today, at a time when we are witnessing a new surge of discrimination in the face of the overwhelming tide of displaced people around the world. The new insistent question seems to be one that the black community experienced a long time ago, one, in a word, fully implemented in Morrison's work: How can one man grow to be a man when deprived of the elements which until today have helped men grow—roots, a land, cultural traditions, language? How can broken communities strengthen themselves from within, without rejecting the others, the strangers outside? How can people establish relationships based on human understanding rather than oppositions of races, colors, religions, languages? As she tried to explore the many meanings of a project she called *The Foreigner's Home,* playing on the ambivalence of the phrase as a possessive (*the home of the foreigner*) and/or a statement (*the foreigner is home!*), Morrison addressed the contemporary problems of states and borders, citizenship and immigration, integration and discrimination, belonging and exile, identity and foreignness as expressed by artists throughout history. Questioning categories and stereotypes, she encouraged a new, revived approach to works of art whose meaning seemed to have been solidified by time. This, in a way, sums up the importance and appropriateness of Morrison's work and the vitality of her message to our time. Morrison is not only a politically engaged writer; she is a philosopher who explored the black character's psyche in relation to such questions as love and hatred, identity and dispossession, alienation and belonging, religion and faith. She always has a question at the back of her mind when she begins working on a novel. Some African Americans may resent the idea of Morrison as a curator and grand master of ceremonies at the Louvre as a betrayal of her race, but it would only mean that they underestimate their own progress and wisdom.

It all began with the reflection of a face in a mirror. Who has not, one day, looked into a mirror and wanted to be someone else, dreaming of a place where the burden of life would vanish, taking away the unbearable feeling of isolation that seizes one the minute birth tears away the infant from his mother? What painful intensity this profoundly human feeling reaches when in the mirror appears the counter image or negation of what Western civilization has for centuries called beauty: a black face? In Toni Morrison's novels, little black girls peer into their mirrors for the bluest eyes or find there, with a shiver, the evidence of their own ugliness. Whereas Pecola dreams of being Shirley Temple (*The Bluest Eye*, 1970), Nel discovers that she *is* Nel because she is neither as beautiful nor as creamy as her mother (*Sula*, 1973).

In the United States that is the backdrop of Morrison's work, there are for the African American only two ways of existing: running away or imitating the white. However, flight, the central metaphor of *Song of Solomon*, turns into a fall, whereas imitating the white man leads to complete alienation. The wish to be someone else ultimately leads to madness and death: This is the sad conclusion of Morrison's first two novels, none of which offer any answer to *The Bluest Eye's* Claudia's initial "why?"

In *Song of Solomon* (1977) and *Tar Baby* (1981), Morrison attempts to go beyond the lie to which appearances condemn the African American by a return to the origins. It is necessary to go beyond the *letter* toward the authenticity of the *spirit* in order to link the African American to his principle. The Scriptures, in particular Saint Paul, quoted by Morrison as epigraph to *Tar Baby,* are used, together with African American folklore, to debunk the white man. Going back to a mythical South—Shalimar (Virginia) for Milkman, Eloe (Florida) for Son—rediscovering there the ancestral wisdom of Pilate or Therese, becomes the means for the African American to find his roots and assert his own difference. However, whether such a regressive trip to the realm of childhood enables him to face his own responsibilities, to meet the Other and build a future, remains doubtful. The African American hero appears to revel in a dream of innocence far from the stark realities of life. As for the contemporary African American woman that Jadine embodies, such a return to her "ancient properties" can only mean giving up herself for the benefit of a patriarchal system in which she is little more than a slave, if not of her male companion, at least of her nurturing function.

At the end of *Tar Baby,* one is bound to come up with this evidence: the black character has to get rid of the poetic illusion of an Arcadian past. Whether dressed in myth, as in *Song of Solomon,* or introduced as a pastoral, as in *Tar Baby,* the past is unable to give coherence to and hold together the elements of the present. The African American man will not find himself by developing new illusions or new lies about himself. Neither will he find his true nature by imitating the solitary, egotistic quest of the white hero, as Milkman's life demonstrates.

If her fiction is to be true and political, Morrison has to go further than mere literary themes and make the perilous dive into the real past of the black race in an attempt to find the *why* of its alienation. In *Beloved* (1987), her characters eventually discover the bonds of solidarity, which help them face evil and share a common destiny. One cannot save oneself without the help of the Other. Paul D's words best sum up this new evidence:

> Sethe, if I'm here with you, with Denver, you can go anywhere you want. Jump, if you want to, 'cause I'll catch you, girl. I'll catch you 'fore you fall. Go as far inside as you need to, I'll hold your ankles. Make sure you get back out. (*Beloved* 46)

The haunting memory of a traumatic past, the necessary fall within oneself may not be deadly, provided someone is there holding you. Putting one's faith into someone else triggers the dialogue which, in turn, permits life to go on. As he listens to you, he enables you to discover the other within yourself. With *Jazz* (1992), this identity quest also means for Morrison the discovery of a spirituality that translates the inner search into a patient progress leading to gradual transformation of the individual. The *Nag Hammadi,* which is quoted as epigraph to the novel, opens an inner kingdom which owes nothing to the miraculous intervention of the Lord. To understand the attraction of these texts and their link with Eastern metaphysics, let us quote Emile Gillabert on the Gospel of Saint Thomas: "The Self is realized in as much as the *me* lets go and opens his self to the other. It is all about giving up, relinquishing one's self, unlearning and being free not to act but to be acted upon, being vulnerable, welcoming, willing to accept sufferings as well as joys" (*Paroles de Jésus et pensée orientale* 70).

Is there any better way to express Violet's spiritual progress as she ends up killing her revengeful *me* to discover her true *Me* (*Jazz* 209)? Such discovery presupposes shedding everything that burdens the soul in order to go beyond the dualisms underlying Western Christianity, in particular the fruitless confrontation of the flesh and the spirit. In front of the possessive madness of

Joe, Violet's progress, beginning with the most spectacular anti-act (killing a corpse) appears as a true conversion. She finds herself by renouncing herself and thus saves Joe, the man she loves, from death (spiritual death as well as the certain death she is tempted to give him every minute of the day).

With *Paradise* (1997), Morrison enlarges on her religious questioning and pursues still further her spiritual quest of a wisdom born of abnegation and love of the other. She chooses to tackle the subject from a completely new perspective, that of characters who not only have a strong sense of identity, but also strong wills, and unlike the slaves of Sweet Home in *Beloved,* the ability to make plans. Why do these plans fail? Why can't they manage to go to the end of their dream? Is their imagination at fault, as the narrator thinks, or is it once again an inner emptiness that impels them to act against their own welfare? The scope of the novel goes far beyond the problems of shame and intraracism. The deeper problem seems to lie in the fateful division of body and spirit, sex and religion, as if there were no way for men and women ever to find a complete harmony together. Her women, however, seem to overcome this division within themselves and acquire the ability to survive their own demise, even the jealous killing of the men who envy their freedom.

From her first title, *The Bluest Eye,* the thing less likely to be part of the African American's heritage, to *Jazz,* the art that best translates the complexity, generosity, depth, and openness of the African American soul, Morrison's choices have never been insignificant. They translate the move from alienation to inwardness that underlies all her work until the last novel, *Love* (2003), ominously gives birth to a strange hateful love or loving hatred.

From her early assertion: "The search for love and identity runs through most everything I write" (Taylor-Guthrie 96), Morrison has used writing as a way to think the unthinkable, to speak the unspeakable, to body forth the innermost grief and desires of the African American psyche. She did not start out from nothing, since matters of content and style had been debated among her African American predecessors since the Harlem Renaissance. Since Du Bois's *The Souls of Black Folk,* Zora Neale Hurston had led the way to the use of folklore, Langston Hughes had revealed the rhythm of the blues in poetry, Ralph Ellison had pondered over the meaning of a name in the search for identity, which he considered the American theme, and Margaret Walker had paved the way for the use of historicized fiction in the search for African American identity. Morrison could avail herself of a wide range of subjects and manners that would speak to the people she was addressing: at first, those of her race. Her specificity lies perhaps in the fact that she went further and beyond all of her predecessors in the use of these elements, which she treated on a par with Western mythology and other literary loci. As Ellison put it: "Too many books by Negro writers are addressed to a white audience. By doing this the authors run the risk of limiting themselves to the audience's presumptions of what a Negro is or should be; the tendency is to become involved in polemics, to plead the Negro's humanity" (*Shadow and Act* 177). Morrison understood very early that in order to become a writer, she had to be very careful not to fall under the control of the white man's vision of the African American; she had to get free from the fetters of sociopolitical slogans and could not narrow her scope to the vindication of race only.

To avoid such pitfalls, Morrison first decided to write "as though there was nobody in the world but me and the characters, as though I was talking to them" (Taylor-Guthrie 96). She, like most modern authors, was influenced by the finality of analysis, looking for an inner causal link likely to account for the origin and nature of identity. She did not want to reproduce stereotypes. More than anyone, perhaps, the African American character is looking for coherence and understanding through narrative. The ambition of the writer is therefore to find "The Words to Say It," as Morrison herself explains in *Playing in the Dark* (1992). These five words speak "the full agenda and unequivocal goal of a novelist" (3), she says, acknowledging the analogy between Marie Cardinal's and her own preoccupations. "To make chaos coherent" (*Playing in the Dark* 5) is the way she sums up the common goals of both literature and psychoanalysis, and we cannot doubt that the reading of Cardinal influenced the new direction taken by Morrison in *Beloved* and *Jazz*. In *Beloved*, she metaphorically transcribes the traumatic separation of Africans from their Mother, Africa, whereas in *Jazz* she provides a series of variations on the freeing, cathartic effect of jazz, a music that springs from the depth of the soul and of the wounded body of African Americans and which appears to be, already in *The Bluest Eye*, the only way to express oneself when words are lacking. It seems that Morrison has recognized in Cardinal a process that has long been hers.

As early as *The Bluest Eye*, the narrative voice tries to capture the *how* of the tragic events that led young Pecola to madness through the analytical structure of recollection and going back over one's past. The novel begins with a breach in the process of identification: the ideal family depicted by the primer is distorted by repetition and acceleration of the phrase that loses its structure, words tumbling on each other, until all meaning is lost. The identity of the characters disappears into chaos and the reader learns that in the Breedlove family (an antiphrastic name), the daughter bears the father's child. Such monstrous oedipal transgression upsets Claudia's expectations, and it is her desire to find an explanation that launches the narrative: How did it happen? Who are these people? These questions in turn lead to questioning Claudia's own identity, since rejecting the Breedloves on account of the ideal family pattern would mean accepting the white man's definition of what family is. Claudia, who is the narrator and most probably the author's voice, is eventually the only character who becomes aware of the bad faith at work in the community. Her feeling of guilt also fuels the narrative as the only way to speak the shameful, not so much to exonerate herself as to explain the ill inflicted on Pecola by those who should have supported her. The question that underlies all the other questions is, How can the African American community have reached such a lack of self-knowledge as to ignore and condemn its own members instead of attempting to save them? The novel also reveals how, through the personal stories of Pauline and Cholly, two individuals can reach such a state of alienation as to deny their own child. The strongest biological links are annihilated and have become meaningless. But Claudia's uneasiness at Pecola's rejection by the community cannot be a satisfying answer to her desire to know the truth.

It seems that Sula's provocations are a new way to put the same question. The inversion contained in the name "Bottom" for the top of the hill allotted to the black community takes over the initial breach of the first novel only to interiorize it. Nothing is what it seems in this small, isolated world and the young girl intent on knowing herself and looking for freedom keeps colliding with the nonsense of a life where love kills, motherhood annihilates, and heroes, like Ajax or Jude, are irresponsible. Sula, like Baldwin when he flew to Europe, runs away only to find that she is totally alone, isolated from Negroes and whites alike, because she has not understood that her scorn and rejection of the blacks were unconsciously dictated by whites. The importance of roots and ancestors has escaped her and she eventually disperses herself geographically and sexually, denying herself as surely as she denies Eva, her grandmother.

The same analytical structures are at work in all the novels, but with *Song of Solomon,* the process is enriched by mythical references, which take the plot beyond its usual limits and give it a universal resonance far beyond the trivial news item that started it all. Looking for oneself becomes a geographical and historical search imitating classical models. The peregrinations of the hero that appeared as a negative experience in *Sula* here become enriched with the myths of Ulysses and Jason, opening up the fate of the hero and making it fit the aspirations of a whole community. The trip south also provides the quest for oneself with a dynamic that agrees with the love of movement of the male hero. The journey to maturity takes Milkman, in agreement with the analytic process, to the land of his ancestors, the land of his origins, which initiates a return of the repressed in his consciousness. Milkman's desire is fuelled by the wish to find the gold which his father had lost, that is to say, by a wish to correct, even to understand, his enigmatic past. His adventures are as many stages in his own understanding of himself, until he reaches the revelation, which belongs to the past as much as to the future. In the end, the discovery of his filiation gives Milkman the courage of jumping into the air toward an ambiguous epiphany: Either he becomes the mythical Flying African or tumbles down in a fantastical fall into the arms of his alter ego. The desperation that arose from the first two novels becomes, thanks to the myth, an eloquent message that hovers on the edge of truth, now a matter of belief. The reader has to decide for herself.

With *Tar Baby,* the psychoanalytical model becomes allegory with Son, the eternal son and Jadine the independent daughter, as hard as her name Jade, rushing together toward an end that seems to be a repetition of their beginning, as neither one has been able to launch the dialogue that would have enabled maturing and transformation. The narrative structure has obviously reached a threshold, a resistance level. If the end is in the beginning, if the narrative is nothing more than a succession of obstacles and repetitions that simply postpone the conclusion, if the latter simply obeys the determinism of the libido, there is little hope for a happy future. The characters can only cross each other's paths without any real meeting or dialogue between them. The psychoanalytical process cannot be reduced to primary feelings, to predetermined desires. Evolution requires a consciousness that can act upon life. The character has to discover his own free will in order to discover his own self. Now, this is exactly what Sartre attempted to demonstrate. He opposed existential psychoanalysis to Freud's idea: "existential psychoanalysis knows nothing but the primary surge of human freedom" (*L'être et le néant* 629). Instead of an unconscious psyche that escapes the subject's intuition, it makes the psychic fact coextensive with consciousness. It seems that Morrison's characters undergo precisely such an evolution. Gradually, they become conscious of their freedom of choice. Gradually we see them appropriating memory and language, which first belonged to the narrator, or the ancestor, in order to assert their own freedom of choice and responsibility toward the other.

In *Beloved*, Paul D performs a complete turn on himself when he decides to come back to Sethe freely. His will to stay by her side in the hope of better days appears the only way to stop the destructive mechanism initiated by the white man, even if the reader is entitled to doubt the possibility of happiness for a tormented character like Sethe. Such freedom of choice is what fuels *Jazz,* where even the narrator is seen hesitating, doubting, improvising like a jazz musician, finally recognizing that she has been beaten by the characters, who have been able to surprise her in deciding their own destiny without regard for her prognostication. An existential interpretation of freedom replaces the Freudian determinism of the origins. Acts are not simply understood in the light of the deeds and reactions that led to them, but in the light of the end assigned to them by the conscious subject. This move happens when a character becomes conscious of his physical, affective, psychological, and social ties, all of which support self-esteem, and ultimately the building of identity. "One has to be conscious in order to choose and one has to choose in order to be conscious. Choice and consciousness are one and the same thing" (517) wrote Sartre. This, of course, as *Paradise* and *Love* demonstrate, is by no means an assurance of peace and happiness. Self-consciousness, which is also self-knowledge, enables the individual not to be the slave of motivations that are beyond him and to project himself forward. But once again, the willful father does not necessarily pass on the wisdom he has acquired. After the long progress from alienation to self-consciousness, from renunciation to action, from possession to love, marking the difference between Cholly Breedlove and Joe Trace, there remains for the black male not to forget the lessons of slavery and not to lose the spirit, which he has acquired with so much suffering. The risk is of course to forget the spirit and revert to a close interpretation of the letter. The risk is to confound memory and commemoration, power and authoritarianism, love and comfort. With *Paradise* and *Love,* the quest goes on among successful members of the community who too easily forget the Other that is in them and next to them.

For Morrison, narrative is necessary. It is a psychic process that enables humanity to conceive and satisfy its fundamental need for coherence and understanding. The model of psychoanalysis throws light on the progress of characters looking for themselves as well as on the peculiar link the narrative creates between them. Such a relationship, reflected in the reciprocal link between narrator and reader, finds its model in the relationship shared by the analyst and its patient. The narrative of the one is stimulated by the patient listening of the other. Wisdom, if it emerges from such relation, is the work of both. The narrative process, like the analysis, tries to decipher and re-member the past, thanks to the traces left by memory or dream. In both cases, the aim is to discover the power of the desire that fuels the story, its origins, in order to master the process that, by elucidating the past, will lead to maturity. For the American black community, whose past is more easily read on the mutilated bodies or in the unfathomable eyes than in libraries, whose present is most often synonymous with alienation, telling stories is above all the way to refigure and to understand, to accept and to master a dismembered history made of holes and omissions.

Two of the novels reveal in a particularly meaningful way the complementary aspects of this assumption: *Sula* is built in circles around an empty center, the 10 years Sula has been away, absent from the community. Other omissions, like the mysterious disappearance of Eva for 18 months, provide an echo to this one. Things happen, like people, with no apparent reason. No explanation is ever given for gestures or reactions and events take on an absurd, meaningless stance, as if they partook of fate, as in Ancient Greece. In front of fatality, revolt is deadly. The characters of *Sula* can only accept and survive: "The purpose of evil was to survive it and they determined (without ever knowing they had made up their minds to do it) to survive floods, white people, tuberculosis, famine and ignorance" (*Sula* 90).

Such determination is probably what gives the slaves of Sweet Home their life strength. However, when the paroxysm of suffering and annihilation is reached, acceptance is sometimes simply impossible. Then we get Sethe's pure and bloody revolt. The novel *Beloved* is built around her extreme, unspeakable act, which all of the characters attempt, bit by bit, to decipher and to understand. The whole narrative, made up of all the personal narratives of the characters throughout the novel, is meant to get to the *how* of Sethe's gesture, for lack of getting a rational understanding of the *why.*

Whereas *Sula* offers a diagnosis of the illness, *Beloved* offers a cure that will enable the character to assume her own life again. By refiguring, rewriting their history, the characters can eventually recognize one another as belonging to a community. In *Beloved*, the narrative is truly there to re-member the past, to speak the unspeakable and give a meaning to what is meaningless. Its therapeutic effect comprehends the narrator and the reader as well as the character—who end up appropriating the narrative in *Jazz*. One can apply to Morrison's work what Brooks says of *Absalom, Absalom!*

> The seemingly universal compulsion to narrate the past in *Absalom, Absalom!*, and to transmit its words, may speak both of an unmasterable past and of a dynamic narrative present dedicated to an interminable analysis of the past. Faulkner's present is a kind of tortured utopia of unending narrative dialogue informed by the desire for "revelatory knowledge." That knowledge never will come, yet that desire never will cease to activate the telling voices. (*Reading for the Plot* 312)

Morrison's open endings, the unexplained pieces of evidence in her plots and the intriguing presence of white people in the building of the narrative arouse the wish to know more and often make a second reading necessary for the puzzled reader. He has to go back over obscure passages to interpret them retrospectively. Such outline, moreover, finds its justification in the African American tradition as Morrison herself explains:

> The open-ended quality that is sometimes problematic in the novel form reminds me of the uses to which the stories are put in the black community. The stories are constantly being retold, constantly being imagined within a framework. And I hook into this like a life-support system....
>
> Classical music satisfies and closes. Black music, does not do that. Jazz always keeps you on the edge. There is no final chord.... There is something underneath [spirituals] that is incomplete. There is always something else that you want from the music. I want my books to be like that-because I want that feeling of something held in reserve and the sense that there is more-that you can't have it all right now. (Taylor-Guthrie 153, 155)

It is as if African Americans, in the suffering created by the rupture that is at the heart of their history, had discovered, long before Freud, the therapeutic and social value of storytelling, verbal or musical. Morrison very skillfully brings together the literary text, psychoanalytical structures, and the African American tradition in order to produce a masterful corpus which has initiated a revaluation of African American literary production as a whole.

This analysis is made even more pertinent by the deliberate use of a narrative voice reflecting the orality of the African American tradition. It has to be heard and like the preacher's voice, it has "to make you stand up out of your seat, make you lose yourself and hear yourself" (Taylor-Guthrie 123–24). The reader, like the congregation, is expected "to participate, approve, disapprove and interject" (Taylor-Guthrie 146) along the way. Both reader and narrator participate in the exchange and are engaged in seeking the truth. Like Walter

Benjamin, Morrison does not conceive of the novel as something to be con-sumed in solitude. There is an almost erotic link between narrator and listener that permits the transmission/transference of a kind of reciprocal wisdom:

> My language has to have holes and spaces so the reader can come into it. He or she can feel something visceral, see something striking. Then we (you, the reader, and I, the author) come together to make this book, to feel this experience. It doesn't matter what happens. (Taylor-Guthrie 164)

The narrative itself becomes the product of the love relationship between the novelist/storyteller and the reader/listener. Its truth is a matter of conviction. But Morrison's warm, cello-like voice knows all too well how to charm and convince her audiences. This talent was surely enhanced by her acting experi-ence when she was a student.

Because language is both the tool and the method, it is the measure of the rise to consciousness of the characters. They will suddenly feel impelled to trust a character, to speak to her or him. They will build a story together, interpreting silences and blanks, making up an imaginary world together in which memory will slowly come back to life and be transcended. This is not an easy task, rather an ever-repeated attempt, and few characters manage to find that sort of confidence.

It is necessary to understand the complexity of influences on the building of identity in order to measure the lacks of a child born in an alienated envi-ronment. Culture and biology are altered in such a way, emotional bonds so perverted, that the child is unable to recognize a parental bond. The father does not feel like a father and even the mother is unable to be a mother. It is such a dislocated world that Morrison offers her reader. In her first novel, the most basic parental ties have been destroyed and the child, who belongs to nobody, remains in the margin of a society which offers him no support and no emotional links in order to develop his own character. Cholly is such a child, abandoned by his mother for a crime he cannot understand, soiled from birth by this rejection, which kills in him the right to be. His unhappy daughter, Pecola, inherits her father's alienation. The process of belonging is, of course, made more difficult by the position of the African American com-munity in relation to the white world. Even when the family bonds are strong, to conform to the rules of a marginal group adjusting mimetically to the sur-rounding dominant world is a way for the African American character to lose her identity. To counterbalance the annihilation provoked by the white man's look, there is only the mother's breast. When even that is absent, when the child is deprived of the first emotional bond, only the look remains to keep the African American child forever subservient.

Before Cholly, the first of a long list of lost souls, the Shadracks of the world, there was this peculiar, destructive institution that Morrison compares to 200 years of war. The black man, deprived of freedom, of his name, of memory, deprived of his responsibilities, separated from his family, turned into a thing deprived of language, was systematically dehumanized and reified. No communication, no ties could remind him that he was a human being. How then could he think, speak, write his lost history? How could the slave whose subjectivity had been broken to pieces recover a sense of his own being? The mother remained, even for a brief moment, the only secure link. The fathers having been killed, or sold, the mothers alone had to assume the responsibility of bringing her children up, knowing all the while that they would sooner or later be taken from them. In *Beloved,* the mother's milk becomes the metonymic symbol of mother-child love which is declined in all the tenses: the milk the child has had, has, will have, or dream of having, missing milk, denied, stolen milk. The uncertainty of life, the impossibility of making a plan for a future that can only be equated with suffering, perverts the most elementary feelings. The mother's love is fundamental, but when her love is exacerbated owing to the absence of the father, it may become the first obstacle to the growth of the child. When it does not exist, the emptiness it creates in the child sends him on a regressive quest for the original oneness; when it is exclusive, it stifles or sends the child running away. The child is the last fragment of love for the exhausted and suffering mother. When Baby Suggs exclaims, "A man ain't nothing but a man, but a son? Well now, that's *somebody*" (*Beloved* 27), she is not a possessive mother, but simply a disillusioned woman who has lost all her men one after the other and is able to assess the miracle of having kept the last one for 20 years, a lifetime for a slave. The temptation is great to replace the missing man by a wider love for the child, a love so dense sometimes that it borders on madness.

In the violent, chaotic world of slavery, therefore, the mother remains the first bond, sometimes delegated to another woman from the community, a sister, an aunt, a grandmother. The privileged Other is not primarily a question of gender. Morrison's best creations are perhaps her gallery of ancestors, those indescribable women, grandmothers, midwives, storytellers, who embody the wisdom of the community and its traditions. M'Dear, Eva, Baby Suggs, and Pilate are not independent women in the modern sense of the word; they are women who have accepted their past and turned it into strength, women whose liberation comes from their full knowledge of what they are instead of a rejection of it. Pilate is perhaps the most accomplished character in that sense, although her marginality may be seen as paradoxical. Her living in the margins of the community certainly reveals the limits of her power within the community, while it may be interpreted as a way of belonging both to the group and to herself. Pilate is without doubt the strongest woman character created by Morrison; she has learned to disregard the disapproving look of other people, men or women, and finds her strength within herself and in the private conversations she has with her dead father's spirit. In her turn, she is a storyteller and demands a disciplined, attentive audience.

As the novels develop, the narratives of men and women become more and more discordant. The solitary quest or drifting of the man is opposed to the double bond that ties the woman to her children. Her freedom is conditioned by theirs: If she leaves them behind, she cuts a part of herself away. If she chooses to assume them, she may be forced into awful sacrifices that cripple her. In *Beloved,* mother, daughter, sister, are merged in a possessive desire of the other that annihilates them. In most of Morrison's tales, the absence of the fathers, both as a cause and a consequence, conditions the mother's possessive love. Sons, with no father image to guide them, are unable to become fathers. From generation to generation, the tragedy is reproduced, one father leading us back to his father and so on, until we reach the legendary figure of the Flying African, which conveys the same drifting and unstable image, that of a father who disappeared, leaving 21 sons behind. Ryna, like Niobe, "screamed and screamed, lost her mind completely" (*Song of Solomon* 13), not for the loss of the man she loved, as Susan Byrd tells Milkman, but for having to take care of the children by herself. The reader understands that between Ryna, Baby Suggs, Rose Dear, there is no difference. In the moans of Ryna's Gulch is found the epitome of forsaken women's grief for a multitude of fatherless children. This is probably one of the most recurrent themes of Morrison's writing, her first novel being somehow the direct consequence of her own divorce, as if her husband's failure had sent her on her own identity quest.

At one point, Morrison seems to have imagined the ideal scenario as being an egalitarian, matriarchal society in which free women would live independently with their children while choosing a companion for the night when necessary. The feminine trio formed by the grandmother, the mother, and the daughter, found in *Sula, Song of Solomon, Beloved,* and briefly in *Jazz,* tends to establish a feminine filiation. The ancestor passes the songs, the gestures, the tales, and the legends from generation to generation. She is the pillar of the community, a large "tree hanging in some princely but protective way over a row of smaller trees" (*Sula* 18). This structure, however, is soon weakened by the tensions between mothers and daughters and the absence of a stable, masculine presence. With the third generation, it collapses. Young Hagar lets herself die for the love of her cousin Milkman and her flaw cannot be wholly explained by a lash at Hollywood and MGM romantic love. Weeping Ryna's despair, when she is abandoned by her man, belongs to a time in the African American past when Hollywood did not exist. The legend seems to belie Pilate's self-contained character. Similarly, Sethe's resentment at Halle's failure contradicts the wishful camaraderie between men and women that was supposed to exist during slavery time.

Man's desertion, unexplained and often unexplainable, is an offence for the woman who has given him her life. In her novels, Morrison gives a very harsh picture of men, most of whom are immature and irresponsible. All the mothers lament the absence of their children's fathers and their lack of support. If women are brought together, it is not for any feminist claim, but for survival, because they cannot share their burden with the men who are unfit or have run away. Women, apart from Pilate, have not chosen to be alone; it is a fate that has been forced upon them. Now, this community of women undergoes a change as the novels evolve. The woman ancestor may represent the past and its authentic values but she rarely ever manages to pass on her strength to her daughters. As already pointed out, the authority of the mother hampers the consciousness that is necessary for the daughters to develop their own characters. The mother stifles the son and pushes the daughter to revolt.

From *Sula* to *Love,* the black man appears to be the most desired of men because he is the most missing, and women are willing to go to the end of the world, to kill one another for him. Even the puritanical Alice Manfred, who does not understand vindictive women like Violet, has to own to having been once thirsty for the blood of her rival for the love of a man.

Finding herself requires the woman to free herself from the masculine look that divides her; she has to recognize her link with other women, accept her mother and motherhood as being parts of her definition of herself. The dialogue that will nurture identity takes place between peers and a family by affinity replaces the biological family. The Convent in *Paradise* is a particularly strong, if extreme, symbol of such extended family.

It is the choice by the woman of opening the dialogue and being responsible that may eventually bring the man back home, but after what sacrifice, what ordeal? In order to go from Pilate's last wish ("I wish I'd a knowed more people. I would of loved 'em all" [*Song of Solomon* 336]) to the simple reality of the couple Violet and Joe at the end of *Jazz,* in order to replace the deadly passion by a wider, more generous love, the reader will have gone through Paul D's Hell and Sethe's animal love, Joe's crime and Violet's madness, and in both cases, one evidence remains: one cannot live alone and if there is one person left to love, one has to love him or her. Such Christian wisdom is reached after a long, painful progress. Generations of women have loved and suffered before the feminine characters of Morrison can start to be themselves without the protective support of a man.

When each character has gone to the end of herself, when she has given up expecting from the other what she cannot give, man and woman, delivered from the evil of possession, conscious of their belonging to a community and of the responsibilities that ensue from it, can eventually hope to put side by side their histories.

A HISTORY OF ALIENATION

Whereas it seems necessary to envision the identity quest of Morrison's characters in the order of their creation, in order to throw light on their evolution and the maturing of her work, it seems necessary to follow the historical chronology to look for the causes of their alienation. Each novel is situated at a turning point of Afro-American history. The starting point is *Beloved,* with the attempt of the slaves to escape from a Kentucky Plantation, Sweet Home. Eighteen years later, the narrative voice tries, through partial and circular analepsis, to put words on their experience. Haunted by their painful past, they try hopelessly to stifle it. *Jazz* and *Sula* take place during the great waves of migration to the North between the wars. *Jazz* begins in 1925 but, like *Beloved*, looks back into the past to find the wounds that provoked the present scars. *Sula* covers the years from 1919 to 1941. The end of the novel in 1965 is a sour sweet coda on the meaning of the word *integration*. The *Bluest Eye* grows with the seasons of the year 1941, whereas *Song of Solomon* can be superposed with the life of the author, from the birth of the hero in 1931 to the 1960s and the Civil Rights Movement. *Tar Baby* takes place at the end of the 1970s, offering a very modern image of the identity quest of the Afro-Americans. Morrison launches her great epic with *Paradise*, taking her reader over three generations and dozens of characters along their exodus and founding of their own black city in the midst of Oklahoma. *Love* is even closer to us, with an invisible narrator who weaves her own rememory of a dream love from the 1940s to this day, while she tells the story of the women of Bill Cosey's household, all entranced, fascinated, held captive by the charm of the now absent man whom they all loved. The word *alienation* naturally evolves with the time, and over almost two centuries of history, what we call black community also undergoes sociological and geographical changes. But Morrison's aim remains to capture the soul of her people and give them an identity in the world of letters as well as in history.

Dedicated to the 60 millions and more who died in the Middle Passage, *Beloved* does not try to give a full account of African deportation over the centuries. The slaves have already written much about their enslavement, but in many slave narratives, the veil is dropped as soon as the tale becomes too terrible to relate. They found no words to express the distress of the child who is deprived of his mother, no words to relate the mutilation of the mother, the stealing of her milk or of her babies. The black woman was doubly enslaved to the whites and to the black male: the violence, which generally meant sexual exploitation, remained unspeakable. Who, then, would want to remember those events? Morrison, facing the dead end of Jadine and Son's relationships, decides to lift the veil and tell the true unspoken story of the black woman.

No chapter better expresses this attempt than the third monologue in the central part of *Beloved*. It occurs in the plot when Sethe is attempting to re-appropriate her past and to resurrect metaphorically the original fusion with her child. Beloved's monologue offers, out of the vortex of the unconscious, a perspective on the psychic and temporal annihilation she underwent during the Middle Passage. Her voice becomes the voice of all those who have not survived. The polyphony of voices, reflecting a common memory, culminates in the next chapter with the trio of Sethe, Denver, and Beloved, in the tradition of the spiritual, the only tradition capable of giving voice to the ineffable conversation of their desires. Before this, however, the inexpressible nature of Beloved has given rise to modulations that express, beyond the young child-woman's consciousness, the consciousness of 60 million lost souls. The clear voice of the little girl, speaking of the suffering of so many dead people, dominates the composition by her innocence. As in a dream, images ebb and flow, without resolutions, nor punctuation, expressing the child's desire and her fear, both amplified by the absence of the mother. It is the obsessive delirium of a psyche shocked by the endlessness of suffering. The blanks in the text, as if she were panting, gasping for breath, literally translate her unbearable physical and mental suffering: "All of it is now it is always now there will never be a time when I am not crouching" (*Beloved* 248–53). Past and future merge in an intolerable present. Immured in the silence of an encounter with death, her face against the face of a corpse, the girl clings to her difference ("his face is not mine" [*Beloved* 248–53]), which is also her lack ("the face I want the face that is mine"), as it is her mother's face she yearns for ("I am not separate from her there is no place where I stop her face is my own" [*Beloved* 248–53]). But a cloud separates her from her she loves, the gun smoke of a subdued rebellion that has earned her mother an iron collar. Is this the punishment for her resistance? The innocent child mingles, in metaphoric language, what she sees and what she feels, her anguish at not finding her mother and her precise observation of what is happening around her, managing to describe these terrible deeds, as it were without lifting the veil, and painting the most fearsome and detailed tableau of the Middle Passage.

Beloved's monologue superposes other moments of the young woman's life to the suffering of the slave ship, becoming a metaphoric representation of all the losses and all the separations. What extreme abuse, what cruelty can drive a mother to forsake her child, to choose death for herself, for the child, or both? In what inverted, perverted world is death preferable to what is best in a woman, her motherly love? Morrison chooses the deadly perversion of motherhood, the original place of love and life, as the borderline paradigm of the monstrous reversal effected by slavery.

This unspeakable wound, deeply repressed and lived as life denial, as self-disintegration, only accidentally emerges through the words of the narrative, which then acquires the characteristics of the historical and analytical process: from traces, clues, dream images, it is to refigure the past and re-member the bits and fragments of torn individual beings. Slowly, in a haunting fashion, Sethe's murderous act is merged with her own search for her mother's hat, the only clue she had, and with Beloved's own hunger for her face. Gradually, almost without our paying attention, the black females' fatal transgression is given words, and the reader is made to accept infanticide as being the most charitable deed in such an upside down world.

The thing which, for Sethe, counters all the despair of her past is Nan's revelation:

> She threw them all away but you. The one from the crew she threw away on the island. The others from more whites she also threw away. Without names, she threw them. You she gave the name of the black man. She put her arms around him. The others she did not put her arms around. Never. Never. Telling you. I am telling you, small girl Sethe. (*Beloved* 62)

Sethe was loved, and she has, like Pilate, a name that signifies her father, a name that signifies life, like the child Seth granted by God to Eve. In the jungle that is their life, the slaves cling to the smallest bit of significance, a tree, a bird, a name, even the most ridiculous, provided it has a meaning. The power to name is godly, granted by God to Adam who asserts his dominion over the animals and all living creatures. The white man claims for himself the right to name and to define, which is the right of the master; the slave, being denied his manhood, is like all things, defined by the white man. As Sixo discovers when he dares reply with a logical argument, the white man sets the rules, just as he gives names. When Sixo understands that reasoning is being denied to him, he follows his own logic and ceases to speak English "because there was no future in it" (*Beloved* 25). Like Caliban before him he sees no profit in learning a language that can't be used, but when he is led to death, he does not forget to name his heir "Seven-O!" as a challenge to his master. Beloved is first a name on a tomb, a symbol of remembrance that marks her brief life and death.

Those 60 million and more now are like ghosts, they have left no trace of themselves behind and among those who have survived there are those who believe that they are animals. For a long time, Paul D's only friends have been trees. Whenever he has a name, the slave's name marks the master's possession like a regimental number. His father's name has been erased; the new name tells him that he has no past, no genealogy, his memory has been wiped out. In some African tribes, the giving of a name also gives a soul for the child. Banned from humanity, the slave has no soul. Such dispossession leads to what Ellison has called "the Negro's complicated assertions and denials of identity." The risk for him is to drift away, without beacon, undergoing multiple sea changes like Son, this son who has not been named by his father and therefore is ignorant of the law of the father, "A man without rites: unbaptized, uncircumcised, minus puberty rites or the formal rites of manhood" (*Tar Baby* 165). His various names do not call him to be, but are as many disguises, camouflaging. Faced with the negation of himself, Son clings to the only thing he knows: he must be someone's son. Similarly, Baby Suggs keeps the only name that means anything for her, the nickname given to her by the last man who loved her. Naturally, such a name no longer registers the bearer in a group, which explains Baby Suggs's abortive quest for her lost children. However, those who have known her will recognize her better than if she were called Jenny Whitlow, a white marker that only carries evidence of her slavery.

The importance of the name is such that Morrison dedicates a whole novel to it, to what she calls "the feeling of anonymity, the feeling of orphanage" (Taylor-Guthrie 25). At one level, the quest is that of Milkman, the hero of the novel who hates his family name, gotten by mistake when a drunken Yankee at the Freedmen's Bureau filled in the wrong spaces in the registration book. His name "dead," symbolic of his nonsensical genealogy, may be socially useful, but it cannot be part of who he is. The problem is that his nickname is not an evidence of love either, but a shameful mark he has to bear all his life for having been spied at his mother's breast at an unreasonable age. Milkman has to bear his mother's transgression: he likes her milk too much, but there is also a sexual undertone to his name, as the only milk he can give is his sperm. Like Oedipus, he is a transgressor without knowing it. Helped by Pilate, he embarks on a quest for himself and his true meaning. Leaving civilization behind, he rediscovers his roots in the soil of Virginia "by simply walking the earth" (*Song of Solomon* 329–30). He does not limp anymore; he becomes whole and can at last decipher the riddle of his own life. By rediscovering his past and his sap, Milkman discovers that he is not *Dead*, that under the official name is another one, hidden, mysterious, containing the secret of life.

The other aspect of the quest is the masterful creation of Pilate, a character with Shakespearean dimensions. Her name, first, is a whole story beginning on the day her illiterate father, opening the Bible, points haphazardly to a name that looks beautiful to him. The name of Christ-killing Pilate is a heavy burden to bear for a little girl, but as an adolescent, she decides to keep as a treasure the piece of paper on which her father has inscribed the name, knowing intuitively that it is her sesame to the symbolic world of language. It is also the only trace left by her father, her own roots as well as the only way for her to be recognized by him once dead. Macon Dead Sr. has in fact redefined the name according to its written form and phonetics. It looks like a beautiful tree and to him resounds like leader. The murderous association only comes third and Pilate's father does not really care, since a name taken out of a sacred book is sacred anyway. If God has allowed providence to choose this name for him, it simply means that God lacks authority since He has not saved his wife either. The little girl, therefore, has to bear unconsciously the punishment for the death of her mother; her guilt is later embodied by her smooth belly. Discovering that she has no navel, she gets the proof of her own self-generated creation.

Now, Pilate could, like her brother, be ashamed of that name (Miss Pilate Dead, what a bastard name!), she could also, like Malcolm, deny it and choose to be called X. She decides, against all expectations, to bear it proudly, like a jewel, to make it her own, and through her posture, gives us a beautiful instance of "Signifyin(g)" (cf. Gates Jr., *The Signifying Monkey*), an indirect way to assert her own character and identity, to mock the official interpretations of the Bible, none of which really care for the spirit of the letter. Her posture gives Pilate "a local habitation and a name" (Shakespeare, *A Midsummer Night's Dream* 5.1.7) so powerful that the reader forgets that there has ever been another Pilate before her. Whether the person identifies with the name or is defined by it, the meaning of the name has to be determined. As Pilate demonstrates, power does not lie in acquiring names, but in defining what these names mean. The black community has to impart names, then words, with new significations, just as the novelist has "to clean the language up and give words back their original meaning" (Taylor-Guthrie 165), a meaning that is not necessarily immediate as irony and paradox often hide a subversive use of language, which has to be untangled and interpreted.

In a hostile world where most values are negated or inverted for the black community, the *Signifyin(g) Monkey* is working at all levels, as the first chapter to *Song of Solomon* reveals. Whether we deal with individuals, their names or the city where they live, the direction is always the same: One has to dig deep down and in the past to exhume, behind the lies of the letter, the authenticity of the spirit. In this light, the *Two Cities* of Saint Augustine, founded like *Beloved* on the distinction made by Paul between the letter of the ;aw and temporal life, on the one hand, and the spirit and the promise, on the other, can adequately symbolize the striving toward significance of all Morrison's work.

There is no doubt that such opposition is at work, even though implicitly, as early as *The Bluest Eye*. After bitterly realizing the impossibility for African Americans to find a structuring model for themselves in the letter of a civilization that negates them, the novelist turns, from *Song of Solomon* onward, toward a quest for the spirit that will enable the African American community to find itself in the unity and intimacy of an invisible city, all the stronger as its impalpability cannot be reached by the destructive powers of the whites.

Names, as symbols of dispossession, actively participate both as letter and spirit, to the quest of meaning at work throughout Morrison's novels. To give meaning to meaningless things and make absence visible, to speak the unspeakable, led to the creation ex nihilo of Beloved. The letters B.E.L.O.V.E.D. engraved on the tomb of the little girl represent the quintessence of the process of nomination as well as its greatest paradox, since they immortalize the love of a mother for her nameless little girl who is called "crawling-already? Baby" (*Beloved* 187) until her death. Why this child, who unlike most other children in Morrison's work, had a loving father, never received a name remains a mystery. The only thing we get to know is that she was loved, which, in the nothingness of dispossession, appears to be the supreme gift. Is it not what Pilate premonitorily shouts at Hagar's funeral: "My baby girl... And she was *loved*!" (*Song of Solomon* 319).

As an epitaph, such a personal and anonymous inscription as Beloved becomes a symbol of collective memory, the expression of the living's desire and of the dead's lack. Without love, there is no true name, without name, there is no memory, without memory, there is no past, without which the present itself becomes meaningless and the future remains empty:

> Everybody knew what she was called, but nobody anywhere knew her name. Disremembered and unaccounted for, she cannot be lost because no one is looking for her if they don't know her name? Although she has claim, she is not claimed. In the place where the long grass opens, the girl who waited to be loved and cry shame erupts into her separate parts, to make it easy for the chewing laughter to swallow her all away. (*Beloved* 274)

Without a name, Beloved cannot be called: "For he whose name has not been spoken is ignorant. Indeed, how is one to hear if his name has not been called? For he who is ignorant until the end is a creature of oblivion, and he will vanish along with it" (Robinson 42). If the beloved is a creature of oblivion, she takes love away with her, she carries away the spiritual part of men, without which there is no morrow. It is the reason why she has to come back to haunt the hearts of those whose name bear the trace of a wound. At the end of the novel, Beloved is inscribed as a call and an epitaph.

It is another Beloved who is being buried at the beginning of *Jazz*, murdered for love by Joe Trace who has chosen for his own name the trace his parents have left behind, himself. By his name, Joe Trace sanctions the absence of his parents and becomes their epitaph. He finds a substitute father with Henry Lestroy, who teaches him hunting. He learns to follow the trace and his destiny becomes metaphorically that of a hunter. We may attempt an interpretation of the name Lestroy and its variant Lestory, as symbols of the life story that both Joe and Golden Gray are trying to discover. Whereas Beloved embodied the memory of the black people, Henry Lestory may be its narrator-archeologist, uncovering the traces of a past that renders people their true identity. With him, Golden Gray finds the true history of his life; as for Joe, he follows the traces of Wild, a most elusive character who may be an avatar of Beloved as well as his possible mother. Joe would then be Beloved and Paul D's son, a tangible evidence of the reality of Beloved, which Morrison calls "making memory real" (Taylor-Guthrie 249).

That narrative, reached by following the traces and remnants engraved by the past into memory, provides us, through name giving, with an allegory of literary creation according to Morrison. Wild and Beloved represent the spontaneity and authenticity as well as the bestiality and dereliction of a past that is difficult to accept for African Americans. In *Jazz*, the Beloved who haunts the imagination is no longer the child, but the mother, Joe's silent mother whom he cannot recognize shamelessly, yet has to accept as the deep, rebellious part of himself.

The wild woman within each one has to be recognized and embraced for life to go on; such seems to be the lesson given by the narrative voice in *Jazz*: "I'd love to close myself in the peace left by the woman who lived there and scared everybody. Unseen because she knows better than to be seen.... I am touched by her. Released in secret" (*Jazz* 221). Wild may be one of the figures of *Thunder*, in the *Nag Hammadi*, with the ability to bring the contraries together and to create unity out of discord:

> For I am the first and the last.
> I am the honoured one and the scorned one.
> I am the whore and the holy one.
> I am the wife and the virgin.
> I am (the mother) and the daughter.
> I am the members of my mother. (*The Nag Hammadi Library* 297–303)

These lines evoke Beloved's final fragmentation, fusing with the elementary forces of nature. Since Morrison herself points to it, the assimilation of Beloved and Wild to Thunder is not unjustified. Wild could even be the sum of her mother's members, which would make her Beloved's daughter, Joe being her and Paul D's grandson, sharing with the latter the weakness of being manipulated by a girl young enough to be his own daughter.

> Why, you who hate me, do you love me
> And hate those who love me? [...]
> You who know me, be ignorant of me,
> And those who have not known me, let them know me.
> For I am knowledge and ignorance.
> I am shame and boldness.
> I am shameless; I am ashamed.
> I am strength and I am fear.
> I am war and peace.
> Give heed to me.
> I am the one who is disgraced and the great one.
> [...]
> I am the speech that cannot be grasped.
> I am the name of the sound
> And the sound of the name.
> I am the sign of the letter
> And the designation of the division. (*The Nag Hammadi Library* 297–303)

Wild, this name which is not a name, perfectly evokes this other name of the sound and sound of the name so characteristic of Black culture: *jazz.* The famous onomatopoeia whose origin remains unknown seems to sum up in a single word the problem of naming of African Americans. Jazz is both voice and sex, joy and pain, harmony and discord, wildness turned perfection; it is the most ill-defined word of the language, whereas it expresses the deepest truth, because in Jazz precisely, signified and signifier are one.

Morrison has a Renaissance-like ability to turn words and ideas upside down and to create harmony out of discord. *Paradise* and *Love* open new directions to her investigation without losing sight of her lifelong purpose. Her very titles are antinomic, since *Paradise*, originally meant to be *War*, is a conflictual saga in which love is once again the desire that drives people to act more than a realized state of happiness, whereas *Love* tells a tale of hatred that flowers into love in the last minutes before total annihilation. The paradox that is staged in these novels lies in Morrison's desire to suppress references to color in her narrative. This she manages by reaching further down to the mimetic desire which is at work in all human relationships, at all levels between races, and inside them between men and women. Such desire is so intense that its color makes the individual blind to the color of the skin, when the latter has not already been erased by the violence of mimetic rivalries. Whereas the eight-rocks demonize all light-skinned people while being haunted by the vision of creamy and luminous ladies, two women wage war on each other for the possession of the same object that escapes them until death. Meanwhile, Morrison pursues her spiritual quest of good and evil, investigating further the contentions she detected as early as *Tar Baby* among the members of the House of Chloe—her own community, of course. When all has been said about the dispossession and fragmentation engendered by slavery, about shame and intraracism, when her characters reveal strong wills and forceful identities, when, unlike the slaves at Sweet Home, they can make plans and go a long way toward fulfilling their dreams, what mechanism turns their accomplishment upside down and ruins all their hopes of harmony is now the issue. Meanwhile, the paradise of Bill Cosey testifies to the ability of the black man to be also rich and intelligent and even the host of white people. It is his way to "contradict history" (*Love* 54) and to refuse segregation. In his world, the opposition between white and black has dissolved into a new undifferentiated term: colored. Everybody is colored, which tends to emphasize the resemblance between races. When Peter Paul asks Junior if she is colored, she replies that she does not know: "he said it didn't matter, because he couldn't invite Gentiles to his house anyway" (*Love* 56). One form of discrimination hides another; the color line is blurred in both novels by religious beliefs that become more and more obtrusive.

In *Paradise,* the proliferation of doubles, the abnormal presence of twins, appears as a way to confuse the issue of identity. This aspect is stressed by the narrator's refusal to give the reader any clue as to the identity of the white girl who is killed in the opening line of the novel, and the choice of a particularly mimetic historical context as the narrative is permeated by Booker T. Washington's uplift ideology. After having explored and attempted to find the causes of the opposition between whites and blacks—something incomprehensible for Baby Suggs and Stamp Paid in *Beloved*—after having sung the multiple shades of black, risking the temptation to demonize white, after having gone to the origins of slavery, it seems that Morrison is now going even farther back in history to the myth of the origins in order to uncover its mimetic mechanism. Like Shakespeare, she seems to attribute original sin to the deed that attracted the "primal eldest curse" (Shakespeare, *Hamlet* 3.3.37), a brother's hatred, rather than to the temptation of Eve. She will now investigate siblings' jealousy and rivalry, sisterly love stained and broken by the irresponsibility of a father whose figure charms and bewitches everyone.

Paradise tells the epic story of the eight-rocks as they evolve into a monstrous double of the white civilization. The citizens of Ruby have become perfect copies of the Pilgrim Fathers, with whom they share pride and the conviction of divine election. Ruby itself is like a piece of New England— puritanical, industrious, as white and deserted as a Hopper painting—in the midst of Oklahoma. It is the success story of the twins Deacon and Steward, who carefully maintain its mythical origin. Forty years before, their grandfather Zechariah led the small troop in an exodus from Louisiana to Oklahoma in order to run away from white hatred. Following Moses, they walk in the desert expecting a sign from above. They are black, blue black, and want to preserve the purity of their blood. Such fundamentalism is later explained by the denial of Fairly, another black town whose colored inhabitants are afraid of the raggedy newcomers.

What few Ruby inhabitants know and the reader only discovers late in the novel is that Big Papa, nicknamed Coffee, had a twin called Tea. Those names probably reveal the different shades of black of the brothers and will ultimately call for a revaluation of the Fairly initial trauma. If Coffee is the darker brother, he is also the most successful, with a government position that arouses the envy of those around him. The text leaves us no doubt as to the reason why he is a scapegoat: He is too successful and much too white for the community, whereas his black skin is highly visible in a mulatto world. It is remarkable that both blacks and whites dislike him. The episode tells us how the two brothers are mocked by white men and asked to play the minstrels. Tea accommodates the whites whose pistol is a convincing argument, whereas Coffee takes a bullet in his foot and "from that moment they weren't brothers anymore" (*Paradise* 302). According to René Girard, desire is essentially mimetic, and all the stronger as it is doubled. What should we think of twins' desires? "When Coffee got the statehouse job, Tea seemed pleased as everybody else," says the narrator (*Paradise* 302). This *seemed,* however, opens the space for doubt that is confirmed by the episode just quoted. Tea, obviously, is all too ready to obey the white man and has probably wanted to imitate him like his brother. He certainly envied his position as a legislator. Each of them has answered in his way to the white man's desire. Tea, whose skin is lighter, may even be mocking his brother while dancing, just as Remus mocked his brother Romulus by dancing on the boundaries of his city.

From this moment on, the story becomes a myth, and nobody in Ruby has ever heard of Tea, for Coffee has taken great care to revise history by changing his own name and erasing all the traces of violence that could have shocked his followers. In history as in a law case, the only evidence is the wound. Coffee is wounded. Like Oedipus, he becomes a tragic hero. Deacon's explaining that Grand Papa Coffee has been wrong in what he did to his brother comes as a shock. Whose guilt is it after all?

The contemptuous dismissal of Fairly, shocking as it may have been, cannot be the real cause of the trauma. It had to come from the victim's community itself, a community so mixed racially that it was undifferentiated: "He [Coffee] was an embarrassment to the Negroes and both a threat and a joke to whites. No one, black or white, could or would help him find other work" (*Paradise* 302). His own brother is probably among them. Every man envies Coffee's good fortune and expresses his frustration through violence against Coffee, who has acquired all the characteristics of the scapegoat. He was probably hunted out of the city like a lame dog. His pierced foot remains the trace of his brother's hatred as much as the sign of his own transgression, for he was the first to emulate the whites.

In order to gather a new community around himself, he had to find a cohesive idea, he had to change his guilt into something more universal, more primitive like the stain that has burdened the black race since the beginning of times and which, in history, justified racism. The Fairly episode does just this, mixing together the sin—inner stain—with the disallowing—external stain.

With Coffee, however, Morrison twists the process of mythical crystallization that normally concluded the sacrificial crisis. The victim brings back prosperity through his death and the newly recovered peace of the community turns him into a God. Coffee is in a sense deified and founds his own community under the name Zechariah, but this is a different community and he does not die, leaving Tea, who becomes the victim, behind.

Ruby's founding myth is a lie and the racial war waged by Zechariah and his descendants over three generations is a politic pretext hiding Zechariah's resentment of his lighter-skinned brother. As Misner's sermon reveals, the inhabitants of Ruby understand little of the meaning of the cross and Zechariah's so-called prophetic message is not one of love. It is only by willingly accepting his part as a scapegoat, his sacrifice, that he could have worked toward reconciliation, smothering the will to revenge. Zechariah runs the risk of seeing the mimetic forces that animate his group develop into new violence once the outer enemies have been overcome. Who then will bear the brunt of their quarrels and dissensions? Since blackness is their badge of honor and purity, since no stranger to the town is welcome, all lighter-skinned babies can only come from a woman's betrayal. Ruby has gradually re-created inside the community the frustrations and jealousies of the origins. Transgressions multiply, twins proliferate until even different characters are paired in the eyes of the community (Fleet and Jeff, Zechariah and Rector, Misner and Pulliam, etc.). Such confusing sameness, indicative of intermarrying, is a bad omen for the future of a place living in total isolation. Everybody ends up suspecting everybody, even the twins, Deek and Stewart who have always been able to read each other's mind and share the same secret desire for elegant, creamy women, suspect each other. The pastel vision that occupies their minds becomes the absolute Other for which they transgressed their father's law. It is there, implicit, as a watermark, in the narrative of their life.

When Stewart, suspecting his brother of betrayal, kills the golden woman who has thrown a spell on his brother, the color is once again a pretext, which as convincing as it may be within the context of racist America, is again a trap for the reader to lose himself. The true cause is to be found in the fear of both brothers of losing their status and their power, and even deeper, the resentment and desire born of their resemblance. To prevent his brother from getting what he himself dreams of, Stewart organizes a hunt similar to that which chased Coffee out of town. The difference is in their hunting females, which an honorable hunter knows he cannot do. By killing the white girl first, they simply reveal the transgression of their own desire.

Love replaces the epic dimension by the intimacy of the novel, the desert wilderness by the affluence of a fashionable resort and the gothic extravagance of the Convent by the intimacy of a town house where rivalries are aggravated. The close relationship of the characters intensifies the similarity of their desires and their confrontation. The time is now one of freedom and casualness in which young innocent girls have all gone through a sad story with a monster who has turned them into hard, scandalous women. In the background, the narrative voice generalizes on situations she witnesses and disapproves of, blurring differentiation in a community where everyone is looking for a culprit outside. The Police-heads are, in that light, both real and mythical, very convenient props for all the grievances and all the wrongs, the accidental drowning as well as the ultimate bankruptcy of the resort. Facing the bad faith and the blindness of all the characters, the narrative voice L—Love, but also "she" or "her" in French—which may be Morrison herself—is revealed as an arch-manipulator, who alone possesses the truth.

In this novel, color has the violence of desire, like the two orange squares in Baby Suggs's blanket, it screams in the greyness of everyday lives. The colors of landscape seem to make people drunk, troubles their judgment so much that they confound the innocence of a child's love with the childish whims of the rich who follow the last capitalistic fashion. If Cosey's family resort cannot stand the competition of Hiltons and cruises, can it resist the self-destructive desire of its members?

Like the Morgan brothers, Cosey, obeying B. T. Washington's philosophy, has become a successful businessman whom everyone envies and emulates. Yet, in spite of the hatred he sometimes generates, he has no rival because he is so much above the others. The power of desire that seems to rule the novel never quite manages to conceal the oppositions between races, sexes, social classes, but it manages at its climax to blur the references, to transgress generations. Where the Morgan twins had to deal with the rigid law of the father, the candidates to the title "sweet Cosey child" have very early to steer a delicate course between treasons and traps, lust and lies that darken the truth and the innocence of their love. To them, the color of their skin and their antagonistic social classes are of no account. Christine and Heed fall in each other's arms until the perversity of an adult separates them forever. By marrying the best friend of his granddaughter, Cosey initiates a lifelong rivalry between them. Christine is not only deprived of her friend, she is deprived of a home. Revenge becomes her goal and when she comes back for Cosey's funeral, Christine and Heed are pitted against each other, "Standing there, one to the right, one to the left, of Bill Cosey's casket, their faces, as different as honey from soot, looked identical. Hate does that. Burns off everything but itself, so whatever your grievance is, your face looks just like your enemy's" (*Love* 34). What clearer summary of René Girard's conclusions on the violence of mimetic desire? Their hatred, kindled by a few cryptic words on a paper napkin, turns each of them into the double of the other. Although Heed is black and Christine white, they have become twins. Bill, who may one day have been a god for them, is dead, but their rivalry is kindled anew, fed by violence only, showing that he was not its object after all.

Both women fight till death for the inheritance of Bill Cosey: a name, "Sweet Cosey Child," and a house where they spy on each other, plotting the destruction of their rival until they end up realizing that they have killed each other for nothing:

> We could have been living our lives hand in hand instead of looking for Big Daddy everywhere.
> —He was everywhere. And nowhere.
> —We make him up?...
> —Only a devil could think him up. (*Love* 189)

The devil is, of course, the mimetic desire that has chained them together. Like the last word of a lifelong meditation on slavery, racism, and possession, Morrison concludes as a humanist on the responsibility of each one to provoke dialogue. Desire gives life its color, its perfume too, but desire also triggers death when passion and possession become obsessions. Free from the yoke of slavery, Morrison's characters get giddy with the freedom of love, like Sethe. Desire is what creates and kills. In the rivalries, the only link between people is language. When Christine and Heed finally begin to speak, they understand their illusion and their misfortune. After what seems a large loop into the mechanism of desire, Morrison comes back to language and the necessary dialogue that can help each of us to be. She holds everyone responsible. If the Ruby men had tried to speak with the Convent women, if Heed and Christine had recovered their youthful intimacy, violence would have been avoided and a richer world would have been born. As the old blind woman says to the young boys mocking her: "I don't know whether the bird you are holding is dead or alive, but what I do know is that it is in your hands. It is in your hands" (*Nobel Lecture* 11).

Morrison's last novel, *A Mercy* (2008) appears as the quintessence of her work. In this beautiful short novel, her language is so clean and so apt that it becomes poetry without effort. Her main character's orality is no longer a combination of words emerging out of the ungrammatical mastery of written language, but the simple, straightforward expression of sensory, and sensual, impressions, the language of a child who has not yet been conditioned by a system. But this is not a child's book, and there is nothing mawkish about it. Morrison simply implements the condition of the foreigner's experience when arriving in an unknown land, whose languages, codes, rules, he does not master. Your senses then become your only means of apprehension of a world which may be frightening and dangerous. What you see, hear, smell, taste, touch, what Florens calls reading the signs, become the condition of your survival in a chaotic world already corrupted by gold and the desire for power. Morrison goes back a very long time to the foundation of the land, when most immigrants were exiles and foreigners looking for home in the new world, when racism had not yet become the peculiar institution that would shame America. Her characters are once again mostly women centered on a male protector. The narrative subtly reveals the workings of desire, fear, and strength, in a world marked by ignorance and the first "lawless laws" that would corrupt the "wish for permanent happiness" that had first fuelled the discovery of America. The recurring question remains: Who's responsible? but Morrison's pen does not—should we say no longer?—moralize, neither does it accuse; her imagination has acquired the negative capability of poets and she leaves it to the reader to make up her mind and engage herself. The bird is more than ever in her hand to be saved or killed.

BELOVED

Beloved, a neo–slave narrative published in 1987, is Morrison's iconic Pulitzer Prize–winning fifth novel. The novel emerged at the height of what many critics have called the black women's literary renaissance, a great upsurge of black women's writing that occurred in the 1970s and 1980s. By the time Morrison published *Beloved,* several other black female authors, including Maya Angelou, Lucille Clifton, Gloria Naylor, Sonia Sanchez, and Alice Walker, among others, had also risen to prominence on the literary scene. However, while Morrison shares company with an illustrious group of black women writers, none of their works have achieved the critical acclaim or global iconic status as her novel, *Beloved.*

Most reviewers hailed *Beloved* as an artistic achievement and Morrison's best work. *New York Times* reviewer Michiko Kakutani applauded Morrison's "magisterial yet sensuous prose," pronouncing *Beloved* a "dazzling novel" (C24). Novelist Margaret Atwood called Morrison's work a "triumph" and contended that her "versatility and technical and emotional range appear to know no bounds. If there were any doubts about her stature as a preeminent American novelist, of her own or any other generation, 'Beloved' will put them to rest" (560). Others were less adulatory in their praise. Although Ann Snitow ultimately endorsed the novel, she found the ghost story element weak and unpersuasive and the romance narrative between Paul D and Sethe clichéd and problematic, contending that in the end, the novel "fails in its ambitions" (50). Like Snitow, Judith Thurman commended the novel overall, but found Morrison's use of language "powerful but manipulative" (75), contending that her prose is subject to operatic melodramatic excess (77). Stanley Crouch was perhaps the most negative reviewer by far; he lambasted the work as a "blackface holocaust novel" and decried Morrison for what he saw as her "almost always [losing] control" (205) and giving in to "the temptation of the trite or the sentimental" (209). Most scholars and critics agree that Crouch's vehement attacks on the novel miss the mark in understanding *Beloved*'s timeliness and enduring appeal. Indeed, the few instances of harsh criticism notwithstanding, *Beloved* is not only considered Morrison's masterpiece, but one of the finest pieces of literature ever written.

Despite its acclaim and almost immediate iconic status, *Beloved* won neither the National Book Award nor the National Book Critics Circle Award in 1987. This sparked large controversy and outrage from literary circles. One of the ensuing results was that 48 preeminent African American authors and critics, such as June Jordan, Ernest J. Gaines, Henry Louis Gates Jr., and Alice Walker, among others, wrote a tribute to Morrison and in defense of *Beloved*'s merits in the January 24, 1988, edition of the *New York Times*. In the piece "Black Writers in Praise of Toni Morrison," the authors argued that the "legitimate need for our own critical voice in relation to our own literature can no longer be denied" and condemned what they saw as the "oversight and harmful whimsy" of the selection committees of the National Book Award and the Pulitzer Prize (BR36). While some applauded the authors' stance, others, such as novelist Charles Johnson, accused them of manipulation and attempting to incite white guilt. Nevertheless, in the face of this controversy, *Beloved* did eventually go on to win the Pulitzer Prize in 1988.

Because of its status as a literary icon, *Beloved* has garnered significant interest from literary scholars since its publication. *Beloved* is a complex novel, with themes ranging from slavery and the Middle Passage to the importance of memory (or "rememory") and the role of community, to the illustration of spirituality and the possibility of romantic love. However, because Morrison foregrounds many themes connected to motherhood, literary critics have discussed these particular aspects of the novel in great detail. Commenting on Sethe as an archetypal strong maternal figure, Trudier Harris contends that Morrison has crafted the novel's protagonist in the "tradition of so many of those who walked to freedom with Harriet Tubman, and [Sethe] takes her chances with her own very pregnant body" (70). Along those lines, Andrea O'Reilly argues that "Sethe claims a maternal subjectivity in defiance of the construction of slave mothers as breeders, in order to instill in her children a loved sense of self so that they may be subjects in a culture that commodifies them as objects" (127). Harris and O'Reilly are among many other critics who have noted the significance of strong maternal figures in *Beloved*, arguing that Morrison is challenging the notion that slavery completely disrupted familial love or care.

Several scholars have discussed the importance of history and memory in *Beloved*. Barbara Christian, for example, has claimed that in the novel, "the adventure is not an exterior one, but the more dangerous internal one of the self remembering and even understanding its past" (340). She lists characters such as Paul D, Sethe, Denver, and Beloved, who all struggle, some more successfully than others, with the persistence of painful personal and collective memories. Likewise, Cheryl A. Wall contends that "*Beloved* itself is rememory; it imagines the pictures that women like Margaret Garner might have carried around in their heads and the stories they might have told about them had there been anyone able to listen" (98). As Christian and Wall, among others, have emphasized, the role of memory is an important theme in *Beloved*, one that greatly informs the other themes of the novel.

Morrison's novels are noted often for their intricate and demanding prose, and *Beloved* is no different. In particular, the novel has been heralded for its emphasis on oral culture and storytelling. Yvonne Atkinson foregrounds the trope of "call and response," a type of verbal exchange in African American culture, is interweaved throughout *Beloved*. She states that "Morrison's 'Sixty Million and more' and the epigraph of Beloved are powerful, in part, because they Call forth an emotional Response from the reader, who has cultural, historical, and personal knowledge of the institution of slavery" (252). DoVeanna S. Fulton also sees Morrison's prose as grounded in African American oral traditions, contending that "Morrison employs a variety of oral traditions grounded in Black culture that, taken together, recalls the Jazz singing form of scatting. The piece-by-piece method Morrison chooses to reveal the experiences of the residents of 124 Bluestone Road simulates the note-by-note...form of scatting" (105). Fulton cites *Beloved* as a type jazz novel, where Morrison's conveys the characters' stories as multilayered testimonies that build off each other to create a new set of histories. Atkinson and Fulton are just two examples of the many scholarly pieces devoted to the role of language in *Beloved*.

Beloved's structure is important in understanding its content. The novel consists of 28 chapters, comparable to the days of a lunar month and a women's menstrual cycle. The structure also invokes the 28 days of freedom Sethe experiences when she arrives in Cincinnati. Aside from the 28 chapters, the novel is divided into three main sections of varying length. Each section opens with an extensive chapter describing 124 Bluestone Road. In section one, 124 is "spiteful," in section two it is "loud," and in section three it is "quiet." These words signal the shifting action throughout the text. It has somewhat of an inverted pyramid structure: section one has 18 chapters, section two has 7 chapters, and section three has 3 chapters.

Section two features four chapters that offer first-person, stream-of-consciousness narration. Sethe, Beloved, and Denver alternately narrate their views and feelings about themselves and their relationship to one another. Chapter 20 is Sethe's opportunity to reflect on her life and her role as a mother. Sethe remembers telling Mrs. Garner about her violation with schoolteacher's nephews and caring for Mrs. Garner as if she were her own mother. Most of Sethe's rumination is about Beloved and Sethe's happiness at her return. Chapter 21 is Denver's stream-of-consciousness chapter. In it, she remembers her childhood (and adult) fears about her mother and wonders what lead her to kill her sister. Chapter 22 is by far the most complex and perplexing segment. Beloved narrates this chapter and recalls her experiences in death and in the Middle Passage. During death it is as if she merges with the "60 million or more" who perished on the transatlantic journey to the Americas and thus recounts their experience along with her own. Morrison bypasses punctuation and uses irregular syntax to reflect Beloved's childlike speech and the horror of the slavery. The chapter transmits Beloved's undying longing for her mother and her desire to return to her. Chapter 23 is a polyphony of Sethe, Denver, and Beloved's perspectives, detailing the desire each has to possess the other. Morrison repeats the phrase "You are mine" to denote the possessiveness and obsession that characterizes this trio.

Community is one of the most significant themes of Beloved. Upon Sethe's escape from slavery, she experiences 28 days of freedom in her community. She has women and men friends, she enjoys meeting others, and relishes being with her family. However, disharmony ensues after Sethe's violent reaction to Schoolteacher's return. While some characters insist that they abhor her infanticide, the community's main issue with Sethe is her pride. Because she does not immediately seek their help, the community rejects her, while Sethe resents the community's attitude and further distances herself. The result is an 18-year estrangement between Sethe and the African American community.

Motherhood is one of the most resonant themes in the text. For Sethe, motherhood is the site of both her greatest pain and joy. She is unable to know her mother and even sees her murdered because of rebellion. She runs away because she fears her children will be sold from her. She eventually murders her daughter rather than see her re-enslaved. Sethe also believes her children to be her "best thing," the part of her that remains unsullied by slavery and white oppression. Nonetheless, this emphasis on motherhood effaces Sethe's positive image of herself as anything besides a mother. Indeed, throughout most of the novel, she fails to recognize that she is her own "best thing"; when Paul D asserts this to be the case, Sethe replies with a skeptical "Me?" (*Beloved* 322). The dialogue ends there and it is up to the reader to decide whether Sethe believes this or continues to mourn the loss of Beloved. Ultimately, Sethe's life is lived in reaction to the realities of black motherhood during slavery and soon after.

Slavery is a major thematic issue in the novel. However, the novel is less about the daily realities of the institution—although it does include that—and more about the consequences of slavery: the tenuous and tenacious slave family, the importance of community, the impossibility of being free while chained to the past, and the resilience of the self despite persistent and malicious oppression. Morrison accomplishes the difficult task of illustrating slave experiences without reducing the characters to uncomplicated victims. Instead, she creates complex and even troubled individuals who are survivors.

Memory is often called "rememory" in the novel. Morrison crafts a world where time does not simply exist linearly, but where past and present coexist. Indeed, the past constantly intrudes on the present and is slowly revealed to the reader in pieces, asserting the fragmentary nature of memory. Many characters do their best to avoid their past and banish their memories, but as the presence of Beloved reveals, the past must be dealt with. The last lines of Beloved sum up the novel's preoccupation with memory: it ends with an exclamation that the story is not one to "pass on." Clearly, this phrase has a double meaning. On the one hand, it refers to the novel as a story that should not be shared. On the other hand, the phrase also asks the reader not to cast the story aside. Taken together, the phrase suggests that the reader remember the horrors of slavery and not replicate them.

Because *Beloved* is in part a ghost story, ghosts and spirits are important symbols. Much of Morrison's fiction, including *Song of Solomon* and *Jazz,* has been classified as magical realism, a literary device that mixes elements of magic and fantasy with realism to underscore the importance of the fantastic in everyday life. Magical realism often rejects the constraints of logic, infusing seemingly irrational occurrences into otherwise normal life. Morrison's use of magical realism also connects to Latin American authors such as Isabelle Allende and Gabriel García Márquez, who similarly use the fantastic in seemingly ordinary settings. To that end, characters are undisturbed by the appearance of the supernatural. Indeed, the border between the natural and supernatural is rather porous and permeable in *Beloved*. When Paul D walks into 124 Bluestone Road and experiences the baby ghost's fury, he is not taken aback at the existence of the ghost, but rather is surprised by its vehemence. Likewise, Baby Suggs perceives the haunting as nothing surprising, reminding Sethe that the country is peopled with the angry dead, the souls of African Americans unable to rest. Nevertheless, some critics resist aligning Morrison's work with magical realism because, as they argue, Morrison does not ask the reader to suspend their disbelief (and believe that ghosts are real in the novel), but rather that she posits ghost are real within the novel and without.

As in much of Morrison's fiction, naming is critical in *Beloved*. "Sethe" is a feminine version of "Seth," who in the Judeo-Christian tradition is the third son of Adam and Eve, the child who replaces Cain and Abel, and helps to people humanity. Paul D has the same name, save a middle initial, as his brothers Paul A and Paul F. The sequential order of the Pauls' names suggests that perhaps there were other brothers (Pauls B, C, and E) that previously died or who were sold away. The naming also suggests a certain amount of interchangeableness between the men, as if the men are slightly different versions of the same product. Paul may allude to the Apostle Paul, author of several chapters of the New Testament and early Christian missionary. Unlike the biblical Paul, Paul D is not particularly religious; however, the two both experience extensive travels. Denver is named for Amy Denver, the white woman who helped birth her. Stamp Paid is born Joshua, but renames himself after enduring a year of his wife Vashti as his master's concubine. Baby Suggs also renames herself. While enslaved she is called "Jenny," but when she is freed she names herself "Baby" because that is what her husband called her. She also dismisses her slave last name of "Whitlow" and takes her husband's last names of "Suggs." Beloved's name is particularly significant. It is important to note that the reader is never privy to her name as a baby. She is described as a "crawling already?" baby (*Beloved* 187) and only as Beloved once she appears as an adult. "Dearly Beloved," are the two words Sethe remembers from her murdered daughter's funeral. She goes so far as get "Beloved" engraved on a tombstone commemorating her child.

Although media mogul Oprah Winfrey acquired film rights to *Beloved* soon after the novel was published, it did not appear in theatres until 1998. During the more than decadelong delay, several writers, including Akosua Busia, Richard LaGravenese, and Adam Brooks, attempted to translate Morrison's masterpiece to film. Once the script was settled on in 1997, Winfrey was able to get her first choice for director, Jonathan Demme, on board. Although Demme was the respected director of *Silence of the Lambs* (1991), *Philadelphia* (1993), and other successful films, Winfrey experienced some backlash for not hiring an African American director. Winfrey starred as "Sethe," in her first film role since playing "Sofia" in Steven Spielberg's adaptation of Alice Walker's *The Color Purple* (1985). Joining her was her *Color Purple* cast mate Danny Glover as Paul D, Kimberly Elise as Denver, and Thandie Newton as Beloved.

Although highly anticipated, *Beloved* did not garner wholesale acclaim with critics or movie-going audiences. The film opened in a lackluster fifth slot and disappeared from the box office after soon. Some film critics faulted Oprah Winfrey's influence as both producer and star, one contending that perhaps "Jonathan Demme found himself quite unable to challenge Winfrey's vision of how this story should be told," which resulted in a haphazard "*Roots*-meets-*The X Files* viewing experience" (Orr 5). Other reviewers applauded Demme's skill, but still found the film unconvincing, especially when compared to the book. Reviewers generally praised Winfrey, Glover, and Elise for their acting; however, Newton's portrayal of Beloved garnered mixed reviews. Some critics thought her rendering of this ghost-turned-young-woman affecting and powerful, while others described her garbled voice and lurching actions as disturbing and repulsive. Whether it was the film's protracted length (at nearly three hours), its content (mainstream dramas featuring African American casts have a history of doing poorly in theatres), or the style (confusing flashbacks without voiceovers to narrate the events), *Beloved*'s success as a film has in no way matched the novel's acclaim.

Despite *Beloved* the film's critical and commercial failings, *Beloved* the novel remains an iconic text. It is frequently cited as one of the best pieces of literature ever published, listed as one of *Time* magazine's top 100 novels, and included on several other influential book lists.

Ultimately, *Beloved* remains a literary icon not only in spite of the critical firestorm at its publication and a lackluster film version in its wake, but because of its wide-ranging appeal and enduring cultural relevance.

Beloved

Beloved, *whose publication gave Morrison the Nobel Prize for Literature, was made into a film directed by Jonathan Demme, starring Oprah Winfrey as Sethe and Danny Glover as Paul D (1998).*

BIBLIOGRAPHY

Beloved. New York: Knopf, 1987.

The Bluest Eye. New York: Holt, 1970.

The Dancing Mind. New York: Knopf, 1996.

Jazz. New York: Knopf, 1992.

Love. New York: Knopf, 2003.

A Mercy. New York. Knopf, 2008.

The Nobel Lecture. New York: Knopf, 1993.

Paradise. New York: Knopf, 1997.

Playing in the Dark. New York: Knopf, 1992.

Remember: The Journey to School Integration. Boston: Houghton Mifflin, 2004.

Song of Solomon. New York: Knopf, 1977.

Sula. New York: Knopf, 1973.

Tar Baby. New York: Knopf, 1981.

Toni Morrison invitée au Louvre *Etranger chez soi*. Paris: Christian Bourgois, 2006.

What Moves in the Margin: Selected Fiction. Ed. and with an introduction by Carolyn C. Denard. Jackson: UP of Mississippi, 2008.

Theatre

Dreaming Emmett, performed at SUNY, Albany, in 1986.

Critical Works, Articles

"Behind the Making of the Black Book." *Black World* 23 (1974): 86–90.

Birth of a Nation'hood. Intro. by Toni Morrison, ed. with Claudia Lacour. New York: Pantheon, 1997.

The Black Book: A Scrapbook of 300 Years of the Folk Journey of Black America. New York: Random House, 1974 (a compilation by Middleton Harris). Morrison edited this book at Random House and contributed some family photos and texts.

"Black Matter(s)." *Grand Street* 10.4 1991: 205–25.

"City Limits, Village Values: Concepts of the Neighborhood in Black Fiction." *Literature and the Urban Experience: Essays on the City and Literature*. Ed. Michael C. Jaye and Ann Chalmers Watts. Piscataway, NJ: Rutgers UP, 1981. 35–43.

"Faulkner and Women." *Faulkner and Women: Faulkner and Yoknapatawpha*. Ed. Doreen Fowler and Ann J. Abadie. Jackson: U of Mississippi P, 1986: 285–302.

"I Will Always Be A Writer." *Essence* December 1976: 54–56, 90.

"A Knowing So Deep." *Essence* May 1985: 230.

"Memory, Creation and Writing." *Thought* 59 (December 1984): 385–90

The Nobel Lecture in Literature. 1993. New York: Knopf, 1994.

"Of Unspeakable Things Unspoken; The Afro-American Presence in American Literature." *Michigan Quarterly Review* 28 (Winter 1989): 9–34.

"On Behalf of Henry Dumas." *Black American Literature Forum* 22.2 (Summer 1988): 310–12.

Playing in the Dark: Whiteness and the Literary Imagination. Cambridge: Harvard UP, 1992.

"Reading." *Mademoiselle* May 1975: 14.

"Rediscovering Black History." *New York Times Magazine* August 11, 1974: 14, 16, 18, 20, 22, 24.

"Rootedness: The Ancestor as Foundation." *Black Women Writers*. Ed. Mari Evans. Garden City, NJ: Anchor, 1984. 339–45.

"The Site of Memory." *Inventing the Truth: The Art and Craft of Memoir.* Ed. W. Zinsser. Boston: Houghton-Mifflin, 1987: 103–24.

"A Slow Walk of a Tree (as Grandmother Would say), Hopeless (as Grandfather Would Say)." *New York Times Magazine* July 4, 1976. 104+.

Conversations and Interviews

Angelo, Bonnie. "The Pain of Being Black." *Time* 133 (May 22, 1989): 120–23.

Taylor-Guthrie, Danille, ed. *Conversations with Toni Morrison.* Jackson: UP of Mississippi, 1994.

Opera

Margaret Garner, with composer Richard Danielpour. World Premiere on May 7, 2005.

FURTHER READING

Denard, Carolyn C., ed. *Toni Morrison: What Moves at the Margin, Selected Nonfiction.* Jackson: UP of Mississippi, 2008.

Fultz, Lucille P. *Toni Morrison: Playing with Difference.* Urbana: U of Illinois P, 2003.

Grewal, Gurleen. *Circles of Sorrow, Lines of Struggle: The Novels of Toni Morrison.* Baton Rouge: Louisiana State UP, 1998.

Kubitschek, Missy Dehn. *Toni Morrison: A Critical Companion.* Westport, CT: Greenwood, 1998.

Mitchell, Angelyn. *The Freedom to Remember: Narrative, Slavery, and Gender in Contemporary Black Women's Fiction.* Piscataway, NJ: Rutgers UP, 2000.

Morrison, Toni. *Playing in the Dark: Whiteness and the Literary Imagination.* Cambridge: Harvard UP, 1992.

Peach, Linden. *Toni Morrison.* 2nd ed. New York: St. Martin's, 2000.

Peterson, Nancy J., ed. *Toni Morrison: Critical and Theoretical Approaches.* Baltimore, MD: Johns Hopkins UP, 1987.

Robinson, James M., ed. "The Gospel of Truth." *The Nag Hammadi.* 3rd rev. ed. San Francisco: Harper, 1990. 21, 30–38.

Weisenburger, Steven. *Modern Medea: A Family Story of Slavery and Child-Murder from the Old South.* New York: Hill, 1998.

Zauitu-Selassie, K. *African Spiritual Traditions in the Novels of Toni Morrison.* Gainesville: UP of Florida, 2009.

Annie-Paule Mielle de Prinsac and Susana M. Morris

Walter Mosley attends the 80th anniversary celebration of Harlem's Schomburg Center at the Lincoln Center in New York, 2006. (AP/Wide World Photos)

Walter Mosley

Walter Mosley (1952–) may be most familiar as the writer of *Devil in a Blue Dress,* which was turned into a 1995 film starring Denzel Washington. His Easy Rawlins series is extremely popular and extremely loved; even former President Bill Clinton was a fan. Mosley is a prolific writer, averaging more than a book a year in the 20 years he has been publishing. Mosley is also a writer who crosses boundaries—of genre, of race, of time—to produce his fiction. In addition to the Easy Rawlins series, Mosley has written two other mystery series, science fiction, literary fiction, a young adult novel, and several nonfiction books. His latest novel, *The Last Days of Ptolemy Grey,* was published in November 2010, and explores memory, old age, and love. Walter Mosley is an icon not only for being the writer who brought African American mystery fiction to a broader audience (book reviewers have given him credit for integrating the genre), but also for accomplishing a rare feat: having great mainstream success in genre fiction while still being taken very seriously by literary critics and the broader literary establishment. His books have sold hundreds of thousands of copies and been translated into 21 languages. Several of the Easy Rawlins books were *New York Times* bestsellers, as are the two Leonid McGill mysteries and *The Last Days of Ptolemy Grey.* His books have also been Edgar Award nominees, and Mosley has won the Anisfield Wolf Award, an O. Henry Award for short fiction, the Sundance Rick-Takers Award, and the PEN American Center's Lifetime Achievement Award.

His reputation as a serious writer of the first rank is due to both his literary fiction, like his latest novel and 2004's *The Man in My Basement,* and the complex protagonists and lush recreations of mid-century Los Angeles found in his first two mystery series, the Easy Rawlins and Fearless Jones books. His reputation has also been built on his unflinching and realistic depictions of race and racism throughout his body of work. With his current mystery series, the Leonid McGill series, planned for 10 books, Mosley has moved the action from L.A. to New York City and moved from the midcentury setting of many of his works to the contemporary age, but these books, like Mosley's work in other genres, carry on the thematic issues found in his early work. Mosley has also parlayed his critical and commercial success into aiding the development of other writers of color and the publishing industry. He offered the Easy Rawlins prequel, *Gone Fishin',* to Black Classic Press rather than one of the larger publishing houses with which he had worked. He also worked with NYU on the "Black Geniuses" lecture series, worked within PEN (Poets Essayists and Novelists) to establish the Open Book Program, and worked with City University of New York to open the Publishing Institute at City College, which helps young urban residents to learn the publishing industry.

Mosley drew more African American mystery readers and writers and helped integrate the genre by disproving what prospective publishers told him at the start of his writing career: "White people don't read about black people, black women don't read about black men, and black men don't read" (Wilson 1). As he told the *Seattle Post-Intelligencer* in an interview, Mosley wanted to write books that everybody reads but that black men can enjoy and feel connected to (qtd. in Marshall). And he achieved this as both his iconic stature and bestselling status testify. As an extremely successful mystery writer in a genre (the hard-boiled mystery especially) most associated with white writers, Mosley helped to integrate the genre and also drew African American readers and writers to it by exploring a multifaceted African American community in which African Americans were not only perpetrators or victims, even though Easy Rawlins recognizes the pervasiveness of that stereotype in *Little Scarlet*: "He was a cop by trade and I was a criminal by color" (10). Several other writers, including Barbara Neely, Eleanor Taylor Bland, Nichelle Tramble, and Valerie Wilson Wesley, would publish mystery series with African American detectives soon after Mosley's *Devil in a Blue Dress* appeared in 1990. While the series differ in many respects, there are similarities that help illuminate Mosley's iconic status. While Neely and Wilson Wesley both have female protagonists, their novels share concerns with Mosley's work. Wilson Wesley's Tamara Hayle is a single parent like Easy Rawlins, and shares his concern both with family and with helping those in the community (Rawlins trades in favors), and her books examine life in inner-city New Jersey for African Americans in a way that is reminiscent of Mosley's examinations of African American communities in Los Angeles. Neely shares Mosley's concern with an exploration of race and identity on the national, familial, and individual levels.

All of Mosley's work, across genres, is connected in its explorations of identity. Mosley crafts complex protagonists who actively question who they are and how they fit in their worlds, an exploration that gives the protagonists an almost existential edge in many of the books. And Mosley creates lush and detailed worlds in which the protagonists maneuver; readers see not just who the characters are, but truly get to know their worlds as well, which gives their examinations of identity a stronger context and weight because, for the length of the book, the reader inhabits that world as well. The works are also linked by the sense of history and the importance of setting, whether that setting is 20th-century L.A., or more narrowly, a basement in a beloved but endangered family home in Sag Harbor. The final element that links all of Mosley's work is the protagonists themselves. Mosley centers his novels on ordinary, working-class African American men, true black everyman figures who worry about mortgages and bank accounts and fights with their loved ones and friends. But in Mosley's hands, these everyman characters have a heroic nature. Some of them save women and children from fates worse than death (or simply from actual death); some of them heroically fight an internal weakness or sense of doom. And Mosley said in an interview with *Moment* magazine that he writes about black male heroes because so few authors have—there have been, according to Mosley, black male protagonists and supporting characters, but few actual heroes. But Mosley heroes are not one-dimensional good guys. They are deeply human characters who are often reluctantly heroic, doing what needs to be done because someone has to. They are often outsiders because of race, class, and basic personality—they don't always truly connect with the people around them or they fail to recognize the importance of the connections they have. In short, they are fully realized people with flaws, vices that go along with their virtues, and personalities that make the reader feel like he could be sitting with a neighbor, coworker, or friend. Heroic actions notwithstanding, the reader gets to know these characters, and so can't help but root for them, can't help wanting to know more. The search for identity developed through protagonists who are black everyman figures explored in settings that shape them and reflect broader history centers Mosley's work and makes him the iconic figure that he is.

Of the kinds of fiction Mosley has written, his science fiction is probably the least well known. Yet, the concerns and themes that permeate his work and make him an iconic writer are visible here as well. *Blue Light* shows how the linking themes and motifs of Mosley's works appear in his science fiction. The novel presents the story of a group of people who have been touched by the blue light as it came to earth over California in the late 1960s. One of the people transformed by the light is Ordé, who preaches to followers in the park, a group called the Close Congregation. The narrator, Chance, is also our protagonist. He is the everyman figure—he did not see the blue light and has been following Ordé not because he truly understands the message he preaches, but because he met Ordé on the day he was going to attempt suicide. His first attempt had been the night the blue light came to earth. Chance is a washed out PhD candidate in Ancient Studies from Berkeley who is trying to make sense of his life. He's done everything right— gotten good grades, listened to his mother and tried to fit into her white world and expectations, gotten into a prestigious graduate program, but he doesn't feel a sense of true purpose—he isn't sure who he is. He's drawn to the Close Congregation and Ordé because the message from the blue light is that humans are the sleeping, walking dead. Chance sees himself in this: "It seemed true to me. I felt lifeless; I felt inconsequential" (*Blue Light* 24). He is just one of the many drifting through San Francisco in the late 1960s, seeking something but unsure what that something is, and uncertain of how he fits into the world of his mother, of the academy, of a country that is often made uncomfortable because he is a big black man.

The novel follows Chance as members of the Close Congregation start to go missing and then to be found dead and as Ordé and the group are investigated. Some of the members have died as Ordé tried to make them stronger, by having them drink a mixture of his blood and theirs, a concoction that poisons most of them. Chance, however, survives this ritual and has his senses enhanced by it. He is still, however, human; he is not and cannot be one of the Blues who have been transformed by the blue light into superhumans or demigods. Even this, however, while it does give him a stronger feeling of belonging, does not truly give him a sense of purpose. That purpose, and the heroic nature that has been seeking an outlet, come as the true threat to the Blues becomes clear. On the night the blue light came to earth, Horace LaFontaine died of cancer while looking out his bedroom window. He dies before he can truly see the blue light, but it is so powerful that its effect on his open eyes is enough to reanimate his corpse. He becomes a Blue, but an evil one called the Gray Man, who exists to bring only pain and death. Gray Man is behind the murders of the Blues and attacks them in the park during a meeting of the Close Congregation. Ordé and many of the Blues are killed during this confrontation, but three special Blues, all children, escape due to Chance's actions. Chance finds his purpose in keeping these three Blues safe and helping them achieve their purpose of regenerating the world. Chance lacks the power to defeat Gray Man, but that is the point of his heroism. He does not have special power or strength, just the human impulse to protect the young girl Gray Man is about to kill. He acts because he has to, but he acts heroically because he has put his purpose and his world before his fear. This is typical behavior for Mosley's everyday heroes; they are both loners and protectors, finding purpose in their relationships and in what they can contribute to the world around them, even when that contribution may seem inconsequential or mundane.

The importance of history also permeates *Blue Light* in quite explicit ways. Chance has been studying to become a historian, specifically focusing on Thucydides's *Peloponnesian War*. He is drawn to it because Thucydides not only wrote history, "he *was* history" (*Blue Light* 46). Ultimately, Chance follows this same path. When he has to leave his graduate program because of his suicide attempt, he wanders San Francisco writing a *History of Love,* a chronicle of the life in the city at the time. Once he becomes a part of the Close Congregation, this changes to a chronicle of a different sort, *A History of the Coming of the Blue Light.* As readers, we are immersed in that history; in reading Chance's story, we are reading the history of the blue light and the effects it has had on the world and on Chance. He becomes that history as he helps the Blue children escape the Gray Man and then to fight him in Treaty, a magical world in the woods in Northern California overseen by Juan Thrombone, the most powerful of the Blues. While he cannot defeat Gray Man alone, the Blues can't do it without him either; he is the human force that gives the history meaning. For Mosley, history is a human force, a human story, not just dates and events. Chance gives dimension to the history of the blue light and the Blues. The Blues are flat, traits more than people with personalities; they are the Warrior, the Pathfinder, the Dreamer, the embodiment of kinds of knowledge. They are "the philosopher without humanity, the lover who felt no love" (*Blue Light* 245). Without Chance, they are ideals and ideas but not really history. Due to this very human dimension to history, it is also not neutral for Mosley. History impacts people, shapes them; it is not simply a timeline or the province of a few great and unusual men. Chance finds his purpose, finds himself, in crafting the history of the blue light, in action and in words, but he is crafted by history as well—and this is at the heart of Mosley's grounding of his characters in personal and broader histories. His protagonists, like Chance, are "at the center of history and paying the price" (*Blue Light* 234).

What price those histories exact from Mosley's characters has everything to do with the particular place and time they inhabit. For Chance, that setting is both a recognizable California in the late 1960s and a fantasy world of singing trees, children who become women in a week or who never age beyond 10, and a nature that both protects and threatens humans. The believability of the fantasy world—it is as real and tangible and vivid as the descriptions of San Francisco—is a testament to Mosley's ability to recreate the world on the page. While there is an almost fairy-tale quality to Treaty, the details are drawn so specifically that the reader is there, inhabiting the woods with Chance. The trees exude their pine scent; the bears are bears, scary and wild and menacing. The trees also sing and have consciousness; the bears are Thrombone's beasts of burden who work for honey and wrestle with the warrior Blue and lose. Yet, the reader does not question that this is reality for Chance and his band of superhumans. The way that this setting provides him with peace and purpose is unmistakable. Mosley's heroes are who they are because of where they are—and where they've been. And when the moment comes when Chance must leave so the Blues can fight Gray Man, his leaving and entering the everyday woods makes him who he is as well. He has been at the center of history, and when the Blues push him to the margins so they can fight their epic fight, he resists because in his introspection he has realized the value of connections. He knows in a deep way that history is no history without the human connection. And so he returns and enters the end of the battle with the Blues. And what is left in the charred remains of treaty is only the human—only the everyman survives.

But this is a Mosley novel and not a fairy tale. When Treaty has been burned to the ground, Chance must return to the world we know. And here, too, he is shaped by his surroundings. In a fairy tale, the forces of evil would have been defeated, and Chance and the Blues would have lived happily ever after. But Mosley's talent lies not in providing readers with a happily ever after, a pleasant escape from the real world, but in giving them a real world in all its complexity and pain and joy and not-so-happy endings. Chance enters back into our world telling the history of the blue light, and the world is not accepting. His history ends not with the triumphal spreading of the gospel of the blue light but with disbelief. Chance is charged with arson for setting a national forest on fire and is sentenced to a mental hospital. His heroism, as is all too often true in the world, is unrecognized and called insanity. And he is torn between his knowing—his purpose, his identity—and being like everyone else, fitting into his world without question. The existential edge that made him question, that helped him know his world, keeps him from being regular, from knowing but not being history.

The kind of outsider perspective that Chance represents as a science fiction protagonist is also apparent in the protagonists in Mosley's literary fiction, particularly Socrates Fortlow in *Always Outnumbered, Always Outgunned* and Charles Blakey in *The Man in My Basement*. Socrates Fortlow is an ex-con in his mid 50s, living in a broken-down alley apartment in Watts (Los Angeles). He's moved to Watts after a 27-year term in jail for killing a man and woman and raping the woman. He's killed other men while in jail. But like many of Mosley's heroes who know violence, who have committed acts of violence and taken lives, the violence is not all there is to him. It has shaped him, but that shaping influence has made him value words and the world around him. He is, as his name suggests, a thinking man. He is prepared for poverty, prepared to make his own way, but he is also prepared to make atonement by living right and by contributing something other than violence to the world around him.

The reader first meets Socrates in the alley outside his apartment early one morning. He has come outside to check on the neighbor's rooster, Billy, who has not crowed that morning. What he finds is a young boy, Darryl, who has killed the rooster and is stealing it to sell. It's not Socrates's rooster, and he could have simply let the boy run. Instead, he drags Darryl into his apartment and makes him pluck the chicken. Darryl thinks Socrates is crazy, but he does what he's been told because he is scared of Socrates and the strength in his hands. Socrates starts cooking a breakfast of the chicken and asks Darryl if he's hungry. The exchange they have about being hungry shows readers how Socrates is both an ordinary man and also an extraordinary one.

> "Boys should be hungry. Yeah. Boys is always hungry. That's how they get to be men."
>
> "What the fuck you mean, man? You just crazy. That's all."
>
> "If you know you hungry then you know you need sumpin'. Sumpin' missin' an' hungry tell you what it is."
>
> "That's some kinda friend to you too?" Darryl sneered. "Hungry yo' friend?"
>
> "Hungry, horny, hello and how come. They all my friends, my best friends." (*Always Outnumbered* 17)

Socrates has learned the hard way—doing hard time—about being a man, particularly about being a poor black man in a society in which he is not valued. He drags Darryl in both out of anger at what Darryl has done and out of a desire to help a throwaway boy become a man, a man fit for but not conquered by his environment.

This element of giving to and helping build the community is woven throughout the stories about Socrates Fortlow. His violent past both sets him apart from his neighbors and makes him a valued member of the community. He can help Darryl see the problems in not setting something right—whether it's killing a chicken or being involved in killing and dumping the body of a young retarded boy from the neighborhood while he's with some friends. But he is not a moralistic figure who turns people over to the police or simply opines on how they've done wrong. He actively works to make it better; he mentors Darryl and helps get him out of the neighborhood when it becomes apparent that the neighborhood might swallow him. When the men in the neighborhood turn to him to help deal with a junkie who is robbing and killing people, Socrates knows that they expect him to kill Pettis and thus end the problem. But Socrates doesn't want more blood on his hands because he recognizes the futility of that violence. He doesn't turn Pettis over to the police either. His own experiences of jail, and his feeling for the community and how the racism of the justice system damages it means that this is not an option. Instead, he scares Pettis into leaving. He has conversations in his head with other young toughs from the neighborhood whom he wishes that he could save. His heroism is not evident in splashy acts but in working every day, despite—or perhaps because of—his own bloody and criminal past, to make things better for himself and for his community.

He has come to L.A. on being released from prison because it's warm (prison was cold) and because of its anonymity. He has wanted to blend in, to be one of a thousand passing faces. But his introspective nature, his existential awareness of himself, makes him reach out in myriad small ways to combat the bleak prospects of life in his neighborhood. His acts are sometimes for himself and sometimes on behalf of others, but they are always involve a principle. This is seen in one of the stories from *Always Outnumbered, Always Outgunned* called "Equal Opportunity." Socrates has gone to apply for a job at a supermarket. The assistant manager asks his age—which Socrates points out is illegal—and then tells him to come back in the fall. Socrates can tell that the young white man has judged him and doesn't want to give him the application, which Socrates points out is also illegal. Finally, the store manager gives him the application, but after he has filled it out suggests that because Socrates does not have a phone, they won't be able to consider the application. After some back and forth, she finally says she'll pass it to the chain's head office. Socrates returns and is told that they haven't heard anything. He understands that they are simply trying to get him to go away, and he even sees his actions as foolish since "It didn't take a hero to make a fool out of himself" (*Always Outnumbered* 74), but he tells them he will keep coming back each day until they have an answer for him. He keeps returning, and the store manager says that if he comes back one more day, she'll call the cops. He decides to go back despite this threat because the right thing to do is to fight for a fair chance. He's called the chain headquarters and knows the manager has not turned in his application, so he is standing on the principle. When he returns on the day the police may be there, waiting instead is the store's private security—two former policemen—who Socrates is finally able to talk to. And this is at the heart of his action; he knows that he will never be able to work for this store and this manager—she's terrified of him—but what is important is the principle: "because he knew that he was telling the truth and that those men believed him" (*Always Outnumbered* 77).

The setting and its details are also important to the development of Fortlow's character and to Mosley's literary fiction. The L.A. of the late 20th century is re-created in its poverty and drugs and gangs and crime, both petty and serious. But this bleak outlook on the seamier side of L.A. (one of the things most often remarked on about Mosley's writings) is also balanced by details of environment that provide more hope and insight into the complexity of Socrates as a character. The alley where we first find Socrates is filled with trash, but even that trash, broken bottles and the like, "shone like murky emeralds" in the early morning light (*Always Outnumbered* 13). Even more important is what is behind the fence that separates Socrates's house from the alley itself. He is growing string beans and tomatoes, nurturing life and nourishment in the midst of the concrete bleakness. This small detail demonstrates both the richness of the actual environments Mosley creates—no detail is too small to add to the scene in which his action and his characters unfold—and also how those details of scene give us insight into character. The violence that exists in Socrates's hands, which are how he has killed in the past, is balanced with the fact that they are also used to nurture growing things, the plants first and then Darryl. Within the first page of his story, the details have set us up to see more than a violent ex-con trying to make it in the mean streets of an anonymous city. The environmental details evoke the complexity readers can later see in Socrates's speech and actions. But they are not details that sugarcoat who he is or what he's done; he's growing something practical, vegetables, not something simply pretty or ornamental like flowers.

This connection between the worlds they inhabit and the characters themselves is also seen in Socrates's first experience of the ocean. He had been having one of his internal conversations with his mental version of one of the young men he can't save. In this imagined conversation, the young man tells him that he is nothing and can't go anywhere, and that Socrates is just the same as him. Socrates declares out loud, on a bus full of people, that indeed he can go wherever he wishes. The next Saturday morning, he takes the bus out to Santa Monica to see the ocean. On the bus trip out, he is the only passenger, and he talks to the driver. They discuss her kids and how they see racism. Then she asks what he's doing out there and if he's going to work. Socrates tells her he's just out there because he wants to be:

> "You don't have to spend yo' whole life livin' in a cave like some goddam caveman. I wanna see the ocean. I been in L.A. for eight and a half years an' I ain't seen the ocean once."
>
> "Hm! Well at least you know it," the driver said, sneering with the satisfaction of the truth. "That's what wrong wit' so many people. Here they got the whole world right in front'a them an' they complainin' that they ain't nuthin' they could do. I'm wit' you. Pay your fare and see what's what." (*Always Outnumbered* 113)

He is acting on his principle, proving to himself that he can go anywhere. But this is not just a respite in nature from an ugly concrete city. It is Socrates engaging in the world, walking for miles in the sand, sitting and eating fruit and sandwiches he's carried along in his pockets. Exchanging greetings with other walkers, he's seeking something that he isn't even sure exists. But he is seeking. And one of the things he finds is a feeling of "freedom that he only ever dreamt about when he was a child" (*Always Outnumbered* 115). He also meets a couple, a Vietnam vet and a beautiful teenage girl, with whom he shares some wine and the evening. The evening with them, and the beach, and the canyon, give Socrates what he, and we, didn't know he was seeking: the understanding that he already has everything he needs. As he learns about his world—in its bleakness and its beauty and in how the two bleed into each other—he learns about himself. Mosley makes us see the complexity at the heart of Socrates' easily caricatured world and at the heart of Socrates himself—expanding our ideas of who can be a hero and what a black male hero might look like.

While the world Socrates inhabits is deeply informed by race, the issue itself is most often obliquely addressed. It is more explicitly addressed through the plot and world of another of Mosley's literary novels, *The Man in My Basement.* This is the story of Charles Blakey, who is out of work, drinks too much, and is behind on the mortgage payments on his home in Sag Harbor, which he has borrowed money against and allowed to fall into disrepair, and which has been in his family for generations. He has lost his job at the bank in town, and hasn't looked much for another, assuming that he'll be able to pick something up when he really needs it. When he goes to try to get a construction job, he is turned down and then discovers it is because the bank has fired him for stealing money but has decided not to prosecute. One evening, a white man shows up at his door and asks to rent his basement for the summer. He initially turns him down, but when he discovers he won't be able to find work since no one in town will hire a thief, he considers it. He doesn't really want to do it, but he does need to find the money to pay the mortgage. He gets back in touch with the white man, Anniston Bennet, who is quite wealthy, and Bennet offers him roughly $50,000 to spend two months in the cellar.

Once he and Bennet come to an agreement and Blakey receives the down payment, he starts to clean up the house and discovers elements of his family history—some African masks for instance. This, and eventually Bennet's presence and what he requires of Blakey, starts Blakey on a journey of self-discovery, a journey into how his roots have shaped who he is. Like many Americans, and like most of Mosley's protagonists, Blakey is aware of, but in many ways cut off from, his roots. One of the effects of this in this novel, and in much of Mosley's fiction, is that the protagonists feel somewhat isolated; while they have many people around them who in some cases have known them for their entire lives, they often feel that no one really knows them. It is this, as much as the money, which drives Blakey to accept Bennet's offer. Even when he understands that Bennet is going to live in a jail cell, as Blakey's prisoner, in the basement, even when he understands that Bennet has chosen him because he knows all of his misdeeds and how he has been blacklisted in the business community in the town and how his family has given up on him, he agrees because of this need for self-identity and the need for that identity to be acknowledged. Blakey explains:

> I agreed because of knowledge and intimacy. Anniston Bennet knew
> more about me than any other person—and he was still willing to enter

this business deal. Those shocking blue eyes looked right into mine and knew what they were seeing…. If he felt he was better than me, it was only because he felt better than everyone, and that, in some strange whiskey-soaked way, made me an equal in the world. (*The Man* 124)

While Blakey is less self-consciously introspective than Socrates, as well as the characters at the center of Mosley's mystery series, his search for identity and his feelings of being both so deeply rooted it's smothering and being so rootless as to not know how he fits into the world make him deeply relatable.

And while his search is not one that takes place on anonymous and uncaring city streets, as is true in much of Mosley's fiction, it is still deeply shaped by his surroundings and by the history reflected in those surroundings. Blakey points out that while he can say and mean good morning to the white business owners and people in his town, there is a separation between them, and it's one that they both want to maintain. He also understands that his personal history—family lore suggests that Blakey's ancestors came to America by choice as indentured servants and that one of them may even have been a slaver—is not enough to set him outside the history of the broader world he lives in:

Many of my relatives didn't like to think that they were a part of the mass of blacks in this country. They would say, secretly, that they were no different from the English or Irish immigrants. But most Negroes, even the old families that dotted our neighborhood, understood that racism doesn't ask for a pedigree. I knew that many white people didn't like me because of my dark skin. I wasn't stupid. (*The Man* 125)

And it is this, in part, that he will explore on the journey into which being Bennet's warden forces him. His understanding of his town, and even of his house and its history, changes as he becomes Bennet's jailer and seeks to understand Bennet's history as well. Why would a wealthy white man want to spend his summer in the Hamptons in captivity doing penance rather than being on vacation? Initially, he dismisses the oddness of the situation and the secrecy involved as simply the eccentricity of the white and wealthy. But ultimately, this is not a satisfactory answer. He needs to know more because in learning about Bennet, he is learning about himself. He feels basically disconnected from family history and from the world, even from his friends, but Bennet's presence in the basement as he pays for what he terms his crimes against humanity makes Blakey confront his past and present, caught up in a moral dilemma he has not asked for and doesn't understand.

While he doesn't understand Bennet or his crimes, having him in the basement changes Blakey's view of the world and of himself. He starts thinking about his parents, taking better care of the house, and most importantly, he starts contemplating the African masks, passport masks, that he has found in cleaning out his home. He starts wondering about and appreciating his ancestors both near and far, wearing his father's suits and seeing the world rather than sleepwalking through it to the next drink or girl. Blakey sees that he is on a journey, that it matters to him whether the men Bennet has killed were black or white, that the things from the house that he saw simply as antiques that could bring him some money instead have a different and more intrinsic value. Even his relationship to his home changes. He has initially been afraid of having Bennet in the basement, afraid someone will find out and call the police, afraid of Bennet's power. And he hasn't seen the family home as truly his; he still refers to the rooms as his uncle's or his parents', and Bennet's presence has initially pervaded the house, keeping Blakey from sleeping and making him nervous. But as he travels farther on his journey into himself, he changes the rules for Bennet. He has been acting more as manservant and host than as jailer, but as he comes more fully into his identity, he imposes new rules on Bennet because it is his house, and so Bennet must learn to play by Blakey's rules, to truly be a prisoner rather than simply playing at it.

This newfound sense of self and history makes Blakey reconsider selling all the antiques he has cleaned out from the basement to make room for Bennet's cell. He begins to see value not just in money, from Bennet or elsewhere, but in his everyday life and the connections he has missed out on. He finally makes Bennet explain why he has chosen Blakey's house and Blakey as his warden. Bennet points out that there was a joke in it, with the "whitest white man" jailed by a black man who is actually a "blue blood in American history" (*The Man* 219). Blakey begins to appreciate his own history because he has been forced to see it, and seeing it opens the world and his own nature to Blakey. He realizes that even though Bennet, an extremely powerful man who understands the hidden workings of governments and corporations, believes that no one can be saved, that we are even incapable of saving ourselves, Blakey believes that people can be redeemed. And through his journey of identity, his understanding of his home and those who created it, Blakey redeems himself. He turns his home into a museum and reconnects with everyday life, keeping in mind that Bennet has always been wrong, that some people do live "according to love and being loved" (*The Man* 248). And so his heroism is not in anything grand but in fighting the bleakness that can take any of us over.

This fight against the bleakness of the world, and of ourselves, is seen most strongly in the work Mosley is most known for, his mystery fiction. Easy Rawlins, Paris Minton (the protagonist of the Fearless Jones series), and Leonid McGill, Mosley's most recent mystery protagonist, are all those black heroes Mosley wants to create because so few other authors have. The worlds these men inhabit—midcentury L.A. for Rawlins and Minton, modern New York City for McGill—are in many ways hostile. Mosley's L.A. has often been compared to the L.A. of Raymond Chandler's novels, a seamy world of sex and crime and manipulation. Mosley's portrayal of contemporary New York is less overtly racist but no kinder, with the odds stacked against those outside the circles of power and violence pervasive. Yet they struggle through, helping themselves, helping others, and trying to become better men. Like the protagonists of his science fiction and literary novels, these men are outsiders to the corridors of power—Rawlins and Minton because of their race, McGill because of his criminal past, and all three due to both their socioeconomic class and, in some ways, their introspective natures. None of the three see themselves as heroes, or even as unusual; they are working men concerned with the everyday realities of mortgage payments, family troubles, and their luck (or often lack thereof) in love.

Paris Minton, the protagonist of the Fearless Jones series, is the owner of a used bookstore that sells library castoffs. He has a weakness for pretty women and wants a life where he can read books and basically be left alone. He is far from a tough guy, a role filled in the series by Fearless Jones himself, one of Minton's closest friends. While the series is named for him, Minton is really the heart of the novels. Paris narrates the novels, and so what we see we see through his eyes. Fearless is exactly that, and he has the capacity of violence that makes the mystery plotting work in the hostile world they inhabit. But it is Paris Minton who draws Fearless into the mysteries and who centers the novels with his introspection. In the first novel of the series, simply titled *Fearless Jones,* Paris is visited in his bookshop by a beautiful woman, the typical femme fatale of the hardboiled tradition. This visit leads to a later visit by some men intent on finding the woman and hurting or killing Paris to do so. This pulls Paris, and by extension Fearless, into a world of police corruption, money, racism, and other outsiders. Fearless is the more obviously heroic of the two men: he is streetwise, deeply loyal, physically courageous, and strong. Fearless can knock out the bad guys and will gladly do so for a friend. He maneuvers through a world that does not value him, despite his exemplary war service, by using his street smarts and his fists when necessary. Paris, on the other hand, does not seem heroic at all: he is an admitted coward, not particularly strong, book smart but not particularly crafty, and not unquestioningly loyal. But we see the story through his eyes, and hear it through his words, and so he is the shaping consciousness of the series. He is also heroic in his own, less physical, ways. He is able to penetrate the mysteries, to talk his way into and out of situations, and to care about the broader world and how it impacts outsiders in a way that Fearless cannot. The two men complement and balance each other:

> "You plenty smart, Paris," Fearless said pouring himself another shot of cognac. "It's like you look at everything like one'a them books you read."
>
> "Yeah," I said. "I know enough to jump in the Pacific but I don't know how to swim."
>
> Fearless brightened at that.
>
> "That's where I come in," he said. "You know I can swim like a dolphin. Yes, I can." (*Fear of the Dark* 224–25)

The men, Paris in particular, realize that part of their identity comes from their partnership. Their connections help create their community and so shape them.

Paris recognizes that while he is a typical man, he is living in an atypical situation. At the beginning of *Fear of the Dark,* the third novel in the series, Paris is explaining why he needs to take extra precautions for security in his bookshop. It is, after all, America in the 1950s, not a war-torn country or the Wild West. In Mosley's inimitable way, he weaves race and Paris's heroism into this discussion. Paris needs to take precautions that others don't because "most Americans weren't black and they sure didn't live in South Central L.A." (*Fear of the Dark* 2). Furthermore, even if they shared Paris' race and socioeconomic status, they didn't share his propensity for sticky situations—which most often occur because Paris wants, or feels he needs, to help someone. And it is in this desire to help that Paris's heroism lies. He could simply have the life of a moderately successful business owner, reading his books, and living his life. Instead, he fights through his fears and works for whatever justice he can help to achieve. This means that despite the everyday nature of his life and even of his personality, he becomes heroic in the eyes of the readers if not his own. He explains:

> Through no fault of my own I often found myself in the company of desperate and dangerous men—and women. I associate with murderers, kidnappers, extortionists, and fools of all colors, ages, and temperaments. By nature I am a peaceful man, some might even say cowardly. I don't care what they say. It does not shame me to admit that I would rather run than fight. (*Fear of the Dark* 2)

But Paris does fight, with words and logic, and physically when necessary. He fights criminals and racist cops, his own fears and weaknesses, and a system that doesn't look kindly on black business owners or intellects.

And the world that Mosley situates Paris and Fearless in, 1950s L.A., makes Paris's heroism both possible and poignant. It is a world that means Fearless has to fight and that Paris can't simply run his business. Mosley's genius in presenting this world to readers is in the way it is never didactic; the characters simply accept that it is the way of their world, however much they dislike it and know that it is wrong, and so the reader does too. Mosley also has the ability to present the racism of 20th-century America in a way that doesn't overwhelm the lives of the characters; their race matters, but it is not the only thing that matters. They deal with racism, subtle and overt, but do not become consumed by it. They live and love and eat and play and grieve and hate the system and care for their communities in the way that people have to if they want to survive. Paris ponders how race and racism have been shaping forces for him and for Fearless, which forces the reader to ponder it as well, but the racial politics are always blended with the page-turning mystery plots and with the stories of relationship and identity that elevate Mosley's work beyond so much of the available genre fiction.

When Paris recounts the story of being searched by police in a robbery investigation and being arrested despite his innocence and a complete lack

of any evidence turned up in the search, or when he tells us of the complete
indifference the police show about the arson that razes his first shop and
their suspicion of where he would get books to sell to begin with, it never
turns into a polemic against racism. Instead, it simply provides a context in
which his actions, and Fearless's, make sense. Paris comments that they do
what they do because "we were poor and black and so either we fought or
we lost ground. That's all there was to it" (*Fear of the Dark* 193). The reader
understands why Paris and Fearless have to create their own justice. Whether
its because the cops use the word "Jew" like an epithet when speaking to the
elderly Fanny Tannenbaum in *Fearless Jones* or because they suspect Paris
and Fearless themselves of being up to no good simply for being black, the
world that they inhabit makes the reader see why "a life worth remembering
is hell to live" (*Fear of the Dark* 317), and why Paris cannot not simply be
the mild-mannered bookworm. L.A. in the '50s demands both introspection
and heroism, and Paris has no choice but to be an everyman hero if he doesn't
want to give in entirely.

Some of the same demands are placed on Leonid McGill, the private investigator at the heart of Mosley's current mystery series. The time and place
have changed, but the questions largely remain the same—How do I fit into
my world? Who am I in that world? Does any of it even matter? McGill is a
private eye with a long history of working on the wrong side of the law. He
was trained as a boxer, has a wife who doesn't love him, kids who aren't related to him by blood, and a desire to go from being fully crooked to "slightly
bent," the best he can hope to do with his past. In the first book in the series,
2009's *The Long Fall*, we meet him in the reception area of a high-priced
financial firm, being stonewalled by the young and hip receptionist. Mosley
immediately establishes him as an everyman: "All the secretaries and gofers
that worked for Berg, Lewis & Takayama were young and pretty, regardless of their gender. All except one. There was a chubby woman who sat in
a far corner to the left, under an exit sign. She had bad skin and a utilitarian
fashion sense. She was looking down, working hard. I immediately identified
with her" (*Long Fall* 1). McGill not only notices her, he sees himself as her,
not quite fitting in the high-money, high-power world around her. He, too, is
uncertain of how he fits into the straight world he is trying to enter, unsure
how he fits in his family, worried about the things he has done in his job.

As the novel opens, he is working a seemingly straightforward case of
locating four childhood friends for another P.I. who works out of Albany
rather than out of New York City. This detective has provided McGill with
the street names the men were known by two decades ago. Three of the
men are easily found due to adult criminal records and McGill's contacts in
the police, who are willing to bend the rules and look at sealed juvenile cases.
The fourth, Roger Brown, however, gives McGill some pause. He works for
the high-powered firm filled with the young and beautiful. Something about
his connection to the other three, petty criminals all, fills McGill with misgivings, as does the fear in the man's voice when he learns someone is looking for

the four of them. But McGill needs to pay the rent on his offices and support his wife and kids, and so he takes the money and gives the other P.I. the information. This leads to three murders—the Albany P.I., the young financial advisor, and one of the petty criminals. And in true Mosley fashion, McGill can't let this rest. Brown's death weighs on his mind, and he feels he has to do something. Here, too, Mosley weaves in history as a shaping force in his characters' lives. McGill is feeling pinned to his chair by the murders and his association, however unintentional, with them. While trying to decide what he can do about them, he reminisces about his father:

> "It's the housewives and the plumbers," my father had told me and my brother, Nikita, "the law-abiding and pious, that allow the most heinous crimes to continue. They raise their children and pray to God, while soldiers slaughter dark-skinned families in their country's name."
>
> I wished my father were standing there before me right then. If he was, I could rise to my feet and slap his face. I'd tell him that his lessons put Nikita in prison and nailed me to that chair, wishing I had become a plumber voting the Republican ticket and saluting the Stars and Stripes. (*Long Fall* 101)

McGill is not who he is by chance or even simply by his choices; he has been molded by his father's Communism, by the history (and contemporary reality; as he says, it's not 2008 everywhere in America) of race, by the city in which he lives and the opportunities it offers, both legal and illegal.

While McGill is an everyman figure, struggling with bills and an unfaithful wife, he is also essentially introspective. He worries about the implications of the jobs he does; he wonders how to connect with and save Twill, his son in bond if not in blood, from himself. He won't leave his wife, even though she has left him and he loves another woman, because staying is part of doing the right thing, which he is trying so hard to do as he turns over a new, and law-abiding, leaf. He, like Blakey in *The Man in My Basement,* sees some possibility for redemption if not for salvation. His dreams are haunted because of the life he has led, but he knows that the long fall out of a burning building that is his nightmare does not have to be his life. He can act to redeem himself and to save some others along the way as long as he keeps living his mantra: "I'm alive and safe, ambulatory and able to think" (*Long Fall* 109).

And it is this idea that centers all of Mosley's protagonists—reluctant heroes who are drawn into dilemmas not because they know they are heroes or even because they want to behave heroically or even bravely in many cases. They are not only alive, surviving a world that is indifferent to their survival, but thinking and acting. Their ability to think is not simply in a traditional detective sense; it is not simply the ability to recognize clues and reason them out à la Sherlock Holmes. Their thinking is both introspective and worldly at the same time. They make choices and see the answers to puzzles not out of astronomically high IQs or lots of formal education but out of a desire to be the men they want to be in a world that doesn't behave justly or ethically and that privileges power drawn from racism and wealth and greed and heartlessness. They think with their hearts and guts as well as their minds. They make use of their surroundings, their environments, to help combat the bleakness of their worlds. And so McGill can make use not only of his own strength and smarts (he in many ways combines the traits of both Fearless and Paris from the earlier series) but also the technologies of 21st-century Manhattan and the foibles of the power structure—whether that power structure is that of mobsters like Tony Towers or the NYPD and the legal system. McGill traces emails and uses electronic surveillance the way that Paris and Fearless used street connections. He bargains with Tony for respectful treatment of one of his female employees and understands that "the blood was part of our dialogue" with Detective Kitteridge, with whom he shares a grudging respect and a mutual distrust (*Long Fall* 125).

This is also what allows Mosley's worlds to ultimately be less bleak than they may originally seem. This is crime fiction, so there will and must be violence, but even when exploring the seamiest parts of L.A. and New York, when looking at the absolute atrocities one person is capable of visiting on another, there is hope in Mosley's worlds. There is McGill's appreciation of the sky outside his office window, his appreciation of the beautiful art deco office building itself. There is love and connection between people, McGill and his son Twill for instance, even in the face of the chaos and violence around them. There is growth in the characters; these are not cartoon heroes, perfect and unchanging, but men who have flaws as well as their better impulses and traits, men who make mistakes but who can make up for them. New York City is the environment for much wrongdoing, some of it McGill's own, but it is also the space for his redemption, an arena in which he can right wrongs. And ultimately it is a world in which falling can be both terrifying and liberating, where dreams and nightmares are not always mutually exclusive.

This hope and bleakness and complexity in the everyman and everyday are what have made Mosley's best known hero, Easy Rawlins, so iconic. The short story collection and 10 novels in the series follow Easy from his young adulthood in Houston in the late 1930s through his life in L.A. from when he returns after his service in World War II through the late 1960s. Through the series, both Easy and L.A. change. *Devil in a Blue Dress* was the first of the series published, although it's chronologically the second book. (*Gone Fishin'*, which takes place before *Devil in a Blue Dress*, tells a story of Easy's early life and how he ended in up L.A. It's the only one of the series not set primarily in Los Angeles.) It's L.A. in 1948, and Ezekiel "Easy" Rawlins, a World War II veteran, has just been fired from his job at a military aircraft fabrication plant. He is drinking away his afternoon and his troubles in a dive above a butcher's, when he is "surprised to see a white man walk into Joppy's bar" (*Devil in a*

Blue Dress 45). The white man exudes an aura of power, and initially makes Rawlins uneasy:

> When he looked at me I felt a thrill of fear, but that went away quickly because I was used to white people by 1948.
>
> I had spent five years with white men, and women, from Africa to Italy, through Paris, and into the Fatherland itself. I ate with them and slept with them, and I killed enough blue-eyed young men to know that they were just as afraid to die as I was. (*Devil in a Blue Dress* 45)

Easy is immediately both like and different from thousands of other black men in his time and place—he is struggling economically, concerned with his joblessness, a veteran who loves his country, and touched but not deterred by racism. Yet he is also hyperaware of his thoughts about his own fears and how racism affects him—a luxury (or curse depending on your point of view) for most men, who need to be primarily concerned with keeping body and soul together. He is Mosley's exemplar of the black hero, an everyman with that existential edge that gives him, and readers, a deeper insight into his world and himself as a man.

The white man in the bar, Dewitt Albright, seems to have the solution to Easy's immediate problem with being unemployed. He'd like Easy to look for a white woman who frequents the jazz clubs of black L.A., and will pay handsomely for information about where this woman is. Albright's explanation for why he can't find her himself—he would not be welcome or easily able to navigate the world of black nightclubs and speakeasies—gives a nod to the racial divisions in Easy's world, but also makes Easy a bit nervous. Eventually, with a bit of persuasion from Joppy, Easy decides to take the job, and his explanation of why shows us he is no superhero figure but an everyman. It is not only the promise of money to pay his mortgage that draws Easy into his first favor; it is his character and its flaws: "Whether he knew it or not, DeWitt Albright had me caught by my own pride. The more I was afraid of him, I was that much more certain to take the job he offered" (*Devil in a Blue Dress* 57). Easy is touched by the same foibles and pitfalls all of us are tempted by, and he's a young man in this book, putting pride before caution and so getting drawn into violence and betrayal in his own neighborhood and the halls of the powerful in the city—and in true noir fashion, it all centers around a woman.

Mosley's depiction of L.A. is often also described in noir terms—bleak and seamy, filled with criminals both petty and grand, and ultimately hostile to our main character. While all these things are true of the city Easy inhabits, Mosley's depiction of the city and of Easy are more complex than this. Easy's L.A. is a place of community and beauty, of friendship and opportunity, as much as it is dark and uncaring. Easy's house—one he owns and loves—is evocative of this. He knows his neighbors and loves his little plot of land filled with fruit trees and peace. When he is feeling the pressures the city brings to bear, his house and his strong desire to keep it at all costs, to not let the house he loves down, helps carry him through. After a particularly bad night when the city is feeling like too much and he has reached out to his friend Mouse, a violent man he has been avoiding, he describes this effect:

> I put my chair in front of my window so I could look out into my yard. I sat there for a long time, balling my hands together and taking deep breaths when I could remember to. Finally the fear passed and I fell asleep. The last thing I remember was looking at my apple tree in the predawn. (*Devil in a Blue Dress* 154)

Easy's mundane concerns and the beauty that most often coexists with the bleakness in Mosley's creations centers him and the book in a vision of the world that allows as much room for joy as it does for terror.

And it is a world that contains terror, particularly for African American men like Easy. Race is a real and persistent factor in determining opportunity and even safety. The police are racist and brutal, willing to both beat men like Easy and use them as patsies. The criminals, both black and white, will as soon kill Easy as look at him if they think he is getting in their way or has outlived his usefulness, and his acquaintances will betray him over a pretty woman. There are dangers in talking to or being seen with white women or going into the wrong neighborhood or business. And in taking us along on Easy's journey as he navigates these terrors, we understand the sense of history that permeates this world and this journey. It is a world where white teens feel justified in threatening Easy for responding to a greeting from one of the young girls in their group. It is a world in which a woman cannot be with the man she loves because she can pass for, but never be, white. It is a world where Easy needs the voice that first came to him when he was in mortal danger in the war, because his world still is at war against its enemies of racism and circumscribed opportunity: "The voice is hard. It never cares if I'm scared or in danger. It just looks at the facts and tells me what I need to do" (*Devil in a Blue Dress* 143).

But ultimately, it is also a world that is shifting, that has some hope and some real connections. *Devil in a Blue Dress* ends with Easy having stood up to a racist boss, found his calling in doing detective work—favors for those in need—and being able to sit with a good man, a friend. The book closes on a conversation between Easy and Odell, a friend from the neighborhood:

> "Odell?"
>
> "Yeah, Easy."
>
> "If you know a man is wrong, I mean, if you know he did somethin' bad but you don't turn him in to the law because he's your friend, do you think that's right?"
>
> "All you got is your friends, Easy."

"But then you what if you know somebody else who did something wrong but not so bad as the first man, but you turn this other guy in?"

"I guess you figure that that other guy got ahold of some bad luck."

We laughed for a long time. (*Devil in a Blue Dress* 263)

Mosley's complex world and complex men allow for both laughter and anger, betrayal and loyalty. And the world grows as Easy does over the series.

The series takes us through both historical and personal events: the McCarthy-era Red Scare (*A Red Death*), the Watts Riots and Summer of Love (*Cinnamon Kiss*), and through Easy's drinking and not drinking, his marriages and the growth of his adopted children. And Easy becomes an icon—a working man in a city that is sometimes too much, who loves and fears, saves and loses, who is a hero. Easy, and Mosley, ask and allow us to step into a world both familiar and absolutely new. Easy's struggles and triumphs, his city and his character in the face of tragedy, terror, friendship, and love embody why Walter Mosley is an iconic and beloved figure in the African American literary tradition.

Film Adaptations

Devil in a Blue Dress. *Dir. and screenplay by Carl Franklin. Perf. Denzel Washington, Don Cheadle, and Jennifer Beals. 1995.*
Always Outnumbered, Always Outgunned. *Dir. Michael Apted. Perf. Laurence Fishburne, Cicely Tyson, and Natalie Cole. 1998.*

BIBLIOGRAPHY

Easy Rawlins Mysteries

Bad Boy Brawly Brown. New York: Washington Square, 2002.
Black Betty. New York: Washington Square, 1994.
Blonde Faith. New York: Washington Square, 2007.
Cinnamon Kiss. New York: Little, Brown, 2008.
Devil in a Blue Dress. New York: Washington Square, 1990.
Gone Fishin'. New York: Black Classic, 1997.
Little Scarlet. New York: Washington Square, 2004.
A Little Yellow Dog. New York: Washington Square, 1996.
A Red Death. New York: Washington Square, 1991.
Six Easy Pieces. New York: Washington Square, 2003.
White Butterfly. New York: Washington Square, 1992.

Fearless Jones Mysteries

Fear Itself. New York: Grand Central, 2003.
Fearless Jones. New York: Grand Central, 2001.
Fear of the Dark. New York: Grand Central, 2006.

Leonld McGill Mysterics

Known to Evil. New York: Riverhead, 2010.
The Long Fall. New York: Riverhead, 2009.

Science Fiction

Blue Light. New York: Little, Brown, 1998.
Futureland: Nine Stories of an Imminent World. New York: Grand Central, 2001.
The Wave. New York: Grand Central, 2005.

Socrates Fortlow Books

Always Outnumbered, Always Outgunned. New York: Washington Square, 1998.
The Right Mistake. New York: Basic Civitas, 2008.
Walkin' the Dog. New York: Little, Brown, 1999.

Literary Fiction

Fortunate Son. New York: Little, Brown, 2006.
The Last Days of Ptolemy Grey. New York: Riverhead, 2010.
The Man in My Basement. Boston: Little, Brown, 2004
RL's Dream. New York: Washington Square, 1995.
The Tempest Tales. New York: Washington Square, 2008.

FURTHER READING

Brady, Owen E., and Derek C. Maus. *Finding a Way Home: A Critical Assessment of Walter Mosley's Fiction.* Jackson: UP of Mississippi, 2008.

Marshall, John. "Investigator Rawlins is Hard at Work Again in Walter Mosley's Latest Entry." *Seattle Post-Intelligencer* July 23, 2002. Web.

Wilson, Charles E. *Walter Mosley: A Critical Companion.* Westport, CT: Greenwood, 2003.

Jessica Parker

Richard Wright (photographed in 1939) is best known for his first published novel, *Native Son*, which introduced a new realism to literary treatments of America's racial problems, rendering sympathetically the always fearful, sometimes violent psychology of the oppressed. (Library of Congress)

Native Son

Richard Wright, author of *Native Son* (1940), is considered one of the lions of African American letters and mentor to an entire generation of emerging authors, but had truly inauspicious origins. Born to an illiterate sharecropper and a quiet and pious schoolteacher in Roxie, Mississippi, young Richard overcame Herculean obstacles in his pursuit of literary greatness. As Wright biographer Michel Fabre notes, Wright "accomplished the social progress of three generations in one lifetime" (xvi).

Wright's early years were anything but blissful. Plagued by financial hardships, his mother and father relocated first to Natchez and then to Memphis, Tennessee, where his mother labored as a cook and his father became increasingly absent from his young family, eventually deserting them. Wright's mother, Ella, then suffered several serious physical maladies, including a stroke that left her partially paralyzed, forcing Wright and his younger brother into an orphanage. In *Black Boy*, Wright remembers the orphanage as a horrific place under the martial rule of a cruel and perverse woman who delighted in her young charges' vulnerability (33–37). Wright ran away at his first opportunity, only to be returned until his mother's health temporarily improved and she was able to piece together enough money to once again relocate her family, first to Jackson, Mississippi, and then again to Elaine, Arkansas (16–17). After bouncing around the South for a number of years, Wright eventually saved enough money to move to New York by way of Chicago, taking over the responsibility of supporting his mother and brother (and often additional relatives, as well). Later in life, Wright moved abroad, distancing himself physically, though never emotionally, from the painful scenes of his youth.

Although his most famous novel is set in Chicago, those formative years spent in the South provide the violent racial backgrounds to many of his novels and short stories. While a youth in Arkansas, as Wright relates in "The Ethics of Living Jim Crow," he began learning the incredibly hard lessons of surviving in the segregated South, lessons including the brutal assault upon him and his black friends by young white boys, a painful encounter worsened by his own mother's insistence that he assume the appropriate subservience to these whites rather than fight them (1411). Further, as readers learn in the full text of Wright's autobiography, Wright's Uncle Silas Hoskins, the husband of beloved Aunt Maggie, was killed by Elaine, Arkansas whites who were jaded by the minimal economic success of a black man in their midst (*Black Boy* 63). Wright's mother and aunt quickly fled to West Helena, Arkansas, taking the terrified young Richard physically, though never emotionally, away from the scene of his uncle's lynching (63–64).

This brutal killing of his uncle likely initiated Wright's lifelong contemplation of the constant threat of death haunting black men. Certainly, this was the first family member known to Wright who was lynched, though Wright's young life would be peppered with threats of lynchings as well as actual lynchings of friends and acquaintances. In *Exorcising Blackness*, critic Trudier Harris notes that Wright deals repeatedly with scenes of lynching in his fiction, and Abdul R. JanMohamed argues that this obsession with what he terms "the death-bound-subject" is central to Wright's literary project. As JanMo-hamed explains, "lynching, murder, and violent struggles to the death are the leitmotifs that tie his novels and short stories together into a coherent body of work. Wright was clearly obsessed with death and lynching" (1). Wright's central characters, especially his black male characters, are threatened by the noose at every turn, baptized into violence and constricted by the haunting specter of their own pending deaths, an apt description for Bigger Thomas, *Native Son*'s main character.

Published in 1940, *Native Son* is Richard Wright's best-known and most acclaimed novel. Critic Irving Howe perhaps penned the most iconic review of the book when he wrote in 1963: "The day *Native Son* appeared, American culture was changed forever. No matter how much qualifying the book might later need, it made impossible a repetition of the old lies. In all its crudeness, melodrama and claustrophobia of vision, Richard Wright's novel brought out in the open, as no one ever had before, the hatred, fear and violence that have crippled and may yet destroy our culture" (63). Within four months of the novel's appearance, multiple reviews appeared in such publications as the *New York Times,* the *New York Sun,* the *Boston Evening Transcript,* and the *New Masses,* to name a few. In addition, it was the first novel by an African American writer to be selected by the Book-of-the-Month Club. In the pages of *Kabloona Book of the Month Club News,* Henry Seidel Canby qualified the novel as the "finest novel written by an American Negro" (February 1940). In the *New York Herald Tribune Review of Books,* Milton Rugoff praised Wright's skillful ability to "connect one individual's pathology to the whole tragedy of the Negro spirit in a white world" (March 3, 1940), while Sterling Brown called it a "literary phenomenon" and the first African American novel to probe the psychology of "the consciousness of the outcast, the disinherited, the generation lost in the slum jungles of an American civilization" (*Crisis,* June 1940).

Reviews that condemned the book did so because they considered it aes-thetically lacking and melodramatic, and they dubbed it a protest novel and a political document for the promotion of the author's communist ideology. Furthermore, in the minds of some people, the novel did not realistically represent African American life, which was said to be better than the book suggested. For example, James Baldwin, in a 1949 essay titled "Everybody's Protest Novel," questioned the credibility and complexity of Richard Wright's characters. In another essay titled "Many Thousand Gone," he characterized the novel as protest literature that perpetuated racial stereotypes and did not reflect the complexity and richness of the black experience in America. For him, *Native Son* was too melodramatic and its main character, Bigger Thomas, a "symbolical monster" (55). Ralph Ellison, the author of the acclaimed *Invisible Man* (1952), in an essay called "The World and the Jug," written in response to Howe's praise of Wright, condemned *Native Son* as an aesthetically lacking and narrow sociological explanation of African American experience that did not reflect the diversity and complexity of African American life.

The Black Arts Movement of the 1960s saw in Richard Wright's Bigger Thomas a revolutionary character. In its embrace of cultural nationalism, the movement liked Bigger as an iconoclastic character who did away with the old stereotypical view of the black man in mainstream American literature as a childish, lazy, subservient, innocent, and sentimental being. Bigger Thomas is the opposite of Uncle Tom in Harriet Beecher Stowe's *Uncle Tom's Cabin.* Unlike Uncle Tom, Bigger is a rebel, a grown-up Tom, who refuses victimization. As perverse as his crimes are, he uses them to create himself and force acknowledgment by a society that has denied him true existence. Writers who paid tribute to Richard Wright in this period include Eldridge Cleaver in a chapter titled "Notes on a Native Son," in the book *Soul on Ice* (1968), Edward Margolies in his book *Native Sons* (1968), Arthur P. Davis in *Dark Tower* (1974), and Addison Gayle in *The Way of the New World: The Black Novel in America* (1975). In a sense, the Black Arts Movement period marked the beginning of a new appreciation of Richard Wright, not just as a social thinker but also as a literary craftsman. In general, post-1970s literary studies on *Native Son* have focused on Richard Wright's literary art. Examples include Michel Fabre's *The World of Richard Wright* (1985), Joyce Ann Joyce's *Richard Wright's Art of Tragedy* (1986), Margaret Walker's *Richard Wright: Daemonic Genius* (1988), Keneth Kinnamon's edited volume *New Essays on Native Son* (1990), and Robert Butler's *Native Son: The Emergence of a New Black Hero* (1991).

The publication of Richard Wright's seminal novel inspired a new generation of African American men and women of letters such as William Attaway, Chester Himes, Ann Petry, Ralph Ellison, James Baldwin, Margaret Walker, Gwendolyn Brooks, and Lorraine Hansberry, all of whom more or less experimented with modernism and naturalism, not just as literary movements but mostly as literary perspectives native to their own lives. If American writers of the early 20th century had explored the literary potential of these two movements, for Richard Wright and his African American contemporaries, the modernist themes of alienation, exclusion, fragmentation, despair, and apocalyptic doom and the naturalistic idea of determinism were part of the forces that had shaped their lives and threatened to destroy them and thus did not have to be imagined, as Theodore Dreiser, Stephen Crane, or Jack London had to imagine them as a matter of literary exercise. Richard Wright woke and shocked America to the ravages of centuries-old racism that produced Bigger Thomas and, as Irving Howe argued in 1963, threatened to destroy America if more Bigger Thomases were allowed to continue to be born. In so doing, he inspired generations of African American writers, provided literary critics with a windfall for their pens, and created himself a place in the pantheon of American letters.

Native Son is the story of Bigger Thomas, a 20-year-old African American who, as the novel opens, lives with his mother, brother (Buddy), and sister (Vera) in a rat-infested apartment in the black belt of South Side Chicago in the 1930s. The story begins with the sound of an alarm clock, literally to wake the family but symbolically to wake up America to witness the fear and frustration that centuries of racism have wrought on a young black man and his whole race. The sudden eruption of a rat in the room and Bigger's exasperating chase of the rodent before he kills it with an iron skillet foreshadows a later scene in the novel when Bigger himself is cornered and arrested by the police. The scene also highlights Bigger Thomas's psychology: he eventually kills the rat and dangles its dead body in front of his sister, who faints, which prompts the mother's intervention to scold Bigger for his action. Bigger Thomas's uncaring act is an expression of his frustration over his family's poverty and his inability to do anything about it.

Much of the first book, fittingly titled "Fear," familiarizes the reader with the life of Bigger Thomas and the historical, economic, and political forces that have shaped and will continue to shape him. His is a world that tells him that as a black man, he is very restricted in what he can do; he cannot learn to fly an airplane, even though it is his dream, and his employment is limited to menial jobs. He spends time at the poolroom where his meets his friends Gus, G. H., and Jack. They also go to the theatre, where they watch a newsreel featuring vacationing rich white people and the rhythmic tom-toms of primitive Africans, but they know that both worlds are out of their reach. The plot to rob a white man's store aborts when, calculating to get out of the scheme because of the danger usually associated with crimes against whites (unlike black-on-black crimes, which hardly get the attention of the police), Bigger picks a fight with Gus, accusing him of being afraid of robbing the white man's store.

Even though he is apprehensive of the move, the same evening he crosses out of the black belt into the affluent world of Mr. Dalton to get a new job, only because his family needs him. Bigger's uncomfortable attitude at the Daltons' reflects the two separate worlds they inhabit; Bigger has literally crossed into unknown, dangerous territory, and Mr. Dalton has unknowingly invited into his world a person that his race and status have ignored, even though he gives money to the National Association for the Advancement of Colored People (NAACP) to assuage his conscience for renting to black people in the black belt at exorbitant prices for rundown apartments. As much as Mr. Dalton and his blind wife, as well as their daughter Mary and their servant Peggy, try to make him comfortable, Bigger is too confused to understand all they are telling him. They cannot see clearly that they and Bigger inhabit two different worlds—that they know too little about each other.

Mr. Dalton gives Bigger the duty of driving his daughter Mary to the university. The first night on the job, he drives Mary, but instead of going to the university, she directs him to her Communist friend, Jan Erlone. The two make him even more uncomfortable by sitting him between them, talking to him, calling on him to address them by their first names, asking him to take them to an African American diner where his friends are present, and insisting on him eating with them, thus humiliating him in front of his friends. After dinner, the drunk Mary and Jan make out in the back seat. After the car drops off Jan, Mary and Bigger drive back home, but Mary is so drunk that she needs Bigger's help to go to her room. Even though he knows of the dangers involved, he takes her in his arms to her room, where he starts to kiss and fondle her. Mrs. Dalton, who is blind, enters the room. Afraid of being found in Mary's room, in a scene reminiscent of Othello smothering Desdemona in William Shakespeare's tragedy *Othello, the Moor of Venice,* Bigger puts a pillow over Mary's face as he waits for Mrs. Dalton to exit the room; when she finally does, Mary is dead. To get rid of the body, he cuts off Mary's head so she can fit into the furnace, and he burns her. He later accuses Jan and the Communists of the crime, adding a ransom note to make the kidnap plausible.

Bigger's scheme seems to be working for a while, especially because the capitalists (Mr. Dalton is one of them) hate and distrust the Communists; moreover, Bigger is able to manipulate the Daltons and the police because of their internalized view that Bigger is incapable of intelligent schemes such as writing ransom notes. His flight starts when an investigative journalist discovers Mary's bones in the furnace. After telling his girlfriend Bessie the whole story, Bigger involves her in his flight. Then, after raping her in an abandoned building, he murders her by hitting her several times with a brick. In his flight through the city, he realizes that his crime has become sensational in the newspapers. He has a sense of empowerment, as everybody is talking about him: whites have reverted to stereotypes about blacks (he is called an ape), and blacks hate him because he has given the police a good excuse to terrorize them and the other undesired groups such as the Communists, members of labor unions, and workers' organizations. In the process, feeling a sense of power, he rationalizes that he actually did kill Mary, that it was not accidental. After a frantic chase, and in a fashion that is reminiscent of the rat scene at the beginning of the novel, the police finally corner him on a rooftop and arrest him.

In book three, titled "Fate," Bigger Thomas is in prison. Initially, he does not want to talk to anybody or drink or eat anything. In spite of Bigger's early accusation, Jan visits him in prison and proposes to him the services of a Jewish Communist lawyer, Boris Max. Following Max's spirited plea, Bigger Thomas is still condemned to death, an outcome that was expected given the social and legal context of the 1930s, embodied in the stereotypical language of the state attorney, Mr. Buckley. What is more, Richard Wright's choice of naturalism, a literary movement that usually involves characters victimized by natural, social, political, and economic forces that are too overwhelming to overcome, prepares the reader to understand that Bigger Thomas is doomed even before the story unfolds, because he cannot control the forces that shaped him and continue to control him. The story ends with the condemnation of Bigger to the electric chair, but not before he completes his individual, internal journey and affirms his humanity, as if to suggest that he is going to die as a human being, not as an animal (an ape), as the media and State Attorney Buckley have portrayed him during his flight and at this trial.

The shock value of Bigger Thomas's killings, the condemnation of the book by many writers and critics, particularly in the months following its publication, and certainly the use of a literary philosophy (naturalism) judged pessimistic, fatalistic, and out of fashion, as well as the overt political social protest, have often obfuscated the more enduring literary values of Richard Wright's novel *Native Son*. Yet it is probably the case that these negative qualifications signaled that America was not ready for Wright's unprecedented fearless and shameless depiction of race matters. After he published *Uncle Tom's Children* in 1938 and read its reviews, he concluded, as he wrote in "How 'Bigger' Was Born," that he "had made an awfully naïve mistake": "I found that I had written a book which even bankers' daughters could read and weep over and feel good about. I swore to myself that if I ever wrote another book, no one would weep over it; that it would be so hard and deep that they would have to face it without the consolation of tears" (40). To achieve this goal, he utilized a combination of literary and philosophical traditions to portray the main character, Bigger Thomas. These include modernism, naturalism, dialectical materialism, and existentialism. From a naturalistic perspective, Bigger Thomas is a product of his environment, a native son of a racist America that has closed all doors of opportunity for this young black man, originally from the Deep South, but now living in a northern urban setting, the poor, lowly ghetto of South Side Chicago. Dealing with social, political, and economic forces that he cannot control and that, in fact, overwhelm him, his behavior is controlled by fear, anger, and frustration, which largely deny him his free will. Furthermore, these factors make him a victim of the social Darwinist idea of biological determinism (the survival of the fittest) and Marxist determinism, or class struggle, in which the bourgeoisie, represented by Mr. Dalton, is now an overwhelming force that destroys the like of Bigger Thomas.

As a result, the main theme of the novel is racism, a force so powerful and overwhelming that it turns Bigger Thomas into a fearful and frustrated individual whose only option is to respond with violence. This racism largely affects the African American community, but it does not spare the oppressor, who, through Wright's ingenious use of irony, sometimes falls prey to his own tricks. Even the most liberal oppressors are blind to reality, an idea captured by the aptly named Daltons, who fail to see their part in the tragedy of Bigger Thomas. The other major themes of the novel, also associated with racism, include the parody of justice in the third part: In the 1930s, a black man who is accused of killing a white woman is already guilty, no matter what the circumstances are. What is more, the novel clearly demonstrates that justice is caught up between the media frenzy and sensationalism, on the one hand, and on the other the ambitions of a politician, State Attorney Buckley, who rushes the case to give himself the advantage in an election season. The stereotypical language used by the media and the state attorney, both of which are part of the overarching system that has oppressed Bigger Thomas, ironically prove Boris Max's long argument that Buckley qualifies as below the dignity of the court.

One may easily find reasons to qualify naturalism as somehow simplistic, notably because of its high predictability, but this is more a cognitive judgment and hardly a measure of artistic value. One may even contend that Bigger Thomas's accidental killing of Mary Dalton turns him into a dangerous psychopath who loses the sympathy that naturalistic writing often imposes on the reader. After all, over centuries, African Americans suffered all kinds of exploitation, injustice, and annihilation, but still did not take Bigger Thomas's path. However, the scene is central to Wright's art in *Native Son*: the moment Bigger Thomas puts the pillow on the drunk Mary Dalton, irony becomes the major creator of meaning. In this tense scene, Wright summons the dead Uncle Tom from Harriet Beecher Stowe's *Uncle Tom's Cabin* (1852), along with his less subservient incarnations in Wright's own *Uncle Tom's Children* (1938), and place him in a situation where Bigger Thomas knows that it could be death if he is found alone with a white girl in her room. At Bigger's trial, State Attorney Buckley indeed echoes what swarmed Bigger Thomas's mind when he saw the white silhouette of Mrs. Dalton, saying, "Mind you, Your Honor, the central crime here is rape!" (481). In a remarkable intertextual networking, Bigger Thomas refuses the victimization that Stowe's Uncle Tom so gladly worships as he proclaims that the cruel Simon Legree is actually helping his ascent to heaven. Richard Wright's text summons Uncle Tom and transforms him from childish, innocent, subservient, sentimental slave to a bigger Tom, a Tom who grows to act with extreme harshness and cruelty, a Tom who perversely refuses victimization. Bigger Thomas is a bigger Tom because he refuses to be treated like a cliché, a dead sign. In fact, his perverse act becomes an act of creation, as he will ascertain at the end of the story: "I didn't know I was really alive in this world until I felt things hard enough to kill for 'em" (501).

The grammatical categories of subject and object can also be used to describe Bigger's transformation after the murder of Mary Dalton. The subject is the doer of the action, whereas the object is the sufferer, the patient of the action (carried by the verb). While the premurder Bigger Thomas was the patient of a system that he watched oppress him, trap him, and contain his ambitions, the after-murder Bigger is a doer, and others suffer his gained power to allegorize and reduce them through his manipulation of his knowledge, at least for a moment. He knows what happened to Mary; he becomes the center of attention, as he is questioned by different people and most importantly as he leads them where he wants, as he writes the ransom note, and more. This twist of irony dramatically empowers him: he has knowledge and he uses it to stall the discovery of his murderous act. Because of this dramatic irony, the reader shares Bigger Thomas's secret as well as condemning it.

When Bigger's girlfriend, Bessie, shares his knowledge, she threatens his survival, his power to continue to be the actor, the subject. When many people know, Bigger loses his power. His salvation is not in communal sharing of knowledge and power, but in the individual possession and manipulation of his knowledge. When Bigger is guided by communal elements (stereotypes, for example), he is less powerful; when he is led by individual "rationalization" of his crime, he gains in power. Thus, after the murder, he starts to rationalize his actions, even though the reader knows Bigger's lack of motive. In the second part of the book, "Flight," he continuously tries to take ownership of his crime by ascertaining that as a black man in a white girl's room, he has killed her anyway. He believes his utmost sense of individuality when, toward the end of the novel, he makes an existentialist pronouncement: "What I killed for, *I am*!" (501). Here is a statement that, remarkably, simultaneously reflects two contradictory philosophies: rationalism and existentialism. It almost reads, "I killed, therefore I am," thus parodying René Descartes's "Cogito ergo sum" (I think, therefore I am), a pronouncement that embodies the Enlightenment philosophy. Bigger Thomas has grown to be a philosopher of kinds who generalizes, universalizes about his actions. At the same time, he affirms the existentialist idea that existence determines essence, that individual actions determine the identity of an individual. Bigger's statement reconciles two apparently irreconcilable philosophies; he has discovered his deepest sense of life as well as his individual existence, marked mostly by murder, starting at the end of book one of the novel and lasting throughout the rest of the story. Turned existentialist, he tries to deal with the anguish and despair of life by assuming responsibility for his actions, even as he is waiting for the electric chair.

Bigger's murder of Mary Dalton is accidental; it is also heavily charged with irony. Bigger knows that the white society has determined that a black man found in a white woman's room has necessarily raped her. The bedroom scene produces a web of ironies that make the reader both horrified with and sympathetic to Bigger's situation. Perhaps more than any other scene in the novel, the murder scene is an introduction to the failures of race relations in America; what is wrong between the white and black races culminates in this episode and produces and amplifies Bigger's tragic life. A drunk, helpless white woman needs assistance from a black man, who is also drunk and who has just witnessed the woman and her boyfriend making out in the car. While helping Mary Dalton, Bigger is certainly aroused and once in Mary's bedroom, he exploits her drunkenness, kisses her and fondles her. When he perceives the white silhouette of the blind Mrs. Dalton, his move is dictated by the aforementioned premise, and he proceeds to muffle Mary by putting a pillow on her mouth. This moment summons all kinds of ironic signification. First, Mary, the flower of white womanhood, does not live up to this expectation. More than once, she has transgressed the cult of true womanhood by compromising her virtue, as seen in the newsreel scene in which she is visible on the Florida beach. She is conspiring against her capitalist society by associating with her Communist boyfriend Jan Erlone and embracing and promoting the Communist ideology. More importantly, she is helpless and vulnerable in the hands of a black man, and she allows herself, albeit in unconscious drunkenness, to be kissed and fondled. So the whole scene becomes both subversive and ironic. The premise was established to protect white womanhood,

which hardly applies to Mary Dalton, and Bigger Thomas, intent on countering the consequences of breaking that rule raises the stakes by complicating
the situation. The very thing that prevents him from committing the crime of
rape causes him to commit murder. Yet Bigger knows that if he is ever connected to the murder in Mary's bedroom, he will be accused of rape. Without
the appearance of Mrs. Dalton, Bigger would have raped Mary—she does not
have the right mind to consent. Ironically, in the second part of the novel, Bigger convinces himself and us that he did not accidentally kill Mary, while rape
becomes the state attorney's central argument during the trial episode.

 This cluster of ironic instances starts an ironic cycle in the novel. The murder prompts Bigger Thomas to think about how to dissociate himself from it,
by constructing scenarios to elude the law. He burns Mary's body to get rid
of evidence; he is smart enough to think about fingerprints. He uses all the
knowledge he has about the Daltons—for example, "Hadn't Mr. Dalton said
that they did not get up early on Sunday morning? Hadn't Mary said that
she was going to Detroit? If Mary were missing when they got up, would
they not think that she had already gone to Detroit?" (110). He then frames
Jan Erlone, an easy target since he is a Communist, loathed by the Chicago
capitalists, including Mr. Dalton. To make the whole plan plausible, he writes
a ransom note signed "Red" for Communists. Bigger Thomas later starts to
rationalize his murderous action. Dramatic irony occurs with this rationalization when he goes back to his family, but his mind keeps working. When his
brother Buddy says, "Oh, yeah. I met Jack last night. He said you almost murdered Old Gus" (117), Bigger Thomas is aware of the irony of the situation:
"Here he was sitting with them and they did not know that he had murdered
a white girl and cut her head off and burnt her body" (118). Of course, the
reader knows because the next paragraph reads: "Though he had killed by
accident, not once did he feel the need to tell himself that it had been an accident. He was black and he had been alone in a room where a white girl had
been killed; therefore, he had killed her … he had killed many times before,
only on those other times there had been no handy victim or circumstance to
make visible or dramatic his will to kill" (119). Buddy notices Bigger's nervousness, which somehow underscores the ironic force of the previous moment: the brief argument with Vera about Bigger looking at him (123) and the
conversation with Buddy (124).

 In the moments that follow, Bigger Thomas is intensely concerned about
his survival, as he reasons about the forces he is battling. He blames Mary
for her death (128) and invokes the naturalistic justification of his action,
claiming that white people are "not really people; they were a sort of great
natural force, like a stormy sky looming ahead, or like a deep swirling river
stretching suddenly at one's feet in the dark" (129). Bigger's subsequent dealings with the Daltons, the police and the press constitute a dramatic case of
role reversal. Now, Bigger, the stereotypical dumb black boy, is the one with
knowledge about Mary's disappearance. Equipped with this knowledge, he
manipulates. He becomes the knower, the dissembler, the deceiver, the smart

one, the trickster, the typical *eiron*. Only he and the reader knows. The white side is the one left with stereotypes to work with. This ironic moment somehow temporarily suspends Bigger's naturalistic determinism, because he has the knowledge and the possibility to manipulate those interested in Mary's whereabouts.

Bigger succeeds in manipulating everybody because of the assumptions about him. He basically makes the police and the Daltons believe that he has nothing to do with Mary's disappearance, that Jan Erlone probably knows where she is. He writes a ransom note to drag Jan Erlone and the Communists into this, and he thus succeeds in keeping suspicion away because as a black boy he is not supposed to be smart enough to plan Mary's disappearance. So the knowledge he has empowers him to the extent that he becomes convinced of the empowering effect of his actions. Murdering has made his life meaningful, and he is even ready to "live out the consequences of his actions" (277).

This whole episode in which Mr. and Mrs. Dalton and the police are trying to figure out what happened to Mary, Bigger detains power, and they are helpless. He is the subject, the doer, the one who can move things one way or another. This moment that puts him on top of events also undermines, in an ironic twist, the forces that he is battling. His fate will catch up with him when his misdeed is discovered. Even in his flight, the story that he brings about is the newspaper headline. Bigger Thomas, the unknown brute so far, enters the collective landscape. Perversely it is true, but nobody can avoid reading him now as a story, empowered by his temporary triumph over the societal stereotypes that created him in the first place. After his capture, he directly confronts the forces that shaped him, through their representative institutions: the police, the prosecutor, the court, and the media, as well as the mob outside that would like to lynch him for raping and murdering a white woman.

Bigger's trial becomes a forum where society and its institutions show their power and crush the individual whom they had already reduced to poverty and humiliation. In a way that shows Richard Wright as a man who thought ahead of his time, Bigger Thomas's defense attorney, Boris Max, indulges in what is known today as critical race theory. He uses one of the strategies of critical race theory in legal practice: storytelling. Stemming from the conviction by some scholars that the Civil Rights Movement of the 1950s and 1960s did not eradicate racism from the American society and certainly not from the courtroom, and that truth is contingent on one's racial experience and perceptions, critical race theory appeals to extralegal strategies to make up for the perceived injustices of the dominant race. There is an underlying belief that the dominant center cannot impart impartial justice, and thus the defense lawyer and indeed common people are justified in having recourse to extralegal practices and narratives. Storytelling is an extralegal strategy in that it seeks to mitigate individual responsibility in a court of law in the overall, historical, and current suffering of the group to which the defendant belongs.

Even before this extralegal strategy had the name of critical race theory, Richard Wright has his character Boris Max use it in his defense of Bigger

Thomas. Here is an individual accused of murdering Mary Dalton (and Bessie Mairs), and who thus in normal proceedings would be asked to address these two murders. Instead, Boris Max constructs a long narrative that dismisses Bigger's responsibility in the centuries-long exploitation and oppression of African Americans during slavery and afterward and in the prevailing racism in America. He also includes other groups victimized by the current political and economic system—the Communists, labor union members, and workers' organizations (448). Boris Max concludes his long speech with an indictment of the society that, through its racism and stereotypes, produced Bigger Thomas. "We planned the murder of Mary Dalton," Max argues, "and today we come to court and say: 'We had nothing to do with it!'" (459). Later on, he adds, "the most pathetic aspect of this case is that a young white woman, a student at a university, ignorant and thoughtless, though educated, tried to undo as an individual a gigantic wrong accomplished by a nation through three hundred long years, and was misunderstood and is now dead because of that misunderstanding" (462). From an ideological vantage point, Max's argument makes sense, but his use of storytelling is ineffective in this context. For decades, the white society lynched black men for any alleged whistling at a white woman or any accusation of attack of a white woman by a black man. The media has largely presented Bigger as a rapist and a murderer—ironically, the only genuine, calculated victim of rape and murder, Bessie (Bigger's girlfriend) is hardly mentioned, and if so, only as circumstantial evidence. Because of the sensation created by the media, emotions are high, and there is a mob outside ready to lynch Bigger Thomas. In this context, Boris Max, a Jew and a Communist (two not-so-desirable categories in 1930s Chicago, and the whole country, for that matter) cannot be convincing with his logical appeal.

The state attorney's intervention is no more of a truly legal act. It simply piles past and current prejudices against the black man to reinforce what the reader already knows at the very beginning of the novel: Bigger Thomas is irreversibly doomed! Buckley goes back to the Enlightenment and pulls out its philosophers' justification of the inferiority of the black man in order to establish white superiority. Such philosophers as David Hume, Immanuel Kant, Sir Francis Bacon, and others asserted that blacks (and other people outside the European civilization) were inferior to whites and justified their position by saying that these people did not have arts and sciences, the manifestations of reason, the ultimate measure of one's humanity during the Age of Reason. This idea was very much used by slave traders and slave owners to justify the inhumane and unspeakable treatment they were inflicting on Africans taken to the Americas and to Europe.

Buckley's prosecution of Bigger Thomas becomes an occasion for Richard Wright to bring forth the philosophical, historical, social, political, and economic ideologies that shaped Bigger Thomas's life as an African American. Buckley's immediate goal is to present the defendant as less than a man, a brute, closer (according to the Great Chain of Being) to the animal world. It is no surprise, indeed, that Buckley keeps using the adjective "black" or its synonyms: "and not tremble with fear that at this very moment some half-human black ape may be climbing through the windows of our homes to rape, murder, and burn our daughters!" (476); "this black mad dog who sits here today, telling him that he must report for work" (477); "but the plight of his mother ... had no effect upon this hardened black thing" (477–78); "what black thoughts passed through that Negro's scheming brain the first few moments after he saw that trusting while girl standing before him?" (479); "for we have only this black cur's bare word for it" (480); "Again, we have but the bare word of this worthless ape to go on" (482); "So eager was this demented savage to rape"(483); "and a crime as black and bloody as this is committed" (483); and more.

In his speech, Buckley underscores the Enlightenment dichotomy of "Us Europeans" versus blacks and other races. "Us" belongs to the center defined in terms of arts and sciences, law-abiding citizens, "Us" with our "finest and most delicate flowers of our womanhood" (476) versus "They," the savages, the brutes, the people with no reason, the people without arts and sciences, the rapists, and the murderers. "I represent the forces which allow the arts and sciences to flourish in freedom and peace, thereby enriching the lives of us all" (475), Buckley says, obviously excluding the blacks (who were all bothered when the search for Bigger Thomas was going on, as well as the Communists and the trade union members who work against the capitalistic values of the center. The others, represented by Bigger Thomas, are "men who know no law, no self-control, and no sense of reason" (475) and who "are sub-human" (477). While "Us" (the center) represents civilization, law, and order, the "others" represent subhumanity, marginality, disorder, chaos, savagery, barbarism, cannibalism, rape, and murder—a great danger to American civilization.

Another stereotype that Buckley pulls from the past and the present American white collective consciousness is the idea that a black man in the presence of a white woman will rape her. This was a powerful idea that led to the lynching of many blacks since the post-Reconstruction period. For example, in Charles W. Chesnutt's *The Marrow of Tradition* (1901), a historical novel based on the 1898 Wilmington, North Carolina, race riot, there is an episode in which a black, loyal servant named Sandy Campbell is almost mob lynched. An old woman, Mrs. Ochiltree, is robbed and dies, probably of a heart attack. The robbery, however, is not the main reason that Sandy Campbell, mistakenly arrested, is to die. The galvanizing element that attracts the mob—grave and cheering men, women, and children—is that white womanhood has to be protected. Sandy is saved in extremis after it is discovered that a young white man, Tom Delamere, nephew of Sandy's dignified, liberal Old Delamere, is the real culprit. Furthermore, the 1880s and 1890s and afterwards provide us with multiple cases in which black men were severely dealt with for gratuitous accusations of having raped white women, simply because they were in their presence, and accusations of whistling or staring at white women. Richard Wright was very familiar with the Scottsboro Boys' case, about nine black boys accused of gang-raping two white girls in the Deep South on a railroad freight car on March 25, 1931. The case gripped the nation and the world. The Robert Nixon and Earl Hicks case was another sensational case in the *Chicago Tribune* in 1938 that Richard Wright used in his novel: the two black men were arrested for killing a white woman with a brick in her apartment. In the pages of the *Tribune,* the case was, without any proof, immediately dubbed a sex crime. Furthermore, in 1955, a 14-year-old boy from Chicago named Emmett Till, visiting relatives in the Mississippi Delta region, was brutally murdered after allegedly whistling or simply talking to a white woman in a store. This was another cause célèbre that showed the precarious life of a black man when put in the presence of a white woman.

Buckley knows very well the power of this stereotype in the 1930s white collective mind, and he makes it the primary crime to play on the emotional appeal of the case: "It is a sad day for American civilization when a white man will try to stay the hand of justice from a bestial monstrosity who has ravished and struck down of one of the finest and most delicate flowers of our womanhood" (476). Later, Buckley insists:

> He planned to rape, to kill, to collect! He burned the body to get rid of evidences of rape! … He killed her because he raped her! Mind you, Your Honor, the central crime here is rape! Every action points toward that! (481)

Buckley's intervention reverses the status of subject/doer/agent that Bigger Thomas had achieved in "Flight." When Buckley is speaking, the history of African Americans is retraced from a philosophical vantage point. Ironically, while Buckley refutes Boris Max's narrative, the keen readers know they are both invoking the same discourse: the first to condemn the defendant, the second to save him. The irony of the situation is that Buckley justifies Max's speech, even if the latter fails to achieve its end. The idea of rape that Buckley brandishes so forcefully is an accusation that the black man knows too well in the 1930s. As Richard Wright writes in "How 'Bigger' Was Born," so volatile and tense are these relations that if a Negro rebels against rule and taboo, he is lynched and the reason for the lynching is usually called "rape," that catchword which has garnered such vile connotations that it can raise a mob anywhere in the South pretty quickly, even today (26). Later on, Wright adds:

> Any Negro who has lived in the North or the South knows that times without number he has heard of some Negro boy being picked up on the streets and carted off to jail and charged with "rape." This thing happens so often that to my mind it had become a representative symbol of the Negro's uncertain position in America. (40)

Everybody involved in the trial of Bigger Thomas (himself included) knows about the bias that governs race relations and the judicial system. The reader certainly gets a high dose of irony during this trial. In fact, the trial constitutes the climax of what I have called the ironic cycle. We saw Bigger Thomas suffocating Mary Dalton. We witnessed Boris Max trying the extralegal strategy of storytelling to save Bigger Thomas, and—the irony of all—Buckley actually agreeing with both Bigger Thomas and Boris Max about the social ideas that led to Mary's murder. The only difference is that they put their agreement to different uses—Bigger to kill, Max to defend him, and Buckley to have him taken to the electric chair.

Buckley's intervention annihilates Bigger's ontological determination by calling him a brute, a savage, a crawling animal that could cause another fall of mankind (American civilization), and Buckley calls on the "civilized," "decent white man in America" to crush that serpent (476). His unapologetic invocation of the great chain of being stands in sharp contrast to Bigger's keen manipulation of Buckley and his men earlier on. In the stages of human development that the great chain of being refers to, Bigger Thomas belongs, in the eyes of the state attorney and the white men he appeals to, if not to the bottom stage where animals are, but hardly in the first stage of human development. Bigger Thomas may not catch this part of Buckley's reasoning, but his lawyer, Boris Max, will tell him later, as if to refute Buckley's claim: "You're human, Bigger.... In the work I'm doing, I look at the world in a way that shows no whites and no blacks, no civilized and no savages" (495). Ironically, it is after Buckley's refutation of Bigger's humanity that the latter completes the "act of creation" that he started with the unintentional murder of Mary. He fully reclaims his humanity in a manner that is consistent with other protagonists in the African American literary tradition.

The novel in general and the trial in particular allow Richard Wright to inscribe his work in the broad literary tradition of African American letters inaugurated by the slave narratives. Naturalism then becomes a powerful literary tool in Wright's literary project to depict, beyond the obvious sociopolitical protest, a critical paradigm in African American literature, that is, the liberation paradigm. Naturalism allows Richard Wright to do what Frederick Douglass did with clusters of negatives in the first chapter of *Narrative in the Life of Frederick Douglass* (1845). In that opening chapter, Frederick Douglass knows only where he was born, but he does not know about the other dimensions of human definition—his mother, his father, or his date of birth. The peculiar institution has made sure that no records concerning his early life were kept. What the text of the opening chapter does is to convey a sense of nothingness. Frederick Douglass's narrative then traces the trajectory from this nothingness to being. It certainly is an ontological exercise of extreme urgency to a man who was denied humanity by slavery. His autobiographical writing is, no doubt, an act of creation, particularly sealed in chapter 10 in which we read his soliloquy to the ships he observes from the Chesapeake Bay, and importantly, his famous chiasmus: "You have seen how a man was made a slave; you shall see how a slave was made a man" (75). Chapter 10 of Frederick Douglass's narrative is the climactic moment of the story. It is a revolutionary moment that I have called the Douglassian moment (in *Race and Gender in the Making of an African American Literary Tradition*) and would subsequently be reenacted by other African American writers including Harriet Jacobs, Harriet Wilson, James Weldon Johnson, Zora Neale Hurston, Richard Wright, Ralph Ellison, and Alice Walker, among others. In *Native Son,* Buckley overtly repeats or echoes European literary texts and philosophical treatises from the 16th century to the 20th century that provided the intellectual frame wherein the enslavement of blacks and the colonization of people outside Western Europe were justified.

Even though Bigger Thomas does not have a life after his own revolutionary pronouncement, we have witnessed his trajectory from nothingness to being, if in a perverse manner. Naturalism allows Richard Wright to duplicate the slave narrative's sense of annihilation: the rat-infested apartment, the impossibility of Bigger pursuing any real dream, his life within a gang, his helplessness, his entrapment by the snowstorm that bars all ways out of the city, his frustration, and his violence are all elements that annihilate Bigger Thomas (and other blacks). The overwhelming crushing of naturalistic elements over Bigger Thomas shows him as a victim, an object/patient of forces he cannot control. Unlike the slave narrative, naturalism in Richard Wright's hands signals that Bigger Thomas is doomed, crushed, annihilated by superior forces. On the other hand, like Frederick Douglass and other slaves, Bigger Thomas has to liberate himself, and this needs to be an autogenic exercise, generated by his own free will. After all the trials (metaphorically and judicially speaking), Bigger Thomas is about to be executed, but he has reached a higher level of humanity best expressed in a surprisingly oxymoronic association of rationalism and existentialism: "But what I killed for, I am!" (501). This assertion counters the otherwise irreversible annihilation wrought by naturalistic elements. This is indeed a highly philosophical statement that reconciles reason as creative agency and existence as the true measure of one's essence. Bigger makes his life and his actions (existence) the prelude of his essence. "I killed, therefore I am" is Bigger Thomas's own paradigm. His act of killing starts him on a journey to defeat being a cliché, a stereotype, a dead sign. He refuses to continue being acted on, being the victim. He acts instead; he becomes the agent, the subject, the doer. "I always wanted to do something" (499), he tells his lawyer, something significant, that would redeem him, or at least allow him who belongs to the periphery to meet the center in a thunderous manner. Even though his action also leads to his condemnation to death, before this happens he reclaims his human identity by revising the rationalist motto that has much to do with the social forces represented by the state attorney. "'I am!' not because I think, but because of my actions." In this existentialist moment, Bigger Thomas assumes responsibility and takes ownership of his actions and their consequences.

In another instance that shows his avant-garde flair, Richard Wright explored the possibilities of the existentialist philosophy in literature before Jean-Paul Sartre, Albert Camus, and others during and after World War II popularized it again. He later met and became friends with both French writers when he moved to Paris in 1947, but he was already familiar with Fyodor Dostoevsky's work, particular *Notes from Underground* (1864), with its emphasis on the meaninglessness, absurdity, and alienation of urban life—Wright has been called the "Black Dostoevsky" (*Conversations with Richard Wright* 133). Existentialism, particularly Sartre's version, contends that a person becomes his or her action, that existence precedes essence, that a man becomes what he does. Reacting to the positivist, totalizing rationalism of the Enlightenment, Søren Kierkegaard, Dutch theologian and philosopher, proposed that truth is subjective, not in the sense that it is dependent on individual whims, but rather on the individual's experience in the world. It is not the preconceived ideas or institutions that give meaning to a person's existence. Ideas such as reason, the Church, and society may well be parts of an individual's life, but they should not dictate his existence. Existing somehow means being aware of this possibility. Existence, Jean-Paul Sartre tells us, simply means becoming aware of one's presence in the world—an accidental presence. Existence, he suggests in *Nausea,* is simply being there, among other existences. Antoine Roquentin, the main character in *Nausea,* becomes aware of his accidentality by experiencing the presence and resistance of other existences such as a piece of paper that resists being picked, a door knob that resists turning, a chestnut tree that imposes its being in the world in a backyard. "To exist is simply to be there" (131), Roquentin says. One is constantly facing the anguish, despair, and absurdity of this life. Jean-Paul Sartre affirms that the resolution to anguish is free will, responsibility for one's actions, and freedom. Albert Camus himself experimented with existentialism in literature in his acclaimed novel *The Stranger.* Initially published in 1942 as *L'Etranger* in France, it shows echoes of Richard Wright's *Native Son.* After Bigger's trial and condemnation, his mother and brother and sister try to visit him in prison, but he tells them to stay away (488). Reverend Hammond, Bigger's mother's pastor, is treated in the same manner. Bigger has already rejected him by throwing away the cross Hammond gave him; Bigger has simply concluded that it is a symbol of the Ku Klux Klan. Furthermore, he looks at religion as a way of escaping problems, not dealing with them, just like his mother or Bessie, who used to drink whiskey to drown her problems. Bigger also deals harshly with a white priest who tells him to turn to religion to deal with his trouble: he throws hot coffee at him (488). This scene echoes the ending of Camus's novel two years after the publication of Wright's novel. Meursault, the main character, also condemned to death for murder, refuses the consolation of religion that the chaplain tries hard to impose on him. Meursault has lived a typically existentialist life, refusing to adhere to preconceived, societal institutions, and living a moment-by-moment life. After the trial, while awaiting his execution, he accepts the responsibility of his murdering the Arab, but he still refutes religion (one of the preconceived ideas) and deals with the last moment of his life resolving once and for all the absurdity and anguish of life. He is facing the ultimate anguish in life: death. Interestingly enough, in his existentialist credo, like Bigger Thomas he rationalizes his death and in so doing gains a sense of freedom.

The absurdity and meaninglessness of life, developed by Sartre and Camus in their work in the 1940s and 1950s, are already forces that shape Bigger Thomas's life in *Native Son*. Bigger Thomas's accidental killing of Mary Dalton sets him on a journey to self-discovery by rendering him aware of the precariousness of his existence. Even though his life was previously very much precarious, his perverse actions make him intensely aware of his existence. His life becomes a succession of tense moments, each being potentially the last one of his life. His flight is just reflective of his anguish. Everything threatens his survival, and he deals with it accordingly. His manipulation of the Daltons and the police, Bessie Mears, the ransom plot: all these dealings are specific moments in Bigger's new intense life. As shown earlier, his capture and trial bring about the climax of the ironic cycle closed at the end by Bigger's oxymoronic link of rationalism and existentialism in "What I killed for, *I am*!"—a parody of the Cartesian philosophy as well as an enactment of the existentialist (especially Sartrean) acceptance of the responsibility of one's actions. Before his death, Bigger Thomas fully assumes his humanity by accepting this responsibility. He is going to die as a man, not as an ape, a realization that Ernest Gaines would later reenact in his 1993 novel *A Lesson before Dying*. Both *Native Son* and *A Lesson before Dying* show dehumanized black men claiming their full humanity, and like Albert Camus's Meursault, finding freedom at a time when life is about to end.

Richard Wright's forceful and unique take on racism in America in *Native Son* also attracted stage and film adaptations. Orson Welles did a stage adaptation of *Native Son* featuring Canada Lee as Bigger Thomas. It opened on March 24, 1941, at the St. James Theatre, New York. The play was later produced in other places, including European cities. Kent Gash's 2005 adaptation and direction featured Ato Essandoh as Bigger Thomas. Film adaptations include the 1951 and 1986 films (the 1986 film, directed by Jerrold Freedman, featured Oprah Winfrey as Mrs. Thomas, Bigger's mother); the first was filmed in Argentina, with Richard Wright playing Bigger Thomas (visibly double the age of the protagonist). Unlike the novel itself, the two movies were not well received.

Native Son has also influenced contemporary American literature and popular culture. For example, in the episode "Far beyond the Stars" of the *Star Trek: Deep Space Nine*, Benny Russell praises *Native Son* as a noteworthy African American book. In a novel set in post-Depression California and heavily shaped by the author's own turbulent life, problem child Alex Hammond, the main character in Edward Bunker's novel *Little Boy Blue* (1998), reads *Native Son* in his solitary confinement. His fascination with Wright's novel is understandable, since Alex Hammond also reacts to his life's frustration with rage and violence. Percival Everett's satirical novel *Erasure* (2001) has a section titled "My Pafology," a ghetto fiction that parodies *Native Son*. The novel is also mentioned in *American History X*, a Tony Kaye movie (1998) that deals with white-black race relations. Lemony Snicket uses Boris Max's words (in his defense of Bigger Thomas) in his book *The Penultimate Peril*

(2005): "Who knows when some slight shock, disturbing the delicate balance between social order and thirsty aspiration, shall send the skyscrapers in our cities toppling?" (*Native Son* 469), warning against what he calls the "looming image of violence" if the system condemns Bigger Thomas when it is not interested in knowing what he symbolizes in the racist American society of the 1930s (469). Saul Williams used two lines about Bigger Thomas putting a corpse (Mary Dalton's) in a furnace in the lyrics of his song "The Ritual," which is part of the album *The Inevitable Rise and Liberation of Niggytardust* (2007). In 2008, the HBO program *Brave New Voices* had a Chicago team reciting the poem "Lost Count: A Love Story," in which "Bigger Thomas's town," "Native Sons," "Chicago," and "anyone under age 20," all direct references to Richard Wright's novel, are mentioned in this strong plea against youth-on-youth crime.

Little Known Facts about Native Son

- *The novel sold 250,000 hardcover copies within three weeks of publication, thus quickly becoming a bestseller.*
- *Wright's importance in American letters was sealed with the publication of* Native Son, *for the novel was the first authored by an African American to be selected by the Book-of-the-Month Club in March 1940, an honor bringing with it an incredibly large circulation (*Unfinished Quest *177–78).*
- Native Son *was adapted for the stage where it was again a wild success. Working with Paul Green, Wright co-authored the dramatic transformation of* Native Son, *eventually partnering with United Productions and Orson Welles, John Houseman, and John Mankievicz (*Unfinished Quest *207). Canada Lee's renowned portrayal of Bigger Thomas fused exceptionally well with Welles's flamboyant set design, and the play was a commercial and critical success (*Unfinished Quest *211–12).*
- *In 1949, James Baldwin famously called the novel "Everybody's Protest Novel," in an essay of this title. Later, Baldwin included this essay and "Many Thousand Gone" in his collection of essays* Notes of a Native Son *(1955).*
- *Although Wright turned down many attempts to purchase the film rights to* Native Son, *when he finally agreed to the making of the movie, he was swayed more by a desire to maintain truth to the novel's text than by stellar casting and directing. Wright's concerns about the text's integrity were well founded, for an early offer from Metro-Goldwyn-Mayer had proposed an entire transformation of the novel's plot, substituting white characters for Bigger Thomas and the rest of the black characters. However, dedication to the precise letter of the text may have led Wright*

to sacrifice experience and talent in the end. Wright himself ended up playing the role of Bigger Thomas, and although an incredibly dedicated participant, he only sometimes captured a convincing protagonist. Throughout much of the film, as Fabre notes, Wright was awkward and uncomfortable in the role (338–49). The movie was the joint project of Wright and a French producer, Pierre Chenal, and was filmed in Argentina and Chicago (Unfinished Quest 336–40). Because the film exceeded the expected budget three times over, ran into trouble with censors in multiple countries, and suffered from many amateur performances in the supporting cast, Native Son *was never a smashing success as a film. Perhaps most upsetting to Wright, American censors excised approximately 2,500 feet of film, apparently damaging part of the sound track in the process so that much of the trial scene initially played to American audiences without sound (Unfinished Quest 348). Although the sound track and some of the missing footage were eventually restored, the damage was irreparable as far as Wright was concerned.*

- *In 1991, the Library of America published the restored text of the novel. This edition also contains Richard Wright's essay "How 'Bigger' Was Born."*
- *The American Library Association has placed the novel on the list of the Most Frequently Challenged Books of 1990–2000, and the Modern Library on its list of the 100 best novels of the 20th century.*

RICHARD WRIGHT: *NATIVE SON*

Many writers think that it is not their business to offer interpretations of their works, but Richard Wright did not shy away from offering insights about *Native Son*. The first two of the following excerpts were taken from a lecture ("How Bigger Was Born") that he delivered a few times (before it was added to post-1940 editions of the novel); the next two extracts are from a collection of conversations that Keneth Kinnamon and Michel Fabre, two Wright scholars, had with the author.

- The birth of Bigger Thomas goes back to my childhood, and there was not just one Bigger, but many of them, more than I could count and more than you suspect. ("How Bigger Was Born" 22)
- I made the discovery that Bigger Thomas was not black all the time; he was white, too, and there were literally millions of him, everywhere. ("How Bigger Was Born" 28)
- There were Negroes who felt that the book didn't present the best side of the race—something that has been said over and over again. The white

parallel to this reaction was, "Mr. Wright, you don't really think that we do these things, do you?" As you no doubt know from your own experience, the artist is sometimes caught up in no-man's land. He gets shots on both sides. (*Conversations with Richard Wright* 145)

- Hollywood will continue being as it is now, "the industry of pure fiction." For example, my book *Native Son* should have been turned into a film there. I sold the rights, but I withdrew the script because they wanted to turn Bigger Thomas, a black boy marked by fatalistic destiny, into a white character. That is to say, they were only interested in the political plot of the affair, causing the social meaning of the drama and the racial problem to disappear. (*Conversations with Richard Wright* 35)

NATIVE SON ON STAGE

When *Native Son* was adapted for the stage, it was again a wild success. Working with Paul Green, Wright co-authored the dramatic transformation of *Native Son,* eventually partnering with United Productions and Orson Welles, John Houseman, and John Mankievicz. Canada Lee's renowned portrayal of Bigger Thomas fused exceptionally well with Welles's flamboyant set design, and the play was a commercial and critical success.

NATIVE SON ON THE BIG SCREEN

Although Wright turned down many attempts to purchase the film rights to *Native Son,* when he finally agreed to the making of the movie, he was swayed more by a desire to maintain truth to the novel's text than by stellar casting and directing. Wright's concerns about the text's integrity were well-founded, for an early offer from Metro-Goldwyn-Mayer had proposed an entire trans-formation of the novel's plot, substituting white characters for Bigger Thomas and the rest of the black characters. However, dedication to the precise letter of the text may have led Wright to sacrifice experience and talent in the end. Wright himself ended up playing the role of Bigger Thomas, and although an incredibly dedicated participant, he only sometimes captured a convincing protagonist. Throughout much of the film, as Fabre notes, Wright was awk-ward and uncomfortable in the role (338–49). The movie was the joint project of Wright and a French producer, Pierre Chenal, and was filmed in Argentina and Chicago. Because the film exceeded the expected budget three times over, ran into trouble with censors in multiple countries, and suffered from many amateur performances in the supporting cast, *Native Son* was never a smash-ing success as a film. Perhaps most upsetting to Wright, American censors excised approximately 2,500 feet of film, apparently damaging part of the soundtrack in the process so that much of the trial scene initially played to

American audiences without sound. Although the soundtrack and some of the missing footage were eventually restored, the damage was irreparable as far as Wright was concerned.

THE CENSORING OF *NATIVE SON*

After its publication, *Native Son* was censored in America. The reason for the American censorship can be found in roughly the last 150 pages of the 400-page novel, the part of the novel dealing with Bigger's arrest and trial. The problem, it seems, was the Communist attorney provided Bigger in the novel, Mr. Boris Max. Max, a man who defends Bigger valiantly, makes statements such as the following: "Your Honor, another civil war in these states is not impossible; and if the misunderstanding of what this boy's life means is an indication of how men of wealth and property are misreading the consciousness of the submerged millions today, one may truly come" (*Native Son* 369). Thus, one of Wright's philosophical lenses through which to interrogate race and racism in America, Communism, also presented one of the biggest obstacles in getting his message to the masses.

Wright, like many of his peers in African American arts and letters at the time, was courted by the Communist Party when other political avenues seemed mostly closed to African Americans. And since so much of the deprivation experienced by black America at the time was economic, Communism provided a plausible solution to many of the challenges faced by the Biggers of the 1940s and '50s. Wright, therefore, aligns himself with Communism in *Native Son* with fairly bold fervor, taking a strong Marxist Communist stance throughout the novel. This is not, however, to suggest that Wright saw no potential problems with Communism. Like his protégé, James Baldwin, and his friend Ralph Ellison, Wright understood the dangers of losing individuals in political movements, and by the time *Native Son* was published, Wright was already beginning to question the motives of Communists in embracing African Americans. Indeed, several of the Communists in the novel—most notably Jan and Mary—are guilty of failing to practice what they preach, experiencing the comforts of their capitalist families' extravagant lifestyles while proclaiming themselves opposed to the doctrines providing their privilege. Further, some of the other party members in the novel, particularly those who appear on the scene shortly after Bigger's arrest, seem quite willing to risk the lives of individuals for their cause. However, the strongest proponent of Communism in the novel, Max, the attorney defending Bigger, provides Bigger with some of the first genuine support and sympathy he has known from whites, and Max argues as well for the economic leveling of the playing field across racial lines, something that seems likely to have an impact on future generations of black men if they are able to access the education and opportunity that was denied Bigger Thomas. Even Max is guilty of losing sight of the individual as he seeks the bigger picture, though, and as the end of the novel reveals, Max ends up perplexed by Bigger's behavior and insistence on his own destruction, mostly because Max has failed to listen to Bigger, never truly seeing him as an individual but only as a representative for the cause. Max is arguing for Bigger's life, seeking for him a legal punishment of life in prison rather than execution. Having experienced the prison house of economic disparity and seriously restricted mobility via Jim Crow segregation, Bigger Thomas is ready to have his life ended quickly rather than have the noose of incarceration slowly suffocate him. Max, despite his best intentions, cannot see the needs of his client because the Communist cause overshadows the individual's desires and needs. Max is particularly baffled (and even horrified) by Bigger's ultimate declaration that what he "killed for must've been good" (392), and by extension, the killing itself was therefore good. These two men are unable to communicate their new understandings because Bigger is focusing exclusively on the means (the killing), while Max is focusing on the end (Communist consciousness-raising, and perhaps revolution).

Although Communism offered an avenue for addressing economic disparities experienced by blacks, Wright felt that the Communist Party was too quick to sacrifice the entire black community in the interest of promoting party philosophies. In his 1949 essay "I Tried to Be a Communist," Wright explores the shortcomings of the party's solutions to the problems plaguing 20th-century blacks, chief among them, the lack of admission that race was at least a complication of the single-minded Communist focus on economics as the root of all social ills.

FURTHER READING

Austin, John. *How to Do Things with Words*. Cambridge: Harvard UP, 1962.

Baldwin, James. "Many Thousand Gone." *Twentieth Interpretations of* Native Son. Ed. Houston A. Baker Jr. Englewood Cliffs, NJ: Prentice-Hall, 1972. 48–62. *Black Boy: A Record of Childhood and Youth*. 1945. New York: HarperCollins, 1993.

Bloom, Harold, ed. *Modern Critical Views: Richard Wright*. New York: Chelsea House, 1987.

Butler, Robert. Native Son: *The Emergence of a New Black Hero*. Boston: Twayne, 1991.

Camus, Albert. *The Stranger*. Trans. Matthew Ward. New York: Vintage, 1989.

Chomsky, Noam. *Aspects of the Theory of Syntax*. Cambridge, MA: MIT P, 1965.

Douglass, Frederick. *Narrative of the Life of Frederick Douglass, An American Slave, By Himself*. Boston: Bedford, 1995.

"The Ethics of Living Jim Crow, an Autobiographical Sketch." 1937. *The Norton Anthology of African American Literature*. Ed. Henry Louis Gates, Jr. and Nellie Y. McKay. Second Edition. New York: W.W. Norton, 2004. 1411–19.

Fabre, Michel. *The World of Richard Wright*. Jackson: UP of Mississippi, 1985.

Grice, Paul. "Logic and Convention." *Syntax and Semantics: Speech Acts*. Vol. 3. Ed. P. Cole and J. Morgan. New York: Academic, 1975.

Gumperz, J. J. *Discourse Strategies*. Cambridge: Cambridge UP, 1982.

Hakutani, Yoshinobu. "Richard Wright's The Long Dream as Racial and Sexual Discourse." *African American Review* 30.2 (1996): 267–80.

Hakutani, Yoshinobu. *Critical Essays on Richard Wright*. Boston: Hall, 1982.

Harris, Trudier. *Exorcising Blackness: Historical and Literary Lynching and Burning Rituals*. Bloomington: Indiana UP, 1984.

Howe, Irving. "Black Boys and Native Sons." *Twentieth Century Interpretations of Native Son*. Ed. Houston A. Baker Jr. Englewood Cliffs, NJ: Prentice-Hall, 1972. 63–70.

Hutcheon, *Linda. Irony's Edge: The Theory and Politics of Irony*. London: Routledge, 1994.

Joyce, Joyce Ann. *Richard Wright's Art of Tragedy*. Iowa City: U of Iowa P, 1986.

Kenner, H. "Irony of Ironies." *Times Literary Supplement* October 17, 1986: 1151–52.

Kinnamon, Keneth, ed. *New Essays on* Native Son. Cambridge: Cambridge UP, 1990.

Kinnamon, Keneth, and Michel Fabre, eds. *Conversations with Richard Wright with Richard Wright*. Jackson: UP of Mississippi, 1993.

Reilly, John, ed. *Richard Wright: The Critical Reception*. New York: Franklin, 1978.

Sartre, Jean-Paul. *Nausea*. Trans. Lloyd Alexander. New York: New Directions, 1964.

Smith, Valerie. *Self-Discovery and Authority in Afro-American Narrative*. Cambridge, MA: Harvard UP, 1987.

Twagilimana, Aimable. *Race and Gender in the Making of an African American Literary Tradition*. New York: Garland, 1997.

Walker, Margaret. *Richard Wright: Daemonic Genius*. New York: Warner Books, 1988.

Wright, Richard. "How Bigger Was Born." *Twentieth Century Interpretations of Native Son*. Ed. Houston A. Baker Jr. Englewood Cliffs, N J: Prentice-Hall, 1972. 21–47.

Wright, Richard. *Native Son*. 1940. New York: HarperPerennial, 1993.

Aimable Twagilimana and Cammie M. Sublette

Lorraine Hansberry, a playwright and civil rights activist, wrote the first play by an African American woman to appear on Broadway. (Library of Congress)

A Raisin in the Sun

Lorraine Vivian Hansberry (1930–1965) allowed neither the inequalities in the world nor the perspectives of others to taint the work that she had taken on as her mission. Hansberry's writing sought to identify and incite the greater good in all of humanity. As an artist, she'd been absorbed in her training and craft. As a woman, she pushed for a greater equality and appreciation of her artistry. As an African American, she'd lived through an era of many brands of injustice and fought for permanent social changes. And as a human being, Hansberry wrote to inspire a better future for all of mankind to inherit. For all of these reasons she is a true icon of African American dramatic literature. Hansberry shied away from the expectations of her affluent upbringing. Born on May 19, 1930, she writes in *To Be Young, Gifted and Black* of the distance between her family members, whose shows of emotion were awkward and embarrassing (*To Be Young* 48). It stands to reason that while it was not the most comforting environment in which to grow, the development of her analytical and critical mind was far from neglected. She was the youngest of four children, with a seven-year difference from the closest in age to her. Instead of attending a historically black college like her parents and siblings, she chose the University of Wisconsin, where she was a minority and an unknown. Eventually bored with the routine of school, she dropped out of college (with her mother's permission) in 1950 to become a writer. Lorraine Hansberry had been studying visual art, but so greatly influenced was she by Sean O'Casey's work that she decided to work in a new medium—theatre. O'Casey, an Irish playwright, made dramatic the experiences of the average working-class family and explored the foibles of living in a Dublin slum in the early 20th century. His adherence to realism in theatre would later prove crucial as Hansberry developed her style as a playwright and crafted her most successful works. For Hansberry, the move to New York City, epicenter of American theatre, facilitated her immersion into the world of writing and brought her closer to many highly regarded African American thinkers, artists, and activists of the time.

A Raisin in the Sun: *Important Dates*

1959   A Raisin in the Sun *first appeared on Broadway. It won the Drama Critic's Circle Desk Award for Best Play of the Year. In addition to being the first Broadway play written by an African American woman, it was also the first Broadway play directed by a black man, Canadian, Lloyd Richards.*

1961   *The iconic film version of* A Raisin in the Sun *was directed by Daniel Petrie and starred Sidney Poitier as Walter Lee Younger, Ruby Dee as Ruth Younger, Diana Sands as Beneatha, and Claudia McNeil as Lena Younger.*

1973   Raisin *opened on Broadway. Robert Nemiroff produced and wrote the book for the musical treatment of* A Raisin in the Sun. *It went on to win a Tony Award for Best Musical in 1974 and Virginia Capers, the first African American to do so, won Best Actress in a Musical for her portrayal of Lena Younger.*

2004   *The Broadway revival of* A Raisin in the Sun *directed by Kenny Leon, starred actors from stage, screen, and even the music industry. Phylicia Rashad and Audra McDonald both won Tony Awards for their performances as Lena Younger and Ruth Younger, respectively. Especially notable, Rashad was the first African American to win a Tony for Leading Actress in a Play. Also featured in the production was film star Sanaa Lathan as Beneatha. In the role of Walter Lee Younger was hip-hop producer and business mogul Sean Combs. His being cast in the role was met with controversy and criticism by theatre traditionalists, particularly since many great black actors have played the part—Sidney Poitier, most famously, Danny Glover, and scores of other trained actors—yet Combs's performance earned positive reviews from many camps.*

2008   *A TV movie of* A Raisin in the Sun, *also directed by Kenny Leon, was broadcast on ABC with the 2004 Broadway cast reprising their roles.*

Hansberry was able to synthesize two of her passions by studying African history under W.E.B. Du Bois at the Jefferson School for Social Sciences and working as an associate editor with Paul Robeson's *Freedom* newspaper. Neither man was a stranger to her, as she was introduced to them both in her youth. Her parents' position in Chicago's affluent African American community and her uncle, William Leo Hansberry, an early African scholar, allowed her greater exposure to politically progressive circles and supported her study of the politics of black people in Africa and America. Opinionated and outspoken, Hansberry's political stance on many issues was considered subversive during the Red Scare, when the possibility of being blacklisted loomed large on the horizon for every intellectual who dared to agree with any passage or concept associated with Communism. Her views on other social justice issues such as civil rights were like many African Americans of her time, considerably progressive. Under investigation due to her political views, Hansberry earned an FBI file, as did many other artists who spoke out against governmental injustice, human rights abuses, and international policies. This was especially so as she traveled to Uruguay in Paul Robeson's stead after his passport had been revoked by the U.S. government. Lorraine Hansberry could have jeopardized her young career for believing so strongly that the world should be a better place. Though she published many articles using her own name in lieu of a pseudonym, she was never called to testify in any trials. Perhaps she was not considered to be enough of a threat, being black, a woman, and not yet a household name. Hansberry did not, however, cease to be a mouthpiece for her ideals. Through her body of work, Hansberry tapped into many political issues, whether or not they were the hot topic at the time.

Inspired by Langston Hughes's poem "Harlem," *A Raisin in the Sun* debuted on stage March 11, 1959, at the Ethel Barrymore Theatre, where it ran for 530 performances. It chronicles the experiences of the working-class Younger family as they confront the struggles and frustrations of surviving daily life on Chicago's South Side and details their efforts toward social mobility and maintaining hope for a better future in that racially segregated city. Contributing to the play's iconic status is that it thematically addresses both the national debate about racial segregation as manifested through real estate covenants in cities like Chicago and Los Angeles and its relationship to social mobility ongoing at the time of its initial production that had not been previously addressed on stage. The significance of *A Raisin in the Sun*'s commentary on the struggles of working-class African Americans was not lost on writer James Baldwin, who after seeing the play in Philadelphia in 1959 alongside more African Americans than "he had ever seen in his life at the theatre," asserted that "never before, in the entire history of American theatre has so much of the truth of black people's lives been seen on stage" (Baldwin xii). Adding to its iconic status is the play's prefiguring of both interracial and intraracial discussions around the politics of racial oppression and race representation, which took on greater significance during the expansion of the Civil Rights Movement following the its debut. Writer Amiri Baraka confirms, "as a document reflecting the essence of [civil rights] struggles, the play is unexcelled...it remains the quintessential civil rights drama" (41). Further, *A Raisin in the Sun* offers a parallel critique of the American dream that another iconic domestic drama of the postwar era—Arthur Miller's 1949 play *Death of a Salesman*—advances through the family relationships depicted. Miller's attention to the duplicity inherent in the American dream as detailed through his protagonist, Willy Loman, shares continuities with Hansberry's play and its protagonist, Walter Lee Younger. Still, as Hansberry argued, though both Younger and Loman might be figured as victims of a detour of the American dream, Walter Lee departs from Willy in his ultimate rejection of some of his culture's values (Hansberry 194). While Willy Loman appears to accept American cultural values, Walter Lee Younger, "draws on the strength of an incredible people, who historically, have simply refused to give up" (194) in order to fuel his rejection of segregation and its implications for the Younger family.

Though the play's themes contribute to the significance of its groundbreaking Broadway debut and its iconic status, its production history, its reception by critics at its debut, as well as its influence in the careers of African American actors and actresses heightens its impact and longevity. Hansberry's play was initially produced in New Haven, Philadelphia, and Chicago because its producer, Philip Rose, was denied access to Broadway's theatres (Carter 125). After proving its commercial viability in these cities, it opened on Broadway, where it ran for over 19 months (Wilkerson 120). The play went on to win the New York Drama Critics' Circle Award in 1959, making Hansberry the youngest American, the first woman, and first African American to win the award. In addition, though actors Claudia McNeil (Lena Younger), Ruby Dee (Ruth Younger), and Sidney Poitier (Walter Lee Younger) had already appeared in both stage and film productions prior to *A Raisin in the Sun,* the stage debut of the play launched the careers of numerous African Americans in theatre and film, including actors Louis Gossett Jr., Diana Sands, Ivan Dixon, and Glynn Turman, as well as understudies Frances Foster, Douglas Turner Ward, Lonnie Elder III, Beah Richards. Furthermore, it made Lloyd Richards the first African American director on Broadway. Both McNeil and Poitier were nominated for best actor and actress Tony Awards in 1960, and the play was nominated for a best play Tony the same year. The overwhelmingly positive response from both critics and audiences to the play accounts to some degree for its iconic status.

A Raisin in the Sun is drawn from Lorraine Hansberry's own experience with race restrictive real estate covenants in Chicago. In 1937, her family moved into a home in the predominantly white Washington Park (also referred to as South Park) neighborhood, which was bounded on the west and south sides by predominantly black neighborhoods and on the east by the predominantly white Woodlawn neighborhood. Because South Park was viewed as a barrier between Woodlawn and the black neighborhoods, it became a battleground for the Woodlawn Property Owner Association. The association wanted to enforce the race restrictive real estate covenant in place, and sued James and Olive Burke, who sold the home in violation of the covenant to Carl Hansberry, Lorraine Hansberry's father. The Supreme Court of Illinois upheld a lower court injunction that supported the restrictive covenant and Hansberry, with the assistance of the NAACP, appealed the case in the U.S. Supreme Court in *Hansberry v. Lee*; in 1940, the Supreme Court struck down the ruling, saying that it violated the Fourteenth Amendment. Woodlawn Property Owner Association members attempted to intimidate the Hansberrys during the three-year-long court battle through violence including vandalism and mobs surrounding the home. Hansberry's experience in Washington Park is central to *A Raisin in the Sun*.

A Raisin in the Sun traces several weeks in the life of the Younger Family, whose matriarch, Lena, is the beneficiary of her late husband's $10,000 life insurance policy. Living with her son Walter Lee, who works as a chauffeur; daughter Beneatha, a college student; daughter-in-law Ruth, a domestic worker; and grandson Travis in a cramped kitchenette apartment on Chicago's South Side, Lena invests a portion of the funds in a down payment on a home in Clybourne Park, a white Chicago neighborhood, and gives the remainder to her son, asking him to put a portion of it aside for Beneatha's medical school tuition and the remainder to use as he likes. Frustrated by his inability to grasp his dreams of economic freedom through entrepreneurship and material gain for himself and for his family, Walter Lee invests all the money in a dubious plan to buy a liquor store with two acquaintances, Bobo and Willy. When Willy leaves town with all of the money, Walter Lee calls the Clybourne Park Improvement Association representative, Karl Lindner, who had offered to buy the home from the Youngers at a price well above their initial investment so that the neighborhood would not be integrated. In his despair after losing the money, he intends to accept the offer—and by extension—to accept the neighborhood's implication of racial inferiority. However, on Lindner's arrival at their South Side apartment and under his son's gaze, he refuses and restates the family's intention to move into the home because "my father—he earned it" (Hansberry 128) despite the homeowners' misgivings about the Youngers integrating the all-white neighborhood. Following this climactic scene, the Youngers complete their packing, the movers arrive, and as the play ends, Lena Younger, the last of the family to leave the apartment, picks up her symbolic houseplant, which is central to the play's sunlight motif, and closes the door on their cramped apartment to begin the move into their Clybourne Park home.

The relationships between family members foreground themes of integration, the significance of family relationships, family legacy, class mobility, and its relationship to the American dream, as well as gender politics and racial identity. Additionally, the triangulation between Beneatha and her fellow students Joseph Asagai and George Murchison complicates the play's commentary on the intersection of racial identity, class status, and African liberation. Asagai and Murchison embody much of *A Raisin in the Sun*'s treatment of both the American dream and notions of racial identity. However, the struggle within the Younger family itself over the nature of the dream, how to access it, and their competing versions of it deeply informs the play's plot and stage action.

The notion of the American dream—or class mobility and the acquisition of money and material goods—and the ongoing conflicts over it shape the relationships within the Younger family. At the outset of the play, when Ruth refuses to give Travis 50 cents for school because they don't have it to spare, Walter Lee not only admonishes her for telling him the truth about their financial situation, but goes further to give him a dollar and advises that Travis buy himself "some fruit today—or take a taxicab to school or something" (Hansberry 19). Shortly after Travis leaves with the money, Walter Lee pleads with Ruth to use her influence with Lena and encourage her to invest the insurance proceeds in his plans to buy a liquor store. While she resists his pleas, reminding him that the money doesn't belong to them and that he should eat his eggs before they get cold, Walter says "I'm thirty-five years old; I been married eleven years and I got a boy who sleeps in the living room—and all I got to give him is stories about how rich white people live" (Hansberry 22). This scene illustrates the significance of entrepreneurship and social mobility to Walter Lee's version of the dream, but it is also the first of several allusions to the significance of family legacy to his notion of the dream. Throughout the play, Walter Lee references Travis and the possibilities of improving his life chances as the rationale for the primacy of his version of the dream— entrepreneurship as a means of accessing wealth and goods.

However, in the play's climactic scene, Walter Lee's refusal to accept the Clybourne Park Improvement Association payoff as Travis looks on marks the shift in Walter Lee's dream. Rather than continuing his efforts to provide a legacy of money and material goods for his son, he instead demonstrates to Travis that basic human dignity has no price in his rejection of the offer; he also bequeaths to Travis a legacy and cultural inheritance that rejects racist ideologies and that acknowledges the continuities between the past and the present. In his rejection of the offer, Walter Lee traces a family genealogy detailing the Younger's rightful claim to the home in Clybourne Park and the psychological and physical space it offers, which emphasizes their own status as working-class plain people, but also as a proud people; a family who has been in the United States for six generations; and finally a family whose husband, father and grandfather literally paid for the down payment on the home with his life (Hansberry 127). In closing his rejection of Lindner and the Clybourne Park Improvement Association offer with the reference to his father, Walter Lee effectively positions the home as Travis's legacy; at the same time, he figures the family genealogy as serving three rhetorical purposes: as rationale for the rejection, the driving force behind his ability to reject the offer, and finally as part of Travis's cultural inheritance.

Moreover, while Walter Lee outlines a specifically African American cultural genealogy for both Travis and Lindner, it also becomes clear that as potential residents of Clybourne Park, the Youngers share many similarities with the existing residents. By Lindner's own estimation, the community's residents are not wealthy, but rather "just hard-working, honest people who don't have much but those little homes and a dream of the kind of community they want to raise their children in" (Hansberry 97). Consequently, in relating his family's history in the United States and their specific circumstances as African Americans in his rejection of the offer, the continuities across cultures and the universality of the Youngers' experience is revealed, as is the power and seduction of racism, for it is racism that drives the working-class community of Clybourne Park to reject the Youngers. At the same time, his refusal of the offer also serves as a rejection of American cultural values—the same values that dictate that he must measure his worth by class ascendancy and the accumulation of money and goods, as well as a rejection of the racial hierarchies that would lead Lindner and the Clybourne Park Improvement Association to believe the Youngers do not belong there.

Though her version of the American dream differs from Walter Lee's in that she rejects money and material goods as a measure of self-worth and social progress, the most important decision Lena Younger makes in the play—the decision to put a down payment on a home in Clybourne Park—derives from her dream of and commitment to enabling her children to have access to life chances and possibilities that she did not enjoy. For many artists and critics, she reflects the characteristics and qualities of the stereotypical Mammy figure in African American culture—accommodating and passive. However, as Hansberry herself argued, Lena and women like her serve as "the embodiment of the Negro will to transcendence…it is she who, while seeming to cling to traditional restraints, drives the young on into the fire hoses and one day simply refuses to move to the back of the bus in Montgomery" (Hansberry 198). In other words, women like Lena not only help to provide the emotional and psychological support necessary to contend with and survive a society deeply invested in and divided by racial categories and which redistributes resources based on these categories, but are themselves agents of social change. Ultimately, Lena's "will to transcendence" and how it informs her version of the American dream provides the Younger family, and particularly Walter Lee, with the ability to affect change in their own lives and to do so in the face of resistance from the community at large. Her function as an agent of change is apparent during the climactic scene between Walter Lee and Lindner when she advises Walter to make Travis understand what his acceptance of the buyout offer means and to "teach him good" (Hansberry 126). She champions her family throughout the play, and in the same way that Lena nurtures the symbolic "feeble little plant growing doggedly in a pot" that struggles for sunshine in the dark South Side apartment, she cares for her family and provides them with an opportunity to flourish in the new home in Clybourne Park (Hansberry 27).

The stage direction introduces Ruth Younger as a woman for whom "life has been little that she expected, and disappointment has already begun to hang in her face" (Hansberry 12). In many ways, Ruth personifies the weariness that the stage direction says has "won" the Youngers' living room. However, Ruth also functions as an embodiment of hope and possibility in the play because of her pregnancy. Since Lena and Walter Sr. lost an infant son, Claude, to poverty, Walter and Ruth's baby serves as proxy and legacy. Further, the play's preoccupation with legacies shapes the relationship between Ruth and Lena. If weariness has won Ruth in the same way that it has won the Younger's home, then much of Lena's relationship with Ruth is concerned with lifting her weariness and comforting her as she struggles with adversity within their family. Nearly all of their conversations address experiences they share—difficulties in their relationship with Walter Lee, pregnancy, and financial difficulties among others. In a discussion about what Lena will do with the insurance money, she seemingly anticipates and acknowledges Ruth's psychological and physical need for more space and cautiously reveals her intentions to put a down payment on a house for the family. Lena goes on to tell Ruth that she and her husband had planned to save for a house they picked out and that Ruth "ought to know 'bout all the dreams I had…and didn't none of it happen" (Hansberry 32). In response to Lena's stalled dreams, Ruth replies, "life can be a barrel of disappointments sometimes" (32). After Lena makes the down payment on the home in Clybourne Park and shares the news with her family, a jubilant Ruth declares, "Hallelujah and good bye misery, I don't ever want to see your ugly face again" (Hansberry 79–80). Rubbing her hand over her stomach and the "life pulsing therein," she asks Lena one final question about the house—"is there is a whole lot of sunlight?" and Lena, aware of the implications, assures her "yes, child, there's a whole lot of sunlight" (Hansberry 80). These exchanges between Ruth and Lena demonstrate the continuities between the two women in terms of lived experiences and their deferred dreams, but most importantly, Lena's attempt to bequeath to Ruth the means of accessing hope, possibility, and ultimately her dreams binds them to one another. Not unlike Lena's plant that fights for sunlight, Ruth gains access to renewed hope through Lena's sacrifices, generosity, and nurturing. In essence, although Beneatha is Lena's daughter by birth, Ruth is her daughter in both lived experience and ideology, and Lena's legacy to her is the new home.

From the time she appears on stage early in the first scene of the play through to the end, Beneatha seems to be in the midst of a debate or disagreement of some kind. While she strives to become a doctor and that goal is central to her version of the dream, equally significant is the development of cultural identity, and most often, identity sits at the crux of the debates in which she is engaged. As she attempts to define her identity both within and against categories of gender, race, and class, she also encounters conflicts with all of her adult relatives and with both of her suitors over a host of issues ranging from the existence of God, to the use of birth control, to her career choices, to colonialism.

Heightening the play's emphasis on the theme of class mobility as it intersects African American identity is Beneatha's relationship with George Murchison, a fellow college student. The son of a wealthy African American businessman, George is a part of the African American aristocracy, or as Beneatha describes his family, they are "honest-to-God-real-live rich colored people, and the only people in the world who are more snobbish than rich white people are rich colored people" (Hansberry 37). Additionally, George belittles Beneatha, telling her that in order to land a husband, she should downplay her intellect and rely on her physical attributes to attract a partner. He asserts, "you're a nice looking girl…all over. That's all you need, honey, forget the atmosphere. Guys aren't going to go for the atmosphere—they're going to go for what they see. Be glad for that" (Hansberry 82). Adding insult to injury, George points out to her that he doesn't go out with her "to discuss the nature of 'quiet desperation' or to hear all about [her] thoughts—because the world will go on thinking what it's thinking regardless" (Hansberry 83). In response to this assertion, Beneatha asks why they should pursue an education and he sullenly replies, "to learn facts—to get grades—to pass the course—to get a degree. That's all—it has nothing to do with thoughts" (83). This exchange between the two illustrates two significant points. First, it points to the bankruptcy of social and economic privilege when it is not linked to enhancing or advancing a greater social good, and further how this kind of disconnect from a broader community empties one of basic human compassion, connection, and love. In other words, as a member of the upper class African American aristocracy, Murchison not only takes his privileges for granted and fails to see how his own experience can intersect the experiences of people unlike him; he also views his life path as a means to an end rather than a potential path of self-discovery. For all of his financial wealth and the privilege it provides him, Murchison lives an impoverished life in pursuit of wealth and goods for the sake of owning them.

Second, his means-to-an-end worldview forces him to see people, Beneatha in particular, as commodities that are assessed and collected or cast off according to their value. He clearly appreciates Beneatha's physical beauty and implies that if she dropped "the moody stuff" (Hansberry 72) she would become more valuable to him; however, he completely dismisses and devalues her ambition and pursuit of knowledge. His behavior toward both Ruth and Walter Lee demonstrates similar dismissals of their personal goals and desires. When Walter Lee attempts to engage him in conversation about his father's business, Murchison is indifferent and aloof. What he fails to recognize, however, is that Walter Lee is perceptive and insightful enough to understand his indifference and his desire to set himself apart from the Youngers through both his class status and his cultural literacy.

Finally, Murchison makes clear that he refuses any connection, cultural or otherwise to the Youngers or a broader African American cultural genealogy when he tells Beneatha, who is wearing an African wrap given to her by her other suitor, Joseph Asagai, that there is no African American cultural genealogy worth recognition. He posits, "baby your heritage is nothing but a bunch of raggedy-assed spirituals and some grass huts" (Hansberry 68). Murchison's declaration both sets him apart from Beneatha in his emphasis on "your" heritage and simultaneously disconnects him from a broader African American cultural genealogy. In effect, he assesses and discards both Beneatha and her claims to a broader African and African American culture.

Conversely, Nigerian student Joseph Asagai both respects and engages Beneatha's intellectual curiosity, as well as her search for identity. Though he frequently teases her for her earnestness, he also makes it clear that he cares for her and his interest in her goes beyond mere physical attraction; as he tells her, she deeply moves him. When Beneatha shares Walter Lee's botched business plans, the loss of her medical school tuition, and the despair it causes her with Asagai, he challenges her to reframe her dejected reaction to what has occurred. Relentless in her gloom, she tells him that he cannot answer the question of what good is struggle or why people should bother to have dreams and that finally, "there isn't any real progress...there is only one large circle we march, in around and around" (Hansberry 113). Taking her argument further and making a pointedly personal critique of Asagai's commitment to African independence, she asserts, "what about all the crooks and petty thieves and just plain idiots who will come into power to steal and plunder the same as before—only now they will be black and do it in the name of new independence—You cannot answer that" (Hansberry 114). Positioning himself as part of a larger historical continuum, he shouts over her "*I live the answer!*" and continues with his plans to make an impact when he returns to Nigeria, "I will teach and work and things will happen, slowly and swiftly. At times it will seem that nothing changes at all…and then again…the sudden dramatic events which make history leap into the future" (Hansberry 115). As a foil to George Murchison, Asagai envisions himself both as engaged with a broader African cultural genealogy and the long progression of history, which he describes as "a long line that reaches into infinity" (115). Ultimately, as he acknowledges his role in affecting change in his home country—which is to simply live there, connect with the community members in his village, and share his knowledge and life with them—he positions himself as an agent of historical progress rather than an object of it, and encourages Beneatha to view herself, her family, and her current situation in the same light.

In the end, Beneatha's relationship with Asagai foregrounds the ways in which she and her family fall prey to hopelessness and despair after Walter Lee's failed investment in the liquor store, and offers a means of rethinking their despondency through renewed connections. His plea to Beneatha—and by extension the entire Younger family—is to "live the answer" to the doubts and questions of why one continues on in the face of adversity (Hansberry 111). For Asagai, living the answer means facing and contending with the possibilities for both change and regression and by the play's end, this is the challenge that the Youngers take on as a family as they leave the South Side for Clybourne Park. It is important to note that the stage direction makes clear that Walter Lee eavesdrops on Beneatha and Asagai's conversation and that he "visibly respond[s] to the words of his sister and Asagai" and is subsequently inspired to act by what he has heard (Hansberry 112). Although his initial move following Asagai's departure is to make the call to Karl Lindner to accept the association's offer, he cannot follow through on that action precisely because his commitment to both his cultural genealogy and to the long line of history before him—namely his father—and that which will follow him—his son, Travis. Walter Lee's ascent to "living the answer" is revealed in his rejection of the offer, which necessarily entails his willingness to take responsibility for the family's setback. But at the same time, in being accountable for his lapse in judgment, he has cleared the way for committing to being an agent of history, rather than an object of it. In much the same way that Asagai describes the effort to hold on to his power in his home country as one that could inadvertently cause his own death, he figures that possibility as vital renewal, saying that "that such a thing as my own death will be an advance…they who might kill me…even actually replenish me." Likewise, Walter Lee's implicit admission of fault—a death of the entrepreneurial drive in him—also results in his and his family's replenishment in terms of affirming their cultural and human dignity (Hansberry 116). With the help of Asagai and his family, Walter Lee "lives the answer" through the rejection of the offer and grasps Arthur Miller's "golden thread of history" and takes on his "American responsibility" (Hansberry 197).

Though *A Raisin in the Sun*'s production was not the first of a play by an African American playwright on Broadway, the critical reception of the play and its overwhelming success with both black and white audiences predicted its now iconic status during its initial run. This crossover success, however, comes in spite of the play's themes and its critique of legal segregation in the urban North, which had not been addressed on stage before its production. The Civil Rights Movement, often euphemistically referred to in the mainstream press during the time of *A Raisin in the Sun*'s initial production as the "Negro Question," gained media attention in northern urban areas, but primarily in reference to Jim Crow segregation in the South. However, restrictive real estate covenants and other mechanisms used to advance legal segregation in cities such as Chicago were seldom discussed, in spite of multiple firebombing attacks on African American families who sought to move into all-white neighborhoods, thus highlighting the groundbreaking nature of Hansberry's play. Still, while it clearly demonstrates how legal segregation and racism impeded the Youngers' efforts to improve their lives, for critics and viewers it did not utilize confrontational rhetoric or civil actions around segregation that was appearing elsewhere on the national scene. For example, just 18 months before the play's debut, Arkansas governor Orville Faubus called in the National Guard to block the integration of Central High School in Little Rock, and a few months after its opening in August 1959, the first successful drug store counter sit-in occurred in Oklahoma City (Graves 164). In short, many critics and audiences understood the play as neither accusing nor attacking whites for segregation and the racism underpinning it. Mainstream critics in particular read *A Raisin in the Sun* as pointing out the difficulties that segregation presented to the family, but at the same time, did not view the play as an indicting white complicity in real estate covenants and other parallel examples of institutional racism in both the North and the South.

Exploring reviews from the play's debut reveals this tendency among critics to avoid a direct discussion of segregation and instead they consistently demonstrated a concern with the authentic representation of black identity and experience, but at the same time emphasize the ways in which their universal appeal downplays or lessens the significance of their cultural specificity. That is, rather than considering how these representations speak to the racial inequalities that underwrite much of the play's action, critics focus on defusing Hansberry's critique. The reviews of the debut production of *A Raisin in the Sun* reveal how critics responded to and interpreted the representation of blackness in the play and illustrate how the specifics of that particular historical moment shape and inform the critical response to the representations. If the late 1950s and early 1960s are understood as transitional years within the African American freedom struggle that anticipated the later expansion of quest for political and social equality, then the play's 1959 reviews lay bare many of the racial paradoxes that shaped the simultaneous resistance to and embrace of the early Civil Rights Movement and its ideologies, which appear in the play's themes. Ultimately, the critical response to the play at its debut deeply informs the play's reception since its initial production, shapes the way it is interpreted in the current historical moment, and contributes to it status as an icon.

Many of the critics draw parallels between the play and the Negro Question, but stop short of engaging specific issues such as housing access and segregation and instead applaud Hansberry's work because she has "no axe to grind" (Atkinson 12). As critic Stephen Carter observes, "Americans seemed to be embracing the play without fully understanding it—or perhaps wanting to understand it" (Carter 134). The reviews of *A Raisin in the Sun*'s 1959 debut demonstrate the ways in which critics struggle with acknowledging the importance of the play's history-making opening—Hansberry as the first African American woman to have a play produced, as well as Richard's directorial debut—and at the same time minimizing the significant role race plays in the Youngers' predicament.

Of 11 reviews of the play from its opening night, 9 were favorable, 1 unfavorable, and 1 review was mixed. The reviews focus primarily on the honesty of the play, its universal implications, in addition to the sentimental emotions it stirs up in both the audiences and the critics. Several of the favorable reviews also emphasize its integrationist effects—or the idea that the play breaks down barriers between the audience and performers, as well as social barriers between blacks and whites.

Focusing on the play's honesty and its universal implications in his favorable review, Brooks Atkinson notes in the *New York Times* that the play is:

> About human beings who want, on the one hand, to preserve their family and pride and, on the other hand, to break out of the poverty that seems to be their fate. Not having any axe to grind, Miss Hansberry has a wide variety of topics to write about—some of them hilarious, some of them painful in the extreme. (Atkinson 12)

This assessment points at two significant trajectories to consider in terms of cultural mediation and negotiation. First, the universal implications Atkinson ascribes to Hansberry's work and second, the suggestion that there is "no axe to grind" in her representation of blackness; in other words, cultural critique or political agendas are absent from the play. Linked to both these trajectories is the play's realism, which the critics seem to suggest forecloses a specific modality of blackness in its representation and any critique of residential segregation that is underwritten by white racism. In effect, because the play portrays African American life with fidelity that falls in line with his own notions of blackness, Atkinson gives the work universal implications and erases its engagement with African American identity politics and a critique of the larger cultural sphere. For Atkinson then, *A Raisin in the Sun* transcends blackness and the freight of cultural critique, but also marks both an emotional catharsis about the plight of African Americans and posits the universality of the African American experience.

Hansberry, however, rejected such assessments and the omission of the impact of racial identity in the critical evaluations of the play became increasingly problematic for her. Defending the significance of racial oppression in the play, she writes, "the fact of racial oppression, unspoken and unalluded to, other than the fact of how they live, is through the play. It's inescapable. The reason these people are in a ghetto is because they are Negroes. They are discriminated against brutally and horribly…so in that sense it is always distinctly there" (qtd. in Carter 136). Even as the author's intention—a representation of blackness imbued by the lived reality of racial oppression and a critique of that oppression—is recast by critics as universal, it is also figured as an "honest" play with "vigor as well as veracity" (Atkinson 12). This erasure of inescapable racial oppression in the critical assessments suggests a reticence to read Hansberry's representation of blackness as a lived experience, but rather to impose a rubric of universality on the representations that skirts the issue. In effect, the emerging cultural negotiations around representations of blackness as reflected in the critical evaluations fail to fully engage the issue at the core of Hansberry's representation—racial oppression and how it impacts concerns of equal housing access, economic enfranchisement, and African American identity politics.

Additionally, sentimentality figures significantly in the critics' reading of the play. In a favorable review, the *New York Herald Tribune*'s Walter Kerr admonishes the playwright for "driv[ing] her desperation to too unrelenting a pitch in the second act…threaten[ing] [the audience] with a monotone of defeat," but emphasizes the value of sentiment suggesting that Walter Lee's refusal to take the buyout offer marks "a cumulative swell of emotion [that] reaches back over the evening to surround, and bind up, an honest, intelligible, and moving experience" (Kerr 7). He goes on to comment on Claudia McNeil's performance as Lena Younger when her husband's life insurance check arrives at their home and she remarks that the money is more than a check, it represents her husband's life. In response to this scene, Kerr writes, "as she moves away, a lifetime turns over—and so does something or other in your throat" (7). Frank Aston also locates the significance of the play in its appeal to emotions, suggesting that "the number of tears shed by presumably worldly first nighters must have set a new record at the Ethel Barrymore last evening" and adding that "the major weeping comes in two waves," one at the end of the second act, the other in Walter Lee's offer refusal scene near the play's end (Aston 20).

This emotional catharsis for audiences and reviewers alike functions in much the same way critic Karen Sánchez-Eppler describes the workings of antislavery protest novels such as Harriet Beecher Stowe's *Uncle Tom's Cabin* in the mid 19th century. She argues that often, antislavery fiction were tales in which the "tears of the reader" were "pledged as a means of rescuing the bodies of slaves" (Sánchez-Eppler 32) Further, she asserts that antislavery stories written by women abolitionists were marketable because "the horrific events narrated in these tales attract precisely to the extent that the buyers of these representations of slavery are fascinated by the abuses they ostensibly oppose" (32). Obviously, at the time of *A Raisin in the Sun*'s initial production, the United States was almost a century removed from the institution of slavery; however, Sánchez-Eppler's insights into the function of sentiment within the literature and how it served its readers, proves to be a useful tool in considering the review archive of the play because it shows an analogous impulse at work in the reviews of the play. In effect, the reviewers pledge their emotional responses as a means of identifying with the Youngers' experiences within this performance of black identity, but do so without addressing the structural inequalities that shape their experiences.

Since the critical evaluations fail to engage how racial oppression in all its manifestations informs the play, recognition of the emotions and sentiment attached to viewing the play's performance stands in for critical engagement with the truth beyond the text of Hansberry's performance of blackness. What becomes central to critics' assessments, and by extension what then becomes central to their readership is that the emotions and sentiment brought to the fore while viewing *A Raisin in the Sun* allows the tears of the critics and audiences to be pledged as a means of rescuing the bodies of the oppressed. That is, if reviewers and audiences cannot critically engage the issue of racial oppression as it informs the play in their assessments, they can offer emotion and sentiment—tears—as a gesture toward recognizing the play's commentary on racial oppression. Additionally, like readers of antislavery fiction, the audiences and particularly critics, view the representation of an African American family negatively impacted by racial oppression—presumably an institution that those audiences oppose. Interestingly, at least one critic, Tom F. Driver in a favorable review in *New Republic* implies as much, saying:

> If *A Raisin in the Sun* had been written by a white instead of colored woman and if it had been written about a white family it would have done well to recover its investment....As a piece of dramatic writing it is old fashioned. As something near to the conscience of a nation troubled by injustice to Negroes it is emotionally powerful. Much of its success is due to our sentimentality over the "Negro Question." (Driver 44)

Suggesting that the nation is "troubled by injustice to Negroes," Driver binds the play's thematics to what is, in essence, the burgeoning Civil Rights Movement vis-à-vis the Negro Question. Contradicting earlier claims of universal implications by some critics, Driver takes up Hansberry's representation of blackness—albeit reductively—and figures it as central to both the play's success and the emotional responses it elicits from its audiences. This recognition of both the sentimentality and emotion the play's performance underscores, as well as its link to the overriding cultural phenomena—the Negro Question or the nascent Civil Rights Movement—once again speaks to an emerging cultural negotiation of blackness and its representation that critics can only engage on a superficial level. While Driver more closely approaches what

Hansberry calls the "inescapable" evidence of racial oppression represented in the play, his evaluation falls short of engaging the issue. However, along with the other reviews, his assessment brings the issue under a broader cultural lens and marks the start of cultural negotiations between representations of blackness and a communal American identity.

Advancing integration comprises another area of concern for critics. Along with the play's honesty and its emotional significance, the issue of integration and its implications is not fully engaged in terms of how it intersects racial oppression, but is drawn into a developing cultural dialogue about these issues and reflects the early stages of that development. Returning to Driver's evaluation, he suggests that in spite of the function of sentimentality, the play "is a work of theatrical magic in which the usual barriers between audience and stage disappears; the people up there are living among us, and we down here are mixing with those up there of easy terms" (44). Echoing Driver's assertions, John McClain contends in *Journal American*:

> A small hunk of history was made…last night. A play by a Negro about Negroes with an almost all Negro cast opened on Broadway and was a stupendous unsegregated hit. It proved to me at least, that when these people create and participate in something for themselves, they can make the rest of us look silly. (McClain 15)

Seemingly, these critics read the representations of blackness in *A Raisin in the Sun* as a means of eliminating cultural barriers between African Americans and whites. In much the same way that the play's honesty and realism removes the representations from a specifically African American cultural identity, these critics read the integrationist subtext as allowing for mixing with African Americans of easy terms, and along with African American authorship and portrayals, this makes the play an unsegregated hit. Erasing racial oppression from their readings of integration, lays bare the facile premises of the critics' claims: first that integration concerns itself solely with social interaction with whites, rather than access to employment, housing, and educational opportunity, and second, that central to integration is a notion of white cultural acceptance.

However, for African Americans in both the South and the North, integration hinged on questioning white supremacy as a rationale for limited African American access to opportunity. In the South, the 1955 Montgomery Bus Boycott protested segregation in public transit, but more importantly the fact that African Americans were forced to give up their seats to whites—a custom grounded in assumptions of white superiority, even as the majority of the transit system's ridership was African American (Isserman and Kazin 42). Rent strikes and NAACP protests on behalf of African American housing tenants occurred in Chicago and other cities in the North in the mid to late 1950s. As Isserman and Kazin argue, "integration had never been the sole aim of the freedom movement; access to jobs, houses, and commodities mattered far more than did the opportunity to mix with white folks" (42). These critics, then, read integration in the play reductively, and posit those readings in mass cultural forums as part of a developing cultural dialogue on representations of blackness. While those reviewing the play overwhelmingly applaud it, these accolades come at the expense of critical engagement in the central issue informing the work—racial oppression and how it functions in Hansberry's representation of blackness as lived experience.

A Raisin in the Sun has been staged in the United States and around the world almost continuously since its 1959 premiere. In the 1983–1984 season alone, the year of its 25th anniversary, an estimated 200 productions were staged (Wilkerson 119). Three notable revivals of the play have been staged since its debut—at the Yale Repertory Theatre in 1983, the year of its 25th anniversary, off-Broadway at the Roundabout Theatre in 1986, and in 2004 on Broadway at the Royale Theatre.

Lloyd Richards, who was artistic director of the Yale Repertory, brought the 1983 production to the Yale Repertory stage and the production was directed by Dennis Scott. The cast included Mary Alice (Ruth Younger), Troy Streater (Travis Younger), Delroy Lindo (Walter Lee Younger), Sharon Mitchell (Beneatha Younger), Beah Richards (Lena Younger), Tyrone Wilson (Joseph Asagai), and Dennis Green (George Murchison).

The 1986 revival starred Starletta DuPois (Ruth Younger), Kimble Joyner (Travis Younger), James Pickens Jr. (Walter Lee Younger), Kim Yancey (Beneatha Younger), Olivia Cole (Lena Younger), Vondie Curtis-Hall (Joseph Asagai), and Joseph C. Phillips; (George Murchison). Harold Scott directed the play. The significance of this revival is that it contained scenes cut from the original production. Those scenes were staged for the first time in the play's history in this production.

Phylicia Rashad won a Tony Award for her portrayal of Lena Younger in 2004, becoming the first African American woman to win the award for a leading role, and Audra McDonald (Ruth Younger) also won a Tony for Best Featured Actress. Sanaa Lathan (Beneatha Younger) was nominated for the award in the same category. Director Kenny Leon garnered a Drama Desk nomination for Best Director for this successful revival of the play. Though he was not nominated for his portrayal of Walter Lee, Sean Combs's casting in the play did draw a wider demographic to the Royale Theatre and initiated much media attention and discussion of bringing the play to a younger generation, as well as its potential appeal to the hip hop generation because of his long career as a hip hop performer and producer.

A Raisin in the Sun has been adapted for film three times, as well as for a musical. The first film was released by Columbia Pictures in 1961 and starred most of the original 1959 stage cast, including Sidney Poitier, Claudia McNeil, Ruby Dee, Ivan Dixon, and Louis Gossett Jr. However, Glynn Turman, who had played Travis on stage, was replaced by Stephen Perry. Stage producer Philip Rose joined film producer David Susskind in the effort to bring the play to the screen. Hansberry wrote the screenplay for the film, and though

Lloyd Richards was initially hired to direct the film, the studio replaced him with Daniel Petrie. Ruby Dee won the National Board of Review Award for Best Supporting Actress and both McNeil and Poitier gained Golden Globe nominations. Petrie received a special Gary Cooper Award for his direction at the Cannes Film Festival. In 2005, this version of the film was selected by the National Film Registry for preservation by the Library of Congress for its cultural and aesthetic significance.

In 1989, the Public Broadcasting System (PBS) produced an adaptation of the play for the first installment of the eighth season of its series American Playhouse. This production starred Danny Glover (Walter Lee), Esther Rolle (Lena), Starletta DuPois (Ruth), and Kim Yancey (Beneatha), and was directed by Bill Duke. John Fiedler, who played Karl Lindner in the both the 1959 and 1986 stage productions as well as the 1961 film, returned as Lindner once again in the 1989 film.

The most recent film production aired in 2008 on the American Broadcasting Company (ABC) on February 25, 2008. Based on the 2004 Tony Award–winning Broadway revival, which featured Sean Combs (Walter Lee), Phylicia Rashad (Lena), Audra McDonald (Ruth), and Sanaa Lathan (Beneatha), the film premiered out of competition at the Sundance Film Festival in January 2008. Kenny Leon, the director of the 2004 Broadway revival, made his film directorial debut with this production.

Robert Nemiroff, Hansberry's ex-husband and executor of her estate, helped to develop the musical theatre adaptation of the play, *Raisin*. After its premiere in Washington, DC, it then opened on Broadway at the 46th Street Theater on October 18, 1973, and closed on December 8, 1975, after 847 performances. Nemiroff and Charlotte Zaltzberg wrote the book for the musical, Judd Woldin composed the music, and Robert Brittan wrote the lyrics for the production, which won the Tony Award for Best Musical in 1973. *Raisin* starred Joe Morton (Walter Lee), Ernestine Jackson (Ruth), and Debbie Allen (Beneatha).

Clearly, the film and theatre industries saw the potential for financial windfalls in adapting the play due, largely to the financial and critical success of the 1959 stage production. Film critic Mark Reid argues that because of *A Raisin in the Sun*'s success on Broadway, at least six major film producers expressed interest in adapting the play almost immediately after its debut in March and that further, David Susskind, coproducer of the film, lobbied for Sidney Poitier's casting because, following his appearance in *The Defiant Ones* and *Porgy & Bess*, he would "be an important box office element" (Reid 86).

Despite its critical and financial success on the stage and screen, some African American artists and critics rejected the representations of African American identity in the play; however, they and others were nevertheless influenced by and benefited from the groundbreaking production of it. Writer Amiri Baraka, who was critical of the play and its representations at its debut and dismissed it as an assimilationist play that was overly concerned with "moving into white folks' neighborhoods," reconsidered his position on the play on its 28th anniversary, arguing that the Youngers reflected the "black majority" and that further, their concerns illustrate "the essence of black peo-ple's striving and the will to defeat segregation, discrimination and national oppression" (Baraka 41). Theatre critic Samuel G. Freedman suggests that if playwright August Wilson had written *A Raisin in the Sun,* the Youngers would have "joined the Blackstone Rangers street gang or the Nation of Is-lam" rather than Clybourne Park at the play's end; however, Wilson himself, who often cited Baraka and visual artist Romare Bearden as influences in his own work, seemingly acknowledged the ways in which Hansberry's work impacted African American theatrical production, allowing that it "changed everything" for African American theatre (Freedman 49).

Woodie King, a founder and producing director of the New Federal Theatre, goes even further in recognizing the play's influence and relevance. King sug-gests that an entire generation of theatre artists owe much of their success to Hansberry and her impact on theatre. During the making of his documentary, *The Black Theatre Movement:* A Raisin in the Sun *to the Present,* 40 of the over 60 theatre practitioners he interviewed revealed that they had been "in-fluenced, aided, or both by Lorraine Hansberry and her work" (King 126).

Still another example of the play's iconic status lies in subsequent produc-tions that critique its themes and representations through satire. George C. Wolfe's *The Colored Museum* premiered off-Broadway in March 1986 at the Crossroads Theatre in New Brunswick, New Jersey. As critic Harry Elam ar-gues, Wolfe's work "simultaneously celebrates, satirizes and subverts the Afri-can American legacy" parodies representations of African American identity in African American theatre history in eleven vignettes that comprise a tour of "exhibits" of stereotypical representations of "blackness" (Elam 291). Among other images and plays, *The Colored Museum* takes aim at *A Raisin in the Sun* as a representational model for African American drama broadly, as well as the representations of both Walter Lee Younger and Lena Younger specifi-cally in the vignette called "The Last Mamma on the Couch Play." Emphasiz-ing the constraints that domestic realism as a genre has imposed on creativity in African American theatre, Wolfe's parody of Lena Younger, who is simply called Mama, opens the vignette literally attached to the couch as she reads her bible and exerts her matriarchal control over the family. Her son, Walter Lee Beau Willie Jones, an allusion to both Hansberry's play and Ntozake Shange's *for colored girls who have considered suicide when the rainbow is enuf* struggles, not unlike Walter Lee, with taking control of his life and "be-ing" someone (Elam 301). In an interview, Wolfe argued that his work sought to cast off the freight of many stereotypical representations, but that the long shadow of Hansberry's *A Raisin in the Sun* presented particular difficulties because of the ubiquity of some of the representations in the play:

> She's a wonderful playwright and it's a wonderful play, but every Febru-ary all the regional theaters discover black people because of Black His-tory Month and they pull out "Raisin in the Sun." I want to remove these dead, stale, empty, icons blocking me from my own truth. (Kroll 85)

The play won the 1986 Dramatist Guild Award and moved from the Crossroads Theatre in New Jersey to the New York Shakespeare Festival/Public Theatre the same year. It was also produced for PBS's Great Performances in 1991. Though some playwrights and critics like Wolfe critique the influence of *A Raisin in the Sun,* others acknowledge it but elect to move beyond it. Playwright Lynn Nottage's work acknowledges the preeminence of *A Raisin in the Sun*'s domestic realism or the kitchen sink drama within African American theatre history, which often limits the play's action to a single room. While she does not count her work as part of that genre, she refuses to reject them because "they are very important…they were specific kinds of family drama which played out family crises" (Shannon 196).

While the debates around the representations in the play and the timelessness of its craft have endured since its initial production, *A Raisin in the Sun* forever altered American and African American theatrical production and stands as a benchmark in African American and American literary and theatre history because not only did its production mark a number of historic firsts, but it showcased the work of arguably one of the most politically and socially engaged, as well as artistically gifted, writers of the 20th century. Hansberry's insights into the African American experience in America in 1959 continue to resonate for readers and audiences because the Youngers' decision to move into their home marks not only their assertion of the import of their African American cultural inheritance, but also the realization that they are at "crossroads with at least some of [their] culture's values" (Hansberry 197). Their ability to contend and live with these contradictory but inextricably linked impulses and Hansberry's skill in detailing the subtleties and complexities of them underwrite the play's iconic status in both African American and American literature and culture.

BIBLIOGRAPHY

A Raisin in the Sun. New York: Signet, 1959.
A Raisin in the Sun…The Unfilmed Original Screenplay. Ed. Robert Nemiroff. New York: Plume, 1992.
A Raisin in the Sun and *The Sign in Sidney Brustein's Window.* Ed. Robert Nemiroff. New York: Vintage, 1995.

FURTHER READING

Aston, Frank. Rev. of *Raisin in the Sun.* New York: Ethel Barrymore Theatre. *New York World Telegram* March 12, 1959.
Atkinson, Brooks. Rev. of *Raisin in the Sun.* New York. Ethel Barrymore Theatre. *New York Times* March 12, 1959.
Baraka, Amiri Imamu. "A Critical Reevaluation: *A Raisin in the Sun*'s Enduring Passion." *A Raisin in the Sun* and *The Sign in Sidney Brustein's Window.* By Lorraine Hansberry. Ed. Robert Nemiroff. New York: New American Library, 1987.
Baraka, Amiri Imamu. "A Wiser Play than Some of Us Knew." *Los Angeles Times* March 22, 1987, home ed. sec: 41.

Baldwin, James. "Sweet Lorraine." *To Be Young, Gifted, and Black: An Informal Autobiography of Lorraine Hansberry*. By Lorraine Hansberry. New York: Signet, 1969.

Bernstein, Robin. "Inventing a Fishbowl: White Supremacy and the Critical Reception of Lorraine Hansberry's *A Raisin in the Sun.*" *Modern Drama* 42.1 (Spring 1999): 16–27.

Carter, Stephen R. *Hansberry's Drama: Commitment amid Complexity*. Urbana: Illinois UP, 1991.

Domina, Lynn. *Understanding* A Raisin in the Sun: *A Student Casebook to Issues, Sources, and Historical Documents*. Westport, CT: Greenwood, 1998.

Driver, Tom F. "A Raisin in the Sun." *New Republic*, April 13, 1959.

Elam, Harry Justin Jr. "Signifyin(g) on African American Theatre: *The Colored Museum* by George Wolfe." *Theatre Journal* 44 (1992): 291–303.

Freedman, Samuel G. "A Voice from the Streets." *New York Times Magazine* June 10, 1987: 49.

Gordon, Michelle. "'Somewhat Like War': The Aesthetics of Segregation, Black Liberation, and *A Raisin in the Sun.*" *African American Review* 42 (2008): 121–33.

Graves, Carl R. "The Right to be Served." *Chronicles of Oklahoma* 59.2 (1981), 163–68.

Hansberry, Lorraine. "An Author's Reflections: Willy Loman, Walter Younger, and He Who Must Live." *The Village Voice Reader*. Garden City, NY: Doubleday, 1962. 194–99.

Harris, Trudier. *Reading Contemporary African American Drama Fragments of History, Fragments of Self*. New York: Lang, 2007.

Isserman, Maurice, and Michael Kazin. *America Divided: The Civil War of the 1960s*. New York: Oxford UP, 2000.

Jiggetts, Shelby. "Interview with Suzan-Lori Parks." *Callaloo* 19.2 (1996): 309–17.

Kamp, Allen R. "The History behind *Hansberry v. Lee.*" *U.C. Davis Law Review* 20 (1986): 481–99.

Kappel, Lawrence. "Readings on *A Raisin in the Sun.*" *The Greenhaven Press Literary Companion to American Literature*. San Diego, CA: Greenhaven, 2000.

Keppel, Ben. *The Work of Democracy: Ralphe Bunche, Kenneth B. Clark, Lorraine Hansberry and the Cultural Politics of Race*. Cambridge: Harvard UP, 1995.

Kerr, Walter. "No Clear Path and No Retreat." *New York Herald Tribune*, Lively Arts Section, March 22, 1959.

King, Woodie. *The Impact of Race Theatre and Culture*. New York: Applause Theatre & Cinema, 2003.

Kroll, Jack. "Theater: Zapping Black Stereotypes." *Newsweek* November 17, 1986: 85.

Leeson, Richard M. *Lorraine Hansberry: A Research and Production Sourcebook*. Westport, CT: Greenwood, 1997.

Lester, Neal A. "Seasoned with Quiet Strength: Black Womanhood in Lorraine Hansberry's *A Raisin in the Sun.*" *Women in Literature: Reading through the Lens of Gender*. Ed. Barbara Ozieblo. Westport, CT: Greenwood, 2003. 246–49.

Lipari, Lisbeth. "Fearful of the Written Word: White Fear, Black Writing, and Lorraine Hansberry's *A Raisin in the Sun* Screenplay." *Quarterly Journal of Speech* 90.1 (February 2004): 81–102.

Matthews, Kristin L. "The Politics of 'Home' in Lorraine Hansberry's *A Raisin in the Sun.*" *Modern Drama*. 51.4 (Winter 2008): 556–75.

McClain, John. Rev. of *A Raisin in the Sun*. *New York Journal American*, March 12, 1959.

Okafor, Chinyere G. "Location and Separateness of Heroines in African and African American Drama: A Study of Hilda Kuper's *A Witch in My Heart* and Lorraine Hansberry's *A Raisin in the Sun.*" *Postcolonial Perspectives on Women Writers from Africa, the Caribbean, and the U.S.* Ed. Martin Japtok. Trenton, NJ: Africa World, 2003.

Parks, Sheri. "In My Mother's House: Black Feminist Aesthetics, Television, and *A Raisin in the Sun.*" *Black Feminist Cultural Criticism.* Ed. Jacqueline Bobo. Malden, MA: Blackwell, 2001. 106–22.

Reid, Mark. "*Take a Giant Step* and *A Raisin in the Sun*: The U.S. Black Family Film." *Jump Cut: A Review of Contemporary Media* 36 (May 1991): 81–88.

Sánchez-Eppler, Karen. "Bodily Bonds: The Intersecting Rhetorics of Feminism and Abolition." *Representations* 24 (1988): 28–59.

Seaton, Sandra. "A Raisin in the Sun: A Study in Afro-American Culture." *Midwestern Miscellany* 20 (1992): 40–49.

Shannon, Sandra. "An Interview with Lynn Nottage." *Contemporary African American Women Playwrights: A Casebook.* Ed. Philip Kolin. London: Routledge, 2007. 194–201.

Washington, J. Charles. "*A Raisin in the Sun* Revisited." *Black American Literature Forum* 22.1 (Spring 1988): 109–24.

Wilkerson, Margaret B. "Political Radicalism and Artistic Innovation in the Works of Lorraine Hansberry." Ed. Harry Justin Elam and David Krasner. *African American Performance and Theater History A Critical Reader.* Oxford: Oxford UP, 2001. 40–55.

Wilkerson, Margaret B. "*A Raisin in the Sun*: Anniversary of an American Classic." *Performing Feminisms: Feminist Critical Theory and Theatre.* Ed. Sue Ellen Case. Baltimore, MD: Johns Hopkins UP, 1990. 119–30.

Wilkerson, Margaret B. "The Sighted Eyes and Feeling Heart of Lorraine Hansberry." *Black American Literature Forum* 17.1 (Spring 1983): 8–13.

Wilkins, Fanon Che. "Beyond Bandung: The Critical Nationalism of Lorraine Hansberry, 1950–1965." *Radical History Review* 95 (Spring 2006): 191–210.

Carol Bunch Davis and Alexis M. Skinner

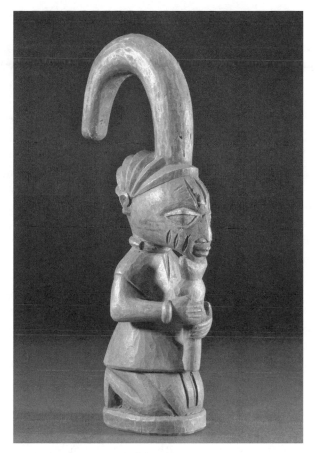

Eshu-Elegba, Yoruba trickster figure known as the Signifying Monkey in African American folklore. (SSPL/Getty Images)

Signifying

In order to fully understand the nature of signifying in African American literature, one must recognize the impact of the oral tradition within African American culture. Verbal signifying refers to the art of taking recognizable words or phrases and giving these words new meanings with the intent of asserting a point of view through innuendo or indirection. In some instances, a speaker might signify in order to criticize or put down an individual or group; at other times, a speaker might signify to elicit humor and laughter among acquaintances. Depending on the context and environment, this language play is written using vernacular spellings or pronunciations. When the -*g* is dropped, the term is known as either signifyin' or siggin'. Additionally, signifying might have altogether different names. Depending on the region or time period, verbal signifying might be called joanin', riffin', reading, or sounding. The act of signifying not only manifests in African and African American oral culture but also in African American literature.

Critic James Snead emphasizes that an inherent part of any culture is its use of repetition. According to Snead, there is a "finite supply of elementary units" that any culture can use and "the need for recognizability" is a principal organization that shows the desire to rely upon "the thing that there is to pick up." Snead maintains that "progress is the sense of avoidance of repetition [and] without organizing principles of repetition, true improvisation would be impossible, since an improvist relies upon the ongoing reoccurrence of a beat" (215). Snead's inclusion of musical terms such as "improvisation" and a reoccurring "beat" are particularly appropriate considering the intimate connections between an oral-based culture and music in African American literature. Snead correlates improvisation with creating new ideas as a prominent feature of what he calls repetition and difference, but we can apply these similar concepts to the art of signifying. In *Talkin and Testifyin: The Language of Black America,* linguist Geneva Smitherman articulates improvisation, in the context of language, as originality. Outstanding signifying, she argues, "involves rhetorical hyperbole, irony, indirection, metaphor, and development of 'semantically or logically unexpected' statements" (70). Claudia Mitchell-Kernan's research on forms of verbal art defines signifying as "a way of encoding messages or meanings, which involves, in most cases, an element of indirection (311). In order to assert a particular point of view, signifying lets the speaker actively and intentionally transform select words or phrases and create new meaning.

A Representative List of African American Works and Their Use of Signifying

- *Charles Chesnutt's* The Conjure Woman *(1899) signifies on the plantation tradition*
- *Frederick Douglass's* Narrative of the Life of Frederick Douglass *(1845) signifies on the autobiography*

- *W.E.B. Du Bois's* The Souls of Black Folk *(1903) and Ralph Ellison's* Invisible Man *(1952) signify on the bildungsroman*
- *Harriet Jacobs's* Incidents in the Life of a Slave Girl *(1861) signifies on Frederick Douglass's* Narrative of the Life of Frederick Douglass
- *James Weldon Johnson's* The Autobiography of an Ex-Colored Man *(1912) signifies on W.E.B. Du Bois's "The Veil."*
- *Toni Morrison's* Beloved *(1987) signifies on the slave narrative*

A legendary illustration of signifying, using Smitherman's term of the "logically unexpected," (103) occurred on April 3, 1964, at the Corey Methodist Church in Cleveland, Ohio. On this date, Malcolm X gave a version of his speech, "The Ballot or the Bullet." His greeting begins with the usual pleasantries, but ends with a clever acknowledgment of oppositional forces against him and his civil rights agenda: "Mr. Moderator, Brotha Lomax, Brothas and Sistas, friends and enemies … I just can't believe that everyone here is a friend, and I don't want to leave anyone out." Malcolm is directly calling out nameless individuals in a critical yet humorous manner.

At other times, a situation might call for a speaker to respond covertly as opposed to overtly. In Zora Neale Hurston's novel *Their Eyes Were Watching God,* Janie retaliates against her husband's assertions concerning her declining youthful appearance. In perhaps the greatest signifying moment in an African American novel, Janie tells her spouse, Joe Starks:

> Naw, Ah ain't no young gal no mo' but den Ah ain't no old wamn neither. Ah reckon I looks mah age too. But Ah'm uh woman every inch of me, and Ah know it. Dat's uh who lot more'n you can say. You bigbellies round here and put out a lot of brag, but 'tain't nothing; to it but yo' big voice. Humph! Talkin' 'bout *me* lookin' old! When you pull down yo' britches, you look lak de change of life. (79)

After Janie's public verbal assault on Joe's manhood, their relationship as husband and wife, unsurprisingly, becomes strained. Thus, a characteristic of signifying is, in fact, a *dis* or a statement of disapproval.

Listening, as well as speaking, represents an important factor in verbal signifying. The more skillful a speaker is at innuendo and implication, the more the listener feels satisfied with her own cleverness when she accurately deciphers the speaker's veiled connotation. For the listener, power lies in successfully interpreting symbolic or metaphorical meaning, especially when it reveals her cleverness. The listener endorses further applications of the speaker's transformed words and this mirrors the situation in Anderson's "Signifying," wherein attempts to get the woman's attention by initially substituting the word "woman" with the more allusive and subtle "day" encourages the others boys to create words to address her indirectly. In this particular case, signifying reaffirms the indeterminacy of language and allows communities to create and maintain their own distinctive semantics systems. If a listener accurately determines the duality behind the speaker's words, the speech act should conclude with an acknowledgment, creating a bond or understanding between the speaker and listener. In African American folk culture, such an act is referred to as call-and-response. When Malcolm X ended his speech "The Ballot or the Bullet," with "friends and *enemies*" the audience responded by clapping and laughing with distinct approval. In *Their Eyes Were Watching God,* Janie's allusion to Joe looking like "the change of life" evokes a boisterous response from one spectator: "Great God from Zion! … Y'all really playing the dozens tuhnight" (79). Such a responder, in this case, finds the verbal duel entertaining.

The purpose of amusement was not always the primary function of signifying for slaves. Research shows that during slavery, it had a more practical purpose. The power of signifying lies in its transformative power. Old words and expressions are given new meaning to persuade or cajole, as well as entertain. Research shows that many slave spirituals used signifying that benefited slaves. Many slaves could not rely on physical aggressiveness against their oppressors, so signifying became a type of semantic manipulation that made use of acute mental processes, providing the speaker with both indirection and implication as the primary means of agency. Mastery of figurative language became a means to achieve a specific type of psychological power over their masters. A rebellion against standardized English is especially important for a people who lost their language and were forced to learn English. Over time, slaves gradually developed new identities and created distinct words for communicating. By making English function for them, slaves achieved legitimacy. The physical impossibility of asserting power in southern slave systems meant that knowledge of language, words, and even intonation of certain phrases could hold great influence and power, not only in the way African Americans communicated with one another, but also the way they communicated with their oppressors. Slavery, Jim Crow Laws, and discrimination, in both the political and employment sectors in the South, soon pushed African Americans into many industrialized cities of the North. During the Great Migration, African Americans carried their southern cultural formations with them to inner cities. Although blacks adapted slightly to meet conditions of an industrial environment, signifying practices persisted, particularly in traditional African American enclaves like Harlem, Chicago, Detroit, and Pittsburgh. Contemporary research into the genesis of African American language, particularly signifying, reveals that the practice originated with groups from western Africa.

In *The Signifying Monkey,* Henry Louis Gates Jr. argues that the origin of signifying has its roots within the indigenous oral traditions of western and sub-Saharan Africa. Gates's analysis of African folklore, such as the Signifying Monkey and Anansi the Spider, connects their origins to the Yoruba and Ashanti. These animals are trickster figures and avatars of Esu-Elegbara, the trickster God (Gates, *Signifying Monkey* 53). Europe and America primarily gathered Yoruba and Ashanti ethnic groups from the western coast of Africa, and Gates asserts that these two groups carried these tales with them. As a result, cultural influences among Yoruba and Ashanti played a larger role in the development of slave culture in America.

Esu's tale and his name varies among people of West African descent, but the gist of his story proceeds with Esu attempting to settle a dispute between two friends through trickery (Gates, *Signifying Monkey* 51). Donning an elaborate disguise, Esu rides through the boundaries separating both acquaintances; on one side, Esu wears a red mask, while on the other side his mask is black. After removing his disguise, Esu returns and questions the two friends, asking them to describe trespassing foreigner; both respond with very different visual descriptions.

What is important here, and what Esu-Elagba's saga ultimately stresses, is the relevance of an individual's perception. The dual visual interpretations of the African leaders mirror the duality of language. Perceptions by both leaders are, in fact, correct, with neither one having more value than the other. In essence, Esu becomes what Gates calls "a metaphor for the uncertainties of explication, for the open-endedness of every literary text" (*Signifying Monkey* 21).

In both the Signifying Monkey and Anansi the Spider stories, the weaker or smaller characters use language to insult and manipulate the larger and stronger animals because of the larger animals' inability to distinguish between figurative and literal words.[1] Their error is one of misunderstanding the conventions of the language game known as signifying. The transatlantic slave trade neither completely destroyed these African-derived folktales nor erased the inherent method of language play within them, especially in terms of their structural form and their transformative lessons regarding the nature of language as figurative.

The very nature of slavery in North America might explain this unique system of establishing double entendres. Transforming words in such a manner reinforces indirection as a means to prevent discovery. More importantly, it might also permit a slave to express himself with little chance of detection. Early forms of double or multiple meanings occur in spirituals, sermons, work songs, and New World folktales. As an oral craft, signifying goes back to Africa, but once in America, people of African descent continued to utilize the art of verbal play within their oral traditions—from folktales to secular rhymes and songs, myths, ballads, preaching, spirituals, work songs, blues, and rap.[2] Through these verbal arts, African Americans became masters of moving from literal meaning to a symbolic, metaphorical, or hidden meaning. Although this requires ingenuity on the part of the speaker, specific listeners, in this case other slaves, must also possess the facilities to decipher select meanings of utterances. Scholars have frequently written about songs that consist of crucial hidden messages to assist, or in some instances, warn other slaves of danger. The former is particularly evident in the spiritual "Steal Away":

Steal away, steal away, steal away to Jesus
Steal away, steal away home,
I ain't got long to stay here. (14)

"Steal Away" and even "Swing Low, Sweet Chariot" employ a figurative use of "home" that creates a useful ambiguity. Home could mean heaven, Africa, or even the northern states and Canada if one perceives home as a safe place away from earthly tribulations.

As explored earlier, signifying may, in fact, suggest sharp criticism of the listener or adversary. A speaker's words create an outlet for articulating specific ideas and values that the audience also shares. This may have far greater psychological implications than physical. For slaves, this mode of understanding would create an indelible sense of knowing and understanding between the participants, while outsiders would be left out. At other times, inside audiences might communicate in a humorous but instructive manner; perhaps going so far as mocking the master or the slave system.

The secular rhyme and song "We Raise de Wheat," for example, uses indirection and implication to criticize dominant systems of white power and white authority:

We raise de wheat
Dey gib us de corn
We bade de bread,
Dey gib us de crust. (27)

Joseph E. Holloway reinforces a prevailing attitude that prayer songs offer dual meanings:

Jesus made de blind to see,
Jesus made the cripple to walk,
Jesus made de deaf to her.
Walk in, kind Jesus!
No man can hinder *me*. (qtd. in Holloway 159)

As Holloway explains, some critical observers presumed the last lines to mean "nothing could prevent access to Jesus." Yet, others considered this song an "aspiration for liberty," particularly if we acknowledge that some versions of the last line of the song include a reference to the collective "we" instead of the singular reference "me" (159).

We can see this indeterminacy of language in the secular blues song, "My Handy Man." The speaker indirectly references pleasure and gratification with her man's lovemaking skill:

He shakes my ashes, greases my griddle,
Churns my butter,
And he strokes my fiddle.
My man is such a handy man. (Razaf and Blake 63)

When one listens to Alberta Hunter's performance of "My Handy Man," pauses and various intonations provide insight into the hidden message or meaning behind the speaker's words, and in all of these instances, covert language relies heavily on performance. The first two examples, one from the sacred and the other from the secular, cite extreme displeasure and criticism with the system of oppression. The third, a blues melody, allows the speaker to express an otherwise unmentionable subject—sexual gratification. All three of these examples in music relate specifically to a person making political and social commentary, and allows an audience to respond in a particular manner. Wordplay gradually became a prominent within written practices. Thus, as African American culture gave rise to written literary traditions, this language play continued, albeit in a different form.

When people of African descent wrote in public spheres, their transformation of Westernized discourse, especially biblical verses, permitted them to construct indirect rhetorical arguments for equality. Phillis Wheatley was an anomaly to many Europeans and Americans.[3] The fact that she could comprehend the written word and create her own distinctive verse contradicted the erroneous presumptions that slaves could not rationalize, demonstrate imagination, or produce original works of art. Her very presence severely undermined the institution of slavery and the belief that Africans were not fully human. As the mother of African American poetry, Wheatley was the first known person of African descent to publish a book. "To Maecenas" and "On Being Brought from Africa to America" apply signifying in printed form and display her intimate knowledge and understanding of both Greek mythology and biblical scriptures. Wheatley's use of people and poems from classical works as well as references to the Bible initially led critics to suspect her of imitation rather than original and creative expression. Wheatley successfully established her credibility as a writer through an examination by judges, lawyers, and clergy.[4] When reading her poems with a signifying method in mind, Wheatley's work becomes an example of originality and subversion, indirectly challenging slavery and the state of other slaves, albeit indirectly, through carefully chosen figures from the classics.

In her poem "To Maecenas," Wheatley conspicuously mentions African Roman poet and playwright Terrance to evoke positive images of Africans. Terrance was African by birth but well respected in Rome. By including Terrance, Wheatley indirectly questions her white audience about the status of Africans. Through associating people of African descent with European civilizations, her work becomes a testimony or argument that if a so-called lowly, black, female slave could effectively call on the grand Greek Muses for inspiration, others like her might achieve similar heights that she and Terence reached if slaves were given the opportunity to experience freedom and equality in America. Perhaps, by including Greek and Roman references such as the Muses, Naiads, Aurora, and other figures, Wheatley was subtly making a point about America's apparent hypocrisy. Elements of paganism remain a part of a society that devalues Africans because of their so-called uncultivated religion; yet, these same forces profess Christianity as their faith. If this is true, then perhaps her fellow Africans, also branded heathens, could become

Christians as well. "On Being Brought" argues that Africans can join the "angelic train" (7) of Christianity.

Although critics sometimes question readings of activism on Wheatley's part as ahistorical interpretations, there is no doubt that she was well aware of the "wanton *Tyranny* with lawless hand" that enslaved the land in which she lived (Gates, *Norton Anthology* 221). Primary references to Christian language such as "redemption," "savior," "angelic train," and "perdition" were accepted modes of discourse during her time. For an African audience (or as Wheatley calls them, "sable race"), these words might have a different significance. Wheatley's older predecessor, Jupiter Hammon, also endured slavery in New England and also used Christianity to make the case against slavery.

Like Wheatley, Hammon's owner also taught him how to read and write using the Bible. To his oppressors, Hammon's sermons complied with the cultural standards of the time. Many northern colonists held that they alone were divinely instructed by God to establish America and were God's chosen people; Hammon's poem "An Evening Thought: Salvation by Christ with Penitential Cries" can be read as countering this myth by signifying on Christian discourse and emphasizing African slaves as a part of God's chosen people. Whereas the word salvation typically implies deliverance from sin, the meaning of salvation in Hammon's context might also refer to Christ as the savior for Africans against the autocratic slave system. Through seeking the Lord Jesus Christ as savior, any person, regardless of color, can be delivered from slavery through devout worship. The word "thy" becomes a key component to the poems signifying, as "thy" can refer to white slave owners and as a subtle berating of the treatment of his fellow slaves (Hammon 163). The phrase "redemption now for every one" in "An Evening Thought with Perennial Cries" engages Africans, whether they are slaves or free. Moreover, the words disarm white slave owners and colonists, while encouraging future generations of African Americans to look to Christianity as a way to achieve freedom.

Hammon's attempts to inspire and communicate with Wheatley, and by extension, younger Africans, are especially evident in "An Address to Miss Phillis Wheatley." In reaching out to converse with Wheatley and dedicating the address to her, Hammon produces the first intertextual writing. Hammon calls attention to their similar ideological perspectives concerning Christianity and freedom by paying tribute to Wheatley's dynamic verse and prose. In many instances, connections between Wheatley and Hammon's poems are primarily based on biblical verse.

While some critics argue that Wheatley and Hammon are too acculturated, passive, and ambiguous to make a case for any argument against slavery, others view their texts as early attempts to promote civil liberties for people of African descent. To these advocates, signifying permits a different approach to reading their literary work. Christianity becomes a veiled and refined way for early black orators and writers to speak publicly, and through their work, to communicate with each other. It seems appropriate to note that Hammon's works, originally presented using the spoken word, connects him within both the oral and written tradition. Hammon and Wheatley counter ideologies of European colonists, theologists, and scientists that insisted on moving Africans out of the human race and into a lower stratification of the great chain of being.

As an accepted discourse for many early African and African American writers, Christian archetypes and tropes emerged within faith communities, linking texts and setting the foundations for African American literature. An archetype is an initial model that causes all things to be representations or copies. As a result, archetypes are effortlessly recognizable. Correspondingly, a trope constitutes a dynamic semantic figure whose fundamental characteristics are repeated but in accordance with the writer's literary imagination or the times. Repetition and originality make use of the inherent qualities of verbal signifying presented earlier. A trope becomes an important feature in tracing the distinctiveness of an African American literary tradition.

Signifying emerged as a rhetorical strategy for writers to express their humanity and ability to reason for themselves; it allowed black writers to attack the institution of slavery indirectly or directly on the grounds that it divided familial ties, dishonored women, and perhaps most influentially, contradicted righteous Christian values set forth by white slave owners. Often, slaves wrote against dominant cultural perceptions that asserted their inhumanity and inability to reason; it is therefore important that African Americans entered the written word.[5]

At other times, writers might indirectly or unknowingly build on a tradition, and this is common because there are limited numbers of recognizable ways to express ideas. A well-recognized biblical story is Moses and his struggle against the pharaoh and Egyptian army. Phillis Wheatley's piece, "To the University of Cambridge, in New England," refers to Egypt as the land of the pharaohs. Since this story conforms, in many ways, to the plight of African Americans, the reader has little trouble identifying subsequent texts that build on a notion of Egypt as a place of oppression and the arrival of a savior. Harriet Tubman, a black woman who brought many slaves to freedom was known as the Black Moses for her status as a messiah-like figure that enabled oppressed slaves to escape the South; on account of her achievements, she is associated with the biblical Moses and his role in assisting the Israelites to escape from bondage. Similarly, "Go Down Moses" and Reverend C. L. Franklin's sermon "The Eagle Stirreth in Her Nest" use Egypt, the pharaoh, Moses, and Israel and its people in a similar context. Signifying is a transcendent semantic method of making people, places, and things emerge in a familiar yet new framework for discourse. Because African American religions identify with the story of Moses, subsequent writers that deal with the idea of freedom sometimes build on this particular story's cultural references. A number of writings have great implications on the development of literature, and the Bible is one such text.

Critics and theorists might analyze or evaluate the manner in which a writer refutes, expands, pays homage to, or parodies not only the language of black folks, but also character types or themes. This includes revealing their imaginative use of irony, satire, parody, pastiche, or burlesque forms of imitation. There are, as Gates suggests, certain inherent tropes within the African American literary tradition. One such tangible trope is the black matriarch, a significant literary device that imbibes identifiable characteristics and has specific functions in African American literature.

Historically, representations of black men and women in literature were relegated to stereotypical, one-dimensional images and directed by the literary imagination of white writers. Novels such as Harriet Beecher Stowe's *Uncle Tom's Cabin* and Thomas Nelson Page's *In Ole Virginia,* as well as minstrel performances, played a role in America's negative view of African Americans. Particularly damaging was the mammy figure.[6] This figure closely resembles Aunt Jemima, whose radiant smile and red headscarf were once used to sell pancake syrup. Aunt Jemima is an extremely well-recognized and well-received commercial figure in America, but the image is one of servitude and hardly representative of the reality that black women encountered on a daily basis. Hattie McDaniel's portrayal of Mammy in *Gone with the Wind* and her role as Beulah in the radio and television show *The Beulah Show* present a mammy-like character without children of her own. Later, in the 1970s, television audiences had to accept a countless number of black women who were the sole caretakers of their offspring in programs like *Julia* (Diahann Carroll), *What's Happening* (Mable King), *That's My Mama* (Theresa Merritt), and (for the majority of its time on the air) *Good Times* (Esther Rolle). Nell Carter even portrayed a contemporary version of the mammy in *Gimme a Break,* a program that aired well into the '80s.[7] African American writers might have consciously or even unconsciously signified on other examples of black mammies or matriarchs in the construction of their characters. Like writers who are influenced by culture, readers also come to a text with presuppositions, primarily from other literary and media sources. If a postmodern condition truly exists, then we cannot limit our observation to the confines of literature, for the conditions of postmodernism do not permit limiting representation to simply literature. Therefore, any analysis of signifying should consider the ways in which other literary genres and media represent this character.

Black writers have signified on the mammy figure and essentially reconstructed this character to exemplify positive characteristics such as dignity. These characters are perhaps more appropriately referred to as matriarchs. In many communities, black women have been the spiritual and physical healers in their families, and such an important presence laid the foundation for positive, more realistic, and diverse portrayals. Even 21st-century writers continue to build on productions of earlier writers, reinforcing literature as an intertextual endeavor, and this too is a form of signifying.

While the archetype of the black matriarch is ambiguous, representations of black women in literature can be traced from the first novel by an African American writer. From Harriet Wilson's *Sketches from the Life of a Free Black* to Terry McMillan's *Mama,* the strength of black women is revered. Recognizable distinctiveness and divergences, Langston Hughes's *Not Without Laughter,* Gloria Naylor's *Mama Day,* and Ishmael Reed's *Flight to Canada* all involve depictions of resilient black women and the role they play within their families.

In *Saints, Sinners, Saviors: Strong Black Women in African American Literature,* Trudier Harris draws attention to the one-dimensional representations of black women wherein "strength becomes their reason for being" (110).[8] Harris maintains that many black writers have relegated black women into a particular function that rarely goes beyond that of caretaker:

> Black writers inadvertently created another stereotype—that of the Black woman who was more superhuman than human, more introspective than involved, more silently working out what she perceived to be best for her children than actively and warmly communicating those desires to them. (Harris, "This Disease as Strength" 110)

Striking similarities between Hughes's Aunt Hagar and Naylor's Miranda "Mama" Day include their physical and psychological strength, their compassionate attitude toward people in their communities, and spiritual faith. Aunt Hagar's appearance in literature is earlier; therefore, she might be considered a modern representation of a matriarch rather than an imitation of the mammy from plantation literary writers. Hagar becomes a prototype for other matriarchal figures like Mama Day. Both Hagar and Miranda possess an innate ability to physically and spiritually restore people to health. The intuition and wisdom that they exhibit allows them to have an acute understanding about their immediate environment and the larger world. Hagar's wisdom passes on to her daughter Harriett, while in *Mama Day,* Miranda ensures that her knowledge passes to her great niece, Cocoa, the last of the Day lineage.[9]

Mama Day presents readers with a sustained, more complex characterization. Mama Day's sexual awareness is a prominent feature and black matriarchs rarely act in ways that give emphasis to sexuality. She primarily functions as a trickster figure, a trope derived from Esu-Elegba. Mama Day takes great pleasure in humiliating Dr. Buzzard in making him believe that he is being chased by ghosts. The delight she displays in alarming Dr. Buzzard, and her frequent rivalry with him, may suggest a personal rivalry or that he is a former lover. Mama Day's acknowledgment of sexuality is most evident when she enters a theatre to see a film called "The Milkman and the Old Maid." The place turns out to be a pornographic movie theatre, but she sees the movie twice just to "be sure she could believe [her] own eyes" (Naylor 306). Her spirit is playfully wicked and one would not necessarily consider her an old spinster. Aunt Hagar, however, shares none of these characteristics.

Mama Day embodies many of the characteristics of caretaker and magical women in black literature. Using the supernatural as a plot device for expressing magical realism, Charles W. Chesnutt's "The Conjure Woman" includes a conjurer named Aunt Peggy. She functions behind the scenes and is "denied textual presence of any serious import" (Tucker 154). Mama Day, on the other hand, is a prominent character.

Ishmael Reed, on the other hand, takes a radically different approach to the mammy figure in *Flight to Canada* (1998). Instead of using the common vocation of servitude, Reed employs satire or parody by making Mammy Barracuda a subversive character. Reed treads the line between humor and a serious positioning that stresses the ridiculousness of the character's existence from film and television. When we look at literary and nonliterary representations of black matriarchs, we can trace their development in African American literature as a significant trope.

The second literary mode of signifying refers to allusions or influences that manifest themselves consciously and sometimes even unintentionally between texts. One might describe such an approach with the term *intertextuality*. Intertextuality calls attention to a particular method where African American writers allude to or take inspiration from other texts while, at the same time, expressing singular inventiveness. This second mode relates to verbal signifying, but the implications are on a greater scale. Instead of taking general words and phrases and giving them fresh meanings, signifying in literature involves using allusions to well-established or obscure texts that writers find particularly inspiring and either building on these texts or countering them through literary modes of signifying such as parody.

Resembling verbal signifying in many ways, signifying in literature relies on audiences having certain knowledge or experiences within African, African American, or Euro-American culture and texts. One's awareness and comprehension of other texts, whether or not it is African American–derived or from somewhere else, enables readers to enjoy the significance of specific allusions or references, as well as to evaluate their own broad intelligence and understanding.[10] Toni Morrison's novel *Tar Baby,* for instance, illustrates the reverence for oral traditions in African American literature. Her novel is a tribute to the West African story called "Tar Baby." Throughout her novel, Morrison places references to Jadine's skin as looking like tar. Later, Son criticizes Jadine through innuendo by retelling the story to insult her. At the end of the novel, Son searches for Jadine, but his quest is reminiscent of the last lines in the Tar Baby folktale: "Then he ran. Lickety-split. Lickety-split. Looking neither to the left nor to the right. Lickety-split. Lickety-split. Lickety-lickety-lickety-split" (Morrison 306). This is Morrison's direct allusion to Son as the rabbit ensnared by his love for Jadine. Morrison's story is original because it is a love story and is her reinterpretation of the original Tar Baby story. Similarly, Morrison's *Song of Solomon* signifies on two texts—the biblical "Song of Solomon" and the African American folktale of the flying Africans. Unlike *Tar Baby, Song of Solomon* augments the antecedent text rather than replicating its structure. *Song of Solomon* and "The People Could Fly" both convey a story about Africans who had the power to fly and escape slavery, but Morrison's novel spins off from the original folktale.

While Gates maintains that *The Color Purple* is a re-envisioning of Hurston's *Their Eyes Were Watching God,* there are other forms and genres of literature that African American writers have signified on. Frederick Douglass's *Narrative of the Life of Frederick Douglass: An American Slave, Written by Himself* signifies on the autobiographies of English and American figures, particularly such autobiographies by prominent figures such as Benjamin Franklin. Plantation literature, popularized in the late 19th century and usually set in the South, conveys a romanticized view of slavery. As envisioned by Thomas Nelson Page and Harry Stillwell Edwards, Charles Chesnutt, in his collection of short stories *The Conjure Woman,* signifies on this tradition. Ishmael Reed's *Flight to Canada,* Octavia Butler's *Kindred,* and Morrison's *Beloved* signify by responding to the oral tradition of Africa and American slaves and American literary archetypes. The novel is not the only literary form that holds the possibilities of signifying; poetry holds connections as well.

Within the context of modern and postmodern African American literature, signifying possesses two meanings. The first denotes a manner in which writers accentuate black vernacular forms of language and communication within a text instead of emphasizing standardized English ones. Whereas verbal signifying changes language and asserts a particular perspective or argument, signifying in written traditions inserts these forms within writing and connects these writings to create a vivid, living tradition. Writers such as Charles Chesnutt, Langston Hughes, Sterling Brown, and Zora Neale Hurston emphasize a narrator's voice or a character's words and phraseology in order to establish a connection between written words and oral traditions typically spoken and heard in African American communities. African American language varies depending on time and place and includes Black Vernacular English (BVE), folk sayings, narrative sequencing (storytelling), tonal semantics, intonational contouring, sermons, testifying, toasts, the dozens, snaps, or African American song titles or lyrics in written form. In other words, certain writers signify on written traditions by drawing attention to oral forms of communication. Gates calls this method of black writing a *speakerly text.* He argues that these texts are concerned "with the possibilities of representing the speaking black voice in writing" (Gates, *Signifying Monkey* xxv).[11]

Hughes persistently argued for the expressions of black folk culture in his essay "The Negro Artists and the Racial Mountain."[12] Hughes emphasizes black vernacular forms of language and communication, and frequently utilizes such forms in his first novel, *Not Without Laughter.*

Sociologists Richard Majors and Janet Mancini Billson observe that black males commonly use signifying as a form of verbal play to establish social bonding and their dominance within peer groups. In their book, *Cool Pose: The Dilemmas of Black Manhood in America,* Majors and Billson observe verbal dexterity as a highly valued component within many male peer groups. In fact, in many cases, one's mastery of words becomes as valued as one's physical prowess. The dozens, as affirmed earlier with the verbal signifying of Janie Crawford against her husband's manhood in *Their Eyes Were Watching*

God, is a form of signifying that makes direct or indirect statements by bait-
ing their opponent. The essence of the dozens is to make fun of another's
appearance, relatives (especially one's mother), or situation. These are verbal
rather than physical duels.

Hughes captures a timeless socialization process that many inner-city black
men experience with Sandy Rodgers, the young protagonist in *Not Without
Laughter*.[13] Sandy's rite of passage includes learning the rules of communicating places where black men gather, such as the barbershop and pool hall.
Women kinfolk influence Sandy's home life, but as the narrator asserts, "the
barbershop [is] a man's world" (198) and here Sandy acquires a different
mode of discourse. The narrator explains that "the patrons liked him and
often kidded him about his sandy hair." Gradually, Sandy would then "blush"
because he did not like to be "kidded" about his hair. The patrons tell him:
"Boy, you's too dark to have hair like that. Ain't nobody but white folks supposed to have sandy-colored hair. An' it yours nappy at that!!" This is before
Sandy learns the oral manipulation of "turning back a joke"; the next time
a patron teases Sandy about his hair being "sandy and nappy," he quickly
replies, "So's your pa's" (Hughes 200).

Boasting and telling tall tales are included within the socializations of black
males. Hughes bears witness to this with Uncle Dan, another character in *Not
Without Laughter* who has lived under southern slavery. Uncle Dan is called
"the worlds champion liar" and when he boasts about his status as the man
on his plantation whose virility and ability to have babies was rewarded, his
tale becomes suspect:

> You all want to know wht dey called me when I was yo' age … De called
> me de stud n—! Yes, dey did! On 'count o' de kind o' slave-time work
> I was doing' –I was breedin' babies fo' to sell! … An' it warn't no time
> befo' little yaller chillens an' black chillens an' red chillens an' all kinds
> of chillens was runnin' round de yard eaten out o' de hog-pen an' a-
> callin' me pappy. (250)

Although Uncle Dan attempts to tell his story in a humorous way, his version
does not convey the exploitation and humiliation that men like Dan must
have endured. However problematic Uncle Dan's statements might be, it was
Hughes's intent to describe the manner in which Dan takes a deplorable situation and turns the situation to his ability to reproduce. Even today, some rap
artists continue this trend by exaggerating about their superior lovemaking
skills, their many sexual liaisons, and their wealth. Hughes's inclusion of vernacular traditions, such as the dozens, tall tales, and blues music in his first
novel successfully captures realistic and authentic realties involving the black
speaking voice.

In 1899, Paul Laurence Dunbar's poem "Sympathy" appeared in *Lyrics of
the Hearthside*. A central image in "Sympathy" is a bird in a cage and its
struggle for release. Despite its rigid confinement, the bird resists by beating its

wings against the cage and singing an exquisite perennial cry to the heavens. The final lines of Dunbar's poem serve as the inspiration for Maya Angelou's autobiography, *I Know Why the Caged Bird Sings*. The theme of Dunbar's poem adds relevance to Angelou's story. As a young girl, Angelou was molested by a family friend and thereafter refused to speak. It was only through exposure to reading and writing poetry that she reclaimed her voice, and was able to express her anger and desires. A connection between these two works provides insight into the nature of signifying in the context of African American literature.

In a similar manner, Lorraine Hansberry's theatrical production *A Raisin in the Sun* derives its title from the opening lines of "Harlem," a poem by Hughes. Hughes's poem questions the effect time has on dreams that are postponed. Hansberry's play depicts the deferred dreams of each member of the Younger family. This is particularly true for Walter Lee Younger, and is expressed in a conversation between Walter and his mother regarding his seemingly bleak future:

Sometimes it's like I can see the future stretched out in front of me—just as plain as day. The future, Mama. Hanging over there at the edge of my days. Just waiting for me—a big, looming blank space—full of nothing. Just waiting for me. (Hansberry 1799)

Walter desires to own a liquor store; Beneatha, his sister, wants to go to college and become a doctor; and Ruth, his wife, wants to leave the "rat-trap" (Hansberry 22) they call home.

Signifying is also present in African American musical traditions; however, when musicians and singers employ previous lyrics and melodies from other artists in their own music, it is more properly identified as sampling. In 2005, rapper Kanye West released "Gold Digger," a song that utilized lyrics and music from Ray Charles's 1955 hit, "I Got a Woman." West's popular interpolation of Charles's music and lyrics also made clever use of actor and singer Jamie Foxx, who portrayed Ray Charles in the 2004 motion picture biopic *Ray*. Foxx introduces the number by imitating Ray Charles's voice and combines the original refrain with a slight difference. While "I Got a Woman" celebrates a man's love for a woman who "treats [him] right," Fox and West use the song to criticize women who date or get married to successful men, not out of love, but for their eminence, monetary status, and the security their money affords. Not knowing the contemporary's connection to the original does not diminish one's appreciation of West's song in this instance, but adds to its artistic meaning and import. The very nature of call-and-response within African American oral culture places "Gold Digger" within a long tradition of creative music. West's song presents more than a response or elaboration on Charles's composition—it is a signifying, self-reflective production that critiques the nature of its visual and musical presence as art. "Gold Digger" confirms a tradition within African American culture, specifically within musical traditions, that those melodic and lyrical forms of signifying, otherwise known as sampling, are also a treasured and traditional art. Musical forms of signifying are not merely limited to compositions and artists; one can draw a variety of direct links between music and African American prose.

Music has always had (and probably always will have) some type of an influence on African American literature. *The Narrative of the Life of Frederick Douglass,* an early African American slave narrative, incorporates music and chronicles a song created by slaves as they are selected to work in their master's house:

> While on their way, they would make the dense old woods, for miles around, reverberate with their wild songs, revealing at once the highest joy and deepest sadness. They would compose and sing as they went along, consulting neither time nor tune. The thought that came up, came out—if not in the word, in the sound;—and as frequently in the one as in the other. They would sometimes sing the most pathetic sentiment in the most rapturous tone, and the most rapturous sentiment in the most pathetic tone. Into all of their songs they would manage to weave something of the Great House Farm ... [t]hey would sing most exultingly the following words;—
> "I am going away to the Great House Farm!
> O, yea! O, yea! O!" (31)

Today, many contemporary African American writers elaborately signify on various musical genres by including spirituals, work songs, gospel music, blues, jazz, rhythm and blues (R&B), rap, and hip hop. Even legendary artists that sing this music—Billie Holiday, John Coltrane, Ella Fitzgerald, or Bob Marley occasionally become figures of signification in African American literature.

Perhaps the most recognizable music-to-literary form of signifying comes from Ralph Ellison, whose lines from a blues song made famous by Louis Armstrong titled "(What Did I Do to Be So) Black and Blue" appears in the prologue to his modernist novel *Invisible Man* (12). The initial words in *Invisible Man* mirror the lyrics of the song. The concluding section of the prologue, however, uses the lines with a slight variation. "But what did I do to be so *blue?* Bear with me" (14). The slightly revised lines do not accentuate the narrator's racialized differences with the outside world; rather, it reinforces his despondency and is a precursor to the remaining chapters of the unidentified narrator's troubled and complicated past. While the original lyrics to "(What Did I Do to Be So) Black and Blue" reflect everyday loneliness, Ellison's revision explores another interpretation of the song, revealing its existential qualities, as existentialism figures prominently in Ellison's novel. More contemporary African American writers have employed similar strategies by using African American lyrics and music to reinforce written words on a page.

Two of John Edgar Wideman's novels use African American music as an inspiration. His 1983 novel, *Sent for You Yesterday,* signifies on the jazz song "Sent for You Yesterday (Here You Come Today)." The song, made popular by Count Basie, and later Jimmy Rushing, reinforces the opening protagonist's homecoming to the Pittsburgh area called Homewood. The jazz tune supports the novel's overall tone as well as its improvisational, jazz-influenced structure and dialogue. In fact, blues and jazz melodies become supporting characters in the novel. Drugs, violence, and inner-city poverty within a former bustling and industrial community reveal their suffering and convey the manner in which these characters cope with the sadness, loneliness, and despair through a rich musical heritage.

In a similar manner, Wideman's reflective piece *Fatheralong: A Meditation on Fathers and Sons, Race and Society* is a reference to the spiritual "Fartheralong." During his youth, Wideman misheard the song as "*Father*along" rather than "*Farther*along." Not only does his title reinforce the nature of language as interpretative, but it also permits the oral as well as the aural tradition to become as imprecise as written communication. In his reflection, Wideman recollects his father's emotional, and later, physical absence during his childhood and he discovers that he must eventually come to terms with his resentment for his father, not as a child, but as an adult. This interaction subsequently permits a greater self understanding of Wideman's role as a black man and as a father. The topic of masculine identity figures prominently in African American literature, and more recently male writers have begun to approach sexuality and gender in provocative and innovative ways.

Contemporary gay writer E. Lynn Harris signifies on traditional stories of manhood in his novels *Invisible Life* and *Just as I Am*. These novels reference earlier novels by African American male writers such as *Autobiography of an Ex-Colored Man, Native Son, Go Tell It on the Mountain,* and as a result of the title, *Invisible Man*. Harris also signifies on musical compositions, such as in his 1998 novel *If This World Were Mine*. Harris's title is a direct reference to a number originally sung by Marvin Gaye and Tammy Terrell in the late '60s, but later made famous by influential R&B writer and singer Luther Vandross in 1982. Harris's sixth novel details the lives of four former college classmates and their journal club over a 20-year period of regular gatherings. The novel's title directly alludes to the song by comparing and contrasting the foursome's dreams as young adults to their current status as 40-something mature adults.

Harris maintains a signifying practice of black music once again with his 2006 novel *I Say a Little Prayer*. Here, Harris repeats songwriters Burt Bacharach and Hal David's signature song, "I Say a Little Prayer," as sung by Dionne Warwick (and later, Aretha Franklin) as an inspiration. Again, interpretive aspects of "I Say a Little Prayer" and its lyrics become a prominent feature of Harris's use of the song. On the one hand, one can listen to the song as a woman's devotion for a man. On the other hand, one can also hear the lyrics as a sacred testimony or plea to God. Harris alludes to an interpretation grounded in Christian faith, and such a reading lends itself to a critical assessment of the black church and its paradoxical relationship with homosexuals within their congregation. Similar to my preceding illustrations of the relationship between music and literature, songs, when used appropriately, frequently reinforce textual themes and structures with a creative difference. Thus, Harris complicates the initial pretext of the song by making the novel a reference to romance between a gay man and his church as opposed to the heterosexual relationship alluded to in the original song. Clearly, literary modes of signifying draw attention to the significance of African American oral tradition, particularly music, and this had a direct affect on the developing elements of African American literature. One must be aware or have some understanding of African American cultural traditions in order to effectively decipher and reinforce a novel's text and subtext.

Signifying plays a tremendous role in the African American oral tradition. The act of signifying has been around a long time and can be traced to West African oral tales. The idea also transforms particular meanings of words to assert a point of view or position. As a result of the close relationship between the oral and written tradition, African American writers frequently employ signifying practices in their work. Early African American writers relied heavily on Christianity and the Bible. Phillis Wheatley, Jupiter Hammon, and Harriet Wilson are three writers who successfully wrote by signifying on America's religious traditions. Wheatley also dabbled in Roman and Catholic works, another prevalent discourse in America's search for a national identity. By employing signifying, one can read these works as making direct, and at other times subtle statements about slavery and freedom. The emphasis on Christianity gave rise to intertextual themes and an authentic and more realistic look at the language of black folks. In literature, signifying emphasizes an interconnectedness between texts by using various themes and tropes. Many writers also highlight the inherent beauty and power of the black voices in their works to enhance black character, consciousness, and culture. Signifying is therefore a complex figure in African American literature and culture.

NOTES

1. "The Signifying Monkey": In this tale, a monkey goads a lion (and in some versions, an elephant), insulting him and his family. The motivation behind the monkey's behavior is to trick the larger animals in the jungle to kill each other. "Anansi the Spider" (also Aunt Nancy in South Carolina): A story that originated in Africa with the Ashanti, and later with the Gullah and Akan. In this story, a spider tricks various animals using language.

2. See Bernard Bell's *The African American Novel and its Traditions* and *The Contemporary African American Novel: Its Folk Roots and Modern Literary Branches* for more information on the way the oral tradition influences African American literature.

3. Phillis Wheatley-Peters was taken from Africa at a young age and put aboard a ship named *Phillis*. Her owner named her after the ship and gave her his last name.

4. In "Notes on the State of Virginia," Thomas Jefferson said of Wheatley's poems: "Religion indeed has produced a Phyllis Whately [*sic*] but it could not produce a poet. The compositions published under her name are below the dignity of criticism."

5. Harriet E. Wilson's *Our Nig or Sketches from the Life of a Free Black* signifies by using biblical scripture that is frequently revised to express her own individual ideas of race and gender.

6. In his essay "The Negro Character as Seen by White Authors," Sterling Brown discusses the prevalence and history of seven stereotypes of black characters in literature: (1) The Contented Slave, (2) the Wretched Freeman, (3) the Comic, (4) the Brute, (5) the Tragic Mulatto/Mulatta, (6) Urban and Local Color, and (7) the Exotic Primitive.

7. For a look at stereotypes of African Americans in American culture, see the documentary *Ethnic Notions* by Marlon Riggs.

8. Trudier Harris's essay "This Disease Called Strength" analyzes the representation of black women in literature: "The landscape of African American literature is peopled with Black women who are almost too strong for their own good, whether that strength is moral or physical or both. Historically, Black writers have assumed that strength was the one useable characteristic they could apply to Black women."

9. In the film *Daughters of the Dust,* Nana Peazant, a similar matriarchal figure, passes on her legacy to her daughter-in-law Eula Peazant and that knowledge will be passed down to her child. August Wilson's *Gem of he Ocean* also reinforces the idea of passing on knowledge to a new generation with Aunt Esther.

10. Several of Toni Morrison's novels employ signifying in the context of the written word. *Tar Baby* is a reworking of the folktale "Tar Baby," which is derived from African and African American communities. *Song of Solomon* is a revision of the myth of the Flying Africans called "The People Could Fly" and "All God Chillen Had Wings."

11. In *The Signifying Monkey,* Henry Louis Gates Jr. assesses the dual nature of language in Hurston's *Their Eyes Were Watching God.* The narrator's Standard English vernacular sometimes comes in direct opposition to Janie's Black Vernacular English. As the primary narrator of the novel, Janie's voice overshadows the narrator. Such a dichotomy represents Hurston's legacy to African American written traditions. The dual voices are in tension with each other. Other writers have achieved similar dual voices in their novels, but not with the originality, complexity, and authenticity that Hurston conveys.

12. Hughes wrote "The Negro Artist" (1926) in response to George Schulyer's essay "The Negro Art Hokum."

13. Although primarily known for his poetry, *Not Without Laugher* is Langston Hughes's first novel (1927). It tells the story of a young boy, Sandy Rogers, who must choose between sacred and secular and the past and the present.

FURTHER READING

Abrahams, Rodger. D. *Deep Down in the Jungle: Negro Narrative Folklore from the Streets of Philadelphia.* New York: Aldine, 1970.

Angelou, Maya. *I Know Why The Caged Bird Sings.* New York: Bantam, 1993.

Armstrong, Louis. "What Did I Do to Be So (Black and Blue)." Decca, 1955. Record.

Baker, Houston. *Modernism and the Harlem Renaissance.* Chicago: U of Chicago P, 1987.

Charles, Ray. "I Got a Woman." *The Very Best of Ray Charles.* Rhino, 2000. CD.

Daughters of the Dust. Dir. Julie Dash. Perf. Cora Lee Day and Alva Rodgers. 1991. New Press, 1999. DVD.

Douglass. Frederick. *The Narrative in the Life of Frederick Douglass: An American Slave, Written by Himself*. New York: Signet, 1968.

Dunbar, Paul Laurence. "Sympathy." Gates 922.

Dundes, Alan. *Mother Wit from the Laughing Barrel*. New York: Garland, 1981.

Ellison, Ralph. *Invisible Man*. New York: Vintage, 1995.

Franklin, Aretha. "I Say a Little Prayer." *Aretha's Best*. Atlantic, 2001. CD.

Franklin. C. L. "The Eagle Stirreth in Her Nest." *The Norton Anthology of African American Literature*. Ed. H. L. Gates and N. Y. McKay. New York: Norton, 1984. 98–104.

Gates, Henry Louis, Jr. *The Signifying Monkey: A Theory of African American Literary Criticism*. New York: Oxford UP, 1989.

Gates, Henry Louis, Jr., and Nellie Y. McKay, eds. *The Norton Anthology of African American Literature*. New York: Norton, 1984.

"Go Down Moses." Gates 12.

Hammon, Jupiter. "An Evening Thought with Perennial Cries." Gates 163–65.

Hansberry, Lorraine. *A Raisin in the Sun*. Gates 1771–1830.

Harris, E. Lynn. *If This World Were Mine*. New York. Time Warner, 1999.

Harris, E. Lynn. *I Say a Little Prayer: A Novel*. New York: Doubleday, 2006.

Harris, Trudier. "This Disease Called Strength: Some Observations on the Compensating Construction of Black Female Character." *Literature and Medicine* 14.1 (Spring 1995): 109–26.

Harris, Trudier. *Saints, Sinners and Saviors: Strong Black Women in African American Literature*. New York: Palgrave, 2001.

Holloway, Joseph, ed. *Africanisms in American Culture*. Indiana: Indiana UP, 2005.

Holton, Sylvia Wallace. *Down Home and Uptown: The Representation of Black Speech in American Fiction*. Madison, NJ: Fairleigh Dickinson UP, 1984.

Hughes, Langston. *Not Without Laughter*. New York: Simon, 1995.

Hurston, Zora Neale. *Their Eyes Were Watching God*. New York: HarperPerennial, 2006.

King, Martin Luther, Jr. "I've Been to the Mountaintop." Gates 110–16.

Majors, Richard, and Janet Billson. *Cool Pose: The Dilemma of Black Manhood in America*. New York: Touchstone, 1993.

Mitchell-Kernan, Claudia. "Signfiying." *Mother Wit from the Laughing Barrel: Readings in the Interpretation of African American Folklore*. Ed. Alan Dundes. Upper Saddle River, NJ: Prentice Hall, 1973. 310–28.

Naylor, Gloria. *Mama Day*. New York: Vintage, 1993.

Nero, Charles. "Towards a Black Gay Aesthetic: Signifying in Contemporary Black Gay Literature." *Brother to Brother: New Writings by Black Gay Men*. Ed. Joseph Beam and Essex Hemphill. Boston: Alyson, 1991. 229–52.

O'Neale, Sondra. *Jupiter Hammon and the Biblical Beginnings of African American Literature*. New York: Scarecrow, 1993.

Razaf, Andy, and Eubie Blake. Perf. Alberta Hunter. "My Handy Man." Amtrak Blues, 1978. LP.

Rushing, Jimmy, Eddie Durham, and Count Basie. "Sent for You Yesterday (Here You Come Today)." *The Essential Jimmy Rushing*. Vanguard, 1974. LP.

Smitherman, Geneva. *Black Talk: Words and Phrases from the Hood to the Amen Corner*. Boston: Houghton Mifflin, 2000.

Smitherman, Geneva. *Talkin and Testifyin: The Language of Black America*. Detroit: Wayne State UP, 1977.

Smitherman, Geneva. *Word from the Mother: Language and African Americans.* New York: Routledge, 2006.

Snead, James. "Repetition as a Figure of Black Culture." *Black Literature and Literary Theory.* Ed. Henry Louis Gates Jr. New York: Methuen, 1984. 59–79.

"Steal Away to Jesus." Gates 14.

"Swing Low, Sweet Chariot." Gates 14.

Tucker, Lindsey. "Recovering the Conjure Woman: Texts and Contexts in Gloria Naylor's *Mama Day.*" *African American Review* 28.2 (1995): 174.

"We Raise the Wheat." Gates 27.

West, Kanye. "Gold Digger." *Late Registration.* Perf. Kanye West and Jamie Foxx Roc-a-fella, 2005. CD.

Wheatley, Phillis. "On Being Brought From Africa to America." Gates 219–20.

Wideman, John Edgar. *Fatheralong: A Meditation on Fathers, Songs, Race and Society.* New York: Vintage, 1995.

Wideman, John Edgar. *Sent for You Yesterday.* Boston: Houghton Mifflin, 1983.

Wilson, Harriet E. *Our Nig or Sketches from the Life of a Free Black.* New York: Penguin, 2005.

X, Malcolm. "The Ballot or the Bullet." Web. http://www.historicaldocuments.com/BallotortheBulletMalcolmX.htm.

Timothy Mark Robinson

Captured in the interior of West Africa as a young boy and sold to Europeans as a slave, Olaudah Equiano endured many years of enslavement before eventually purchasing his own freedom. After publishing an autobiographical account of his travels and speaking publicly against slavery and the slave trade, Equiano became an important figure of the 18th-century British abolition movement. Frontispiece and title page from *The Interesting Narrative of the Life of Olaudah Equiano*. (Library of Congress)

Slave Narrative

The slave narrative, one of the most unique genres in American literature, affords the reader an intimate view into the life of the slave in the history of the United States. Like any narrative, the slave narrative tells a story, in this case an autobiography or memoir capturing that part of the author's life as a slave. The earliest known slave narrative is that of James Albert Ukawsaw Gronniosaw: *A Narrative of the Most Remarkable Particulars in the Life of James Albert Ukawsaw Gronniosaw, an African Prince, as Related by Himself* (1772). Gronniosaw's brief 18th-century narrative illustrates the beginnings of both slavery and the slave narrative in what was soon to become the United States; his narrative commences in Africa, moves to a slave ship, onto American soil, and eventually to England, where the narrative is published. Setting the stage for other slave narratives to follow, the impoverished Gronniosaw dictates his story to a white Christian woman of means and weaves the message of Christianity as critical to the salvation of the slave into his narrative. In addition, Gronniosaw's narrative includes a preface by a white person of both means and stature in society, in this case, the Reverend Walter Shirley.

While one finds many interesting elements in the slave narrative, those particulars set into place by Gronniosaw become especially important to the genre. The act of dictating one's story to another, a scribe, comes from necessity, of course. The writer in this case simply could not pen his own words. While the work of the scribe is critical to the very existence of the slave narrative, it also makes the narrative suspect to some degree. How much liberty did the scribe take in committing the former slave's words to paper? Did the scribe have any particular agenda—such as religious proselytizing—that transcended her need to be accurate in the transcription? In the absence of a scribe—that is, in the many instances where the narrative writer is literate and thus able to pen his or her own work—there is often an editor present, usually a sympathetic white person, again of social standing and importance, who may act with some degree of influence on the content of the narrative. This leads the reader to the same type of questions as addressed above. One finds such questions throughout the canon of the slave narrative.

Chronology of Important Slave Narratives in African American Literature and Significant Historical Events

1641—Massachusetts legalizes slavery in the colony

1772—Publication of A Narrative of the Most Remarkable Particulars in the Life of James Albert Ukawsaw Gronniosaw, an African Prince, as related by Himself

1776—Declaration of Independence

1787—Northwest Ordinance (banned slavery in parts of the United States)

1789—Publication of The Interesting Narrative of the Life of Olaudah Equiano, or Gustavus Vassa, the African, Written by Himself

1793—Fugitive Slave Law (decreed that runaway slaves in the North may be pursued and returned)

1807—Congress ends slave trade

1817—The American Colonization Society is founded (mission: send freed blacks back to Africa)

1820—Missouri Compromise (Missouri admitted to the Union as a slave state, Maine as free)

1831—Publication of The History of Mary Prince, a West Indian Slave, Related by Herself

1831—Slave insurrection of Nat Turner

1837—The first national Anti-Slavery Society Convention, New York City

*1845—*Narrative of the Life of Frederick Douglass, an American Slave, Written by Himself

*1847—*Narrative of William W. Brown, a Fugitive Slave. Written by Himself

*1850—*Narrative of Sojourner Truth, a Northern Slave, Emancipated from Bodily Servitude by the State of New York, in 1828.

1850—Fugitive Slave Act

1854—Repeal of the Missouri Compromise

*1857—*Dred Scott *case (denied the citizenship of slaves and former slaves)*

*1860—*Running a Thousand Miles for Freedom; or the Escape of William and Ellen Craft from Slavery

*1861—*Incidents in the Life of a Slave Girl, Written by Herself

1863—The Emancipation Proclamation

1865—Thirteenth Amendment (abolished slavery in the United States)

Another element of the slave narrative that Gronniosaw's work sets in motion is the testimony to the character of the writer and the veracity of the writer's story. This becomes a critical part of the selling and sharing of the slave narrative for many writers. The better known the author of the testimony, the better chance the narrative would enjoy strong sales. Analyzing the societal importance of the particular testimony's author becomes an interesting exercise that leads the reader to an enhanced understanding of the execution of the narrative. One gains a firmer understanding of both the author herself and the conditions under which the author is attempting to publish the narrative.

Other elements found in Gronniosaw's case follow into subsequent slave narratives. The reader often finds deep financial struggles plaguing the narrative writer and his family. The reader also often finds Christianity an increasingly important part of the narrative writer's life, even when those who originally taught the writer Christianity are portrayed as unfamiliar in their own life with the basic tenets of Christianity. Additionally, the reader inevitably encounters a delicate balance between the races, with the black writer is most often careful not to offend the presumed white reader and the definite white supporter, with the black writer often revealing intimate relations between the races—sometimes freely chosen and many times forced.

Despite the restrictive conditions faced by some of the slave narrative writers, these narratives play a vital role in both the larger African American literary canon and the American literary canon. Those slave narratives published in the 18th and 19th centuries helped the classes of power, those who were educated and able to influence legislation and social change, to understand the layers of complications that faced the slave. The narratives put a face on the issue of slavery and worked on the sympathies of the reader to begin to effect legal and social change. These works also literally put a face on the African American in the midst of crude caricatures of the race and incredible misunderstandings on a sociological and psychological level. Although some readers held the narrative writers up as a rare example of excellence, many others used those same writers as symbols of the race at large.

Publishing a successful slave narrative sometimes led to a career in speaking, as it did with Frederick Douglass. Such writers went on the lecture circuit to more widely spread their tales of slavery and to work for the abolition movement. Some, again, like Douglass, became abolitionist leaders in their own right. Overall, the slave narrative opened up many creative possibilities for the African American. It also led to a series of fictionalized slave narratives and novels that revolved around the issues of slavery. Sometimes it led to white writers attempting to hijack the genre in order to find success in the publishing world.

While some slave narratives never found their way to publication, others were published but faced minimal sales. Some of these were lost to literary history for years. Recent decades have led to more and more exciting discoveries of formerly forgotten African American literature texts, slave narratives included. On the other hand, several slave narratives enjoyed critical and sustaining success and found their way into literary studies early on in the 20th century. It is these texts that are viewed as icons of the genre.

The first critically important slave narrative, and the narrative that continues to serve as example and template in contemporary studies of the genre, is *The Interesting Narrative of the Life of Olaudah Equiano, or Gustavus Vassa, the African, Written by Himself.* Published in 1789 in London, Equiano's slave narrative both compares and contrasts to that of Gronniosaw. Certainly both men use long titles lending to self-description, a practice that was common in 18th-century British and then American literature. Unlike Gronniosaw, Equiano was literate and penned his narrative himself. While Equiano's narrative does include a preface, it is a preface written by the author himself rather than by a white supporter. Unlike slave narratives that were to follow, Equiano's published narrative does not include any testimony to veracity by any person other than Equiano himself. This seemingly trite fact sets Equiano's narrative apart from other slave narratives, as does Equiano's background, situation, and education. A list of subscribers—people who purchased copies of the volume in advance of publication—is included in at least one edition of Equiano's narrative. Though this is not quite the same as including testimonies by the wealthy and respected, it does serve as testimony nonetheless, in that the names of the powerful, the wealthy, and the respected in society appear on this list, helping Equiano with both marketing and the appeasing of questioners. Like Gronniosaw's narrative, Equiano's narrative was first published in England. Equiano also touches upon Christianity in his narrative, although with slightly less unadulterated passion than does Gronniosaw. Another difference, major in scope, lies in the fact that Equiano was not struggling financially, as was Gronniosaw. Equiano lacked desperation, which surely affected the writing of his narrative. Because of Equiano's circumstances, the writer also found himself in a position to work for abolition in both Britain and the United States. Although some viewed him as an abomination, Equiano's education and polished presence served to earn him more respect than the average African turned American slave was afforded. Another interesting comparison between the two men, a fact that will prove to lead to increasing treatment of the subject in future works of African American literature, is that both men chose white Englishwomen as their spouses. While this would have been not only outlawed but condemned in the United States, Equiano and Gronniosaw found in England more acceptance on a variety of levels. Although Britain itself was a major player in the slave trade and was still decades from abolishing slavery, sympathy, or at the very least, humane curiosity, was easier to find in Britain than in the United States. It is important to note that the publication of Equiano's narrative in England helped spur increased efforts on the part of abolitionists.

Equiano's narrative is separated into 12 chapters, each of which begins with a list of summary phrases for that chapter. In his first chapter, Equiano introduces the reader to his native land, revealing that he was born in the village of Essaka, in the district of Eboe, hundreds of miles from the coast and the flourishing slave trade. This region is known as Nigeria today. Equiano treats the reader to an anthropological view of his homeland, discussing marriage, the arts community, the simplicity of life in the agrarian village, religious beliefs and ceremonies, and so on. From this very first chapter the reader becomes aware of a difference in Equiano from what one had perhaps expected: This is not the portrayal of an Africa that the white American or British reader is expecting. Rather than a description of a community of savages living without benefit of culture, manners, or God, Equiano's description paints a picture of absolute civilization, beyond the boundaries of Europe and America.

The reader, no doubt wondering how Equiano ended up enslaved in America from such a seemingly stable childhood, discovers in the next chapter the unfortunate event that eventually leads to Equiano's misfortune. Again, no doubt surprising to the reader, Equiano tells of being kidnapped with his sister, both home alone in the village at the time while the others were out work- ing, by members of another tribe. Thus begins Equiano's journey into slavery, although at first this is slavery confined to his native continent. The slavery he encounters in Africa is distinctly different than that he discovers upon be- ing taken hostage on a slave ship bound for America. In Africa, although he is moved from one place to another, and although he mourns the separation from his family and village, Equiano—and his sister, with whom he is briefly reunited—faces masters who, despite expecting work of him, treat him almost like a member of the family. His education continues and he becomes adept at speaking more than one language. It is when Equiano is carried to a slave ship bound for Virginia that the horrors of Western-style slavery meet him.

Equiano's descriptions of the harsh, inhumane, and often deadly conditions on the slave ship mark the first explicitly written account of this part of slav- ery; the horrific details that help shape Equiano's slave narrative also helped fuel the passions of abolitionists in Britain and the United States who read the narrative. Equiano's narrative goes on to describe his sale from one master to another, as well as his astonishment at life in the West in general and the con- dition of enslaved Africans in the West specifically. The reader finds Equiano depicting himself as at once obedient and firm in his desire to remain his own man, even if only spiritually and mentally. Equiano is taught the Christian religion, is baptized, and embraces the religion as a way of depending on a higher power to help him through his struggles, much as did the members of his native land. Unusual in slave narratives—or in slavery, in general, for that matter—is the relative liberty given to Equiano as he becomes a skillful sailor, depended on greatly by his master. Also unusual is Equiano's determination to make his own money by setting upon entrepreneurial endeavors while also performing his duties to his master. These endeavors are at first seen as prob- lematic; Equiano's strong argument for his case, coupled with the respect for his skills that his master possesses, indeed allows Equiano to earn his own money. It is this initiative of Equiano's that leads him to being able to buy his own freedom. The discussion of manumission and the inclusion of the legal manumission form in the narrative lends to an important understanding of the crucial difference between slave and freeman, even though racial prejudice still often continued to plague the freeman. Interestingly, the narrative does not end on Equiano's manumission. Rather, the author continues to relate the tales of his adventures on the seas, as well as his deepened faith in God. Much is made of his Christian faith in the latter third of Equiano's narrative, to the point of the author requesting to be sent to Africa as a missionary. This strong faith correlates to the theme of spirituality that readers so often encounter in later works of the African American literary canon, from autobiography (including slave narratives) to sermons and novels and poetry.

Equiano's slave narrative is important on a number of counts. The au- thor relates critical information about native Africans, as well as about the act of Western slave traders stealing Africans into slavery. He also portrays himself—and thus Africans in general—as an educated, thinking, industrious, and enterprising man, thus helping to shatter racial stereotypes that had already begun to settle into the minds of Westerners. Perhaps most importantly, Equiano uses his narrative as an epistle against the practice of slavery, using his Christian faith as the foundation of that epistle.

Several decades after Equiano's narrative, *The History of Mary Prince, a West Indian Slave, Related by Herself* was published. Like both Gronniosaw's and Equiano's narratives, Prince's slave narrative was first published in London. Thomas Pringle, secretary of the Anti-Slavery Society, assures the reader in his preface to the 1831 volume that, although the narrative has been transcribed by "a lady visitor" to Pringle's home, the words are exactly those of Prince, who herself initiated the telling and publishing of her story. Unlike the previous two authors discussed, Mary Prince was born a slave in Bermuda. With Mary Prince's narrative, literary history is given the first known slave narrative written from the point of view of a woman and written outside of the realm of slavery on U.S. soil. The tale Prince tells correlates quite closely to later tales told by slaves or abolitionist sympathizers about slavery on U.S. soil, making her story a critical work in the slave narrative genre.

Particularly striking about Prince's narrative are her tales of physical brutality and her rendering of slaves being sold or sent to work away from their families. The young Prince recalls her first placement, with her mother and some of her siblings in the Williams household, as rather comfortable—that is, as long as Mr. Williams is away at sea. While her husband is away, Mrs. Williams runs a congenial and kind household. Once Mr. Williams returns, everything changes for everyone—including Mrs. Williams. It is when the very young Mary Prince is sent to work for another family that she first experiences one of the most inhumane aspects of slavery, being separated from her mother. Her situation is not completely dire, however, as she is able to maintain contact with her mother until Mrs. Williams dies and Mr. Williams, eager to remarry, sells Mary and two of her siblings in order to pay for his wedding. The bitterness of separation that ensues is second only in shocking detail to Prince's description (and her editor's additional graphic description) of the slave auction block. The 19th-century reader unfamiliar with the horrors of slavery must have cringed at these descriptions and then cringed even more upon reading of the heinous physical brutality visited upon the young Mary Prince in the home of her new master and mistress, brutality experienced daily with such ferocity that the reader is left to wonder how Prince managed to live through the ordeal. When she is sold from this situation, Prince finds herself in yet another brutal, control-addicted household.

Equally important to Prince's narrative is her relation of running away to her mother out of desperation, being returned by her father, and falling into a psychological struggle that proves the cold-heartedness of her slaveholders. Even when Prince finds someone to lend her the money to buy her freedom, her master refuses to grant her manumission, committed to total control over another human being as he is. Prince escapes her bondage only when she is taken to England with her master and mistress and finds the opportunity to leave them. With help from the Anti-Slavery Society, she secures places of safety and ends up employed by the Pringle family; this family helps her to get her narrative published.

Prince's slave narrative is relatively short and includes the author's relation of her acceptance of Christianity, through her friends at the Anti-Slavery Society, as well as her relation of learning to read and write. While Prince gives God and her faith their due, this is not what the reader most takes away from the narrative. Rather, the reader takes the disturbing effect of Prince's physical abuse, bordering on sexual abuse, even after she marries a freeman. The reader also takes away the sobering realization that Prince is never free—not through marriage, not through her Anti-Slavery Society connections, not through her working in the Pringle household. She is always someone else's property, and therefore never at ease. The basic human right to freedom remains one of the recurring themes of Prince's narrative; she strongly disparages the notion that anyone enslaved can be truly happy.

One-fourth of Mary Prince's narrative is written by the book's editor as a "Supplement to the History of Mary Prince." This supplement adds interesting information to Prince's story, including her initial outreach to members of the Anti-Slavery Society as well as letters between members of the society and Mr. Woods, Prince's legal owner. While Prince's narrative does not include outright testimonies by respected white members of society the way later slave narratives do, the addition of this supplement, along with the preface by Pringle, certainly serve much the same purpose. Clearly, Prince's story will not be doubted, a fact that is especially important in light of the Prince's gender and what she chooses to relate about her abuse at the hands of white slaveholders.

Perhaps the best known slave narrative, published a decade after Mary Prince's narrative, is the *Narrative of the Life of Frederick Douglass, an American Slave, Written by Himself.* Following the established pattern, Douglass's narrative was published by Boston's Anti-Slavery Office in 1845. Also following an established pattern, Douglass's narrative includes prefaces by two respected white men of the time, which attest to the veracity of Douglass's tale and to the necessity of taking his narrative seriously. The first preface is penned by the famous editor and abolitionist William Lloyd Garrison, publisher of the abolitionist newspaper *The Liberator,* the second by Wendell Phillips, lawyer, abolitionist, and writer. In 19th-century Boston, one couldn't hope for better in terms of endorsement for a slave narrative. As Garrison explains in his preface, he met the newly escaped Douglass at an antislavery convention in Massachusetts, where Douglass was urged by a fellow abolitionist to share his tale. Garrison, like many others after him, found himself absolutely impressed with the intelligence, stature, grace, and passion that shone through Douglass's oratorical skills. The stage was set for a long career as orator for Douglass, first as a spokesperson for abolition, then for women's rights and suffrage, believing that freedom and equality for all, regardless of race, gender or any other divisions, were irrefutable rights. Realizing Douglass's ability to read and write exceptionally well, Garrison and the other area abolitionists were eager to have him write his narrative, knowing the impact such would have on those still uncertain about the issue of slavery in the nation.

And write Douglass did. He followed *Narrative of the Life* with *My Bondage and Freedom* (1855) and *The Life and Times of Frederick Douglass* (1881); all belong to the slave narrative genre. In addition, Douglass began his own newspaper, *The North Star*, in 1848. The prolific and highly intelligent Douglass set the standard for the slave narrative in the 19th century with his *Narrative of the Life*. Douglass begins this narrative with an almost journalistic tone, clearly concerned with relating facts without the advantage of storytelling techniques. The first chapter of his narrative immediately makes Douglass's early situation clear to the reader: born to an enslaved woman from whom he is separated soon after birth and whom he sees only sporadically and only under the cover of night in the next several years, Douglass is orphaned of his mother at age seven. The identity of his white father remains a mystery to him. The fact that Douglass devotes significant space to the discussion of his parentage is an important addition to the slave narrative genre that readers do not see so blatantly in the previous slave narratives. The issue of separating mothers from children, husbands from wives, brothers from sisters was a real and bitter part of the American slave experience. In Douglass's case, the separation of mother from child is compounded by the fact of Douglass's age at separation and the deliberateness with which his master acts in parting infants and mothers in order to prevent any lasting, permanent bonds. Although Douglass's mother does make several nighttime visits to her young son, the master's intent is realized: The child feels little loss when he hears of his mother's death, for he hardly knows her. Likewise, Douglass's discussion of his white father, whom many presume to be the master, underscores the act of sexual possession that many slaveholders saw as their right. In bringing these issues to light, Douglass opens to discussion some of the most horrific facts of slavery that had lain hidden from the observation of the white majority. Family abuses spur sympathy unlike almost anything else; Douglass's treatment of these issues served the abolitionist movement well.

When Douglass is old enough to work for his master and leave the shelter of his grandmother's quarters, he immediately encounters the extreme cruelty of Captain Anthony, the master, as he viciously whips Douglass's aunt for having disobeyed him by going to see a male friend. Witnessing this scene traumatizes the child and sets the stage for his bleak expectations.

Douglass's graphic descriptions of brutality are reminiscent of those of Mary Prince, but Douglass goes beyond Prince to successfully attempt a look at some of the specifics of day-to-day slavery that had not before been recorded in the slave narrative genre. Douglass gives an account of the meager food and clothing allowance given to the slaves and their living conditions, as well as of the daily schedule demanded of them. When he describes Mr. Severe, the aptly named overseer working for the owner of the large plantation,

Colonel Lloyd, the author describes a man of utmost cruelty. Again, Douglass goes into graphic detail without taking the time to display overt emotion. The sharing of such information becomes important to the slave narrative genre specifically because it laid the groundwork for a truer understanding of slavery on the part of sympathetic citizens, northerners who had little or no primary knowledge of slavery. Equally important is Douglass's brief treatment of the seemingly benign and even silly songs the slaves sang, songs which Douglass soon came to realize resounded with hidden and comforting meaning. Many of these songs would find a place in the later known genre of the Negro spiritual.

As Douglass's slave narrative progresses, the reader becomes increasingly aware of the horrors of slavery. The cruelty of overseers, that is, those men hired by the master to oversee the slaves, making sure that each is working to maximum capacity and that each stays in line or is severely punished in order to maintain a perverse order, along with the anxiety almost constantly felt by the slave, become cornerstones of Douglass's narrative. When Douglass describes how a slave who does not know his master by sight is tricked into confessing that his master works him too hard and cares too little for him and the others, the reader gasps to learn that slave is sold away from family and friends into the deeper South. After so much misery treated in the first part of the narrative, the reader with relief discovers Douglass leaving Colonel Lloyd for a seemingly better, kinder situation with the Aulds. It is in this household that Douglass begins to learn to read, with the assistance of Mrs. Auld. This critical situation in the narrative shows Mrs. Auld being caught in the act of teaching Douglass by her husband, who lectures her about the dangers of teaching a slave to read and write, thus opening the slave to the possibility of discontent and restlessness, further leading to trouble for the master. While Auld's words have the desired effect on his wife, they have an even more profound effect on Douglass, who suddenly sees the importance of knowledge and determines to obtain that for himself, somehow. While Equiano's narrative clearly shows the advantages of education and literacy, Douglass's narrative does so in a more pointed, poignant way. Illustrating the fear a white man feels upon reflecting on the education of a slave and the desperate need a slave feels upon tasting the possibilities of the power of education, and thus, a very real form of freedom, Douglass masterfully sets forth a precedent in the slave narrative genre, forcing the reader to acknowledge not only the power of education for all but also the basic humanity of a slave whose very soul thirsts for education and enlightenment. As with the other slave narratives, it is when the white reader of the time realizes that basic humanity that the effect of the slave narrative takes hold and rises to its higher purpose and readership.

Having become aware of the possibilities of being literate, Douglass relies on his wits to continue his lessons without the help of Mrs. Auld, whom he credits with having opened his eyes. Douglass in part continues his lessons by teaching himself; he also, however, trades knowledge for bread with some of the poorer white boys in the vicinity. Approaching his teen years, Douglass speaks philosophically of realizing two things: first, the bitterness of knowing he is destined to be a slave for life, and then the existence of abolitionists. It is this second realization that leads Douglass to begin to hope that he can perhaps obtain freedom some day. This realization spurs Douglass to learn to write along with his learning to read. Using his young master's schoolbooks and schoolwork as guides, Douglass succeeds in this goal as well.

As Douglass's narrative progresses and as the reader witnesses Douglass maturing into a young man, he relates going from one master to another, ending up back with his original master's son upon the slaveholder's death, and being hired out to a slave breaker, Mr. Covey, to prepare him to better serve his new master. Again, Douglass deals vividly with the physical brutalities of slavery. He also treats his attempts at escape with a group of other slaves. That first attempt fails, but eventually, of course, Douglass makes it to freedom. Before that point, his narrative touches on the hypocrisies of Christianity in the hands of southern slaveholders, a topic that is to become of critical importance not only to slave narrative, but also to speeches and sermons based on the principles of abolition and the purer theological messages. When Douglass writes of the Sabbath and of attempting to teach his fellow slaves the true message of Christianity, he must end that portion of his tale with the relation of violence upon the part of white Christian men incensed by the slave's attempt to educate on theological and philosophical matters. Douglass illustrates the dangers of being an educated slave: As Mr. Auld had feared, an educated slave leads to trouble for the slaveholder in that he feels discontent; as Douglass himself discovers, being an educated slave not only leads to discontent but to an impossible situation, that of knowing that his circumstances are intolerable and unjust, while at the same time knowing that the chances for escape are slim.

When Douglass writes of his eventual successful attempt at fleeing slavery, he underscores his position that it is unwise to reveal the specifics of his escape. To do so, he maintains, would put those still enslaved at risk. In a move that most likely proved unpopular with some segments of abolitionist society and that is little discussed even today, Douglass asserts that the methods of the Underground Railroad, while noble in their core, put many lives at risk by making escape trails and safe houses too well known. Again, Douglass serves to open an important discussion about slavery and abolition, making his slave narrative at once unique and pressing in its message.

Douglass ends his narrative with an appendix that caps his affinity for going against the norm. In this appendix he discusses what he calls "slaveholding religion"; that is, the special brand of unorthodox Christianity espoused by the South. Douglass uses scathing rhetoric to bring the hypocrisies of religion to the forefront, but he also makes it known that he himself is a Christian, although not of the same brand as the slaveholders. Douglass's religion is based on the true tenets of the religion, not on tenets twisted for the purpose of making slavery not only just but a God-given right of the white man. This discussion in the slave narrative paves the way for another important part of the larger slavery and abolition discussions: how people pit God against each other, and how the Christian God is used to further slavery in the South. With this final discussion, Douglass cements his place as perhaps the most significant slave narrative author of the 19th century.

Douglass is not alone in shocking 19th-century readers into realizing the perversions of slavery, however. Harriet Ann Jacobs's *Incidents in the Life of a Slave Girl, Written by Herself,* published in 1861, takes the brutalities against women slaves described by Douglass to another level, that of deliberate sexual abuse and sexual ownership of the female slave, in this case, Jacobs herself. Jacobs's narrative is unique in that she changes her name and that of all the key players in her life in the narrative. In the preface to her slave narrative, Jacobs, using the pen name Linda Brent, attests to the veracity of her tale, and on behalf of enslaved women in the South, calls for the sympathy and assistance of free women in the North. This appeal to women by a woman is a first for the slave narrative genre and certainly sets Jacobs's narrative apart from that of Douglass and the other earlier narrative writers. This is also an appeal uniquely suited to the mid-19th-century American readership. Made up largely of women of some means and education, the readers of this time in history were accustomed to sentimental literature. Along with the plea for help, Jacobs also includes in her brief preface an explanation of her slow writing process, due to being in her situation as a woman on her own, left to her own devices to support her children. Such is the stuff of which sentimental literature is made, and such is the stuff certain to strike a chord of sympathy in the reader of Jacobs's time.

Following Jacobs/Brent's preface is an introduction "by the editor," in this case the famous abolitionist and women's rights activist Lydia Maria Child. Just as the other slave narrative authors discussion depended on the validation and support of white citizens and friends of means and stature in society, so did that of Jacobs, and just as having William Lloyd Garrison vouch for him was a coup for Douglass, so was having Child vouch for Jacobs a coup for her. Child's assistance was especially important to Jacobs because of the central topic she deals with in her slave narrative: that of the sexual abuse and ownership of an enslaved black woman by a Christian white male slaveholder. Without such support, Jacobs's tale would have been largely unbelievable, an affront to the white Christian female readers of the time, who would have had a very difficult time reconciling the reported behavior of that white Christian man with their own deep-seated beliefs in how Christian males acted or did not act. To help the case of believability, Child adds an appendix with testimony by the esteemed Amy Post, who was a member of the Society of Friends, commonly known as Quakers. The Quakers were indeed friends to the abolitionist movement and to escaped slaves. Post was also an especial friend to the escaped Jacobs, a friend who urged Jacobs to pen her narrative. Highly unusual for testimonials in a slave narrative, Child also includes in the appendix a statement by George W. Lowther, "a highly respectable colored citizen of Boston" (Jacobs 158), who attests to having known Jacobs from childhood and to knowing the circumstances of her sad tale well. The addition of a black voice as testimony stands as both unique and interesting in this slave narrative.

Testimonies aside, Jacobs's narrative supplies the reader with a chilling account of ownership and desperation that had not previously been seen in the slave narrative—or in any genre, for that matter. Jacobs begins her narrative by describing a fairly benign and idyllic early childhood. Jacobs describes her parents by shades of color, a new phenomenon in the slave narrative. While Douglass makes the reader aware of his biracial (or mulatto, using 19th-century terminology) heritage, he does not do this to the extent that Jacobs does. In the case of Jacobs's narrative, this distinction between shades of color clearly also becomes a distinction of class and privilege among members of the enslaved race. Her description of her family includes the admission that the all members of the family were enslaved, but also leaves the reader clear about the status of the family as one living much like any other of the majority race—almost a family of certain privilege, as it were. Beginning her narrative in this way allows Jacobs to immediately gain the sympathy of her 19th-century readers, who would have related to the intact family unit living together in the same way as were the majority of white families of their acquaintance. Jacobs's legal position in life is not clear to her until her mother's death, when Jacobs is six and sent to live in the home of her mistress. Still, Jacobs's life is a fairly good one; she enjoys kind treatment by this family that had looked upon her mother as more human than would have many slaveholders. It is when Jacobs is nearing her teenage years that her life takes a drastic and bitter turn: her mistress dies and wills Jacobs to the mistress's very young niece. Being sent to the Flint family (Flint being the pseudonym for the Norcom family in the book) begins the trauma that defines Jacobs's life in the narrative of her life as a slave. Almost immediately thereafter Jacobs's father dies, leaving her and her brother orphans as well as slaves of the Flint family. Their grandmother, who lived as independently as could be imagined for a woman of any color, let alone a black woman legally a slave, and who made her own living, vowed to be a parent to her grandchildren, and so she was—as much as was allowed by law and by the Flint family. Revealing such family tragedies and confirming the blockade that slavery put on permitting one family member to take care of others, even children, became an important revelation and a clever rhetorical method in the slave narrative, as it allowed for natural sympathy by the readers. With her honesty and her ability to write in the sentimental style of the day, Jacobs succeeds in bringing the reader to her side very early on in her narrative, cleverly setting the stage as a writer for the depth of sympathy necessary before she approaches the more horrific details of her life as a slave.

It is but a couple of years into Jacobs's residence with the Flint family that Dr. Flint first lets Jacobs know that he expects her to be obedient to him in all things, for he owns her in all ways. The results of his persistence and his inevitable power over her are many, not the least of which is the displeasure of the mistress of the house. In touching upon the jealousy experienced by a white mistress over the sexual attentions her husband shows toward a female slave, Jacobs opens up a critical topic heretofore untouched in the slave narrative genre. Powerless before her master, the female slave subject to such attentions had little in the way of ammunition in her arsenal of protection against her chastity and the wrath of her mistress. While the white mistress was also fairly powerless in the face of her husband's planned or executed sexual transgressions, she did possess the ability to make the female slave, and any offspring that slave might produce, miserable beyond that misery the slave and her children would already have felt in light of their situation. Jacobs shows an admirable level of courage in admitting such situations and thus opening them to the discussion and scrutiny of her readers, many of whom were abolitionists increasingly on the lookout for further proof of the evils of slavery. Part of this discussion inevitably led to the questioning of the morals of the female slave, even when she had been duly Christianized, as had her family members before her. There existed a tender and tentative line between the sympathetic reader's wish to take pity on the poor female slave and the reader's need to believe that no Christian white man, especially one of means, could possibly stoop to such perversions. In taking on the task of her slave narrative, Jacobs strikes at the exact center of such debate. In her case, that discussion becomes even more powerful due to the crux of Jacob's story: its veracity.

Jacobs, as Linda Brent, feels compelled to take drastic measures to keep her master from sexually abusing her. Begging the pardon of her readers and asserting that the slave woman cannot always be held to the same moral standards as the free woman, for to do so would be to put her life at greater risk, Jacobs relates the kindnesses visited upon her by the unmarried white neighbor, Mr. Sands (her pseudonym for Samuel Tredwell Sawyer). A desperate 15-year-old girl, Jacobs thinks it better to succumb to Mr. Sands's gentle overtures as a way of dissuading her master. Her hope is that Mr. Sands will eventually buy her freedom and will also free any children they may have. Jacobs does indeed become pregnant, twice, by Sands, but he does not buy her freedom. Any thoughts of such are dashed by Dr. Flint, who refuses to sell his property. When Jacobs introduces the reader to the extent of one slaveholder's perverse need to own his slave as fully as possible, she begins an important education into the psychological trauma of slavery with which many to this point had not yet been aware. Jacobs's trials lead her to the desperate measure of hiding in an attic crawl space of her grandmother's house, a space that allowed for minimal movement—no standing, no sitting allowed. Jacobs remains hidden away for several years while her grandmother, swearing innocence of her whereabouts, tends to the children. The reader certainly marvels at Jacobs's ability to remain quiet and prone in her coffin-like confines, but marvels perhaps even more at Jacobs's ability to see and hear her children through slight cracks in the boards of the house and yet remain silent, despite her aching heart, in order to secure a safe future for the entire family. Through trickery, Jacobs's children, as well as her brother, are sold to Sands, although they remain with their great-grandmother. All do indeed make it safely north eventually, Jacobs as a fugitive slave, but Jacobs's story is far from over. She still has the tale of Dr. Flint's continued pursuit of her, his death, and then the attempt of his now-grown daughter and her husband to reclaim Jacobs by seizing her from the North and returning her to their southern home. This pursuit is made possible by the passage of the Fugitive Slave Law, a law with which her readers would have still been contending. Much to the deep shame and sorrow of Jacobs, it is only through her northern friends' intervention by purchasing her from her pursuers that she is free of her former masters.

Among the issues Jacobs brings to the forefront in her narrative are slave insurrections and Christianity and slavery. Nat Turner's famous insurrection occurred in 1831 about 40 miles from Jacobs's hometown of Edenton, North Carolina. Much press was given to the horrific violence Turner and his gang of escaped slaves visited upon whites in the vicinity, and the white community in the South reacted with violence in turn. The point of view of slaves during this time was not actively sought. Jacobs, however, lends exactly that point of view to the historical perspective, making extremely clear the dangers that befell slaves throughout the Southern states in the aftermath of the insurrection. Her description of the violence done to her grandmother's house by lower-class white citizens who suddenly felt empowered by their ability to wreak havoc on anyone of color, in the name of justice and with the silent blessing of more powerful, wealthy white citizens, serves as a chilling account of the depths to which racism and prejudice could fall. Having already gained the sympathy of the reader for herself and her grandmother, the insurrection portion of her narrative adds to the necessary topics of discovery she offers her readers. She follows this scene with illustration of the reaction of the white clergy, who begin in earnest to renew one of their favorite tactics with slaves, to preach that God demands obedience of servants. Like Douglass before her, Jacobs serves a scathing diatribe against such Christianity, all the while making it clear that she considers herself a Christian, but like Douglass, a true rather than contrived Christian.

While Jacobs's narrative brings forth many important aspects of slavery to the reading public of her time, perhaps most important is her point of view as an enslaved woman struggling first to maintain her chastity then to save her children from the continued horrors of slavery. Though Jacobs does not have the horrific tales of physical abuse to share with the readers that Douglass and others had, what she does have is of critical importance. Psychologists have time and again proven that mental and emotional abuse can be more of a strain than physical abuse; Jacobs, through her pseudonym Linda Brent, proves just that. As she continually illustrates the abhorrence of knowing that one can be owned physically, emotionally, sexually—any way—by another during slavery, she makes the horrors of such clear to the reader, who cannot help but ponder what that type of control and feeling of ownership over another must do to another human being.

The popularity the slave narrative attained by the middle of the 19th century led to a romanticizing of the genre that in turn led to fictionalized accounts of slave narratives. Some of these fictions are now attributed to white writers who were attempting to profit in one way or another from the works. Some have been discovered in recent years by scholars of African American literature and then have been dismissed by others after further research and investigation. Such has been the case with *The Bondwoman's Narrative,* written by Hannah Craft in the 19th century and rediscovered in the late 20th century by scholar Henry Louis Gates Jr. Other white writers of the 19th century were also influenced by the slave narrative. Harriet Beecher Stowe rose to fame as "the little lady who started the big war" upon the publication of the 1852 *Uncle Tom's Cabin.* Stowe's novel draws on many of the devices used in the writing of slave narratives, although she never purported to be writing anything other than fiction and never presented herself as intimately knowledgeable about the life of a slave. It is interesting to note that Harriet Ann Jacobs approached the famous and respected Stowe for her assistance with the writing of her narrative. Finding Jacobs's tale of sexual abuse by her former master too incredible to be true, Stowe sought verification of the tale from Jacobs's dearest white friend, who had not yet been entrusted with Jacobs's tale. Stowe herself was not to be trusted by Jacobs after that.

Although not considered a true slave narrative, Harriet E. Wilson's *Our Nig* (1859) continues the slave narrative tradition with the autobiographical tale of a young African American girl of mixed parentage who is abandoned by her mother and left at the door of a cruel family that takes her in as an indentured servant at best, a slave at worst. The family's treatment of the young Frado is abominable, yet she is bound to them until she comes of age. Many parallels can be drawn between the revelations of the slave narratives and those of Wilson's story. Wilson also adds to the discussion of the hypocrisy of white Christians who preach one thing for themselves and another for those of other races. Especially important to Wilson's book is the fact that Frado is living in the North, not in the South, yet she is treated as abysmally as are her counterparts in the South. While this makes for interesting commentary and discussion in our contemporary age, it unfortunately led largely to disbelief in Wilson's own time, the time for which it was most critical that Wilson's message be heeded. Like the authors of the slave narratives, Wilson sought the acknowledgment of respected members of white society to help validate and sell her book. Unlike the others, though, Wilson did not have supporters with strong social influence. The preface Wilson includes in her book appeals to the generosity of readers to help her financially by purchasing her book; she speaks especially to her "colored brethren" (Wilson 3), something not done by the slave narrative authors.

Equally important to the genre of the slave narrative is the work done by the Federal Works Progress Administration in the 1930s to collect evidence of the oral histories of former slaves. Transcripts of interviews with these former slaves as well as recordings of the interviews still exist, and though not written slave narratives as are those of Equiano, Prince, Douglass, and Jacobs, the oral tradition adds strength, validity, and vitality to the genre of written narratives. Many of the same themes treated by the slave narrative writers are also treated by the oral narrators, with the added attraction and poignancy of being able to hear the voices of some of these former slaves.

For every slave narrative that has been published and forgotten, forgotten and rediscovered, contemplated, discussed, and studied over the years, there are surely others still waiting to be found. The slave narrative has come to be viewed as a fluid entity, capable of surprising and enlightening with each new discovery. The slave narrative authors we have come to know well share similar themes: the inherent humanity of the enslaved African/African American; the dispelling of the happy slave myth—for who does not instinctively love and yearn for freedom?—the issue of mixed race, as perpetuated by the violence of the male slaveholder against the female slave; the hypocrisy of self-professed Christians and the yearning of those enslaved for a true bond to a good and loving God; the brutality that one person seeing herself as superior to another is capable of visiting upon that other; and the ability of one person to convince himself of a right to complete and total ownership over another. While these themes speak clearly and significantly to the era of slavery in America, they also continue to speak to contemporary struggles with race issues in the United States.

FURTHER READING

Berlin, Ira, Marc Favreau, and Steven F. Miller, eds. *Remembering Slavery: African Americans Talk about Their Personal Experiences of Slavery and Freedom.* New York: New Press, 1998.

Equiano, Olaudah. *The Interesting Narrative of the Life of Olaudah Equiano, Written by Himself.* Ed. and Intro. by Robert J. Allison. Boston: Bedford, 1995.

Jacobs, Harriet A. *Incidents in the Life of a Slave Girl, Written by Herself.* Ed. Jean Fagan Yellin. Cambridge: Harvard UP, 1987.

Six Women's Slave Narratives. Intro. by William L. Andrews. New York: Oxford UP, 1988.

Slave Narratives. Notes by William L. Andrews and Henry Louis Gates Jr. New York: Library of America, 2000.

Terry Novak

W.E.B. Du Bois, called the father of Pan-Africanism for his work on behalf of the emerging African nations, devoted his life to the struggle for equality for African Americans and all people of color. (Library of Congress)

The Souls of Black Folk

Since its publication more than 100 years ago, *The Souls of Black Folk* has provided readers with an intimate glimpse not only into its author's, W.E.B Du Bois's (1868–1963) life, but also into the complex, conflicting, and competing psychological, material, and ideological conditions that African Americans survived through, triumphed over, and continue to endure. Notwithstanding the facts that the Emancipation Proclamation freed the formerly enslaved African Americans, the Thirteenth Amendment abolished slavery, the Fourteenth Amendment ensured due process and equal protection under the law, and the Fifteenth Amendment guaranteed black men voting rights, in the 30-year period following slavery, African Americans painstakingly realized that the fetters of racism extended beyond chattel slavery. The end of Reconstruction, the rise of the Ku Klux Klan and other white supremacist organizations, the revocation of voting rights through literacy tests, grandfather clauses, and physical violence, the reinforcement of segregation through the 1896 *Plessy v. Ferguson* Supreme Court decision, and the increase in lynchings and race riots undoubtedly reinforced America's commitment to racism and inequality. This historical and political climate contextualizes why, in *The Negro in American Life and Thought: The Nadir 1877–1901* (1954), historian Rayford Logan has termed the turn of the 20th century the nadir of race relations in American history. Despite America's persistent unwillingness to extend to African Americans the democratic ideals the Constitution promises, they have remained optimistic about obtaining full citizenship rights and opportunities in America. *The Souls of Black Folk* captures these rich and complicated aspects of American history, rendering legible the multiple experiences and cultural practices that constitute African American history and culture. Inasmuch as the book records a history past, it prophesies a future coming; while *The Souls of Black Folk*, from beginning to end, remains entrenched in history-based sociological, political, and cultural analyses, the text uses that history to project an empowered future. In doing so, it articulates the aspirations and longings that African Americans had had and continued to have, as well as the tangible ways in which African Americans have contributed to the economic, spiritual, and cultural development and progress of American society.

Interesting Facts about Du Bois

Du Bois was the first African American to earn a PhD at Harvard University. He finished his dissertation, "The Suppression of the Slave Trade," in 1895.

After publishing The Souls of Black Folk *in 1903, Du Bois continued his goal to enfranchise African Americans by founding the Niagara Movement in 1905 and working with the newly founded National Association for the Advancement of Colored People (NAACP) in 1909. Du Bois's work with the NAACP, as the director of publicity and research, gave him a prominent voice in the early 20th-century African American Civil Rights Movement. During this time, he also founded and edited* Crisis.

Between 1920 and his death in 1963, Du Bois involved himself in a variety of projects that aimed to improve America, African America, and Africa. After the NAACP dismissed him in 1945, he became the chairman of the Council on African Affairs. As a result of Du Bois's growing concern for Africa and Pan-Africanism, as well as his disenchantment with the U.S. government, which accused him of being a communist and denied him a passport until 1958, he renounced his American citizenship in 1962 and became a citizen of Ghana. He died in Ghana in 1963 and is buried there.

The progressive ideas in this seemingly radical text garnered both hostile and receptive responses. For example, the famed and prophetic opening line of the book, "the problem of the 20th century is the problem of the color line" (3), foregrounds America's racist ideologies and practices as central to the work. In an equally provocative way, Du Bois unequivocally asserts that America's economic, social, and cultural prosperities are all predicated on African Americans' labor. And finally, Du Bois, unlike his contemporary Booker T. Washington, demands immediate voting rights for African American males in southern states, where white Americans invested their own power in denying African Americans rights. Such arguments did not elicit laudatory reviews from white Americans. In Georgia, for example, the *Atlanta Journal Constitution* (*AJC*) reports that *The Souls of Black Folk* "is the thought of a negro of northern education who has lived among his brethren of the South, yet who cannot fully feel the meaning of some things which these brethren know by instinct—and which the southern-bred white knows by a similar instinct—certain things which are by both accepted as facts" (*Chicken Bones*). It is not surprising per se that the column writer resists changing a system, in the South in particular, that expects and trains black people to occupy subservient positions and to be contented in so doing. The paradigm shift for which Du Bois calls subverts the unearned privilege that keeps the racial power dynamic institutionalized, and the column writer therefore scoffs at *The Souls of Black Folk*. The language the writer uses, however, illustrates how ingrained and naturalized these racist ideas and social practices were. By using the word "instinct" to describe socially constructed relationships between white and black people in the South, the writer perniciously argues that the social hierarchy is biologically determined and therefore socially immutable. In other words, pseudoscientific racism laces itself throughout the argument. The *Nashville Banner* furthers the *AJC*'s sentiment, arguing, "This book is dangerous for the Negro to read, for it will only excite discontent and fill his imagination with things that do not exist, or things that should not bear upon his mind" (*Chicken Bones*). Although Du Bois's attitude toward race relations changes later in his life, in 1903 he believed that the racial attitudes that perpetuated slavery and persisted in America following emancipation could be changed through a reeducation of Americans. At the heart of *The Banner*'s criticism of *The Souls of Black Folk* lies the fear that African Americans might read this book, follows its suggestions, become empowered, and dismantle the racial hierarchy. While Du Bois would later discover that such a transformation would not readily come, he sincerely believed that his text would at least inaugurate the necessary dialogue for that change to begin. Together, the *AJC* and *Nashville Banner* stories representatively elucidate a particular type of southern racist ideology that Du Bois hoped *The Souls of Black Folk* would counteract.

Within African American and northern contexts, however, the book receives praise for its astuteness, acuity, and audacity. Composer of "Lift Every Voice and Sing," popularly known as the "Negro National Anthem," and author of *The Autobiography of an Ex-Colored Man* (1912), James Weldon Johnson proclaims that *The Souls of Black Folk* "had a greater effect upon and within the Negro race in America than any other single book published in this country since *Uncle Tom's Cabin*" (Johnson 282). *The Souls of Black Folk*'s vestiges emerge in the works of Du Bois's contemporaries, including Johnson's own *The Autobiography of an Ex-Colored Man,* as well as those of several other African American writers, including Jean Toomer, Ralph Ellison, and Toni Morrison, to name a few. About *The Souls of Black Folk,* the *New York Times* appends that it "throws light upon the complexities of the negro problem, for it shows the key note of at least some negro aspiration is still the abolition of the social color-line" (*Souls* 205). As Johnson and the *New York Times* suggest, *The Souls of Black Folk* inaugurated in-depth discussions about African American and American life and race relationships that up until its publication had not been as thoroughly, candidly, and systematically discussed. Although several abolitionist texts, autobiographical narratives of formerly enslaved African Americans, essays, and sermons had illuminated the persistence of racial discord, *The Souls of Black Folk* became one of a kind in its formal structure and explicit demands.

Structurally, *The Souls of Black Folk* is divided into 14 chapters, some of which had been published previously as individual essays, and addresses a range of topics, including racism, family, education, history, culture, and politics, that are especially important to African American empowerment efforts. While each of these issues remains meaningful, Du Bois's articulation that the problem of the 20th century is the problem of the color line, definition of the concept of double-consciousness, promotion of the idea of the Talented Tenth, and critique of Booker T. Washington's political strategies and decisions canonize the text as a paradigmatic manifesto of black life and intellectual history. Moreover, in terms of literary devices, Du Bois frames each chapter with musical scores, inverts the ascent narrative commonly deployed in African American literature, and manipulates the literary conventions that typify emancipatory narratives.[1] Through his inversion of tropes that typically characterized African American literature, Du Bois situates *The Souls of Black Folk* firmly within African American literary production, paying homage to the already-forming tradition, while charting new directions for its future development. African American literary texts in particular, and other cultural texts more generally, have continued to invoke Du Bois and the ideas he proffers with *The Souls of Black Folk*.

Du Bois's prophetic declaration that "the problem of the 20th century is the problem of the color line—the relation of the darker to the lighter races of men in Asia and Africa, in American and the islands of the sea" (*Souls* 9) foregrounds racial imperialism as a global issue that adversely affects all the communities it infects. Although Du Bois focuses on race relations in the United States, he acknowledges the ubiquity of colonialism, racism, and imperialism throughout the world. His declaration nevertheless remains prophetic in the 21st century, where racism, while having improved, remains a long way from being solved. Indeed, in as much as *The Souls of Black Folk* outlines the historical problems that have caused and maintained a problematic color line, it also proposes a variety of solutions, including voting rights and a liberal arts education, that Du Bois believed would alleviate or outright ameliorate the problem. Du Bois's optimism declines, however, and as he sees America's continued unwillingness to live up to its democratic principles, he becomes progressively less faithful to the view that education can fundamentally alter racist attitudes and practices.

Du Bois's notion of double consciousness, which results at least partially because of the color line, explains the psychological effects that racism has on black subjects, and demonstrates the coping mechanisms blacks have used to resist such debilitating experiences. Double consciousness is a psychological state in which black subjects realize that they have two seemingly distinct selves, one black and one American, both of which remain at odds in a racist American society; these two selves must repair or reconcile the psychological rifts that they experience in a country where both law and custom attempt to deny African Americans their citizenship and personhood. As Du Bois explains, "it is a peculiar sensation, this double-consciousness, this sense of always looking at one's self through the eyes of others, of measuring one's soul by the tape of a world that looks on in amused contempt and pity. One ever feels his two-ness,—an American, a Negro; two souls, two thoughts, two unreconciled strivings; two warring ideals in one dark body, whose dogged strength alone keeps it from being torn asunder" (9). As Du Bois's own words reveal, double-consciousness, while providing African Americans unique insight into the American experience, is not a preferred state of mind. On the contrary, it is a defense or coping mechanism that African Americans enact to withstand the psychological fracturing that racism might cause. Without it, the persistent contemptuous white pitying gaze would succeed in doing what chattel slavery had aimed to do—break African Americans' spirits. Du Bois emphasizes this notion of African American resilience here, as well as when he urges African Americans not to follow back-to-Africa emigration movements.

Arguing for African Americans' rightful inclusion into the American body politic, for example, Du Bois also suggests that it is African Americans' very exclusion, their Negro status, that gives them the fortitude to endure a psychological state that might otherwise cause their demise. The result, or argu-ably the consequence, of this double consciousness is the gift of a veil, a second sight that provides African Americans with special insights into race relations within American society. It is from behind this veil that Du Bois writes, and it is behind this veil that Du Bois hopes to bring his audience, both black and white. By revealing this intimate aspect of black people's lives, Du Bois strives, as he articulates in his introductory forethought, to gain empathy that will incite change. For Du Bois, neither pity nor inaction is an acceptable option.

Although Du Bois identifies white and black people as working coopera-tively to better the social and political ills African Americans face, he outlines programs of action for African Americans in particular. Specifically, he calls for a talented tenth, an elite group of educated black men who would lead the African American masses to political and economic enfranchisement. Du Bois's notion of a talented tenth reflects his belief that there is an unequal dis-tribution of materials, opportunities, time, and talents within African Ameri-can communities. Interestingly enough, his talented tenth program attempted to diminish these gaps, while arguably needing them in order to function. As articulated here, for example, at no point does everyone get to become talented; some sort of stratification persists. After slavery's end, the dispari-ties between African American communities became increasingly clear as the government and benevolent societies worked to figure out how to integrate African Americans into a society that had purposefully and systematically excluded them. Du Bois proffered that education was the key tool to trans-forming Africa America, yet firmly understood that educational inequity was difficult, if not impossible, to conquer.

Recognizing the incongruity in schools in the South following emanci-pation, as well as the disparity in educational preparedness among black people in general, Du Bois conceded that only a select portion of African Americans would obtain a liberal arts education. This select group then would be responsible for leading what we might rightfully call Civil Rights Movements. As Du Bois elaborates in a separately published article, "The Talented Tenth" (1903):

> Men of America, the problem is plain before you.... Education and work are the levers to uplift a people. Work alone will not do it unless inspired by the right ideals and guided by intelligence. Education must not simply teach work—it must teach Life. The Talented Tenth of the Negro race must be made leaders of thought and missionaries of culture among their people. No others can do this work and Negro colleges must train men for it. The Negro race, like all other races, is going to be saved by its exceptional men. (861)

As Du Bois's comments elucidate, he counteracts any notion that African Americans are incapable of succeeding in America. On the contrary, their men, like the men of all other races, will lead the journey toward empowerment. While the chapter summaries will demonstrate Du Bois's at least nominal understanding of how gender compounds experiences of racial disenfranchisement, it seems that he remains invested in the notion that men are best suited to be leaders.

Contemporary critics of Du Bois argue that the concept of the talented tenth is elitist and sexist, thereby calling into question its effectiveness as a viable political solution to the problems affecting black men and women. As black feminist critics have observed, for example, this idea reinforced patriarchal gender notions, and specifically limited the role of black leadership and racial uplift to black men. Such a notion is ironic, if not preposterous, because as Du Bois knew, through his general knowledge and specific relationships with African American women activists Anna Julia Cooper and Ida B. Wells, African American women had begun the Black Women's Club Movement. Arguably, the Club Movement, demanding dignity and respect, was one of the largest racial uplift movements in the 19th century. This tendency to fight racism, while condoning or promoting sexism, either explicitly or implicitly, led Anna Julia Cooper to conclude: "while our men (black men) seem thoroughly abreast of the times on almost every other subject, when they strike the woman question they drop back into sixteenth century logic" (Cooper 75). Whereas some critics have argued that Du Bois's treatment of women in *The Souls of Black Folk* is sincere and sympathetic, others have maintained that Du Bois's treatment of black women falls short of the real analysis that he might have offered. Accordingly, critics have disagreed as to whether or not to categorize Du Bois as a sexist, or to regard his analysis as a reflection of the broader cultural time period. In "Profeminism and Gender Elites: W.E.B. Du Bois, Anna Julia Cooper, and Ida B. Wells Barnett," feminist Joy James identifies Du Bois as a profeminist, one who opposes gender oppression and patriarchy. At the same time, she maintains he has a masculinist view, which replicates masculine values and privileges that contribute to women's oppression. James maintains that this tension between masculinism and profeminism characterizes Du Bois's writings more generally. In "The Souls of Black Men," cultural critic Hazel Carby is less forgiving than James, arguing that in *The Souls of Black Folk,* Du Bois deliberately promotes male privilege and domination.

Furthermore, as cultural critic and philosopher Cornel West reminds, the notion of a talented tenth does not include the majority of African Americans, who must be a part of any African American civil rights project. By definition, the talented tenth excludes 90 percent of the African American population. Requiring a select group of leaders to train the masses, this model does not promote cooperative politics between the leader and the masses, and presumes that the leaders have an interest in uplifting the masses. But Du Bois himself was not oblivious to the notion's elitism, for in 1948 he reconsiders: "When I came out of college into the world of work, I realized it was quite possible that my plan of training a talented tenth might put in control and power, a group of selfish, self-indulgent, well-to-do men, whose basic interest in solving the Negro Problem was personal; personal freedom and unhampered enjoyment and use of the world, without any real care, or certainly no arousing care, as to what became of the mass of American Negroes, or of the mass of any people. My Talented Tenth, I could see, might result in a sort of interracial free-for-all, with the devil taking the hindmost and the foremost taking anything they could lay hands on" (West 96). Although Du Bois never explicitly names the gender bias inscribed within his definition as having been problematic, he demonstrates an understanding at least of the notion's limiting parameters. This later reflection admits his realization that the talented tenth might have been more interested in further enhancing its privilege than helping the overwhelming majority of disenfranchised and disempowered black communities. Notwithstanding these valid criticisms leveled against Du Bois's notion of a talented tenth and the concept's inherent difficulties in implementation, it provided a solution for obtaining the education and leadership African American communities sorely needed. Furthermore, it emphasized the importance of education (literacy) to freedom and rights, a concept that has governed African American writings and literature throughout slavery and well into the 20th century.

While the concepts of double consciousness, the veil, the talented tenth, and the color line certainly have helped to maintain *The Souls of Black Folk*'s iconic status in African American Studies, Du Bois's castigation of Booker T. Washington's political strategies and ideologies is one of the most widely discussed aspects of the text. Analyzing *The Souls of Black Folk,* however, illuminates the common misperception that Washington and Du Bois directly oppose one another on issues of political, economic, and cultural enfranchisement. Author of his autobiographical narrative *Up from Slavery* (1875) and principal of the Tuskegee Institute, Booker T. Washington became (in)famous for his Atlanta Exposition speech (1895), which is often referred to as the "Atlanta Compromise Speech." Here, Washington concedes to white southern politicians the idea that African Americans do not need voting rights until they became more politically savvy and could exercise those rights responsibly. In the interim, he felt that African Americans should learn a trade and build their own resources, while learning politics. His assertion, "In all things purely social we can be as separate as the fingers, yet one as the hand in all things essential to mutual progress" (Washington 585), garnered support from white segregationists, earned him the title of accommodationist, and aroused disdain from northern African American integrationists such as Du Bois. Washington knew, to invoke the language of the previously discussed *AJC* article, "by instinct" the relationship that black and white people were to have. Washington's desire for racial progress, financial support for antisegregationist organizations, and leadership and commitment to a historically black college make it difficult to dismissively classify him as an accommodationist. Even if one disagrees with the public tactics he used in his 1895 speech, one has to consider the possibility that Washington appealed to white racism as a way to obtain the financial support that he needed to run Tuskegee. In doing so, he reinforces racist perceptions of blacks in white minds. Yet, he uses the Tuskegee Institute to train blacks who could later dismantle that system. Rather than offering a sympathetic reading of Washington's "Atlanta Compromise

Speech," this analysis illuminates the complex politics undergirding Washington's empowerment agenda.

In *The Souls of Black Folk*, Du Bois clarifies his perturbation with Washington's politics. Du Bois's concern originates from his belief that voting rights specifically, and lawfully protected rights more generally, are essential for African Americans to be enfranchised. If African Americans lack rights, or to borrow a phrase from slavery, do not have any rights that a white man (woman, child, or law) has to respect/uphold, building up resources seems futile; and as Du Bois himself wonders, "what good is it to build one's own home if that house could be lawfully usurped at any time?" (*Souls* 39–40). This criticism certainly does not suggest that Du Bois is against an industrial education; inasmuch as Du Bois believes that only a select portion of the population would/could obtain a college education, and that African Americans should be productive citizens who take responsibility for themselves, he supports industrial education. He does not, however, believe that African Americans should be limited only to an industrial/vocational education or that voting rights ought to be delayed any further. For, as Du Bois sincerely believes, the ballot will help African Americans to achieve their enfranchisement.

Whereas the previous overview has introduced the key concepts that have helped *The Souls of Black Folk* to maintain its iconic status in the general field of African American studies, the following analysis focuses particularly on the ways in which it has shaped and was shaped by African American literary studies. *The Souls of Black Folk* has had a profound influence on the African American literary tradition, perhaps functioning as a model for a significant portion of the literature written after its publication. Literary critic Arnold Rampersad confirms the pervasiveness of *The Souls of Black Folk*'s impact, arguing, "If all the nation's literature may stem from one book, as Hemingway implied about *The Adventures of Huckleberry Finn*, then it can accurately be said that all of Afro-American literature of a creative nature has proceeded from Du Bois' comprehensive statement on the nature of people in *The Souls of Black Folk*" (Rampersad, "Slavery and the Literary" 89). Reinforcing Rampersad's idea that *The Souls of Black Folk* is a literary progenitor, literary critic Cheryl Wall further maintains that its "pre-eminent statement of modern black consciousness" contributes to its having "unsurpassed influence among texts" (217). This influence, as Robert Gooding-Williams explains, is precisely because of the text's ability to use the literary art to make a political statement: *The Souls of Black Folk* "conceptualizes these modes of authority (literary and political) as convergent, which is one reason why appreciating Du Bois' text as literary art is essential to appreciating its political influence" (205). Gooding-Williams's articulation of the interrelationship between arts and politics reflects Du Bois's own point of view that art must have political significance. Eschewing the notion that literature must be apolitical, for example, Du Bois has elsewhere opined: "All art is propaganda and ever must be" ("Criteria of Negro Art" 66). To that end, the formal techniques that Du Bois employs in the text also help to offer political critiques and to establish the text's literary authority. Du Bois's use of African American expressive culture, including music and rhetoric, as well as European musical scores, and allegory, allusion, and the picturesque create multilayering and multidisciplinarity that contribute to the text's iconic stature.

While analyses of *The Souls of Black Folk* have positioned it as a founding text of 20th century African American literature, the text is indebted to the 19th century emancipatory narrative. The formal features of the emancipatory narrative, for example, often contain a preface, where a white person (benefactor) attests to the authenticity of the narrative. The authenticator verifies that the author indeed wrote the text, that the details are accurate, and that the only changes he/she has made have been stylistic. These prefaces are then followed by a second preface by the author who articulates his/her reasons and goals for writing. Although Du Bois's text does not possess an authenticating preface, the faming "forethought" alludes to this tradition. Appealing to a sympathetic and engaged audience, a "Gentle Reader," Du Bois asks the readers, including his white audience, to "receive [his] little book in all due charity," "forgive mistake and foible for sake of the faith and passion that is in [him]," and "seek the grain of truth hidden there" (*Souls* 3). This opening, undoubtedly, is similar to those narratives of formerly enslaved African Americans,[2] whose authors beg forgiveness for their putative stylistic deficiencies and enlist the readers' empathy and action. Take for example Harriet Jacobs's plea at the beginning of *Incidents in the Life of a Slave Girl, Written by Herself* (1861), where Jacobs writes, "I wish I were more competent to the task I have undertaken. But I trust my readers will excuse deficiencies in consideration of circumstances.... But I do earnestly desire to arouse the women of the North to a realizing sense of the condition of two millions of women at the South.... I want to add my testimony to that of abler pens to convince the people of the Free States of what Slavery really is" (120). Despite differences in historical period and circumstances, both authors employ a sentimental apologetic tone to elicit support from the reader. The significant difference, however, is that, whereas Jacobs's text has an authenticating document, Du Bois's text is self-authenticated.

Moreover, Du Bois uses black American spirituals, which he prefers to calls sorrow songs, to frame each chapter of the text, thus foregrounding black American music as an essential component of American (literary) culture. As Du Bois himself explains, "they [enslaved African Americans] that worked in darkness sang songs in the olden days—sorrow songs—for they were weary at heart. And so before each thought that I have written in this book, I have set a phrase, a haunting echo of these weird old songs which the souls of the black slave spoke to men" (177). As Du Bois insinuates, these songs bear witness to the enslaved African Americans' ability to maintain hope and dignity in a system that intended to strip them of their personhood. These songs, therefore, are both "the sole American music" and "the most beautiful expression of human experience" (178); they record both the history of enslavement and the will to triumph over it. Beyond this point, these songs grapple with the emergent discourses in African American protestant theology. Relying on biblical tropes, stories, and archetypes, the sorrow songs depict the image of an omnipotent, justice-seeking God who will liberate oppressed peoples. Enslaved African Americans, then, sang the songs because of their multiple significations. They were religious and secular, focusing on contemporary material conditions as well as spiritual afterlife ones. The broad cultural significance of the sorrow songs challenges extant notions that enslaved African Americans sang these songs because they enjoyed their status as chattel. Despite the success of the Fisk Jubilee singers, whose soulful renditions of these sorrow songs throughout America helped them to raise enough money to construct the school's first permanent building, Jubilee Hall, Americans generally misunderstood or had limited understandings of these songs' multiple meanings.

Interpretations of the spirituals as testaments to enslaved African Americans' happiness, as well as minstrel caricatures of the songs, demonstrate how American society denigrated this particular form of cultural expression. Despite the hope embedded within the songs, "they are the music of an unhappy people, of children of disappointment; they tell of death and suffering and unvoiced longings toward a truer world, of misty wanderings and hidden ways" (179). Reinforcing the multilayeredness of the sorrow songs' meanings, Du Bois illustrates how the spirituals employ allusions to effectively mask their double meaning and help to subvert the existing order. Take, for example, the spiritual, "Swing Low, Sweet Chariot." Although one might argue that it is otherworldly, that is, it focuses on an afterlife in heaven but does not consider the contemporary experience of slavery as problematic, such a limited interpretation of this spiritual neglects the worldly focus. While the promise of a Christian resurrection pervades this song, and the spirituals more generally, the song is also deeply embedded with contemporary meaning and symbolism. As scholars have aptly demonstrated, the song also provides information about escape routes from slavery—the chariot is a person coming to lead the African Americans out of their current bondage into a promised land of freedom—the North. Besides their historical and cultural significances, the spirituals embedded in Du Bois's text reflect their broader importance within the context of African American literature, which had oral beginnings that the spirituals began.[3]

The musicality and aurality of The Souls of Black Folk situate it squarely within the larger African American literary tradition, reflecting the intimate relationship that exists between oral and written forms of communication in the literary tradition. Whereas Frederick Douglass's Narrative of the Life of Frederick Douglass, an American Slave, Written by Himself (1845) discusses the spirituals and their significance to enslaved African Americans' lives, Du Bois's text explores their formal qualities, as well as connecting the spirituals to a larger cultural context. Following Du Bois, and extending musical forms to include the blues, jazz, and gospel, James Weldon Johnson's The Autobiography of an Ex-Colored Man (1912), Jean Toomer's Cane (1923), Ralph Ellison's Invisible Man (1951), Gayl Jones's Corregidora (1975), Toni

Morrison's *Song of Solomon* (1977), and Toni Morrison's *Jazz* (1992) all are examples of texts that self-consciously integrate different musical forms into the texts, and consider how those forms shape the texts' overall meaning in a broader cultural context. Building on the motifs that Du Bois employs, these texts often revise the musical image, reflecting different cultural contexts and concerns.[4]

Furthermore, Du Bois's concern with double consciousness, the recognition of one's self as Other and how that identification informs one's self-understanding, inaugurates an interrogation of identity formation in African American literature, for which texts remain indebted to *The Souls of Black Folk*. For example, contemporary writer Toni Morrison's entire corpus of work can be said to engage the double (triple, quadruple) consciousness. In particular, her earliest book, *The Bluest Eye* (1970), and her second novel, *Sula* (1973), examine racial, gender, and sexual triple consciousnesses that shape young black girls' self-images. Earlier African American letters, during the Harlem Renaissance, examine a similar motif. Nella Larsen's *Quicksand* (1928) and *Passing* (1929) show that the protagonists understand themselves through their perceptions of race, class, gender, and sexuality, which are sometimes at war with each other. In both Adrienne Kennedy's and August Wilson's respective plays, *Funny House of a Negro* (1964) and *Fences* (1985), an analogous interrogation drives the plot. Undoubtedly, this list could extend further, but demonstrates Cornel West's notion that the modifier double in the term double consciousness inadequately grasps the multiple categories that mold people's identities.

When *The Souls of Black Folk* celebrated its 100th year of publication in 2003, publishing houses reprinted anniversary issues of the text, academic organizations held conferences that examined the text's continued impact, public intellectuals went on NPR to discuss its lasting effect, and scholarly journals and university presses alike published new essays that analyzed the book using contemporary theoretical paradigms and methodologies. These productions, both symbolically and materially, attest to the book's initial importance and lasting significance. Du Bois's analysis has proven itself useful to people interested in African American studies and should to those interested in American studies as well. The book's continued presence across disciplines and relevance to contemporary culture suggests that in 2103, on its 200th year anniversary, its iconic stature will not have waned. Undoubtedly, the institutionalization of African American studies as an academic discipline in the late 1960s has contributed to making Du Bois and *The Souls of Black Folk* a founding figure and text of this discipline. As its first century in existence demonstrates, both the text and its author are central figures within American history, culture, and thought. But the optimistic tone and hope that characterizes *The Souls of Black Folk* mutates by the end of Du Bois's career. Continued racism and failure to adhere to the country's democratic ideals impacted even the man who arguably was most committed to African Americans' subscribing to America's ideals. In the 21st century, where progress has been made, there exists a cautionary tale from *The Souls of Black Folk;* improved conditions are not solved problems. A warring consciousness can withstand only so much.

CHAPTER SUMMARIES

The first chapter of *The Souls of Black Folk,* "Of Our Spiritual Strivings," recounts a personal encounter that introduced Du Bois to racism, and frames this incident as awakening his racial consciousness that had until that point remained unconscious. As an elementary school student, Du Bois attempts to give his white female classmate a visiting card as a sign of his affection. Her refusal to accept the card because he is black, as well as the accompanying contemptuous gaze she gives, compels Du Bois to wonder: how does it feel to be a problem? Yet, more accurately stated, Du Bois considers how it feels to be *perceived* as a problem? This distinction is important because it emphasizes the fact that Du Bois never accepts the notion that he is a problem. Rather, his whole notion of double consciousness considers the relationship between perception and reality, and recognizes that his treatment is based on that perception. Following this personal anecdote, Du Bois defines the concepts of double consciousness and the veil, articulates why voting rights are important to African Americans' enfranchisement, and argues for African Americans' rightful place in the American body politic despite their continued disenfranchisement.

Chapter 2, "Of the Dawn of Freedom," explores the economic, social, and political conditions that enslaved African Americans found themselves in immediately preceding the Civil War, as well as in the years following. By no means does Du Bois romanticize African Americans' living conditions prior to the Civil War. By contrasting life before the war with life after it, however, Du Bois demonstrates how the failed promises of freedom struck African Americans who had envisioned significantly altered material conditions in the wake of emancipation. Honing his attention on The Freedmen's Bureau, Du Bois particularly analyzes how the bureau's lack of financial and material resources rendered its project of assisting African Americans ineffective. Moreover, Du Bois argues persuasively that the expectations of the bureau were unrealistic and that, from the outset, it was set up to fail. Charged with the responsibility of supervising all formerly enslaved African Americans, the Freedmen's Bureau established schools, functioned as a legal protector and arbiter, recorded and filed vital statistics, and helped to secure employment. However, with its structural limitations, that is, funding and staffing shortages, and resistance from white southerners, the Freedmen's Bureau ceased to exist after 1870 and the freed African Americans' dreams of full citizenship remained deferred.

Chapter 3, "Of Mr. Booker T. Washington and Others," argues that Booker T. Washington's political strategy of accommodation will ultimately undermine African Americans' political progress because it will not grant

African Americans any rights or property that the law protects. Du Bois demonstrates that he is not against Washington's notion of an industrial education, for industrial education will provide African Americans who do not obtain a liberal arts education with a viable means to work and be productive citizens. Rather, he disdains the notion that an industrial education is the *only* type of education that African Americans should obtain. Furthermore, he highlights the irony of Washington's dismissive attitude about the usefulness of a liberal arts education by arguing that it is through a liberal arts education that teachers are trained to run the Tuskegee Institute that Washington leads. Although this chapter certainly criticizes what Du Bois views as Washington's counterprogressive politics, it also commends Washington for encouraging personal responsibility and strong work ethics as essential to racial self-help ideas. Although Washington and Du Bois disagree on strategy, they agree that African Americans need to work to improve their social, political, and economic statuses.

Chapter 4, "Of the Meaning of Progress," shifts Du Bois's focus from a discussion of black men to an examination of the specific ways in which eclipsed opportunity affects black women and their strivings. Recounting his experience of meeting families while attending a teacher's institute in Tennessee, Du Bois memorializes Josie, a young black woman who dies as a consequence of her family's size and correlative poverty. In Du Bois's representation of Josie, her responsibilities to her family and community, and her corresponding willingness to sacrifice herself, ultimately cause her premature death. Through this characterization of Josie's life and death, Du Bois criticizes how unbalanced gender expectations within families and societies prevent Josie from fulfilling her dreams and aspirations. For example, as a woman, Josie is expected to be a caregiver for her brothers and sisters in ways that her brothers are not. In adhering to these gender roles, Josie relinquishes her dreams and perhaps unknowingly accepts her impending demise. In doing so, Josie ultimately symbolizes the true face of underrealized dreams and aspirations in a society that limits the possibilities and quality of life for black people. By casting Josie as the true face of underrealized dreams, Du Bois suggests that gender and class statuses further complicate the racial oppression she experiences. Unlike his discussion of black men's eclipsed opportunities, however, Du Bois does not call for an end to gender oppression per se. Yet, this discussion of Josie perhaps explains why some critics resist classifying Du Bois as sexist.

Chapter 5, "Of the Wings of Atalanta," invokes a maiden of Greek mythology, Atalanta, to critique the greed, the mammonism, that Du Bois claims plagues the South. Consistent with European Enlightenment theories, Du Bois argues that education can compel citizens to be better people and eschew the temptation of greed. For this reason, he maintains that the rise of universities in and throughout the South will counteract this cultural trend. Of particular interest in this chapter is Du Bois's assertion that not all black men are destined for college and that some ought to get an industrial education. This assertion not only corroborates the point that Du Bois is not wholly against vocational education, but also anticipates his notion of a talented tenth, an elite group of black men who would obtain a liberal arts education and then cultivate the masses.

Chapter 6, "Of the Training of Black Men," traces the development of Negro schools, criticizing what Du Bois deems inefficiencies and short-comings within those systems in particular, and American education more generally. Du Bois argues that schools must train men to become leaders in their communities and to train other men. Noting the professions that black graduates of historically black colleges and universities like Hampton, Tuskegee, Fisk, and historically white colleges and universities like Harvard, Yale, and Oberlin have undertaken, Du Bois reinforces the centrality of education to the uplift and advancement of African Americans. As the chapter title suggests, Du Bois conceptualizes this leadership in particularly masculinist terms.

Chapter 7, "Of the Black Belt," compares the beauty of certain places in Georgia, including Atlanta and Albany, with the destituteness of other counties like Dougherty to highlight the disparity between black and white people's resources. The richness of land in the white part of Doughterty County further contrasts with the hardness of the soil in the black counties, where one-room cabins house entire families. This narration of his drive through Georgia provides a statistical and sociological analysis of the economic and structural barriers that keep African Americans economically disempowered and foregrounds the arguments that Du Bois explains further in chapter 8.

Chapter 8, "Of the Quest of the Golden Fleece," extends the argument Du Bois proffers in chapter 7, focusing on the particular ways in which housing markets and sharecropping contribute to African Americans' economic plights. For Du Bois, houses represent the more pervasive economic conditions of a people; consequently, one-room cabins underscore the economic despair that African Americans face. Furthermore, Du Bois maintains that sharecropping perpetuates African American disenfranchisement by providing meager wages, and forcing African Americans to remain forever dependent on white employers, who hold earnings to pay for the land and tools. That landlords require sharecroppers to pay them in cotton further exacerbates this situation, because cotton is the most profitable crop. As such, its payment to the land lord reduces African Americans' chances of using it to make a profit, become less dependent on white people, and gain economic freedom.

Chapter 9, "Of the Sons of Master and Man," considers the multiple ways in which American chattel slavery and the pervasiveness of racism have shaped race relations in the United States. Conceptualizing segregation and separation as further distancing black and white people, Du Bois also believes that the color-line contradicts Christian principles of equality. Du Bois suggests that both black and white people must change their understanding of the color line; black people cannot argue that racism is the only reason for their social condition and white people cannot argue that they are prejudiced against black people because of that social condition. Such arguments, Du Bois claims are futile and do not offer solutions that improve the lives of African Americans.

Chapter 10, "Of the Faith of the Fathers," proffers that both black people's faith in God and their participation in black churches have been central aspects of African Americans' socialization in the United States. Although Du Bois positions himself as an outsider in relation to the black church, he conceptualizes the black church as the social and political center of black life. Du Bois does not argue that there is a uniform black church experience, but he does rightfully locate the black church as a powerful and pervasive institution in black communities. Beyond spiritual enlightenment, black churches functioned as major socializing institutions, providing leadership and educational opportunities that black people were unable to obtain in other sectors of American communities.

Chapter 11, "Of the Passing of the First-Born," laments the death of Du Bois's firstborn son, whose untimely passing ironically saves him from the veil behind which he would otherwise live. Du Bois's tone in this chapter is at once sad and relieved. On the one hand, at birth, this son represents the possibilities for a future that would extend beyond the problems of the color line. His death therefore saddens Du Bois; the dream of his progeny succeeding is deferred. On the other hand, his untimely death stops Du Bois's son from experiencing the personal and systemic racism that circumscribes the lives of African Americans. For this reason, Du Bois interprets his son's death within the Christian typology of freedom. As Du Bois explains, "Not dead, not dead, but escaped; not bond, but free" (151). Death emerges as a sure way through which black people can escape America's racism.

Chapter 12, "Of Alexander Crummell," contrasts Du Bois's son's death with that of Alexander Crummell, whose life embodies the inherent difficulties of being a black man in a racist American society. Du Bois proffers that Crummell's life was divided into three stages: hate, despair, and doubt. As a black man whose desire to be a priest met resistance by the diocese because of his race, Crummell hates America. He subsequently feels despair, and refusing to be segregated and banned from the Catholic Church, Crummell founded his own church, but later moved to Africa. According to Du Bois, Crummell's migration to Africa symbolizes Crummell's search within his soul for a better earth. This move counteracts the despair he experienced as a result of his exclusion from the American politic. Du Bois asserts that Crummell's final return to America marks his triumph over hate, despair, and any doubt he had about his humanity. Although Crummell was an accomplished black man, Du Bois feels that he has not received his proper recognition in American society. This chapter memorializes Crummell and corrects this historical omission. In a somewhat ironic way, it anticipates a parallel cycle in Du Bois's life, although when he moves to Ghana he never returns.

Chapter 13, "Of the Coming of John," contrasts two Johns, a black John and a white one, to demonstrate how systematic and personal racism and prejudice keep black people behind the veil. Black John leaves his southern home and goes to the North, where he is educated. When John returns to the South, both black and white communities ostracize him. Whereas black communities find John's new ideas and idiom foreign and therefore do not embrace him, white communities believe John has gotten out of his place.

When John takes a job as a local school teacher, the white judge limits his curriculum to ensure that he does not teach black children any ideas that might unsettle the social order. After the judge closes John's school, John realizes he cannot remain in the South. This decision is reinforced when John sees the white John attempting to sexually assault black John's sister. This final catastrophe compels John to leave the South forever, as he can no longer tolerate southern white attitudes toward black people's education and sexuality. This chapter elucidates why appeasing/accommodating southern racism is problematic; doing so does not dismantle the underlying racial system.

Chapter 14, "Of the Sorrow Songs," explains the significance that Negro spirituals have in American society, and argues that they are the only authentic form of American music. Countering any notion that enslaved African Americans sang because they were happy or content with their social statuses, Du Bois rather conceptualizes the songs as the epitome of sorrow and hope. Moreover, although Du Bois admits that he is not a musicologist, he does consider how the songs' rhythms and melodies evoke pathos that contributes to their meaning. And finally, the chapter ends with a discussion of the three phases through which Du Bois maintains black music has gone: African, African American, and African American and American. Du Bois believes that these blends contribute to the meaning, hope, and authenticity embedded in African Americans' personal, religious, and spiritual journeys.

NOTES

1. Building upon Angelyn Mitchell's formulation of emancipatory and liberatory narratives in *The Freedom to Remember: Narrative, Slavery, and Gender in Contemporary Black Women's Fiction,* the term emancipatory narrative illuminates the fact that slave narratives are focusing on the construct of freedom, that is, emancipation, more so than the construction of slavery. The term invokes an epistemological shift wherein those narratives provide insights as to what freedom means, as well as the different types of freedom that enslaved African Americans sought.

2. The phrase *formerly enslaved African Americans* reinforces the fact that bonded African Americans were indeed people who had lost their rights. Unlike the term *slave,* which suggests the sum total of their existence was defined by their status as slaves, *enslaved African American* suggests that their status was temporally defined and reinforces the idea that enslaved African Americans were people and not merely objects.

3. For a thorough discussion of how African American literature specifically, and Anglo-American literature generally, are indebted to oral forms of communication, see Gayl Jones's *Liberating Voices: Oral Tradition in African American Literature,* where she theorizes the relationships that different forms of oral culture have to African American literary texts.

4. Literary critic Henry Louis Gates Jr. uses the term *signifyin'* to discuss the ways in which African American literary texts deploy and revise the motifs, which he calls tropes, that an earlier text employs. This tropological revision, as Gates describes it, can serve to criticize the limitations of, or further enhance the initial trope. See *The Signifying Monkey: A Theory of Literary Criticism* (1989).

FURTHER READING

Andrews, William. *Critical Essays on W.E.B. Du Bois*. Boston: Hall, 1985.

The Atlanta Journal Constitution. Chicken Bones: A Journal for African American Literary and Artistic Expression. Ed. Nathaniel Turner. Web. 27 Jan. 2008. http://www.nathanielturner.com/soulsofblackfolk2.

Blum, Edward J. *W.E.B. Du Bois: American Prophet*. Philadelphia: U of Pennsylvania P, 2007.

Byerman, Keith. *Seizing the Word: History, Art, and Self in the Work of W.E.B. Du Bois*. Athens: U of Georgia P, 1994.

Carby, Hazel. "The Souls of Black Men." *Next to the Color Line: Gender, Sexuality, and W.E.B. Du Bois*. Ed. Susan Gillman and Alys Eve Weinbaum. Minneapolis: U of Minnesota P, 2007. 234–68.

Cooper, Anna Julia. *A Voice from the South*. New York: Oxford UP, 1988.

Cooppan, Vilashini. "The Double Politics of Double Consciousness: Nationalism and Globalism in *The Souls of Black Folk*." *Public Culture* 17.2 (2005): 299–318.

Du Bois, W.E.B. "Criteria of Negro Art." *Within the Circle: An Anthology of Literary Criticism from the Harlem Renaissance to the Present*. Ed. Angelyn Mitchell. Durham: Duke UP, 1994. 60–68.

Du Bois, W.E.B. *The Cornel West Reader*. Ed. Cornel West. New York: Basic Civitas, 2000.

Du Bois, W.E.B. *The Souls of Black Folk*. New York: Barnes and Nobles Classics, 2003.

Du Bois, W.E.B. "The Talented Tenth." *W.E.B. Du Bois: Writings*. New York: Library of America, 1986.

Gates, Henry L. *The Signifying Monkey: A Theory of African American Literary Criticism*. New York: Oxford UP, 1988.

Gilkes, Cheryl T. "The Margin as the Center of a Theory of History: African-America Women, Social Change, and the Sociology of W.E.B. Du Bois." *W.E.B. Du Bois on Race and Culture: Philosophy, Politics, and Poetics*. Ed. Bernard Bell, Emily Grosholz, and James Stewart. New York: Routledge, 1996. 111–40.

Gooding-Williams, Robert. "Du Bois, Politics, Aesthetics: An Introduction." *Public Culture* 17.2 (2005): 203–15.

Hubbard, Dolan, ed. The Souls of Black Folk *One Hundred Years Later*. Columbia: U of Missouri P, 2003.

Jacobs, Harriet. *Incidents in the Life of a Slave Girl: Written by Herself*. Ed. Kwame Anthony Appiah. New York: Random House, 2000.

James, Joy. "Profeminism and Gender Elites: W.E.B. Du Bois, Anna Julia Cooper, and Ida B. Wells-Barnett." *Next to the Color Line: Gender, Sexuality, and W.E.B. Du Bois*. Ed. Susan Gillman and Alys Eve Weinbaum. Minneapolis: U of Minnesota P, 2007. 69–95.

Johnson, James Weldon. *Black Voices: An Anthology of Afro-American Literature*. Ed. Abraham Chapman. New York: Signet, 1968.

Jones, Gayl. *Liberating Voices: Oral Tradition in African American Literature*. Cambridge: Harvard UP, 1991.

Joy, James. *Transcending the Talented Tenth*. New York: Routledge, 1997.

Keller, Mary, and Charles Fontenot Jr., eds. *Re-Cognizing W. E. B. Du Bois in the Twenty-First Century: Essays on W. E. B. Du Bois*. Athens: Mercer UP, 2007.

Lewis, David. *W.E.B. Du Bois: Biography of a Race, 1868–1919.* New York: Holt, 1993.

Lewis, David. *W.E.B. Du Bois: The Fight for Equality and the American Century, 1919–1963.* New York: Holt, 2000.

Logan, Rayford. *The Negro in American Life and Thought: The Nadir 1877–1901.* New York: Dial, 1954.

Mitchell, Angelyn. *The Freedom to Remember: Narrative, Slavery, and Gender in Contemporary Black Women's Fiction.* New Brunswick, NJ: Rutgers UP, 2002.

Nashville Banner. Chicken Bones: A Journal for African American Literary and Artistic Expression. Ed. Nathaniel Turner. Web. 27 Jan. 2008. http://www.nathaniel turner.com/soulsofblackfolk2.

Nero, Charles. "Queering *The Souls of Black Folk.*" *Public Culture* 17.2 (2005): 255–76.

Rampersad, Arnold. *The Art and Imagination of W.E.B. Du Bois.* Cambridge: Harvard UP, 1976.

Rampersad, Arnold. "Slavery and the Literary Imagination: Du Bois's *The Souls of Black Folk.*" *Slavery and the Literary Imagination.* Ed. Deborah McDowell. Baltimore, MD: Johns Hopkins UP, 1987. 104–24.

Reed, Adolph, Jr. *W.E.B. Du Bois and American Political Thought: Fabianism and the Color Line.* Oxford: Oxford UP, 1997.

Wall, Cheryl A. "Resounding *Souls*: Du Bois and the African American Literary Tradition." *Public Culture* 17.2 (2005): 217–34.

Washington, Booker T. *The Booker T. Washington Papers.* Vol. 3. Ed. Louis Harlan. Urbana: U of Illinois P, 1974.

Zamir, Shamoon. "'The Sorrow Songs'/'Song of Myself': Du Bois, the Crisis of Leadership and Prophetic Imagination." *The Black Columbiad: Defining Moments in African American Literature and Culture.* Cambridge: Harvard UP, 1994.

Robert J. Patterson

Born a slave in 1856, Booker T. Washington became a staunch civil rights activist and one of the most influential educators in American history. (Library of Congress)

Up from Slavery

Booker T. Washington's *Up from Slavery* (1901) presents his life story from his birth to a slave mother by an unknown white father through his experiences as a child laborer set on getting an education at any cost, to his successful founding and fostering of the Tuskegee Institute and his rise to national prominence. The book details Washington's personal hard work and sacrifice to become educated, including his work in a salt-furnace and a coal mine and his arduous 500-mile journey from West Virginia and his family to the Hampton Institute in Virginia in the hopes of being admitted as a student, and the benevolent treatment he received at the hands of the many and varied benefactors who helped to make his education possible. It is not only a classic African American text, but also a classic American rags-to-riches story. As such, it has been compared to both Horatio Alger's novels and Benjamin Franklin's autobiography.

Thematically, the text focuses on the importance of self-reliance and hard work and the benefits that will come to those that act on these virtues. At each stage of Washington's journey from illiterate slave to principal of Tuskegee and nationally known representative of his race, Washington prospers from his own labor and is granted help through the proving of his worth through his work ethic. This is best demonstrated by his entrance exam to the Hampton Institute. He arrives at Hampton hungry, dirty from working his way there and from sleeping on the ground under a sidewalk, and unable to pay tuition or board. The head teacher is unimpressed and does not immediately admit him as a student. Rather, she asks him to sweep a recitation room. Washington recognizes that he can impress this head teacher with his ability to work hard, so he sweeps and dusts every inch of the room, including closets and woodwork, several times before reporting back to her that the task has been completed. After examining the room for any dust by running a handkerchief over areas of the room she suspects he has missed, she decides that he will do well as a student and admits him. This strong work ethic also provides the means for Washington to stay at Hampton, despite his inability to pay, because due to his exemplary work in cleaning the room, he is offered a position as a janitor, which allows him to work off the cost of boarding at the school. While Washington portrays this head teacher, Miss Mackie, as one of his best friends and supporters, it is his own virtues that make her so. Her benevolence and help is the direct result of Washington's ability and desire to work hard in order to improve himself.

Washington describes his time at Hampton as being an education both in the traditional sense—becoming literate—and as an education in the ways to live—the value of regular meals eaten at a dining table, the value of the bath and toothbrush, of sleeping between sheets, the value in choosing the best men to emulate. His portrayal of the teachers and of the head of the school, General Samuel C. Armstrong, emphasizes their tireless work to make their students fit to do the work of uplifting their race. Armstrong, in particular, is presented as a role model and benefactor to Washington. He found Washington a patron to pay his tuition during his entire stay at Hampton and later recommended that he start and run Tuskegee. Once again, this is a reward for Washington's own virtues of hard work and loyalty. He prospered through his time as a student at Hampton despite the long hours required by his job as a janitor, and was willing to do anything for the general and for his project— including giving up his room to sleep in a tent to make Hampton able to accept a larger number of students despite their limited dormitory space. This loyalty extends throughout the general's life, as he spends a few of his last months, paralyzed and needing care, at Washington's home. These interactions with the General were also the foundation of Washington's own educational models that placed industry and skilled labor as more important than traditional higher education for the development of his race.

After graduating from Hampton, Washington is out of money but again demonstrates his perseverance, working as a waiter for the summer (a job he had neither the training nor aptitude to do) before returning to his family's hometown and being given the job of teacher for the African American school. After two years in this position, he spends a year studying in Washington, DC, at an institution that does not offer industrial education in addition to its academic programs. He finds the students there lacking in self-reliance and overly concerned with the superficial. For Washington, this cements the wisdom of the general and his model of education in the trades for African Americans as the best path to follow for racial uplift. After this time of supplemental study, Washington is asked back to Hampton as a teacher, undertaking the running of two new programs—a night school and the overseeing of Native American education—at the general's request. His success in these programs is once again rewarded by his benefactor. When General Armstrong is asked by some colleagues in Alabama to recommend a white man to start a school for African Americans in the town of Tuskegee, he provides the opportunity to Washington. Upon this recommendation, Washington is accepted as the head and founder of this new venture and begins his life work of building the Tuskegee Institute.

The bulk of *Up from Slavery* details the development of Tuskegee, literally from the ground up. The state of Alabama had provided $2,000 a year for the school, but this covered only teacher salaries. There were no appropriate buildings in which to hold classes, only a dilapidated shack and church. There were no dormitories for students to live in. In short, there was an idea for a school, but no school itself, and no money to build the necessary accommodations for students and teachers in which to live and work. The book is in some ways as much a history of the development of the school as it is an autobiography of Washington himself. And this was a part of Washington's design and rhetorical mastery. *Up From Slavery* worked not only to provide a picture of Washington's rise to prominence and his uplifting of the race along the way, but also to promote the value of the school, and others modeled after it, to the southern whites who were these schools' neighbors and to the northern whites who could be benefactors and patrons for Tuskegee and schools that followed the Tuskegee model. The book posits the value that graduates from industrial institutes such as Tuskegee can have in crafting a New South economy while satisfying liberal northern desires for the progression of African Americans—all in the guise of a classic American story of the travails and successes of a humble, rugged individualist hero.

Yet as an autobiography, it presents a much clearer picture of the man's work than of the man himself. This, too, is part of the rhetorical cleverness of the book. The man who emerges from the description of the work itself is the creation as much of the audience as it is of Washington himself. This allowed *Up from Slavery* to simultaneously work effectively for three different audiences, with very different worldviews and goals. Washington effectively addresses southern whites who are skeptical of education for African Americans, northern whites who could help the school financially, and African American readers whom he wanted to convince of the effectiveness of his program in creating progress. White southerners could read the text, focus on Washington's portrayals of loyalty and work to earn rights at some unnamed point in the future, and feel that the man himself was not a radical or an agitator but rather a force against political agitation. These readers could create a Washington who was content with the social and political conditions as they existed and who would train other African Americans into appropriate workers and contributors to the southern economy. Wealthy northern whites who were interested in supporting some progress could read the text and find a Washington who was a businessman, someone who would use donations wisely, and who understood the situation well. African American readers could find a Washington who could lead them to better days, both economically and socially, a Washington who worked tirelessly to help not just himself but his entire race, who was a representative and a voice for them, and who was well respected in both the North and the South.

Up from Slavery sold widely and well and created fans and friends for Washington in all three of these divergent audiences. And the crafting of his rhetoric with all three in mind was no accident. *Up from Slavery* was actually Washington's second autobiography. The first, *The Story of My Life and Work* (1900), was originally ghostwritten for Washington by African American journalist Edgar Webber, who produced the manuscript with little oversight and drew heavily on published speeches and schedules. It was published by J. L. Nichols and Company, a subscription publisher that sold primarily to African American readers, and was cheaply produced and rife with errors. Later editions removed Webber's name from the index and picture from the text and were heavily corrected by Washington. Dissatisfied with this work, and hoping to reach a broader, and wealthier, audience, Washington almost immediately began work on the second book, this time making arrangements with the much more prestigious Doubleday to publish the book in 1901 after it had appeared serially in *Outlook,* a popular family magazine, from November 1900 to February 1901. Washington also employed a ghostwriter this time, but chose a white journalist, Max Thrasher, who came with stronger, more reliable recommendations and experience. Washington would also not repeat the mistake of lax oversight and dictated much of the book to Thrasher. These choices in ghostwriter and publisher are indicative of the new audience Washington envisioned for *Up from Slavery*.

The rhetoric that Washington uses throughout the text is also indicative of his awareness of his various readers and what they would want to hear. Southern whites read a message of contentment with current structures, northern whites read a message of racial conciliation, amity, and progress, and African American readers could read a message of hope and forward movement. A short passage from chapter 10, "A Harder Task than Making Bricks without Straw," illustrates this rhetorical balancing act. Washington is describing the creation, by the students themselves, of a dining room and kitchen. Because there is no room in the main building itself for these facilities, the students dig out a basement room beneath the living quarters and use this uncomfortable and dimly lit area for both cooking and eating. Rather than decrying the extremely humble conditions they had to start in, Washington recalls this as a valuable part of the school and students' development: "Had we started in a fine, attractive, convenient room, I fear we would have 'lost our heads' and become 'stuck up.' It means a great deal, I think, to start off on a foundation which one has made for one's self ... they are glad that we started as we did, and built ourselves up year by year, by a slow and natural process of growth" (75). Southern whites, worried about African Americans agitating for political rights or getting educations and "forgetting their place" or becoming "stuck up," can see in this event Washington's conservative racial policies that emphasize hard work and remaining humble and content. More progressive readers, African American or white, could find Washington's emphasis instead on the idea of growth and the fulfillment of desires—whether for an attractive dining room or economic prosperity or civil and social rights. Indeed, they could see that progress, forward movement, is the natural, and thus inevitable, outcome, as it was in the building of Tuskegee itself. This balancing act is possible in part because of the text's focus on the work more than the man. Washington remains the driving force of the work (both the book and the development of Tuskegee, and by extension the uplift of the race), but what drives him—personal power and prestige or the drive for racial equality or conservative racial politics—remains enigmatic and open to the interpretations of both followers and critics alike.

One of Washington's important choices *Up from Slavery* was the use of many of the conventions of one of the most popular and prevalent forms from 19th-century African American literature—the slave narrative. However, Washington uses these conventions in ways suited to his postbellum environment and his own educational and political agenda. Slave narratives had created and cemented the reputations and leadership positions of others before him, such as Frederick Douglass, a figure Washington was sometimes compared to (and he draws this comparison himself in his descriptions of letters he received calling on him to be the spokesperson for his race upon Douglass's death in 1895). Antebellum slave narratives were used as abolitionist propaganda;

Washington used his latter-day slave narrative as propaganda for his vision of the proper path to civil rights and equality. Traditionally, slave narratives followed a particular pattern and relied on common motifs to enlighten white readers about the realities of slavery as a hell on earth and demonstrate the innate humanity and dignity of African Americans, as well as how African Americans deserved their full human rights. This pattern showed the slave being ripped from his home and plunged into the evil of slavery, dehumanized at the hands of masters, falling into despair, but then experiencing a growth of self-reliance and providential help that leads to the slave achieving freedom. The slave's story is presented less as her individual story than as a story than represents the feelings and ambitions of all members of the oppressed group. The motifs most often represented in the slave narratives include the physical and spiritual deprivations of slavery, slaves' innate resilience and skills, and the quest for literacy as often integral to the quest for freedom. Frances Smith Foster, in *Witnessing Slavery: The Development of Ante-bellum Slave Narratives,* describes the narrative arc of traditional slave narratives: "The action moves from the idyllic life of a garden of Eden into the wilderness, the struggle for survival, the providential help, and the arrival into the Promised Land" (84). Conventionally, the idyllic life is in Africa, the wilderness is the enslaved life, and the Promised Land is freedom in the North.

Washington takes this narrative arc and puts it to use in ways that fit his own story (his birth into slavery for instance) and his agenda of appealing to skeptical as well as sympathetic white audiences. Slavery was not a hell on earth, but a school in which African Americans learned skilled trades, "the industries at their doors" (42), and developed the ability to work hard and persevere through any difficulty, two of Washington's most cherished virtues. African Americans are dehumanized and led astray not by cruel masters, but by ambitions above their skills or economic means, which Washington demonstrates in his stories of African American youths in Washington DC who consistently went into debt or spent half their weekly wages on fancy carriage rides or other things that enhanced only their image, or more famously in his anecdote of the young man dressed in rags and living in squalor who is spending his time studying a French grammar rather than improving his physical situation. They fall into despair not because they are oppressed but because they have followed the path of folly—agitation rather than diligent work for a strong economic foundation—or because the true road to the Promised Land is so difficult for those, like Washington himself, trying to pull themselves up from poverty. *Up from Slavery* represents this in Washington's own difficult, dirty, and hungry journey to school at Hampton, and in the times at Tuskegee when he is nearly out of money and it seems as though the progress at the school must end. *Up from Slavery* repeatedly strikes the chord of self-reliance being rewarded with providential help—it consistently embodies the proverb that "God helps those who help themselves"—with the providential help coming in the form of benevolent white patrons who make the Promised Land a possibility for Washington himself and later for his students at Tuskegee.

These patrons are both those white people who helped Washington by mentoring him and paying his tuition while he was a student at Hampton Institute and the patrons of Tuskegee, including famous men such as Andrew Carnegie, who donated both large and small sums to help build the school. Throughout the text, Washington often recounts how these donations came truly providentially, often with little to no indication that they were coming and most often arriving just when things looked most bleak because a bill was due or the bank accounts were truly empty. He closes the narrative arc not just with an arrival to a Promised Land, which is how he describes his first vision of Hampton Institute, but with the creation of a new one, a new Eden carved out of the "Black Belt" of Alabama, Tuskegee Institute itself. The movement Smith describes is fully represented with the idyllic life being Washington's life with his family in which they all work together to survive poverty, the wilderness and struggle represented in his struggles to become educated and then to build a school, quite literally out of the wilderness, since Tuskegee's main campus was carved out of an abandoned farm, and the Promised Land being Tuskegee itself, the school which valorized labor—Washington's own being foremost despite his humble presentation of himself.

Washington also makes use of the motifs common to the antebellum slave narratives but again molds them to his own needs. The early chapters focus on Washington's desire to learn to read both while working in the salt furnace and coal mine and when given the opportunity to go to a day school in his hometown. He describes literacy as one of his strongest desires, but focuses much less strongly on the path to and importance of literacy than many of the antebellum slave narratives had. In fact, he rarely mentions reading once he has learned to do so, and the importance of books is strongly overshadowed by the centrality of productive work. Furthermore, because his own educational agenda was so strongly industrial in nature, he also emphasizes the dangers that come along with an overemphasis on book learning, including misplaced priorities and the hazards of just a little knowledge, while highlighting the importance of learning directly from great men like General Armstrong, and points out that education of African Americans would benefit from not just studying books, but "learn[ing] to study men and things" (30). Because the bulk of *Up from Slavery* describes Washington's life after emancipation, he focuses less on the deprivations of slavery, although these are addressed somewhat in the early chapters, than on the deprivations of the poverty that was a reality for Washington and many others after emancipation. He points out that his living conditions were not materially improved by freedom—the house they lived in after being freed was much the same as their house in the slave quarters, and the hard work required by slaves simply became the hard work required to support himself and his family. It is lack of economic stability and prosperity that serves to deprive Washington, and in his view other African Americans, of the life they desire, much more so than it is racial hatred or oppression. This is a view that provides hope by making the possibility for the life one wants available to any African American who is willing to work and sacrifice, as Washington's brother John does in working to support the family while Washington receives his education. It is also a view that is soothing to white readers because it makes no accusations and places no blame and reassures them that Washington, and by extension other African Americans, bear no ill feeling and carry no race prejudice.

While he makes use of all three of the major motifs, he emphasizes most strongly the innate resilience and skill of the African American population, in part as a point of racial pride and in part as a clear message to southern whites that their future economic prosperity was tied to the future of African Americans. Washington consistently points out the value that African Americans had in the development of the New South. This idea is truly the core theme of *Up from Slavery* and a central tenet of Washington's educational (and some would argue political) philosophy. The importance Washington placed on this resilience and skill and his use of the motif appears quite strongly in chapter 14, "The Atlanta Exposition Address," which presents the text of the speech that brought Washington to truly national fame and cemented his role as the leader of his race in the minds of many white Americans. In 1895, Washington was invited to speak at the Atlanta Cotton States and International Exposition, which was going to have a full building devoted to a Negro exhibit. Washington had spoken before Congress as part of a delegation seeking help in putting on the exhibition, and the board had been so impressed with his message there that they invited him to speak to the exposition on opening day. The speech that he gave highlighted the importance of the African American to the South and the importance of the South to African American progress, as this was where Washington believed true economic and industrial opportunity for African Americans existed, as exemplified in the exposition itself. The speech was greeted with many accolades, including recognition from President Grover Cleveland, which extolled the hope and determination that African Americans must certainly have taken from the speech.

Washington's Famous Quote

"Cast down your bucket where you are" may be Washington's most famous quote from the Atlanta Exposition Address. It sums up his philosophy: African Americans needed to make friends with their white neighbors in the South rather than seek to please people in the North.

Major Works

The Future of the American Negro. *1899. Charleston: Nabu, 2010.*
My Larger Education. *1911. New York: Cornell UP, 2009.*
The Story of My Life and Work. *Charleston: Nabu, 2010.*
Up from Slavery. *1901. New York: Dover, 1995.*

The "Atlanta Exposition Address" highlights Washington's educational agenda, as well as his rhetorical mastery. It references the proven loyalty of African Americans, who did not rise up in slave revolts but rather endured slavery and built wealth for the white South by highlighting how African Americans had helped "lift the load" (101) both before and after emancipation in a way no other workers (particularly foreign workers or workers with union ties) could be relied on to do. This can be read as either a racially conservative acceptance of the subservient role of African Americans or as a celebration of intrinsic strength and great ability to persevere and prosper through adversity, a point of pride for the race. Two of the most famous quotes from the address also highlight both the trope of resilience and skill and Washington's rhetorical slipperiness, where one can find either a highly conservative or a progressive view of race and race relations. Both address segregation in the social rather than the economic arena. The first explicitly addresses the codependence of southern whites and African Americans: "In all things that are purely social we can be as separate as the fingers, yet one as the hand in all things essential to mutual progress" (100). Those happy with the social order of the time certainly heard this as an affirmation that segregation as practiced under Jim Crow laws could continue apace, with the blessing of the leader of the African American race, as long as economic opportunities, which could be envisioned simply as manual and skilled labor jobs, were provided to ensure the material wellbeing of all the citizens of the South. However, the metaphor of the hand also implies the deep and inextricable linkages of white and African American southerners. None of the fingers can be eliminated or injured without an impact to the full hand, and the discrimination and racism that led to lack of opportunities in education, for instance, or worse to violence and lynching, were quite definitely injuries. This shored up the need and support for schools like Tuskegee, even for those racial conservatives who worried about the implications of educating African Americans, and furthered Washington's own projects of further expanding Tuskegee and of garnering support for other schools modeled after it throughout the South.

Washington's educational program, while it included academic classes, focused heavily on education in the trades—carpentry, brickmaking, construction, sewing, and laundering—and agriculture, the connection to the land of the South itself. And in this as well, he makes use of the trope of the resilience and skill of freed African American slaves and their descendants. The second oft-quoted line from the address highlights the importance of that type of work while obliquely addressing social segregation. This line also demonstrates the balancing act that Washington engaged in to effectively address his divergent audiences: "The opportunity to earn a dollar in a factory just now is worth infinitely more than the opportunity to spend a dollar in an operahouse" (101–2). Once again, this has a comforting, accommodationist ring for the conservative white Southern audience at the exposition. However, in the context of the full address, and of the full text of *Up from Slavery*, which mentions the importance of recognizing the full rights of African Americans as citizens, a more progressive reading remains possible. The inclusion of "just now," two small words easily glossed over by a listener or reader who wants to be reassured that the current situation is stable and acceptable, indicates that the situation is only satisfactory for the time being. This reading is consistent with Washington's belief that rewards come through work. As African Americans work and achieve economic prosperity and independence, the natural order will also demand that they are not discriminated against in other arenas. In fact, in other places in the text, Washington points out that those who have made themselves economically essential cannot long be socially discriminated against. While demanding full exercise of their rights—political, economic, and social—might "just now" be out of reach, the day was coming when it would be fully and rightfully in their grasp.

This chapter also explicitly mentions that there were some in the African American community who felt that the address had not been strong enough in its call for rights and had been too forgiving of southern whites and the damages they had inflicted on African Americans as individuals and as a race. Here, too, Washington is able to turn a potential liability into an asset. After briefly mentioning the criticism, he claims the critics have come around to his way of seeing things and provides an anecdote of a similar time in the past when he and Tuskegee were criticized. He points out that through forbearance—he neither defended himself nor retracted his statements—he was eventually proved right in the eyes of his critics and the world. This not only works with the slave narrative trope of resilience, since Washington both survives the criticism and has his reputation enhanced both by his ultimate rightness and by his diplomacy in handling his critics, but it also serves to reinforce that Washington's models for the education of African Americans and their racial uplift and progress in civil rights can weather the storm of any criticism or skepticism.

Washington's insistence on the rightness of his ideas might lead a reader to expect an arrogance or superiority in the tone in the text itself. Instead, in perhaps the most impressive indication of his mastery of rhetoric and audience awareness, Washington comes across as humble and down to earth, even folksy in places, throughout his description of his, objectively, quite amazing life. As the title suggests, Washington had indeed come up in the world. The text may have started with Washington enslaved, and then impoverished, but it ends with him having built a thriving school, enjoying European vacations, meeting presidents, and being welcomed triumphantly as an honored guest into Richmond, the city where he had once had to sleep under a sidewalk because he was so poor and friendless. Yet throughout his recounting of this truly unusual journey to prominence, there is little direct celebration of himself (although he does frequently include excerpts of letters of praise or other accolades he received). Washington does not ascribe his success to any special talent or brilliance of his own, or to any quality not accessible to any of his readers. He attributes it to hard work, something anyone is capable of, and to the help of benevolent friends and mentors, which he describes as being available to anyone who will go looking for help without expectation but with loyalty. This everyman tone is established from the first page of *Up from Slavery*, when he points out that while he does not know the particulars of his birth, "I suspect I must have been born somewhere and at some time" (1). The focus on the very obscurity of the beginnings of his life suggests that the great are not born but crafted through effort and circumstance, which makes him much like his readers. The gentle attempt at humor and the inauspicious beginning to his life provide hope to African American audiences; they, too, could achieve success, could pull themselves up by following his example. And for white audiences it demonstrated a deferential, self-deprecating character that did not threaten the established order but wanted only to work to better himself, and through his work, to better the opportunities available to others of his race as well.

Ultimately, this tone and the focus on these key values of self-reliance, hope and aspiration, hard work and loyalty allowed Washington to craft a deeply American story of opportunity and success. It is a classic American rags-to-riches story that speaks to and of the pioneer spirit and work ethic that is so fundamental to the broader American story. Yet it accomplishes this while still discussing in both explicit and implicit ways the additional struggle that African Americans were burdened with, the struggle against a history (and in *Up from Slavery*, Washington presents it mostly as a history rather than a contemporary reality) that had disadvantaged African Americans in both material and spiritual ways. This ability to craft a story that gained the trust and respect of both white and African American audiences in a time of deep and obvious racial division is at the heart of the iconic status that *Up from Slavery* had at the time and has continued to have. While it is not the strong call for political rights that some hoped for, neither is it an unqualified acceptance of second-class citizenship that some have accused it of being. It stands not just as the story of Washington's life or of his work, but as a barometer of the time in which it was written, a time when the way forward toward civil rights was just beginning to be forged.

What that path was in Washington's view is made most evident in the program he followed at Tuskegee. Washington's status as an icon is due not simply to *Up from Slavery* and Washington's other books, but also to the legacy of the work that *Up from Slavery* detailed. While Tuskegee was not the first school for African Americans, nor was it even the first run by African Americans, it was and is one of the best known. The work Washington describes in his autobiography turned a legislative appropriation for a school into an actuality. Washington's labor took a dream for the education of his people and created an institution that today has more than 3,000 students and more than 100 major buildings. Tuskegee University today has five colleges: Agricultural, Environmental, and Natural Sciences; Business and Information Science; Engineering and Physical Sciences; Liberal Arts and Education; and Veterinary Medicine, Nursing, and Allied Health. Tuskegee now grants bachelor's, master's, and doctoral degrees while still saying true to Washington's desire to educate not only the minds of his students but their hearts and, most importantly, hands as well. *Up from Slavery* describes not just the life of Washington as a man, but the birth and development of one of the nation's best-known historically black universities.

When Washington arrived in Tuskegee, he found that there wasn't truly a school for him to run. The legislative act that created Tuskegee Institute only provided state money to pay teachers' salaries. A local church donated a dilapidated building in which to hold classes, but there was nothing that was recognizably a school. Those key themes of *Up from Slavery*, self-reliance and hard work, allowed Washington to take the idea of a school and make it into a thriving bricks-and-mortar reality. He opened the school on July 4, 1881, with himself as the only teacher for the 30 students drawn from the surrounding county. These students were all receiving training to be teachers, a job some of them already held, and varied widely both in age and in academic preparation. This emphasis on teacher training helped build Tuskegee's, and Washington's, legacy. Much as Washington himself had been trained to teach at Hampton and then took these skills to not only teach but also build an institution, many of Tuskegee's graduates went out and taught, and some built small schools of their own across the South. This was *Up from Slavery*'s principle of the value of helping others rather than simply oneself—the reason Washington gives in the text for not becoming a politician—in action.

And Washington's ambitions were much greater than training a few dozen teachers at a time in a shanty. His autobiography details his desire to reach more students and to include the industrial and craft training that he believed was of such central importance. This meant the school itself had to grow. It needed a location and land of its own. But with the state monies dedicated entirely to instructor salaries, and no further help from that quarter, Washington had to find another way to grow the institution. Washington found land on which to start building, an abandoned plantation near town, and he borrowed the money needed to purchase it from the treasurer of the Hampton Institute. This move to land of their own in the second year of the school's existence allowed Washington to truly put in place his threefold educational policy: educating minds through academic classes and teacher training; industrial, hands-on education through the development of trades; and the civilizing areas he had learned in his time at the Hampton Institute—personal hygiene, proper etiquette, and spiritual training.

Up from Slavery documents how the industrial programs grew in an organic order by what was dictated by the needs of the school and students. The agricultural program was the first to develop because the school needed to provide food for its students and teachers, so they began to farm. The next program to develop was brickmaking and building because the school needed buildings. The majority of the buildings were built wholly by the students and faculty in residence at the time. The brickmaking program illustrates how Washington's awareness of his audience existed not just in the text of the autobiography but in the practical decisions that he made while running the school itself. Chapter 10 of the text details how the brickmaking program was designed not only to supply the bricks needed to build the institute's own buildings, but also to supply a broader community need. The town of Tuskegee didn't have a brick-works, and so there was a gap in the supply chain. Washington determined to fill this gap with high-quality bricks, understanding, as he explains in the text, that supplying this need would make the white neighbors skeptical about educating African Americans see that education under Washington's model would not create racial tensions or agitation for rights, but rather create African American citizens who could make solid contributions to the economy and material comfort of the community. As he details both the hard work necessary to learn the dirty and difficult job of creating high-quality bricks and the way this created friends among their white neighbors, Washington again weaves the rhetoric of racial pride in hard-won accomplishments with the rhetoric of the inextricable economic linkages between the African American and white communities. This continual underscoring of his themes in ways that played to both audiences furthered his status and his agenda.

This educational agenda itself blended traditional academic training and practical education for all students. Students could work for their tuition and board, but no student, even if he could afford to pay these fees, could simply study books. All the students who attended Tuskegee were involved in the labor of the school. Students grew the food that the student body ate, built the buildings in which they studied and lived, made the bricks to make those buildings, cooked the food, and did the laundry. Washington had no desire to create what his white neighbors feared Tuskegee would produce: graduates obsessed with presenting a fancy image and without any interest in or ability to work, the kind of man "who was determined to live by his wits" (57) and not by work that contributed to the community. He felt that producing graduates who had a useful skill was of the most benefit. They would leave Tuskegee with the means to support themselves well, to contribute to the African American community by providing necessary goods and services and appropriate leadership, and to develop the southern community as a whole by their solid economic contribution and value. This was the cause for some complaint among some students and their parents. But as was his pattern, Washington turned this potential liability to his own use. He details these complaints in the text but then emphasizes that he did not change his plans due to them but rather was spurred to travel across the state speaking to parents about the value of industrial education and convincing them of the rightness of his agenda. The students also come to see the value in the labor, and the school attracts more and more students. Here in the text, as elsewhere, Washington mentions criticisms in order to dismiss them and suggests that he does not need to adapt his agenda because the critics eventually come to his way of seeing things. In the text, the criticism serves to burnish rather than tarnish his program and legacy—it, too, is resilient and can stand against all storms.

As Washington attracted more students and got more financial support, the number of buildings and programs at Tuskegee increased, as did the profile of the school. In addition to training brickmakers and carpenters, he details that the students became skilled enough to do everything needed to construct the new buildings without bringing in any outside help or workmen, displaying the value of the self-reliance the text so consistently preaches. The agricultural program also exemplified his emphasis on helping the community as its students and graduates not only implemented advanced agricultural techniques at the school, but also taught those techniques to others who couldn't study at Tuskegee through extension programs. In this area in particular, the school gained fame when Washington invited George Washington Carver to come to Tuskegee as the head of the new Department of Agriculture in 1896.

The growth of Tuskegee was possible due to the virtues of hard work and sacrifice that Washington celebrated in *Up from Slavery*. Because the state funding covered so few of the needs of developing a new institution, much less making it prosper, all the other monies needed—for food for students who boarded, materials to build furniture, books, and so forth—had to be raised. Many students couldn't afford board or tuition, so the money had to come from patrons and donations. Washington's tireless efforts as a fundraiser and his willingness to ask friends for personal loans made the growth of Tuskegee beyond a one-room schoolhouse possible. He traveled and spoke widely in both the North and the South and solicited donations both large and small. This combination of fundraising and the labor of the students, which meant more could be done with less, meant that Tuskegee could continue to add to its facilities and also to its student body and staff.

Washington was a tireless fundraiser who sought help for the school both near and far. His descriptions of the schools' donors throughout the later chapters of *Up from Slavery* rely once again on his desire to reach his three-fold audience. He points out the pride African Americans in the community took in the school, donating eggs and hogs when they had no money to contribute. He details how the white members of the community never turned him away when he needed something to further the growth of the school, giving examples of not only monetary donations but the help provided with building materials and food purchased on his word of future payment alone. He also details the contributions of northern philanthropists, both large and small, to help pay for the erection of buildings, including a $20,000 contribution from Andrew Carnegie to cover the building of a library in 1900, when the school had grown to 1,100 students and 86 faculty members. These varied descriptions allowed the text to portray the school as belonging not just to those studying and working there, but to the broader Tuskegee and Alabama communities—both black and white. It also demonstrated the role the school, and by extension Washington himself, played in working toward the end of not only racial divides, but also sectional divides. This strategy helped to cement Washington's role as a spokesperson for his race and for the South in a way that addressed the needs and desires of each of his audiences. The text shows how Washington was simultaneously one with the poorest African Americans in his community and rubbing shoulders with captains of industry and presidents. It showed how he was a proud son of the South while still capable of being a dignified spokesperson who could successfully navigate northern culture. The text shows him deferring to the segregation laws of the South in stories of issues that arose on trains and in hotels while still being comfortable in his dealings with the most important white men in the land—including presidents. *Up from Slavery* details the ability of African Americans to deftly adapt to full integration while not demanding it outright, and so it is a text that demonstrates the possibilities of blurring the color line while simultaneously arguing that the line must be kept in place for the time being.

As Washington's fundraising brought him into contact with many important and famous people in both the South and the North, and as his personal reputation and the reputation of the Tuskegee Institute grew, Washington found himself with a great deal of political power. While *Up from Slavery* was in some ways designed to enhance and cement that power and Washington's leadership role amongst African Americans, Washington's subtle portrayal of that power in the text serves to underscore his mastery of tone. While he can command audiences with presidents and visit Carnegie at his home, this power is presented in the same everyman tone as the inauspicious story of his birth that opens the book. The reference to his relationship with Carnegie is simply presented in the letter he sent him soliciting funding for the library; he portrays his first meeting with President McKinley as the result of the kindness of the president's secretary in facilitating a meeting on a day when many people of many kinds were wishing to meet with him. McKinley's discussion of the state of race relations with Washington on his second meeting is ascribed not to Washington's position or power, but to McKinley's heavy heart due to race riots and his interest in demonstrating his faith in African Americans in deed rather than word. This leads to McKinley's visit to Tuskegee in December 1900. Washington does not congratulate himself in this chapter—he allows the president and the secretary of the navy to do it. He publishes their kind words of praise—McKinley recognized Washington's "genius and perseverance" in his speech—and so maintains his everyman tone (140).

Up from Slavery closes by returning to the scene of one of Washington's moments of despair before he had reached the Promised Land of the Hampton Institute, Richmond, Virginia, the capital of the Confederacy. But this is a triumphal visit. Washington is an honored guest, invited to speak to both races, and welcomed by not only the African American community and its leaders, but also by the white City Council and state legislature. He speaks in a hall previously barred to the use of African Americans and gives his message of hope and thanks to both races of the state in which he was born into slavery. The slave narrative trope has come full circle, and been transformed, through Washington's inventive use for it. The cradle of his slavery is also his Promised Land—it has welcomed him back with open arms. And the text shows the American Dream—even a slave uncertain of the details of his own beginnings, with no knowledge of his father, and no advantages of birth, cannot just survive but can build his own Eden, and can share that Eden with others. Washington's portrayal of himself and his work, the flourishing of Tuskegee and industrial education, live in the text to show how far up African Americans could come. *Up from Slavery* becomes a classic by embodying that dream.

However, Washington's dream embodied was not without its detractors. While the white press had largely glowingly reviewed *Up from Slavery,* and some positive reviews had appeared in the African American press, Washington's program and his leadership were not universally embraced. Part of the importance of *Up from Slavery,* and Washington himself, in the African American canon lies in the response the book and Washington's educational program engendered in the African American community. While the text itself suggests that Washington's critics were won over to his viewpoint and that he rarely felt anything but support, there was a larger critical response to Washington and the Tuskegee model. Washington obliquely acknowledges other models of progress for his race when he discusses the folly of political agitation and demands for immediate full implementation of rights rather than the gradual earning of them that Washington's model advocates. While he doesn't specifically name other leaders or movements, this model of political activism fits the ideas posited by Washington's most well-known critic, W.E.B. Du Bois. Du Bois's path had been distinctly different from Washington's. While he had also experienced childhood poverty, he had been born free and went on to be Harvard educated, earning the first doctorate Harvard granted to an African American. His concern was that Washington's emphasis on industrial education held African Americans in a subservient position, so a stronger emphasis on traditional higher education was required, and that his accommodationist rhetoric set back the progress toward full civil rights and true civil liberty for African Americans.

Du Bois's criticisms of Washington and the program he lays forth so explicitly in *Up from Slavery* is put forward in chapter 3 of Du Bois's book, *The Souls of Black Folk* (1903). In this essay, titled "Of Mr. Booker T. Washington and Others," Du Bois details the criticisms of Washington that have existed, but have been silenced because of Washington's popularity and power, in the African American community. Thus, part of the importance of Washington and his books in the canon of African American literature exists in this dialogue between his position and Du Bois's position. This dialogue would continue in the assessments of the two leaders and their programs for progress throughout the 20th century. As a testimony to the power of Washington and the following his work and his autobiography had created, Du Bois starts out with a balancing act of his own. The first part of his critique recognizes Washington's need for and success in balancing the expectations of his northern and southern audiences in such a way as to win applause and admiration in both sections while the work "silenced if it did not convert the Negroes themselves" (31). He also recognizes that Washington had achieved much in building Tuskegee.

However, the Tuskegee model of education is portrayed as narrow and dependent on the teachers trained by the university educations that Washington has devalued. Furthermore, Du Bois contrasts Washington with that other iconic African American leader that many saw as comparable: Frederick Douglass. Du Bois points out that Douglass valued "assimilation through self-assertion" rather than the tacit acceptance of racial inferiority put forth in Washington's program (35). Du Bois characterizes the picture that Washington presents of the current state of race relations and the development of African Americans as "a dangerous half-truth" (41). He claims that remaining silent in the face of the short comings of Washington's program and leadership is a shirking of duties and suggests that not resisting is sitting by "while the inevitable seeds are sown for a harvest of disaster to our children, black and white" (40). This division will continue through the peak of Washington's political power, the first decade of the 20th century. During this period, he advised President Roosevelt on the appointments of African Americans to government positions, guided philanthropists in choosing which African American schools and organizations would receive their money, and advised politicians on questions of race. The divide becomes even more clear when Du Bois helps found the Niagara Movement in 1905, which fails in part due to the widespread belief in Washington's position, and then in the founding of the NAACP in 1909. Ida Wells, one of the founding members of the NAACP, recalled in her 1928 autobiography that the organization was concerned with the ascendancy of Washington's program and worried that it constricted the aspirations of an entire race to a too-narrow industrial education.

Washington explicitly addressed these criticisms—though he never names Du Bois himself—in his third autobiography, *My Larger Education* (1911). Chapter 5, "The Intellectuals and the Boston Mob," describes the criticisms "the Intellectuals" or the "Talented Tenth," a direct nod to Du Bois, make and the depths to which they would sink in order to disrupt Washington's program. Washington dismisses the criticisms as out of touch with the realities of African American life for any but the most elite, college-educated, northern African Americans and again points to how the majority of the critics had become ashamed of themselves and joined his cause. This dismissals of the criticisms, while rhetorically effective in Washington's texts themselves, did not actually stem the tide of criticism. And Washington was unwilling to put in print the work he had done behind the scenes, sometimes anonymously, to achieve legal and political rights. He makes one quick reference to antilynching activity at the end of *Up from Slavery*, but this did not combat the characterization growing through the 20th century of Washington as an accommodationist.

One of the places where this criticism again arises is in one of the most famous African American novels of the 20th century, Ralph Ellison's *Invisible Man*. The narrator describes the statue of the founder of the Collegea statue essentially identical to the actual Booker T. Washington memorial. It is a statue of the founder lifting the veil from the face of a slave kneeling at his feet. Yet as the narrator ponders the statue, he is puzzled and cannot decide if the founder is actually lifting the veil or lowering it, if he is "witnessing a revelation or a more efficient blinding" (Ellison 36). The college is clearly based on Tuskegee (which Ellison himself attended for a time), and the Founder is clearly based on Washington, as can be seen in the biography of the Founder given in Reverend Barbee's speech. This question of whether the Founder is helping or hurting the slave at his feet, and by extension all African Americans, is a representation of the conflicting views of Washington's program itself. And Dr. Bledsoe, the president of the college when the Invisible Man is a student there, is often read as a satire of Washington and his pragmatism, his tempering of his message for white audiences. Dr. Bledsoe is willing to sell out his people if it maintains his personal power; he has aligned himself with white interests by accommodating white racism for personal gain. And this criticism of Washington as a type of Uncle Tom figure is a note struck often in reactions to him and his books in the latter half of the 20th century.

Ultimately, questions about who Washington was and how effective his program of education was would remain. While there are schools across American named after him, and while he is recognized as an important part of African American history, his reputation largely suffered through the 20th century. Du Bois became more celebrated as the NAACP became recognized and as more and more Americans valued direct protest against racism during the civil rights era. Scholars have continued to study him and *Up from Slavery,* and their interpretations and assessments continue to vary. The most recent biography of Booker T. Washington was published in 2009. Two things are certain: first, that Tuskegee University is a tangible legacy of Washington's work ethic and the diplomacy he exhibited in garnishing the support, financial and otherwise, needed to build it; and second, that no matter whether his program was the best road to follow or not, what he accomplished in building Tuskegee was a worthy achievement.

Discussions of the appropriate response by African Americans to systemic racism and discussions of Washington himself often refer to masking. Responses to racism could be a mask of submission or a mask of protest. Ellison's fictionalized descriptions of Washington use the trope of masking as well: Is the founder masking or unmasking those who come to him for education? Who is Dr. Bledsoe behind the mask of subservience and concern he wears for patrons like Mr. Norton, or the mask of rage he wears with the narrator and other students? When we read autobiography, we often expect the writer to unmask himself, to show us the truth behind the public image and actions we already know. In this, as in so much in his life itself, Booker T. Washington confounds the expectations of him. His humble beginnings could not lead to expectations that he would become called to be the leader of his race. His origins did not create the expectations he would build a famous institution and advise presidents and captains of business and industry. And *Up from Slavery* confounds our expectations that Washington the man will be truly revealed. It is autobiography as mask, a carefully created image to help him achieve the full implementation of his image, to ensure his legacy. When the readers close the book, whether they walk away as followers or critics, whether they see Washington as a gradualist who helped African Americans' economic prospects but stunted their political ones, or as a leader who served his race well and walked the tightrope of the conflicting expectations and needs of whites in the South, whites in the North, and his own people, says as much about the readers as it does about Washington. *Up from Slavery* reveals the work, the program, but the man remains masked.

Washington literally turned himself into an icon—a symbol or emblem—through *Up from Slavery*. He does not present himself as a man but as a symbol of the possibilities he saw available to African Americans. The reality of his life and success was figured not as an individual story but as the possible story of any African American who embraced his program, his virtues of hard work, self-reliance, and perseverance. And while some of the criticisms of Washington and of his text are justified, and the text certainly presented a rosier picture of the possibilities than many African Americans in his time, or after, could actually live, *Up from Slavery* is in the classic idealistic American tradition of stories that celebrate a pioneer forging a life for himself and his community out of the soil of America itself, the story of Washington, and Tuskegee, and African Americans, rising up from the soil of the Black Belt into a Promised Land of their own creation.

FURTHER READING

Du Bois, W.E.B. *The Souls of Black Folk*. 1903. New York: Bantam Classics, 1989. Web. University of Virginia Library.

Ellison, Ralph. *Invisible Man*. New York: Vintage International, 1995.

Foster, Francis Smith. *Witnessing Slavery: The Development of Ante-bellum Slave Narratives*. 2nd ed. Baltimore: U of Washington P, 1994.

Harlan, Louis R. *The Making of a Black Leader, 1856–1901*. New York: Oxford UP, 1975.

Harlan, Louis R. *The Wizard of Tuskegee, 1901–1915*. New York: Oxford UP, 1986.

Washington, Booker T. *Up from Slavery*. 1901. Norton Critical ed. Ed. William L. Andrews. New York: Norton, 1996.

Jessica Parker

One of the best and most influential writers of her generation, Alice Walker (seen here in 1990) has affected modern American life not only through her brilliant poetry and novels, but through her actions as a black feminist ("womanist") and social activist. Her novel *The Color Purple* is perhaps her most popular work so far. It was made into a movie starring Oprah Winfrey in 1985. (AP/Wide World Photos)

Alice Walker

Alice Walker (1944–) is probably best known as the author of the novel on which the film *The Color Purple* is based, and nearly every American student who has opened the pages of a literature anthology is familiar with her name as the author of the short story "Everyday Use" and the poem "Revolutionary Petunias." While these works figure among her most popular, she has an entire body of work that has contributed to her status as an icon of African American literature. That body of work is guided by a spirit of effecting personal and societal change. Above all else, Alice Walker is a champion of learning how to love the self and showing anyone who will listen how to do the same. It is this mission that has established and continually reaffirms her status as an icon.

Film and Stage Adaptations

Film Adaptations

The Color Purple. *Directed by Steven Spielberg. Screenplay by Menno Meyjes. 1985.*
Warrior Marks. *Directed by Pratibha Parmar. 1993.*

Stage Adaptations

The Color Purple *(Broadway musical). Produced by Oprah Winfrey and Scott Sanders. Directed by Gary Griffin. Songwriter: Brenda Russell. Dramatist: Marsha Norman. First staged in 2005, the show is currently on tour.*
Walker's first published short story, "To Hell with Dying" (1976), was published as a children's book in 1988.
Walker is credited for introducing academia to one of the first African American women's literature courses (Wellesley 1977).
The Color Purple *was on the* New York Times *bestseller list for 25 weeks.*
Walker coined the phrase womanism, *which refers to African American feminism.*

Since 1968, Alice Walker has been writing about healing personal and community wounds. Part of this healing process she writes about demands that the causes of both physical and psychological wounds be confronted. One cause Walker elucidates is the relationship between psychological and physical trauma. She investigates the vicious cycle of oppression, victimization, and self-loathing and its effects on individuals and communities. What ultimately results from this cycle is a rupture between the mind and the body, an inac-curate self-image usually defined by a dominant force, and a lack of agency. Whether a particular work focuses on an individual's story or that of a com-munity, Walker always shows the process her characters go through in extract-ing themselves from this cycle. Most importantly, merely surviving in a world where such a cycle is the norm is not enough, for mere survival signals acqui-escence to oppression and domination of form. From her earliest poems to her most recent publication, Alice Walker celebrates a dynamic spirit of human triumph, and that is, perhaps, what continues to draw readers to her work.

One of the ways that Walker demonstrates triumph and transformation is through a focus on language: she represents black voices, investigates etymol-ogies, and constructs characters, narrators, and speakers who are especially concerned with rejecting an external definition in favor of a self-definition. Walker focuses on language because it has been the means whereby so many individuals and groups have been oppressed. Language can be manipulated to create stereotypes and negative self-concepts, and it is especially malevolent when individuals let someone else define them or set the limits to their lives. But if individuals take responsibility for the language they use and the terms by which they define themselves, they can remake the self and the world.

Of particular interest to Walker is the development of self-definition within the context of a community. In all of her work, she gives careful attention to the process of working through the complications of the individual's assertion of self in tension with the community. A common pitfall here is the develop-ment of a shifting self rather than a dynamic self. The shifting self is a self that changes depending on context and is always threatened as an individual by a community. Furthermore, when definition exists only at the community level, linguistic ground is fertile for the development of stereotypes and oppres-sion. To empower the self to grow and change rather than to let context dic-tate one's behaviors and one's thoughts about the self is the struggle through which Walker would have all readers triumph.

Alice Walker's entire body of work—novels, poems, essays, and a documentary—is actively engaged in the mission of freeing up the body and language so that they are threatened neither by discourses nor communities. The novels, in particular, call and respond to those of other writers as well as to her own work. And while at first glance it might appear that *The Color Purple* is her main experiment with form, Walker has consistently modified structure, perspective, language, and memory to reflect the concerns not only of African American women but of humanity. Her characters are dynamic beings who either learn to love their own bodies or who demonstrate the physical and psychic trauma of self-loathing. Though not all of her characters learn how or are willing to redeem themselves, true to the mission she has often stated, Walker never abandons faith in that possibility for the future and the reader. In the careful construction of her characters' consciousnesses and their attitudes toward their bodies, Walker creates a refrain that plays again and again in her novels.

In this refrain, there is an abiding concern with not only the acceptance but also the enjoyment of the divinity of one's body. While this concern is nascent in early works such as *The Third Life of Grange Copeland* and *Meridian,* it is fully embodied in the character of Shug Avery in *The Color Purple* and becomes conflict and theme in Walker's later novels. Self-inflicted transgressions against the body are of such great concern in *Possessing the Secret of Joy* and *By the Light of My Father's Smile* that Walker starts to seem singularly obsessed. If her novels are considered as a coherent body of work, however, they reveal a pattern of repetition, a refrain that sings the praises of the interconnectedness of all life. Walker is going to keep on repeating the refrain, with variation, until the world gets her message that the human body is an extraordinary instrument. And though her last novel, *Now Is the Time to Open Your Heart,* is strikingly less concerned with body modification, it presents an African American woman at peace with her body and her choices. In fact, this novel serves as a literary coda to the themes developed from *The Third Life of Grange Copeland* to *By the Light of My Father's Smile.*

Walker's novels are not, however, mere repetitions of other African American women's novels. Though Walker's novels talk to her own and other authors' work, each novel is an individual expression of her refrain and a dynamic development of her style. Walker has moved increasingly toward the theoretical with each novel. Both her message and her concerns have become more global in nature, while her conclusions have grown more prophetic and optimistic. She is deeply attuned with the divine, and many of her characters are as well, but the supernatural or fantastic is either limited to the world of dreams or presented as an extension of characters' personalities. One last hallmark of her style speaks to the role of personal history in being a doer of the living word. Being a doer of the living word means experiencing transformation for yourself and then sharing your testimony, thus helping others to experience transformation. In *Doers of the Word*, Carla Peterson identifies the implications of this phrase for African American women:

> Adapting a verse from the Epistle of James to describe their self-appointed cultural mission, they [19th-century African American women preachers, speakers, and writers] thought of themselves as "doers of the word." In invoking themselves as such, these women recognized the extent to which their efforts to "elevate the race" and achieve "racial uplift" lay not only in their engagement in specific political and social activities but also in their faith in the performative power of the word—both spoken and written. For these and other activists … speaking and writing constituted a form of doing, of social action continuous with their social, political and cultural work. (366)

For Walker, being a doer of the living word entails experiencing transformation and sharing it through her creative, expressive acts and her social activism. She does not merely tell us that we need to change; she inspires and empowers us to change because in her nonfiction, she shows us how she has done it herself. And in her fiction, Walker shows her characters living through their painful pasts rather than only showing them *dealing* with their painful pasts. As Janie tells Pheoby at the end of Zora Neale Hurston's *Their Eyes Were Watching God,* we see Walker's characters "go there" and watch them learn to "know there" (191).

Although Walker does not simply retell the stories of her literary foremothers through a contemporary lens, she is quick to acknowledge her indebtedness, especially to Zora Neale Hurston:

> When Toni Morrison said she writes the kind of books she wants to read, she was acknowledging the fact that in a society in which "accepted literature" is so often sexist and racist and otherwise irrelevant or offensive to so many lives, she must do the work of two. She must be her own model as well as the artist attending, creating, learning from, realizing the model, which is to say, herself....
>
> Well, I thought, where are the *black* collectors of folklore? Where is the *black* anthropologist? ...
>
> And that is when I first saw, in a *footnote* to the white voices of authority, the name of Zora Neale Hurston....
>
> And having found *that* Zora ... I was hooked. What I had discovered, of course, was a model. A model, who, as it happened, provided more than voodoo for my story, more than one of the greatest novels America had produced—though, being America, it did not realize this. She had provided, as if she knew someday I would come along wandering in the wilderness, a nearly complete record of her life. And though her life sprouted an occasional wart, I am eternally grateful for that life, warts and all. (*In Search of Our Mothers' Gardens* 8–12)

This indebtedness is an acknowledgment of another icon who inspired and empowered her. It is a testimony to Walker's belief in the power of creativity, especially the living word. In the development of an African American women's literary tradition, Hurston provides a necessary bridge from suppression of self—and the woman's voice—in the service of racial uplift to the assertion of self-liberation from the constrictions of language and gender. Janie Crawford had to first listen to her own voice and assert her right to her body in order for any of Walker's characters to give voice to the divinity of their bodies.

Both Hurston and Walker join text with body to signal the healing of that rupture between body and mind. The expressivity of the body becomes the expressivity of the text. In key moments, where stereotypes are destroyed and the language of the dominant culture is subverted, the body of a character speaks. Both Janie and Celie experience moments of self-negation, and both Janie and Celie are able to regain that presence through the expressive capabilities of the body. In the chapter "Color Me Zora: Alice Walker's (Re)

Writing of the Speakerly Text" from *The Signifying Monkey,* Henry Louis Gates Jr. attributes the self-assertion in both novels to a linguistic act: "[C]elie's written voice to God, her reader, tropes the written yet never uttered voice of free indirect discourse which is the predominant vehicle of narrative commentary in Hurston's novel.... Janie and her narrator speak themselves into being; Celie, in her letters, writes herself into being" (243). These characters, however, would not have been able to complete these linguistic acts if they had not first recognized the divinity of their bodies possible only when reunited with the mind.

Walker's novels are also in conversation with each other. Among the themes repeated with variation are redemption, thwarted communication, and the miseducation of children. Probing these themes in different contexts—and in some cases, with the same characters—allows Walker to accomplish several purposes. While responding to the call issued by her literary foremothers, including Hurston, Walker voices her own call and creates her own tradition.

The Third Life of Grange Copeland (1970) and *The Color Purple* (1982) focus on the themes of miseducation, miscommunication, and redemption. In the pairings of both Mr. _____ and Grange Copeland and Harpo and Brownfield Copeland, the reader can see a conversation on these themes. Though the first pair of characters consists of fathers who experience redemption and the second pair are sons who suffer the consequences of a miseducation, the striking differences from the first character to the repetition and variation in the next underscore individuality and the individual's choice of whether or not to be a doer of the living word.

In his first life, Grange Copeland is a sharecropper nearly obliterated by the futility of his situation. He is oppressive, humorless, contentious, and verbally abusive. His life is a weekly repetition of the same activities that end in the same result every weekend: a drunken brawl with his wife. Both he and his wife, Margaret, take lovers and are so dedicated to the dysfunction of their life that they fail to realize the life they lead results in a tragic miseducation for their son, Brownfield.

In frustration, Grange deserts the family and moves to the North. Margaret poisons herself and her baby, leaving Brownfield to try to make a life on his own based on the things his parents have taught him. The second life of Grange Copeland is spent in New York City, where Walker develops the dynamic quality of his character. As he wrestles with identity and the surprising northern white oppression, he also grapples with how to redeem himself. And while Walker allows Grange to correct some of the mistakes of his first life, she uses Brownfield's resistance to demonstrate the destructive potential of believing someone else's story for your life.

Earlier in the novel, it is clear that Brownfield has expectations for his father to demonstrate his love. As a child, he blames his father for the changes in his mother's personality, but he also holds both of them accountable for their abysmal parenting and selfish examples: "What Brownfield could not forgive was that in the drama of their lives his father and mother forgot they were not alone" (20). He yearns for authentic communication, both physical and verbal, with his parents. After one particularly dramatic encounter between his parents that ends with Grange's departure, Brownfield presents Grange with the opportunity to be secretly tender toward him. On some level, Brownfield clearly understands the codes of masculine behavior that keep a black man from demonstrating affection and/or tenderness: To do so would signal weakness and threaten emasculation. But Brownfield also understands that he needs this from his father. More importantly, the reader understands that Grange has a deep need to honor tenderness and affection. When Grange returns, Brownfield pretends to be asleep. He has tears on his face as his father bends down to look at him. Brownfield yearns for his touch, wanting Grange to touch the physical evidence of his pain, but also wanting him to be the gentle man that his world tells him he should not be:

> He saw his hand stop, just before it reached his cheek. Brownfield was crying silently and wanted his father to touch the tears. He moved toward his father's hand, as if moving unconsciously in his sleep. He saw his father's hand draw back, without touching him. He saw him turn sharply and leave the room. And he knew, even before he realized his father would never be back, that he hated him for everything and always would. And he most hated him because even in private and in the dark and with Brownfield presumably asleep, Grange could not bear to touch his son with his hand. (21)

This is perhaps one of Walker's most explicit uses of an African American literary trope, that of God the father wiping the tears from His children's eyes. This trope is drawn from prophetic passages in the Bible that detail a divinity so concerned with human suffering that he would note their sorrow and wipe it away with the touch of His hand: "He will swallow up death in victory; and the Lord God will wipe away tears from off all faces; and the rebuke of his people shall he take away from off all the earth: for the Lord hath spoken *it*" (Isaiah 25:8); "For the Lamb which is in the midst of the throne shall feed them, and shall lead them unto living fountains of waters: and God shall wipe away all tears from their eyes" (Revelation 7:17); "And God shall wipe away all tears from their eyes; and there shall be no more death, neither sorrow, nor crying, neither shall there be any more pain: for the former things are passed away" (Revelation 21:4). This is a God who is fearsome, all-powerful, and yet tender enough to *touch* his creation. Brownfield wants his father to be powerful, to end the sorrow, and to communicate love through touching him. But this simply is not possible for Grange has not overcome his own miseducation and redeemed himself. Walker's use of this trope significantly questions the possibility of such a prophecy if people do not first learn to love themselves. With his father gone north and his mother and baby sister dead, Brownfield is catapulted alone into adulthood with a series of painful examples and miscommunications that reinforce oppressive forms and self-degradation.

One hopes that Walker will not have Brownfield make the same mistakes she had his parents make. She has included nothing in his education or experience that allows him to acknowledge the divinity of his own body and its capacity for good, however. In fact, his father's refusal to wipe the tears from his eyes is a denial of divinity and communication with the divine. Brownfield has a chance to make his own life, but his father's rejection of him and his mother's surrender leave him ill-equipped to break the patterns of the past. Even though Brownfield is determined to be his own man when he leaves home, he immediately begins repeating his father's mistakes. He starts out in the wrong direction by sleeping with his father's old girlfriend, Josie, who gives him a version of the past that Walker later reveals is false. When faced with white oppression and the recurring sensation that he is a "sissy," and that his manhood is invalidated, he becomes mired in debt to the white landowner Shipley, is ruthless in his physical and verbal abuse to both wife and children, and eventually murders his wife. Even after all of this, when Grange returns from the North, he represents the possibility and opportunity for Brownfield's redemption. Brownfield, however, is too embittered and emasculated to break the pattern he has fallen into.

After tragedy strikes Brownfield's family, Grange redeems himself and offers a correction to the miseducation he gave Brownfield. Although Brownfield refuses to accept redemption, Grange fights to raise Brownfield's daughter Ruth. The education he gives her provides her the choice to assert her individuality, defend the sanctity of her body, and promote community change through her fight against injustice. In a confrontation involving his daughter, Josie, Grange, and himself, Brownfield reveals the source of his bitterness, "But *you was no daddy to me*" (206). This bitterness runs so deep with him that he is jealous that Grange has decided to give Ruth a proper education in humanity. Grange responds that the true source of emasculation is found in lack of personal accountability and forms created by an oppressively structured language:

> "By George, I *know* the danger of putting all the blame on somebody else for the mess you make out of your life. I fell into that trap myself! And I'm bound to believe that that's the way the white folks can corrupt you even when you done held up before. [...] You can't do nothing wrong without them being behind it. You gits just as weak as water, no feeling of doing *nothing* yourself. Then you begins to think up evil and begins to destroy everybody around you, and you blames it on the crackers. *Shit*! Nobody's as powerful as we make them out to be. We got our own *souls*, don't we?" ... "I mean," he said, "the crackers could make me run away from my wife, but where was the *man* in me that let me sneak off, never telling her nothing about where I was going, never telling her that I forgave her, never telling her how wrong I was myself?" (207)

In this powerful self-revelation, Alice Walker reveals the evils of miseducation and miscommunication, but she also declares that blame is not the way out. Redemption is only possible if each individual takes responsibility for remaking his or her life. Brownfield still will not redeem himself, but Grange is determined to end the cycle. Instead of redeeming his son, he kills him when Brownfield attempts to ruin Ruth's life. Although Grange admits to Ruth that he knows he doesn't have a chance at survival, he has made the way for her to have a chance. After he is shot by the police, Grange maneuvers his body into a prayer pose. Instead of praying—which we are told he cannot do— Grange ministers to himself, saying "Oh, you poor thing, you poor thing" (*Third Life of Grange Copeland* 247), and rocks himself in his own arms. In this final scene, Walker suggests that Grange has become his own creator, his own divinity in his third life. Like the Old Testament God, he destroys his creation that is beyond redemption. But like a man, he is at last alone, praying to himself, and yet in control of his own form. He has righted his wrongs, taken responsibility for them, and at least for this fictional family, ended the cycle of physical and psychological abuse.

Twelve years after *The Third Life of Grange Copeland,* Alice Walker offered a repetition and variation on this type of character with Mr. ____ in *The Color Purple.* Though these two characters make very different choices, they are faced with similar patterns to break and pitfalls to avoid. Mr. ____ is also thwarted in love, and because he cannot assert himself to his father, he creates a life of misery not only for himself, but for his first wife, his children, and Celie. He most grievously wounds his son Harpo through miseducation and miscommunication; his advice is for Harpo to beat his wife into submission. Brownfield has also learned this lesson through the observation of his parent's relationship. The redemption that comes near the end of this novel is much different. Here, communication is redirected through ministry to the body from the son to the father.

Throughout his early years, Harpo is described in domestic terms. He likes to cook, clean house, and care for the children. Seemingly, Sofia is the perfect partner for him: she is more aligned with the physically demanding chores of their life. Sofia has a strong sense of self, and she knows how to fight. Because Harpo has felt the effects of a miseducation, this marriage suffers. Harpo's mother was shot by her lover, and she dies in Harpo's arms; Harpo's stepmother Celie suppresses her voice and will to avoid beatings from Mr. ____; Mr.____ tells Harpo that women need to be treated like children; Celie tells Harpo to beat Sofia when he asks Celie how to make Sofia mind. Sofia gives Harpo a beating he didn't count on, and in response he tries to eat himself into physical bigness.

Harpo and Sofia suffer a lifetime of verbal and physical miscommunication. The combined efforts of the women in this novel serve to reeducate Harpo. When faced with a battle with Sofia over her acting as pallbearer at her mother's funeral, Harpo's redemption becomes complete. It is clear that Harpo fears emasculation when gendered norms are upset. Sofia demonstrates to Harpo that her decisions are not about breaking with gendered norms or trying to emasculate men; her choices are about remaking things in her way.

Walker uses Harpo's redemption to demonstrate the importance of sharing that experience; it is the thing that allows Harpo to reeducate and redeem his own father. Sofia and Harpo tell Celie that Mr. ____ has started to work in his fields and "clean that house just like a woman" (229). Celie cannot believe this is the truth until both Sofia and Mr. ____ himself convince her of the change. After Celie curses Mr. ____ and leaves for Memphis with Shug, he retreats to his house where he lives "like a pig" (231). After suffering delusions and fearing his own misdeeds, Mr. ____ experiences redeeming grace ministered by Harpo. Harpo cleans the house, cooks for him, and gives his father a bath. Though their lives have been inscribed by miscommunication and miseducation, Harpo baptizes his father allowing him to "enter into Creation" (231). One evening, Sofia goes to Mr.'s____ house to talk to Harpo, and she sees the thing that awakens her love for him (224). In a repetition and variation on the ending of *The Third Life of Grange Copeland*, Harpo holds his father in his arms as they sleep.

One of the key elements in Walker's philosophy of being a doer of the word is that personal transformation is passed on to the community. This does not signal the individual's capitulation to dominant ideologies or the community's will. Rather, it is through the individual's experience in defining and asserting the self that he or she participates in community healing and building. In her second novel, *Meridian* (1976), Alice Walker combines all of the elements of her earlier work in poetry, and in both short and long fiction. For in telling Meridian Hill's story, Walker unabashedly faces the taboo, demonstrates a path to redemption for a woman who does not always make choices that fit in with the dominant moral code, weaves specific autobiographical elements that miraculously speak to a diverse group of women, attends to the spiritual well-being of her characters, and calls out to her readers with the poetry of human speech and self-reflection.

One of the ways Walker infuses Meridian Hill's story with poetry is through song. Song is present in three pivotal moments in Meridian Hill's developing consciousness. All of these moments depict the community's reaction to death. The first instance involves the funeral of Wile Chile who appears in the slum near Meridian's college when she is estimated to be five or six. Wile Chile had no parents, friends, relatives, or language. She could not tell her story or even tell anyone her age. Over the years, the neighbors attempt to take her in and civilize her. She resists all attempts until she is found to be pregnant. Meridian succeeds in capturing her by luring her with cake, colored beads, and fresh cigarettes. While Meridian bathes her, Wile Chile reveals her linguistic ability in the form of obscenities. She is uncouth, farting "as if to music," and upsets the peace of Meridian's college dorm. Meridian attempts to find a home for her, but Wile Chile escapes and is killed by a speeding car. While Wile Chile and her story represent a number of stories of oppression and abuse in the American past, the aftermath of her death provokes in Meridian a struggle over how she will define herself in relation to her community.

Meridian and her friends band together to buy a casket and hold a funeral for Wile Chile. They are met with administrative opposition as they attempt to enter the chapel. In response, the women begin expressing their resistance in a number of ways:

> For five minutes the air rang with shouts and the polite curses of young ladies.... They were so ashamed and angry they began to boo and stamp their feet and stick out their tongues through their tears. In the heat of their emotion they began to take off their jewelry and fling it to the ground [all symbols by which their culture would inscribe them].... They shook loose their straightened hair, and all the while they glared at the locked chapel door with a ferocity that was close to hatred. (47)

Without speaking a word, the women move the casket to the symbolic tree, The Sojourner. They begin to sing "We Shall Overcome" with tears and grief streaming down their faces and bury Wile Chile in an overgrown corner of the black cemetery. It would seem that these women have learned to resist oppression and exterior definition.

In reality, the very act of capturing Wile Chile leads to her destruction. Similarly, when they riot in response to administrative oppression, they mistake the meaning of The Sojourner and saw down the "mighty, ancient, sheltering music tree" (48). Meridian does not participate in this act, and attempts to persuade the women to dismantle the president's house instead. The narrator writes that their act was done in "a fury of confusion and frustration" (47). They have mistaken the symbols, mistaken who Wile Chile is, and have destroyed their mothers rather than their oppressors. Though they express their anger with their bodies and sing a hymn of protest, the meaning is lost on all but Meridian. The sense of guilt weighs so heavily upon her that she is catapulted back through a series of reflections in which the meaning of guilt as defined by someone else has led her to misunderstand her own self. She has believed someone else's story for her life, and she has tried to fit Wile Chile into this mold rather than try to understand what Wile Chile has attempted to communicate. The significant use of the symbol and poetry in the song make Meridian confront her own humanity and how she has defined that.

The second key instance of song is much later in Meridian's life when she attends the funeral of Martin Luther King Jr. After the service, the "pitiable crowd of nobodies" (186) follows the casket singing "In the Garden." The song, a favorite of Dr. King's, seems neutral to Meridian. She then notices that the crowd is absorbed in all things except for obvious mourning, and they cease the song: "Those who had never known it anyway dropped the favorite song, and there was a feeling of relief in the air, of liberation that was repulsive" (186). Though the song is about the individual soul's communion with the deity, her revulsion at their seeming lack of decorum nearly forces Meridian to misunderstand the community.

As she turns in shame, she hears a young black man offer an explanation to a white couple. Here Walker recalls Grange Copeland's speech about getting trapped in someone else's definition for your life: "'It's a black characteristic, man,' a skinny black boy tapping on an imaginary drum was saying. 'We don't go on over death the way whiteys do.' He was speaking to a white couple who hung on guiltily to every word. Behind her a black woman was laughing, laughing as if her cares, at last, had flown away" (186). Their behavior at a funeral is a thing of resistance itself; they will not subscribe to white notions of grief and loss and let those dictate their behavior. But Meridian is obviously troubled by this explanation; she looks within herself and within the institutions of the black community for answers.

Meridian then reflects on a series of questions she discussed with her sometimes lover Truman Held. What she struggles with is the differentiation between the right thing and the correct thing to do when it comes to killing. She knows that people do whatever is necessary to survive without counting the cost. This, the narrator tells us, is what differentiates most people from Meridian. In Meridian, however, Walker embodies the notion of the physical action requisite for the spoken word: if Meridian says she would be willing to kill, then she had better be able to do it. Barbara Christian identifies this as Meridian's "persistent identification of her body with her soul, her past with her present" ("Novels for Everyday Use" 77). Through the character of Meridian, Walker illustrates the organic process of engaging with the living word.

When Meridian is unable to find answers through her solitary suffering, she starts visiting different churches. On one particular Sunday, she visits a Baptist church. Feeling her usual revulsion at the containment, the formality, and the sameness of the service, she is also surprised when she cannot remember the words to a very familiar tune. Meridian remembers the melody, but cannot remember the words. In fact, the words seem to be associated with Meridian's search for self:

> But now she could not remember the words; they seemed stuck in some pinched-over groove in her memory. She stared at the people behind the altar, distractedly clutching the back of the bench in front or her. She did not want to find right then whatever it was she was looking for. She had no idea, really, what it was. And yet, she was *there*. (194)

Meridian tries to sing but realizes the words are new to her. Just then, a red-eyed man whose son was killed in the civil rights struggle starts to whisper to the people around him, and another man asks for someone to lead in prayer. The prayer delivered is more of a declaration thanking the community for its solidarity but resolving not to pray any longer because of the amount of work—the action of the living word—required in the community. Speaking the words without resolve for personal action is no longer enough. This interaction with language is representative of a fundamental shift in the Civil Rights Movement from the ideology of the 1960s to that of the 1970s, and the setting for Meridian's contemplation establishes the importance of her role as a redefined self interacting in a community context. Again, Barbara Christian elucidates the importance of the connection between mind, or thought and language, and body, a necessary instrument for articulating that which cannot otherwise be articulated:

> Meridian insists that to be whole, there must be a unity of body and mind. So, too, the central action of the Civil Rights Movement, body resistance to manifest the protest of the mind, attempted to demonstrate this oneness. The process of putting one's body on the line, of resisting oppression without inflicting violence, is crucial to the Movement's spirit—the desire to change without destroying, to maintain the integration of body and spirit, to resist separation and alienation. ("Novels for Everyday Use" 79)

In *Meridian,* Walker issues a call about the cultural oppression that separates the body from the mind; the refrain here is very personal and particular. Walker responds to her own call with *Possessing the Secret of Joy,* in which the reader sees both the personal and the political reunification and revision of form.

After Meridian is given the chance to ponder how the unfamiliar familiar reflects her own purpose, another song with unfamiliar words is sung. This time, however, Meridian abandons the search for words as her consciousness merges with "the triumphant forcefulness of the oddly death-defying music" (195). After this song, the minister, who sounds a lot like Dr. King, begins to preach. Meridian initially questions his imitation, attributing it to mockery. She suddenly realizes that the imitation is a deliberate signification designed to keep lost voices alive: "It struck Meridian that he was deliberately imitating King, that he and all his congregation *knew* he was consciously keeping that voice alive.... [T]he preacher's voice—not his own voice at all, but rather the voice of millions who could no longer speak" (196). The congregation responds to this call in the nature of their "Amens." Meridian notices that the responses are neither resigned nor desperate; the "Amens" calmly convey the message "We are fed up." The red-eyed man then delivers his three word speech that he delivers every year, "My son died" (193). He stands on display and then falls heavily into his chair, communicating the "inarticulate grief" that his speech could not. The service is concluded with music that further communicates this inarticulate grief, the passing of the collection plate for the prison fund, and the preacher urging the congregation to vote. Meridian's experience in this church service ends with her contemplation of the stained glass. Rather than the traditional stained glass image, this one is titled "B. B., With Sword."

This experience leaves Meridian puzzled. She is puzzled that the church, once so reliable for its forms, has changed. She is puzzled about the changes in the community's behavior in church. She is puzzled about how to show love for someone already dead. She is puzzled about the meaning of the ceremony at the church. Meridian at first sees it all as a defamiliarizing event, but she soon realizes the meaning of the linguistic and corporeal acts and this allows her to understand her role in the community.

As she makes out the meaning of the unfamiliar songs, the signifyin(g) preacher, the new "Amen," the physical expression of the red-eyed man, and the stained glass image of B. B. King, Meridian comes to understand the meaning of the communal body. The last two instances of song and death have signified on her first experience with Wile Chile:

> The people in the church were saying to the red-eyed man that his son had not died for nothing, and that if his son should come again they would protect his life with their own. "Look," they were saying, "we are slow to awaken to the notion that we are only as other women and men, and even slower to move in anger, but we are gathering ourselves to fight for and protect what your son fought for on behalf of us. If you will let us weave your story and your son's life and death into what we already know—into the songs, the sermons, the 'brother and sister'—we will soon be so angry that we cannot help but move." (199)

Here, Walker delineates the fundamental principles of telling one's own story and being a doer of the living word. There are no strict forms to adhere to; the self and the community are dependent on the new forms that develop each time a new story is added to the communal song. This is the point at which Meridian faces what she was looking for:

> The respect she owed her life was to continue, against whatever obstacles, to live it, and not to give up any particle of it without a fight to the death, preferably *not* her own. And that this existence extended beyond herself to those around her because, in fact, the years in America had created them One Life. (200)

She believes then that she *would* kill before she allowed a member of the community to be murdered. Walker brings Meridian to the point where she, like the church, is going to be a proactive rather than a reactive body.

Meridian also realizes that she is a minister rather than a revolutionary of the future because she really could not kill. This does not bring despair; rather it allows her to affirm her value as an individual within the community. She likens herself to the old music and understands its purpose:

> It will be my part to walk behind the real revolutionaries ... and when they stop to wash off the blood and find their throats too choked with the smell of murdered flesh to sing, I will come forward and sing from memory songs they will need once more to hear. For it is the song of the

people, transformed by the experiences of each generation, that holds them together, and if any part of it is lost the people suffer and are without soul. (201)

Each person's song and each person's body are required for the perpetuation of a healthy community body. In her essay "Novels for Everyday Use," Barbara Christian defines Walker's construction of Meridian Hill as a device that articulates the quest for the individual's voice within a communal context:

> The question that permeates this book and her [Meridian's] life is the nature of social change and its relationship to the past and the future, a question that is at the crux of the Civil Rights Movement. In other words, what does one take from the past, which is still often present, to create a new future? ... In *Meridian*, Walker encompassed the past, the present, and the future as her major character uses her heritage to change her society, even as she seeks her own expression. Meridian then is not only a character, she is the embodiment of the novel's major concept, the relationship between personal and social change. (72–73)

This relationship between the individual and society is also the major concept in investing forms with new meaning.

In addition to repeating themes and rhetorical strategies within and among her novels, Alice Walker also employs the strategy of repetition with a group of characters in three novels. Although she has expressly stated that these novels are not sequels to *The Color Purple,* the repetition of the characters demonstrates their dynamic qualities, their influence on the community, and the way in which Walker subverts language and Western literary structures through the disruption of a linear concept of time. One character repetition is central to Walker's entire project. Shug Avery figures largely in *The Color Purple* and makes appearances in *Possessing the Secret of Joy* and *The Temple of My Familiar.* Her presence in all three of these novels serves to reinforce the importance of the process of personal transformation and passing that on to the community.

In *The Color Purple,* the reader sees Shug Avery's concept of God as a dynamic, individually defined construct that allows Celie to rout oppression and assert her voice. Celie's transformation and self-assertion in turn inspire other transformations in her community. The God that Shug and Celie believe in is everywhere, in everything, and craves a personal relationship with creation. It is this animism and link between divinity and creativity that connects us all to—as Walker has elsewhere stated—"the Source." Through creative and expressive acts, our connections to humanity and divinity are affirmed. In Walker's work, there is a close link between the creative impulse and the identification of the divinity within the self.

Walker gives this creative impulse to Shug Avery, both in her role as a blues singer and as a "minister" and the author of a pamphlet, *The Gospel According to Shug,* in *The Temple of My Familiar.* Olivia, Celie's daughter, is the first character who addresses Shug's publication and her religion:

> Mama Shug had decided to found her own religion.... Everyone who came brought information about their own path and journey. They exchanged and shared this information. That was the substance of the church. Some of these people worshipped Isis. Some worshipped trees. Some thought the air, because it is alone everywhere, is God.... Mama Shug felt there was only one thing anyone could say about G-O-D, and that was—it had no name.... I was telling them, Mama Celie and Miss Shug, about how the Olinka use humming instead of words sometimes and that that accounts for the musicality of their speech. The hum has meaning, but it expresses something that is fundamentally inexpressible in words. Then the listener gets to interpret the hum, out of his own experience, and to know that there is a commonality of understanding possible but that true comprehension will always be a matter of degree. (170)

Walker's use of Olivia to repeat Shug's gospel is as significant as the repetition of the character Shug herself. Shug articulates a belief that Olivia connects to a West African linguistic maneuver. Furthermore, Olivia understands the dynamic and individual nature of the gospel as she repeats it to her own daughter who is much in need of a strategy for breaking free from forms.

Much later in the novel, Walker textually reproduces the pamphlet. It reads much like the Beatitudes. But rather than declaring the doers of the words as "blessed," Walker remakes the meaning of the form by asserting the doers are "helped": "'HELPED' are those who are shown the existence of the Creator's magic in the Universe; they shall experience delight and astonishment without ceasing" (289). In all, there are 27 tenets that comprise this gospel. They articulate Walker's concerns and themes from *The Third Life of Grange Copeland* to *The Way Forward is With a Broken Heart.* Furthermore, they represent the union of word with action, they reconstruct a scriptural form and the Christian ideology, and they are the counterpart to the physical Shug that Walker presented in *The Color Purple.*

In this group of novels, Walker is also concerned with how assertion of the self and individual expressivity are stymied by mutilation of the body. In fact, Walker explores the cycle of abuse, the damaged psyche, mutilation, and lack of agency in all of her novels. She moves beyond female circumcision to include any alteration or marking of the body resulting from shame, oppression, or an attempt to conform to a dominant standard. Whether sexuality is suppressed or the body is mutilated, Walker elucidates the connections between body image and expression. The body becomes either a passive text to be written on, or an instrument through which the self is expressed. For the latter to happen, characters have to remake their form and tell how they did it.

Possessing the Secret of Joy is a novel that in form and content reveals the divided consciousness of Tashi. The clearest indication of Tashi's fragmentation is the varying headings of her sections: Tashi, Evelyn, Tashi-Evelyn, Evelyn-Tashi, Tashi-Evelyn-Mrs. Johnson. In these sections, Walker uses these conflicting fragments of Tashi to give voice to the corporeal and psychological damage of the circumcision in particular. Ultimately, Tashi murders the *tsunga* (ritual circumciser) who circumcised her, and is condemned to death for her deed. In the end, she is Tashi Evelyn Johnson Soul, no longer fragmented, reborn to spread the living word through her voice in the text.

In her journey to this point, however, Tashi experiences an unfathomable amount of physical and emotional pain. Walker draws upon her research of female circumcision rites to paint a grim picture in which Tashi is subjected to not only a clitoridectomy, but her labia are also removed and the gaping wound is sewn shut with a thorn. She suffers from the pain and stench of a blocked menstrual flow, unsuccessful surgical attempts at reconstruction, and a distorted birth canal that damages the brain of her son, Benny. In *The Color Purple,* Walker has Tashi relate her worst fears: "I fear Adam will be distracted by one of these naked looking women and desert me. Then I would have no country, no people, no mother, and no husband and brother" (286). In fact, Adam engages in a sexual relationship with a French woman, Lisette, and has a son with her.

It is this son, Pierre, who ministers to Tashi by researching the origins of female circumcision rites. Tashi has been plagued by a nightmare of a tower, and this nightmare has become the sole obsession of Lisette. Pierre uncovers the meaning of this tower and reaches out to help Tashi heal. Female circumcision is revealed as a mutilation of the female form borne out of the male need to dominate. Furthermore, both male and female circumcision are attempts to create an unnatural gender division: the clitoris is masculine in its protrusion from the body, and the foreskin is feminine in its enclosure of the penis. From his research, Pierre asserts that the original human beings were endowed with two souls of different sex, but the desire for definite categories and forceful domination led man to circumcision.

After learning this, Tashi remarks that it is no surprise to her that Pierre is biracial and bisexual. He fully accepts all of the parts and urges of his body. As a character similar to Shug Avery, Pierre helps Tashi to unlock the pain of her nightmares, her divided consciousness, and to learn the meaning of a ritual to which she is so blindly capitulated. It is a mystery, Tashi writes in a letter, "that kept me enmeshed" (277). The mystery threatens to destroy her until she learns that there was a tribe of African women who loved their bodies: "They liked their genitals. So much so that they were observed from birth stroking and 'pulling' on them. By the time they reached puberty, well, they had acquired what was to become known, at least among European anthropologists, as 'the Hottentot apron'" (277–78). Before patriarchy and theories of race difference, there were women not ashamed of their flesh. Pierre's research opens up the meaning of the tradition and allows Tashi to be free of its inscription. Though she cannot recover her clitoris or labia, Walker creates a woman who can remake herself and spread the gospel. As Tashi is executed she reads the banner that her people have made for her "RESISTANCE IS THE SECRET OF JOY!" (281). Her very resistance to form and oppression inspires her fellow countrywomen.

As Tashi makes her way to her execution, she is met by women protesters. The meaning of their presence is not recognized by the men facing them with machine guns. They have been warned not to sing. Unbeknownst to the men, their corporeal presence is a song of sorts to Tashi. By asserting their right to a physical presence in a culture that devalued them and denied them pleasure for reasons long forgotten, these characters whom Walker places at Tashi's execution stand for resistance. In the face of a government that has completely convoluted oppression and reinforced sexism through the separation of a woman's body from her spirit through ritual female circumcision, Tashi's fragmentation drives her to violence. But Walker allows Tashi to be remade whole, and the women who meet her at her execution remake this violent act into a scene of resistance and unification. They communicate in a way that is incomprehensible to their oppressors, and they remake meaning for their own forms:

> The women along the way have been warned they must not sing. Rock-jawed men with machine guns stand facing them. But women will be women. Each woman standing beside the path holds a red-beribboned, closely swaddled baby in her arms, and as I pass, the bottom wrappings fall. The women then place the babies on their shoulders or on their heads, where they kick their naked legs, smile with pleasure, screech with terror, or occasionally wave. It is a protest and celebration the men threatening them do not even recognize. (280)

In true antiphonal fashion, Walker has Tashi call to her fellow countrywomen through her actions and insistence on the divinity of the body, and Walker has the women respond with their bodies. Furthermore, while the presence of the women represents resistance, the nonviolent act of removing the swaddling—forms that bind—from their babies' bodies indicates the reintegration of body and spirit and positive resistance for the future.

In her first two novels, Walker uses a third person omniscient narrator to tell the stories of characters defining themselves. With *The Color Purple,* she uses the epistolary form to tell the story from Celie's perspective and signifies on the way in which Janie finds her voice in *Their Eyes Were Watching God.* The next novel, *The Temple of My Familiar,* has a third person narrator. Due to the number of characters and the global nature of the material, omniscience is necessary. The lives of these characters are all intertwined, and Walker uses the third-person narrator to mediate the activity and fill in gaps. *Possessing the Secret of Joy,* though involving many characters, is focused on the story of Tashi. The narration of this novel is patterned after the gospel song, where polyvocality and antiphony blend to create a master narrative. As the voices blend together, they are also distinct, sharing their individual experience in the narrative of the community.

Walker combines these narrative styles in *By the Light of My Father's Smile.* The reader first encounters what seems to be a third-person omniscient narrator. Walker soon reveals that he is the spirit of Susannah and Pauline's father. This voice then blends with those of other characters as they each relate their stories in response to the voice of this father. Although the father watches over the events of his daughters' lives, it is not in a spirit of dominion or control. He is a restless spirit, forced to watch the consequences of the domineering actions of his earthly life. He is an absent presence felt by his daughters, seeking their forgiveness and trying to do for them in death what he could not do in life.

The father here is a clever repetition of Grange Copeland and Mr. ___. He is unable to redeem himself in this life and attain peace after death because he has sinned against the spirits and bodies of his daughters. His adherence to a patriarchal system that denies love of the body and expression thereof leads him to severely beat Pauline for her sexuality. Susannah witnesses this transgression against the body. Both daughters suppress the self and either abuse or mutilate the body throughout the rest of their lives. As a spirit, the father is able to restore a sense of wholeness, acceptance of the body, and acceptance of the self to his daughters.

In an interview with Alice Walker, Evelyn C. White asked her about the spirit of the father watching the sexual development of his daughters. Quite candidly, Walker asserts that women most want to be blessed in their sexuality by their parents. This allows the parents to know the entire child and to love him or her in entirety. Walker has clearly written this novel to especially touch the lives of fathers:

> They need to know how deeply their daughters are wounded by their apparent incomprehension that their daughters have sexual feelings. I think young girls are hurt when they come to understand that just because they are female, their fathers don't believe they have sexual passions or interests. Meanwhile, they get to watch their brothers be encouraged to sow his wild oats and be affirmed in their manhood.... I think they should be made aware of the tenderness that is required from fathers in raising daughters. They should embrace the whole female child in a way that makes her feel affirmed in her body.

Love of the entire self is essential to a healthy self-image and healthy behavior. Throughout her novels, Walker repeats the theme that self-loathing is at the root of oppression, racism, and violence. Later in the interview, Walker comments on the intended reader of this novel: "My novel is really a call to fathers to stand with their daughters and help protect them in a world where they are vulnerable. If a child has a strong mother, she's very lucky. But barring that, she gets faulty information and becomes a victim.... The system has already told the woman that she is to submit. We need to break this." Alice Walker calls to readers to be doers of her words, to reeducate themselves, to remake language, to break the final chains of a broken system. Until that happens, she will continue to give us the living word.

In her seven volumes of poetry from 1968 to 2003, Alice Walker has confronted what we fear—what we fear to ask, to say, to do, and to become—with unflinching honesty and a firm commitment to share with readers how she continues to grow and learn from life. In her introductions to the volumes, as well as in several of her essays, she refers to the decision to quit writing that she has made several times. Yet every time she makes this decision, she is reminded that such a decision denies her life. Her latest volume of poetry, *A Poem Traveled down My Arm*, was borne out of such an experience. Walker introduces the poems with a confession that they evolved, almost unconsciously, from an attempt to relieve her boredom in signing autograph sheets:

> As I began signing sheets of the quite high stack of blank paper, my pen joined me in boredom at writing my name. It began to draw things instead. I was delighted. There was an elephant! A giraffe! A sun! A moon! Hair! And at the same time, as if completely *over* the mundane task of writing my name, we, my pen and I, began to write poems.... And that, dear reader, is the story. Not all of it, of course. *Because*. It is really a story about exhaustion. About deciding to quit. About attempting to give up what is not in one's power to give up: one's connection to the Source. Being taught this lesson. Ultimately it is a story about Creativity, the force that surges and ebbs in all of us, and links us to the Divine. (xii–xiv)

Though sometimes criticized for their lack of originality and formal experimentation, or ridiculed for their amount of self-disclosure, Alice Walker's poems represent a writer's response to affirm the full extent of life in herself and in her readers.

As a body of work, her poems also testify to the continual process of achieving balance. In fact, in her first volume, *Once,* Walker used an epigraph from Camus to invoke an understanding of the necessity of balance: "To correct a natural indifference I was placed half-way between misery and the sun. Misery kept me from believing that all was well under the sun, and the sun taught me that history wasn't everything" (Camus, qtd. in *Once*). In the poems that follow, Walker expresses the misery of people not included in history, she questions the beliefs of her society, and she celebrates the fact that she has come through both of these experiences recognizing the fact that they have made her more alive.

Walker's second volume of poetry, *Revolutionary Petunias*, continues this thread, focusing particularly on liminal periods, experiences of change, and of course revolutions, both personal and political. Nearly halfway through the volume, the poet voices her need to learn to embrace change in the poem "Reassurance. For in learning to love the questions, she is becoming, attending to what the soul seeks rather than seeking the answers. It is a reassurance that allows her to declare in conclusion of the volume that she will not only survive; she will thrive amidst the change.

In subsequent volumes, through all of her life's changes, Walker continues to ask the questions and revel in them. Beginning with *Good Night Willie Lee, I'll See You in the Morning*, she offers more lessons to readers as she honors her losses and the losses of her world while she experiences the fact that even forgiveness is a celebration of life. She articulates her understanding of forgiveness as the final segment in the cycle of change, the segment that assures her both of "blooming gloriously" and of future change. *Horses Make the Landscape Look More Beautiful* is both a testament to yet another cycle of change and Walker's meditation on her mission in life. In this way, her poetry becomes fully personal and political. While she has written freely about her social activism and her mission as a writer in her prose, this volume of poetry marks the first meditation on poetry as a means of working through change for the poet while at the same time having a full awareness of her poems' transformative effects on her readers. Again, she returns to the theme of balance, learning to recognize and love all parts of herself, including those ancestors of hers whose actions repulse her. All of these ancestors, her sorrows, her triumphs, and her changes contribute to the person she is becoming. More than anything, this volume of poetry is witness to the forgiveness in "Good Night, Willie Lee, I'll See You in the Morning," for Walker writes of learning to forgive her white, rapist great-great-grandfather and herself so that she can experience transformation and renewal. In "Songless," she writes of saving her own life, and in "These Days," she writes of saving the earth for the people she loves. Surely saving her own life is closely connected to saving the earth.

And saving the earth is clearly the theme of her last full-length collection of poems, *Absolute Trust in the Goodness of the Earth*. In the preface to the poems, she again writes of having sworn off writing. Walker differentiates between "writing" and poems, implying that "writing" is a more active, deliberate process, while poems are inspired: "Unlike 'writing,' poetry chooses when it will be expressed, how it will be expressed, and under what circumstances" (xii). The inspiration for these poems, she writes, was the American cultural aftermath of 9/11. With startling clarity, Walker realizes that one of the effects of the attacks on the American psyche was being thrust into a cycle of questions and change. These poems, then, arose as a way to "learn to feel our way among and through shockingly unfamiliar and unexpected shadows. To discover and endure a time of sorrow, yes, but also of determination to survive and thrive" (xii). True to her iconic status as wise woman, activist, spiritual medium, and revolutionary, Walker exhorts readers of "Patriot" to love their country. What might otherwise sound preachy or didactic simply does not. It is because we know that Alice Walker is the daughter of sharecroppers; we know she agonized over an abortion; we know that she once felt ashamed of her disfigured eye; we know that she registered voters in Jim Crow Mississippi; we know that she was arrested for protesting the alleged shipment of arms to Central America; and we know that she has suffered and sorrowed. But we also know that she has loved, she has forgiven, and she has gloriously bloomed. We know this because she has told us and we have watched it. And we know that we can suffer loss, and we can change, and we can forgive, and we can love. She shows us how it is done.

One of the more intriguing critical responses to her poetry is to read it as a type of prewriting to the writing of her novels. Given Walker's own view of poetry as something that directs her—for her a process altogether different from the more deliberate process of writing prose—this is a very intriguing view of her poetry. Thadious Davis characterizes the personal nature of her poems in the essay "Poetry as Preface to Fiction":

> A function of her poetry, then, is a psychological exploration of self, a mediating of the consciousness of one's very existence and an attending to the emotional determinants of that existence, which is subsequently reformulated and inscribed in her fiction. For Walker, poetry is the experience of emotional purging, a relation of emotion in expressions usually brief, but occasionally extended over several moods encapsulating one dominant idea, the development of which takes place in the longer fictional pieces. (277–78)

Later, Davis attributes to the poems "a seed of transformative power" (280) that coalesces in her novels. To Davis's interpretation, one might add that in her poems Walker releases the stories of her transformations so that she can expand the stories in the novels. Davis eloquently concludes his essay with a view of Walker that speaks to her iconic status: "Resurgence and resurrection, the simplicity of a soul raised from the dead in a repetitious rite of rebirth, renewal, reproduction, this is the self-mission of Walker's poetry that is the subtext in her novels and her stories. That poetic mission is Alice Walker's preface to fiction and to life" (283).

If poetry is Alice Walker's preface to fiction and to life, then her nonfiction is an extended epilogue to her fiction and a meditation on her life. In her three collections of essays, companion piece to the filming of *The Color Purple*, companion piece to the documentary *Warrior Marks*, and a pamphlet adapted from a post-9/11 speech, Walker traces her influences, comments on her fiction, and confronts her critics, all while demonstrating a life of activism and growth. She is witty, reflective, sometimes sad, triumphant, and always aware of her writerly mission as she shares her losses, loves, and lessons with her readers. What might sometimes appear as artistic eccentricities are, in reality, unbridled and honest insights into the living of life by a woman who has never shied away from the difficult or the forbidden if approaching it meant that she and those she loves would learn and grow from it.

The reader sees Alice Walker defining *womanist* at a time when the Women's Movement was split along racial and sexual orientation lines, giving shelter to stray animals, protesting the shipment of nuclear weapons to Central America, explaining why she would not hold Steven Spielberg's baby for a scene in *The Color Purple*, hugging Fidel Castro, writing to President Clinton to ask him to rethink his position on Cuba, and asking readers to "grow the soul and transform the world" (*Sent by Earth* 55) in the aftermath of the 9/11 attacks. And we might not like some of it. In fact, some of us might not like any of it. We might be offended by her politics or by her desire to mediate her art for the reader. However, there is one thing that Alice Walker's nonfiction does not leave for debate: She asks of no reader what she is not herself willing to undertake. And that is why we love her. We love this icon who, like James Weldon Johnson's God in "The Creation" stepped out and said "I'll make me a world" (4), for she is making a world and living fully in it. She implores us to love ourselves, love the questions, and join in making the world with her.

BIBLIOGRAPHY

Poetry

Absolute Trust in the Goodness of the Earth. New York: Random House, 2003.
Good Night Willie Lee, I'll See You in the Morning. 1979. New York: Harcourt, 1984.
Her Blue Body Everything We Know: Earthling Poems 1965–1990 Complete. New York: Harcourt, 2003.
Horses Make a Landscape Look More Beautiful. 1984. New York: Harcourt, 1986.
Once. 1968. New York: Harcourt, 1976.
A Poem Traveled Down My Arm. New York: Random House, 2003.
Revolutionary Petunias. New York: Harcourt, 1973.
Why War Is Never a Good Idea. New York: HarperCollins, 2007.

Nonfiction

Anything We Love Can Be Saved. New York: Random House, 1998.
Everyday Use. With Barbara Christian. Piscataway, NJ: Rutgers UP, 1994.
In Search of Our Mother's Gardens. 1983. New York: Harcourt, 2003.
Langston Hughes, American Poet. 1974. New York: HarperCollins Children's Books, 2005.
Living By the Word. New York: Harcourt, 1989.
The Same River Twice: Honoring the Difficult. New York: Simon, 1996.
Warrior Marks: Female Genital Mutilation and the Sexual Blindings of Women. With Pratibha Parmar. 1993. Darby, PA: DIANE, 1998.
We Are the Ones We Have Been Waiting For. New York: New Press, 2006.

Collected Short Stories

In Love and Trouble. 1973. New York: Harcourt, 2003.
You Can't Keep A Good Woman Down. 1982. New York: Harcourt, 2003.

Novels

By the Light of My Father's Smile. New York: Random House, 1998.
The Color Purple. 1982. New York: Harcourt, 1992.
Meridian. 1976. New York: Harcourt, 2003.
Now Is The Time to Open Your Heart. New York: Random House, 2004.
Possessing the Secret of Joy. 1993. New York: New Press, 2008.
The Temple of My Familiar. 1990. New York: Simon, 1997.
The Third Life of Grange Copeland. 1970. New York: Harcourt, 2003.
The Way Forward is With a Broken Heart. 2001. New York: New Press, 2008.

Children's Literature (Poetry and Fiction)

Finding the Green Stone. New York: Harcourt Children's Books, 1991.
Langston Hughes, American Poet. New York: Amistad, 2005.
There is a Flower at the Tip of My Nose Smelling Me. New York: HarperCollins, 2006.
To Hell with Dying. Illustrated by Catherine Deeter. San Diego, CA: Harcourt, 1988.

FURTHER READING

Bloom, Harold, ed. *Alice Walker: Modern Critical Views.* New York: Chelsea House, 1989.
Davis, Thadious. "Poetry as Preface to Fiction: Alice Walker's Recurrent Apprenticeship." *Mississippi Quarterly* 44.2 (1991): 133–42.
Dieke, Ikenna, ed. *Critical Essays on Alice Walker.* Westport, CT: Greenwood, 1999.
Gates, Henry Louis, Jr., and K. A. Appiah. *Alice Walker: Critical Perspectives Past and Present.* New York: Amistad, 1993.
White, Evelyn C. *Alice Walker: A Life.* New York: Norton, 2004.
Winchell, Donna Haisty. *Alice Walker.* New York: Twayne, 1992.

R. Erin Huskey

August Wilson poses during a visit to a coffee shop in his Seattle neighborhood, 2003. (AP/Wide World Photos)

August Wilson

August Wilson (1945–2005), a dishwasher-turned-poet-turned-playwright, entered the Broadway theatrical scene in 1984 with a play titled *Ma Rainey's Black Bottom* (1982). In 1987, *Fences* (1983) debuted at the 46th Street Theatre and received great critical acclaim. In 1988, he had the distinction of having two plays run simultaneously on Broadway when *Joe Turner's Come and Gone* (1984) premiered at the Ethel Barrymore Theatre while *Fences* was still enjoying its stint on 46th Street. Opening night for *The Piano Lesson* (1986) was in 1990 at the Walter Kerr Theatre. Two years later, *Two Trains Running* (1990) was produced at the Walter Kerr Theatre and *Seven Guitars* (1995) made its appearance at the Walter Kerr in 1996. In 2001, *King Hedley II* (1999) made its debut at the Virginia Theatre. *Jitney* (1979) opened off-Broadway at the Second Stage Theatre in 2000. *Gem of the Ocean* (2003) opened at the Walter Kerr Theatre in 2004, and *Radio Golf* (2005) made its world premiere at the Yale Repertory Theatre in 2005.

Wilson Important Facts

Black Bart and the Sacred Hills—*the first play Wilson penned.*

"The Ground on Which I Stand"—Wilson's infamous speech before the Theatre Communications Group in Princeton, NJ. Among other things, the speech articulated his position regarding the appropriate function of black art, particularly black theatre, his stance against colorblind casting to accommodate multiculturalism initiatives, and his belief that black theatre is alive but underfunded.

Wilson is only the seventh dramatist to attain the honor of winning the Pulitzer Prize for Drama twice. He won a Pulitzer in 1987 for Fences *and in 1990 for* The Piano Lesson.

Wilson is the only American dramatist with the honor of having two plays running simultaneously on Broadway. In 1988, both Fences *and* Joe Turner's Come and Gone *played on Broadway.*

In 1995, a television adaptation of The Piano Lesson *debuted as a Hallmark Hall of Fame special. Actor Charles Dutton was cast as Boy Willie, and actress Alfre Woodard was cast as Berniece.*

Wilson enjoyed tremendous commercial success during his lifetime; he won several awards, including the New York Drama Critics' Circle Award, the Drama Desk Award, the Tony Award, and two Pulitzer Prizes for Drama. He has been compared to such great American playwrights as Arthur Miller, Tennessee Williams, and Eugene O'Neill. Hailed as the foremost African American playwright of the 1980s and 1990s, Wilson's dramaturgy spurred a renewed interest in African American theatre; indeed, he almost singlehandedly inspired an African American theatre renaissance.

Wilson's canonical stature is a far cry from his humble beginnings in Pittsburgh. Born the fourth of six children to Daisy Wilson Kittel and Frederick Kittel, a German immigrant, in 1945, Wilson grew up in poverty in Pittsburgh's Hill District after his father deserted his mother (Shafer 4). He dropped out of high school as a 10th grader after being accused of plagiarism and completed his education in the Pittsburgh public library's Negro section, where he discovered such writers as Langston Hughes, Richard Wright, and Ralph Ellison, and dreamed of becoming a writer (Shafer 7). Those dreams did not become true immediately, however, for after having served one year in the army, he returned to his native Pittsburgh where he worked as a short-order cook and porter, among other things. Later, he recalled his desire to become a writer; he tried his hand at poetry but failed because he tried to emulate other writers and stifled his own creative voice.

Although Wilson was unsuccessful at writing poetry, he was quite successful at drama. After he cofounded Pittsburgh's Black Horizon Theater with his friend Rob Penny in 1969, his playwriting career flourished. Since that time, his plays have packed Broadway and regional theatres. Not only do productions of his plays attract large audiences, they have also inspired much scholarly work. To date, hundreds of reviews and essays and several full-length studies have been penned with subject matters varying from the influences on his writing to his controversial views concerning the direction of *Fences*.

Like his predecessors, Wilson started writing plays out of arrogance and frustration (Powers 50). He felt that the work of previous African American dramatists did not fully and truly reflect African American culture. Believing that he could write just as well as other playwrights about the black experience in America, Wilson began his career as a playwright. And his commercial success proved that he could do just that. In the afterword to *August Wilson: Three Plays,* literary critic Paul Carter Harrison calls Wilson's plays "a welcome model for future African American dramaturgy" (Wilson 317).

Wilson credited much of his success at dramaturgy to the four B's from which he found inspiration to write. These four B's—Baraka, Bearden, Borges, and the blues—together functioned as a muse of sorts, providing Wilson with the foundation upon which his plays are created.

When Wilson began writing drama, he used Amiri Baraka's (né LeRoi Jones) work as his model. Baraka was at the height of his career when Wilson began writing. Baraka had enjoyed tremendous success with his plays, *Dutchman* and *The Slave,* and the theatre he founded, the Black Arts Repertory Theatre, was producing plays that were causing audiences, both African American and white, to take notice.

Awe-inspired by the themes and forms of Baraka's plays, Wilson initially adopted Baraka's revolutionary style with its accuse and attack approach.

However, Wilson found that the style did not work for him, so he adopted Baraka's earlier approach of exploring the internal conflict within the characters.

Whereas Baraka influenced Wilson's style of writing, Romare Bearden's art inspired the characters about whom he wrote. Bearden, whose collages depicting African American life gained him national attention in the 1960s and 1970s, was the inspiration for the main character of three of Wilson's plays.

Wilson was first introduced to Bearden's work in 1971 when he saw a copy of *The Prevalence of Ritual,* a collected volume of some of Bearden's collages. Says Wilson about Bearden's work:

> What I saw was black life presented on its own terms, on a grand and epic scale, with all its richness and fullness, in a language that was vibrant and which, made attendant to everyday life, ennobled it, affirmed its value, and exalted its presence. In Bearden I found my artistic mentor and sought, and still aspire, to make my plays the equal of his canvasses. (Schwartzman 8)

The first Bearden collage to provide the inspiration for a Wilson character was *Continuities*. A painting that depicts a large man holding a small baby, *Continuities* provided the inspiration for Troy in *Fences*. The image in the painting mirrors the scene in the play when Troy comes home with Raynell and asks Rose to care for her.

The next play to have a character inspired by a Bearden collage is *Joe Turner's Come and Gone*. Bearden's *Millhand's Lunch Bucket* depicts a large, brooding man sitting at a table within a busy room. Although the room is crowded, the man seems alone and isolated. The man became Herald Loomis, who despite living in Seth and Bertha's boardinghouse, finds himself alone in his quest to find his wife.

Bearden's *The Piano Lesson* is the last play to provide the idea for a Wilson play. Not only did this collage provide the idea for the characters, it also provided the title for the play. In the painting, a woman is instructing a child at the piano. The woman and child became Berniece and Maretha in *the Piano Lesson*.

Wilson credited his storytelling ability to the Argentine poet and fiction writer Jorge Luis Borges. From Borges Wilson learned that it's not what happens that counts but how, so in Wilson's plays what happens during the course of the action becomes less important than the cause. For example, in *Seven Guitars* (the Wilson play that is most like Borges's style in that the audience knows what will happen upfront) it is not Floyd's death that is the focal point but the circumstances that lead to his death.

As Mary Friedman notes, Borges's stories have "central characters who travel twisted paths always to a point of little hope ... at this juncture ... some fantastic, irrational event occurs, offering the possibility of spiritual salvation, of release from the world of oppression and death." (6) The same can be said for Wilson's plays, for during the course of his plays, all of his protagonists seem to be burdened by the details of their lives and on the path toward dismal futures, but then experience a redeeming moment that affirms them.

The B that the most influenced Wilson's work is the blues. In countless interviews, he acknowledged the blues as the wellspring of his art. Wilson's use of the blues motif in his work is the result of an appreciation for the blues, which he discovered when he bought a stack of old 78s, including Bessie Smith's "Nobody in Town Can Make This Sweet Jelly Roll Like Mine." Wilson says that when he played the record,

> Everything fell to a new place. I lived in a rooming house at the time with this odd assortment of people. I had never connected them to anything of value. I began to look at these people differently, and at myself differently. I realized that I had history and connection—the everyday poetry of the people I'd grown up with. (Plummer and Kahn 66)

Since that time, Wilson acknowledged that he made a conscious effort to include the blues in his plays. He readily admitted that his plays were "entirely based on the ideas and attributes that come out of the blues" (Moyers 14).

Similar to Ralph Ellison, who emphasized that the blues does not skirt the painful facts of human experience, but works through them to an artistic transcendence (Bone 46), Wilson also believed the Blues contains a philosophy of life. Embedded in the blues are instructions on how to live life as an African American in a white world. And, as such, the blues became the African American community's cultural response to the world in which they found themselves (Powers 50). This response was passed on from generation to generation and became a link between them. Similarly, Wilson wishes for his plays to become a connective force that links the past with the present and the present with the future.

In an interview with Bill Moyers, Wilson said,

> Blues are important primarily because they contain the cultural responses of blacks in America to the situation that they find themselves in. Contained in the blues is a philosophical system at work. You get the ideas and attitudes of people as part of the oral tradition. That is a way of passing along information.... The music provides you an emotional reference for the information, and it is sanctioned by the community in the sense that if someone sings the song, other people sing the song. (14)

These strong emotional overtones in the blues find varied expressions in Wilson's plays. In some instances, the blues is an integral part of the subject (*Ma Rainey*), while in others, it takes on a more symbolic role (*Piano Lesson*). In *Joe Turner's Come and Gone,* the sense of the music being inextricably woven with the cultural identity of African Americans is given a symbolic shape as the characters search for their "song." Wilson says that in *Joe Turner's*

Come and Gone, the song Loomis seeks is his African identity; "understanding who you are ... you can (then) go out and sing your song as an African" (Moyers 16). Or, as Bynum tells Loomis in the same play, "All you got to do is sing it.... Then you be free" (Wilson 287). In finding his own song—his Africanness, his roots—the African American discovers his own identity and the value of his true self. In *Ma Rainey's Black Bottom,* Levee's frustration at not being allowed to write a song his way reaches such a fervor that he kills one of his fellow musicians. In *The Piano Lesson,* Wining Boy is driven almost to desperation by the attempts to suck the music from him:

> Go to a place and they find out you play piano, the first thing they want to do is give you a drink, find you a piano and sit you right down.... They ain't gonna let you get up! ... You look up one day ... and you hate the piano. But that's all you got. You can't do nothing else. All you know how to do is play that piano. Now, who am I? Am I me ... or am I the piano player? Sometimes it seem like the only thing to do is shoot the piano player cause he's the cause of all the trouble I'm having. (41)

Like the blues, history also plays an important role in Wilson's plays. When he began writing, he planned to complete a 10-play cycle that documented the African American experience during the 20th century. His intention was that the plays would explore some of the historical choices that have confronted African Americans since their emancipation from slavery. Wilson does not do this in the traditional sense, however. According to Jay Plum, instead of "writing" history Wilson "rights" it in that he alters his audience's perception of reality to give status to what American history has denied is "real" (562). By contextualizing African American cultural experience, Wilson in turn created an opportunity for the African American community to examine and define itself.

In an interview with David Savron, Wilson explained his reasons for redrawing the American past, and in doing so explained his dramatic vision:

> Writing our own history has been a very valuable tool, because if we're going to be pointed toward a future, we must know our past. This is so basic and simple, yet it's a thing that Africans in America disregard.... One of the things I'm trying to say in my writing is that we can never really begin to make a contribution to the society except as Africans. (295–96)

Wilson wanted his audience to accept and take pride in its Africanness. Like his characters who come to realize that they are primarily African Americans rather than Americans who happen to be of African descent, so too did he want the members of his audience to have this understanding. To Wilson, the only way this knowledge would be acquired was through African Americans' recognition and embracement of their African and slave past. By looking to the past and incorporating its knotty, conflicted legacy of language, custom, history, slavery, and deep pain, Wilson saw an affirmation that could inform, strengthen, and empower. His plays tell African Americans that strength does not lie in avoidance of the past, even one as laden with complexity as the slave past is. This avoidance of the past, believed Wilson, was one of the key reasons why the African American community flounders. In his opinion, rather than looking the past head-on and learning from it, African Americans have turned their backs to it, and as a result, they have remained uninformed and misinformed, repeating the same mistakes from generation-to-generation.

For Wilson, the biggest mistake African Americans made was leaving the South for the North. As he saw it, the migration north removed them from a distinctively African American culture that had already been founded. Wilson believed African Americans would have been a stronger people if they had stayed in the South and viewed the migration north as the root of all the problems they have experienced, and uses his dramaturgy to express this opinion. As Sandra Shannon points out in her essay, "A Transplant That Did Not Take: August Wilson's Views on the Great Migration," the theme of the Great Migration as an enormous mistake seems to be present in all his published plays (660); this may be the reason he sets his plays in Pittsburgh, to depict the evils that plague people in the North.

Joe Turner's Come and Gone, Ma Rainey's Black Bottom, The Piano Lesson, Fences, and *Gem of the Ocean* demonstrate the crippling effect of the slave past. The plays' protagonists are haunted by the ghosts of a past they would rather forget, and because they would rather forget their pasts, they refuse to acknowledge them. Instead, they try to relegate them to the far corners of their minds, but find that this consignment becomes disempowering, affecting them mentally, emotionally, and spiritually. This suppression informs their actions and reactions to people and situations, prohibiting them from developing healthy and nurturing relationships.

In *Joe Turner's Come and Gone,* Herald Loomis would rather forget his seven-year imprisonment on Joe Turner's chain gang, but his suppression of this experience causes him to have visions. The vision of the bones people causes the other boarders to view him as insane and prevents him from finding his "starting place in the world." In *Ma Rainey's Black Bottom,* Levee would like to forget the gang rape of his mother by white men, and his father's vigilantism and ultimate death at the hands of those same men. Because of his containment of these atrocities, he fails to relate to his fellow band members and Ma, and by dissociation, fails to succeed as a musician. In *The Piano Lesson* Boy Willie and Berniece would like to forget that the piano in her living room is a symbol of the splitting of their family, both from the sale of their great-grandmother and grandfather for its purchase and the murder of their father during his attempt to return it to their family. It causes them to squabble amongst themselves, almost to the point of a permanent severance of the familial bond through fratricide. In *Fences,* Troy struggles with two aspects of the slave past, a domineering father hardened by the southern sharecropping system and a rejection by the major leagues formerly governed by its Gentleman's Agreement. Troy's failure to realize the effect these actions have on his life and relationships proves detrimental to his familial bond. In *Gem of the Ocean,* a deeply troubled Citizen Barlow seeks out Aunt Ester for help and sanctuary after committing a crime. He's troubled because he has allowed his crime to be pinned on another man, who drowned himself rather than be falsely convicted.

In order to rid themselves of their ghosts, the protagonists of each play must come to terms with their pasts, and this occurs via an acknowledgment of it, but a simple recognition of it is insufficient. They must also accept it and establish a bond with it.

Herald Loomis realizes that he can only rid himself of the visions of the bones people by acknowledging and accepting the slave past, both his and that of his ancestors, for they are one and the same. He makes this connection once he hears Bynum sing the "Joe Turner Song," for he realizes that his experience with Joe Turner is not his alone. There have been many Joe Turners who have imprisoned African Americans and separated families.

Berniece and Boy Willie discover that they must acknowledge the piano as their legacy, a legacy that can neither be sold nor neglected. They make this connection when Boy Willie engages the ghost in a wrestling match and Berniece plays the piano to exorcise Sutter's ghost, calling on the ancestors, and thereby forming a four-generation familial force to destroy the hold the Sutter family has had on them.

After boarding the slave ship, the Gem of the Ocean, and voyaging to the City of Bones, Citizen Barlow learns that one is affected by his history whether or not he knows that history.

Unlike Herald Loomis, the Charles siblings, and Citizen Barlow, Levee and Troy do not recognize and accept their pasts. While Ma in *Ma Rainey's Black Bottom* stays connected to her roots through the blues music she sings, Levee disconnects himself by refusing to play that "old jug music" and opting for the new swing sound that Sturdyvant prefers. When he does this he unknowingly connects with that same racist past that is responsible for his parents' death and will lead him to commit murder.

Troy, too, tries to disconnect himself from the past, and in doing so disconnects himself from his family. Fearing that Cory will also be slighted by the sport in which he depicts athleticism, Troy thwarts all chances of Cory obtaining a football scholarship. In doing so he ostracizes his son, forever. His disconnection also causes him to feel repressed in his role as husband, father and provider, leading him to infidelity with Alberta in an attempt to forget the "problems and pressures" of the world. Too, wanting to be unlike his father, he no longer sings the "blue song," the one legacy his father passed on to him, but one that is a testament to loyalty.

With the exception of Levee and Troy, after the protagonists of each play accept their past and establish a bond with it, they are able to move on and live productive lives. Herald Loomis finds his starting place in life and begins a relationship with Mattie Campbell. Boy Willie and Berniece reconnect and agree that the best use of the piano is in the family's living room where it can both be used both to generate income and revered by future Charles generations. Levee, however, because he was unable to bond with his past, will probably spend the rest of his life in prison for Toledo's murder, and Troy dies estranged from Cory and Rose, not having heeded the lesson in the song.

Another subject upon which Wilson was quite vocal was the African American theatre. Like his predecessors of the Harlem Renaissance and the 1960s, Wilson pushed for an African American theatre movement. He, too, believed that African Americans should be writing, directing, and acting in plays that depicted the African American way of life. As he put it, for too long African Americans had relied upon "others" to represent them, and usually those depictions had been stereotypical (Freedman 36). Hackneyed, perhaps, not out of insensitivity, but out of unfamiliarity with the culture. This unawareness is one of the main reasons for Wilson's push for an African American theatre. This was one of the reasons that Wilson refused to hire anyone other than an African American to direct the screen adaptation of *Fences*. He felt that a white director would not understand the play and see the possibilities of the film (Wilson, "I Want" 200). Also, he insisted that only an African American director would approach the work with the same amount of passion and respect with which he had approached it (200).

Wilson's ideas concerning the direction of *Fences* and an institutionalized African American theatre spurred lots of censure from critics, many of whom saw his views as hypocritical. Writing in response to Wilson's 1998 address to the Theatre Communications Group, in which he denounced the American theatre as an instrument of white cultural hegemony and called for a separate African American stage (Wilson, "The Ground On Which I Stand," 486–88), literary critic Henry Louis Gates, Jr. said that Wilson's comments and views were duplicitous, for he failed to acknowledge his own power within the same world of American theatre that he condemned (134). He also pointed out that none of Wilson's plays had premiered at an African American theatre (134).

Historically, *Joe Turner's Come and Gone,* which is set in 1911, is the first play in Wilson's 10-play cycle. In the play, Wilson returns to the beginning of the Great Migration and explores the genesis of what was really a journey toward self-affirmation. He depicts the influence of the migration on the identity of each character; how their quests for lost lovers and new loves reflect a deeper search for themselves. He then raises crucial questions about the nature of the African American experience in America, probing the blending of two cultures that have informed the sensibilities of African Americans—their African heritage and the Christian tradition into which they were thrust. Wilson investigates their poignant yearnings for meaningful relationships and their struggle to sing the song of their true identity. He also concentrates on the ways in which separation and migration launched the 20th-century destinies of African Americans in urban America. In focusing on these ideas, Wilson demonstrates that the path to self-discovery lies in establishing bonds with the past.

Although the storyline of *Joe Turner's Come and Gone* follows Herald Loomis's search for his lost wife, its underlying action is his odyssey toward self-empowerment. Set in a boardinghouse in Pittsburgh that is run by Seth and Bertha Holly, the play begins in 1911, at the start of the decade in which began the massive influx of southern African Americans into northern cities.

Ma Rainey's Black Bottom is set in Chicago in 1927 during a recording session by blues singer Ma Rainey and the four musicians who accompany her. The significance of the date echoes strongly throughout the play, for much of the action flows from a conflict between proponents of the old and new forms of black music: blues and jazz.

Wilson makes this division apparent early in the play through the characters' stage directions. He draws a sharp distinction between the three older musicians and the younger musician: Cutler, the trombonist and guitar player, is the "most sensible," with a playing style that is "solid and almost totally unembellished (13); Toledo, the pianist, "recognizes that his instrument's limitations are an extension of himself" and "his insights are thought-provoking" (14); and Slow Drag, the bassist, is "deceptively intelligent, though, as his name implies, he appears to be slow" (13–14). Levee is more flamboyant and "somewhat of a buffoon," with a "rakish and bright" temper and strident voice. Their personalities also reflect their attitudes toward music: The older three favor the more plaintive, deeply emotional sounds of the blues; Levee is attracted to the flashier rhythms of swing.

As the play progresses and the audience learns more about the characters' past experiences through their stories, Wilson allows the audience to explore the individual psychologies of the characters and shows their efforts to survive the injustices, social and economic, that beset African Americans during the 1920s. Since music is an integral part of the lives and racial identity of these characters, much of the conflict centers on their music.

The Piano Lesson, set in 1936 and the third play in the 10-play cycle, is the story of the Charles family and the conflict surrounding a piano the family owns. Berniece and her brother, Boy Willie, fight over the piano in her house in Pittsburgh—he wants to sell it and she wants it left there. There is also a ghost that wants the piano and roams Berniece's house in search of it.

In *The Piano Lesson,* Wilson continues to develop the themes of self-affirmation and empowerment that he develops in *Joe Turner's Come and Gone* and *Ma Rainey's Black Bottom.* However, *The Piano Lesson* more closely parallels *Joe Turner's Come and Gone* in that in both plays, Wilson sets forth the idea that the relationship of the past to the present for African Americans promotes an active lineage kinship bond between the living and their ancestors. In this sense, the transmission of history becomes a binding ritual, through which the characters obtain an empowering self-knowledge, a tangible sense of their own self-worth and identity, that gives them strength to manage the future on their own terms. In both plays, meaningful progress toward the future and self-affirmation are achieved only by establishing connections to the past—connections represented as the power of the ancestors.

In *The Piano Lesson,* the link to the past is the piano that sits in Berniece's living room. It has played a pivotal role in the Charles family's fight for freedom, and its very presence in the household is a powerful testament to the success of that effort. Its history is a direct reflection of the struggle that engendered the blues.

The piano is a visual symbol of the family and its history. On it are carved weddings, births, funerals, and the sale of Berniece's and Boy Willie's great grandmother and grandfather. Thus, the carvings on the piano pictorially preserve important events of the family's history, as well as the images of ancestors themselves.

Fences, which is set in 1957, focuses on former Negro League baseball player Troy Maxson. Even though he had a prolific career in the Negro League, Troy is disgruntled because the social climate of his day denied him an opportunity to play in the major league. When the play opens, major league baseball has been integrated, but he is still disenchanted with America's social terrain and feels that things are no better for the African American male at that time than they were when he was in his prime. Thus, part of the action in *Fences* concentrates on Troy's skepticism and refusal to accept the fact that social conditions are changing for the African American, especially the African American male. This creates much of the dramatic conflict, leading to problems between him and his family, particularly his son Cory. Troy's obstinacy springs from his bitterness over the fact that, despite his great talent, he could not play major league baseball, while lesser white players became stars. He will not let Cory go to college on a football scholarship, arguing that there is no future in sports for the boy as there was no future for him. His wife, Rose, reminds him that since Jackie Robinson broke the color barrier, things are a little different, but Troy will not be persuaded. Convinced of no professional future for African American athletes, he is determined to direct his son into a more practical career, at the A&P, or perhaps hauling garbage as he does.

Whereas *Joe Turner's Come and Gone, Ma Rainey's Black Bottom, The Piano Lesson,* and *Fences* focus on the effects of the slave past, Wilson shifts focus in *Two Trains Running, Seven Guitars, Jitney, King Hedley II,* and *Radio Golf.* Their focus is the effects of assimilation and migration to the North. They are concerned with the contemporary issues the African American has found himself faced with since relocating to the North: the breakdown of the African American family (*Jitney* and *King Hedley II*), urban decay (*Two Trains Running* and *Radio Golf*), imprisonment (*Two Trains Running, Jitney,* and *King Hedley II*), and crime (*Two Trains Running, Seven Guitars, Jitney,* and *King Hedley II*).

With a historical setting of 1969, *Two Trains Running* primarily focuses on the disintegration of the city. Early into the play, there is mention that the block on which Memphis's restaurant is located is a wasteland of empty and boarded buildings. However, this neighborhood was not always that way. It once flourished. Memphis remembers a time when there would be a line of people waiting to get into his restaurant, and he would cook four cases of chicken over the course of a weekend. But all of that has changed. Now he's lucky to cook one case of chicken per week, and the restaurant is empty with the exception of the regulars: Holloway, West, Hambone, and Wolf.

As Memphis sees it, all of his troubles began when the city of Pittsburgh began buying out business owners. Slowly, the business owners began to accept the city's offer for a buyout, and now with the exception of the restaurant and West's funeral parlor, all of the other businesses—the supermarket, the drugstore, the five and ten—have closed. Even the doctor and dentist's offices have closed. The city has offered to purchase his restaurant, and although Memphis knows that it is no longer profitable for him to stay in business, he refuses to sell. As he sees it, because the city has taken away his livelihood, it will have to meet or beat his asking price of $25,000.

Unlike Memphis's restaurant, West's funeral parlor is profitable. The interment business is the only business that thrives in this wasteland. As a matter of fact, business is better than ever for West. As Memphis points out, as long as "the niggers are killing one another West will get richer" (9) Burying his fellow African Americans has made West a very wealthy man. He is a millionaire and other than Hartzberger, he owns every other building in the neighborhood. But West's wealth stands in stark contrast to the economic situation of those around him. The others in the neighborhood live in utter destitution and must scrape to get by, which often entails criminal activity.

Crime is increasing in the neighborhood as its inhabitants try to find any means to survive. Some turn to "running the numbers" and gambling—Wolf and Holloway—while others turn to theft—Sterling. Still others turn to crime to acquire the material trappings of West and Prophet Samuel—Cadillacs, color TVs and furs. Whatever the reason, the commission of such crimes usually leads to one of two results—death or imprisonment. Imprisonment seems to be the most common by far, for as Wolf states, "you can … walk down the street and ask people … every nigger you see done been to jail one time or another" (56). However, death is running a close second, and that is the result West prefers.

Death allows West to maximize his profits. Over the years, West has learned that death lends itself to manipulation. He has made a business of taking advantage of his customers' grief. Stories abound about him convincing the bereaved to purchase a more expensive "satin-lined" (*Two Trains* 12) casket and swapping it out for a less expensive pine one before burying the body. However, his exploitative methods don't stop there. For an additional $100 per feature, he also persuades them to purchase a casket that locks and is leakproof. Thus, through the character of West, Wilson ingeniously allows himself to bring to the audience's attention two problems of northern life—crime and exploitation

In *Two Trains Running,* Wilson depicts not only a decaying city, but also the cycle of death, crime, and imprisonment associated with it. By the end of the play, the audience witnesses the closure of yet another business as the city beats Memphis's asking price by offering him $35,000 for the restaurant; Hambone dies a pauper, never receiving his ham; and Sterling, wanting to provide closure to Hambone's nine-year request, breaks into Lutz's meat market and steals one, a certain indication that he will soon return to the penitentiary.

With a setting of 1948, *Seven Guitars* is Wilson's first play, according to historical setting, to shift from the theme of reconciliation with the past. Described by Peter Wolfe as Wilson's most "bewildering and threatening play" (152), it is a murder mystery that focuses on the events leading to the protagonist's death. But Wilson does much more than simply depict the events leading to Floyd's death; he also brings to the audience's attention problems that were starting to infiltrate the African American community at that time.

One problem is black-on-black crime. Not only is there Floyd's murder at the hands of Hedley, but Canewell mentions that he is lucky to be alive, for he has known "six or seven men that got killed" at the hands of other African American men (21). Later, it is learned through Hedley's conversation with Ruby that Floyd is not the first African American male Hedley has killed, for as he tells her, he once killed a man for refusing to call him by his name, King. And, of course, Ruby has come to Pittsburgh because one of her lovers shot the other, seemingly without provocation. Thus, from the first scene of the play to the last, there is the mention of or actual commission of 10 acts of black-on-black crime. Of course, in the larger world, 10 murders is not a large number and would not be a reason for alarm, but in the world of the play it is and seems to be Wilson's way of indicating that black-on-black on crime has become an epidemic that plagues the community.

Wilson also seems to point to the cause of this plague, the proliferation of weapons in the community. Weapons abound in *Seven Guitars.* All of the male characters carry some form of weapon: Red Carter and Floyd carry guns, Canewell and Hedley knives. There is even a conversation about which form of weapon—gun or knife—is better. To possess a weapon is not gender specific, however. Louise, the matron voice of the play, also has a gun that she sleeps with and professes to being "all the man she needs" (19). And these characters do not keep weapons in their possession because it is in vogue. They believe that a knife or gun can right any wrong. Floyd constantly rants about solving his woes with his .38; Hedley believes that the machete Joe Roberts gives to him will prevent him from being sent to the sanitarium; and Louise tells Vera to shoot a man before letting him use her up.

Through all this discussion about weapons and violence, Wilson seems to be attempting to diffuse the idea that violence cannot solve one's problems; but instead, violence begets more violence. Floyd and Poochie rob the store, which results in Poochie's death. The robbery, by implication, leads to Floyd's death because Hedley, in a drunken stupor, seeing Floyd with the money from the robbery, mistakes him for Buddy Bolden and kills Floyd/Buddy for refusing to give him the money.

As in *Two Trains Running,* all of the male characters in *Seven Guitars,* with the exception of Hedley, have been imprisoned. Although the charges were trumped—varying from worthlessness (Floyd) to laziness (Canewell) and having too much money (Red Carter)—man has served time, and by having each one mention his experience, Wilson seems to be bringing attention to the increasing number of African American men in prison, and the reason behind that increase, racism.

Told in flashback, the plot of *Seven Guitars* has been described as transgressive, challenging, and difficult. It is referred to in this way, perhaps, because Wilson's use of flashback allows him to shift the audience's attention more toward the issues he is addressing. Unlike in the other plays, with *Seven Guitars* Wilson seems to be making a more direct appeal to the audience to recognize black-on-black crime and the high incidence of African American male imprisonment as problems that require not only our full and undivided attention, but resolution as well.

Although *Jitney* is the seventh play produced in the 10-play cycle, it was the first written. Penned in 1979, *Jitney* is set in 1971 and is the story of five Pittsburgh jitney drivers. As Joan Herrington relates, Wilson wrote the play after having hailed a jitney for transportation one day during a visit to Pittsburgh (114).

Much like *Two Trains Running,* the backdrop of *Jitney*'s action is a place of business slated for closure. The city of Pittsburgh has earmarked the storefront from which the jitney station is run for demolition. But unlike in *Two Trains Running,* this time the city is not offering compensation, so with the building's obliteration comes unemployment for Becker, Doub, Fielding, and Youngblood. Thus, it seems that not only does Wilson continue to address the problem of urban decay in *Jitney,* but he also addresses the increasing rate of unemployment in the African American community.

While *Jitney* has many similarities with *Two Trains Running,* it reads more like a companion piece to *Fences.* Like in *Fences,* one of the play's central conflicts is the father-son relationship, but unlike in *Fences* where the estrangement occurs during the course of the play, in Jitney the estrangement occurs before the play's opening scene.

Twenty-five years before the play's first scene, Booster was imprisoned for murdering a woman who accused him of rape. Soon after his sentence, Booster's mother died of a broken heart. Not only does Becker blame Booster for Becker's wife's death; he also blames Booster for killing all the aspirations he had for him when he committed the murder. And like Troy, these events have soured Becker, so much so that when Booster visits him at the Jitney station after being released from prison, he rejects his son. When Booster returns a second time, he rejects him again and dies thereafter. Thus, like Troy, Becker dies estranged from his son.

Although *Jitney* did not enjoy the commercial success of Wilson's other plays, with its continuation of the themes of urban decay and the father-son relationship, it tackles major Wilson issues.

If *Jitney* can be viewed as a companion piece to *Fences,* then *King Hedley II* can be viewed as the sequel to *Seven Guitars.* Set in 1985, *King Hedley II* finishes the story begun 37 years earlier in *Seven Guitars.*

While *King Hedley II* has its own plot, it is essentially a resolution to *Seven Guitars,* for throughout the play the audience receives answers to some of the questions left unanswered at the end of *Seven Guitars.* For example, the audience learns that Canewell informs the police that Hedley murdered Floyd. As a result of his "stooling," Ruby and the other characters begin to call him Stool Pigeon, hence the name by which he is referred in *King Hedley II.*

As Ruby tells Louise in *Seven Guitars,* she allows Hedley to believe he is the father of her unborn child and names the child in his honor. Ruby pursues a career as a blues singer, is very successful at it, and leaves the young King to be raised by Louise when Hedley succumbs to pneumonia.

Much like *Seven Guitars, King Hedley II* has as its major theme crime in the African American community. King has done a stint in prison for killing Pernell. Although his act was one of self-defense (Pernell had tried to kill King), King has no regrets about having another man's blood on his hands. There is also Elmore, who in *Seven Guitars,* kills Leroy. His gun is his best friend, and he has killed plenty of men, as he proudly boasts throughout the play. As a matter of fact, there is so much violence and disregard for the value of human life that Tonya, King's wife, would rather abort their unborn child than give birth and have it grow up in such an environment.

In addition to the violence in the play, there is also larceny. King and his best friend Mister have aspirations of opening a video store and sell stolen refrigerators as a way of reaching that goal. However, feeling that it will take them too long to acquire the money they need through the sale of the refrigerators, like Floyd and Poochie in *Seven Guitars,* they commit a robbery.

Despite the bleak picture *King Hedley II* seems to paint of the 1980s, and though like *Seven Guitars* it ends with the commission of murder, it also ends with an impending birth, certain indication that there is indeed a future for the people of Pittsburgh's Hill District.

Radio Golf, which takes place in 1997 in Pittsburgh's Hill District (the setting for many of Wilson's plays), concerns middle-class blacks, a first for Wilson. The characters are educated people who have not necessarily suffered the consequences of what other African Americans have suffered; the main character, Harmond Wilks, is the son of a wealthy father. Ivy League educated, Wilks returns to the blighted neighborhood with plans to gentrify it. His plans include constructing a high-rise apartment building that includes a Starbucks coffee shop, Barnes and Noble bookstore, and Whole Foods grocery store. His plans are thwarted, however, when the locals challenge his decision to demolish the building located at 1839 Wylie, which is the former home of Aunt Ester, the neighborhood's sage. Through his dealings with the neighborhood denizens, Harmond realizes that there is more to life than earning money, status, or reputation. It is about finding the center of your soul—who you are, where you've been, and where you're going.

Through his use of history and the blues motif, Wilson has fashioned an ocuvre of plays that pry at the deepest sensibilities of the African American community—the slave past and what it means to be a person of African descent in America. It was Wilson's wish that his audience, like his characters, would leave his plays with the realization that in order to become in tune with themselves they must look to their past.

BIBLIOGRAPHY

Fences: A Play. New York: New American Library, 1986.

Gem of the Ocean. New York: Theatre Communications Group, 2008.

The Ground on Which I Stand: Dramatics Contexts. New York: Theatre Communications Group, 2001.

"I Want a Black Director." *May All Your Fences Have Gates: Essays on the Drama of August Wilson.* Ed. Alan Nadel. Iowa City: U of Iowa P, 1994.

Jitney. Woodstock, NY: Overlook, 2001.

Joe Turner's Come and Gone: A Play in Two Acts. New York: New American Library, 1988.

King Hedley II. New York: Theatre Communications Group, 2005.

Ma Rainey's Black Bottom: A Play in Two Acts. New York: New American Library, 1985.

The Piano Lesson. New York: Dutton, 1990.

Radio Golf. New York: Theatre Communications Group, 2008.

Seven Guitars. New York: Dutton, 1996.

Three Plays. Pittsburgh: U of Pittsburgh P, 1991.

Two Trains Running. New York: Dutton, 1992.

FURTHER READING

Bogumil, Mary L. *Understanding August Wilson.* Columbia: U of South Carolina P, 1999.

Bryer, Jackson R., and Mary C. Hartig. *Conversations with August Wilson.* Oxford, MS: UP of Mississippi, 2006.

Elam, Harry Justin. *The Past as Present in the Drama of August Wilson.* Ann Arbor: U of Michigan P, 2004.

Elkins, Mary. *August Wilson: A Casebook.* New York: Garland, 2000.

Herrington, Joan. *I Ain't Sorry for Nothin' I Done: August Wilson's Process of Playwrighting.* New York: Limelight Editions, 1998.

Menson-Furr, Ladrica C. *August Wilson's Fences.* New York: Continuum, 2008.

Nadel, Alan. *May All Your Fences Have Gates: Essays on the Drama of August Wilson.* Iowa City: U of Iowa P, 1994.

Pereira, Kim. *August Wilson and the African American Odyssey.* Urbana: U of Illinois P, 1995.

Plum, Jay. "Blues, History and the Dramaturgy of August Wilson." *African American Review* 27.4 (Winter 1993): 561–567.

Rocha, Mark William. "A Conversation with August Wilson." *Diversity: A Journal of Multicultural Issues* (Fall 1992): 24–42.

Savron, David. "August Wilson." *In Their Own Words: Contemporary Playwrights.* New York: Theatre Communications Group, 1988.

Shafer, Yvonne. *August Wilson: A Research and Production Sourcebook.* Westport, CT: Greenwood, 1998.

Shannon, Sandra and Dana Williams, eds. *August Wilson and Black Aesthetics.* New York: Palgrave, 2004.

Shannon, Sandra, and Dana Williams, eds. *The Dramatic Vision of August Wilson.* Washington, DC: Howard UP, 1995.

Snodgrass, Mary Ellen. *August Wilson: A Literary Companion.* Jefferson, NC: McFarland, 2004.

Wang, Qun. *An In-Depth Study of the Major Plays of African American Playwright August Wilson: Vernacularizing the Blues on Stage.* Lewiston, NY: Mellen, 1999.

Wolfe, Peter. *August Wilson.* New York: Twayne, 1999.

Yolanda Williams Page

About the Editor and Contributors

THE EDITOR

YOLANDA WILLIAMS PAGE is an associate professor of English at the University of Arkansas at Pine Bluff, where she also serves as dean of the School of Arts and Sciences. She has presented literary papers, published chapters in books, and written several articles on African American literature. *Encyclopedia of African American Women Writers* (Westport, CT: Greenwood Press, 2007), a sourcebook that she edited, was named a New York Library Association Best of Reference.

THE CONTRIBUTORS

KARINE BLIGNY, presently taking the famous French *concours* (a national competitive exam), is a postgraduate student in the University of Burgundy. Her research is focused on African American literature and its musical dimension—and has also developed in relation to her artistic activities (guitar and salsa). She has recently written a master's paper on the subject and published an article in the Sorbonne review *Afram*.

REGINA N. BRADLEY is a doctoral candidate in African American literature at Florida State University. Her research interests include African American literature, identity politics, African American humor, and popular culture. Her current research project investigates negotiations of whiteness and privilege in the late 20th- and 21st-century black consciousness.

WARREN J. CARSON is professor of English and African American Studies at the University of South Carolina Upstate, where he also serves as associate vice chancellor of academic affairs. He holds a doctorate in English from the University of South Carolina, where he wrote his dissertation on Zora Neale Hurston's early works. He has published widely in a variety of journals and most recently contributed a chapter to the *Cambridge History of African*

American Literature (2011). Dr. Carson presently serves as president of the College Language Association.

THOMAS CASSIDY is a professor of English in the Department of English and Modern Languages at South Carolina State University, where, for 20 years, he has taught composition, world literature, and American literature. He holds a BA in English from Bard College, and an MA and PhD in English from Binghamton University. His department, which he has served since 1991, has twice selected him to be their Professor of the Year, most recently in November of 2009. He has published and presented to professional organizations on a wide variety of topics related to American and African American literature. He has published essays in the *CLA Journal* and the *African American Review,* among other places, and has written entries in several standard reference works, including *The Greenwood Encyclopedia of African American Literature.*

CAROL BUNCH DAVIS is an assistant professor of English at Texas A&M University at Galveston where she teaches African American literature. Her current research examines the ways in which the representation of race in the drama and performance of the 1960s informs current discussions about race and relations in the United States.

ANNIE-PAULE MIELLE DE PRINSAC is a PhD and musician who first studied Elizabethan music and taught at the University of Sussex (England). She obtained a research scholarship at the University of Harvard, where she worked on metaphor and metamorphosis in Shakespeare's Last Plays. She taught at the University of Madagascar and later became a specialist of African American Literature with a book on Toni Morrison: *De l'un à l'autre. L'identité dans les romans de Toni Morrison* (Edition Universitaires de Dijon, 1999). She has contributed many articles on Shakespeare and African American literature (Morrison, Harriet Jacobs, Langston Hughes, E. J. Gaines) to *Etudes Anglaises* and *Ellipses.* She was a fellow of the Du Bois Institute at Harvard (Summer-Fall 2002). She is currently assistant professor at the University of Bourgogne.

MARIAN C. DILLAHUNT is an assistant professor of developmental English and reading at Vance-Granville Community College in North Carolina, and she was the recipient of the North Carolina Community College System 2011 Teaching Excellence Award. She received her BA from North Carolina Agricultural and Technical State University, MA from North Carolina Central University, and an MLS from East Carolina University. She is a doctoral student at Indiana University of Pennsylvania. Her research interests include contemporary African American literature, comparative literature, and pre-curriculum English studies.

R. ERIN HUSKEY, PhD, teaches English at Valdosta State University in Valdosta, Georgia, where she is an assistant professor in the Department of English and the African American studies program. Her areas of specialization include

African American women's literature, modern and contemporary American literature, and autobiography theory. Her publications include a pedagogical essay on collaborative writing in *Notes on Teaching English,* a review of Yolanda Barnes's novel *When It Burned to the Ground,* and forthcoming essays on Toni Morrison's novels and *The Color Purple.* Currently, she is working on an essay on quantum physics in Toni Morrison's novels, and a book-length manuscript that discusses the gospel ideology in the works of Alice Walker, Toni Morrison, and Suzan-Lori Parks.

MARK S. JAMES currently works as a visiting instructor at the University of West Florida, where he teaches American and African American literature. His research interests include the representation of intellectuals in popular and academic cultures, the history and status of liberal education in the United States, and the impact of consumer culture on education, democracy, and the life of the mind in general.

KARIMA K. JEFFREY is an assistant professor of English at Hampton University, where she teaches courses in African American, Caribbean, and American literatures. She is interested in interdisciplinary studies and literary theory—especially postcolonialism—and has published and/or presented papers on Langston Hughes, Edwidge Danticat, George Lamming, Jamaica Kincaid, Paule Marshall, James Joyce, Frantz Fanon, Jean Toomer, James Baldwin, and Gloria Naylor.

SUSANA M. MORRIS is an assistant professor of English at Auburn University where she teaches contemporary African American literature and women's studies. She received her PhD from Emory University. Her research interests include motherhood, gender and feminist theory, and black sexuality. She is currently completing a monograph titled *Loosened Tongues: Motherhood and Storytelling in Black Women's Literature* about the roles of storytelling and motherhood in contemporary African American and African Caribbean women's literature.

TERRY NOVAK is a professor of English and director of the Collaborative Learning Program at Johnson & Wales University, Providence campus, where she teaches introductory composition and literature courses, as well as African American literature. Her research and publications focus on 19th-century African American writers, 19th-century women writers, collaboration, and learning communities.

KIMBERLY ODEN is an English PhD candidate at Morgan State University. She received her BA and MA in English at North Carolina Central University, in Durham, NC. Kimberly's scholarly interests include African American literature, women's studies, and popular culture studies.

LAKISHA ODLUM is a graduate student of English education at Columbia University's Teachers College. Her research interests are African American literature, feminist theory, and urban education reform.

JESSICA PARKER has a PhD from the University of Denver in English, literary studies concentration. She currently is a visiting assistant professor in the English department at Metropolitan State College of Denver, teaching coursework in African American and American literatures. Her own research is in African American literatures and music, particularly hip hop, and other popular culture and literary genres, such as the detective novel.

ROBERT J. PATTERSON, PhD, is an assistant professor of English at Florida State University, where he specializes in African American literary and cultural studies. He currently is completing his first book project, *Literary Activism: Civil Rights Discourses in Contemporary African American Literature and Culture,* which analyzes the ways in which four contemporary African American writers' fictive texts have shaped the discourses on civil rights in the post–civil rights era. As he finishes this book, he is beginning a second project, tentatively titled, *Why I Did (Not) Get Married: The Representational Politics of Marriage, Gender, and Sexuality in Contemporary African American Literature and Culture.* This book is an interdisciplinary study that analyzes how and why the institution of marriage has been represented in particular ways and what the implications of those representations are. In addition to literary studies, Dr. Patterson's research and teaching interests include African American, American, cultural, and gender studies, as well as liberation and womanist theologies.

TIMOTHY MARK ROBINSON received his undergraduate degree from SUNY Brockport and his MA and PhD in literature at Pennsylvania State University. After graduation, he was awarded a postdoctoral fellowship from the Consortium for Faculty Diversity at Liberal Arts Colleges. He has taught rhetoric and composition and a variety of courses in American literature at Penn State University, Southwestern University in Georgetown, Texas and Huston-Tillotson University in Austin, Texas. Timothy is currently a visiting assistant professor at Bates College in Lewiston, Maine where he teaches African American literature. He is in the process of completing his first book, *In the Presence of the Ancestor: History, Culture, and the Literary Imagination in African American Fiction* and is the general editor of *The Encyclopedia of Slavery and Freedom in American Literature* (2010).

DOLORES V. SISCO holds a BA and MA in English literature, and has taught a wide range of literature courses in American, British, African, and Caribbean literature and culture. She has published articles on Terry McMillan, Gloria Naylor, Ralph Ellison, and Paul Laurence Dunbar, and is currently planning a study of African American female detective fiction. Dr. Sisco received a PhD in English literature from Michigan State University, where she also taught courses on the immigrant and the black migration experiences. Currently, she teaches a wide range of multicultural literature course at Youngstown State University, and is currently researching popular detective fiction by black women authors.

ALEXIS M. SKINNER grew up in community theater and went on to study at Temple University in Pennsylvania. She received her master's degree in Arts Administration and Cultural Policy from Goldsmith's College, University of London. While working at the Theatre Royal Stratford East, a premiere theater that produces original programming for the broad spectrum of minorities in the UK, Ms. Skinner studied the theater archival process. She is currently a theater instructor at the University of Arkansas at Pine Bluff.

RASHELL R. SMITH-SPEARS grew up in Memphis, Tennessee. She received her BA from Spelman College and her graduate degrees from the University of Memphis and University of Missouri-Columbia. Currently, she teaches American, African American, and world literature classes at Jackson State University. In addition to presenting at numerous conferences, she has published in *Writing African American Women, Encyclopedia of Hip Hop Literature, Short Story, Black Magnolias*, and *A Lime Jewel: Anthology of Poems and Stories in Aid of Haiti*. Her research interests are cultural studies, particularly film and television and issues of identity in American literature.

CAMMIE M. SUBLETTE is an associate professor of English at the University of Arkansas—Fort Smith. She teaches African American literature, popular culture, postmodern literature, genre studies, 20th-century American literature, composition, and literary theory.

ORDNER W. TAYLOR III is a doctoral candidate at Morgan State University in Baltimore, Maryland. He is particularly interested in comparative criticism, British Romanticism, African American literature, and literature of the African diaspora. His current research and doctoral dissertation focus on the influence of British Romanticism on specific African American literary selections.

AIMABLE TWAGILIMANA is professor of English and director of the African and African American Studies Interdisciplinary Unit at Buffalo State College. He is also vice-chair of the Association of African Studies Programs.

JASMIN J. VANN currently teaches sophomore and senior English at Alvin High School in Alvin, Texas. She also teaches English composition at Houston Community College.

LYNN WASHINGTON is currently a Fulbright scholar and a doctoral candidate in English at Morgan State University. Her Fulbright research, focusing on the reggae aesthetic in literature, is being conducted at the University of the West Indies in Mona, Jamaica. Her other research and teaching interests are passing narratives from 1850 to 1950, 20th-century African American women writers, African American and Caribbean literature, literary criticism, and musico-literary aesthetics.

Index